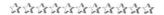

Also by David Rosengarten

David Rosengarten Entertains
Taste
The Dean & DeLuca Cookbook
Red Wine with Fish

It's
All American
Food

*The Best Recipes for More Than
400 New American Classics*

David Rosengarten

Little, Brown and Company

New York   Boston

Little, Brown and Company
Time Warner Book Group
1271 Avenue of the Americas, New York, NY 10020
Visit our Web site at www.twbookmark.com

Originally published in hardcover by Little, Brown and Company, October 2003
First paperback edition, May 2005

Library of Congress Cataloging-in-Publication Data

Rosengarten, David.
    It's all American food : the best recipes for more than 400 new American classics /
by David Rosengarten.
        p. cm.
    ISBN 0-316-05315-5 (hc) / 0-316-15920-4 (pb)
    I. Cookery, American. 2. Cookery, International. I. Title.

TX715 .R83635 2003
641.5973 — dc21

                                                                    2002043647

10 9 8 7 6 5 4 3 2 I

Q-FF

BOOK DESIGN AND ILLUSTRATIONS BY LILLY LANGOTSKY

Printed in the United States of America

To Connie —
Who gave me all
the best things in life

Contents

✩✩✩✩✩✩✩✩✩✩✩

☆☆☆

Part Three: Classic America

Introduction:
It's All American Food

★☆★☆★☆★☆★☆★☆★☆

Some years ago, I had the pleasure of speaking with Alain Ducasse, arguably the best-known, most highly respected chef in France today, during one of his first visits to America. He wanted my dining recommendations for New York City. Rather than give him the address of a fancy restaurant, I decided to pick him up, drive him out to Queens, and sit him down at a dive called Pearson's Texas Barbecue before a plate of Southern barbecued ribs.

He wasn't mildly impressed; he wasn't merely being polite. He sat there beaming, licking the barbecue sauce off his fingers, muttering, *"Je l'adore, je l'adore!"*

This is a book about what we eat in America and everything that we remember eating. It revisits and reinvents all those foods from our grandmothers' kitchens that we once found mildly embarrassing. For some time now, happily, we have been returning home, discovering not only the potency of American regional and home cooking of the past but also the unexpected foods that have arrived on our shores over the past hundred years — and will be shaping the way we think about American cooking for some time to come.

I set out to write this book with the intention of discovering America all over again. To do so, I had to look at the American table in some unaccustomed ways. For the real subject of this book is not the usual cookbook fare, nor is it the idealized fantasy food of a photostylist's imagination. Rather, it is the vital, almost invisible American food that is eaten every day from the bayous to Boston, from east Texas to the shore of Lake Michigan, from Biscayne Bay to San Francisco Bay. This book not only includes the panoply of traditional regional cooking, and Mama's comfort classics, but also embraces the mongrel cooking of our endlessly hyphenated romance with ethnic food. From Italian-American to Cuban-Chinese — and not usually in fancy restaurants! — what we eat has been enlivened by the influence of the corner deli, the corner takeout, and those who, newly arrived in America, struggled to make sense of our ingredients.

Most important, this book focuses on what Americans really like to eat — which isn't often celebrated. Not too long ago, I was a judge at a chef's competition in Reykjavík, Iceland. At the start of the competition the judges followed the chefs through a large, very bright, American-style supermarket in the ingredient-gathering phase of the event. As we left the store,

☆☆☆

I noticed that another judge, Pierre Hermé, had bought some groceries. Hermé is justifiably considered the pastry and chocolate god of Paris.

"You bought something," I said, somewhat curious.

"Oui," he said.

"What is it?" I inquired.

"Ell-mann's," he said simply.

"Hellmann's mayonnaise?" I repeated, somewhat startled at the thought.

"It is the best," said his wife.

"As good as the mayonnaise you make at home?" I asked.

"Much, much, bett-AIR! We cannot find it in France, so we buy a lot wherever we can."

If this was a surprise to me, imagine what a shock it would be to many American foodies! I am certain that were they to host the Hermés at their home, out would come the mixing bowl, the whisk, the egg yolks, the Provençal olive oil, and a half hour of vigorous beating and emulsifying would ensue. Pierre is a gentleman. You would never know how disappointed he was.

Why must we feel guilty about using crowd-pleasing convenience products? We use them in cooking for ourselves, but when company is expected, out comes the Cuisinart. Does it really make sense to jump through contorted gastronomic hoops to impart a small bit of fresh garlic flavor to a sauce when you can simply sprinkle on a little garlic powder? Let your taste buds find the difference. Imagine how your mother, and your grandmother, must have welcomed these products, how liberated and modern they felt, and if they were immigrants, how American they must have thought themselves to be! Why put yourself back into kitchen drudgery? Used properly, these ingredients are among the elements that made this country's cooking great.

Here are just a few "cheating" ingredients that most foodies secretly love, that have the ability to make foods taste wonderful . . . and that should by all rights come out of the cupboard.

Hellmann's, or Best Foods, mayonnaise. Can you imagine a tuna salad sandwich made with homemade mayo? I'm not saying it'd be bad — but it sure wouldn't be what most of us expect. The homemade mayo has a great place in classical European cuisines; when it's used as an almost-runny sauce, to coat, say, room-temperature poached chicken breasts, I'm all for it. But the stiffer American Hellmann's version, with a less-pronounced oily taste — first marketed in 1912 and today called Best Foods mayonnaise west of the Rockies — is much better suited for the delicious kinds of salads and sandwiches that we make in this country.

Heinz ketchup. Can you imagine a hamburger without ketchup on it, particularly the kind of rich, sweet, tomatoey stuff exemplified by Heinz ketchup? Starting in the 1980s, many a New Wave do-it-yourselfer embarked on homemade ketchup projects because there was a stigma attached to the Heinz product. It seemed too mundane. Well, I've liked many a homemade ketchup — but they're always different from Heinz, usually mucked up a bit, never as simply satisfying on a burger. The shrimp cocktail sauces on page 417 and the Thousand Island Dressing on page 420 just wouldn't be the same without Heinz.

French's mustard. You probably won't hear too many foodies confessing, even under duress, to a secret preference for French's mustard. To many palates, the darker, spicier Dijon-style mustard is superior. However, the thin, vinegary, turmeric-scented French's product is delicious in its proper American context. It's a perfect fit on ballpark hot dogs (see the amazing combo of ingredients that add up to the Chicago Hot Dog on page 368), and no tart Southern Mustard Slaw (like the one on page 321) could be taken seriously with Dijon mustard in it.

Garlic powder. Many food snobs abhor the idea of using garlic powder when garlic is called for in a recipe. I would go so far as to say, in fact, that Cajun/Creole cuisine took a public relations hit around the country when cooks discovered that both garlic powder and onion powder are used extensively in Louisiana cooking. But there's no real reason for this unease, especially when you apply a most important principle: a "convenience" product should never be viewed as a substitute for the "real" product. Yes, if you think about the ways in which you enjoy "real" garlic, and then think about substituting garlic powder, you may well be resistant to the switch. I, for instance, love the taste of fresh garlic in Linguine with White Clam Sauce (see the garlic-engorged recipe on page 16) and would never dream of substituting garlic powder there. But, for example, in the dry rub for Blackened Redfish (a modern Cajun classic on page 350) or in the Maryland steamed crab coating (see Crabhouse Spice Blend on page 293) or in the seasoning for Southern Fried Chicken (page 308), a good garlic powder is just the thing you want. It's not just that it's easier to use — it also carries the flavor better.

Margarine. Once upon a time, margarine was touted as a healthy alternative to butter — and it was during this period that many learned to use the old oleo. Then came the fall: the revelation that margarine is not better for you than butter is. So ask a foodie today about margarine, and you'll probably be told that he or she hasn't purchased any in twenty years. Typical. In reality, there are some good uses for margarine. It adds color to pastry. It keeps its flavor better than butter does after long cooking. In some situations, food cooked with margarine, or part margarine, seems less greasy than food cooked with butter alone (see Classic Grilled Cheese on page 427). Lastly — and most important — it has a higher smoking point than butter, so you run a lower risk with margarine of burning or overbrowning food. Paul Prudhomme — an American master of bringing food in a pan to its peak — wrote in *Paul Prudhomme's Louisiana Kitchen:* "I use margarine, often with butter, instead of oil. . . . I usually prefer the taste of margarine to olive or vegetable oil for frying when butter is also being used."

As a California friend recently said to me: "I've had it with screening out 'gastronomically incorrect' ingredients. It's silly. I now feel this: If it tastes good, use it."

During my years as a restaurant critic, I would spend my nights in luxury restaurants, watching plate after plate of fancy, creative, expensive food come out of the kitchen. Sometimes I would love the food. Sometimes I'd find it all right. Sometimes I'd hate it. But at all times, soon after I returned to my apartment, I'd start thinking about the hamburger I could make or the tuna salad sandwich or the leftover ribs or the quesadilla fixin's sitting in the refrigerator.

When I indulged at midnight (which I usually did), I'd often find myself enjoying the late snack far more than I enjoyed dinner. Nevertheless, I fell into the trap. I never had the notion that my snack food was in any way equivalent or superior to the dinner food I'd had earlier in the evening. I was slumming, in my mind — taking perverse, even guilty pleasure in something obviously inferior. Perhaps the fact that it wasn't pretentious is precisely what delighted me. It couldn't have been, I believed, that it was the tuna sandwich itself that delighted me more than the tuna tartare with beet oil and house-made taro gaufrettes.

I was wrong. I have finally come to feel that it is precisely the tuna sandwich itself. Why did I — why do we — assign some kind of quality hierarchy to different types of food? I can love a great dish in a three-star restaurant in France as much as the next palate does — but am I on some different plane of being when my palate lights up over a BLT? Is it a different order of experience? I think not! We're not comparing different forms of, say, love: parental, platonic, devotional, romantic. We're talking about sensations experienced on your tongue! There's nothing "better" or "finer" about great food at a three-star restaurant compared with great food in your kitchen. It certainly is different food — but why should the taste sensations at one place make you feel that you're living correctly, while the taste sensations in your kitchen make you feel like an aesthetic miscreant?

These days, I think it's more important than ever to preserve our informal, down-home traditions. For, what you can get in the fancy restaurants of New York, Chicago, Las Vegas, and San Francisco, is not awfully different anymore from what you can get in the fancy restaurants of Paris, Madrid, Tokyo, and Sydney! What you cannot get outside the United States is American barbecue, Maryland crab feasts, Chicago hot dogs, Santa Fe comfort food, Pacific Northwest salmon roasts, Cal-Mex burritos and tacos, delicious American pies and cakes.

I'll never forget my conversation a few years back with Umberto Eco, renowned Italian novelist and grand gourmand from the city of Bologna. I met him at a book party in New York as he was completing a publicity tour across the United States. He'd been wined and dined for weeks in fancy restaurants across the country — but apparently had found the time to slip in a few other things as well. "What did you think of American food?" I asked.

"America," he intoned, "has given two great gifts to world gastronomy."

I was all ears.

"The Reuben sandwich," said Eco, "and the pecan pie."

Yes, this food is familiar to us; yes, this food is our everyday fare. But why do we differ from other nations in our most intimate feelings about our real food? If you think the answer is "our real food is inferior" — you've never sat with a visiting European gourmand who is startled and delighted upon tasting a deep-fried soft-shell crab sandwich on toast, a mess of Buffalo chicken wings with blue cheese dressing, a Caesar salad, a juicy cheeseburger, or Mom's apple pie.

The real and simple foods of other places work well enough for us. If we can learn to apprehend a perfect tomato in the south of Italy topped with a gorgeous drop of olive oil and a terrific grain of coarse salt as great food, the kind that deserves respect, the kind that's ennobling to eat — can't we learn to think the same way about a New England Lobster Roll made with Hellmann's mayonnaise?

Finally, my pet theory about Americanized ethnic food. For years, some Americans have felt that there's something "wrong" with our versions of Italian food, Chinese food, Mexican food. That doesn't mean we don't consume our versions of these things; far from it. But it does mean that we don't boast about them — about a great Veal Parmigiana, about a fabulous Egg Foo Yung, about a rather un-Indian Lamb Vindaloo, about a terrific casserole of Cheese Enchiladas, about a New Yorker's version of Cheesecake. This is unnatural on the world stage. Cuisine is an evolving cultural artifact. Most cultures accept that. Throughout history, culinary ideas have traveled from one country to another, leading to the ultimate birth in the second country of a new cuisine. No one in Japan thinks less of Japanese Tonkatsu, the great fried pork cutlet inspired by the Portuguese, because it's different from Portuguese cuisine in Portugal. No one disparages spinach-based dishes in France described as Florentine because they're not authentically Tuscan.

The simple fact is you cannot serve "authentic" foreign food in the United States. Any diaspora will produce hybrids, and America, having been on the receiving end of numerous populations from every possible part of the world for generations, has more hybrids than most. Now, some chefs who have great familiarity with the original ethnic cuisines can come close to authenticity. But even the best attempts cannot be truly authentic. The ingredients are different here. The water is different. The air is different. Even the *metaphoric* air is different — for it takes both a physical and an emotional environment to create a national cuisine. When ethnic cuisines land on these shores . . . it's *all* American food.

And that's just fine and dandy with me.

In my view, no one should think poorly of our American conversions of ethnic culinary ideas. However, in that typical American mode of gastronomic self-effacement, many Americans most certainly do look down on these inventive adaptations.

Why?

If that rich and fabulous American version of Lasagna (see page 24) gives pleasure, makes diners swoon, why should we think that American lasagna is not as fine as the plate of wide green noodles with a Ragu Bolognese consisting of chicken livers and sweetbreads that you find in Emilia-Romagna? Because they've been doing their version of lasagna longer?

Doesn't seventy-five years across a country of two hundred million and more count for something? In my view, the Italian-American immigrants simply did what travelers always do. They worked old ideas into a new form here — and created what I like to call one of the tastiest Italian regional cuisines. The region just happens to be a little far from Rome.

This denigration of adapted ethnic foods has implications. Most important of these is the fact that the denigration itself spells the food's demise. Once upon a time, for example, great, vital versions of Italian-American cuisine were available in restaurants across the country, prepared by the people who invented this cuisine and, later, by their children. Today? An "Italian" chef in America looking for praise and prestige wouldn't be caught dead in the same kitchen as a meatball; he or she is usually focused on weaving radicchio and strozzapreti pasta into something the world has never seen before. Oh, there are plenty of places still serving spaghetti and meatballs — but because no one gives this cuisine the respect it deserves, these old-fashioned manicotti places don't attract the top cooking talent. So people sample their mediocre versions and come away with the notion that Italian-American cuisine is an inferior thing. And the next generation of chefs eschews the great Italian-American cuisine of the 1940s and 1950s, preferring to climb ever higher mountains of arborio rice and arugula.

This is a problem with all our real American food. There are so many bad versions of it around because we treat it as a lesser thing, a guilty pleasure, merely an everyday convenience, a gastronomic trifle. Because of this, few pay attention to what it can be at its best. And if you don't believe that a Chile Relleno Casserole from New Mexico or a New York Reuben or a Cuban sandwich from Miami or a transnational dish of scalloped potatoes with ham can be great food, chances are strong you'll never take the time to figure out how to make these things taste delicious.

And that's precisely where this book comes in.

Above all, this is a cookbook — a living, breathing, modern cookbook. I wouldn't want to anthologize some awful 1940s dish just because it says something about who we were as a people then. Each recipe came into this book because I believe in it, because I believe that if you take the time to figure out a great way to make it, you will be rewarded with great food. In many cases, for me, that meant preserving all the traditional details about a dish; if you can make the best damned chicken gumbo ever (see page 347), you don't need to get creative and add elements. In some recipes, there are some tweaks — but only because I felt that small tweaks, as long as they remain in the spirit of the dish, could actually make the dish better. Adding a little Chinese sausage to wontons vastly improves their flavor but doesn't take them in a different direction (see page 163); cooking shrimp-cocktail shrimp in salted, sugared water that's not boiling improves the shrimp immeasurably; steaming a Reuben sandwich (rather than griddling it) makes it even more tender, melting, and irresistible.

My core sentiment toward every recipe in this book was respect. This spawned a desire to get each recipe to your table in the greatest possible form — from fancy Americanized French food to the blue plate special at the local diner.

So . . . should I wish you *bon appétit?*

I don't think so.

I far prefer "Chow down, dude!"

It's
All
American

Food

★☆★☆★☆★☆★☆★☆☆

Part One

Ethnic America

✦☆

It would not be accurate to think of America's cuisine as the only cuisine in the world shot through with ethnic influences. There is simply no country on the planet that has a "pure" national cuisine; influences from other cuisines, other cultures, have always blended with indigenous cooking ideas. Just a few random examples:

- ✪ The ancient Romans brought to Rome an amazing proliferation of foods and ideas from all over their far-flung empire (and beyond) — ranging from British oysters to Spanish rabbits to Indonesian spices.
- ✪ Later, in the Middle Ages, the desire to blend spices from Indonesia and other Asian locales into local European cuisines drove the Age of Exploration, launching a thousand commercial ships.
- ✪ When Catherine de Médicis left Florence and arrived in France in 1533 to marry the French dauphin, she brought about a grand infusion of Italian cooking ideas into French cuisine.
- ✪ India's culinary history is particularly rich with absorptions: Muslim ideas in the north, Portuguese ideas in Goa (leading to such dishes as vindaloo), Persian ideas in Maharashtra (the Parsi cuisine of Bombay).
- ✪ Starting in the fifteenth century in Malacca, and later in Penang, in Malaysia, Chinese immigrants developed their own cuisine, which later combined with the cuisine of native Malaysians (as the Chinese men and Malaysian women intermarried), creating the still-vibrant Nonya cuisine of Singapore.
- ✪ In the seventeenth century, Europe was rocked by the importation of a new dish from the Americas: hot chocolate from Mexico, which led to the creation of public drinking establishments called chocolate houses across the continent, and a new European fixation.

Obviously, history abounds with examples of "ethnic influence." However, despite the manifold historical precedents, I firmly believe that what modern Americans eat every day has been more significantly affected by ethnic influence than has the daily fare of any other nation in the history of the world.

This is so, I would argue, because more than any other nation in the world, we are a nation of immigrants — immigrants who didn't just transmogrify a cuisine but forged one.

This is decisively less so elsewhere. When we speak of ethnic ideas' being incorporated into the mainstreams of other countries, we assume that there were "mainstream" traditions there to begin with! There was an already defined French cuisine in France before Catherine arrived; there was a Malaysian cuisine before the Chinese straits immigrants altered it.

America started with a much cleaner plate, so to speak. For many centuries before the arrival of Europeans, of course, the land belonged to the Native Americans. Did they establish a culinary base here that one would recognize today as a national cuisine? No. Certainly not in the same sense that the French did in France, Italians in Italy, Chinese in China, Persians in Persia.

For one thing, given the vastness of America, the Native Americans were more broadly dispersed than were, say, enclaves of French people in France. In old France, a culinary idea could blow into Paris with the weekly mail from Lyon — but the likelihood of culinary ideas from the Seminoles in Florida and the Pueblos in the Rocky Mountains merging into something national was far more remote.

Additionally, American cooking always lacked the motivating drive of royalty (which is part of our national charm!). Cuisines in France, in Italy, Spain, Persia, in northern India, Thailand, Peking, were all heavily inspired by the necessity of creating "national" food for the royal court. This not only unified the cooking in those countries but also boosted its complexities — as chefs attempted to outdo each other in pursuit of royal approval. Though the masses in 1788 certainly were not eating what Louis XVI ate (as his famous wife acknowledged in her most famous utterance), the cooking ideas and dishes that developed at Versailles and other royal venues over many centuries were later incorporated into what every French citizen eats everywhere in France.

Lacking such a galvanizing force, before the European arrivals American food never merged into a unified coast-to-coast phenomenon. Of course, the Native Americans made major ingredient contributions to what we eat today, particularly corn. It's fascinating to think that so many things that we do consider part of our national gastronomic life — such as corn on the cob, creamed corn, corn dogs, corn flakes, grits, tortilla chips, even our cheap American beer brewed from corn — are grounded in this ingredient preference of the early Native Americans. But did that preference lead to a "national cuisine"? By looking at neighboring Mexico — where it did lead to one — I think we can see that the answer is no. The Spaniards who started arriving in Mexico in the sixteenth century didn't merely grab a good ingredient and do something else with it; they truly blended their ideas with the native Mexican Indian ideas. Tacos al carbòn? The Spaniards brought the pork; the Indians supplied the tacos. When you eat in Mexico today, you'll find every table laid with modern versions of Indian ingredients, and Indian culinary ideas for those ingredients. You cannot say the same about the modern American table.

The modern American table was shaped, to a large degree, by the immigrants who began arriving in the United States about the time of the Civil War — and who continue to arrive today. They did not find a strongly defined national cuisine to belly up to when they arrived. So they brought their own ideas, and they held on to them — and they changed the food of America in the process. That's the key difference between the arrival of immigrants in America over the last 150 years and the arrival of immigrants in most other places. In that great American spirit of individual creativity, immigrants changed the national menu by simply adding their food to it.

There are two main ways in which this occurred. In one model, immigrants arrive and simply reproduce here what they ate at home. I call this a late-vintage phenomenon, because in order to do so the immigrants need access to the key ingredients they used back home. And it is only in the modern world of jet travel and international commerce that this has become possible. Had Japanese people arrived in 1750, they'd have had a hell of a time making sushi; arriving Greeks could not have enjoyed taramasalata; arriving Koreans wouldn't have had a prayer with kimchi. Today, to the contrary, Japanese-American communities produce sushi and Greek-American communities produce taramasalata and Korean-American communities produce kimchi — all of which taste a great deal as they do back in the original countries. Then, it goes further. Adventurous eaters notice the good food of ethnic persuasion. They get curious. They want some. Ethnic restaurants start welcoming guests who have nothing to do with the ethnicity, and before you know it, all Americans are sitting around at home saying, "Do you feel like Thai tonight? . . . or Brazilian? Or Ethiopian?" Those ethnic cuisines become part of our national menu, our national set of options. They become American food. Perhaps they do so even more when creative American chefs start grabbing those ideas, mixing them with others, and presenting them in high-end "American" restaurants. One of the most famous chefs in the Pacific Northwest — of English heritage, I believe — once served me a great dish of local scallops on a bed of hummus. How many American chefs today of all ethnic origins are serving Moroccan charmoula, Argentinian chimichurri, Scandinavian gravlax, Indonesian satays, and Russian zakuski — not to mention transmogrified Italian risottos, French sauces, and Spanish shellfish stews?

But there's another path. It's an older path but possibly one that leads even more significantly into our lives. Long before an immigrant from Tokyo could arrive here, go to the neighborhood market in New York or San Francisco or Dallas and buy sticky rice for sushi and marinated ginger, immigrants arrived from Canton who could not find oyster sauce and peanut oil. In the late nineteenth century, immigrants arrived from Naples who could not find San

Marzano tomatoes and buffalo-milk mozzarella. These groups wanted to bring their food to America, and the lack of an overarching American gastronomic order made a clear path for them to do so — but how do you make the food of your homeland in 1890 when no food from your home is here? You adapt. The early Chinese-American food, and the early Italian-American food, were not very much like the food of China and the food of Italy. But clever chefs made it similar enough — and in the process invented new cuisines that still stand one hundred years later. Purist foodies sometimes scoff at these cuisines, but I believe that's because they haven't had the opportunity to taste great versions of them. There is no stronger proof of America's uniqueness as a country of "ethnic" gastronomic influences than the way in which egg rolls, spareribs, fortune cookies, pizza, pasta, and minestrone have woven their way into our daily lives, even in our homes.

Italian Food

There's no question about it: the ethnic cuisine that has most significantly penetrated our everyday American habits is the cuisine of Italy. Frankly, nothing else has even come close.

Let's put it this way: it wouldn't be bizarre to call spaghetti, pizza, and lasagna just as American as milk shakes, hot dogs, and hamburgers.

Of course, what we call Italian food in the United States has taken its own course and has veered significantly from food in Italy. Nothing to apologize for there: Italian-American food, when cooked right, is some of the most delicious food in the world.

The intriguing metamorphosis began with the first great wave of immigrants from Italy in the 1880s and 1890s. What emerged from these years was a clearly defined cuisine — Italian-American food — that delighted diners in the United States when it was lovingly prepared, throughout the 1940s, 1950s, 1960s, and into the 1970s.

It did feature more meat than the cuisine that spawned it. In Italy, appetizers and primi (usually pasta) were the first two courses, often meatless. Secondi, or what we'd call the main course, was almost an afterthought: a little bit of simply cooked fish or meat to round out the meal. In Italian-American cooking, meat was likely to appear anywhere in the meal order; meatballs, sausages, and veal cutlets abounded. And the main meat course was no afterthought: I remember going to great "Italian" restaurants in the 1950s where, after the spaghetti with meat sauce, they'd serve a huge platter of steak pizzaiola, good steak in a tomato–and–green pepper sauce.

Lots of sauce, in fact — and therein lies another key difference. Italian cooking in Italy has traditionally called for a little sauce to moisten the main ingredient. Pasta is a great case in point. In Italy you never see a pool of sauce underneath the pasta; the cook adds just enough sauce for it to cling to the pasta and no more. In the United States, saucing is summed up by the word *abbondanza;* more is more to us, and more sauce is surely what you get on your pasta. Purists denounce it — but if the sauce is great, what's wrong with having a lot of it?

Americans, in fact, turn their bowls of pasta into such elaborate affairs that Italian-American cuisine has spawned a whole new use for pasta: as a main course! This was never done in Italy, but here — where sauce, vegetables, meat, cheese, all kinds of things, may accompany the pasta — why not?

Along with these major shifts come a whole host of subsidiary ones. We tend to use a lot more garlic in Italian-American cooking than they do in Italy. Our Italian-American food is a lot more cooked-in, generally speaking, than food in Italy. Oh, there are long-cooked dishes there, to be sure, but the two-minute light and fresh pizza of

Naples becomes a heavier, more cooked-in ten-minute affair in New York; many pasta dishes follow suit. Then comes the cheese; just as Mexican-American cooking features much more melted cheese than Mexican cooking does, so does Italian-American cooking severely up the formàggio ante. So what? That bubbly, flavorful stuff running all over my lasagna, turning into stretchy strings as I raise it to my lips, is delicious! More cheese, more meat . . . and, oh yes, fewer vegetables. I don't suppose you can make a virtue out of that. But I can tell you that never, ever in 1959 after my garlic bread, lobster fra diàvolo, spaghetti with meat sauce, and chicken cacciatore did I ever ask for spinach.

✰ Pre-Bruschetta ✰ Garlic Bread

Garlic bread — that's what going to an Italian-American restaurant meant in 1959. No trendy grill was used for the bread, no infusion of garlic, no fancy or authentic methods. The guy in the kitchen just piled a load of chopped garlic on slices of bread, drizzled olive oil over all, and baked the slices in a hot oven. If you ate the slices with the garlic still on them, you couldn't get close to anyone for three days. But most people knocked the garlic off before eating — and I'm still crazy about the fresh but subtle taste of garlic left behind in that garlic-evacuated bread. You may remember other pre-bruschetta garlic-bread options — such as soaking a whole bread with butter and garlic, wrapping it in foil, and baking it in the oven. But the following version is my best memory of garlic bread in Italian-American innocent paradise.

Yield: 12 slices

1 loaf basic Italian bread
1 cup fruity olive oil
8 tablespoons chopped garlic (about 16 large cloves)

1. Cut bread on a slight diagonal into 12 slices that are each about 1 inch thick; ideally, the slices should also be about 3 inches long and 1½ inches wide. Place slices on a baking pan. Break the surface of each slice with the tip of a spoon in a few spots. Drizzle 2 teaspoons of the olive oil over each slice. Top each slice with a heaping ½ tablespoon of the garlic. Drizzle 2 teaspoons more of the olive oil evenly over each slice. Let bread rest, covered, for 1 to 2 hours.
2. When ready to cook, preheat oven to 425 degrees. When oven is hot, place baking pan in oven, uncovered. Let bread heat until it is warmed through and crunchy around the edges — about 7 to 8 minutes. If you like the bread to be browned on top, pass it for a moment under a hot broiler. Serve immediately.

✰ Postlapsarian Bruschetta ✰ with Parsley, Red Pepper, Olive, and Caper Topping

The paradise of great, simple Italian-American food in U.S. restaurants was lost when the restaurants became ristoranti and garlic bread became bruschetta (pronounced brew-SKET-ta). All right, I've overstated the case. The real problem with bruschetta is the attitude that sometimes comes with it; I have no problems whatsoever with the dish itself! In fact, I really do love the simplicity of the old peasant notion of grilling bread slices, rubbing them with garlic cloves, then dousing the grilled slices with good olive oil. In most American restaurants that serve bruschetta, a topping usually comes with the simply grilled bread (some logical, some baroque). Most common is a topping of chopped tomatoes with basil and garlic. The following topping's a little more complicated but also basic and delicious. If you want real austerity, as I sometimes do . . . just follow the directions for the bread, garlic, and oil and leave out the topping.

Yield: 12 slices

6 smashed and 3 whole garlic cloves
1 cup packed parsley leaves (washed and
        plucked from the stems)
2 cups roasted red bell pepper
        (home roasted or from a jar)
¼ cup capers, drained
1 cup kalamata olives, pitted
1 round loaf country bread, not too dense,
        about 8 to 10 inches in diameter
1 cup extra-virgin olive oil (preferably young
        Tuscan)
Coarse salt

1. Prepare a medium-hot charcoal fire.
2. In a food processor combine the 3 whole garlic cloves (peeled) and the parsley. Process until they are fine. Add the roasted red peppers, capers, and olives and pulse the mixture a few times until it is chunky. Season with salt and pepper to taste. Reserve at room temperature.

3. Cut the middle portion of the round loaf into 6 long slices, each one almost an inch thick. Cut these slices in half, making 12 half slices that are roughly 4 by 3 by 1 inch.
4. When the fire is ready, place the 12 slices over it in a single layer. Cook, turning once, until the outsides of the bread are golden brown (with grill marks, if possible). This should take about 2 minutes per side; check frequently to make sure the bread isn't burning.
5. When the bread slices are done, rub them along the edges with the smashed garlic cloves. You can rub lightly or heavily, depending on your garlic preference — but you will need about 6 smashed cloves to reach all spots. Place the bread slices on a large platter in a single layer. Sprinkle each slice with 2 teaspoons of the olive oil, breaking the surface of the bread lightly with the tip of a spoon to let the oil soak in. Season with coarse salt. Turn the slices over and repeat the oil-and-salt procedure. Top with the parsley–red pepper mixture and serve.

☆ Mozzarella in Carrozza ☆

I'll never forget the first time I saw this dish on a menu at an Italian-American restaurant. The menu read "Mozzarell im Garutz," and I had no idea what this thing was. It was, of course, a phonetic spelling of the dish, written by someone with a healthy Italian-American accent (which tends to soften the *c*'s and drop the final vowels). In the original Italian, it means "mozzarella in a carriage" — the carriage being two slices of white bread that carry the cheese into deep oil. The "garutz" place served it with tomato sauce, as do so many Italian-American restaurants today. But another saucing option has been popular since at least the seventies at more-upscale Italian-American places, the kind that used to be called northern Italian — anchovy and caper sauce. I prefer it. The following version of this sauce is made with cream and white wine; this particular carriage makes a terrific starter for any Italian dinner, in any dialect.

Yield: 6 first-course servings

1½ cups heavy cream
4 anchovies, chopped
1 large garlic clove, minced
2 teaspoons whole capers, plus 1 teaspoon
      minced capers
2 tablespoons dry white wine
6 slices good white bread, each slice about
      ½ inch thick
4 ounces mozzarella cheese, cut into
      ¼-inch slices
4 ounces provolone cheese, cut into ¼-inch slices
Canola oil for deep-frying
4 tablespoons grated Parmigiano-Reggiano
      cheese
3 jumbo eggs, beaten
¾ cup fresh bread crumbs or panko crumbs
      (see sidebar on page 9), crushed with
      your fingers

1. Place the cream, anchovies, garlic, the 1 teaspoon of minced capers, and the white wine in a heavy-bottomed saucepan. Bring to a boil, making sure the cream doesn't rise out of the saucepan. Lower heat and simmer for 25 minutes.

2. Meanwhile, line up 3 slices of the bread on a counter. Divide the mozzarella cheese among the 3 slices, laying the cheese evenly on top of the bread. Leave a thin border of bread showing around the cheese. Do the same with the provolone cheese, laying it on top of the mozzarella. Top each sandwich with another slice of bread, making 3 sandwiches in all. Working all around each sandwich with your fingers, pinch each one closed. Reserve.

3. Place canola oil in wide pot to a depth of about ½ inch. Heat oil to about 350 degrees.

4. While oil is heating, add Parmigiano-Reggiano to eggs in wide, shallow bowl and blend together well. In another wide, shallow bowl place bread crumbs.

5. When oil is ready, dip the sandwiches in the egg mixture. Coat well on all sides and edges. Dip the sandwiches in the bread crumbs. Coat well on all sides and edges. Immerse sandwiches in hot oil (not all at once if the pot isn't wide enough). Cook sandwiches about 2 minutes per side, or until golden brown. Remove sandwiches and drain on paper towels.

6. Finish the sauce: Pass the sauce through a sieve into a clean saucepan and add the remaining 2 teaspoons of whole capers. Keep warm.

7. Assemble: Cut each sandwich in half, diagonally, and cut each half into 2 triangles; you will have 12 triangles. Place 2 triangles on a plate, nestled against each other. Top with a few tablespoons of sauce, including a few capers. Repeat five times and serve immediately.

Bread Crumbs

Many recipes in the Italian-American idiom — and in other cuisines — rely on bread crumbs. As you select your crumbs, you have several options:

1. The option most home chefs choose is the store-bought can of bread crumbs, plain or seasoned. I dislike this option; these crumbs often lead to heavy, pasty coatings without any magic in flavor or texture.

2. The only store-bought crumbs I love are panko crumbs, a Japanese product that you can buy in Asian grocery stores. The crumbs are light, puffy, shot through with air — and when used for coating deep-fried foods, they make miraculously light and crispy exteriors. The only problem with panko crumbs is that their texture in deep-frying is so specifically Japanese; an Italian-American dish, for example, made with panko crumbs won't seem traditional. I have, however, found a way around this: if you crush the panko crumbs between your fingers, you'll get less of that frilly Japanese feel. The result when you use these crushed panko crumbs is much closer to the results of using regular crumbs — and much, much better than using any other store-bought crumbs.

3. The best option of all, in my opinion, for most dishes — unless you're trying to get that frilly panko coating — is to make your own bread crumbs at home. Here's a great recipe that's very easy to do.

Homemade Bread Crumbs

Yield: About 4½ cups

1 (1-pound) loaf Italian bread

1. Preheat oven to 300 degrees.
2. Cut bread (with the crust on) into 1-inch cubes and lay them in a single layer on 2 large sheet pans. Bake for 30 minutes. Turn oven off but do not remove sheet pans. Leave bread cubes in oven for 1 hour more. Remove from oven and let them sit until dried out (about 3 hours).
3. Working in batches, place crumbs in work bowl of food processor. Process until fine. Use soon, or wrap tightly and freeze.

✩ Deep-Fried Calamari, ✩ Checkered-Tablecloth Style

Once an exotic Little Italy treat, deep-fried squid with spicy tomato sauce has taken off in all kinds of Italian and quasi-Italian restaurants around the country. But the quality problems are still the same: it isn't easy to fry this thing perfectly. Sometimes the finished product is oily; sometimes it's dry; sometimes it's heavy or bready. Add to that the additional peril of tough, rubbery squid. The following recipe should solve all these problems: By avoiding bread crumbs and using only a bubbly froth of flour and club soda, you will make the lightest, most elegant fried calamari imaginable. By cooking it very quickly in hot oil (375 degrees), you will likely avoid the "rubbery" problem (and using fresh, not frozen, squid also helps). The high heat has another virtue: it brings out an additional flavor dimension in squid, something bordering on an attractive cheesiness. Lastly, I would urge you to avoid pouring the tomato sauce over the delicate fried squid before serving it; this will obviously deflate the crunch. It's much better to dip the cephalopod morsels into the sauce just before poppin' them into your mouth.

Yield: 4 first-course servings

*Vegetable oil for deep-frying (such as
    canola)*
¾ cup all-purpose flour
¾ teaspoon salt
1 cup plus 2 tablespoons club soda
*1 pound cleaned, very fresh, medium-size
    squid, including tentacles*
*2 cups marinara sauce (I like the
    Longer-Cooked, Very Garlicky
    Marinara Sauce on page 11)*
1 to 3 teaspoons crushed red pepper

1. Place the vegetable oil in an appropriate vessel for deep-frying, making sure the oil's at least 2 inches deep. Heat to 375 degrees.

2. Place the flour and salt in a large bowl. Working with a fork, slowly stir in the club soda. Do not overmix; the flour and club soda should be just blended into a medium-thick batter.

3. Cut the squid bodies into rings about ⅓ inch wide; leave the tentacles as they are (unless they're very large). When the oil is at the proper temperature, dip the pieces of squid into the batter with a fork, let drip over the batter bowl for a moment, then immerse the squid in the oil. You will need to work in batches, because adding too much squid all at once will lower the temperature of the oil. The pieces of squid are done when they turn golden brown; this should take no more than 1 to 2 minutes.

4. While the squid are cooking, place the marinara sauce in a saucepan and add the desired amount of crushed red pepper. Heat and serve as a dip for fried calamari.

☆ Italian Baked Clams ☆

One of the great Italian-American restaurant treats can be baked clams — but so often this dish comes to the table with fatal problems. More often than not, the clams are rubbery. And more often than not, the breading is unattractively dense, with nary a lick of clam flavor. The following recipe rectifies all. By chopping the clams and cooking them quickly, you help them to retain the more pleasing texture of raw clams. And by covering them with a thin mantle of homemade bread crumbs, you avoid the gunky quality that usually comes with the territory. To my taste, the benefits are maximized when you cook the clams very quickly indeed; after just two minutes under the broiler, the clams are still slightly raw, brimming with flavor. For me — perfect! You may like them cooked a little more or, if your broiler's weak, they may need additional time. It all depends on your broiler and your taste.

Yield: 36 baked clams, enough for
6 first-course servings

1 cup Homemade Bread Crumbs (page 9)
¼ cup finely grated Parmigiano-Reggiano cheese
¼ cup finely minced parsley leaves
4 large garlic cloves, finely minced
3 tablespoons extra-virgin olive oil
*36 cherrystone clams (each about
    2½ inches across)*
*4½ teaspoons fresh lemon juice,
    plus lemon wedges for garnish,
    if desired*
*6 tablespoons (¾ stick) unsalted butter,
    melted*

1. Combine the bread crumbs, Parmigiano-Reggiano, parsley, garlic, and olive oil in a bowl. Season to taste with salt and pepper. Reserve.

2. Scrub the clams under running cold water. Shuck each one with a clam knife, reserving clam juice for another use. Reserve 36 half shells. Chop the meat of each clam into 8 pieces and put in a small bowl. Toss with the lemon juice.

3. Divide the chopped clams evenly among the 36 reserved shells. Top each shell with 2 teaspoons of the bread crumb–cheese mixture. Then drizzle the butter evenly over the crumbs, about ½ teaspoon of butter per clam. Pat down lightly with your fingers.

4. Place clams on a sheet pan and cook under a broiler until breading is golden brown. If the clams are too close to the broiler, the crumbs will brown before the clams get cooked. If they're too far away, the clams may cook too much before the crumbs brown. Experiment and find the perfect distance from your broiler. In mine, they take about 2 minutes to cook and brown perfectly. Serve with lemon wedges, if desired.

☆ Quick Marinara Sauce ☆

It is possible to find something called marinara sauce in Italy — but it isn't easy. It's another story on this side of the pond; every checkered-tablecloth Italian restaurant has marinara sauce on the menu. The great thing about the Italian-American version is that it's so quick and easy to make; it has to be a short-cooked sauce or it will have a totally different flavor. Why open a can of sauce when you can have something so much better with little effort and in practically the same amount of time? There's one more advantage to the following recipe: it freezes well, so you might want to double or triple it and stock up.

Yield: 2 to 3 cups

3 tablespoons olive oil
2 large garlic cloves, chopped
½ teaspoon dried oregano
⅛ teaspoon red pepper flakes
3 (14½-ounce) cans plum tomatoes
2 tablespoons chopped parsley
½ teaspoon red wine vinegar
½ teaspoon sugar

1. In a saucepan, heat olive oil over low heat. Add the garlic, oregano, and red pepper flakes, stirring until garlic just begins to color.

2. Remove tomatoes from can and squeeze them into coarse chunks with your hands. Reserve the squeezed-out liquid and the liquid from the can. Place tomato chunks in saucepan. Add parsley, vinegar, and sugar. Bring to a boil, reduce heat, and simmer uncovered until thickened, about 20 to 30 minutes.

3. If you'd like a thinner sauce, add some tomato liquid. If you'd like a thicker sauce, add some tomato paste. If you'd like a smoother sauce, run sauce through a food mill or process with a hand blender. Season to taste with salt and pepper.

☆ Longer-Cooked, ☆ Very Garlicky Marinara Sauce

If you cook marinara sauce a little longer, you lose the bright tomato taste. But if you make up for that by adding a megadose of garlic . . . the results are delicious!

The following is a version of the sauce developed at Trio's Ravioli Shoppe in Boston.

☆☆☆

Yield: About 9 cups

¾ cup olive oil
¾ cup finely minced garlic
2 (28-ounce) cans tomatoes in tomato puree
6 cups water
2 tablespoons chopped fresh basil
1 tablespoon minced fresh parsley
1½ tablespoons sugar
2 teaspoons salt
1 teaspoon freshly ground pepper

1. Place the olive oil in a large, heavy pot over medium-high heat. Add the garlic and sauté, stirring occasionally, until it's lightly golden. 2. Add the contents of the tomato cans, juice and all, squeezing the tomatoes with your hands to break them up as you drop them into the pot. Add the water, basil, parsley, sugar, salt, and pepper. Bring to a boil, then lower heat and simmer, stirring occasionally, for 45 minutes. Serve immediately, or freeze for future use.

☆ All-Purpose Bright Red ☆ Tomato Sauce

This sunny, good-natured tomato sauce has neither the fresh, chunky impact of the marinara sauces nor the depth of the long-cooked Four-Hour Epic Sauce. It is easy to make and works well in almost any recipe that calls for a tomato sauce. You could well make it the workhorse of your Italian-American kitchen. Incidentally, if you'd like a smoother, more pureed workhorse, simply whizz this sauce in the food processor for a few seconds.

Yield: Approximately 5 cups

¼ cup olive oil
1½ cups finely chopped onion
1 tablespoon very finely chopped garlic
1 (35-ounce) can Italian tomatoes, undrained
1 (6-ounce) can tomato paste
¼ cup chopped fresh basil
2 tablespoons chopped parsley
1 tablespoon salt
1 tablespoon sugar
1½ teaspoons dried oregano
½ teaspoon pepper
1½ cups water

In a large saucepan, heat olive oil over medium heat. Sauté onion and garlic 5 minutes. Put tomatoes in a food processor and pulse on and off for a few seconds. Leave chunky. Add to saucepan along with the tomato paste and all remaining ingredients and bring to a boil. Reduce heat, cover mixture, and simmer, stirring occasionally, for 1 hour.

☆ The Four-Hour Epic Sauce: ☆ Grandma's Long-Cooked Tomato Gravy

When I was growing up, all my Italian friends had grandmas who'd spend all day making tomato sauce — or what many of my friends called gravy. The name confused me, since gravy, to me, was a brown thing, not a red thing. But there was no confusing that Italian-American gravy taste: deep, sweet, subtle, evocative, like something from another century. I didn't have one of those grandmothers. Worse, I have trouble today finding an Italian-American restaurant that pays homage to that kind of grandma and takes the time to make an old-fashioned gravy like hers. But if you have the time to throw some tomatoes and bones together in a pot — having something meaty in the sauce is what officially makes it "gravy" — you will be delighted by the atavistic wonder of the following recipe. I make huge quantities of it, freeze it, and use it as my basic tomato sauce. It's fabulous just by itself on pasta (simply heaven on macaroni with lots of grated pecorino Romano cheese) or as a building block in any meat-friendly dish that calls for tomato sauce as an ingredient. I love the romantic notion of Grandma cooking all day in the kitchen. Truth is . . . this particular recipe (and I've cooked it as long as seven hours!) tastes best to me at three and one-half to four hours of simmering. At that point it's on the cusp between a tomato sauce and a meat sauce and it's still runny. As you increase the cooking time, it becomes a thick meat sauce — and finally, at about seven hours, an incredible thing that's practically a meat stew. I'm going with the four-hour sauce.

Yield: About 4 quarts

½ cup olive oil
½ cup finely minced garlic
3 pounds onions, peeled and finely minced
3 medium-large carrots, peeled and
    finely minced
3 large stalks celery, finely minced
5 (28-ounce) cans whole tomatoes
4 (6-ounce) cans tomato paste
1 cup shredded fresh basil leaves,
    firmly packed
2 tablespoons dried oregano
Sugar
12 cups water

5 pounds beef bones (I like to use some marrow
    bones)
5 pounds meaty pork bones (I like to use about
    a pound of pig's feet as part of the mix)
½ pound piece of rind from pecorino Romano
    cheese

1. Place the olive oil in a very large stockpot over high heat. Add the garlic and onions and sauté, stirring occasionally, for 7 minutes. Add the carrots and celery and sauté, stirring occasionally, for another 5 minutes.

2. Pour the tomatoes and their juices into the stockpot. Add the tomato paste, basil, and oregano. Taste for sweetness; if the sauce seems a little tart, adjust with sugar (I usually add about 1 tablespoon). Add water. Bring sauce to a simmer.

3. Add the beef bones, pork bones, and pecorino Romano rind. Stir well. Keep sauce at an active simmer for 3½ to 4 hours, stirring occasionally. The sauce is done when it's medium-thick but runny, and when you like the balance of tomato and meat flavors. If it's too thin at 4 hours, raise the heat and reduce the sauce a bit.

4. When the sauce is done, let it rest in the pot until it cools off slightly. Then remove most of the dark red oil swimming on top. Discard.

5. Place the sauce in a large roasting pan. You may need several roasting pans, or you may need to do this in a few batches. When the sauce is cool enough, run your hands through the sauce, picking out and discarding any bones that you find. Use the sauce immediately, or freeze for future use.

☆ Classic Brooklyn-Italian ☆ Meat Sauce

If the previous sauce is a slightly meaty tomato sauce, this one is a slightly tomatoey meat sauce. There's nothing all-purpose about it: you serve it on pasta when you want a few ladlefuls of liquid meat! It is exactly what I grew up with in Brooklyn, when the choice at most Italian restaurants for spaghetti sauce was either tomato sauce or meat sauce. Later we all learned that this meat sauce has its roots in the renowned Bolognese ragú. But you'd never mistake one for the other. The ancestor from Bologna has a mix of meats in it (sometimes including chicken liver), and much less meat. This Brooklyn-Italian meat sauce has tons of ground beef alone — and, after an hour or so of cooking, a surprising amount of wonderful, hearty flavor.

Yield: About 3 quarts

> 2 tablespoons olive oil
> ½ cup finely minced garlic
> ½ pound onions, peeled and
>   finely minced
> 1 carrot, peeled and finely minced
> 1 stalk celery, finely minced
> 3 pounds ground beef
> Salt
> 2 (28-ounce) cans tomatoes in juice
> 1 (6-ounce) can tomato paste
> 1 teaspoon sugar
> 2 tablespoons dried oregano

1. Place the olive oil in a large, heavy Dutch oven over medium-high heat. Add the garlic and onions and sauté, stirring occasionally, for 5 minutes. Add the carrot and celery and sauté, stirring occasionally, for another 5 minutes.

2. Push vegetables to one side of the pot and add about one-third of the ground beef. Salt the beef to taste. Cook until starting to brown, about 3 to 5 minutes. Stir the beef occasionally, breaking it up as you do. Push it to the side (or over the vegetables) and repeat with the second third of the beef. After that starts to brown, push it aside and repeat with the remainder of the beef. When all the beef is done, mix the beef and vegetables together.

3. Add the tomatoes with their juice to the pot. Add the tomato paste, sugar, and oregano. Mix well. Simmer for 1½ hours, stirring occasionally, breaking up the tomatoes against the side of the pot as you do.

4. When the sauce is done cooking, season to taste with salt and pepper. Serve immediately, or freeze.

☆ Minestrone ☆

For many decades this great vegetable soup — a specialty of Liguria — has been the headliner soup in Italian-American restaurants, and has been simmering in the pot of many an Italian-American grandma. There are many, many forms of it — both there and here — but the American minestrone most typically includes tomatoes, beans, cabbage, and small pasta. The following version — one of the most haunting and delicious I've ever had anywhere — owes its success to the inclusion of a rind (just the outer part) of Parmigiano-Reggiano in the soup pot (which deepens the flavor immeasurably) and a last-minute swirl of basil, garlic, and oil (sort of a thin pesto, recalling both Liguria and the pistou that's swirled into a similar soup in the south of France).

Yield: 6 servings

1 cup good-quality extra-virgin
olive oil

1 medium leek, pale green and white parts
only, split, washed, and sliced ½
inch thick (about ⅔ cup)

1 small onion, cut into ½-inch pieces
(about ½ cup)

2 small carrots, peeled and cut into
½-inch pieces (about ⅔ cup)

1 small russet potato, peeled and cut into
½-inch pieces (about ¾ cup)

1 small zucchini, cut into ½-inch pieces
(about ⅔ cup)

6 large garlic cloves, minced,
plus 2 large garlic cloves, minced

4 tablespoons tomato paste

1 small head escarole, washed and
chopped coarsely (about 2½ cups,
loosely packed)

½ small head savoy cabbage, cored and
chopped coarsely (about 4 cups,
loosely packed)

1 (28-ounce) can tomatoes, drained
and chopped coarsely

5 cups chicken stock

5 cups water

1 rind of Parmigiano-Reggiano cheese
(about 5 by 5 inches)

1 cup firmly packed fresh
basil leaves, rinsed, dried,
and finely chopped

¾ cup ditalini or small elbow macaroni or
other small pasta shape

1 (14-ounce) can navy or cannellini beans,
drained and rinsed

3 ounces Parmigiano-Reggiano cheese

1. Place ½ cup of the olive oil in a large stockpot over high heat. Add the leek, onion, carrots, potato, zucchini, and the 6 minced garlic cloves. Cook without stirring for about 4 minutes to allow the vegetables to begin browning. Reduce the heat to medium-high and continue cooking, stirring occasionally, until the edges of the vegetables have begun to turn golden, reducing the heat if the vegetables threaten to burn, about 5 to 6 minutes more. Add the tomato paste and cook for an additional 2 minutes, stirring regularly. Add the escarole, cabbage, tomatoes, chicken stock, water, and cheese rind and bring to a boil over high heat. Taste for seasoning (if your chicken stock is not salty, you may need as much as 2 teaspoons of salt). Reduce heat to a bare simmer and cook for 45 minutes, stirring occasionally.

2. Meanwhile, in a small bowl, combine the remaining 2 minced garlic cloves, the remaining ½ cup of olive oil, and the basil. Blend well. Cover with plastic wrap and set aside.

3. After the soup has cooked for 45 minutes, stir in the small pasta and cook for 5 minutes. Stir in the beans. Taste the broth and adjust the seasoning with salt. When the pasta is just cooked through, ladle the soup into large bowls and garnish each serving with a heaping tablespoon of basil-garlic oil, dribbled over the entire surface. Grate a tablespoon of Parmigiano-Reggiano cheese in the center of each bowl and serve, passing the grater with the remaining cheese at the table.

☆ Pesto ☆

Pesto played a big role in the modern evolution of Italian food in America: in the 1970s it was one of the "new" dishes from Italy that pointed the way to life beyond red sauce. But the typical American version is one of the few Italian-American transplants that I'm not so crazy about. Why? Because we often use large, bitter leaves of basil — not the sweet little guys they use in Liguria, on pesto's home turf. We also usually overpower it with garlic. Then we overpower the pasta with the pesto, serving way too much thick pesto per strand. In Liguria, to prevent that, they water the pesto down with water from the pasta pot! The following recipe is an attempt to clear up some of the usual problems — but for the best possible pesto, please don't make it unless you have lovely, in-season basil. For those off-season needs: pesto freezes well, as long as you freeze it before you've added cheese to it; when you defrost it, add the cheese then.

Yield: 1 cup

7 tablespoons fruity olive oil
1 tablespoon minced garlic
2 tablespoons pine nuts
1½ cups very firmly packed washed and
    dried basil leaves
4 teaspoons firmly packed grated
    Parmigiano-Reggiano cheese

1. Place 1 tablespoon of the olive oil in a small, heavy skillet over medium heat. Add the garlic and sauté for 30 seconds. Place the garlic in the work bowl of a food processor. Turn heat under the skillet to high and add the pine nuts. Sauté for a minute or so, just until they begin to color. Place pine nuts in the food processor.

2. Add the basil to the food processor and process for 10 seconds. With the motor running, quickly pour the remaining 6 tablespoons of olive oil through the feed tube, over the course of 5 seconds or so. The mixture should be a bright green, not entirely smooth puree.

3. Transfer the pesto to a bowl. Add Parmigiano-Reggiano cheese and stir in with a fork. Add salt to taste.

NOTE: Pesto is great on pasta, but it's a good idea to thin it with a little hot water from the pasta pot. Also keep in mind that cold or room-temperature pesto makes a superb condiment; if you have, for example, fresh tomatoes and fresh mozzarella, they would love to meet a little of your pesto.

☆ Linguine ☆ with White Clam Sauce

The combination of dried pasta and clams is a staple all over southern Italy. But the dish is usually different from what we see here in two significant ways. First of all, though Italian-American restaurants almost always choose linguine for clam sauce, in Italy you are much more likely to be served spaghetti with clam sauce; the Italians claim it holds the sauce better, and they may be right (you may substitute spaghetti for linguine in the following recipe if you wish to test the theory yourself). Second, they don't make the distinction, as we do, between white clam sauce and red clam sauce. In Italy you simply order "spaghetti con vongole" and out comes a bowl of pasta with clams, oil, garlic, and a few pieces of tomato tossed in; the standard spaghetti with clam sauce of Italy is somewhere between red and white. I love it there — but I'm also nuts about the clamlike, saline purity of the classic Italian-American white clam sauce. The following recipe captures that quality perfectly; it is a feast for clam lovers.

Yield: 4 servings

⅔ cup plus 2 tablespoons olive oil
½ cup thinly sliced garlic plus 2 heaping
    tablespoons minced garlic
24 large cherrystone clams (or a few more,
    if necessary; see Note)
12 ounces linguine
4 teaspoons finely minced parsley

1. Place the 2 tablespoons of olive oil in a large, nonreactive sauté pan over medium-high heat. Add the 2 tablespoons of minced garlic and sauté, stirring occasionally, until the garlic is light golden brown (about 2 minutes). Remove garlic and reserve at room temperature. Spill oil out of pan and wipe clean with a dry paper towel.

2. Return pan to medium heat. Add the ⅔ cup of olive oil and the ½ cup of sliced garlic. Sauté, stirring occasionally, until the garlic is just starting to color (about 3 minutes). Remove pan from heat and reserve, covered, at room temperature, for at least 4 hours (and no more than 8 hours).

3. Either ask your fishmonger to shuck the clams for you, reserving the juice, or shuck them yourself. Cut the clam bellies into coarse chunks (about 3 pieces per belly). When done, you should have about 2 cups of fresh clam juice and about 1⅓ cups of minced clams. You will need all the clams and 1½ cups of the clam juice. If you have

less, you must make up the difference by shucking a few more clams.

4. When ready to cook, bring a large pot of salted water to the boil. Add the linguine and cook until al dente, about 8 to 9 minutes.

5. Toward the end of the linguine cooking time, place the reserved pan of olive oil with the thinly sliced garlic over medium-high heat. As soon as it starts to sizzle, add 1½ cups of the fresh clam juice (reserve the rest for another use). Whisk it together with the oil, bring almost to a boil, then turn heat off.

6. When the linguine is done, drain it in a colander. Return it to the pasta cooking pot over medium-high heat, along with the 1⅓

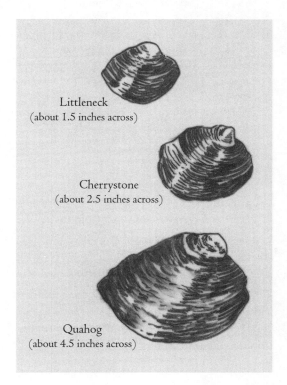

Littleneck
(about 1.5 inches across)

Cherrystone
(about 2.5 inches across)

Quahog
(about 4.5 inches across)

Whole Clams in Your Bowl?

Some restaurants and cooks like to serve whole clams, in their shells, in the bowl of linguine. It certainly looks pretty and festive. But it has been my experience that when you steam open the most widely available clams — littlenecks or cherrystones — they get rubbery very fast. That's why I choose to chop them up and cook them very, very briefly just with the rewarming pasta.

However, if you can find Pacific clams — either Manilla clams or New Zealand cockles, both of which have come into our markets — you can steam them open, because they don't toughen up. I like to put about two dozen of them in a wide, heavy pot, douse them with one-half cup of water or so, bring them to a boil — keeping them covered — and remove the clams from the pot as soon as they open (you can lift the lid to peek). Then you can divide them among the four bowls. They make a lovely garnish.

cups of minced clams. Toss in the pot for 1 minute. Add the hot clam juice with oil and garlic and toss for 1 minute more. Divide the linguine with white clam sauce among four wide, shallow bowls, making sure the pasta, clams, and sauce are divided evenly. Sprinkle each bowl with a quarter of the reserved minced garlic and 1 teaspoon of the minced parsley. Serve immediately.

NOTE: Though this recipe calls for twenty-four cherrystone clams, the really important ingredients are the one and one-third cups of coarsely chopped clams and the one and one-half cups of fresh clam juice. I specify twenty-four cherrystones because I know that they will usually yield what you need. But if you have access only to smaller or larger clams, don't hesitate to use those — as long as you extract the required quantity of coarsely chopped clams and fresh clam juice. If you do not have access to fresh clams — only to canned clams and bottled clam juice — you can still make this dish using the same proportions of meat and juice. It just won't have the same level of sea-bright flavor.

✻ Linguine ✻ with Red Clam Sauce

Italian-American Red Clam Sauce has its charms too. To the disappointment of some clam freaks, it is typically less clammy, less salty, and sometimes less oily than White Clam Sauce. But the consolation is the comfort of tomatoes and basil, those old friends, helping the clams along. If you're not a fanatic clam lover but would like an exotic twist on tomato sauce, this could be the clam sauce for you.

Yield: 4 servings

24 cherrystone clams (or a few more,
　　　if necessary; see Note this page)
12 ounces linguine
6 tablespoons olive oil
½ cup thinly sliced garlic
1 (28-ounce) can whole tomatoes
4 tablespoons tomato paste
½ cup shredded fresh basil
4 teaspoons minced parsley

1. Either ask your fishmonger to shuck the clams for you, reserving the juice, or shuck them yourself. Cut the clam bellies into

coarse chunks (about 3 pieces per belly). When done, you should have about 2 cups of fresh clam juice and about 1⅓ cups of minced clams. You will need all the clams and 1 cup of the clam juice. If you have less, you must make up the difference by shucking a few more clams.

2. Place the linguine in a large pot of boiling, salted water. Cook until the pasta is al dente, about 8 to 9 minutes.

3. While the pasta is cooking, place 4 tablespoons of the olive oil in a wide saucepan over medium-high heat. Add the garlic and sauté, stirring occasionally, until the garlic is golden brown, about 3 minutes. Immediately start adding tomatoes by crushing each one in your hands over the saucepan; let the tomato and its juice fall into the pan. Do not use the tomato liquid left in the can. When all the tomatoes are added, stir in the tomato paste, blending well. Simmer for 2 minutes. If the pasta's not ready, remove tomato sauce from heat.

4. When the linguine is ready, drain it in a colander. Pour the 1 cup of clam juice into the tomato mixture over high heat. Add the basil. Place the empty pasta cooking pot over medium-high heat and add the remaining 2 tablespoons of olive oil. Add the 1⅓ cups of clams. Cook for 30 seconds, stirring. Return the pasta to the pasta pot, stirring to mix in the clams, about 30 seconds. Now add the tomato–clam juice mixture to the pasta, stirring well to mix everything together. Cook for 1 minute. Divide among four wide, shallow bowls. Sprinkle 1 teaspoon of parsley over each and serve immediately.

✸ Ravioli ✸

Ravioli is one of those rare dishes that — at least in its classic form — are not so different in Italy from their U.S. version. Cheese-filled ravioli and meat-filled ravioli are common in Italia, as is a tomato sauce to surround them; here, of course, they are practically emblematic of Italian-American food. The only problem is that ravioli, here, got trivialized over the years. Probably a high percentage of Americans first had it out of a can. A later generation first had it out of the freezer. Today, if home cooks are going to make it, there's a high probability that they'll buy premade, unsauced, frozen ravioli and boil them up at home. This is the main difference between the two countries: in Italy, freshness still rules. So why not turn the clock back to the way things were when Italians first arrived here — pre-Chef Boyardee (an actual Cleveland resident named Boiardi) — and work your way through the following wonderful from-scratch recipes that result in steaming, magnificent bowls of ravioli?

★ Pasta Dough for Ravioli ★

You could, of course, just buy sheets of fresh pasta dough, roll them out, and personalize them with your own filling. But if you feel like going all the way with ravioli, this is a great and simple recipe for the dough. All you need is a pasta machine. . . .

Yield: Enough dough for
4 to 5 dozen ravioli, 6 servings

2 cups all-purpose flour
2 large eggs
½ tablespoon milk (or water)
¼ teaspoon salt

1. Place the flour in a large bowl and create a well in the center of the flour. In a small bowl, mix eggs, milk, and salt with a fork until egg is well beaten.

2. Pour egg mixture into flour well. With a fork, bring flour into the well a little at a time until a sticky dough is formed (there will still be a lot of flour left around the well). Remove the sticky dough from the center of the bowl and place on a floured counter. Knead dough, adding more of the flour from the bowl as needed, until the dough is very smooth and elastic, about 10 minutes. Wrap in plastic wrap and refrigerate for at least 30 minutes before rolling.

3. To roll, set pasta machine at the widest setting. Divide dough into 4 pieces; keep unrolled pieces covered with a kitchen towel as you roll. Take the first piece, flour it lightly, and roll through the first setting. You will have a quasi rectangle. Lay it on the counter left to right. Picking up the dough on the left, fold one-third of it toward the right onto half the remaining dough. Picking up the dough on the right, fold one-third toward the left, overlapping the double-layered remaining dough. (You are folding the dough like a letter.) You will now have a piece of dough with two sides closed and two ends open. Feed the dough back into the machine, feeding an open end first. Repeat three more times on this setting, folding the pasta like a letter each time it comes out.

4. Now you want to roll the sheet of pasta through all the remaining settings on the machine. On each setting (except the last one) you roll the pasta through twice, without folding the pasta between the roll-throughs. Keep working through all the settings, ratcheting down each time, until you have rolled through the next-to-last setting. Then roll the dough through the last setting one time only. Your finished sheet will be a long quasi rectangle, probably about 6 inches wide. Repeat with the three remaining pieces of pasta. As strips are finished, cover with plastic wrap.

★ Cheese Filling for Ravioli ★

Yield: Enough for 1 batch of pasta dough

1 pound good-quality whole-milk ricotta cheese
1 cup grated Parmigiano-Reggiano cheese
1 large egg
2 tablespoons finely chopped parsley
2 tablespoons fresh bread crumbs
1 tablespoon fresh lemon juice
⅛ teaspoon grated nutmeg

Combine all ingredients in a bowl, blending well. Season to taste with salt and freshly ground black pepper.

NOTE: If a good-quality "homemade" style ricotta is not available, you can use a standard brand — but drain it overnight in a cheesecloth-lined strainer to remove excess liquid.

★ Meat Filling for Ravioli ★

This recipe has to be made in quantities that make enough filling for two batches of pasta dough. But do not double the pasta dough recipe on page 20, as it will be too difficult to knead. So . . . you can either make two single recipes of pasta dough and use all the meat filling (which will yield eight to ten dozen freezable ravioli), or you can freeze half the meat filling for next time. I love the deep, mysterious flavor of this filling; the wide range of ingredients gives you great layers of flavor. I also love the slightly soft texture; the filling, with its old-fashioned grinding of the meat in a grinder, or by hand, is a big improvement over fillings that start with store-bought ground meat. You have the option of using spinach in this filling: if you do, the filling will be lighter but a little less meaty tasting.

Yield: Enough for 2 batches of pasta dough

2 tablespoons olive oil
½ pound beef stew meat
½ pound veal stew meat
½ pound veal bones
1 small onion, peeled and quartered
1 small carrot, scraped and
    coarsely chopped
2 garlic cloves, crushed and peeled
1 bay leaf
½ cup white wine
1½ cups chicken stock
⅛ pound chicken livers
2 thin slices prosciutto
2 thin slices mortadella

¾ cup grated Parmigiano-Reggiano cheese
½ cup cooked, well-drained, chopped fresh spinach
    (optional; frozen, thawed spinach is fine)
1 egg yolk
⅛ teaspoon ground nutmeg

I. In a Dutch oven, heat olive oil over medium-high heat. Add beef and veal in small batches, browning evenly on all sides. Remove meat and reserve. Add bones, onion, carrot, garlic, and bay leaf. Sauté for 5 minutes, stirring occasionally. Add wine, bring to a boil, and boil until wine is reduced by half. Return meat to pot and add chicken stock. Cover and simmer until meat is tender, about I to I½ hours. Add chicken livers and simmer about 5 minutes more, or until livers are just cooked. Strain broth, reserve meats and livers, discard remaining solids. Degrease stock and reserve.

2. Using a meat grinder, grind reserved meats and then livers through coarsest setting into

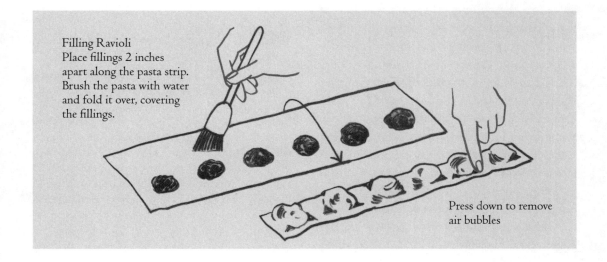

Filling Ravioli
Place fillings 2 inches apart along the pasta strip. Brush the pasta with water and fold it over, covering the fillings.

Press down to remove air bubbles

a large bowl. Grind prosciutto and mortadella. (Alternatively, you could chop all the meats by hand.) To the bowl, add the cheese, spinach (if using), egg yolk, and nutmeg. Mix well. Add reserved stock a few tablespoons at a time until mixture holds together when pressed in the palm of your hand (you'll probably need about ¼ cup to ½ cup broth). Season to taste with salt and pepper.

★ Final Preparation of Ravioli ★ (Cheese or Meat) with Tomato Sauce

Yield: 4 to 5 dozen ravioli, 6 servings

1 batch pasta dough for ravioli
(4 rolled-out strips)
1 batch cheese filling or ½ batch meat filling
3 cups Four-Hour Epic Sauce (page 12),
heated in large pot
Grated Parmigiano-Reggiano cheese (optional)

1. To fill ravioli, lay out 1 of the 4 pasta strips on the counter, the long way left to right. Place about 2 teaspoons of filling from left to right at 2-inch intervals on the strip of pasta, placing them at a spot about a quarter of the way from the lower margin of the pasta strip to the top margin of the pasta strip. Using your fingers or a pastry brush, paint around the fillings with water. Working from the top margin to the bottom margin (toward you), fold over remaining pasta, pressing down to remove air bubbles from around filling. Make sure you don't press on the fillings themselves. Press down on the edge to seal. Cut into square ravioli, making sure the cut edges are sealed. Place on a floured sheet pan while you proceed with the remaining 3 pieces of dough.

2. Bring a large pot of salted water to a boil. Immerse ravioli in the water. Cover pot and bring water back to a gentle boil as quickly as possible, checking to make sure the ravioli are not sticking to each other or to the sides of the pot. As soon as water comes back to a gentle boil, remove cover. Continue boiling gently until the pasta is just cooked through, about 4 minutes.

3. Pour the contents of the pot into a large colander, draining the water. Toss ravioli in colander to shake off moisture. Toss very well.

4. Place heated tomato sauce into pasta pot over medium-high heat. Add ravioli and toss in sauce for 30 seconds. Serve immediately as is, or blend in the grated Parmigiano-Reggiano to taste.

⁂ Saint Louis Toasted Ravioli ⁂

One of America's great Italian communities is on the Hill in Saint Louis — and this very particular ravioli dish, unlike anything made in Italy, is one of the specialties there. "Toasted" is misleading — the ravioli are actually coated in flour, eggs, and bread crumbs and deep-fried. Sauce is served on the side, for dipping. If you've never had them, you must try them! They are wonderful, large, golden, toasty-crisp pillows that puff up with big air pockets during the frying. The flavor interaction between the fried pasta dough and the filling inside is surprising and delicious.

Yield: 4 appetizer portions

2 dozen meat- or cheese-filled ravioli,
    uncooked
1 cup all-purpose flour
2 large eggs, beaten with 1 tablespoon water
1 cup fresh bread crumbs
2 tablespoons grated Parmesan cheese
Vegetable oil for frying
1½ cups marinara sauce for dipping

1. Bring a large pot of salted water to a boil. Add ravioli and quickly bring back to a simmer. Simmer for 2 minutes more. Drain and rinse under cold water. Pat dry.

2. In three separate bowls, place flour, eggs, and bread crumbs. Mix the cheese into bread crumbs. Season each bowl with a little salt and pepper. Heat about 2 inches of oil to 365 degrees in a large pot.

3. Dredge each ravioli in flour, then egg, then bread crumbs. Place on a sheet pan. Fry in small batches (about 6 per batch) for about 3 minutes, or until golden brown. Drain on paper towels. Serve with warm marinara sauce on the side for dipping.

✯ Baked Manicotti with ✯ Cheese Filling and Tomato Sauce

This casserole classic appears to be a purely Italian-American invention. But there are two ways of making it in America. Much more common, especially these days, is a casserole of dried pasta tubes stuffed with cheese. But old-timers prefer to stuff the cheese into homemade crepes, yielding a lighter, more delicate dish. I like it better that way. Moreover, the crepes make more sense of one theory explaining the dish's name: some say *manicotti* has something to do with "cooked hands," which apparently got burned during the making of the crepes in a hot pan. Others insist that the name comes from the Latin word *manica*, which means "sleeves" — and could describe either the dried-pasta tube or the crepe. Whichever way you make it, I prefer to remove the cooked sleeves from the casserole at the end of cooking, place them on individual plates, sprinkle extra cheese on top, and pass them under the broiler until they're bubbly brown.

Yield: Approximately
24 manicotti, 8 servings

8 large eggs, at room temperature
1½ cups unsifted all-purpose flour
1¼ teaspoons salt
1½ cups water
2 pounds ricotta cheese
8 ounces commercial mozzarella cheese, grated
1 cup grated Parmigiano-Reggiano cheese
¼ teaspoon pepper
2 tablespoons finely chopped parsley
About 5 cups tomato sauce (I prefer the
    All-Purpose Bright Red Tomato Sauce
    on page 12)
4 cups assorted grated cheeses for melting
    (see Note)

1. Make manicotti crepes: Combine 6 of the eggs, the flour, ¼ teaspoon of the salt, and the water in a large bowl. Using an electric hand mixer or egg beater, beat just until smooth. Let stand ½ hour or longer.

2. Heat an 8-inch nonstick skillet over medium heat. Pour in 3 tablespoons batter. Tilt the skillet quickly to cover the bottom of the

pan. Cook for about 1 minute. The edges will start to pull away from the pan. With a fork, loosen an edge and flip the crepe over using your fingers. After a few seconds, remove to a plate. Continue cooking manicotti crepes and stacking them between pieces of waxed paper. They can be made a day in advance and kept in the refrigerator, covered.

3. Make the filling: In a large bowl, beat the remaining 2 eggs. Add and combine the ricotta, mozzarella, ½ cup of the Parmigiano-Reggiano, the remaining 1 teaspoon of salt, pepper, and parsley.

4. Preheat oven to 350 degrees.

5. Spread ¼ cup filling down the center of each manicotti and roll up.

6. Spread 1½ cups sauce in each of two 13 by 9 by 2-inch pans. Place half of the rolled manicotti, seam side down, close together in each of the pans. There will probably be a few that will not fit comfortably in a single layer. These can be laid on top.

7. Cover each pan with the remaining sauce, about 1 cup per pan. Sprinkle with the remaining Parmigiano-Reggiano and bake, uncovered, until bubbly, about ½ hour. Remove from oven.

8. To serve, place 3 manicotti on each of eight dinner plates. Top each trio of manicotti with ½ cup assorted cheeses. Run each plate under a hot broiler until the cheese is browned. Serve immediately.

NOTE: For the assorted cheeses that melt over the manicotti just before it's served, I like to use about one-third commercial mozzarella, one-third provolone, one-third Parmigiano-Reggiano.

✷ Classic American Lasagna ✷

Lasagna is near the top of the all-time pantheon of Italian-American dishes. Oh, it has its antecedents in Italy, of course. But things are different there. For one: when they say "lasagna," they are usually referring to the noodle itself. And that noodle can be sauced and served in a multitude of ways — most of them outside the oven. Yes, when it's layered with meat and cheese and baked, it's called lasagne al forno, designating that it goes into the oven. But it's still quite different from ours: not as cheesy, not as saucy, not as meaty, and with a wider variety of meats in the mix. I love the rich, gooey, meaty American version — and the following recipe incorporates everything I love about it. Pure 1957 in a lasagna pan.

Yield: 8 main-course servings

1 (1-pound) box lasagna noodles, preferably curly at the edges
1 (15-ounce) container whole-milk ricotta cheese
1 large egg, beaten
¼ cup chopped fresh parsley leaves
2 quarts Classic Brooklyn-Italian Meat Sauce (use two-thirds of recipe on page 14)
1 pound grated commercial mozzarella cheese (not soft, freshly-made mozzarella)
1½ cups grated Parmigiano-Reggiano cheese

1. Preheat oven to 350 degrees.

2. In a very large pot of boiling salted water, cook lasagna noodles 10 minutes, carefully stirring to separate. They should remain al dente. Drain and cool under running water. Lay noodles flat on a sheet pan, separating

layers with parchment or waxed paper. You will probably not need all the noodles in the box, but do cook them all, as some break or stick together or tear.

3. In a large bowl, stir together ricotta, egg, and parsley. Season mixture with salt and pepper.

4. Select a lasagna pan that is roughly 14 by 10 by 3 inches.

5. To assemble the lasagna, place 1 cup of meat sauce in the bottom of the lasagna pan. Top with a single layer of noodles that fit perfectly in the pan and cover the sauce; if you have to cut them a bit and reconfigure them to cover the sauce, that's fine. Top the noodles with half of the ricotta mixture, spreading evenly with a spatula. Top that with a third of the grated mozzarella, a third of the remaining meat sauce, and a third of the Parmigiano-Reggiano. Cover with another single layer of noodles. Top the noodles with the remaining half of the ricotta mixture, spreading evenly with a spatula. Top that with half of the remaining mozzarella, half of the remaining meat sauce, and half of the remaining Parmigiano-Reggiano. Top with another single layer of noodles that covers all. Top noodles with remaining sauce, mozzarella, and Parmigiano-Reggiano. Remember to season layers with salt and pepper as you go.

6. Bake uncovered for about 1 hour, or until lasagna is browned, bubbling, and hot in the center. Remove from oven and let sit 15 minutes to ensure nice clean slices. Cut into 8 portions and serve immediately.

✳ Spaghetti and Meatballs ✳

You will find meatballs in Italy — polpettone — but you will not likely find those meatballs with spaghetti. Why? Because the pairing appears to have been devised here, under some very unusual circumstances. In the early twentieth century, Italian immigrants to America were merrily preparing their healthy, Mediterranean cuisine — so the story goes — when government social workers became concerned about the lack of protein in this immigrant diet. "Just carbohydrates and tomatoes? You need to add some meat to that diet, make it healthier!" This may well have been the birth of spaghetti and meatballs. By the end of the century, of course, the original plate of spaghetti alone was deemed healthier — and nothing was more firmly buried in the dustbin of outdated dishes than spaghetti and meatballs. Nevertheless, when it's made properly — with light, fluffy meatballs, not the bread crumb–dense belly bombers one is usually served — it's a treat as delightful as it is nostalgic. Forget your white-truffle-and-pasta-fresca ways for a few hours and innocently relive the 1950s experience.

Yield: 6 servings

1 large egg
⅓ cup milk
1½ cups soft bread cubes (torn or cut from plain slices of white bread with crust)
1 pound ground beef
½ cup grated pecorino Romano cheese, plus extra for serving
1 teaspoon very finely minced garlic
¼ cup very finely minced parsley
¼ cup olive oil
6 cups tomato sauce, warmed (my choice: the Longer-Cooked, Very Garlicky Marinara Sauce on page 11)
1 pound spaghetti
2 tablespoons butter

1. Beat the egg in a large bowl, then blend in the milk. Add the bread cubes, stirring to coat them well. Let sit for 15 minutes.

2. Using a fork, mash the bread cubes until they've formed a rough paste. Add the ground beef to the bowl and, working with your hands, incorporate the rough paste into the beef. Add the pecorino Romano, garlic, and parsley and blend evenly with the meat mixture. Add salt and pepper to taste (you can taste by frying a little bit of the meat mixture).

3. Using wet hands, form the meat into balls the size of golf balls or a little smaller. Place the olive oil in a large, heavy sauté pan over medium-high heat. Add the meatballs to the oil to brown on all sides. Don't crowd them in the pan; you may have to brown them in batches. As they are finished browning, transfer them to the saucepan that holds the warmed tomato sauce. Bring sauce to gentle simmer and cook for 45 minutes.

4. When the meatballs are nearly done, drop the spaghetti into a large pot of boiling salted water. Cook until spaghetti is al dente, about 8 to 9 minutes. Drain spaghetti in a colander, then return it to the pasta cooking pot over medium heat. Ladle enough sauce from the saucepan to just coat the pasta; stir well. Add the butter and stir well. Keep the pasta in the pot for a total of about 1 minute. Then divide the pasta among six wide, shallow bowls. Top each mound of pasta with a few meatballs, then ladle some more sauce over all. Serve with grated pecorino Romano on the side.

☆ Pasta Primavera ☆

In the 1970s the Italian-American restaurant dish that announced "We have moved beyond red-sauce Italian" was Pasta Primavera, a combination of pasta, cream, and vegetables. It was when your local Italian restaurant became a "ristorante." Le Cirque in New York City made the dish famous, but it became a nationwide menu staple soon after that. Oddly, the dish may have had less to do with real Italian food than the red-sauce stuff did. As the myth of some unified "northern Italian" food spread, many Americans assumed the cuisine was rich in cream — which it never had been. Nevertheless, Pasta Primavera usually featured not only cream but lots of cream — for this was still the era when pasta in America carried too much sauce, no matter what the sauce was. The following version certainly has its fair share of cream, to be true to its Upper East Side roots — but you will find, I hope, a much more up-to-date sensibility in it, which I think makes the dish much better.

Yield: 6 pasta-course servings

Salt

8 medium asparagus spears, ends trimmed and sliced on the bias in ½-inch lengths (about 1 cup)

1 bunch of broccoli, bite-size florets only (about 1 cup)

2 small zucchini, quartered lengthwise and cut into ⅓-inch-wide pieces (about 1½ cups)

½ pound string beans, trimmed and cut into ½-inch lengths

1 pound fresh green peas in the pod, shelled (about 1 cup), or 1 cup frozen peas

6 tablespoons pine nuts

2 tablespoons olive oil

½ pound small white mushrooms, thinly sliced (about 2 cups)

1¾ cups whipping cream
2 medium shallots, minced
    (about 2 tablespoons)
2 large garlic cloves, minced
Finely grated zest of 1 lemon
⅛ teaspoon cayenne
5 tablespoons unsalted butter,
    cut into small pieces
2 tablespoons lemon juice
1 pound spaghetti
½ cup grated Parmigiano-Reggiano cheese
1 cup firmly packed shredded basil leaves,
    plus 6 sprigs for garnish

1. Bring a large stockpot of very well salted water to a boil. (Add enough salt to the pot so it tastes almost as salty as seawater.) Have ready a medium-size strainer and a large bowl of ice water. Cook the asparagus, broccoli, zucchini, and green beans, one group of vegetables at a time, in the boiling water until each group is tender but still a bit crisp, about 3 to 4 minutes for each one. As each group of vegetables finishes cooking, collect the pieces in the strainer and immediately immerse the strainer in the bowl of ice water to stop the cooking and set the color. Once the vegetables are cool (about a minute), transfer them to a bowl lined with paper towels (to absorb excess water). Cook the peas for about 30 seconds and cool in the same way. Combine the cooked vegetables and set aside. Cover the pot and the water and set it aside for cooking the pasta.

2. In a large sauté pan over medium heat, add the pine nuts and, shaking the pan occasionally, allow them to toast lightly, taking care not to let them burn. When they become golden brown in spots, about 3 to 5 minutes, remove them from the pan and set aside.

3. Add the olive oil to the pan. When the oil shimmers and slides easily in the pan, add the mushrooms and stir them to coat with the oil. Cook until the mushrooms are just tender and cooked through, about 5 minutes. Salt mushrooms to taste, remove from the heat, and drain on paper towels. Let cool, then combine with the other vegetables.

4. In a small saucepan over medium-high heat, bring the cream to a boil, reduce to a brisk simmer, and cook until reduced by about half and slightly thickened. Be careful not to let the cream boil over. Add the shallots, garlic, lemon zest, cayenne, and a few grinds of black pepper. Whisk in the butter until the sauce is well blended and creamy. It should easily coat the back of a spoon. Whisk in the lemon juice and add salt to taste. Simmer and whisk for another minute or so to rethicken slightly. Remove from heat and set aside on a warm part of the stove. Check frequently to make sure the sauce is holding; whisk it together if it isn't.

5. Return the large pot of water to a boil and add the spaghetti, stirring occasionally to prevent sticking. When the pasta is tender but still firm (al dente), reserve a cup of the pasta water, drain the pasta, and return pasta to the pot. Add the reserved vegetables, the cream sauce, pine nuts, cheese, and shredded basil and toss thoroughly over low heat. If the sauce seems a bit thick — each strand of pasta should glisten with a little medium-runny sauce — add some of the reserved

cooking water and toss again. Taste for seasoning. Serve in warmed bowls, garnished with basil sprigs.

☆ Lobster Fra Diàvolo ☆

There is real controversy about the origins of this spicy, tomatoey, garlicky dish. Some old-timers claim that it's a southern Italian tradition, made with spiny lobster. Others say that it's a dish made up by rich restaurateurs in the United States, using southern Italian sauce ideas; they had access to Maine lobster, and they had clients willing to pay for it. You can never unravel the puzzle today; I recently had the dish near Palermo, and when I asked where the lobster came from, they said Boston. I can guarantee that that wasn't going on in 1750 or so. But there is one big point of difference between the dish in America and the one in Italy today: here, many restaurants serve it on a bed of pasta. In Italy, of course, the separation of main course and pasta is more sacrosanct than the separation of church and state. I actually prefer it the Italian way, which puts more focus on the lobster. By all means, however, feel free to lay a base of sauced linguine under this great dish.

Yield: 2 main-course servings

2 (1½-pound) lobsters
Vegetable oil for filming roasting pan
4 tablespoons olive oil
10 large garlic cloves
½ cup dry white wine
2 (28-ounce) cans whole tomatoes
2 dried hot red chilies
1 teaspoon dried oregano
8 torn basil leaves
Crushed red pepper

1. Have your fishmonger split each lobster lengthwise with a long, sharp knife. Ask him to cut each lobster into 8 pieces: 2 chest halves (with legs attached), 2 lobster tail halves, 2 large claws, and 2 knuckles that connect the claws to the body. Make sure he saves any juices that exude from the lobster. Refrigerate tails, claws, and knuckles.

2. Turn on oven broiler. Film a large roasting pan with a little vegetable oil and place the 4 lobster chest halves on it. When oven is hot, place the pan directly under the broiler unit. Cook the lobster chests, turning frequently, for about 10 minutes, or until they are slightly charred.

3. While chests are cooking, place 1 tablespoon of the olive oil in a Dutch oven over medium heat. Peel and mince 6 of the garlic cloves and add to the oil. Sauté, stirring, until the garlic turns golden brown, about 5 minutes.

4. Remove chests from oven and place in the Dutch oven with the garlic and oil. Add the white wine to the roasting pan and deglaze pan for 30 seconds over medium-high heat. Pour the wine into the Dutch oven. Remove the tomatoes from the cans and, one by one, squeeze them over the contents of the Dutch oven, finally dropping in the crushed tomatoes. Reserve tomato juice in cans for possible use later. Add any reserved juices from the lobsters. Add the dried chilies, oregano, and basil. Boil furiously, uncovered, until the tomato mixture starts to thicken, about 5 to 10 minutes. Cover the Dutch oven, remove from heat, and let it rest for at least 1 hour.

5. When ready to cook, pick the shells out of the tomato sauce and discard them. Make sure to pick all bits of tomato and lobster out of the shells before discarding them, and to put the bits into the tomato sauce. Add crushed red pepper to taste.

6. In a large heavy skillet, place the remaining 3 tablespoons of olive oil over high heat. Gently peel the remaining 4 cloves of garlic and cut them into broad, thin slices. Add the garlic to the oil and cook until the garlic just starts to burn (about 5 minutes). Add the 4 lobster claws, 4 knuckles, and 4 tail halves (shell side down), and cook, covered, for 4 minutes. Turn the lobster pieces over and cook covered until done, another 3 to 4 minutes. Lower heat to medium, add tomato sauce, and stir well. Taste for seasoning and red pepper. If the sauce seems too thick, thin with a little reserved tomato juice. Cook for 1 minute. Serve immediately.

☆ Eggplant Parmigiana ☆

One of the classics of Italian-American cuisine (and seen far less often in Italy), Eggplant Parmigiana has a confusing history. Why, for starters, is this dish named after Parma, in northern Italy, when it obviously owes so much to southern Italy? You might hypothesize that Parmigiano-Reggiano cheese is the answer — except that many recipes include mozzarella but not Parmigiano-Reggiano. Some have suggested that the "parmigiana" part is actually a reference to a Neapolitan word for louvered shutters, which the overlapping slices of eggplant in the casserole resemble. Wherever the name comes from, I love the method of

first breading and deep-frying the eggplant slices, then burying them with cheese and sauce in the casserole. It does, of course, seem to defeat the purpose of deep-frying, which is usually to turn something crisp — but though the deep-fried eggplant gets soggy in the casserole, the wonderful flavor of frying carries over into the dish. The following version, made with skin-on eggplant, is particularly rustic, delicious, and Italian-American. And it really emphasizes the eggplant itself.

Yield: About 6 main-course servings

3 medium-size eggplants weighing about 3
  pounds total, unpeeled
3 tablespoons plus 2 teaspoons kosher salt
1½ cups regular olive oil, plus ¼ cup
  extra-virgin olive oil
1 cup finely chopped onion
2 (28-ounce) cans whole peeled tomatoes
1 tablespoon tomato paste
⅛ teaspoon crushed red pepper
1 cup loosely packed thinly sliced basil leaves
3 large eggs
3 tablespoons milk
1½ cups plain bread crumbs, preferably
  homemade (page 9)
2 cups finely grated Parmigiano-Reggiano cheese
1 pound mozzarella cheese, thinly sliced

1. Slice the eggplant the long way into ½-inch slices. Sprinkle slices on both sides with the 3 tablespoons of salt. Line a large colander with paper towels and layer eggplant slices in the colander. Cover with paper towels and place a weight on top (a large can or two works just fine). Let rest in the sink for 1 hour.

2. Meanwhile, place the ¼ cup extra-virgin

olive oil in a large, heavy saucepan over medium heat. Sauté the onion in the oil until soft, about 8 minutes.

3. Spill all the liquid out of the tomato cans but keep the tomatoes inside. Reserve liquid for another use. Working with a small, sharp knife, cut the tomatoes into fairly small chunks right in the cans by moving the knife back and forth through them. Add cut tomatoes (and the juice they released) to the saucepan, along with tomato paste and crushed red pepper. Blend well. Bring to a boil, reduce heat, season to taste with salt and pepper, and simmer for 20 minutes. Remove from heat and add basil. You should have about 4 cups of sauce. Reserve.

4. When the eggplant slices have rested for an hour, remove them from colander and wipe them with paper towels to remove excess salt and water. Dry well.

5. In a large, wide bowl, whisk the eggs together with the milk. On a wide, flat plate, mix together the bread crumbs and 1 cup of the Parmigiano-Reggiano.

6. Heat the 1½ cups of regular olive oil in a wide, heavy skillet until the oil reaches 340 to 350 degrees. Dip eggplant slices in the egg-milk mixture, then in the bread crumb–cheese mixture. As they're dipped, place them in the hot oil and cook each slice for about 1 minute on each side; after 2 minutes of cooking, each slice should be golden brown. Remove each slice as it's done and place on paper towels.

7. Preheat oven to 350 degrees.

8. Select a baking pan that's 13 by 9 by at least 2 inches. Cover the bottom evenly with 1 cup of sauce. Cover the sauce with a layer of eggplant slices (about one-third of them); lay them in roughly, not evenly, haphazardly overlapping them, for the most rustic result. Evenly spread one-third of the mozzarella slices over the eggplant. Cover the cheese with 1 cup of sauce. Sprinkle with ⅓ cup of the remaining Parmigiano-Reggiano. Then layer another third of the eggplant slices, another third of the mozzarella, another 1 cup of sauce, and another ⅓ cup of Parmigiano-Reggiano. Finally, add remaining third of the eggplant, the final third of the mozzarella, the last cup of sauce, and the final ⅓ cup of Parmigiano-Reggiano.

9. Bake uncovered for 30 minutes. Remove from oven, let rest 5 minutes, and serve.

✸ Veal Parmigiana ✸

With Veal Parmigiana — since the veal itself is expensive and exclusive — I choose to eschew the Eggplant Parmigiana–type of casserole and focus instead on the deep-fried glory of each individual cutlet. Indeed, many Italian-American chefs of the 1950s and 1960s chose to do the same. It's great to have all that cheesy goodness on top . . . and still see and taste the crispy edges of the veal. The following recipe does just that — and makes sense of the name by deliciously working Parmigiano-Reggiano into the dish in two ways.

Yield: 4 servings

3 large eggs
About ¾ cup finely grated
Parmigiano-Reggiano cheese
2 cups bread crumbs for coating (page 9)

Inexpensive olive oil for deep-frying
4 veal scallops, cut from the top round,
    each a rectangle about 7 to 8 inches long
    and weighing about 2 to 2½ ounces
    (see sidebar)
Several garlic cloves, smashed
About 4 cups warmed tomato sauce
    (my choice: The Four-Hour Epic Sauce
    on page 12 or All-Purpose Bright Red
    Tomato Sauce on page 12)
4 ounces commercial mozzarella, cut into
    broad, fairly thin slices

1. Beat the eggs well in a wide, shallow bowl. Beat in 3 tablespoons of the Parmigiano-Reggiano. Place the bread crumbs in another wide, shallow bowl. Season crumbs with salt to taste.

2. Pour the olive oil into a wide cooking vessel until it comes about ½ inch up the side of the pan. Place over medium heat. Monitor oil with a deep-fry thermometer; the oil is ready when it reaches 365 degrees.

3. Make sure the veal scallops are dry. Rub each one on both sides with the smashed garlic. Dip each one in the egg mixture, coating completely but letting excess egg drip off. Place each scallop, one at a time, on top of the bread crumbs; sprinkle crumbs over each scallop and pat each scallop with a fork to make bread crumbs adhere. Turn each scallop several times and keep patting.

4. When the oil is ready, place the scallops in the oil. (If your pan is large enough, you can do this in one step; otherwise, work in batches.) Cook the scallops, turning occasionally, until they are golden brown (about 3 to 4 minutes). Remove scallops and place on paper towels.

5. Place fried veal scallops on a sheet pan that fits under the broiler. Top each scallop with ½ cup of the tomato sauce; spread sauce out over each scallop but leave a crispy brown border. Top each scallop with a quarter of the mozzarella slices; spread cheese out, but leave that crispy brown border. Sprinkle the remaining Parmigiano-Reggiano evenly over the mozzarella. Pat cheese down. Place the scallops under a hot broiler and cook until the cheese is browned and bubbly. Remove immediately. Place each scallop on a dinner plate and surround each one with a good ½ cup of the warmed tomato sauce. Serve immediately.

The Veal Thing

The quality of the veal makes a big difference in this dish. Veal scallops — related to the word *scallopini* — are properly cut from the top round of the veal leg, then pounded to thinness. The butcher must cut them across the grain, and they must be pounded in such a way that they are not just flattened downward but stretched outward. It has become a standard practice to substitute other cuts of meat for this high-quality, high-priced veal. Worst of all as substitutions, in my opinion, are other cuts of veal, which can be tough and stringy. Cutlets of pork and chicken work much better as substitutes — though you'll be missing the exquisite delicacy of the finest veal. Of course, if you're burying those cutlets in a saucy casserole, who cares?

✹ Chicken Cacciatore ✹

This dish is not as popular in Italy as it is here, but it does exist in the Old Country — in quite a different form. Its literal meaning is "chicken, hunter's style" — and in northern Italy it usually contains wild mushrooms. Tomatoes are optional. The Italian-American version, long a restaurant favorite here, almost always features white mushrooms, green peppers, and lots of tomatoes. I love this dish when it's cooked a short amount of time, a kind of sautéed dish with a sauce; some other recipes cook it for a long time, turning it into a stew. I also prefer making it with chicken thighs but have included both thighs and breasts in the following recipe, so you can please all your guests. If you wish to substitute four more thighs for the breast — be *my* guest!

Yield: 4 main-course servings

2 halves of a chicken breast, skin-on and
  bone-in (about 1½ pounds)
4 chicken thighs, skin-on and bone-in
  (about 1½ pounds)
Flour for coating
5 tablespoons olive oil
2 heaping tablespoons finely minced garlic
¼ pound green bell pepper, seeded and cut into
  1-inch squares
¼ pound red bell pepper, seeded and cut into
  1-inch squares
½ cup red wine
1 (28-ounce) can whole tomatoes
1 tablespoon tomato paste
¼ cup finely minced parsley, plus a little extra
  for garnish
¼ cup finely shredded fresh basil leaves
1 teaspoon dried oregano
2 bay leaves
½ pound white mushrooms, wiped clean and
  cut into medium-thin slices

1. Cut each piece of breast in half crosswise; you will now have 4 pieces of breast roughly the same size as the 4 thighs. Salt and pepper chicken pieces well. Coat lightly with flour. Reserve.

2. Place 4 tablespoons of the olive oil in a large, heavy sauté pan over medium-high heat. Add 1 tablespoon of the garlic and spread evenly across the pan. Immediately add the chicken pieces, skin side down. Cook, turning occasionally, until chicken is golden brown on both sides (about 8 to 10 minutes). Remove chicken and reserve.

3. Add the remaining 1 tablespoon of minced garlic to the pan. Add the green and red bell pepper and toss well in the garlic. Add the red wine and scrape up the browned bits at the bottom of the pan. Simmer for 30 seconds. Remove the tomatoes from their can (reserve tomato juice in can) and, working with your hand, squeeze each tomato into the sauté pan. Add the tomato paste and blend well. Add the parsley, basil, oregano, and bay leaves. Stir well. Return the chicken pieces to the pan, coat with sauce, reduce heat to a simmer, and cook for 15 minutes, covered.

4. While the chicken is cooking, add the remaining 1 tablespoon of olive oil to a wide, heavy skillet over medium-high heat. Add the mushrooms and cook, stirring frequently, until the mushrooms are golden brown and just tender (about 4 to 5 minutes). Salt them to taste. Then, after the chicken has cooked for the 15 minutes in step 3, add the mushrooms to the chicken cacciatore. Stir well to blend in evenly. If the sauce seems too thick, blend in a little of the

saved tomato juice from the can. Season to taste with salt and pepper.

5. Divide chicken among four dinner plates, top with peppers and mushrooms, surround with sauce, sprinkle with parsley, and serve immediately.

✲ Chicken Scallopini ✲ with Prosciutto, Mozzarella, and Marsala

When the "northern Italian" restaurant boom hit in the 1970s, one key change was that Veal Parmigiana went away — and an array of tomatoless veal and chicken cutlet dishes took its place. Veal Marsala became very popular. The Roman Saltimbocca, in which a slice of prosciutto is placed over the veal, had its day. Instead of presenting all the variations (which would take up a book in themselves), I've created the perfect 1970s northern Italian cutlet dish — an omnibus of all the themes that ends up tasting mind-blowingly good. One word of caution: As with any dish that carries prosciutto, there will be some saltiness. If you're sensitive to that, you might want to reduce slightly the amount of Parmigiano-Reggiano that goes on top of the mozzarella, or you could substitute good ham that's less cured — like Italian prosciutto cotto.

Yield: 2 servings

4 pieces of boneless, skinless chicken breast, about 2 ounces each
¼ pound prosciutto, very thinly sliced
2 large eggs
Flour for dredging
10 tablespoons unsalted butter
¼ pound mozzarella cheese, thinly sliced
6 tablespoons finely grated Parmigiano-Reggiano cheese (a good substitute is Grana Padano, another northern Italian grating cheese)
½ cup dry marsala
½ cup unsalty chicken stock

1. Place the chicken breasts between pieces of waxed paper and pound them with a mallet or the back of a cleaver or the back of a heavy pan. They should flatten out to approximately ¼ inch thick, and each piece should be roughly 5 by 5 inches (it doesn't matter if they're a little irregular in shape).

2. Lay out the slices of prosciutto side by side on a counter, with the length of each slice facing away from you. Place one of the chicken cutlets on top of 3 or 4 of the prosciutto slices, laying the cutlet right in the center of those 3 or 4 slices. Using your hands, fold the upper and lower edges of the prosciutto slices in and over the chicken cutlet. The cutlet will be partially covered by prosciutto on the side that faces up; flip it over and it will be totally covered by prosciutto. Make sure the prosciutto is clinging snugly and set that cutlet aside. Repeat until all 4 cutlets are wrapped in prosciutto.

3. Break the eggs into a wide, shallow bowl and beat well. Place enough flour to dust the chicken cutlets in a wide, shallow bowl. Dip each cutlet into the egg, coating each one well. Let them drip off excess egg, then dip them very lightly in the flour.

4. Select 2 medium-size (about 8-inch)

heavy sauté pans, place 3 tablespoons of the butter in each one, and place the pans over medium heat. When the butter is foaming, place 2 cutlets in each pan. Cook the cutlets until they're golden on the outside and just done on the inside (about 2 minutes per side).

5. While the cutlets are cooking, lay a quarter of the mozzarella slices side by side. Working with your fingers, push them and mold them together until they make a "slice" of mozzarella that will cover the top of a cutlet. Sprinkle it with 1½ tablespoons of Parmigiano-Reggiano and push the grated cheese into the mozzarella. You should now have a cheese "slice" that holds together. Repeat until you have 4 "slices."

6. Preheat broiler. When the chicken is done, remove cutlets to a broiler pan. Top each cutlet with a formed "slice" of mozzarella cheese, then place under the broiler. The chicken is ready when the cheese has completely melted and browned slightly.

7. While the cheese is melting, make the sauce. Spill out the butter in each of the two pans, and wipe them out lightly with paper towels. Return pans to high heat and add ¼ cup of the marsala to each one, as well as ¼ cup of the chicken stock. Boil quickly until only 3 to 4 tablespoons of liquid is left in each pan. Turn heat to low and place 2 tablespoons of the butter in each pan. Swirl with a whisk until a creamy brown sauce is formed.

8. Divide the cutlets between two dinner plates and pour the marsala sauce over and around them. Serve immediately.

☆ Grilled Pizza Margherita ☆

In the Italian gastronomic conquest of America, pizza has been the chief weapon. Is there any Italian dish that has infiltrated our lives as thoroughly as this one? Unfortunately, pizza has never been a great dish to make at home. One of the things that make it so good at pizzerias is the high heat of professional pizza ovens, hundreds of degrees beyond the capabilities of home ovens. Some years back, the two great chefs who run Al Forno in Providence, Rhode Island, invented a fabulous new pizza that was soon hailed as the best restaurant pizza in America: the grilled pizza. Unintentionally, they simultaneously solved the home pizza dilemma — because the grilled pizza at home, with a good recipe, can be every bit as otherworldly great as the grilled pizza in a restaurant! Vincent Scotto is a terrific Italian chef who once worked at Al Forno and has gone on to grill pizzas at his own restaurants in New York City. The following recipe is based on his. It has quirks you may find strange: molasses, some whole wheat flour, no mozzarella cheese. But I'm telling you that if you follow this recipe to the letter and grill some pizza in your backyard, you will be amazed at how fantastic a home pizza can be. And it's not difficult. So put down that phone — make it yourself instead.

Yield: 6 individual pizzas, 6 servings

1⅓ cups lukewarm water
1 teaspoon fresh yeast or 1 package active dry yeast
1 tablespoon molasses
2½ tablespoons kosher salt
About 1 cup extra-virgin olive oil
2 cups bread flour
1½ cups unbleached all-purpose flour
½ cup whole wheat flour
3 cups whole, peeled canned plum tomatoes in thick puree

¾ cup chopped fresh basil
2 tablespoons finely chopped garlic
1½ cups grated pecorino Romano cheese (find
the least salty pecorino Romano you can)
1½ cups grated Bel Paese cheese
3 tablespoons chopped fresh parsley

1. In a large bowl, combine the water, yeast, and molasses and stir gently to mix. Set aside for 5 minutes, until bubbly and foamy.

2. Add the salt and 2½ tablespoons of the olive oil to the bowl and stir to mix.

3. In another bowl, whisk together the three kinds of flour. Add the blended flours to the yeast mixture and stir with a wooden spoon until the dough forms a mass and pulls away from the sides of the bowl. Use your hands if necessary to incorporate all the flour . . . but don't knead the dough at all.

4. Form the dough into 6 portions. Roll the portioned dough into balls and place them on a well-oiled baking sheet. Brush the balls lightly with olive oil and cover with plastic wrap. Set aside at warm room temperature for 40 minutes.

5. Place the tomatoes in a colander and drain. Dice the tomatoes. In a bowl, combine the diced tomatoes, basil, ¼ cup of the olive oil, and the garlic. Stir well and set aside at room temperature.

6. Mix together the two kinds of cheese and reserve.

7. Prepare a charcoal or gas fire. Build the fire so that coals on one side are very hot (a concentrated mass) and coals on the other side are only medium-hot (a sparser mass). If using a gas grill with dual controls, maintain a hotter temperature and a cooler temperature. Position the grilling rack 3 to 4 inches from the heat source.

8. While the fire is heating, oil your kitchen counter lightly and flatten 1 ball of dough into a 10- to 12-inch oval, about ⅛ inch thick. It is important to maintain uniform thickness. (Vincent likes to do this by hand, but you might find it easier to do it with a rolling pin, or some combination of pin and hand. Remember: a neat shape is not important, but uniform thickness is!) Continue until all 6 balls are rolled out.

9. Using your fingertips, gently lift one dough (or several doughs, as many as your grill will accommodate) and drape it onto the grill, guiding it carefully onto the rack over the hot part of the coals. Within 1 minute it will puff slightly, the underside will stiffen, and grill marks will appear.

10. Using tongs, immediately flip the dough or doughs over onto the cooler part of the grill. Brush with olive oil.

11. Spread about ½ cup of cheese mixture

Grilled Pizza Margherita

The pizza dough is hand-stretched into an irregular 10- 12-inch oval that's about ⅛ inch thick

over each dough, and then dollop each with 8 to 10 tablespoons of the tomato sauce. Do not spread the sauce over the cheese; leave splotchy pools of sauce. Drizzle each pizza with about a tablespoon of olive oil. Slide the pizza or pizzas back to the edge of the hot section of the grill. Cook for 3 to 4 minutes, until the bottoms are evenly golden brown; make sure not to burn the bottoms. It's not necessary to cover the grill, but feel free to do so if you'd like the toppings to cook down a bit more.

12. Sprinkle with fresh parsley and black pepper and serve immediately. Repeat with remaining doughs.

✴ Focaccia ✴

Focaccia — which derives its name from the hearth, or, in Latin, the *focus* — is a traditional yeast bread most often associated with Liguria in the north of Italy. However, you can find versions of it all over the country (the best one I ever tasted was in Puglia, in the south!). These days, you can also find versions of focaccia all over the United States; for a good fifteen years now it has been one of our hottest, trendiest breads. Why? For one thing, it's easy to make. For another, its style is very recognizable to us — a rectangular pan of soft, airy, slightly spongy focaccia is not altogether different from a rectangular pan of pizza. Lastly, Americans love toppings and variations — and focaccia can be topped with an infinite universe of possibilities. The following recipe is for the basic focaccia, flavored only with olive oil and salt; while the bread is baking the dough almost fries in the oil in the pan, giving it a wonderful crust and a wonderful taste. Recipes for three great toppings — all

of which go on the bread before it's baked — come after the basic recipe. By the way, one more, and very trendy, variation is just a small bottle away: instead of drizzling more olive oil over the focaccia as it's cooling, try drizzling a small quantity of truffle oil.

Yield: 1 loaf (9 by 12 inches)

3½ cups bread flour
1½ cups cool water
½ cup olive oil, plus extra for handling, greasing, and drizzling
1 teaspoon kosher salt, plus more for topping
1¼ cups Bread Starter (recipe follows on page 37)
1¼ teaspoons rapid-rise (instant) yeast
Coarse-ground cornmeal for dusting
Handful of ice cubes

1. Place the bread flour, cool water, ½ cup olive oil, 1 teaspoon salt, bread starter, and yeast in a large bowl of a stand mixer fitted with a dough hook attachment.

2. Mix the ingredients on a very slow speed until all the ingredients are blended together, about 1 minute. This dough is supposed to be very wet, so do not add extra flour. Increase the mixer speed to medium-high and continue to mix until the dough pulls away from the sides of the bowl and starts to come up from the bottom of the bowl, about 15 to 18 minutes. You should be able to grab the dough quickly with your hands, and it shouldn't stick to your fingers.

3. With lightly oiled hands, remove the dough from the mixing bowl and place it in a lightly oiled large bowl. Then coat the dough ball all over with extra olive oil. Cover the

bowl with plastic wrap and place it in a warm area until it has almost tripled in size, about 1 hour. Punch down the dough in the bowl. Cover again and let it rest for 30 minutes more in a warm place. Repeat process, and rest the dough for 30 minutes more (a total of 2 hours' rising time). After the final 30 minutes, lightly oil a 9 by 12 by 2-inch baking pan and dust it lightly with cornmeal. 4. Invert the dough from the bowl onto the baking pan and use your hands to gently flatten out and stretch the dough into every corner of the pan. If the dough is resistant, allow it to rest a couple of minutes, and then finish covering the pan with it. (If using any of the three topping recipes that follow, evenly spread the topping out across the focaccia at this point.) Cover the pan with plastic wrap and let the dough rise in a warm place until it has doubled in size, about 1 hour.

5. Arrange a single rack in the center of the oven and place an ovenproof baking pan in the bottom of the oven. Preheat oven to 475 degrees.

6. Drizzle the focaccia generously with olive oil and sprinkle it with kosher salt. Dimple the focaccia all over by pushing your fingers through the dough to the bottom of the pan. Place the focaccia dough in the oven. Immediately toss a handful of ice cubes into the ovenproof pan on the bottom of the oven. (This will steam the focaccia and allow the bread to expand.)

7. Bake the bread until a golden brown color is reached, approximately 15 to 18 minutes. The internal temperature of the loaf should be 200 degrees. Remove the pan from the oven and sprinkle the focaccia with kosher salt (and additional olive oil if it looks dry). Place the pan on a wire rack and allow the bread to cool. Serve while still a little warm — cut into thick squares possibly cut through the middle of the squares to create thinner "slices."

★ Bread Starter ★

Yield: 3 cups

2 cups cool water
2½ cups all-purpose flour
⅛ teaspoon rapid-rise (instant) yeast
Pinch of sugar

1. In a large mixing bowl combine the water, flour, yeast, and sugar.
2. Use a fork to mix all the ingredients together until they are almost smooth; the mixture should be the consistency of a thick, slightly lumpy pancake batter.
3. Cover the large bowl with plastic wrap. Poke a few holes in the plastic wrap so the mixture can breathe. Let the mixture sit on the countertop to ferment overnight. (It must ferment for a minimum of 12 hours.)
4. Before using the starter in a recipe, use a fork to stir the mixture to take most of the air out of it. This process also homogenizes the mixture, making it easier to work with and more accurate for measuring. Any leftover starter can be kept in a covered jar in the refrigerator for up to 1 week.

★ Gorgonzola and Thyme Topping ★ for Focaccia

A great topping, using a great Italian cheese.

> *3 cups mild Gorgonzola cheese, crumbled*
> *⅔ cup whipping cream*
> *2 teaspoons fresh thyme, chopped*
> *3 tablespoons fresh parsley, chopped*

Place the crumbled cheese and the cream in a medium-size mixing bowl. Using the back of a spoon, blend together the cream and cheese to make a paste. Add the chopped thyme and chopped parsley to the bowl. Blend the mixture with a spoon until all the ingredients are incorporated together. Spread evenly across the top of the focaccia in step 4 of the Focaccia recipe (page 37).

★ Anchovy, Parmesan, and ★ Fresh Oregano Topping for Focaccia

Here's another very Italian and very delicious topping possibility. Shave the Parmigiano-Reggiano with a vegetable peeler.

> *½ cup anchovy fillets (packed in oil), drained*
> *   and coarsely chopped*
> *⅔ cup olive oil*
> *2 cups thinly shaved Parmigiano-Reggiano cheese*
> *¼ cup firmly packed chopped fresh oregano leaves*
> *¼ cup firmly packed chopped parsley leaves*

Place the anchovies, olive oil, shaved cheese, chopped oregano, and chopped parsley in a medium-size bowl. Toss all the ingredients together with a spoon until they are thoroughly blended. Season to taste with pepper. Spread evenly across the top of the focaccia in step 4 of the Focaccia recipe (page 37).

★ Roasted Red Pepper, Cilantro, ★ and Garlic Topping for Focaccia

The cilantro in this delicious topping moves it away from Italy — but it's characteristic of the kind of creative focaccia making that's going on across America.

> *1 cup canned roasted red bell peppers, thinly sliced*
> *1 cup firmly packed minced fresh cilantro*
> *6 large garlic cloves, peeled and very thinly sliced*
> *⅔ cup olive oil*
> *Coarse sea salt*
> *Cracked black pepper*

Place the roasted red peppers, cilantro, and thinly sliced garlic cloves in a medium-size mixing bowl. Add the olive oil to the mixing bowl, tossing all the ingredients together with a spoon until they are thoroughly blended. Season the mixture with the salt and pepper to taste. Set the bowl aside for 15 minutes for all the flavors to blend together. Spread evenly across the top of the focaccia in step 4 of the Focaccia recipe (page 37).

✿ Sesame Bread Sticks ✿

When you go out to dinner in Italy, you're likely to see grissini on the table: long, thin, smooth, bland-tasting bread sticks that originated in Turin. When you go to an Italian-American restaurant, you might see the much more flavorful American cousin: shorter, denser, longer-cooked sticks studded with sesame seeds, which give them a wonderful flavor. It is possible that Middle Eastern and Italian traditions combined to yield this addictive treat.

Yield: 16 bread sticks

3 cups bread flour
2 teaspoons rapid-rise (instant) yeast
1 tablespoon salt
¼ cup olive oil, plus extra for
coating bowl
1 cup warm water
4 ounces sesame seeds

1. Place the flour, yeast, salt, the ¼ cup olive oil, and water in the bowl of a stand mixer. Using the dough hook, blend the ingredients together with the machine on low speed. After the dough comes together, increase speed to medium and knead for 5 minutes. The dough should form a smooth ball; if it's too dry, add a little water, if it's too sticky, add a little flour.
2. Put a small amount of extra olive oil in a bowl and coat the dough in the oil. Cover with plastic wrap and let dough rest for 45 minutes, or until it doubles in bulk.
3. Place the sesame seeds on a sheet pan.
4. Punch down the dough and cut into 16 equal pieces. On a lightly floured countertop, shape into bread sticks, each about 9 by ½ inch. Lightly spray the bread sticks with a water bottle, then coat with sesame seeds. Place the bread sticks on a baking sheet and let rest, uncovered, for 45 minutes.
5. Preheat oven to 350 degrees.

6. Bake the bread sticks in the oven for 40 to 45 minutes, or until golden brown.

☆ Campari–Blood Orange ☆ Sorbet

A number of upscale Italian restaurants in the United States today are offering variations on the sorbet theme — and I've tasted none better than this wonderful iced creation. The best blood oranges come from Sicily, late in the winter. Buy a bunch, squeeze the juice, combine it with Italy's great, bright red, slightly bitter aperitif called Campari — and you've got a sorbet as visually striking as it is devastatingly delicious and refreshing.

Yield: About 1 pint

⅔ cup sugar
⅔ cup water
Zest of 3 blood oranges
1 cup freshly squeezed blood-orange
juice (buy 8 to 10 blood oranges
to be sure)
3 tablespoons Campari

1. Combine the sugar and water in a 1-quart saucepan. Bring to a boil over medium-high heat. Add the blood-orange zest. Set the syrup aside to cool.
2. Mix the syrup with the blood-orange juice. Strain the juice if you prefer a finer texture, or leave in the pulp. Add Campari. Cover with plastic wrap and cool in the refrigerator for 1 hour.
3. Freeze in ice cream machine according to manufacturer's directions.

✶ Cranberry Hazelnut Biscotti ✶ with Chocolate

Along with the coffee boom in the United States came the biscotti boom; rarely seen here until a few decades ago, biscotti today are ubiquitous, being sold in coffee shops, groceries, supermarkets, and by mail order. Their crunchy-firm texture goes extremely well with a cup of coffee — or in a cup of coffee, as the upmarket competition for the classic dunkin' doughnut. The texture comes from the fact that biscotti are actually cooked twice — and so does the name, which in Italian means "cooked twice"! Of course, the Italians do 'em a little differently than we do. In Italy biscotti are usually drier, more austere, not souped up with add-ins. I love the traditional style. But I also unabashedly love the exuberant American-style biscotti. The following example is particularly American, and particularly delicious, with a moister-than-usual texture reminiscent of a good, hard, crumbly cookie. If you'd prefer to leave out the Hershey's Kisses — an all-American touch that works wonderfully well — the recipe can be made without them. Or . . . you can substitute other chunks of chocolate.

Yield: 36 to 48 biscotti

1½ cups sugar
¼ pound (1 stick) unsalted butter at room
temperature
2 eggs, beaten and divided
2 generous teaspoons of freshly grated
orange zest
1 teaspoon baking soda
½ teaspoon salt
3 cups all-purpose flour, plus extra
for working dough
1 cup hazelnuts (skinned and coarsely chopped)
1 cup dried cranberries
20 Hershey's Kisses, each cut in half

1. Preheat oven to 325 degrees.
2. In a mixing bowl with an electric hand mixer, or in the work bowl of a stand mixer, cream together the sugar and butter until it's light and fluffy (about 2 to 3 minutes). Beat in eggs, one at a time, just until incorporated. Mix in orange zest, baking soda, and salt. Add 1½ cups of the flour, the hazelnuts, cranberries, and chocolate. Add the remaining 1½ cups flour.
3. Transfer dough to floured surface; work dough with your hands until the dough just holds together (about 2 minutes).
4. Form the dough into 2 logs of equal size on a baking sheet. Each log should be approximately 14 inches long, 3 inches wide, and about ¾ inch high. (If you have any dough left over, you can form another log on that sheet or on another baking sheet; if you can't get a full log out of the extra dough, make sure that the log you do form is about ¾ inch high.) All logs must be positioned at least 3 inches from other logs.
5. Place baking sheet (or sheets) in the oven and cook until logs are golden brown and firm to the touch (about 55 minutes). Transfer logs from baking sheet to a rack and cool for 5 minutes.
6. On a cutting board, using a serrated knife, cut logs diagonally; each biscotto should be about ¾ inch thick. Place biscotti on their original baking sheet (or sheets); each biscotto must be lying flat on its side.
7. Return biscotti to oven. Bake for 5 minutes, flip biscotti over, and bake for 5 minutes more. The surface of the biscotti should not

Cutting Biscotti

be soft to the touch. Transfer biscotti to a rack and let cool. Eat immediately or store at room temperature in a tightly closed container (they will stay fresh for 2 to 3 weeks). You can also freeze these biscotti, tightly covered.

☆ Tiramisu ☆

This Italian dessert — usually attributed to the Veneto region — took America by storm in the 1980s. Restaurateurs loved it even more than diners; because it's pretty, and so easy to make, a restaurateur could raise the level of his or her dessert menu without even hiring a pastry chef! But even nonpastry chefs like to get creative — and before long, restaurants were turning out newfangled versions of the old classic. I dislike the ones that play with the simple, basic chemistry of the dish. However, the following variation — which substitutes good ole American bourbon for the brandy usually used along with coffee to moisten the ladyfingers — is a new, harmonious creation that I love. I think of this twist as America's return gift to Italy.

Yield: 6 to 8 servings

1 (1 pound) tub of mascarpone
3 large eggs, separated into yolks
    and whites
½ cup confectioners' sugar, sieved
1 cup strong, freshly brewed coffee
4 teaspoons granulated sugar
4 teaspoons bourbon
20 ladyfingers (or savoiardi)
1 tablespoon cocoa powder

I. Take the mascarpone out of the fridge about ½ hour before beginning the recipe. The cheese will be easier to mix with the other ingredients if it has had a chance to soften.
2. Gently whisk the mascarpone with the 3 egg yolks and the sieved confectioners' sugar in a medium-size bowl until blended.
3. In a separate bowl, whisk the 3 egg whites with a pinch of salt until soft peaks form. Stir one-third of the egg whites into the mascarpone, then use a spatula to gently fold in the remaining egg whites.

✩✩✩✩✩✩✩✩✩✩✩✩✩✩✩✩✩✩✩✩✩✩✩✩✩✩✩✩✩✩✩✩✩✩✩✩✩✩

4. Combine the coffee with the granulated sugar and bourbon, making sure the sugar is dissolved. Place mixture in a shallow dish large enough to hold a ladyfinger. Quickly dip both sides of each ladyfinger into the coffee mixture. This takes only a second or two per side; the ladyfingers must be dipped, not soaked.

5. Arrange half of the ladyfingers in a single layer on the bottom of an 8 by 8 by 2-inch pan. (You may have to break them to make them fit.) Cover the ladyfingers with half of the mascarpone mixture, smoothing the top with a spatula.

6. Give the pan a quarter turn on the counter and arrange the other half of the ladyfingers on top of the mascarpone (by giving a quarter turn, you'll now have new ladyfingers covering the spaces left between ladyfingers on the bottom layer). Cover the second layer of ladyfingers with the remaining mascarpone. Smooth the top. Place in the refrigerator for at least 2 hours.

7. Just before serving, sieve the cocoa powder over the top in a decorative pattern.

✩ Hot Zabaglione ✩ with Ladyfingers, Marsala, and Raspberries

Zabaglione — which, in Italian-American dialect, is pronounced za-buy-OWN — got real hot in America's "northern" Italian restaurants of the 1970s. I wish it had stayed hot — because these days you often see "cold" zabaglione being offered on dessert menus. Originally the dish was a hot, eggy foam laced with sweet Sicilian marsala — and I still think that's the way it tastes best. I have grown fond, however — as the following recipe attests — of having a few things at hand to dip and dunk in the hot foam. You will get the foamiest foam from this recipe if you use a handheld electric beater, but a wire whisk could be substituted.

Yield: 4 servings

12 ladyfingers
¾ cup sweet marsala
1 large whole egg, plus the yolks of 4 large eggs
¼ cup sugar
24 raspberries
4 mint sprigs, optional

1. In a pan, sprinkle the ladyfingers evenly with ½ cup of the marsala. Line up 4 martini glasses or old-fashioned champagne glasses. Break 1 of the ladyfingers into 3 pieces and use to form a base layer at the bottom of one glass. Repeat for 3 remaining glasses. Then arrange 2 ladyfingers upright along the opposite sides of each glass. Set aside.

2. Add water to the bottom part of a large, nonreactive double boiler until it is one-quarter filled. (See Note for an alternative.) Bring the water to a boil over high heat, then turn the heat to medium-low and maintain a steady simmer.

3. In the top part of the double boiler, off the heat, combine the whole egg, the 4 egg yolks, and sugar. Using a handheld electric beater, beat on medium speed until the mixture thickens and "forms the ribbon" (about 3 to 4 minutes).

4. Place the top part of the double boiler

over the simmering water and continue to beat on medium speed. Gradually pour in the remaining ½ cup marsala while continuing to beat. From time to time, scrape down the sides of the top pan of the double boiler with a rubber spatula (be aware that the mixture cooks much faster around the edges). Continue to beat until the eggs hold their shape when you lift the beaters. Remove from heat.

5. Immediately place about one-eighth of the zabaglione over the broken ladyfinger base in each glass. Top each zabaglione layer with 3 raspberries. Divide the remaining zabaglione evenly to form a second layer in each glass. Top each second layer of zabaglione with 3 more raspberries. The zabaglione should prop up the 2 standing ladyfingers in each glass. Garnish with mint sprigs, if desired. Serve immediately.

NOTE: The zabaglione can be made either in a double boiler or in a homemade version of a double boiler. If using the latter, add water to a medium saucepan until it is one-quarter filled. Choose a saucepan over which a nonreactive, four-quart, heat-resistant mixing bowl rests steadily.

Greek and Turkish Food

Greek food has never caught on in a big way in America — possibly because citizens of Greek ancestry are not spread out all across the United States. There's a big Greek community in New York City and one in Chicago — but the pita pockets thin out considerably after that. It's a real shame that Greek food hasn't taken root here — because it is some of the most delicious food in the world, perfectly in tune with the times, and not that difficult to reproduce thousands of miles from the motherland.

Indeed, going to inexpensive Greek restaurants in New York or Chicago — especially the old-fashioned ones that lay their dishes out on steam tables, where you make your selections — is not very different from going to similar establishments in Athens.

Greek mezes — including the wonderful whips and dips of Greek cuisine — are similar here to the ones in Greece when made well. The showcase casserole dishes (moussaka, pastitsio) possibly receive a little less care and detail here, but flavors are similar. Vegetables stewed in oil — string beans, potatoes, broad beans — are also quite alike in the two countries.

However, if you take into account all the Greek food that is served in America in restaurants that are not "Greek" restaurants — such as the many diners owned by Greek families that offer, but do not specialize in, Greek food — then you start to see an emerging Greek-American cuisine. Their renditions of Greek dishes are usually saucier, especially the ones that include tomato sauce. There are many great cheeses in Greece, but diner cooks here tend to use Parmigiano-Reggiano when a grated cheese is needed. I suppose that this branch of Greek-American cuisine could be characterized as listing somewhat toward Italian-American cuisine (something, of course, that you'd never see in Greece).

Then there are the upscale Greek restaurants in the United States, of which there are more and more every year. Without access to the amazing fish of Greek waters (though a few labor mightily to bring it in), the outstanding lamb of Greece (particularly the baby lamb, not available here), and the fresh Greek herbs that make you feel like Pan on a Mediterranean hillside, Greek restaurants in America largely substitute American ingredients. This is not a bad thing at all — just a different thing.

Turkish cuisine gets even less attention in the United States. It is, of course, very similar to Greek food in a number of overlapping areas; but there are other parts of Turkish cuisine that seem more Middle Eastern than Greek food does. The Turkish food that's represented in American Turkish restaurants is far more often in the Greek/Turkish overlap area.

What we don't see here, for one thing, is the fantastic street food of Istanbul: amazing breads, both round and European; boiled sheep-head sandwiches; rollable flat-bread "pizza" with ground lamb; fried fish right from the Bosporus; sizzling skewers of innards; wonderfully creamy tripe soup. We do, happily, have versions here of Turkish kebabs — and they are already morphing into Turkish-American creations. What you see in America features larger pieces of meat, usually less pointedly seasoned than the meat

is in Turkey. Once again, this is a good thing; a sense of American muchness and mildness added to the street food of Istanbul gives the food its own brand of deliciousness.

☆ Taramasalata ☆

One of the great features of Greek dining is the array of mezes, or mezedes, that appears at the beginning of a meal — spreads, dips, salads, remarkable little creations that are great with pita bread, olives, and an iced glass of ouzo. In the United States you don't get the same view of the Aegean as you're eating them — but you often do get excellent versions of the mezedes that don't differ a great deal from what you'll find in Greece. One of my favorite "dips" is taramasalata — a whipped puree of carp roe blended with oil, lemon juice, and thickeners (your choice of potato, bread, almonds). The key to making one that tastes as good as it does in Greece is getting good tarama — the carp roe that anchors the dish. You can buy it in refrigerated jars at Greek groceries, it's fine, but for a better result, try to find the light pink version (they call it "white" tarama in Greece). The following recipe is based on the version made by Sotirios Karamouzis, proprietor of the International Grocery in Manhattan — and maker of the best taramasalata I've ever tasted. His secret? Printed here for the first time . . . club soda or seltzer to lighten the puree!

Yield: About 3½ cups, which, along with other dips, is good for a large party (24 to 36 people)

1 (6-ounce) russet potato
4 ounces tarama (Greek-style preserved carp roe)
2 cups vegetable oil

2 tablespoons extra-virgin olive oil
⅓ cup freshly squeezed lemon juice
2 tablespoons very finely minced onion
2 tablespoons finely ground skinless almonds
½ cup club soda or seltzer

1. Boil the potato until tender when pierced with a knife. Remove the potato and let it cool slightly. When cool enough to handle, slip off the skin.

2. Meanwhile, place the tarama in the bowl of a stand mixer outfitted with the whisk attachment. (This could also be done with a big whisk and a strong arm.) Turn on the mixer to medium-high and begin adding the vegetable oil, initially a few drops at a time, then, as the mixture thickens, adding in a very thin stream. This should take about 3 minutes. The mixture will be thickish and appear rather oily. Reduce the speed to medium and add the olive oil and then the lemon juice, which, within a few seconds, will completely emulsify the tarama-oil mixture into a dense mayonnaise-like texture. Blend for about 20 seconds. With the machine still running, add the onion and almonds. Turn off the machine.

3. Pass the potato through a potato ricer (or a food mill fitted with the smallest disk) into the bowl with the tarama-oil mixture. Turn on the mixer to its lowest possible speed and blend in the potato for about 20 seconds. Add the club soda or seltzer and blend on high speed for about 5 seconds. Turn off the machine and scrape down the sides of the bowl with a rubber spatula to incorporate

the watery edges. Blend on high speed for another 10 seconds. The mixture should be dense and a bit fluffy. Serve with warm bread or as part of an assortment of other Greek mezes.

✳ Tzatziki ✳

The great yogurt-and-cucumber combo of Greece and Turkey is very popular in the United States, where it usually does multiple duty. In a thicker form, it's often served on meze appetizer platters (along with hummus, taramasalata, baba ghanouj, and others). When it's a little thinner, it's sometimes served at parties as a dip. And when it's runny, it is often served as a sauce for kebabs, gyros, and lamb dishes. The texture of the following recipe is fully adjustable (by adding or subtracting yogurt) — but, as constituted, it's a thick, garlicky stand-up version.

Yield: 8 to 12 servings as part of a Greek appetizer course

2 cups whole-milk yogurt
2 small cucumbers
1 teaspoon kosher salt
2 tablespoons chopped fresh mint
2 tablespoons chopped fresh dill
1 tablespoon olive oil
2 teaspoons finely chopped garlic
2 teaspoons white wine vinegar
1 teaspoon lemon juice
½ teaspoon sugar

1. Line a strainer with cheesecloth. Add yogurt, cover with plastic wrap, place over bowl, and drain overnight in the refrigerator. After draining you should have about

1¼ cups thick yogurt. Reserve both the yogurt and the liquid that drained off.

2. Peel cucumbers and halve lengthwise. Scoop out seeds with a spoon and discard. Thinly slice cucumbers and place in a strainer over a bowl. Toss cucumbers with the kosher salt and let drain 30 minutes, tossing occasionally. Rinse briefly and dry on a kitchen towel.

3. Place yogurt in a medium bowl. Add cucumbers, the mint, and the remaining ingredients. Stir to combine. Season to taste with salt and pepper.

NOTE: If mixture is too thick for your purpose, add back some of the drained yogurt liquid until you reach the desired consistency.

✩ Skordalia ✩

The famous potato-and-garlic puree of Greece is one of my favorite meze dips at Greek appetizer time; the combo of earthy potato, sharp garlic, tart lemon juice, and fruity olive oil is extraordinary. It can also be served in other ways, such as a warm sauce at main-course time — in which case you'd thin the following recipe out with a bit more hot chicken stock. But I like it at room temperature and very garlicky. If you'd like it even more garlicky — and some people love it at mouth-searing level — by all means, ratchet up that garlic ratio.

Yield: About 2½ cups

1 pound peeled potatoes in large, same-size chunks
2 tablespoons freshly squeezed lemon juice
2 tablespoons fruity olive oil
2 tablespoons garlic paste
  (see Garlic paste note)
4 teaspoons powdered almonds
  (see Powdered almonds note)
2 teaspoons red wine vinegar
Pinch of sugar
At least ¼ cup hot chicken stock

1. Place the potatoes in salted boiling water and cook until they are tender (20 to 30 minutes, depending on the size of your potatoes). Drain in colander and immediately pass potatoes through a ricer (you can break them up in other ways — food mill, hand mashing, and so on — but the ricer yields the best texture for this dish). Place riced potatoes in a large mixing bowl.

2. Immediately add lemon juice, olive oil, garlic paste, powdered almonds, and vinegar. Blend well with a fork. Taste for seasoning; add salt as necessary, and a pinch of sugar.

3. Blending with a fork, pour in the ¼ cup of hot chicken stock. If you'd like a looser consistency, pour in a little more. Serve immediately, or bring to room temperature and serve. Taste for seasoning again just before serving.

GARLIC PASTE NOTE: To make garlic paste, simply chop five to six large cloves of garlic sprinkled with a little salt. When they're finely chopped, pound the garlic on your board with the flat side of a cleaver, or a heavy knife, until they become a kind of puree.

POWDERED ALMONDS NOTE: To make powdered almonds, place blanched, skinless almonds (whole or slices) in the work bowl of a food processor. You'll need to process more almonds than you need for this dish . . . say, at least half a cup or so, depending on the size of your food processor. Run the machine until you have a fine powder.

✳ Ktipiti ✳

The famous Greek mezes above (taramasalata, tzatziki, skordalia), along with the mezes you'll find in the Middle Eastern section starting on page 235 (hummus, baba ghanouj), get most of the play and most of the attention at appetizer time at Greek restaurants in America. But there's a missing link here: the wonderful feta–and–red pepper dip known as ktipiti that's very popular in Greece. It has a beautiful, deep orange color and a fabulous interplay of dairy and red pepper taste. It is finally getting some attention at a few Greek restaurants across the United States — such as at Milos, in New York City, my favorite Greek restaurant of all in America. The owner of Milos, Costas Spiliadis, has been kind enough to share his great recipe. Just remember as you make it: in the small confines of a home food processor, the mixture and the machine are likely to get hot over the course of the 10 minutes it takes to make the dip. So it's a good idea to stop the motor of your food processor every few minutes, whenever the machine becomes hot to the touch.

Yield: 3½ cups

6 tablespoons olive oil (preferably fruity
    Greek oil), plus extra-virgin olive oil
    for drizzling
3 medium-large red bell peppers,
    seeded and thinly sliced
2 large jalapeños, seeded and finely chopped
1¼ pounds feta cheese, crumbled
    (see Note)
½ teaspoon freshly ground black pepper

1. Place the 6 tablespoons of olive oil in a large skillet over low heat. Add bell peppers and jalapeños. Cook, covered, stirring occasionally, until peppers are completely soft but not browned, about 30 minutes. You should be able to break them apart with a wooden spoon.

2. Place peppers in a food processor. Process until smooth. Add the crumbled feta and ground pepper and blend until a smooth, creamy paste is formed. It will take about 10 minutes. Scrape down the sides of the processor with a spatula occasionally as you go.

3. After blending, place dip in a bowl and refrigerate for at least 30 minutes. Taste for seasoning before serving. To serve, drizzle with extra-virgin olive oil.

NOTE: I know it's heresy, but Greek feta cheese — though it makes a very fine ktipiti — may not be the best choice for this dish. Feta that's a little creamier is even better, such as the feta from Bulgaria or France.

✳ Dolmades/Dolmas ✳
Stuffed with Rice,
Pine Nuts, and Raisins

It would be extremely difficult to say whether this dish is more Greek or Turkish; stuffed vine leaves are extremely popular at both Greek and Turkish restaurants in the United States. The name, however, may tell you which kind of restaurant you're in. Greek-American restaurants usually list them as "dolmades," though in Greece you're more likely to see "dolmathes" — where you're also likely to see them called, collectively, dolmadakia. In Turkey the word used most often would be *dolmas*, or *dolmasi*. Now, there are two traditional ways of preparing stuffed vine leaves. They can be hot, filled with meat, and served with a hot egg-lemon sauce. Or they can be stuffed with rice and served at room temperature, as in the following recipe. There is often a word that follows *dolmades* on a menu tipping you off as to which type you've got. Well, two words actually: the room-temperature meatless ones, like the ones below, are called dolmadakia yialantzi in Greece, and dolmasi zeytinyagli in Turkey. Whatever word you use, these scented rolls make a fabulous addition to any spread of Greek and/or Turkish appetizers.

Yield: 36 stuffed vine leaves

¼ cup golden raisins
¼ cup retsina (or other white wine)
36 vine leaves in a jar,
    plus a few extra for lining the pot
10 tablespoons fruity olive oil
    (preferably Greek)
1 medium bunch scallions, finely chopped
    (white and green parts)
1 tablespoon finely chopped parsley
¾ cup long-grain white rice, unwashed
¼ cup lightly toasted pine nuts
2 tablespoons finely chopped dill
2 lemons, individually squeezed
1 cup chicken stock

1. Place raisins in a small dish and cover with the retsina. Soak for 30 minutes.

2. Remove the vine leaves from the jar. Dip each one briefly in a pot of hot water. Cut off stems, pat dry, and place on paper towels with shiny surface down.

3. Place 2 tablespoons of the olive oil in a sauté pan over medium heat. Add the scallions and the parsley. Sauté for 10 minutes, stirring occasionally.

4. Add the rice, pine nuts, and dill to the pan. Sauté for 5 minutes more. Cool.

5. Place a vine leaf on the counter, shiny side down. Position the base of the leaf, where the stem was, closest to you and the tip of the leaf farthest from you. Place a teaspoon of the cooled filling on the leaf, just above the base. Fold the left-hand side of the leaf over the filling; do the same with the right-hand side of the leaf. Now roll away from you, rolling from the base to the tip of the leaf. You should end up with a roll that's about 2 inches wide. Repeat until you have stuffed all 36 vine leaves.

6. Choose a large pot that just holds 18 dolmades in a single layer (lying horizontally)

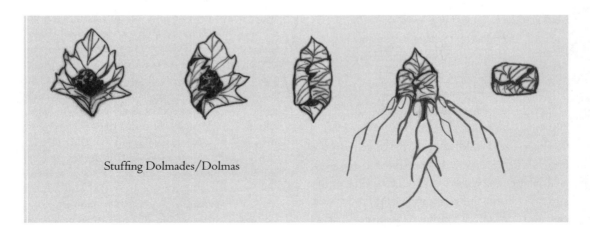

Stuffing Dolmades/Dolmas

on the bottom. Line the bottom with extra vine leaves (if any have broken during the filling process, you can use those). Place 18 of the stuffed dolmades on the bottom of the pot. Fit them in snugly. Sprinkle the juice of 1 lemon and 2 tablespoons of olive oil over the 18 dolmades. Top that layer with a second layer of 18 more dolmades; sprinkle the juice of the 1 remaining lemon and 2 more tablespoons of the olive oil over the second layer. Pour the chicken stock, 1 cup of water, and the remaining ¼ cup of olive oil over all. Place a heavy plate on the two layers of dolmades.

7. Bring liquid to a boil, then turn heat down to very low and cook dolmades, covered, for 50 minutes. Test one; the rice inside should have swelled and should be fully cooked.

8. Remove dolmades from the pot. Drain well. Place on a large platter in a single layer and cover. I like my dolmades kept at room temperature overnight and served at room temperature the next day. Some cooks like to chill them and serve them cold.

☆ Greek Salad / ☆ Shepherd's Salad

The Greek salad doesn't get a lot of respect here. And it probably shouldn't — because most of those refrigerator cases in groceries and delis hold salads that were tossed hours, if not days, ago. The salads often include a bewildering array of "stuff": cheese, olives, low-quality anchovies. I've even seen "Greek salad" with herring in it. The juices run together and make the vegetables watery. Even though I'm fully

dedicated to the virtues of what we eat in America, I cannot give you a recipe for this abomination. However, I can happily report that good Greek and Turkish restaurants in America are now serving something virtually identical to what is called shepherd's salad Over There — a delicious, bright, fresh, crunchy mix of vegetables and parsley with lemon juice and good olive oil. The key is making it just before serving it, not letting it sit. I'm convinced that this is what Greek salad was supposed to be when it came to America — and what it should be now. Irresistible with Greek and Turkish grills of all kinds: fish, fowl, or meat.

Yield: 4 side dish servings

2 cups diced tomatoes (about 4 small ones)
2 cups flat-leaf parsley leaves, whole
1 cup diced green bell pepper, seeded (about 1 large one)
1 cup diced cucumber (about 2 small ones, or half of a large, plastic-wrapped English one)
1 cup diced purple onion
1 teaspoon very finely minced garlic
2 tablespoons freshly squeezed lemon juice
2 tablespoons fruity olive oil

Combine all ingredients in a large bowl. Mix thoroughly. Just before serving, season to taste with salt and pepper.

☆ Chunky Avgolemono Soup ☆

One of the great Greek ideas is the liquid combination of eggs and lemon, sometimes enriched with chicken stock. Avgolemono, as it's called, can be either a soup or a sauce — and it is vastly popular in either form in Greek restaurants in America. The traditional soup is an austere thing, with maybe only a little rice floating in the broth. In America, of course, especially in the current creativity-crazed environment, chefs are complicating their avgolemonos — and I'm not displeased, because this very old warhorse, when served as a soup, can use a little freshening up. The following version adds dill, scallions, and pieces of hard-boiled egg to the traditional recipe — and yields a soul-warming, chunky starter.

Yield: 4 soup servings

1 (3-pound) chicken, quartered
1 onion, peeled and quartered
1 carrot, peeled and roughly chopped
1 stalk celery, roughly chopped
⅓ cup uncooked white rice
2 large eggs, separated
¼ cup lemon juice, plus extra if needed
1 tablespoon unsalted butter
2 tablespoons thinly sliced scallion greens
2 tablespoons chopped dill
3 warm hard-boiled eggs, each cut into about
    8 chunks

1. Place chicken, onion, carrot, and celery in a large Dutch oven. Add water to cover (about 6 to 8 cups) and bring to a simmer. Skim foam from top and discard. Simmer until chicken is falling from the bone and broth is flavorful, at least 2 hours. Strain the broth and reserve. Degrease broth, if desired. Discard vegetables. Pull meat from the chicken and reserve; discard chicken skin and bones.
2. Place reserved broth in a saucepan and boil until reduced to 4 cups of very chickeny broth. Add rice to hot broth and cook, covered, until almost tender, about 12 minutes.
3. Meanwhile, in a medium bowl, whisk the 2 egg whites to soft peaks. Beat and whisk in the 2 egg yolks and the ¼ cup lemon juice. Slowly pour about ½ cup of broth-rice mixture into the egg mixture, whisking constantly. *Very* slowly, pour the rest of the stock into the eggs, whisking the whole time. Pour back into the pan and cook, stirring constantly, over medium heat until mixture thickens slightly (temperature of liquid should be 175 to 180 degrees), about 10 minutes. Whisk in butter.
4. Stir scallion, dill, and reserved chicken meat into soup. Season with salt, pepper, and extra lemon juice to taste. Place 6 chunks of hard-boiled egg into each of four serving bowls and ladle in soup. Serve immediately.

☆ Spanakopita Rolls ☆

Greek cooks love filling their exquisite filo pastry with vegetables or other things, and making pies — known as pitta in Greece. The only one that has gotten onto the American radar screen is the famous spinach-and-cheese-stuffed pie called spanakopitta (but usually spelled with one *t* in the United States). At Greek-American restaurants, if you order it — as an appetizer, or as a side dish, reflecting Cretan practice — you will probably get a square of it cut from a big baking pan of spanakopita. The dish, however, is also popular at American parties — where hosts and hostesses sometimes turn it into hors d'oeuvre finger food, stuffing the filling into filo in such a way as to make individual, triangular pieces (not unlike Indian samosas). I have also seen, at parties, the large roll that's in the following recipe: the spinach-stuffed layers of filo are simply rolled up into a large loaf and baked. This full roll looks absolutely golden-gorgeous when it comes out of the oven.

Yield: 2 rolls, good for 6 appetizer or side dish servings

1½ pounds spinach
At least 5 tablespoons melted butter for
*   brushing filo, plus 2 tablespoons*
*   unmelted butter*
2 large bunches scallions, minced
*   (white and green parts)*
¼ cup grated Parmigiano-Reggiano cheese
2 tablespoons finely minced dill
2 tablespoons olive oil
Dash of freshly grated nutmeg
10 sheets filo pastry, defrosted if the filo was
*   frozen*

1. Wash the spinach. Place it in a large pot with whatever water is clinging to it. Place over medium heat and cook, stirring, until the spinach has drastically reduced in volume (about 5 minutes). Empty pot into colander and let the spinach rest until it's cool enough to handle (a few minutes).

2. Picking up clumps of spinach in your hands, squeeze most of the water out of the spinach. Place the squeezed spinach on a cutting board and coarsely chop it. Reserve in large mixing bowl.

3. Place the 2 tablespoons unmelted butter in a large skillet over medium heat. Add the scallions and sauté, stirring occasionally, until the scallions are soft (about 15 minutes).

4. Add sautéed scallions to spinach in bowl, along with Parmigiano-Reggiano, dill, olive oil, and nutmeg. Stir well to blend completely. Season to taste with salt and pepper.

5. Lay the 10 sheets of filo pastry on the counter; keep them covered with a very lightly damp cloth. Have the 5 tablespoons melted butter and a good, soft pastry brush at hand.

6. Place 1 sheet of filo on the counter, placing the cloth back on the other sheets. Position the sheet so that one of its short sides is directly in front of you. Brush the sheet all over with melted butter, using about 1½ teaspoons. Repeat with 4 more sheets, placing each new sheet exactly on top of the sheet under it. Scoop up half the spinach mixture and place it on the 5 stacked sheets, just above the lower edge that's near you. Spread it out into a log that's about 1½ inches from the lower, left-hand, and right-hand borders.

7. Immediately begin to roll. Fold the left-hand edge of the pastry over the spinach log, making sure that the entire edge of the pastry from bottom to top is folded in (this fold will be about 1½ inches). Do the same thing on the right-hand side. Now, beginning from the short edge right in front of you, start rolling away from you. Keep the pastry tightly filled as you roll. When you reach the top (the short side that's distant from you), you should have a tight roll. Brush a little butter along the seam, if necessary, to seal. Place on a jelly roll pan or a cookie sheet. Hold in refrigerator.

8. Preheat oven to 350 degrees.

9. Repeat with 5 more sheets, more butter, and the remaining half of the spinach mixture to make a second roll. Place second roll on the same sheet as the first (not touching).

10. Place the rolls in the oven. Bake for 25 minutes. Check to make sure they're not sticking or burning. Loosen each on the

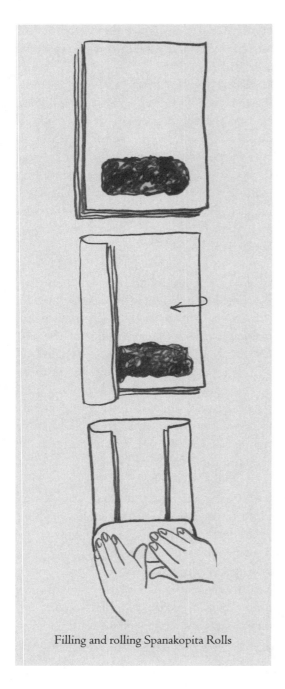

Filling and rolling Spanakopita Rolls

bottom with a spatula. Turn oven up to 400 degrees and cook for 10 minutes more. Remove spanakopita rolls from oven and let them cool for a few minutes. Slice each roll into thirds and serve immediately. They can also be held and served at room temperature.

✯ Marinated Swordfish Kebabs ✯ with Peppers, Tomatoes, Lemon, and Bay Leaf

One of the greatest developments in recent years in Greek and Turkish food in America has been the rise of Greek and Turkish restaurants devoted to grilled seafood. Swordfish kebabs, known as xifias souvlaki in Greece, are highly popular there; they are now, with wonderful reason, growing in popularity in the United States.

Yield: 2 large skewers for 2 main-course servings

1 pound boneless, skinless swordfish, cut 1 inch thick
1 small onion, peeled and grated
1 garlic clove, very finely minced with ½ teaspoon salt
½ teaspoon ground pepper
1 tablespoon lemon juice, plus 1 large lemon
¼ cup olive oil, plus extra for garnish
2 teaspoons tomato paste
1 teaspoon ground cinnamon
1 large green bell pepper
2 medium tomatoes
10 small bay leaves (or 10 pieces of larger bay leaves)

1. Cut the swordfish into 10 (1-inch) chunks.

2. Make the marinade: Combine the onion, garlic, the ½ teaspoon pepper, the 1 tablespoon of lemon juice, the ¼ cup olive oil, tomato paste, and cinnamon. Mix well. Add the swordfish and combine well. Marinate for 5 to 7 hours, covered and refrigerated. After the marination, remove the swordfish chunks, scraping as much marinade back into the bowl as possible. Reserve the marinade. Dry the swordfish chunks with paper towels.

3. Cut the lemon in half lengthwise, then cut each half into four lengthwise slices. Then cut those slices in half crosswise. Reserve 12 of those pieces.

4. Roast the bell pepper over an open flame. Place the charred pepper in a paper bag. Let sit for 15 minutes. Remove blackened skin and seeds from pepper. Cut the bell pepper into 10 pieces, each one about 1 inch square.

5. Cut the tomatoes in half from pole to pole, then into quarters. Scoop out the pulp and seeds (reserve for another use). Cut the remaining tomato flesh into 10 squares of roughly 1 inch.

6. When ready to cook, prepare a medium-hot fire. Make a skewer that contains ingredients in this order: a piece of lemon, a piece of bay leaf, a swordfish chunk, a piece of green pepper, a piece of tomato. Repeat four times, then finish the skewer with a piece of lemon. The skewer will contain 5 chunks of swordfish. Make a second skewer.

7. Salt and pepper the skewers and place them over the fire. Basting with the leftover marinade, cook the skewers 2 to 3 minutes on each of 4 sides, or until the fish is just cooked through.

8. Serve kebabs on a rice pilaf, if desired, with lemon slices as garnish. Drizzle with olive oil and juice from left-over lemon pieces.

✳ Chicken Shish Kebab ✳ with Yogurt Sauce and Hot Buttered Pide

Turkish restaurants have become quite popular in the last decade in many American cities. Though it's a cuisine virtually unknown to most Americans, it shares enough similarities with Greek cuisine to seem not altogether foreign. Of course, it is this very similarity that has the Greeks and Turks perennially arguing about the origins of many shared dishes! The background of the following delicious kebab is pretty clear: though many of the ingredients and ideas are found in Greek cuisine, the notion of slathering cut-up pide (called pitta in Greece, pita in the United States) with yogurt and melted butter, creating a base for grilled meat, is distinctly Turkish. In Istanbul the dish is called Yogurtlu Kebab and is usually made with lamb. I have seen lighter versions, such as the following one made with chicken, in American-Turkish restaurants. I have kept the dish a white-colored one, but it would be quite authentic to garnish it with roasted tomatoes, if you choose.

Yield: 4 main-course servings

FOR THE CHICKEN AND MARINADE:
*1 pound boneless chicken, cut into cubes
    of about 1 inch*
½ teaspoon ground marjoram
¼ cup olive oil, plus extra for the grill
3 garlic cloves, finely minced

¼ cup dry white wine

4 thin slices lemon

¾ teaspoon sweet paprika

1 teaspoon dried oregano

FOR THE YOGURT SAUCE:

2 cups plain yogurt (preferably sheep's milk)

1½ teaspoons very finely minced garlic mixed
    with ¼ teaspoon salt

A little water

FOR THE PIDE:

6 tablespoons butter

3 round, pocketless pide (pita) of about 4-inch
    diameter (see recipe on page 59)

FOR THE GARNISH:

½ cup flat-leaf parsley leaves

1. Season the chicken with salt and pepper. Toss with ground marjoram to coat evenly.

2. Make the marinade: Place the ¼ cup olive oil and minced garlic in a mixing bowl. Whisk in the white wine. Add the lemon slices. Add the chicken and mix thoroughly. Cover and reserve in refrigerator for 5 to 7 hours.

3. When ready to cook, prepare a medium-hot fire. Remove chicken from marinade, reserving marinade, and dry chicken well with paper towels. Thread the chicken onto 4 skewers, about 5 pieces of chicken to a skewer. Season the kebabs with salt and pepper. Sprinkle the kebabs evenly with paprika, on all sides, then sprinkle them evenly with the dried oregano (crush it in your fingers as you apply it). Brush the grill and the kebabs with olive oil. Place the kebabs on the fire, turning to brown on all sides. After the

kebabs have browned a bit on the grill, baste them with the reserved marinade. Cook until they are just past pink, about 2 minutes on each side (8 minutes altogether).

4. Prepare yogurt sauce: Mix together the yogurt and garlic. Add just enough water to make a thick but slightly runny sauce. Season with salt to taste.

5. Prepare the pide: Melt the butter over low heat in a small saucepan. Warm the breads until soft but not toasted (I like to steam them). Cut each pide into four triangles. Place 3 triangles on each of 4 plates. Top the pide triangles on each plate with a tablespoon of melted butter (reserving the other 2 tablespoons of melted butter).

6. Divide the yogurt sauce among the four plates, pouring it directly over the pide triangles. Top the pide on each plate with the chicken from 1 skewer. Divide the remaining 2 tablespoons of butter by pouring it over the chicken on the four plates. Garnish with the parsley.

☆ Adana Kebab on Pide ☆ with Sumac Onions
(Spicy Turkish Ground Meat Kebab)

There is no question about the origins of this terrific dish: Adana, in the south of Turkey, makes a specialty of highly spiced minced meat shaped into rectangular blocks on long, swordlike skewers. Happily, the dish is now starting to turn up in Turkish kebab houses across the United States. We normally do it a little differently here, since the Turkish hot pepper called kirmizi biber is not normally available; paprika or chili powder is used instead. But I highly recommend finding a Middle Eastern grocery store that sells kebab skewers — because making this dish on anything other than a wide, swordlike Adana skewer just wouldn't be the same.

Yield: 4 sandwiches

1 pound ground lamb or beef, not lean
(or a mix of lamb and beef)
2 teaspoons hot paprika (available at gourmet shops) or hot chili powder
1 teaspoon ground cumin
1 teaspoon dried mint, crumbled
½ teaspoon dried oregano, crumbled
¾ teaspoon salt
¼ teaspoon ground pepper
1 egg white
Olive oil, for brushing grill and kebabs
4 pide (see Note)
Sumac Onions (recipe follows)
Plain yogurt for garnish (optional)
Flat-leaf parsley for garnish (optional)

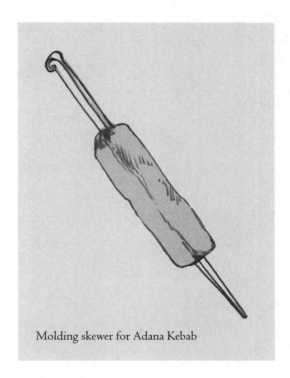

Molding skewer for Adana Kebab

1. Place the ground meat in a mixing bowl and work the paprika, cumin, mint, oregano, salt, and pepper into it with your hands. Add the egg white and pummel the mixture until it's like a paste. (*Note:* The meat will be very wet just after the egg-white addition, but after 5 minutes or so of pummeling it becomes pastelike.)

2. To shape the meat on skewers, it is important to use 2 swordlike skewers with blades that are at least ¾ inch wide. Divide the meat in half. Shape each half onto a skewer, creating a rectangular block on each that is about 6 inches long. The skewer blade should be right in the center of the rectangular block.

Square the meat with your hands. Refrigerate the 2 skewers with their rectangular blocks for 1 to 2 hours.

3. When ready to cook, prepare a hot fire. Brush the grill and the kebabs with olive oil. Cook quickly, about 2 minutes per side (about 8 minutes total). The rectangular block should be crusty on the outside, medium-rare and juicy within. Remove from fire.

4. Cut the kebabs off the skewers, dividing each kebab in half (you'll have a total of 4 halves). Place the kebabs on 4 pide and add sumac onions. You may also add yogurt and flat-leaf parsley.

NOTE: Pide is the Turkish equivalent of Greek pita; in Turkey, pide is made without a pocket. You can make the pitas on page 59 for this recipe, or you can buy pocketless pide at a Turkish or Middle Eastern grocery.

★ Sumac Onions ★

I love using ground sumac either in my Middle Eastern dishes or as a sprinkle on top. The dark garnet powder, made from the sumac berry, looks great, and it adds a delicious, sour, lemony tang. Sumac berries are red and can be purchased whole (in which case you'd grind them yourself), or you can buy ground sumac. Sumac is now widely available in Middle Eastern groceries, and in some fancy groceries. A good and reliable source is Dean and DeLuca, at 800-221-7714. If you can't find it, toss the onions with a little paprika, cayenne, and lemon juice.

> 2 medium-large sweet onions, peeled
> 1½ teaspoons ground sumac

Slice the onions as thinly as possible. Toss with the sumac.

☆ Moussaka ☆

Greeks and Turks hotly dispute the origins of this great casserole dish, but the Greeks have won the PR war in the United States — here, moussaka is not only associated with Greek food but is *the* dish that first comes to mind when Americans think Greek. I think of it as a Greek-Turkish equivalent of lasagna: instead of noodle layers you have eggplant layers; instead of beef and pork you have lamb; instead of oozy cheese on top you have custardy white sauce. Intriguingly, in the same way that lasagna has been transmogrified in Italian-American cuisine, so has moussaka been changed in Greek-American cooking: the emphasis comes off the eggplant (or the pasta), the meat ratio rises, and the sauce emerges as a key

factor in the dish. I love the more austere moussakas of Greece and Turkey — but I also love the tomatoey, exuberant ones of my neighborhood Greek restaurant, reproduced here.

Yield: About 10 main-course servings

> 3 large eggplants
> Olive oil for rubbing the eggplants,
>   plus another 5 tablespoons olive oil
> 2 pounds ground lamb
> 2 large onions, chopped
> 4 garlic cloves, chopped
> 2 teaspoons dried oregano
> 1 teaspoon ground cinnamon
> ½ cup dry red wine
> 2 tablespoons red wine vinegar
> 2 (14½-ounce) cans chopped tomatoes,
>   undrained
> ¼ cup chopped parsley
> 4 tablespoons butter, plus a little extra, melted,
>   for brushing foil
> 6 tablespoons all-purpose flour
> 3 cups milk
> ¼ teaspoon freshly grated nutmeg
> 6 large eggs, separated
> ½ cup dried bread crumbs
> 1 cup grated pecorino Romano cheese

1. Preheat oven to 375 degrees. Rub eggplants with a little olive oil and prick several times with a fork. Place on a sheet pan and roast, turning every 5 minutes or so, until soft, about 20 to 25 minutes. Cool, then slice into ½ inch thick rounds crosswise.

2. Heat a large skillet over high heat and add a little of the 5 tablespoons of olive oil. Brown the eggplant slices in batches on both sides. You will use about 4 tablespoons of

the olive oil altogether. Drain slices on paper towels and season with salt and pepper.

3. Meanwhile, in a large saucepan, heat the remaining 1 tablespoon of olive oil over medium-high heat. Add the lamb, crumbling with a wooden spoon as it cooks. Cook until well browned, about 10 minutes.

4. In the same pan, add the onions and cook until softened, about 5 minutes. Add the garlic, oregano, and cinnamon; blend well and cook until fragrant, about 1 minute. Increase heat to high and add the wine and vinegar. Boil until liquid is reduced by half. Add the tomatoes and parsley, return to a simmer, and cook 20 minutes.

5. Make béchamel sauce. In another large saucepan, melt the 4 tablespoons of butter over low heat. When melted, add the flour and stir to form a smooth paste. Cook, stirring, until raw flour smell is gone, about 2 to 3 minutes. Increase heat to medium and slowly add the milk, whisking to keep smooth. Bring béchamel sauce to a simmer, add nutmeg, and simmer over low heat for 10 minutes. Cool slightly.

6. Place egg yolks in a large bowl and beat. Whisk in about ½ cup of the cooled béchamel sauce in a slow, steady stream. Add the remaining béchamel in a slightly faster stream, whisking constantly.

7. Whip egg whites until soft peaks form. Gently fold egg whites into yolk-béchamel mixture.

8. Preheat oven to 350 degrees.

9. You are now ready to assemble the dish. Select a large baking pan that is roughly 12½ by 9 by 2 inches. Layer as follows:

one-third bread crumbs
one-third eggplant slices (in one layer, overlapping slightly)
one-third cheese
one-third bread crumbs
one-half tomato sauce
one-third eggplant slices
one-half béchamel
one-third cheese
one-third bread crumbs
one-half tomato sauce
one-third eggplant slices
one-half béchamel
one-third cheese

10. You will need to create a foil extension of the sides of your pan to rise above the pan, so the egg whites in the béchamel can puff up as much as possible. Manipulate long pieces of heavy duty aluminum foil, wrapping them around the pan so they stand 2 inches above the top rim of the pan on all sides. Secure foil around pan with a large rubber band or utility tape. Brush lip of foil with melted butter all around. Place pan in the oven and bake 40 to 45 minutes, until top is browned and béchamel is set. Cool at least 15 minutes before slicing.

☆ Butterflied Leg of Lamb, ☆ Greek Style

A venerable Greek tradition is spring lamb for Easter — but what we call spring lamb in the United States is much older than the spring lamb served in Europe. The good news is: lamb is not a seasonal treat for Americans! We have the same cuts available in

October that we have in April. But for emotional reasons only, it still feels right to me to focus on lamb in the spring. For Easter I like the idea of the following butterflied leg of lamb — the butterflying done by your butcher — served in a Greek fashion. In many parts of the country, April is a good time to kick off the barbecue season. So why not kick it off on Easter weekend with this delicious crowd pleaser? I love this lamb with Greek-Style String Beans Stewed in Tomato Sauce and Olive Oil (recipe follows).

Yield: 10 to 12 main-course servings

½ cup olive oil (preferably Greek)
½ cup lemon juice
8 garlic cloves, smashed
½ cup fresh marjoram or oregano, if available
(use ¼ cup dried oregano and
1 tablespoon ground marjoram
blended together if not)
1 tablespoon salt
2 teaspoons freshly ground pepper
1 leg of lamb, butterflied (after your
butcher has removed the bone,
there should be about 4½ to
5 pounds of meat)

1. Combine all ingredients except the lamb, whisking to make sure they're well blended.
2. Spread the butterflied leg out in a large pan and cover with the marinade. Hold in the refrigerator for 24 hours.
3. Prepare a hot fire on your grill. Remove lamb from marinade and dry well with paper towels. Place over fire and cook until desired degree of doneness is reached, turning the meat several times. I like it crispy brown on the outside, medium-rare on the inside (about 130 degrees on a meat thermometer). Remove lamb from fire, let it rest for 10 minutes, then carve on the diagonal into medium-thick slices.

☆ Greek-Style String Beans ☆ Stewed in Tomato Sauce and Olive Oil

Forget about bright green beans. Forget about oil-consumption worries. To appreciate this dish, you have to imagine that you're at a Greek-American restaurant in the 1960s, the kind where all the dishes of the day are laid out on a steam table, the chef ready to ladle up your choice of what was cooked hours ago. Well, dammit, there's a joy, after all, in long-stewed string beans, a wonderful level of flavor the quick-and-green ones never reach. Down with rabbit food! So the key to getting this dish right is making sure the beans cook long enough. Two hours should be about right . . . but if you're not sure, let 'em cook a little longer. You'll be amazed how delicious they become. In the late stages, there will be nothing but oil left around the beans — so add a little water to the pot if you wish to continue cooking. And as you remove the beans from the oil, keep telling yourself that the Mediterranean diet is healthy, the Mediterranean diet is healthy. . . .

Yield: 4 to 6 side dish servings

3 cups water
1 cup smooth purchased tomato sauce
¾ cup olive oil
¼ cup red wine vinegar
1 teaspoon dried marjoram (or oregano)
½ teaspoon ground cinnamon
1 pound fresh string beans, stem ends removed
6 lemon slices
3 tablespoons minced fresh dill leaves for
garnish

1. Mix together the water, tomato sauce, olive oil, vinegar, marjoram, and cinnamon in a stewing pot. Add the string beans and mix again. Place the pot over high heat, until mixture comes to the boil. Then lower heat to reach a medium simmer. Cook, uncovered, for about 2 hours. When done, the beans will be very tender and the sauce will be mostly red-colored oil. Season with salt and pepper. Remove beans from pot, leaving some oil behind, and place on a platter. Let sit for 15 to 20 minutes before serving. Or hold in the refrigerator overnight and serve the next day at room temperature (I think they're even better this way).

2. Just before serving, toss beans with lemon slices and garnish with fresh dill.

☆ Pita Bread ☆

The great round, flat breads of Greece, Turkey, and the Middle East don't usually get a great representation in the United States. Most people know them from the supermarket version. There they are usually called pita pockets, because each bread has a hollow center that can be filled with sandwich stuffings. The worst part about them is that they're usually dry, crumby (literally and metaphorically), way past prime. In the Old World, pita usually does not have a pocket; if it's used to enclose food, it's simply folded over. More important, it is usually hot out of the oven, tender and chewy simultaneously, a baker's delight. The following recipe, I think, features the best of everything. You can separate the walls of these pitas once they're out of the oven, so a pocket is formed if you wish. Or you can keep the walls together and simply fold the pita if you'd like to enclose food that way. Of course, no enclosing or sandwich-making is necessary at all — for these are magical disks, as tender-chewy as what you'll find in Greece or Turkey, as good on their own, as an accompaniment to a Mediterranean meal, as you can get.

Yield: 10 pitas, 6 to 7 inches each

1¼ cups water
1 package active dry yeast
1 teaspoon sugar
6 cups all-purpose flour
2 teaspoons salt
¾ cup whole milk
Olive oil for greasing
Coarse cornmeal

1. Heat water to 110 degrees, using an instant-read thermometer to check temperature. Dissolve yeast and sugar in ½ cup of the water. Let sit for 5 minutes. (Yeast should bubble a bit; if it doesn't, your yeast isn't fresh and you need to start over with fresh yeast.) Set remaining ¾ cup water aside.

2. Combine flour and salt and put in bowl of a stand mixer fitted with a dough hook. Add

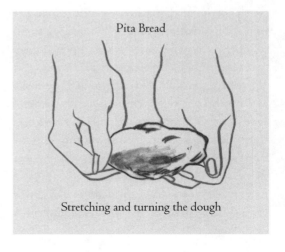

Pita Bread

Stretching and turning the dough

dissolved yeast mixture, remaining water, and milk. Turn mixer on low speed and knead for 10 minutes altogether. Stop the mixer two or three times during the first few minutes and scrape down the sides of the bowl to make sure that all the flour is incorporated. After the dough is kneaded halfway — 5 minutes — turn the dough over in the bowl and continue to knead for an additional 5 minutes. This will ensure that the dough is kneaded uniformly.

3. Remove dough and shape into a ball. Place dough top down in a lightly oiled mixing bowl. Turn dough over so top is greased. Cover bowl with plastic wrap. Let rise in a warm place until dough doubles in size, about 2 hours. Divide dough into 10 equal sections by pulling pieces off the edge of dough and forming each piece into a smooth ball. Place balls on a baking sheet sprinkled with coarse cornmeal and cover with a damp towel. Let rise for 30 minutes.

4. Holding a ball of dough with both hands off the counter, start to stretch the dough gently in both directions by pulling at the edges. This is intuitive work. Continue turning and stretching the dough until a disk is formed about 7 inches in diameter and between ⅛ inch and ¼ inch thick. The disks will not be perfect circles. Cover and let rise again for 30 minutes. (For pitas with a smoother-looking surface and a more circular shape, you can use a rolling pin — but the texture won't be as good.)

5. Preheat oven to 475 degrees. Sprinkle baking stone with coarse cornmeal and place stone in oven.

6. Put dough disks on baking stone, making sure they do not touch each other. If you are not using a baking stone, place disks directly on racks in oven. In 2 to 4 minutes each disk will rise into a mound. As soon as the disks puff up, turn them over using tongs. Cook another minute. Remove from the oven and allow to cool on a wire rack.

☆ Galaktoboureko ☆

Baklava gets most of the buzz at Greek dessert time — but galaktoboureko, or filo pastry filled with custard and soaked in lemony syrup — is always my favorite. It is a staple of Greek restaurants in the United States.

Yield: 12 to 15 servings

1 cup sugar
¾ cup quick-cooking farina (cream of wheat)
6 cups whole milk
3 eggs
1 (1-pound) package filo dough, thawed
About 6 ounces (1½ sticks) unsalted butter, melted
Spiced Syrup for Galaktoboureko (recipe follows)

1. Combine sugar, farina, and milk in a 6-quart saucepan. Bring to a boil over medium-high heat, stirring constantly with a wooden spoon. When the mixture thickens, turn down the heat and cook for 3 minutes more.

2. Whisk eggs in a large bowl. In a thin stream, whisk in about ½ cup of the hot milk mixture. Pour egg-milk mixture into

the saucepan containing the rest of the milk mixture, whisk well, and cook for another minute, stirring. Remove from heat and cover with a sheet of plastic wrap, arranging it so that the film touches the surface of the custard (this will prevent a skin from forming). Place in refrigerator to cool.

3. Preheat oven to 350 degrees.

4. When the custard is cool, take the filo from the package and lay it flat on the counter. Cover with a damp towel so it doesn't dry out. Working quickly, remove one sheet, brush it with melted butter, and lay it in a 9 by 13-inch pan. Don't worry if the filo sheet is too big — just let it hang over the edges of the pan. Repeat with 7 more sheets of filo.

5. Pour the cooled custard over the filo, leveling it with a spatula.

6. Butter another sheet of filo and lay it gently over the custard. Repeat with 7 more layers. When the layering is done, roll the overhanging edges of the 14 filo sheets inward, into the pan, creating a kind of rim around the galaktoboureko. If you have leftover filo, wrap it tightly in plastic wrap and store in the freezer.

7. With a sharp knife, score a diamond pattern on top of the pastry, making sure you don't cut through to the custard. Bake until golden on top, about 40 minutes.

8. Cool the pastry in the pan on a rack for 5 minutes. Strain the hot (or room temperature if made the night before) spiced syrup and pour it over. It may look like a lot, but the pastry will absorb it all.

9. When ready to serve, cut either into squares or into the more traditional diamond shapes. I prefer to eat galaktoboureko when it's still warm, but it will keep perfectly well, unrefrigerated, until the next day. I do not like it cold from the fridge.

★ Spiced Syrup ★ for Galaktoboureko

I recommend making the syrup the night before you make the galaktoboureko; this gives the flavorings a chance to infuse. And what a syrup this is! — with much more flavor than most.

> 1½ cups sugar
> ¼ cup honey
> 1 cup water
> 1 lemon, cut into thick slices
> 1 (3-inch) cinnamon stick
> 2 whole cloves
> 2 whole cardamom pods, slightly crushed

1. Combine all ingredients in a 2-quart saucepan, stirring gently to mix.

2. Bring to a boil over medium heat, then turn heat to low and let simmer for 5 minutes. Remove from heat. Cool to room temperature before using.

Spanish Food

The food of Spain is one of the least understood, and least accurately represented, of the European cuisines in America. It is very rare, even today, to find a "Spanish" restaurant in the United States that even suggests the bounty and variety of dining in Spain.

However, a kind of Spanish-American cuisine did evolve in the lobster restaurants of bohemian Greenwich Village, in New York City, that became quite popular in the 1950s and 1960s — a cuisine that still has a life today throughout our country. Frankly, some of the nights I've spent in those joints over the years have been, for me, some of the most mirthful ethnic-restaurant experiences ever in the United States.

It all starts, of course, with pitchers of sangria that have ice and wooden spoons in them. Never mind that in Spain sangria is made only with red wine; it's got a different taste, and a delicious one, when made with a fruity white, as many Americans like it. The meal then usually proceeds, often through the appetizers and into the main course, to shellfish. This part is accurate: for my money, Spain is the greatest shellfish country on earth. But the Spanish-American takes on the dishes are different. Sometimes they're plain as can be (many of the Spanish restaurants around Fourteenth Street and Twenty-third Street in New York are really broiled-lobster houses with some ethnic trappings). Sometimes they serve shellfish with sauces based on Spanish ideas — but you're likely to see more sauce, with more garlic, than you'd see in Spain. A number of specific Spanish dishes, such as paella, have made it onto the Spanish-American menu — but their emphasis is usually on abundance, not on precise technique or subtlety.

The Spanish-American cuisine is not the cuisine of Spain. But when it's cooked well, and honestly, its good spirit and warm nature mingle beautifully with the delirious bounty of the American table.

✷ Gazpacho ✷

The standard American version of gazpacho is one translation I don't particularly like. In an attempt to make gazpacho "light," chefs here often leave out the bread that is the very heart and soul of the dish (even of its name — that's the *pa* part). The result is sometimes a watery, pulpy tomato mess, threatening to fall apart. I'm happy to report that authentic Spanish gazpacho — in which bread holds everything together in velvety suspension — has finally established a beachhead here and is ever easier to find. So I'm including this Spanish-style gazpacho — but with several American twists.

Yield: 6 first-course servings
(about 6 cups of soup)

1 English cucumber (the long, plastic-wrapped,
*   hothouse kind), peeled and seeded*
1 medium red bell pepper
1 medium green bell pepper
½ cup chopped white onion
1 tablespoon chopped garlic
1 (35-ounce) can Italian peeled tomatoes
1 cup loosely packed diced, crustless white bread
*   (approximately 1 slice)*
1 tablespoon plus 1 teaspoon sherry vinegar
2 tablespoons olive oil
½ cup finely chopped purple onion
½ cup finely chopped hard-boiled egg
½ cup tiny croutons (recipe follows)
3 tablespoons finely minced parsley

1. Cut half of the cucumber into coarse chunks and place them in the work bowl of a blender or food processor; reserve the other cucumber half for garnish. Add to the work bowl half of the red bell pepper, seeded and coarsely chopped, and half of the green bell pepper, seeded and coarsely chopped, reserving the remaining portion of each vegetable for garnish. Add the onion, garlic, the entire can of tomatoes (including juice), the bread, sherry vinegar, and olive oil. Process until very smooth. Season to taste with salt and pepper. Refrigerate for 2 to 4 hours.

2. Meanwhile, prepare the garnishes. Finely dice the remaining cucumber and place it in a small bowl. Finely dice the remaining bell pepper halves and place each in a small bowl. Place the purple onion, the hard-boiled egg, and the croutons in small bowls.

3. When ready to serve, remove gazpacho from refrigerator. Season to taste with additional salt and pepper. Divide among six wide soup bowls and sprinkle with parsley. Serve chilled with garnishes on the side.

★ Tiny Croutons for Gazpacho ★

I created this recipe some years ago for a fancier gazpacho — but these crunchy, flavorful little nubbins remain my favorite croutons for any gazpacho.

8 slices very, very thinly sliced white bread,
  crustless
3 tablespoons olive oil
1 large garlic clove, crushed

1. Dry out the white bread slices either by leaving them on a kitchen counter for 1 to 2 days or by baking them in a warm oven (200 degrees) for about an hour. The bread slices should be dry but not crumbly.

2. Cut the slices into tiny dice, place them in a colander, and shake off the crumbs.

3. Heat the olive oil in a heavy sauté pan over medium-low heat. Add the garlic and sauté for 5 minutes. Add the diced bread to the pan, stirring very gently to coat croutons with oil. Cook them in a single layer over medium-low heat for about 30 minutes, stirring often for even browning. They're done when golden brown. Season well with salt and pepper. Let cool.

☆ Shrimp in Garlic Sauce, ☆ Spanish Style

Almost every tapas bar in Spain serves a made-to-order tapa of shrimp sizzling in garlic sauce; you order it, then they cook it quickly for one person in a small, earthenware crock, which is thought to intensify the flavor. In the United States, shrimp with garlic sauce has been a mainstay at Spanish restaurants for years — even the 1950s kind of places in Greenwich Village. However, in our restaurants you're less likely to see it served in the individual crocks — and if you abandon the crocks, it's much, much easier to make at home for several people at a time. The following recipe is a superb, one-pan version of the dish — with so much flavor you'd never know no crock's involved!

Yield: 4 first-course servings

1 pound small shrimp (40 to 50 shrimp),
  shelled
3 tablespoons extra-virgin olive oil
  (preferably from the south of Spain)

8 to 10 large garlic cloves, peeled and
finely minced

2 dried red chili peppers, each broken into
3 pieces

½ teaspoon sweet paprika (preferably the smoky
kind from Spain; see Note)

3 tablespoons finely minced parsley

I. About ½ hour before cooking, season shrimp well with salt. Place shrimp on paper towels, cover with paper towels, and let rest.

Tapas in America

It was in the 1980s that most Americans became aware of the great Spanish tapas tradition — little nibbles of good things, meant to be consumed before lunch or dinner. And there followed, of course, lots of restaurants here that advertised themselves as tapas bars. However, everyone soon found out that the concept cannot function here as it does in Spain. There, diners start strolling at, say, 8 P.M. from tapas bar to tapas bar in the big cities (such as Madrid), choosing from the selections on the counter, having wine, meeting friends, starting the evening's festivities. At 10 P.M. or later they go for dinner . . . at other restaurants that don't serve tapas. In America, places that served tapas alone couldn't survive, because we don't live the same way; we like to go to one establishment at 7:30 or so and stay there. Tapas have remained with us, in America — but they are today indistinguishable from appetizers in Spanish restaurants. And, of course, they are fabulous pass-around hors d'oeuvres for dinner parties.

2. When ready to cook, place olive oil in a large sauté pan over medium-high heat. Add the garlic and the pieces of chili pepper. Sauté 2 minutes; make sure garlic doesn't brown.

3. Dry the shrimp well. Add them to the hot oil and turn them quickly to coat with oil. Cook, tossing, until the shrimp are just done — no more than 2 minutes. As they finish cooking, sprinkle with the paprika and parsley; stir to blend well. Remove from heat and add salt to taste. Divide among four appetizer plates and serve immediately with good bread for sopping up the oil.

NOTE: This dish will work with any type of sweet, nonbitter paprika. However, if you can get your hands on pimentón — the wonderfully smoky paprika that's made in Spain — so much the better; it will add real dimension to the dish. A good source for it, and all things Spanish, is:

The Spanish Table
1427 Western Avenue
Seattle, WA 98101
206-682-2827

✴ Sautéed Chorizo Tapa ✴

One of the great tapas bar items in Spain is simplicity itself: sautéed slices of the cured, paprika-laden Spanish pork sausage called chorizo. It has increasingly caught on at Spanish restaurants in the United States — especially now that the quality of chorizo available in the United States (made both domestically and in Spain) has risen dramatically. Unfortunately, there's a lot of inferior chorizo out there too — so if you can't find a good one, you should refrain from making this dish (see Chorizo note). If

✫✫✫

you do get your hands on the right stuff, this recipe makes a wonderful party dish, or dinner-party first course. If you're passing the cooked slices around, you could put them on toothpicks or on small skewers with pieces of crusty bread attached. If you're going the sit-down route, a nice presentation involves the careful arrangement of slices on small plates, garnished with a julienne of red bell pepper.

Yield: 8 appetizer servings

1 pound good-quality cured chorizo,
*   not too aged*
½ cup roasted red bell pepper, or roasted red
*   pepper in a jar, julienned (optional)*

1. Cut the chorizo into 48 longish diagonal slices. To do so, lay the sausage from left to right, then angle your knife at about 45 degrees from the tip of the sausage before you begin slicing. Each slice should be about ¼ inch thick.
2. Place a large cast-iron pan over medium heat. If you have more pans, you can heat all the chorizo slices at once; alternatively, you can cook the chorizo in batches. Place the chorizo slices in the pan (or pans) in a single layer. Cook, turning once, until the slices are browned on the outside, heated through on the inside (about 2 minutes per side). Remove and serve. If you're using the roasted red pepper, arrange 6 slices of cooked chorizo in a circle on each of eight appetizer plates, one end of each piece reaching the center of the plate. Top each circle with a tablespoon of room-temperature red pepper julienne at the center, where the ends of each piece meet.

CHORIZO NOTE: Chorizo is a confusing subject because it comes in such a variety of forms. Spanish, or Spanish-style, chorizo, can be anywhere from very lightly cured, and very fresh, to strongly cured and very aged. It can be loaded with paprika and spices or mildly seasoned, tasting mostly of pork. It can be fiery hot or not hot at all. It can be long and thin or short and thick or any other permutation of dimensions (most of the Spanish chorizos in our market are about four inches long and seven-eighths inch in diameter).

To make matters much more confusing, there's the whole world of Mexican chorizo. On the West Coast of the United States, buying chorizo often means buying fresh ground (not cured), strongly seasoned pork — sometimes not even in the casing. There are also plenty of Mexican chorizos in casings, but they usually retain that family character of fresh meat, and a good blast of Mexican spicing.

It is important to know whether your chorizo is a cured, Spanish-style one or a fresh, Mexican-style one: the fresh ones, made from raw pork, *must* be cooked. The cured ones can be sliced and eaten as they are, or they can be cooked.

My choice for this Chorizo Tapa is Spanish, or Spanish-style, chorizo, cured but lightly aged. When you squeeze it, it gives; imagine the feel of squeezing a hard-boiled egg and you've got the idea. Don't expect to find this at your supermarket; most of the Spanish or Spanish-style chorizos now in the major distribution channels are quite aged; many of them taste dry, pebbly, salty, sour, rubbery, and artificial. Don't despair, however. You can find terrific lightly aged chorizo now at many Spanish specialty stores. Additionally, a number of companies will supply you with great chorizo by mail order. Look especially for chorizos from Los Galleguitos (Union City, New Jersey) and for chorizo Bilbao from Dona Juana (Harbor City, California).

Lastly, if you wish to taste the thrill of great Spanish-made, long-aged chorizo, thinly sliced and served uncooked, bursting with pork-paprika-chili flavor, you must try the Palacios Chorizo Picante, available through a Virginia company called La Tienda (just log on to *www.tienda.com*). I can't think of a better tapa than very thin, diagonal, uncooked slices of this amazing stuff served on a platter. Great as a flavor booster for hero sandwiches, too!

★ Zarzuela de Mariscos ★

Zarzuela means "light opera" — and a light shellfish stew of that name (*mariscos* means "shellfish") is made across Spain, with regional variations. "Zarzuela" is also one of the handful of names that made it onto menus at Spanish restaurants in America forty years ago. The classic American zarzuela is different from the Spanish ones. It uses American shellfish, of course. More important, it emphasizes the clichés of Spanish cooking: lots of bell peppers are used, and the Spanish proclivity for sausage and shellfish together is well represented. The result is an easy-to-make, absolutely delicious party showstopper. Garlic toast makes a nice accompaniment.

Yield: 4 servings

½ cup high-quality extra-virgin olive oil
    (preferably Spanish), plus additional
    for drizzling
3 ounces chorizo (cured Spanish sausage) sliced
    ⅛ inch thick, cut into small bite-size
    pieces (see Chorizo Note, page 65)
¾ pound medium shrimp, unpeeled
1 large onion, finely chopped
4 garlic cloves, minced
½ red bell pepper, cut into ¼-inch dice
½ green bell pepper, cut into ¼-inch dice
3 tablespoons brandy (preferably Spanish)
1 cup dry white wine
1 (28-ounce) can good-quality tomatoes,
    chopped
1 teaspoon sweet paprika
⅛ teaspoon cayenne
1 bay leaf
1 cup water
24 small clams, well scrubbed (preferably
    Manilla clams or New Zealand cockles,
    but littlenecks will do)

40 mussels, beards removed and well scrubbed
½ pound medium squid, cleaned, bodies cut
    into ⅜-inch rings, tentacles cut in half
    lengthwise (if large)
30 medium-size high-quality green olives,
    pits removed, coarsely chopped
½ pound bay scallops
6 sprigs parsley, chopped
12 slices baguette, ½ inch thick, lightly toasted,
    rubbed with garlic, and drizzled
    with extra-virgin olive oil

1. In a large straight-sided pan with a tight-fitting lid, heat the olive oil over medium heat. Add the chorizo and cook for about 2 minutes, stirring occasionally. Remove chorizo with a slotted spoon and set aside. Turn the heat to high; when the oil is almost smoking, add the shrimp and sear them for 30 seconds on each side. Immediately remove from the pan and set aside. They should be almost, but not quite, cooked through. Turn off the heat and let the pan cool for at least 2 minutes.

2. In the same pan over medium-low heat, add the onion, garlic, and red and green bell peppers. Cook gently for 10 minutes, stirring occasionally. Do not allow the mixture to color. Raise the heat to medium-high and add the brandy. Carefully ignite the brandy with a match and allow the flame to die. Add the white wine, tomatoes, paprika, cayenne, bay leaf, and water. Cook at a gentle simmer over medium heat for about 5 minutes.

3. Raise the heat to high and add the clams. Cover the pan and cook for 4 minutes, shaking the pan occasionally. Add the mussels

and cover. Cook until the shellfish have opened, about 3 minutes more. Uncover the pan and reduce the heat to medium. Add the squid tentacles and cook for 30 seconds. Add the squid rings, green olives, scallops, reserved chorizo, and reserved shrimp. Cook for 1 minute more, until the squid and scallops are just cooked through and the other ingredients are reheated.

4. Arrange the seafood in four warmed serving bowls. Spoon the tomato mixture and any pan juices over each. Drizzle with additional olive oil and garnish with parsley.

Spanish Paprika

Paprika is one of the glories of Spain — particularly when the chilies are smoked and the paprika comes to the market with a glorious smoky flavor. Smoked Spanish paprika was almost impossible to find in the United States some years ago, but it is widely available now — and adds a huge boost of flavor to any Spanish dish that calls for paprika. See ordering details on page 64.

☆ Crowded Paella ☆ with Shrimp, Clams, Mussels, Lobster, Chicken, and Chorizo

There are huge differences between paella in the United States and paella in Spain — but a good American version, like the one below, is a beautiful thing. Paella is one of those European dishes that draw attention, in Europe, to the primary ingredient. Italians obsess about the pasta, not the sauce. Alsatians obsess about the sauerkraut in choucroute, not the sausages. Gascons obsess about the beans in cassoulet, not the meats. And Spaniards, of course, want the rice in paella to be perfect — which is to say, still a little chewy, and rich (though not as creamy and rich as Italian risotto), and intensely flavored. In Spanish-American restaurants, the rice usually gets secondary attention. There the focus, undoubtedly, is on how much "stuff" is nestled in the rice — usually much more "stuff" than you see in Spain. But here's a curious fact: if you cram a paella with shellfish, all the juices are going to drip into the rice, making it very

flavorful indeed. The following recipe has all those details worked out, yielding one of the most flavorful American-style paellas I've ever tasted — and one with shellfish that's not overcooked, to boot!

Yield: 4 main-course servings

1 (1½-pound) lobster
8 large shrimp, peeled and deveined, tails on, shells reserved
2 cups chicken stock
⅛ teaspoon saffron threads
1 tablespoon olive oil
4 boneless, skinless chicken thighs, each cut into 4 pieces
2 ounces lightly cured chorizo, thinly sliced (see Chorizo note, page 65)
2 shallots, finely chopped
2 garlic cloves, finely chopped
¼ cup chopped parsley, plus additional for garnish
1 cup medium-grain white rice
2 teaspoons sweet paprika

½ teaspoon ground turmeric
8 littleneck clams, scrubbed
½ pound mussels, scrubbed
1 large red bell pepper, roasted, peeled, seeded,
    and cut into strips

1. Ask your fishmonger to kill the lobster and to remove claws and tail from lobster body. When you get the lobster home, wrap each claw in a kitchen towel and crack in several places with a mallet. Set aside. Cut the lobster tail in half lengthwise. Set aside. Chop lobster "chest" section into several pieces.

2. In a small saucepan, combine lobster chest pieces, reserved shrimp shells, chicken stock, and saffron. Bring to a simmer, simmer 20 minutes, then strain. Measure liquid again to be sure you have 2 cups. If not, add a little water.

3. In a large wok, heat olive oil over high heat. Add chicken pieces and brown on all sides, about 4 minutes. Add chorizo and toss. Add shallots, garlic, and ¼ cup parsley, tossing to coat. Quickly add rice, paprika, and turmeric; stir with a wooden spoon to coat all the rice grains with oil. Pour stock over all. Cover wok with foil, then the wok lid. Reduce heat and simmer 5 minutes; add lobster claws and tail pieces, cover the wok with foil and lid, and simmer 5 more minutes.

4. Remove cover and place shrimp, clams, and mussels on top of rice, pressing them into the rice a bit with a wooden spoon. Sprinkle with pepper strips. Cover again with foil and wok lid; simmer another 15 minutes or until clams and mussels have all opened and rice is cooked. Serve garnished with parsley.

French Food

The food of France occupies a unique but paradoxical position in America.

On the one hand, techniques developed in France over the centuries have played as important a role as any foreign culinary ideas have in shaping our cuisine. Probably more. French cooking, for much of the Western world, is the "mother cooking" — and many of our mainstream sauces, salads, ways with fish, ways with vegetables, ways with meats, stews, roasts, breads, cakes, pies, and ice creams came directly to us out of French kitchens.

On the other hand, the food of France is virtually unknown to the average American. Call for a list of Italian dishes, or Chinese dishes, and prepare to hear scores; call for a list of French dishes and prepare to hear hesitation.

There are two reasons for this. For one, with the exception of French migration to Louisiana, there never has been a major influx of French immigrants to our shores; we've got Little Italy, we've got Chinatown, but we certainly have never had Little France or Francetown. Second, the greatness of the food in France — aside from the genius of French technique — firmly rests on the obsessive quality of ingredients. Why is the grand French tradition of cheese only just coming to life in the United States? Because we never had the kind of mind-bending cheese on these shores that they have in France. How come a fabulous dish like choucroute never caught on in America, despite our love of hot dogs and sauerkraut? Because the terrifically fine, delicate sauerkraut that makes the dish in Alsace is simply not available here. The essence of French cooking is hard to transplant.

However, despite the fact that France does not have "breakout" dishes in America, for many years chefs have built an American version of French food in America. These versions really picked up steam after attendees at the 1939 World's Fair in New York City were wowed by the cooking of Le Pavillon. A few years later, a small band of postwar immigrants arrived on the docks of the west side of Manhattan, walked the few blocks toward the theater district, and began building a relatively concentrated neighborhood of simple French restaurants.

What you'd find in those places in the 1950s — which is what you would have found in homes where someone was cooking "French" food at that time, and what you might find today in some "French" restaurants in smaller American cities — is a kind of streamlined version of French food, French food minus the fussy technique. Ratatouille is a good example; unlike the most exalted versions in good restaurants in Provence, where all the vegetables may be sautéed separately, the French-American cook has tended to cook 'em all together in one pot. Similarly, in the fabulous stews of the French heartland, a great deal of technical care is given to each and every ingredient, finally bringing them all together in a symphony of different tastes and textures; typical American home versions of coq au vin or boeuf bourguignon are more like good old-fashioned American stews, simple and direct. Much of this food stays true to the spirit of France — but picks up a kind of winning American innocence.

Later on, a second kind of French-American blending took place: the very most well-known French dishes would go rapidly through the Americanizing machine — often coming out with little resemblance to the originals. This type of Franco-American food is best forgotten. Quiche, for example — an eastern French specialty — had a huge spurt of popularity in the 1960s and 1970s. And along with that came the inevitable. One American magazine in the 1970s published a recipe for Cottage Cheese Quiche with Canned French-Fried Onion Rings; another published Cranberry-Carrot Quiche with Whipped Cream. I didn't taste these dishes, but I'm betting they were not good ideas. At about the same time, crepe restaurants became trendy. Once again, the menus stretched the crepe to accommodate all kinds of wacky things you'd never see in Brittany; I remember being served sirloin tips in a crepe, a coupling I never expect to see again. The crepe should be there to blend with its contents, not to provide a starched jacket for them.

More recently, French-American blending in the United States finally reached its apex — even though most Americans still don't think of the result as French food. The strain of cuisine of which I speak is based on the startling, highly creative ideas that began to appear in France in the 1970s. Heavy sauces were eschewed. Traditional platings were ignored. Escoffier was abandoned. A new generation of French chefs — practicing what the restaurant critics Gault and Millau dubbed "la nouvelle cuisine," or "the new cuisine" — lightened their offerings, painted virtual pictures on plates, and turned to Asia for inspiration. Those chefs forged nothing less than a revolution, showing the world that French technique and new, modern culinary ideas were not incompatible. Traveling American chefs caught the bug and brought those basic principles back to the United States in the 1980s and 1990s. Today, if you go to an "American" restaurant in New York such as Union Pacific, or an "American" restaurant in Chicago such as Charlie Trotter's, you are getting, in essence, an American spin on a set of ideas that came from France. Indeed, much of this creative food in America today — perhaps because of our lack of hidebound tradition — outcreates the French. Let the pundits argue the point, but my point is this: For the first time ever, a diner who didn't know where he or she was — in an expensive restaurant in France or an expensive restaurant in the United States — might, judging by the food alone, not be able to guess.

✳ Escargots ✳ with Garlic Butter

Sizzling snails in their shells, drenched in garlic butter, is just one of a few French dishes in America that most people know about. Happily, this is not a distortion of what people eat in France; all over that food-crazy country restaurants do serve sizzling snails in garlic butter. And, truth be told, many of them do use canned snails, just as we do here. The results are delicious, because the garlic butter is so good. However, the results are even better with large, fresh snails — an impossible dream for most of us. So, with American ingenuity, the following recipe features a quick simmer for the canned snails that brings them a little closer to the earthy flavor of fresh snails. The classic way to make this dish is to stuff the cooked snails, along with a garlic-parsley butter, into empty snail shells; the shells are placed on ovenproof dishes with six indentations in them, each indentation holding one snail. When the snails are cooked, each diner gets one plate of six snails and, using a special tongs that holds the hot snails, extracts the meat with a long, narrow fork. You can dispense with the shells and the equipment by putting the snails in any available small ramekin you have (even edible "ramekins," such as upside-down mushroom caps, will do). Regardless, serve plenty of crusty bread to sop up the hot, garlicky butter.

Yield: 36 snails, 6 appetizer servings

2 cups chicken stock
½ cup dry white wine
¾ cup chopped celery leaves
1 large bay leaf
36 large canned snails
8 medium-large garlic cloves, peeled
1½ cups firmly packed Italian parsley leaves
½ pound (2 sticks) unsalted butter at cool
    room temperature
36 empty snail shells

1. Place the chicken stock, white wine, celery leaves, and bay leaf in a saucepan. Bring to a boil. Add the snails and bring the broth to a gentle simmer. Cook for 5 minutes, then remove from heat. Let the snails cool in the broth. Discard broth (or save for another use).

2. While the snails are cooling, make the snail butter. Finely chop 4 of the garlic cloves, almost to a paste. Do the same with half the parsley leaves. Place 1 stick of the butter in a large bowl and mix well with garlic and parsley. Place the remaining 4 garlic cloves and the other half of the parsley in a food processor. Process until the garlic and parsley have made a kind of puree. Start motor and add the remaining stick of butter through the feed tube, 2 tablespoons at a time, until all butter has been added. Combine the two butters in a bowl, blending thoroughly, and taste for seasoning, adding a bit of salt if desired.

3. Making sure the snail butter is at or near room temperature, stuff the shells. Dip each cooled snail in the snail butter, letting about ½ teaspoon of the butter cling to the snail (this makes it easier to stuff the snail into the shell). Stuff each shell with one buttered snail. Top the snail with additional snail butter, a little less than a teaspoon in each shell. When you're done, there should be a smooth surface of snail butter across the opening of the shell, with no snail visible.

4. Preheat oven to 500 degrees.

5. Place the stuffed snail shells in snail dishes, if available. Place the dishes on one or more cookie sheets. Place the cookie sheets in the oven and bake for about 10 minutes, or until the butter is sizzling. Watch carefully to make sure the butter doesn't burn. Serve immediately.

✵ Basic French Vinaigrette ✵ with Dijon Mustard and Tarragon

Yes, we Americans love our blue cheese dressings, ranch dressings — even our "French" dressing, which has nothing to do with France! But a small trickle of true French vinaigrette — served only in fancy French restaurants decades ago — has now turned into a virtual torrent in both restaurants and homes in America today. There are many ways to make a French vinaigrette. My favorite method starts with a thick, mustardy base; amazingly, as you add vinegar and oil to it, it doesn't get a lot less thick. That's when it's time for the magic: a little tap water to lighten the dressing, harmonize it, and smooth things out. I also love adding fresh tarragon to my basic vinaigrette; it makes the dressing taste very French. If you let the tarragon-flecked vinaigrette sit for 2 to 3 hours in the refrigerator, the results will be even better. This dressing is wonderful on salad but can also be used in a million other ways: on first-course vegetables (asparagus, artichokes), on hard-boiled eggs, on potatoes, on fish, on meats. . . .

Yield: Enough to dress 6 loosely packed cups of greens

4 teaspoons Dijon mustard
4 teaspoons white wine vinegar
5 tablespoons olive oil
1 tablespoon finely minced fresh tarragon
1 tablespoon water
¼ teaspoon salt

1. Place mustard in a bowl. Slowly whisk in vinegar until it's well blended. The mustard should still be creamy thick.

2. Add olive oil, very slowly at first, whisking as you go. When all the oil is blended in, the vinaigrette should be quite thick. Blend in tarragon leaves. Slowly whisk in water, making sure not to "break" the vinaigrette. Whisk in salt and taste to check seasoning. Cover and let rest in refrigerator for a few hours. If necessary, whisk again before serving.

✸ Frisée with Lardons ✸ and Poached Egg

One of the nicest things about French restaurants in America in recent years is that we have finally discovered the French alternative to fancy food: bistro food! Buildings that once housed "trattorias" in the 1980s started switching over to brasseries and bistros in the 1990s. One of the dishes leading the movement across the United States has been the great warm salad in which frilly, bitter frisée leaves get tossed with warm bits of bacon, their hot fat, vinegar, and a few other things included to add interest. When I've had this dish in bistros in France, I've seen either croutons or crispy potato cubes or a poached egg on top as add-ons; here, of course, I've seen all these things simultaneously. As well as raw purple onions! I love this salad as a first course before a hearty bistro main course, or as a main course for a light lunch. To be really French about it: drink a tart red wine, such as a young Beaujolais, and find out for yourself that wine and salad are not natural-born enemies.

Yield: 2 first-course or luncheon servings

4 cups packed frisée (and other lettuces, if desired)
½ cup olive oil (not the expensive stuff)

4 thick slices of smoky bacon
10 large garlic cloves, peeled and cut into thin slices
6 tablespoons white wine vinegar
⅔ cup home fries (see recipe on page 409), crisp and warm
⅔ cup light, garlicky croutons
⅔ cup very thinly sliced purple onion rings
⅓ cup flat-leaf parsley leaves
2 hot poached eggs

1. Thoroughly wash and spin dry the frisée. Reserve.

2. Place the olive oil in a sauté pan over medium-high heat. Cut the bacon into lardoons that are each about 2 inches long, ⅓ inch wide, ⅓ inch thick. Cook until almost browned. Just before finishing, add the garlic. Sauté until the garlic just starts to turn golden, about 1 minute. Remove bacon and garlic, and reserve.

3. Spill 6 tablespoons of pan fat into a mixing bowl. Whisk in the white wine vinegar until a thick emulsion is formed. Season to taste with salt and pepper.

4. Place frisée in a large mixing bowl. Add bacon and garlic. Add the home fries, croutons, purple onion rings, and parsley leaves. Toss all with warm dressing (you may want to add the dressing in increments, making sure that you have just enough to suit your taste). Season to taste.

5. Divide salad between two dinner plates. Top each salad with a poached egg; season with salt and pepper. Serve immediately.

✷ Ratatouille ✷

The great Provençal melange of vegetables, tomatoes, garlic, and olive oil was not wildly popular in America's French restaurants for most of the twentieth century. Perhaps the tide began to turn with the publication in the 1960s of Julia Child's first book, which contained what I still consider to be the finest recipe for a French-style ratatouille. Then came Peter Mayle, Provence mania, and the flood. Today it's the rare informal French restaurant in America that doesn't offer some version of ratatouille. Of course, many of these ratatouilles have been transformed by American chefs. In Provence, a pretty tightly prescribed group of vegetables is used; American chefs throw in other things on a whim (such as the yellow squash below). In the Provençal tradition, ratatouille is served as a room-temperature appetizer; in American restaurants, it may be that, or a hot side dish, or a hot topping or bed for the main course. The following recipe has both French and American elements, but however you classify it or use it . . . it is a terrific ratatouille, rich with the flavors of Provence.

Yield: 6 appetizer or side dish servings

2½ cups unpeeled eggplant cut into ½-inch dice
  (about a 7-ounce eggplant)
1 teaspoon salt
Approximately ⅓ cup good extra-virgin
  olive oil, plus 2 tablespoons
  high-quality extra-virgin
  olive oil for finishing
1 cup yellow squash cut into ½-inch dice
  (about ¼ pound yellow squash)
1 cup zucchini cut into ½-inch dice
  (about ¼ pound zucchini)
½ cup red bell pepper cut into ½-inch dice
  (1 pepper, about 2 ounces)
½ cup green bell pepper cut into ½-inch dice
  (1 pepper, about 2 ounces)

2 cups thinly sliced onion (about 1 large onion)
10 large garlic cloves, finely minced
1 (28-ounce) can peeled Italian tomatoes
½ cup firmly packed torn basil leaves,
  plus 2 tablespoons basil chiffonade
  (very thinly sliced) for garnish

1. Place the diced eggplant in a colander over a bowl. Toss with the 1 teaspoon of salt, cover with waxed paper or paper towels, and weigh down slightly (with heavy cans, for example). Let sit for 30 minutes. Pat dry. (If you prefer less salt, rinse and pat dry.)
2. Meanwhile, heat a large skillet over medium-high heat and add 1 tablespoon of the good olive oil. (You will need to add more during cooking to prevent sticking.) When the skillet is hot, cook the yellow squash and zucchini together until tender and lightly browned, about 6 to 8 minutes. Stir often to prevent sticking; season with salt and pepper to taste while cooking to extract the most flavor. Set squashes aside.
3. In the same skillet, add more of the good olive oil and proceed in the same manner with the red and green bell peppers, cooking for 7 to 9 minutes, until tender and lightly browned but still holding some texture. Set aside.
4. Add more oil to the pan and cook the eggplant for 6 to 8 minutes, until tender and lightly browned. Set aside.
5. Add more oil to the pan and cook the onion for about 5 minutes until softened. Add the garlic and cook another 5 minutes. Add the tomatoes from the can, squeezing them into the skillet as you put them in.

(Save the remaining tomato juice/puree from the can for another use.) Raise the heat to high and cook until the juices have thickened, about 5 to 6 minutes. Add the reserved squash, peppers, and eggplant to the pan. Lower the heat and cook for 3 minutes. Add the torn basil, cook for 1 minute, and turn off heat. Season to taste with salt and pepper.
6. To serve, toss vegetables with the 2 tablespoons high-quality extra-virgin olive oil (or more to taste) and garnish with the basil chiffonade. Serve warm or at room temperature.

✵ Tapenade with Goat Cheese ✵

Thanks in part to Peter Mayle, author of *A Year in Provence*, Provence got hot in the 1990s — and many of the new, informal, bistrolike restaurants in American cities started to incorporate more Provençal cooking ideas, tapenade among them. These days, in the United States, I see tapenade as a trendy "blending" ingredient — something that chefs like to serve in tandem with other things. This is possibly the case because bitterness (which comes from the black olives) is not a taste sensation that Americans generally go for. The following pairing of tapenade and goat cheese, a great product also associated with Provence, has become quite popular — perhaps because the creamy cheese cuts the bitterness of the olives. A tangle of mesclun dressed with oil and vinegar looks and tastes great alongside the dish. You can also eat the tapenade in this recipe (you get about one and one-half cups) by spreading it directly on bread.

Yield: 36 rounds of goat cheese — perfect either for 12 appetizer servings or as a party dish

1 cup pitted black oil-cured olives
3 anchovy fillets
2 tablespoons capers

3 sun-dried tomatoes, coarsely chopped
1 tablespoon lemon juice
¼ teaspoon grated lemon zest (firmly packed)
1 teaspoon balsamic vinegar
1 teaspoon olive oil, plus extra-virgin olive oil
  for drizzling
2 garlic cloves, minced
1 teaspoon coarsely chopped basil
¼ cup finely minced parsley for garnish,
  plus 1 teaspoon coarsely chopped parsley
36 rounds of firm goat cheese, each one about
  ¼ inch thick and 1½ inches in diameter
  (cut from a log of goat cheese)

1. Place the olives, anchovies, capers, sun-dried tomatoes, lemon juice, lemon zest, balsamic vinegar, the 1 teaspoon of olive oil, the garlic, basil, and the 1 teaspoon of parsley in a food processor. Pulse until a coarse paste is formed.
2. Place 3 rounds of goat cheese on each of twelve plates. Top each round with 2 teaspoons of tapenade, leaving a white border of cheese showing. Drizzle with the extra-virgin olive oil; sprinkle with the ¼ cup minced parsley. Serve next to a dressed tangle of mesclun, if desired.

✵ Quiche with Parsnips ✵ and Celery Root

Despite the macho backlash, quiche has had considerable staying power. It may not show up today at as many dinner parties, but it has taken hold on many restaurant menus — particularly those places where "real men" don't eat, such as health- and vegetarian-oriented restaurants. I jest, of course: all that gender coding is extremely silly. The only things that matter with quiche are (1) does yours approach the flaky crust and quivering custard of the best versions? and (2) have you flavored your quiche with something that makes good quiche sense? The following recipe will enable you to answer yes and yes.

Yield: 6 to 8 appetizer portions

FOR THE CRUST:

*7 tablespoons butter, chilled, plus a little extra
    at room temperature for greasing tart pan*

2 tablespoons vegetable shortening

*1½ cups all-purpose flour, plus extra
    for rolling dough*

½ teaspoon salt

*1 large egg yolk mixed with 3 tablespoons ice
    water*

*2 tablespoons freshly grated
    Parmigiano-Reggiano cheese*

FOR THE FILLING:

1½ cups heavy cream

*½ cup peeled and diced parsnip (cut into
    ¼-inch dice, about 3 ounces altogether)*

*½ cup peeled and diced celery root (cut into
    ¼-inch dice, about 3 ounces altogether)*

1 teaspoon olive oil

*½ pound slab bacon, rind removed, cut into
    1 by ¼ by ¼-inch lardoons*

½ cup chopped shallots

2 large eggs plus 2 additional egg yolks

1 tablespoon chopped fresh parsley

1¼ cups grated Gruyère cheese

*4 tablespoons grated Parmigiano-Reggiano
    cheese*

Freshly grated nutmeg

1. Make the crust: Cut the 7 tablespoons butter into small pieces and place in a bowl.

Add the shortening, cover well, and freeze for 15 to 20 minutes.

2. Place the flour and salt in a large bowl and combine. Moving quickly, cut the butter-shortening mixture into the flour with a pastry cutter, or with your fingers, until the mixture resembles coarse meal. Add the egg yolk—ice water mixture and work the dough until it just holds together. Do not overwork. (*Note:* This can also be done in a food processor: Place the flour and salt in the work bowl. Add the butter and shortening and pulse until it resembles coarse meal. Add the egg yolk and ice water mixture through the feeder and continue to pulse until the dough looks like it's coming together.) Form the dough roughly into a disk, and wrap in plastic wrap. Chill for at least 30 minutes. This can be done up to 3 days in advance.

3. Preheat the oven to 375 degrees.

4. Butter a 9½-inch tart pan, preferably one with a false bottom.

5. Remove the dough from the refrigerator. Roll it out on a lightly floured surface into a circle; the circle should be ⅛ inch thick and at least 2 inches larger in diameter than the pan.

6. Carefully lay the dough circle in the pan, centering it. Sprinkle the overhang with the Parmigiano-Reggiano. Fold the overhang back into the pan, to make a rustic edge. Prick the bottom of the crust all over with a fork. Freeze the crust for 10 minutes.

7. Remove crust from freezer. Line the bottom with waxed paper or parchment paper and fill with pie weights or beans. Bake for 10 minutes. Remove the beans and paper and bake for another 5 minutes. Let cool.

8. Meanwhile, make the filling: Boil the cream in a saucepan until slightly thickened, about 2 minutes. Let cool.

9. In a medium saucepan, cook the parsnip and celery root together in boiling salted water until tender, about 10 minutes. Drain and let cool.

10. Meanwhile, heat the olive oil in a medium skillet over medium-high heat. Add the bacon and cook until lightly browned, about

All about Foie Gras

A gastronomically alert Frenchman once said, "The goose is nothing . . . but man has made of it an instrument, a kind of living hothouse in which grows the supreme fruit of gastronomy." He meant, of course, foie gras. Another wag once called foie gras "the Frenchman's cocaine" — expensive, exciting, intoxicating. In translation it sounds somewhat less than intoxicating: "fat liver" (*foie* meaning "liver" and *gras* meaning "fat").

Foie gras is not just any liver: it is the enlarged liver of a goose or a duck that has been specially fattened — force-fed — to produce foie gras. It is a practice that has been around since the ancient Egyptians and Romans — but it was the modern French who perfected the technique, specifically in the regions of Périgord in the southwest and Alsace in the northeast. The bird's diet usually begins with bran and then moves on to cabbage and water, then to grass, then to wheat and oats, and lastly, to corn that has been cooked in milk. The fattening process takes four or five months.

Why go to all this trouble, you ask?

Because the livers that are extracted from these fattened animals produce something that transcends liver or animals; some would argue that it transcends food. My brother intensely dislikes liver, but he'd travel a thousand miles for a bite of foie gras. My sister-in-law detests liver, but the first time she tasted foie gras in France she started to shake, her whole face turned crimson red, and big tears coursed down her cheeks. No, she wasn't disgusted; she was merely in the throes of foie gras ecstasy. I've seen it many times.

Once upon a time, you had to travel to France to know such ecstasy. Fresh foie gras and fresh-cooked foie gras products from other countries were banned in the United States. Until the early 1980s there was no production of fresh foie gras in the United States. So that meant that the only forms of foie gras available in this country were canned. Yuck. No wonder, growing up, I made little distinction between foie gras and liverwurst. Much of the so-called foie gras in cans is not pure foie gras: it contains eggs and fillers and, to boot, has been cooked to death. And the high-priced cans that have a speck of washed-out black truffle in the center may also have an extra dollop of pork liver. Were all this not so, the canned stuff would still be inferior, because it's not fresh. Please, do yourself a favor and don't spend your hard-earned cash on the tins of foie gras you see in the store.

Not anymore. Now fabulous American foie gras is being produced in upstate New York and in California. I've seen many a Frenchman taste our foie gras, expecting to politely patronize it — only to end up sincerely enthusiastic.

10 minutes. Drain bacon on paper towels and set aside. Pour out excess oil from skillet, leaving approximately 1 tablespoon. Cook the shallots in the same pan over medium heat until soft and lightly browned, seasoning with salt and pepper to taste while cooking, about 5 to 7 minutes. Set aside.

11. Preheat oven to 375 degrees. Place the tart pan containing the pie crust on a baking sheet.

12. In a bowl, lightly whisk together the cooled cream and the eggs and egg yolks. Add the reserved parsnip and celery root, the parsley, half of the Gruyère cheese, 2 tablespoons of the Parmigiano-Reggiano, the nutmeg, and salt and pepper to taste. Gently stir to combine.

13. Sprinkle 1 tablespoon of the remaining Parmigiano-Reggiano over the bottom of the crust. Add the bacon, the shallots, then the remaining Gruyère cheese. Pour in the egg-vegetable mixture; it should just about reach the top of the pastry — maybe 1/16 inch below the top. Don't let it come any higher than that. Sprinkle the remaining 1 tablespoon of Parmigiano-Reggiano across the top.

14. Place in oven and bake for 25 to 30 minutes, or until golden, slightly puffed, and set. Do not overcook. Check to see if it's done after about 20 minutes and continue to check every five minutes after that; a knife in the center should just come out clean once it's done. You do not want the custard to get rubbery. Let cool for 5 minutes before serving, or serve at room temperature.

☆ Sautéed Foie Gras ☆ with Herb Salad

When we Americans finally started to raise our own foie gras, about twenty-five years ago, the rage among chefs in French restaurants in America was seared slices of the stuff, served warm. Though we came to realize that turning foie gras into cold terrines is the more traditional way of treating it in France, the seared strategy (foie gras chaud) is still much more common in the United States. The fact that it's much, much easier to do may have something to do with this choice. But in my opinion, there's usually a problem waiting for the seared foie gras on the plate: a thick, sticky fruit sauce. Perhaps inspired by the fine traditional French notion of a little sweet wine to drink with cold foie gras terrine, many American chefs today put sweet food on their hot foie gras. The latter is already insanely rich — why make it richer with a sticky sauce? The best warm foie gras dish I ever had was in Dijon, where the chef served his hot slice simply on top of a sorrel salad — sour greens! Yes! "Sour" complements warm foie gras perfectly, cuts through the richness . . . not "sweet." Having failed to find sorrel recently, even in the spring, I came up with this very tart herb salad, which I think also cuts the foie gras nicely; you can substitute any fresh herb mixture you like, but the salad works best if the herbs are delicate in texture. And one more caveat: make sure you cut thick slices of raw foie gras, at least one inch thick, before you sauté them. Thin slices of foie gras begin leaking their fat very soon after they hit the pan; thick slices shrink slightly, but the interior remains intact. (*Ingredient note:* Almost all of our fresh American foie gras is duck foie gras, though some fresh goose foie gras is now available.)

Yield: 8 first-course servings

1 whole, raw "A" duck foie gras (about 1½ pounds; see sidebar on page 78)
¾ cup firmly packed chervil leaves and stems, plus extra for garnish

½ cup firmly packed 1-inch-long chive pieces

½ cup firmly packed light-colored celery leaves

¼ cup firmly packed flat-leaf parsley leaves

1 tablespoon fresh savory leaves

About ¼ cup Wondra (quick-mixing flour)

Canola oil for sautéeing

1 tablespoon hazelnut or walnut oil

1 tablespoon red wine vinegar

1 teaspoon balsamic vinegar

I. Remove foie gras from refrigerator and cut into slices. You want to get 8 smooth, unbroken chunks of foie gras, each 1 inch thick and weighing about 2 to 3 ounces (the other dimensions will vary, but the chunks must be 1 inch thick). Reserve chunks on counter for 15 minutes or so.

2. Measure the chervil leaves and stems, the chives, and the celery, parsley, and savory leaves and wash them all well. Dry completely in a salad spinner. Place in large bowl.

3. When ready to cook, season the foie gras chunks well with salt and pepper. Sprinkle chunks on all sides with Wondra to make a light coating.

4. Choose a heavy, cast-iron pan that will comfortably hold all 8 foie gras chunks; they must not be touching each other. If you don't have a pan this size, use 2 pans — or cook the foie gras in batches. Place the pan (or pans) over medium heat. Add enough canola oil to make a shallow puddle across

Where to Buy Foie Gras

If you can't find fresh duck foie gras at your neighborhood butcher shop, who you gonna call? D'Artagnan, of course, in New Jersey, the country's leading distributor of foie gras to restaurants and homes. After you've dialed 800-327-8246 and placed your order, a vacuum-packed, refrigerated foie gras will appear at your door the next day. But first you have to decide which grade of foie gras you want.

"A" quality livers, which weigh about one and one-half pounds each, are the best. They are relatively free of veins and have the proper texture; if you push your thumb into the liver, the depression will stay for a few seconds before the foie gras springs back. This resiliency means that the foie gras has the right amount of fat; too much fat, and foie gras isn't resilient, which indicates it won't cook properly. At this writing, "A" quality livers are selling for about fifty dollars a pound.

"B" quality livers are smaller than "A" livers and have many more veins. They cost about forty dollars a pound.

"C" livers, the smallest, least attractive, and least expensive, are sold only to restaurants; they are not available to the public. Chefs puree them and use the puree in sauces and stuffings.

If you've never worked with foie gras before, you might be surprised when you unpack your first liver. It looks nothing like raw liver of other kinds; it is neither red, nor bloody, nor soft. In fact, it looks already cooked — but it's not. It has a firmness to it as well as a fleshy pink color.

Vacuum-packed raw foie gras, if unopened and kept under refrigeration, will remain fresh for about a week and a half.

D'Artagnan also sells the fresh cold terrines of foie gras that they make.

the bottom of the pan (or pans). Heat until the oil just begins to smoke.

5. Immediately add the foie gras chunks. Each chunk will have at least 6 sides, including top and bottom. The trick is to cook each side of each chunk for about 30 seconds. This means that when you put the chunks in the pan, after 30 seconds you must turn each of them onto another side. If the first side hasn't browned considerably in 30 seconds, your oil is not hot enough. Turn the heat up to medium-high. When all the sides are browned, check to make sure that they're browned fairly evenly; you may wish to "touch up" a side or two by placing it in the hot oil for a moment. The total cooking time for each chunk should be about 3 minutes. Remove chunks to paper towels.

6. Toss herb salad with the hazelnut or walnut oil and the red wine and balsamic vinegars. Season with salt and pepper to taste. Divide the salad among eight appetizer plates. Nestle a chunk of foie gras on each salad. Top foie gras with a decorative sprig of chervil, and serve immediately.

☆ Sole Amandine ☆

There are hundreds of classic sole preparations in the French canon (sole Albert, sole Dugléré, sole Marguéry, sole Veronique, and so on). But the two that were most typical of fancy French restaurants in America in the twentieth century were among the very simplest: sole meunière (flour-dusted fish sautéed in butter) and sole amandine (basically the same, but with almond slices added). The old American impulse to be simple was a wise one — since sole is one of the most delectable fish in the ocean, and a great fresh one really needs little dressing up. This is terrific news for home cooks, too — because a minimum of fuss will bring you and your family a maximum of pleasure. Where you must fuss, however, is at the fish market. If there's any way you can obtain fillets of Dover sole (from northern Europe), the special resiliency of that extraordinary fish makes perfect sense of the high price. Most fish markets, truth be told, carry only the Dover sole cousins — such as gray sole or lemon sole. Use those, by all means — for this lovely recipe ennobles any light, delicate, flatfish fillet that it touches.

Yield: 2 main-course servings

2 tablespoons sliced almonds
Flour for dredging (Wondra, a quick-mixing
    flour, works great)
1 tablespoon milk
¾ pound sole fillets (your choice: Dover, gray,
    lemon)
7 tablespoons unsalted butter, cut into 7 pieces
2 tablespoons dry white wine
1 teaspoon very finely minced shallots
1 tablespoon finely chopped parsley leaves
Lemon wedges

1. Place a sauté pan that's large enough to hold the fish fillets in one layer over medium heat and add the almonds. Shaking the pan occasionally, allow the almonds to toast lightly for 3 to 5 minutes, taking care not to let them burn. When they become golden brown in spots, remove them from the pan and set aside.

2. On a large plate, generously season the flour with salt to taste. Rub a few drops of the milk on both sides of each fillet. Dip

each fillet into the flour, coating them but shaking off any excess. Place fillets on a baking rack to dry for 10 minutes.

3. Return the sauté pan to the stove over medium heat and add 4 tablespoons of the butter. When it has melted, allow the foam to subside slightly and add the fish, cooking until lightly golden on one side, about 2 to 3 minutes. Carefully flip the fish and continue cooking until just cooked through, about 1 minute more, depending on the thickness of your fish.

4. Transfer the fish to warmed serving plates. Pour out any butter remaining in the pan and return the pan to the heat. Add the white wine and shallots and allow them to cook for about 20 seconds, until the wine has almost evaporated, scraping up with a spatula any browned bits that may have formed in the pan. Quickly add the remaining 3 tablespoons of butter, the parsley, and the almonds, swirling the pan to combine them. When the butter has melted and begins to foam, pour over the fish, distributing the almonds evenly over each. Garnish with lemon wedges and serve immediately.

✴ Coq au Vin ✴

The following recipe is not intended to make you think of a little farmhouse in France; the intended reference is a French restaurant in America in 1958. Or the home of a good cook of that era. For this is an American take on a great French classic: less winey, a little less fussy in its technique, no last-minute thickening with beurre manié. It is a simple, very homey,

vastly satisfying chicken stew, the chicken enrobed by a luscious liquid somewhere between a sauce and a thick soup. Therefore, I love serving it to each diner in a big bowl. If you cook it the day before and reheat it, you'll find that the chicken tastes even better (having absorbed the wine overnight).

Yield: 4 modest main-course servings

¼ pound slab bacon, cut into ¼-inch cubes
1 (4-pound) chicken, cut into 8 serving pieces
1 tablespoon olive oil
1 onion, roughly chopped
1 carrot, roughly chopped
1 stalk celery, roughly chopped
2 garlic cloves, crushed
1 tablespoon chopped fresh thyme
1 tablespoon chopped fresh parsley,
    plus extra for garnish
2 bay leaves
3 tablespoons all-purpose flour
¼ cup cognac (or any good brandy)
2 cups dry red wine
2 cups chicken stock (preferably homemade)
2 tablespoons tomato paste
½ pound pearl onions (about 20), unpeeled
2 tablespoons butter
½ teaspoon sugar
¾ pound white mushrooms, cleaned and
    quartered

1. Place a quart of water in a saucepan, bring to a boil, add bacon, lower heat slightly, and simmer for 2 minutes. Pour bacon into colander and rinse well. (This removes some of the salt from the bacon.)

2. Dry chicken with a paper towel and season it all over with salt and pepper. Add the olive oil to a large Dutch oven over medium-high

heat. Brown chicken very well on all sides, taking care not to crowd the chicken in the pan. Remove chicken to a plate and pour off all but 2 tablespoons of fat from the pan. Add the onion, carrot, celery, garlic, thyme, the I tablespoon of chopped parsley, and the bay leaves. Cook over medium heat, scraping the bottom of the pan with a wooden spoon, until onion is golden, about 5 minutes.

3. Add flour to vegetables and stir to coat. Cook over medium heat about 2 minutes, or until the raw flour smell is gone. Add cognac, stirring to combine. Boil quickly until cognac is almost completely gone. Add wine, chicken stock, and tomato paste, stirring well. Bring to a simmer. Return the chicken pieces to the pan, coating them well with the liquid. Cover and simmer gently until chicken is just tender, about 35 minutes.

4. Meanwhile, prepare onions. Bring a small saucepan of water to a boil. Add onions and simmer 2 minutes. Drain and rinse in cold water.· Trim the top and root ends away (making sure to leave a bit of the root intact to hold the onion together), then peel off the papery outer layer of skin.

5. In a small skillet, melt I tablespoon of the butter over medium-high heat. Add onions and cook, shaking the pan until the onions begin to brown. Add sugar; toss with onions to blend. Add enough water to come halfway up the sides of the onions. Bring to a simmer, cover, and cook until onions are tender, about 15 to 20 minutes, depending on the size of your onions. When onions are tender, remove cover and bring to a boil over high heat; boil until liquid is syrupy. Roll onions in pan to coat with the syrup. Set onions aside.

6. In a large skillet over high heat, melt the remaining I tablespoon of butter. Add the mushrooms in one layer (you may have to cook them in two batches, depending on the size of your pan; if so, use an additional tablespoon of butter). Cook over high heat, turning mushrooms only once or twice, until browned, about 3 to 4 minutes. Set aside.

7. When chicken is cooked, remove it to a plate, strain solids from the sauce, and return liquid to the pan. Add chicken back to the pan, along with the onions and mushrooms. Heat gently for 5 minutes, then serve immediately garnished with chopped parsley.

☆ Canard a l'Orange ☆

Canard a l'orange has always been a favorite in French-American restaurants, possibly owing to the notorious American sweet tooth; this is one of the few dishes in the classic French repertoire that combine savory and sweet. But American canard a l'orange is a classic example of converting highbrow French technique into homespun American know-how and coming up with an excellent, though different, result. The following recipe requires no long-cooked stock and no delicate operations with orange rind. Still, the result is a rich, flavor-infused dark brown sauce that plays beautifully against the tender duck meat.

Yield: 2 main-course servings

1 (3½-pound) duck, fresh or defrosted, including giblets
2 oranges
Finely grated zest of 3 oranges

2 teaspoons peanut oil
½ cup roughly chopped peeled onion
¼ cup roughly chopped peeled carrot
¼ cup roughly chopped celery
2 cups chicken stock
4 parsley sprigs
2 thyme sprigs
6 whole black peppercorns
1 bay leaf
1 (6-ounce) can frozen orange juice
    concentrate, defrosted, with 3 tablespoons
    of concentrate reserved
1 tablespoon unsalted butter

1. The night before you roast the duck, set the giblets aside and score the duck's skin all over with the tines of a sharp fork, taking care not to puncture the meat underneath. Place duck on a rack and refrigerate overnight, uncovered.

2. The next day, preheat the oven to 350 degrees.

3. Halve the oranges and place them in the cavity of the duck. Loosen the skin on the duck breast and push the orange zest underneath. Season all over, including the cavity, with salt and pepper.

4. Place the duck on a rack in a roasting pan (it's best to use a fairly deep pan, as the duck will release a lot of fat).

5. Roast duck in the lower third of the oven for 2½ hours, occasionally draining fat from the pan.

6. While the duck is roasting, heat the peanut oil in a 2-quart saucepan over medium-high heat. Add the duck giblets, onion, carrot, and celery and cook until the vegetables are almost caramelized. Add the chicken stock, parsley, thyme, peppercorns, and bay leaf.

7. Bring to a boil over high heat. Turn the heat to low and simmer very gently, covered, for 2 hours. Strain and reserve.

8. After the duck has cooked for 2½ hours, remove it from the oven, drain the fat from the pan again, and baste the duck liberally with some of the orange juice concentrate (remembering to keep 3 tablespoons aside for later use). Return duck to oven. After 10 minutes, remove duck and baste again with more orange concentrate. Return to oven. After 10 minutes, remove duck and baste again with more orange juice concentrate. Cook duck for 10 minutes more. Remove the duck from the oven and the pan, place on a platter, and tent loosely with foil.

9. Pour off all the fat in the roasting pan. There will be some brown bits clinging to the bottom. Pour in ½ cup of the reserved warm stock and the remaining 3 tablespoons of the orange juice concentrate. Simmer for 1 minute, loosening the residue with a wooden spoon. Pour the contents of the roasting pan into a saucepan. Measure sauce; there should be about ½ cup, but there may be more. If there is, turn the heat to high and reduce the sauce to ½ cup. Lower heat and whisk in the butter.

10. Meanwhile, cut the duck in half the long way. Discard wings. Remove the legs and reserve. For each portion, cut the breast from the bone and cut boneless breast in half. On each plate, overlap two breast halves and rest leg against them. Nap with sauce and serve.

✴ Blanquette de Veau ✴

This classic, creamy veal stew belongs to the generation of French dishes that Julia Child brought to the American cooking public starting in the 1960s. Though you may occasionally see it on restaurant menus here, it has been more of an obsession with home cooks. The following version is duly velvety but a little more flavorful than most — thanks to an unconventional last-minute addition of mustard and tarragon. I'll never make it any other way again. The recipe does call for an overnight chilling of the stock — to facilitate fat removal — but if you're pressed for time you could eliminate that step and make it on the same day of serving. The dish is traditionally served with buttered white rice.

Yield: 6 servings

6 tablespoons butter

1 tablespoon olive oil

2 pounds veal stew meat, cut into
    1½-inch cubes (shoulder is good,
    or any other tough cut)

2 pounds veal bones (have the butcher
    saw them into 3- or 4-inch pieces)

1 small onion, peeled and quartered,
    stuck with 2 whole cloves

4 medium carrots, peeled

1 stalk celery, cut into large chunks

1 sprig parsley

1 sprig thyme

1 bay leaf

10 whole black peppercorns

6 cups water

8 ounces white mushrooms, cleaned and
    quartered

2 teaspoons lemon juice

12 pearl onions, peeled

¼ cup flour

½ cup whipping cream

Yolks of 3 large eggs

½ cup frozen peas, thawed

1 tablespoon minced fresh
    tarragon leaves

5 teaspoons Dijon mustard

1. Melt 1 tablespoon of the butter and the olive oil in a large Dutch oven over low heat. Season veal stew meat with salt and white pepper. In two batches, sauté the meat in the fat, being careful not to let it brown.

2. Once meat is seared on all sides, add the veal bones, the quartered onion, 1 of the carrots (cut into large chunks), the celery, parsley, thyme, bay leaf, black peppercorns, and water. The water should cover the veal and veal bones completely; if it doesn't, add a bit more water. Bring to a boil. Reduce heat to low and simmer, skimming and discarding foam on top, until veal is tender, about 1½ hours.

3. Cool and refrigerate overnight. The next day, remove congealed fat from the top of the veal stew and discard. Heat the pot gently. When the gelatinous stock has liquefied, strain stock and reserve. Reserve veal stew meat. Discard remaining solids. Bring strained stock to a simmer and reduce to about 3 cups.

4. Meanwhile, prepare vegetables. In a small skillet, melt 1 tablespoon of the butter over low heat. Add mushrooms and 1 teaspoon of the lemon juice (to keep mushrooms white). Cook mushrooms until they release their liquid; increase heat and boil liquid until it evaporates, but be careful not to brown the

mushrooms. Remove from heat; place mushrooms in a bowl and set aside.

5. In the same skillet, melt another 1 tablespoon of the butter. Add the remaining 3 carrots (cut into ½-inch rounds) and water just to cover the carrots. Bring to a simmer and partially cover. Simmer until carrots are tender, about 12 to 15 minutes. Remove lid and bring to a boil; simmer until liquid is evaporated and carrots are glazed but not browned. Place in the bowl with the mushrooms.

6. In the same skillet, melt another 1 tablespoon of the butter. Add pearl onions and water just to cover the onions. Bring to a simmer and partially cover; simmer until onions are tender, about 15 to 17 minutes. Remove lid and bring to a boil; simmer until liquid is evaporated and onions are glazed but not browned. Place in the bowl with the mushrooms and carrots.

7. To finish the stew, melt the remaining 2 tablespoons butter in a large Dutch oven. Add the flour and cook over low heat until raw flour smell is gone, about 3 minutes; do not allow the mixture to brown. Add reduced stock and the cream; increase heat and bring to a simmer to thicken. Simmer 10 minutes.

8. In a medium bowl, whisk egg yolks. Add about ¼ cup of the thickened hot stock to the bowl, whisking constantly. Add another cup of the thickened hot stock slowly, whisking constantly. Pour mixture back into the Dutch oven, continuing to whisk. (This process, called tempering, heats the egg yolks gradually so they won't scramble when added

to the stew.) From this point on, do not allow the stew to go above the merest simmer: more than one or two bubbles and the yolks will scramble.

9. Cook stew over low heat, stirring, until it thickens a bit more, about 5 minutes. Add reserved vegetables, the peas, and reserved veal stew meat. Heat another 5 minutes, or until veal is warmed through. Stir in remaining 1 teaspoon of lemon juice and tarragon leaves. Whisk in mustard and season with salt and white pepper.

✯ Steak au Poivre ✯

There's a story, possibly apocryphal, that Steak au Poivre — an American French-restaurant classic if there ever was one — was actually invented in a bistro in Paris. The story goes that some American guests, before dinner, were guzzling martinis — and the chef, irate at their palate-anesthetizing activity, created (to teach them a lesson) the only kind of dish he thought they'd be able to taste. He studded some steak with peppercorns and called it Steak au Poivre. Truth is, the story makes a kind of sense when you taste a Steak au Poivre that's overpeppercorned — because the result can be hot, bitter, unpleasant. To prevent that result — and to take the dish seriously, making it as friendly to wine as it is delicious — it's a good idea to keep the peppercorn count relatively low. It also helps to nap the steak with a nice, rich, soothing sauce — though I think the heavy cream sauce you sometimes see goes too far. In the end, a good Steak au Poivre is a thing of fine balance — and the following recipe, with its butter-enriched beef sauce, is a fine demonstration of why this classic deserves to live on, no matter how ignominious its origins. Serve with French fries.

Yield: 4 main-course servings

4 cups unsalted beef stock (homemade or
        canned)
1 small onion, peeled and chopped
1 small carrot, peeled and chopped
1 bay leaf
1 sprig thyme
1 teaspoon whole black peppercorns
1 heaping tablespoon coarsely crushed black
        peppercorns
1 heaping tablespoon coarsely crushed
        green peppercorns (dried preferred;
        see Note)
4 strip steaks, 8 to 10 ounces each, cut 1 inch
        thick and trimmed of excess fat
1 tablespoon vegetable oil
4 tablespoons unsalted butter, cut into 4 pieces
2 tablespoons very finely minced shallots
        (about 2 medium shallots)
4 tablespoons cognac or brandy
½ cup dry white wine
2 teaspoons finely chopped parsley

1. Place the beef stock, onion, carrot, bay leaf, thyme, and whole black peppercorns in a medium saucepan and bring to a boil over high heat. Lower the heat to medium and, maintaining a lively simmer, allow the stock to reduce in volume to about ½ cup. Pass the reduction through a fine mesh strainer into a small bowl, pressing lightly on the vegetables to extract any liquid. Discard the solids and set the liquid aside until ready to complete the dish.

2. Meanwhile, combine the crushed black and green peppercorns and firmly press the mixture into the steaks, both the top and bottom sides, coating them evenly. Let the pepper-studded steaks rest at room temperature for 30 minutes. Preheat the oven to 200 degrees.

3. Place a cast-iron skillet (just large enough to hold the steaks without crowding) over medium-high heat and let it warm for 4 minutes. Generously salt the top of each steak. Pour the vegetable oil into the skillet, coating it evenly. When the oil is hot, add the steaks, salt side down; move them slightly after 30 seconds to help browning. Cook for about 3 minutes per side for medium-rare meat; make sure to salt the second side of each steak before flipping. When the steaks are done, place them in a pan or on a platter and hold them in the warmed oven. (The steaks will continue to cook in the oven, so undercook them a bit.)

4. Pour off all but 1 tablespoon of the accumulated fat in the skillet. Return skillet to medium heat, adding 1 tablespoon of the butter and the shallots. Stir until the shallots soften, about 1 minute. Add the cognac and white wine to the skillet, scraping with a wooden spatula to loosen any browned bits. Turn heat to high and reduce the liquid by half. Add the reduced beef broth and reduce liquid by half again; the sauce should begin to thicken slightly. Add any juices that have accumulated beneath the steaks you're holding in the oven and whisk in the remaining 3 tablespoons butter, the parsley, and salt to taste. Place the steaks on dinner plates, spoon the shallots and sauce evenly over and around each one, and serve immediately.

NOTE: I use green peppercorns in this dish only if I can find the dried ones; green peppercorns in brine, also available, don't fit in as well. If the dried green ones are unavailable, I simply eliminate green peppercorns from the dish and double the amount of black peppercorns used in the coating of the steak.

☆ Beef Bourguignon ☆

The following recipe is a close cousin of coq au vin — they're both long-cooked meat stews made with red wine, onions, and mushrooms. As with the Coq au Vin on page 80, however, this is a distinctly American spin on a French classic (you're not likely to see carrots in this dish in France!). It even preserves the standard American misunderstanding of the dish's name; unless you mean to say that the beef is from Burgundy, you should properly call this dish Boeuf à la Bourguignonne (beef in the Burgundy style). No one in America ever will, though. All these details add up to comfort food: an absolutely delicious, no-nonsense, hearty beef stew from another era. Serve it, as we did in the fifties, with noodles, or buttered boiled potatoes. I'd find even more comfort in buttery mashed potatoes — and a good Pinot Noir from California or Oregon.

Yield: 6 main-course servings

2¼ pounds boneless beef chuck, cut into
    2-inch pieces
1 medium carrot, peeled, halved crosswise
1 medium yellow onion, peeled and quartered
1 stalk celery, halved crosswise
5 sprigs parsley, plus minced parsley
    for garnish
5 sprigs thyme
1 bay leaf
1 (750-milliliter) bottle red wine,
    preferably inexpensive Pinot Noir

½ cup all-purpose flour
2 tablespoons vegetable oil
5 slices bacon, diced
4 cups water
10 ounces pearl onions, unpeeled
¼ pound (1 stick) plus 1 tablespoon
    unsalted butter
10 ounces small white mushrooms, halved
5 small carrots, cut into 1-inch pieces
Pinch of sugar

1. In a nonreactive bowl combine the beef, carrot, quartered onion, celery, the 5 parsley sprigs, the thyme, bay leaf, and red wine. Store in the refrigerator for at least 12 hours.
2. Remove the beef and reserve the vegetable-wine mixture. Dry the beef well with paper towels. Season generously with salt and pepper, and toss with the flour.
3. Preheat the oven to 275 degrees. Heat the vegetable oil in a Dutch oven with a tight-fitting lid over medium-high heat. Add the bacon and cook, stirring, until crispy, about 3 minutes. Using a slotted spoon, transfer the bacon to a paper towel–lined plate. Pour two-thirds of the bacon fat into a small bowl.
4. Return the Dutch oven with remaining bacon fat to medium-high heat. Working in three batches, add one-third of the beef to the Dutch oven (leaving behind any excess flour) and cook, stirring occasionally, until well browned, about 5 minutes. Using a slotted spoon, transfer the beef to a plate. Repeat two times with the remaining bacon fat and beef.
5. Wipe out the Dutch oven. Return the beef

to it and add the reserved vegetable-wine mixture. Add the 4 cups of water. Bring stew to a boil, then place in the oven, covered, and cook until the beef is very tender, about 3 hours. Using a slotted spoon, remove and discard the vegetables and herbs. Set the stew aside, covered.

6. While the beef cooks, bring a medium saucepan of salted water to a boil. Add the pearl onions and cook for 2 minutes. Using a slotted spoon, transfer the pearl onions to a bowl of ice water. Using a paring knife, peel the onions, leaving the root ends intact.

7. In a large skillet over medium-high heat, heat 3 tablespoons of the butter. Add the onions and cook, stirring frequently, until well browned and tender, about 7 minutes. Season with salt and pepper to taste and, using a slotted spoon, transfer to the stew. Wipe out the skillet and return to the heat. Heat 3 more tablespoons of the butter. Add the mushrooms and cook, stirring occasionally, until well browned, about 12 minutes. Season with salt and pepper to taste and transfer to the stew. Wipe out the skillet and return to the heat. Heat the remaining 3 tablespoons of butter. Add the carrots and sugar and cook, stirring, until lightly browned and tender, about 7 minutes. Season with salt and pepper to taste and, using a slotted spoon, transfer to the stew.

8. Mix everything together well. Bring the stew to a boil, lower the heat, and simmer, uncovered, until thickened, about 10 minutes. Season with salt and pepper to taste, sprinkle with the minced parsley, and serve.

✧ Crêpes Suzette ✧

Flambéing has always been a significant element in the American perception of French dining. It seems so elegant, so fussy, so . . . French. Never mind that it's relatively rare in France; it certainly wasn't rare in the United States in the elegant French restaurants of the forties, fifties, and sixties. And the most emblematic flambéed dish of all here was Crêpes Suzette, in which the little triangular pancakes get tossed tableside in an orange-and-butter sauce, meeting their incendiary fate in a blaze of Grand Marnier. If there's a showman in you, you too can do it tableside in your dining room. But I've set the recipe up so that you can flame on in the privacy of your kitchen, before bringing the plated dish into the dining room; it's much less pressure. By the way, the crepes in this recipe have an extraordinary, resilient chew — one of the criteria I use for judging this dish — because, unusually, they're made with bread flour.

Yield: 24 crepes,
enough for 6 servings

About ¾ pound (3 sticks) unsalted butter
1 cup bread flour
3 tablespoons granulated sugar
1 teaspoon kosher salt
3 large eggs
⅔ cup whole milk
⅔ cup water
½ cup Grand Marnier
1 tablespoon grated orange zest
16 white sugar cubes (I used
    Domino's Dots)
4 medium-size navel oranges, washed
2 lemons, washed

1. Melt 2 tablespoons of the butter and let it cool.

2. Sieve the flour, I tablespoon of the granulated sugar, and the salt into a medium-size bowl. Using a whisk, make a well in the center.

3. Break the eggs into the well one at a time, gradually incorporating the flour into them with the whisk. Add the milk and water in the same way, gradually whisking in the flour. Add 2 tablespoons of the Grand Marnier. Mix until smooth. If small lumps of flour remain, pass the mixture through a sieve. (*Note:* Steps 2 and 3 can also be accomplished in a food processor.)

4. Mix the cooled melted butter and the orange zest into the batter. Cover the bowl with plastic wrap and let the batter rest for at least I hour.

5. When you're ready to make the crepes, have ready a 6-inch crepe pan or a non-stick 6-inch skillet, 6 tablespoons of the butter, softened (you may have some left over), a ladle for the batter, a cookie sheet to stack the crepes, and a cloth to cover the top crepe so the edges don't dry out. You will also need a spatula to help turn the crepes in the pan.

6. Heat the pan over medium-high heat. Dip a paper towel into the softened butter and use a bit of the butter to lightly film the pan. (Use the butter even if you're using a non-stick pan, as it gives the crepes a nice surface.) Butter the pan in this fashion after every second crepe.

7. Ladle I½ tablespoons of batter into the pan. Swirl the batter quickly to coat the surface evenly. Pour any excess back into the bowl of batter. As soon as the crepe looks solid (about 30 seconds), use the spatula to lift the edges. The underside should be lightly speckled with brown (if the crepe is too dark, or burned, you need to lower the heat). Turn the crepe with the spatula or with your fingers. Cook the second side for I5 seconds. Remove the finished crepe to the cookie sheet and cover it with the cloth. Continue until 24 crepes are made. As each one is finished, stack it on top of the others on the cookie sheet, then cover with the cloth. Once made, the crepes can be stored in the refrigerator or frozen.

8. When you're ready to make the crêpes suzette, rub 12 of the sugar cubes over the oranges to infuse them with the oil in the zest. The cubes will turn orange. Use the same procedure for the remaining 4 cubes and the lemons.

9. Cut the oranges in half and squeeze out juice. Strain to make I cup of juice.

I0. Divide the juice between two 8-inch skillets over medium heat. Add 6 of the orange-flavored sugar cubes and 2 lemon-flavored cubes to each pan, and I tablespoon of the granulated sugar to each pan. Add ¼ pound (I stick) of butter to each pan. When the butter melts, start submerging crepes, one at a time, in the mixture. You can do this by holding the crepes in your fingers and dunking them in the buttery juice. (It's good to work with a buddy: I pan and I2 crepes each.)

II. Remove crepes from the pan as they're moistened. Working on a counter, fold each moistened crepe in half, then in half again to form a triangle. Reserve the 24 folded crepes on a platter or in a pan.

12. Raise the heat under the 2 pans to high and reduce the sauce in each pan to 4 tablespoons. It will look syrupy. Take the pans off the heat and pour 3 tablespoons of the Grand Marnier into each pan. Place 12 crepes in each pan, tucking them under the sauce. Pour any liquid from the holding platter into the pans. Return the pans to medium-low heat and either tilt them gently into the fire or put a match to each one. The Grand Marnier will start to flame. Let it burn out and then divide the crepes, with sauce, among six plates. Serve immediately.

Mittel European Food

People are often startled to learn that the country to which more Americans trace their roots than any other is Germany. The surprise stems in part from our gastronomic landscape: we are a country of Italian restaurants, Chinese restaurants, fancy French restaurants, sushi bars — but certainly not a country of German restaurants. In fact, you usually have to search far and wide to find even one. The days when a fancy German palace like Luchow's in New York City could be esteemed as one of the country's best restaurants are long gone (as is Luchow's).

And yet, when you look a little more closely, you find an insistent Germanic undercurrent in the foods that Americans often eat.

What's more American than a hot dog? Came from Frankfurt.

What's more American than a hamburger? Came from Hamburg.

What's more American than sausages of all types, and all manner of ground-beef dishes with gravies and noodles and potatoes? You expect this food in the great Germanic belt from Ohio through the upper Midwest to Wisconsin — but you actually get it across the country. Not to mention the disarming blend of Teutonic sensibility and cowboy barbecue that occurs in the little-known German population bands throughout central Texas!

Food with Hungarian roots is a bit more esoteric — but two of Hungary's great dishes have crashed onto the roster of foods that home cooks are likely to make at some point: Hungarian goulash and chicken paprikash (both transformed from their parallel dishes in the Old Country). The foods of other middle European countries seem more exotic by comparison but still have a presence. There's a small group of Czech restaurants and an abiding interest in the ways of that part of the world with roast duck. And Polish restaurants draw all kinds of hip city diners; Polish stuffed dumplings, or pierogi, have even become a kind of cult food — one that's threatening to move far beyond the Polish communities in Chicago, Pittsburgh, and the Lower East Side of Manhattan.

✱ Liptauer Cheese ✱

There is a place called Lipto, Hungary, that is apparently the home of this very flavorful cheese spread. But it became popular all over the Austro-Hungarian Empire and, later, all over the pockets of Austrian and Hungarian population in the United States, particularly after World War II, when a new generation of Hungarian immigrants arrived. I've changed the classic recipe a bit — because my dad used to embellish the paprika part of it with the creative addition of some red bell peppers. The result is a little runnier than usual but I think brighter, more flavorful. Great pass-around starter for a dinner party.

Yield: 1½ cups

1 tablespoon sweet paprika
2 teaspoons dry mustard
1 teaspoon caraway seeds
1 teaspoon ground caraway
1 (8-ounce) package cream cheese,
     softened
3 tablespoons butter, softened
¼ cup sour cream
¼ cup drained and chopped roasted
     red bell peppers (bottled)
2 tablespoons lemon juice
3 tablespoons drained capers
4 anchovy fillets, mashed
1 tablespoon grated onion
Cayenne

1. In a small skillet over medium-low heat, toast spices (paprika, mustard, caraway seeds, and ground caraway) until fragrant, about 2 minutes. Cool.
2. In the bowl of a food processor fitted with a metal blade, combine cream cheese, butter, sour cream, roasted red peppers, and lemon juice. Process until smooth. Add capers, anchovies, onion, reserved spices, and cayenne to taste. Process until spices are distributed and mixture is an even color. Season with salt and pepper to taste and refrigerate several hours or overnight to blend flavors. Serve with crackers, bread, or toast.

✱ Sauerkraut Balls ✱

These nifty little deep-fried appetizer num-nums are, I think, pure American in invention — but they do reflect the flavors of central and northern Europe. Americans with roots in those places live all across the Midwest, and that's where you're likely to find these things. There are some regional variations; Ohioans may make 'em with sausage, while Minnesotans go for ham or corned beef. In both places the sauerkraut balls make great bar food or pass-around appetizers at parties.

Yield: About 3 dozen
sauerkraut balls

3 tablespoons butter
½ cup finely chopped onion
1 large garlic clove, chopped
¼ pound chopped baked ham
¼ pound chopped corned beef
1 pound sauerkraut, rinsed, drained,
     and chopped
¼ cup all-purpose flour
2 tablespoons chopped parsley
½ cup beef broth
1 tablespoon Dijon mustard
Pinch of freshly grated nutmeg
Pepper

FOR DREDGING AND FRYING:
½ cup all-purpose flour
2 large eggs
2 tablespoons water
1½ cups dry bread crumbs
½ teaspoon paprika
Canola oil for frying

1. In a medium skillet over medium heat, melt butter; add onion and garlic and cook until onion is softened, about 5 minutes. Add ham and corned beef and cook until lightly browned. Add sauerkraut and simmer until any remaining liquid from the kraut boils away.
2. Add the ¼ cup of flour and the parsley, stirring to coat everything with the flour. Cook about 2 minutes to get rid of the raw flour taste. Add beef broth, bring to a simmer, and cook until thickened, about 2 to 3 minutes. Transfer mixture to a large bowl. Stir in mustard and nutmeg and season with pepper; cool slightly. Cover and chill mixture in the refrigerator until cold, at least ½ hour.
3. Roll mixture into ½-inch balls, placing on a sheet pan as you go. If desired, you can freeze the balls for 15 minutes so they will keep their shape better when you dredge them.
4. For dredging: In a pie plate or bowl, place the ½ cup of flour. Season with salt and pepper. In another pie plate, place eggs and water; season with salt and pepper and beat well. In a third pie plate, place bread crumbs and paprika; season with salt and pepper.
5. In a large, deep saucepan, heat 2 inches of canola oil to 365 degrees. Dredge balls in flour, then egg, then bread crumbs, coating evenly. Fry in oil in several batches until golden, about 2 minutes per batch. Drain on paper towels and serve immediately.

✯ Pierogi ✯

The most famous dish from Poland — Central European ravioli, in essence, with middle European fillings — may be on the verge of breaking out into the American mainstream. There are many inexpensive Polish restaurants across the country that feature pierogi, and there are more pierogi devotees out there than you might imagine. The dumplings are practically a religion among the central Europeans of southwestern Pennsylvania, in and around Pittsburgh. I've been trying hard to become a pierogi fanatic, because I love the idea of the dish — but, as in my search for the perfect gnocchi, I often end up frustrated. Most pierogi I've tried have been heavy, haven't been touched with textural magic. Then a friend in Brooklyn of Polish extraction showed me the following recipe, and the fireworks finally went off. The chew of these pierogi is amazing: flexible, springy, resilient. The fillings — I offer three here — are the essence of comfort food. And the simple topping of sour cream and sautéed onions puts a crown over all. I suggest that you boil these dumplings for maximum comfort, but some Polish chefs like to sauté them in butter.

Yield: About 4 dozen pierogi

3 cups flour, plus extra for rolling dough
1½ teaspoons salt
¾ cup warm water
2 large eggs
1 tablespoon vegetable oil
Pierogi filling (your choice; recipes follow)
Onion topping (page 93)
Sour cream for topping

★☆★

1. In a medium bowl, sift together flour and salt. In another bowl, combine water, 1 of the eggs, and the vegetable oil; beat lightly. Add egg-oil mixture to flour-salt mixture and stir to make a sticky dough. Turn onto a floured surface and knead just until the dough comes together — not more than 1 or 2 minutes. Wrap dough in plastic wrap and let rest in the refrigerator for at least a half hour.

2. Divide dough into 4 pieces. On a floured surface, roll out 1 piece as thinly as possible. Using a 3-inch cookie cutter dipped in flour, cut out rounds of dough. Repeat with remaining dough. Keep cut circles covered as you work so they don't dry out.

3. Beat the 1 remaining egg in a small bowl with a tablespoon of water. Place about 1 tablespoon of filling on one half of a dough circle. Using your finger, wet edges of the circle with the egg wash. Bring dough edges together to form a semicircle. Press edges together with floured fingers to seal, pressing out any air bubbles as you go. At this point the pierogi can be cooked in a large pot of boiling salted water or frozen. Fresh pierogi cook in about 7 to 8 minutes. Add an additional minute to the cooking time for frozen pierogi.

4. When pierogi are cooked, serve them immediately with onion topping and dollops of sour cream.

★ Potato Filling for Pierogi ★

This is my favorite filling of all; pierogi made with this filling taste like great mashed potatoes with extra textural interest.

Yield: Enough for 4 dozen pierogi

1½ pounds russet potatoes, peeled and cut into chunks
6 tablespoons butter
2 cups chopped onion
¼ cup milk

1. Cook potatoes in boiling salted water until tender. Drain and keep warm.

2. In a skillet, melt 4 tablespoons of the butter and add the onion. Cook over low heat until onion is very soft, about 15 minutes.

3. Pass hot potatoes through a ricer or food mill. Add the remaining 2 tablespoons butter and the milk. Stir in the cooked onion and butter. Season with salt and pepper. Cool before using.

★ Sauerkraut Filling for Pierogi ★

This is a great taste of the Old Country.

Yield: Enough for 4 dozen pierogi

8 ounces bacon slices
2 cups chopped onion
2 pounds sauerkraut, rinsed and drained, squeezed dry
1 cup chicken stock

1. In a large skillet, cook bacon until crisp. Drain on paper towels and crumble. Reserve.

2. Pour all but ¼ cup fat from skillet, add onion and cook over medium heat until soft and golden, about 10 minutes. Add sauerkraut, chicken stock, and reserved bacon.

Simmer to reduce chicken stock almost all the way, about 10 minutes. Season with salt and pepper. Cool before using.

★ Cheese Filling for Pierogi ★

This runny, buttery filling puts the pierogi on the cusp between a savory dish and a dessert. If you wish to go in the latter direction, you could serve them with a topping of buttered, sugared bread crumbs, crisped under the broiler.

Yield: Enough for 4 dozen pierogi

2 (16-ounce) containers 2% milkfat (or
    higher) cottage cheese
Yolk of 2 large eggs, beaten
2 tablespoons melted butter
1 tablespoon sugar
⅛ teaspoon salt

1. Place cottage cheese in a strainer lined with cheesecloth over a bowl. Cover and drain in the refrigerator for 24 hours.
2. In a large bowl, combine drained cottage cheese and remaining ingredients. Mix well.

★ Onion Topping for Pierogi ★

Yield: Enough for 4 dozen pierogi

8 tablespoons butter
2 large onions, chopped

In a medium skillet, melt butter. Add onions and cook over low heat until very soft, about 20 minutes. Turn up heat and cook, stirring, until onions are golden, about another 5 minutes.

☆ Chicken Paprikash ☆

There are not a lot of Hungarian restaurants in the United States — New York City's old Yorkville neighborhood, now completely transformed, was once the largest pocket — but the flagship dish of this wonderful cuisine has been assimilated into our mainstream. Many home cooks in America who know little about Hungarian cuisine have had a go at blending chicken, sour cream, and paprika into something delicious. One of the keys is good paprika — and good technique in bringing out its flavor. Try to find a fresh example of a good Hungarian brand (some paprika can be flavorless and bitter). I love a final addition of paprika to the dish as the cooking is complete. The recipe below calls for two tablespoons, but I just keep adding my good stuff until the paprikash seems on the verge of turning gritty.

Yield: 4 main-course servings

1 tablespoon vegetable oil
½ cup all-purpose flour
8 skin-on, bone-in chicken thighs
2 medium onions, finely chopped
2 large red bell peppers, peeled (with a vegetable
    peeler), seeded, and thinly sliced
4 tablespoons sweet Hungarian paprika
2 teaspoons chopped garlic
1 teaspoon chopped fresh thyme
    (or ½ teaspoon dried thyme)
1 cup chicken stock
¾ cup canned tomatoes (undrained), chopped
1 bay leaf
½ cup sour cream

1. Preheat oven to 325 degrees.
2. Add vegetable oil to a large ovenproof skillet (with a lid) over medium heat. Season flour with salt and pepper. Season chicken with salt

and pepper. Dredge chicken all over in flour, tapping off excess. Reserve unused flour. Add chicken to skillet, browning all over (do this in two batches if necessary). As pieces brown, remove them from skillet and set aside.

3. Pour out all but 2 tablespoons of fat from skillet. Add onions and bell peppers and cook, stirring, over medium heat until onions are golden brown and softened, about 10 to 12 minutes. Add 2 tablespoons of the reserved flour, 2 tablespoons of the paprika, the garlic, and thyme and cook 1 to 2 minutes longer to get rid of the raw flour smell.

4. Add chicken stock, tomatoes, and bay leaf. Bring to a simmer, stirring and scraping the bottom of the skillet to loosen any browned bits. Once sauce is simmering, return chicken to skillet, spoon sauce over the chicken, cover skillet, and place in oven; bake until thighs are very tender, about 45 minutes to 1 hour. About halfway through the cooking time, uncover, turn over chicken pieces, replace the cover, and continue baking.

5. Right before serving, place 1 cup of the hot sauce in a small bowl and mix with the sour cream. Pour the mixture back into the pan and stir until smooth. Stir in the remaining 2 tablespoons paprika, blending well. Serve immediately.

☆ Sauerbraten ☆

One of Germany's great home dishes is pot roast with a difference — and the difference is the spice-marinated meat as well as the rich brown sweet-and-sour sauce, usually thickened with crushed gingersnaps. It all seems so medieval — but so delicious to the modern, comfort-craving palate as well. Sometimes, unfortunately, sauerbraten in its modern incarnations is dry, stringy, and tough — but if you follow the directions carefully in this recipe, no such fate will befall you. A fabulous main course alongside buttered spaetzle (see page 96).

Yield: 6 main-course servings

1 cup high-quality white wine vinegar
1 cup dry red wine
3 cups canned beef broth (preferably unsalted or low sodium)
1 large onion, peeled and coarsely chopped, plus ¾ cup finely chopped onion
1 teaspoon dried thyme leaves
1 teaspoon juniper berries, crushed with a cleaver
10 whole cloves
1 teaspoon black peppercorns, crushed with the flat side of a cleaver
3 bay leaves
2 garlic cloves, crushed
1 (4-pound) bottom round roast (ask your butcher to cut the roast from the top part of the bottom round, as this will produce a more tender sauerbraten)
3 tablespoons bacon fat
¾ cup finely chopped carrot
½ cup finely chopped celery
3 tablespoons flour
¾ cup hot water
½ to ¾ cup crushed gingersnaps
½ teaspoon freshly squeezed lemon juice

1. In a large saucepan, combine vinegar, wine, beef broth, the coarsely chopped onion, thyme, juniper berries, cloves, crushed

peppercorns, bay leaves, and crushed garlic. Bring to a boil and simmer 5 minutes to blend flavors. Cool to room temperature.

2. Place roast in a nonreactive container, just large enough to hold the meat and the marinade. Add marinade. Marinate meat in refrigerator, turning twice a day, for 72 hours.

3. On the fourth day, remove meat from the marinade; strain and reserve marinade and discard the solids. Preheat oven to 350 degrees. Thoroughly dry meat. Season with salt and pepper. Place a large Dutch oven or other pot over medium heat. Add bacon fat. When bacon fat is hot, sear meat on all sides until browned, about 15 minutes. Remove meat.

4. Add the ¾ cup finely chopped onion, carrot, and celery to the Dutch oven over low heat; sauté vegetables until tender, about 8 minutes.

5. Sprinkle flour over vegetables and continue to cook, stirring constantly, for another 3 minutes. Add hot water to vegetables in Dutch oven, raise heat to medium, and, scraping bottom, continue to cook for an additional minute.

6. Stir in reserved marinade and remove Dutch oven from the heat. Put the meat in the Dutch oven; it will be partially covered by liquid. Cover Dutch oven and put into oven. Check occasionally to make sure liquid only simmers. If liquid appears to be boiling, lower temperature to 325 degrees. Cook for about 3 hours, or until meat is fork tender.

7. Remove meat from Dutch oven and cover loosely with aluminum foil.

8. The sauce may be strained at this point or left unstrained with the finely chopped vegetables. Allow the sauce to rest for 15 minutes and then skim off fat.

9. Just before serving, add ½ cup of crushed gingersnaps to the sauce over medium heat. Continue to cook until crumbs are dissolved, about 5 minutes. Taste for seasoning. Add more salt and pepper if desired. If a thicker sauce and spicier flavor are desired, add ¼ cup more crushed gingersnaps. If a thinner sauce is desired, additional broth may be added. Stir in lemon juice and remove sauce from the heat.

10. Slice meat and place on platter. Ladle some of the sauce on top, passing the rest in a sauceboat.

☆ "Hungarian" Beef Goulash ☆ with Sauerkraut

Gulyas in Hungary and goulash in the United States are two very different kettles of meat. The Hungarian version was originally a soup; the American version is almost always a stew. Cooks of Hungarian heritage in Ohio like to serve their goulash alongside sauerkraut — a fabulous blend of flavors, with the sauerkraut cutting the richness of the stew. The following "Hungarian" goulash is the finest I've tasted in the United States.

Yield: 6 servings

2¼ pounds beef chuck, cut into 2-inch cubes
½ cup all-purpose flour
6 tablespoons vegetable oil
3 small yellow onions, thinly sliced
4 large garlic cloves, finely chopped

☆★

2 tablespoons hot Hungarian paprika
(or you can substitute a 3:1 blend
of supermarket paprika and cayenne)
2¼ cups chicken broth
¾ cup dry white wine
¼ cup tomato puree
1 teaspoon caraway seeds
2 tablespoons sour cream, plus more for garnish
4½ cups sauerkraut

1. Place the beef in a large bowl, season generously with salt and pepper, and toss with the flour.

2. Place a Dutch oven with a tight-fitting lid over high heat. Add 2 tablespoons of the vegetable oil. Add half the beef (leaving behind any excess flour) to the Dutch oven and cook, stirring occasionally, until well browned, about 5 minutes. Using a slotted spoon, transfer the beef to a bowl. Wipe out the Dutch oven and repeat with 2 more tablespoons of the oil and the remaining beef.

3. Wipe out the Dutch oven, return to high heat, and heat the remaining 2 tablespoons oil. Add the onions and cook, stirring, until lightly browned and soft, about 3 minutes. Add the garlic and paprika and cook, stirring, until fragrant, about 45 seconds. Return the beef to the Dutch oven. Pour in the chicken broth, wine, and tomato puree and bring to just short of a boil. Lower the heat and simmer, covered, stirring occasionally, until the beef is somewhat tender, about 1½ hours.

4. Uncover the Dutch oven, raise the heat slightly, and continue cooking, stirring occasionally, until the beef is very tender and the liquid has thickened, about 30 minutes. Stir in the caraway seeds and the 2 tablespoons of sour cream and cook for 10 minutes more. Season with salt and pepper to taste.

5. While the sour cream and caraway seeds are cooking into the stew, heat the sauerkraut in a medium saucepan over medium heat. Divide the goulash and sauerkraut among six wide soup bowls, serving them side by side, and garnish each bowl with a dollop of sour cream. Serve immediately.

☆ Spaetzle ☆

Spaetzle (pronounced SHPET-sluh, not spetzel!) is one of Germany's major contributions to world cuisine — and is now growing in popularity in the United States too. The name for this specialty of Swabia (southwestern Germany) comes from the German word for "sparrow" — presumably because, to some whimsical wordsmith, these little side dish dumplings resembled birds. What I love about the following version is their lightness, their springiness, and — after their quick turn in hot butter — their browned butteriness. Could there be a better accompaniment to pot roast (see page 441) or sauerbraten (see page 94)? Spaetzle are made by dropping bits of batter into boiling water. There are many ways to cut the batter and drop it in (see sidebar), but this recipe contains a new, no-fuss, impeccably easy method that anyone can master.

Yield: 6 side dish servings

3 large eggs, beaten
1 cup whole milk
¼ teaspoon salt, plus extra for seasoning
2 cups all-purpose flour
2 tablespoons unsalted butter

1. In a large bowl, whisk together the eggs, milk, and salt.

2. Place the flour in a large bowl and form a well in the center; pour in the egg mixture and stir with a strong whisk until a smooth batter is formed.

3. Cut a ¼-inch hole out of a corner of a large, heavy-duty plastic bag. Transfer the batter to the bag.

4. Bring a large pot of salted water to a boil. Hold the plastic bag over the pot, gently squeeze and shake small bits of batter (the size of a kidney bean) into the water, and cook until they rise to the surface, about 1 minute. Make only as many as you can squeeze out within 30 seconds or so, so that doneness will be uniform. Using a slotted spoon, transfer the dumplings to a platter and set aside. Continue until all the batter is cooked.

5. Place 1 tablespoon of the butter in a large nonstick skillet over medium-high heat. Add half the dumplings and cook, stirring occasionally, until lightly browned, about 2 minutes. Season with salt and pepper. Transfer to a platter and repeat with the remaining butter and dumplings. Serve immediately.

Dropping Spaetzle into hot water

☆ Roasted Garlic ☆ and Herb Spaetzle

People sometimes describe spaetzle as a German version of pasta. If you apply that pasta description to the following recipe, it has never been more appropriate. In fact, these little bits of Mediterranean-accented dough have better, more resilient, more Italian texture than almost any fresh pasta I've ever made at home. Give them a try in their traditional German side dish guise — but try them also, some night, as a pasta substitute in an Italian meal.

Yield: 6 side dish servings

Garlic cloves from 2 heads of garlic, peeled
1 teaspoon olive oil
3 large eggs, beaten
½ cup whole milk
¼ teaspoon salt
¼ cup chopped parsley
¼ cup chopped basil
2 cups all-purpose flour
2 tablespoons unsalted butter

The Perfect Spaetzle Method?

There are many different ways to drop the spaetzle batter into the water in the shape of little dumplings. What constitutes a good way? Two factors are involved: (1) the speed with which you can cut and drop (this helps the spaetzle cook evenly), and (2) the ease of cleaning up when you're done.

Tops for speed can be the gadget called a spaetzle maker. Problem is . . . there are many different kinds, and they vary greatly in effectiveness. And they can be a real chore to clean.

Some chefs like to push the batter through the holes of a colander — but you need a colander with very big holes, and then there's that clean-up problem again. The method favored by most German chefs is to simply place the batter on a wooden board and then cut the batter into small dumplings, quickly flicking them with the knife into the water as they're cut. Cleanup's a breeze — but it takes considerable practice to get the classic spaetzle shape with your knife.

My favorite technique is extremely easy. As described in the recipe on this page, you simply snip off one corner of a heavy-duty plastic bag, stuff the bag with batter, and squeeze away into the water. Best of all: the bag gets tossed and there's no cleanup whatsoever.

Remove from the oven, mash the garlic with a fork, and set aside to cool.

2. In a large bowl, whisk together the mashed garlic, eggs, milk, salt, parsley, and basil.

3. Place the flour in a large bowl and form a well in the center; pour in the egg mixture and stir with a strong whisk until a smooth batter is formed.

4. Cut a ¼-inch hole out of a tip of a large heavy-duty plastic bag (see sidebar). Transfer the batter to the bag.

5. Bring a large pot of salted water to a boil. Hold the bag over the pot, gently squeeze and shake small bits of batter (about the size of a kidney bean) into the water, and cook until they rise to the surface, about 1 minute. Make only as many as you can squeeze out within 30 seconds or so, so that doneness will be uniform. Using a slotted spoon, transfer the dumplings to a platter and set aside. Continue until all the batter is cooked.

6. In a large nonstick skillet, over medium-high heat, heat 1 tablespoon of the butter. Add half the dumplings and cook, stirring occasionally, until lightly browned, about 2 minutes. Season with salt and pepper. Transfer to a platter and repeat with the remaining butter and dumplings. Serve immediately.

1. Preheat the oven to 400 degrees. In a small bowl, toss together the garlic and olive oil and transfer to a small square of aluminum foil. Seal the foil around the garlic and bake until very soft, about 35 minutes.

☆ Hot German Potato Salad ☆

I grew up with divided allegiances in the world of potato salad. I loved the mayonnaisey stuff that most of the kids were eating (see page 419) — but watching my father's delight in the hot, sweet-and-sour potato salad of his German heritage moved me mightily in that direction too. It used to be available, room temperature, at New York delis; today you're more likely to find it in a Midwestern home, properly hot. I love it as a side dish with roast pork or, especially, with German-style sausages.

Yield: 6 servings

2 pounds new potatoes
⅓ cup plus 2 tablespoons white wine vinegar
8 thick slices bacon, chopped
Vegetable oil
1 large red onion, chopped
4 long stalks celery, chopped
¼ cup water
1½ tablespoons sugar
1 teaspoon dry mustard
2 tablespoons Dijon mustard
1 tablespoon chopped parsley
1 tablespoon chopped dill

1. In a large saucepan, place potatoes in salted water to cover. Bring to a simmer. Simmer until cooked through but not falling apart. Drain, and cool slightly. Peel the potatoes while they're still hot (as hot as you can handle) and slice them ½ inch thick. Sprinkle them with the 2 tablespoons of vinegar; cover and keep warm.

2. Meanwhile, in a heavy skillet, cook bacon until crisp. Remove bacon and drain on paper towels. Pour fat into a measuring cup and add vegetable oil to total ¼ cup fat.

3. Pour fat into a clean skillet over medium heat. Add onion and celery and cook for 1 minute, stirring.

4. Combine the remaining ⅓ cup of vinegar, the water, sugar, and dry mustard. Add to skillet with onion and celery. Bring to a sim-

mer over high heat, then stir in Dijon mustard. Immediately pour over hot potatoes. Add parsley, dill, and reserved bacon, mix well, and season to taste with salt and pepper. Let stand for 5 minutes before serving to blend flavors.

NOTE: If you're serving this as a party dish, you may want to make it ahead. If so, pour only half of the dressing over the hot potatoes and let sit at room temperature. To reheat, pour remaining dressing over potatoes, toss, and cover; cook in a 375 degree oven for 15 minutes or until hot. Add herbs and bacon after removing from oven.

Jewish Food

There are approximately six million Jews living in America — not a large percentage of the population. This perhaps explains why Jewish cooking has not become a major influence on what people eat across the country — other than in the form of some great ideas that emanate from delis (pickles, rye bread, pastrami, and so on).

It is interesting, however, that Jewish food has another kind of importance — for it carries a disproportionately heavy load of cultural impact. Chopped liver, though very few people eat it, is a punchline. Chicken soup, though rarely prepared in the traditional Jewish manner, has a wide gastroceutical aura, and has even furnished the imagery for a long-running best-selling book. One of the most famous breeding grounds for comedians was long known as the Borscht

Belt, and the beloved potato pancake, the latke, lent a variation of its name to one of the most bizarre sitcom characters ever to appear on television.

All these food references are to one type of Jewish cooking only — the Ashkenazi food, brought here by the central and northern European Jews. There's a wonderful cuisine among the Sephardic, or Mediterranean, Jews — but it has very little presence in the United States outside Sephardic homes. "Jewish" food is always a little tricky to pin down, anyway — because, unlike "Italian" food or "Chinese" food, it does not come from one country; it reflects the cultural history of a religious group that has spent time in a great many countries over the millennia.

☆ Old-Fashioned ☆ Mushroom and Barley Soup

Jewish chicken soup gets all the buzz, but mushroom and barley soup is also a comfort food staple at Jewish delis across America. I usually find its texture to be pleasing — rib-stickingly thick! — but sometimes find it lacking in depth of flavor. You won't experience that deficiency in the following souped-up recipe; plenty of dried mushrooms, chicken broth, and butter at the finish all add depth. Delicious with Jewish rye bread.

Yield: 6 servings

1 ounce dried porcini mushrooms (you may substitute other types of dried mushrooms)
9 cups chicken broth, plus more to thin the soup, if needed
¼ cup vegetable oil
1 medium yellow onion, cut into ½-inch dice
5 large garlic cloves, finely chopped
1 stalk celery, cut into ½-inch dice
1 medium carrot, peeled and cut into ½-inch dice
1 cup pearl barley (not quick-cooking)
¼ cup plus 2 tablespoons all-purpose flour
1 tablespoon cold unsalted butter, diced
Chopped parsley for garnish

1. Place the dried mushrooms in a large bowl. Bring the 9 cups of chicken broth to a boil and pour over the mushrooms. Cover and let the mushrooms soak for 20 minutes.
2. Strain the broth, reserving both the broth and the mushrooms. Roughly chop the mushrooms.
3. In a medium-size pot, over medium-high heat, heat 3 tablespoons of the vegetable oil. Add the onion and cook, stirring, until soft, about 3 minutes. Add the garlic and cook, stirring, until fragrant, about 45 seconds. Add the celery and carrot and cook, stirring, until starting to soften, about 2 minutes. Stir in the reserved mushrooms and the barley and cook, stirring, for 1 minute more. Add the remaining 1 tablespoon vegetable oil and all the flour and cook, stirring, for 30 seconds.
4. Pour in the reserved mushroom broth and bring to a boil, stirring occasionally. Lower the heat and simmer, covered, stirring occasionally, for 1 hour. The barley will be soft, and the liquid should have thickened considerably.
5. If the soup seems too thick (as if the solid ingredients are about to take over the broth), thin with ¼ cup of chicken broth at a time until the desired consistency is achieved. Stir

in the butter, little by little, until fully incorporated. Season with salt and pepper, divide among six soup bowls, and garnish with the parsley.

✻ The Therapeutic ✻ Three-Hour Chicken Soup

Much is made of "Jewish penicillin" — the classic chicken soup that Mom used to make. However, many a home cook comes up with a chicken soup that lacks the full, rich intensity this soup should have. The following recipe, with its almost magical ratios, asks you to stint not on the chicken and vegetables you buy; your reward will be one of the greatest chicken soups you've ever tasted. If you want to serve it as a one-course meal, you might want to consider cooking it for only one and one-half to two hours. At this stage the broth is light, sweet, and chickeny — and the chicken and vegetables in the pot are holding together enough to be served. Divide the broth among six to eight bowls and add some chicken and vegetables to each one. (If you like your vegetables firmer, add fresh ones to the pot about thirty minutes before serving.) Starch? You have your choice of noodles, rice, or matzo balls; add any one of them to the bowls. If you prefer your broth to be richer, deeper, meatier (but less specifically chickeny), with almost consommé-like concentration, you should cook this soup for a total of three hours. The meat and vegetables will be falling apart and not pretty to serve . . . but the liquid will be marvelous. And it makes a perfect base for another great Jewish boiled dish: flanken (recipe follows).

Yield: 10 to 14 cups of soup
(depending on cooking time)

8 pounds cut-up chicken (see Note)
8 stalks celery, including leaves
8 large carrots, peeled and chunked

1 whole clove
2 pounds onions, peeled and quartered
½ pound parsnips, peeled and chunked
1 cup coarsely chopped parsley stems (1 large
*   bunch parsley should yield enough)*
16 cups water

Wash the chicken, if desired. Place it in a stockpot, along with the celery and carrots. Stick the clove into one of the onion quarters and add the onions, parsnips, and parsley. Add water. Bring to a boil, then lower temperature so the liquid is simmering. Skim off scum and discard. Cook 1½ to 2 hours for a sweet, light-tasting soup, or 3 hours total for a deeper-tasting stock (see headnote). Season to taste with salt and pepper.

Defatting Soup

If you wish to serve chicken soup, or flanken, that is lighter and less fatty, you're going to have to defat the soup at some point. The most efficient method is to put the pot of soup, long before serving, into a refrigerator or a freezer; after a few hours, a white layer of solid fat will form across the top. All you need to do is remove this layer, then reheat the soup. If you'd rather serve the soup when it's just cooked, you can always skim the velvety fat off the top of the pot with a ladle; with practice, you'll be able to depress the ladle into the soup and extract a ladleful of liquid that's a good 80 percent fat. Discard the ladleful. You'll lose a little soup when you do this, but it's the quickest way to defat.

NOTE: When I'm buying eight pounds of chicken for soup, I look for the best chicken deal in the market! Often, I find, with the interest these days in chicken parts (even in the lowly wing!), buying whole chickens is the cheapest. There is one other factor to consider: are you making the shorter-cooked soup and planning to eat the chicken? Or are you making the longer-cooked stock and planning to throw the solid contents of the stockpot away? If you're going the shorter-cooked route, obviously you will want to choose parts that you like eating (eight pounds of wings probably won't work in this case). But if you're going the whole three hours and planning to make compost of the solids — anything'll do!

✴ Flanken ✴

I will have a chicken soup dinner if I'm not feeling well — but if I'm really under the weather, particularly in winter, I especially look for therapy in a steaming bowl of flanken. Think of this great dinner as a beef version of Jewish chicken soup, or as a Jewish pot-au-feu. If you've not had it, you can't believe the comfort that comes from the impossibly deep broth, the sweet vegetables, and most of all, the thick, rich, buttery, beefy slabs of short ribs that ride atop your bowl. It's remarkably easy to make: in the classic eastern European Jewish method, you don't even have to brown the meat. The hardest part is getting the right cut of meat from your butcher. "True" flanken comes from the breast of the steer — which, at one point, intersects with the top of the short ribs. It is much easier to ask your butcher for short ribs. But make sure to tell your butcher to cut the ribs flanken style — which means cutting them across the bone, in chunks that are seven to eight inches long and about three inches thick.

Yield: 6 to 8 main-course servings

10 to 12 cups three-hour chicken soup
(page 101)
8 pounds short ribs, cut across the bone into
chunks that are 7 to 8 inches long and
3 inches thick
8 medium-large carrots, each peeled and cut
into 2 to 3 pieces
1 pound large parsnips, each peeled and cut
into 6 chunks
2 cups leek rounds, cut from the white or
yellow-green part, each round
approximately 1 inch thick
Cooked wide egg noodles
Minced parsley for garnish

1. Make sure that the chicken soup is completely strained and defatted (see sidebar). Place it in a clean stockpot.
2. Salt and pepper the short ribs to taste. Add to the chicken stock in the pot and place pot over high heat. As soon as the liquid comes very close to a boil, turn the heat down to medium-low. Skim the scum that rises to the surface and discard. Simmer flanken gently for 2 hours.
3. Add the carrots to the pot and simmer for 10 minutes. Add the parsnips and simmer for 10 minutes. Add the leeks and cook 25 minutes more — a total of 45 minutes of cooking for all the vegetables. The vegetables should be tender but not falling apart. The meat should be extremely tender, ready to come off the bone with the merest prod. Season broth to taste with salt and pepper.
4. Place a cup or so of cooked noodles in each of six to eight bowls. Top noodles with hot broth, chunks of flanken, and a selection of vegetables. Top all with minced parsley and serve immediately. Pass coarse salt to sprinkle on beef.

★ Cholent ★

The Jewish Sabbath begins at sundown on Friday night and lasts until sundown on Saturday night. During the Sabbath, observant Jews must refrain from labor . . . even cooking! So the tradition is to prepare a stew on Friday before sunset, place it in a low-temperature oven, and let it cook overnight until the midday meal on Saturday — when no one has to do any labor in order to enjoy great food! The long-cooked meat-and-bean stew Cholent (pronounced something like "chunt") features beef, of course (pork being proscribed by the kosher laws) — and the short ribs in this recipe melt to an almost unbelievable tenderness. Like buttah! (Which, of course, would also be proscribed.) I think of it as Jewish cassoulet.

Yield: 6 servings

½ cup dried lima beans
½ cup dried kidney beans
½ cup pearl barley
6 tablespoons vegetable oil
6 beef short ribs (about 2½ pounds)
All-purpose flour for dredging
2 medium yellow onions, thinly sliced
6 large garlic cloves, finely chopped
2 teaspoons paprika
1 tablespoon tomato paste
1 large parsnip, peeled and cut into
　　large chunks
1 large carrot, peeled and cut into large chunks
1½ cups canned tomatoes, roughly chopped

I. In a large saucepan, combine the lima and kidney beans and the barley and cover with cold water by 4 inches. Bring to a boil, remove saucepan from heat, and let the beans and barley sit in the water for I hour. Drain beans and barley and set aside.

2. Preheat the oven to 225 degrees. Place 2 tablespoons of the vegetable oil in a 4-quart Dutch oven with a tight-fitting lid over high heat. Season the ribs all over with salt and pepper. Place a cup or so of flour on a plate. Roll 3 of the ribs in the flour until well coated. Add the 3 ribs to the Dutch oven and cook, turning occasionally, until well browned all over, about 4 minutes. Transfer the ribs to a clean plate. Wipe out the Dutch oven and return it to the heat. Add another 2 tablespoons of the vegetable oil and repeat seasoning, flouring, and browning with the remaining 3 ribs.

3. Wipe out the Dutch oven and return it to the range over medium-high heat. Add the remaining 2 tablespoons oil. Add the onions and cook, stirring, until lightly browned, about 4 minutes. Add the garlic and cook, stirring, for I minute more. Add the paprika and tomato paste and cook, stirring, for I minute. Remove the Dutch oven from the heat.

4. Stir in the reserved beans and barley and the parsnip, carrot, and tomatoes; season with salt and pepper and imbed the short ribs in the mixture. Pour in enough cold water to completely cover all the ingredients. Taste the water to see if it needs any salt. Bring to a boil and skim off any scum that rises to the surface. Cover tightly with foil, cover with the lid, and bake for at least 8 hours (overnight, in the traditional manner, is also possible). You want the ribs to be very, very tender and the liquid reduced to a saucelike consistency.

5. When ready to eat, remove the cholent from the oven. If the mixture seems too dry,

you can thin it out with a little water or stock. Season with salt and pepper and serve immediately.

✩ Extra-Crispy Potato Latkes ✩

Potato pancakes — beloved of many cultures — are especially associated with the Jewish Hanukkah table. But no matter who's frying them, you'll see a basic dichotomy in styles: thick, heavy ones versus thin, light, crispy ones. I prefer the latter latkes and find the pancakes from the following recipe to be positively lacy. A classic deli way to serve them is with applesauce as a first course, but I think latkes have no higher calling in life than as a pot roast side dish with a good brown gravy.

Yield: 12 potato pancakes

2¼ pounds Idaho potatoes, peeled and grated
1 small yellow onion, peeled and grated
1 egg, beaten
6 tablespoons matzo meal
1 tablespoon kosher salt
¼ teaspoon freshly ground pepper
Vegetable oil for frying

1. In a large bowl, combine the potatoes, onion, egg, matzo meal, kosher salt, and pepper and mix until well combined.
2. Transfer the mixture to a colander and place the colander in the sink or a large bowl. Press down on the mixture to extract as much liquid as possible. Using your hands, form the mixture into golf ball–size balls, squeezing out any excess moisture.
3. On a work surface, lay out a strip of plastic wrap. Lay the potato balls on the plastic wrap, keeping them spaced apart. Using a perforated spatula, press down firmly on each ball to flatten it and press out any excess moisture. The pancakes should be thin and flat.
4. Pour vegetable oil into a large skillet over medium-high heat until it's about ⅛ inch deep. Working in small batches, transfer the flattened potato balls to the skillet, making sure they don't touch each other. Cook, turning once, until the latkes are browned and crispy, about 2 minutes per side. Transfer them to a paper towel–lined plate and season with table salt. Continue until all 12 are cooked. Serve immediately.

Russian Food

When Americans think of Russian food (which they don't do very often), one image predominates: the mirthful consumption of caviar and vodka. *Vashe zdorovie!* And this stereotype has been reinforced over the years by the one Russian restaurant in America with national impact: New York's Russian Tea Room, now defunct, where for decades wealthy people really have consumed, mirthfully and in elegant surroundings, mountains of caviar and rivers of iced vodka.

But it's a tiny snapshot of a huge canvas. Even at the high end, there is a traditional Russian cuisine — forged through nineteenth- and twentieth-century contacts with French chefs — that has barely been broached in America.

At the people's end there's even more food that we don't know about. Some of it — such as borscht — came here with Russian Jews, and some of it can be had in the wacky party-time Russian restaurants of Brighton Beach, Brooklyn. But most of it — with the exception of a few dishes that had prominence in America thirty years ago (such as chicken Kiev and beef Stroganoff) — has not broken through into the general American consciousness.

Nevertheless, the opportunity to have an insanely indulgent evening of spending or drinking or dancing to "Midnight in Moscow" is always there for us. Even at home.

☆ Blini for Caviar ☆

Most caviar fanatics like only one thing with their caviar: more caviar. But there are ways to consume it — other than killing it with onions — that don't interfere with caviar's subtlety. At the fancy Russian restaurants in New York like Firebird they make a big show of wrapping caviar in butter-drenched buckwheat crepes that the Russians call blini. The following recipe makes wonderfully tender, delicately nutty-tasting blini that go beautifully with caviar.

Yield: About 15 blini

2 cups buckwheat flour

1 cup plus 1 tablespoon all-purpose flour

½ cup sugar

3½ cups plus 2 tablespoons whole milk

3 large eggs, beaten

4 tablespoons (½ stick) butter, melted,
      plus extra melted butter for the pan

½ teaspoon yeast

1. In a medium bowl, mix the buckwheat flour with the all-purpose flour and the sugar. Set aside.

2. In a 2-quart saucepan, combine the milk, eggs, the 4 tablespoons of melted butter, and the yeast and heat to 105 degrees. Remove from heat. Whisk into the dry ingredients, mixing well. Put through a sieve. Let stand at room temperature for one hour.

Putting Together Your Blini and Caviar

If you wish to emulate the pomp of blini-with-caviar service at fancy Russian restaurants, bring a stack of warm blini to the table — along with a sauceboat filled with melted butter and an iced container of caviar. Place one blin on a dinner plate, drizzle a little warm melted butter on it, place some caviar in the middle of it (the quantity is up to you and your accountant, but I like about two tablespoons), fold the blin to enclose the caviar, and drizzle a little more melted butter on top. Eat with knife and fork. Drink icy vodka.

Which kind of caviar should you use? Beluga, the most expensive kind, is a waste in this context; the magnificent texture of great beluga eggs gets lost. Osetra, generally my favorite, is a better choice — but the subtlety of a great osetra would be best on its own. I think that the least expensive of the three sturgeon possibilities — sevruga caviar, with its bracing salinity — is the wisest for blini with caviar.

But I wouldn't send beluga or osetra back to the kitchen.

3. To make the blini, place an 8-inch frying pan (it's easier to use a nonstick pan) over medium heat. Lightly brush the pan with melted butter.

4. Stir the batter and pour ¼ cup into the hot pan, immediately tilting the pan so that the entire surface is covered. Cook for 1 minute, or until small bubbles form on the surface of the blini. Using a spatula, or your fingers, flip the blini over and cook the second side for 30 seconds. Use immediately, or keep in a warm stack covered with towels while you cook the remaining batter.

☆ Russian Salad ☆

Russians love creamy things — sour cream, mayonnaise — and for a long time in the western parts of the former Soviet Union a very popular dish has been cooked vegetables (with beets in the blend) dressed with mayo. Most Russian restaurants in the United States have picked up on this, usually presenting the "Russian salad" as part of an array of appetizers (or zakuski). I love this dish, particularly when it's freshly made.

Yield: 4 appetizer servings

2 medium waxy potatoes, peeled and cut into
⅜-inch dice (about 1 cup)
8 green beans, cut into ⅜-inch lengths
(about ½ cup)
½ cup frozen peas
2 medium carrots, peeled and cut into
⅜-inch dice (about 1 cup)
1 medium beet, peeled and cut into ⅜-inch dice
(about 1 cup)

2 teaspoons cider vinegar
1 cup loosely packed washed and dried flat-leaf
parsley leaves, plus a few extra for
garnish
⅓ cup good-quality store-bought mayonnaise

1. Cook the vegetables separately in a large quantity of rapidly boiling salted water. Start with the lightest in color: cook the potatoes, then the beans, then the peas, then the carrots, then the beet. Cook each until it's just tender. As the potatoes, beans, peas, and carrots are cooked, plunge them into a bowl of ice water for about a minute to stop the cooking process and retain the color. Dry well.

2. Place all the vegetables except the beet in a large bowl. Mix them together gently with the cider vinegar. Season with salt and pepper. Then mix in the beet, turning the vegetables as little as possible. (You won't be able to avoid the beet color running a little.) Chop the parsley leaves and gently mix them in, along with the mayonnaise.

3. Chill before serving. Garnish with additional parsley.

☆ Cold Borscht ☆

Borscht — the beet soup that can be made in both cold and hot versions — came to the United States with Russian and Polish immigrants, many of them Jewish. The Jews, in fact, actually gave it its most commonly used name: *borscht* is Yiddish. (In Russian you would say *borsch*.) The cold version is a wonderful summertime starter — particularly, in my opinion, when your soup bowl is thick with garnishes.

Yield: 6 first-course servings

5 small beets (about 2 pounds)
3¼ cups water
3¼ cups chicken stock
1 medium onion, peeled and quartered
2 garlic cloves, peeled and smashed
1 bay leaf
7 tablespoons lemon juice
3 tablespoons light brown sugar
1½ teaspoons salt

GARNISHES:
4 hard-boiled eggs, quartered
½ cup peeled, seeded, and diced cucumber
½ cup cooked, peeled, and diced red potato
¼ cup chopped dill
½ cup sour cream

1. In a large saucepan, combine beets, water, chicken stock, onion, garlic, and bay leaf. Simmer, covered, until beets are very tender, about 30 minutes. Cool and peel beets. Grate on the coarse holes of a box grater. Reserve.
2. Strain broth and return to saucepan; discard solids. Bring to a simmer. Add lemon juice, brown sugar, and salt. Stir until sugar and salt dissolve; remove from heat. Refrigerate until very cold. Add grated beets.
3. To serve, ladle beets and broth into chilled bowls and top with garnishes.

✳ Hot Ukranian Borscht ✳

As much as I love cold borscht in the summer, I'm even more delirious about hot borscht in winter. But it never hit the mainstream here as the cold borscht did. It is everything you could want from a hearty, one-pot meal: rich broth, lots of wintry vegetables, chunks of meat and sausage. Along with dark bread, butter, and a frozen bottle or two of Russian vodka, borscht makes life beautiful. A little cold still, but beautiful.

Yield: 8 main-course servings

1 tablespoon canola oil
3 pounds beef stew meat with bones
        (cuts such as chuck or shin are good)
½ pound kielbasa, halved lengthwise and then
        sliced ½ inch thick
1 small onion, peeled and coarsely chopped
2 medium carrots, scraped and cut into
        ½-inch dice
2 stalks celery, cut into ½-inch dice
2 sprigs parsley, plus 2 tablespoons chopped
        parsley
2 sprigs fresh thyme, plus 2 teaspoons chopped
        thyme
1½ pounds beets, trimmed with 1 inch
        of stem remaining
2 tablespoons butter
1 medium parsnip, peeled and cut into ½-inch
        dice (about ½ cup)
1 large leek, split, washed, and thinly sliced
        (white and light green parts)
1 large russet potato, peeled and cut into
        ½-inch dice
½ small head green cabbage, cored and finely
        shredded
1 teaspoon sweet paprika
1 large garlic clove, peeled and finely chopped
2 bay leaves
8 allspice berries
15 black peppercorns
3 cups water
2 cups canned tomatoes, chopped

2 cups cooked small white beans (canned is fine)
2 tablespoons red wine vinegar
1 tablespoon sugar
Sour cream for garnish
Chopped dill for garnish

1. Make soup base: Heat canola oil in a Dutch oven over medium-high heat. Add beef in small batches, browning well on all sides; remove and reserve. Brown kielbasa pieces on all sides; remove and reserve. Add beef (not kielbasa) back to the pot, along with the onion, half of the carrots, half of the celery, the 2 sprigs of parsley, and the 2 sprigs of thyme. Add water to cover (about 5 cups). Bring to simmer, then skim the foam that collects at the top and discard it. Simmer until meat is almost fork tender, about 1½ hours. Add kielbasa; simmer until beef is very tender, about ½ hour more.

2. Strain stock, reserving meats and discarding the remaining solids. If time permits, cool the stock and then refrigerate and remove the congealed layer of fat on top. If not, just spoon off as much fat as possible. You should have about 4 cups stock. Reserve. Cool beef slightly and cut or shred into large (about 1-inch) chunks; set aside with kielbasa.

3. Preheat oven to 400 degrees. Place beets on a sheet of heavy-duty foil and season with salt and pepper. Roast until almost tender: about 35 to 50 minutes, depending on the size of the beets. Cool, then peel the beets and grate them on the coarse side of a box grater (you should have about 2 cups). Reserve.

4. In a large Dutch oven over medium heat, melt the butter. Add remaining carrots, remaining celery, the parsnip, leek, potato, cabbage, the 2 tablespoons chopped parsley, the 2 teaspoons chopped thyme, the paprika, and garlic. Cook, stirring, until vegetables are softened but not browned, about 10 minutes. Tie bay leaves, allspice, and peppercorns in a piece of cheesecloth and add to pot. Add reserved stock, water, and tomatoes. Simmer until vegetables are tender, about 30 minutes. Add reserved beets, reserved meats, and the white beans; simmer 10 minutes longer. Add vinegar and sugar; season to taste with salt and pepper. Serve with sour cream and dill.

✹ Pelmeni with Beef Broth ✹

There's a whole galaxy of Russian dumpling possibilities. If the dumplings are made with yeast and stuffed, they're called pirog. If they're made, as this recipe is, with no yeast and stuffed, they're called pelmeni — but only if they're shaped into semicircles. Kolduny are crescent-shaped (which you can do with the following pelmeni, if you wish). Vareniki are like pelmeni, but larger. Lazanki are cut into squares. And on it goes. However, thanks to one of the best dishes for decades at the Russian Tea Room in New York, it is pelmeni that has made an impact in America; generations of Tea Room devotees loved it. Of course, there are many versions of pelmeni. One huge issue involves the background to the dumplings: do they sit in a great deal of broth, or does a little broth just moisten the star of the dish, the pelmeni themselves? I like to serve pelmeni, lots of 'em, as a main-course dish. But I don't include a lot of broth, so the following recipe is not a soup — but what broth I add I like to stud with diced vegetables, such as beets, carrots, and mushrooms (a nontraditional choice). You have three-quarters of a cup of broth to play with per serving; decide for yourself how much you'd like to use.

Yield: 6 main-course servings (¾ cup broth and 12 pelmeni per serving)

2 cups all-purpose flour, plus extra for
    kneading
2 teaspoons salt, plus extra for seasoning
2 large eggs
¼ cup cool water, plus 2½ cups warm water
¾ cup dried mushrooms
¼ pound ground beef
¼ pound ground veal
¼ pound ground pork
2 cups finely chopped onion
1 teaspoon finely minced fresh dill,
    plus extra for garnish (optional)
¼ teaspoon grated lemon zest
½ teaspoon freshly ground pepper
¼ teaspoon ground coriander
1 tablespoon unsalted butter
½ cup finely diced carrot
5 cups beef broth (preferably low sodium
    if using canned broth)
½ cup diced pickled beets
Sour cream for garnish (optional)

1. Place the 2 cups flour and 1 teaspoon of the salt in the work bowl of food processor and pulse to combine. Beat eggs and the ¼ cup cool water together lightly. Turn food processor on and slowly pour in egg mixture. Process until mixture comes together. Turn dough out onto a floured board and knead into a ball. Cover with a cloth and let rest for 1 hour.

2. Cover dried mushrooms with the 2½ cups warm water in a small bowl. Set aside for at least 15 minutes.

3. Combine beef, veal, pork, 1 cup of the chopped onion, the 1 teaspoon of dill, the lemon zest, the remaining 1 teaspoon of salt, the ½ teaspoon pepper, and coriander in a medium-size bowl. Cover and place in refrigerator until ready to make dumplings.

4. Melt the butter in a large pot over low heat. Add the diced carrot and the remaining 1 cup of chopped onion. Cook over low heat for about 10 minutes, stirring occasionally. Do not let them brown.

5. Pour liquid from mushrooms into pot, making sure any dirt or grit from mushrooms remains in the bottom of the bowl. Reserve mushrooms. Add beef broth to pot. Adjust for seasoning with salt and pepper, and set aside.

6. Divide dough into quarters. Roll one piece of dough on a floured surface into ⅛-inch thickness. Cut out circular pieces of dough using a 1½-inch circular cutter. You should have about 18 circles.

7. Put 1 heaping teaspoon of meat mixture in the center of each circle. Using your fingers, pull opposite edges of the dough out and up. Bring the two sides of the dough together over the meat and press to enclose the filling. Working around the edges of the semicircle, pinch edges together tightly. Place pelmeni under a cloth. Repeat with the rest of the

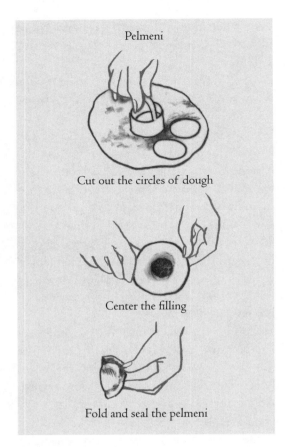

Pelmeni

Cut out the circles of dough

Center the filling

Fold and seal the pelmeni

dough, forming a total of approximately 72 pelmeni.

8. Bring broth to a boil. Add pelmeni. Simmer for about 10 minutes, until pelmeni are tender. Mince reserved mushrooms and add, along with beets. Remove from heat.

9. Divide pelmeni equally among six bowls and ladle an equal amount of broth over each dish (you may use the full ¾ cup per bowl or less). Make sure to divide the solids (carrot, beets, and mushrooms) equally among the bowls. Garnish bowls with dill and a teaspoon of sour cream if desired. Serve immediately.

✿ Chicken Kiev ✿

Though the geographic origins of this dish seem quite specific, no one is really sure how the famous Ukrainian city became connected with Chicken Kiev. All things French were very fashionable around 1900; it is possible that fried chicken cutlets from France inspired someone in Kiev and are really the source of this "Russian" dish. Nevertheless, Chicken Kiev is one of the dishes that Americans think of first when the subject of Russian food comes up: a pounded chicken breast rolled around a core of flavored butter, the whole breaded and deep-fried. The payoff is that when you cut into the cooked chicken, the butter squirts out. I'm going to force this dish to evolve one step further: since the light, crispy, puffy Japanese crumbs called panko are my favorite coating crumbs of all for deep-frying — why not use them here? France meets Russia meets Japan on American ground, logically and deliciously.

Yield: 4 main-course servings

1 stick unsalted butter, at cool room temperature
1 tablespoon chopped parsley
1 tablespoon chopped chives
1½ teaspoons chopped dill
1 tablespoon lemon juice
Finely grated zest of 1 lemon
4 small, boneless, skinless chicken breasts
    (tenders removed and reserved),
    about ⅓ pound each
¼ cup all-purpose flour
2 large eggs, beaten with 2 tablespoons water
1½ cups panko crumbs
Canola oil for frying

1. In a small bowl, mash together butter, parsley, chives, dill, lemon juice, and lemon zest until well blended. Season with salt and

pepper to taste. This could also be done in a mini–food processor.

2. Place a piece of plastic wrap (about 16 inches long) on the counter, place the flavored butter in the middle, and shape into a narrow log. Roll in plastic wrap, then roll wrap on the counter to extend the length of the log to about 10 inches. Twist the ends of the wrap to seal and place in the freezer. Freeze until solid.

3. Place a piece of plastic wrap (about 12 inches long) on the counter, sprinkle lightly with water, and place 1 of the chicken breasts in the center. Place another piece of plastic wrap on top. Pound with a meat mallet until chicken is about ¼ inch thick. Repeat with remaining chicken breasts.

4. Cut or pull the white tendon from each of the 4 chicken tenders, taking care not to remove any meat. Discard tendons. Using the same method as above, pound tenders until about ¼ inch thick.

5. Cut frozen butter into 4 equal pieces. Place a chicken breast on the counter, with the longest part running horizontally on the counter. Season with salt and pepper. Place a piece of butter in the middle and place a pounded tender over the butter, hiding as much of the butter as possible. Use your fingers to smooth the tender over the butter. Fold the long edges of the chicken over the tender, then roll up the breast, tucking in the short edges. Repeat with remaining breasts, placing each breast in the refrigerator after it is rolled so the butter remains hard.

6. In 3 pie plates, place the flour, egg mixture, and panko crumbs. Season each with

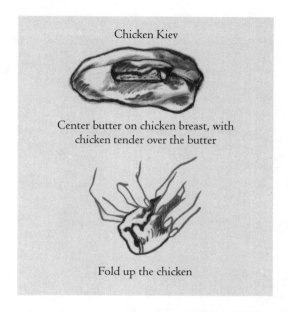

Chicken Kiev

Center butter on chicken breast, with chicken tender over the butter

Fold up the chicken

salt and pepper. Dip the rolled breasts in flour, then egg, then panko crumbs, coating each one completely in each step. Place on a sheet pan and return to the refrigerator for at least a half hour to let the crumbs set.

7. Preheat oven to 400 degrees. In a deep saucepan, heat canola oil to 365 degrees. Deep-fry chicken, two at a time, until golden, about 5 minutes. Place on a sheet pan and place in the oven to finish cooking, approximately 15 to 16 minutes. Serve immediately.

✶ Beef Stroganoff ✶

This cream-sauce-and-beef affair became a wildly popular party dish in the United States in the 1940s and 1950s. Surprisingly — for it seems so much like an American invention — it really has roots in Russian cuisine, having been named for the affluent Stroganov family from Novgorod in northern Russia. There are many different ways to approach this much-anthologized dish, but the central question is this: Do you cook the beef quickly, or do you stew it? James Beard came down firmly on the side of quick cooking, and so do I; to me, it's what gives the dish its distinction. In order to pull this off, however, you need really tender meat — hence the use of filet mignon here. A traditional accompaniment is fried matchstick potatoes.

Yield: 6 main-course servings

2 tablespoons vegetable oil
1¼ pounds beef tenderloin or filet mignon,
    cut into thin, 1-inch-long strips
½ cup plus 3 tablespoons unsalted butter
10 ounces small white mushrooms, quartered
5 medium yellow onions, thinly sliced
4 large garlic cloves, minced
2 tablespoons tomato paste
3 tablespoons all-purpose flour
1 cup dry white wine
3 tablespoons sour cream
1 tablespoon Dijon mustard
2 teaspoons freshly squeezed lemon juice
2 tablespoons chopped flat-leaf parsley
2 tablespoons chopped chives
1 (12-ounce) package extra-wide egg noodles

1. In a large skillet over high heat, heat 1 tablespoon of the vegetable oil. Season half the beef generously with salt and pepper and cook, without stirring, until well browned on one side and still pink on the other, about 1 minute. Transfer to a plate and set aside. Repeat with the remaining oil and beef. Drain beef and reserve.

2. Return the skillet to the burner and lower heat to medium-high. Add the ½ cup of butter, and when the foaming begins to subside, add the mushrooms and onions. Cook, stirring, until browned and soft, about 10 minutes. Add the garlic and cook, stirring, until lightly browned and fragrant, about 2 minutes. Add the tomato paste and cook, stirring, about 2 minutes. Add the flour and cook, stirring, for 2 minutes. Pour in the wine, bring to a boil, and cook, stirring occasionally, for 2 minutes. Add 2 cups of water and bring to a boil. Lower heat and simmer, stirring, for 2 minutes. Stir in the sour cream, mustard, lemon juice, parsley, and chives. Season with salt and pepper to taste. Set aside.

3. Cook the noodles according to package instructions. Drain and reserve ¼ cup cooking liquid. Put the noodles back in their cooking pot and toss with the remaining 3 tablespoons butter and the reserved cooking liquid. Keep warm.

4. Reheat the beef in the sour cream sauce over medium heat just until the beef is warm. Make sure the sour cream doesn't curdle. Divide the noodles among six plates and top with the beef mixture. Serve immediately.

Scandinavian Food

The fresh, clean food of Scandinavia has had a minimal impact on the general cuisine of America. Certainly, in pockets of Scandinavian population — in Minnesota, in Kansas, and, surprisingly, near Santa Barbara,

California — there has been a much greater impact, but it hasn't spread much. At least on the plate. The mind is something else. For I think the image of Scandinavian food floats in the imagination of many culinary Americans as they contemplate a kind of cooking — particularly with fish — that relies on great ingredients and minimal kitchen transformation. Though few have done it — and though there are precious few opportunities to do it in the United States — most people would be delighted to spend time at a smorgasbord. Forward-thinking foodies feed off a mental smorgasbord instead.

☆ Gravlax with ☆ Coriander Seed, Cardamom, Aquavit, and Dill

The Scandinavian idea of simply sprinkling salmon with salt and sugar and flavorings, then letting it sit under a weight for a few days, creating a kind of cured salmon, became more popular in the United States in the 1970s and 1980s than any other Scandinavian dish. It is de rigueur today at Scandinavian restaurants across the country but has also achieved some popularity among home cooks in the United States. The following recipe is the best home version I've ever tasted. There are several things about it that I love. Many gravlax recipes feature a large volume of salt and pepper in the rub — so much that the rub has to be knocked off at serving time to enjoy the fish. I prefer to lessen the amount of salt and pepper, setting things up so that you can leave the coating on when you eat the fish. Most recipes call for skin-on salmon, with, therefore, maximum flavor permeation on one side only; my low-quantity salt and pepper can go on both sides of a skinned salmon fillet, vastly increasing the flavor. And what flavor is it, exactly? Well, I admit that the following recipe is Americanized, in that it has more flavor than what you might find in Sweden. *But . . .* the flavors are intrinsically Scandinavian, drawing on a group of spices often used in other ways in traditional Swedish cooking. I like this gravlax best when it has sat, weighted, in the refrigerator for four days; that's when the texture is ideal. But it also tastes good at three days, two days, even twenty-four hours after putting it up. Serve with thin slices of dark bread and, especially, icy glasses of aquavit.

Yield: 6 first-course servings

1 (1½-pound) very fresh center-cut salmon
*   fillet (see Salmon note)*
2 tablespoons aquavit (see Aquavit note)
2 tablespoons light brown sugar
1 tablespoon plus 1 teaspoon kosher salt
2 teaspoons whole coriander seeds
½ teaspoon whole white peppercorns
¼ teaspoon cardamom seeds, removed from pods
*   (see Cardamom note)*
⅛ teaspoon ground cloves
1 tablespoon grated lemon zest
*   (see Lemon zest note)*
½ cup firmly packed finely chopped fresh dill

1. Have the fishmonger remove the salmon skin or do it yourself. One edge of the salmon fillet will be thinner than the rest; cut it away and reserve for another use (you're cutting away about one-sixth of the fish). You should now be left with a skinless chunk of salmon that has even thickness and weighs approximately 1¼ pounds.

2. Place the salmon fillet on a large sheet of plastic wrap. Sprinkle 1 tablespoon of the

aquavit over one side of the salmon and rub it in. Flip the salmon over and repeat with the remaining 1 tablespoon of aquavit.

3. Place the brown sugar and kosher salt in a bowl. Mix together well. If the sugar is lumpy, break it up with your fingers until it's granulated. Sprinkle half of the mixture over one side of the salmon, spreading it out evenly with your fingers. Flip the salmon over and repeat with the remaining half of the sugar-salt mixture.

4. Place the coriander seeds, peppercorns, cardamom seeds, and ground cloves in a spice grinder or in a mortar with a pestle. Grind until the mixture is fairly fine but not powdered. Sprinkle half of the mixture over one side of the salmon, spreading it out evenly with your fingers. Flip the salmon over and repeat with the remaining half of the spice mixture.

5. Spread half of the lemon zest evenly on each side of the salmon. Spread half of the chopped dill evenly on each side of the salmon. Fold the plastic wrap over the salmon on all sides, wrapping it tightly. Place the salmon on a wide plate, cover with another plate, and place weights (such as heavy cans) on top of the top plate. Place in refrigerator and let sit for half of the curing time (as the headnote indicates, half of the curing time can be anywhere from half a day to 2 days). Remove weights, turn salmon over, reweight, then return to refrigerator for second half of curing time. (An example would be turning salmon over after 2 days, curing for 2 more.)

6. When ready to serve, remove gravlax from plastic wrap. Leave coatings on. Slice on the diagonal into broad, thin slices. Let stand, covered, for 10 minutes at room temperature, and serve.

SALMON NOTE: Buying salmon for this dish is very easy: you just want to purchase a center-cut salmon fillet. But a couple of tweaks can make things even better. Most important: a hunk of salmon fillet is pretty evenly thick right across the fillet — except for a thin, fatty flap on one edge. I recommend in the recipe that you cut that thin flap off, because it will cure at such a different rate and probably turn salty. I also recommend removing the skin of the fillet so that the flavors can penetrate from two sides. And this is why I suggest that you buy a one-and-one-half-pound fillet; after the various trimmings, you should be left with a recipe-ready piece that's about one and one-fourth pounds.

AQUAVIT NOTE: When you make gravlax, some type of spirit is used to augment the flavor — and chefs today choose many different spirits to do the job. The spirit that I find to be in the best key for this dish — no surprise! — is Scandinavian aquavit, a clear spirit with a hint of caraway flavor. There are good examples in our stores from Norway and Sweden — but my favorite one, the Aalborg Akvavit, is from Denmark. Make sure to drink some a few days later with the dish!

CARDAMOM NOTE: These seeds come to the market with either black pods or green pods. The higher-toned green pods work better here. Make sure to break the pods and extract the pebbly little seeds that live inside them; these are what you use in the dish. Discard the pods themselves.

LEMON ZEST NOTE: It is important, when you grate the lemon to remove the zest, that you grate only the yellow part of the skin. Just below the yellow part lies the white pith; this is bitter and will spoil the dish. The very best tool to remove the yellow zest, I've found, is a new-fangled one called the micrograter; it pulls the zest off in soft, curly little loops that seem less bitter than zest extracted in other ways.

✳ Split Pea Soup ✳ with Rye Croutons

Pea soup comes from a number of ethnic directions and is popular in many parts of the country. But the most famous pea soup of all, in America, is from a large restaurant called Andersen's, in an incongruous hotbed of Danish culture just north of Santa Barbara. Their smooth, pureed soup — made with split green peas, unlike the yellow peas you often see in Scandinavia — is very good. The following recipe is like theirs in many ways — except that I like pea soup better when the monolithic puree is broken up by little texture surprises. So this one has lots of hammy bits in it (as well as the unmistakable taste of pork) and a topping of crunchy rye croutons.

Yield: 6 servings

> 2 tablespoons unsalted butter
> 1 cup chopped leeks (white part only)
> ½ cup peeled and finely chopped carrot
> ½ cup finely chopped celery
> 1 small russet potato, peeled and diced
>   (about ½ cup)
> ¼ cup minced fresh parsley leaves
> 1 teaspoon minced fresh thyme leaves
> 2 bay leaves
> ¼ teaspoon hot pepper sauce
> 2 cups split green peas, rinsed
> 8 cups water
> 2 ham hocks
> *Rye croutons (recipe follows)*

1. Melt butter in a large saucepan over low heat. Add leeks, carrot, celery, and potato. Sauté until vegetables are softened but not browned, about 12 minutes.

2. Add parsley, thyme, bay leaves, and hot pepper sauce. Add split peas and stir to coat with butter. Add water and ham hocks. Bring to a boil, reduce heat, and simmer about 1 hour, or until peas mash easily with a spoon. During cooking, skim and discard any foam that accumulates on top of the soup.

3. Remove ham hocks and bay leaves. Once ham hocks are cool, pull off meat and chop fine. Reserve. Puree soup until completely smooth using an immersion blender or a regular blender. Return chopped ham to soup and simmer until heated through. Season to taste with salt and pepper. Serve with rye croutons.

★ Rye Croutons ★

Yield: About 2 cups

> 6 slices seeded rye bread
> 2 tablespoons butter

1. Preheat oven to 350 degrees. Using a serrated knife, cut crusts from bread and then cut bread into ½-inch cubes.

2. Heat a large ovenproof skillet over medium heat; add butter. When butter is melted, add bread cubes, tossing and turning croutons with tongs to coat evenly with butter. Continue to cook and toss over medium heat until bread begins to get crisp on the outside, about 3 to 4 minutes. Place skillet in the oven and bake until croutons are golden and crispy throughout, another 5 to 7 minutes. Season immediately with salt and pepper.

★ Swedish Meatballs ★

Of all the Scandinavian delights, this is probably the one name that's recognized most by Americans. Ironically, the versions you see in the United States don't usually resemble what you see in Sweden. Over there, the meatballs are served in a dark brown sauce, often with lingonberry jelly on the side. The classic Swedish-American Meatball is accompanied by a cream sauce — sometimes a quite light-colored one. The following recipe, which features remarkably tender little meatballs, splits the difference: there's cream, but it creates a deep, hearty, tan sauce, like the mushroom cream soup of your dreams. You're more likely to see something like this in the United States — but it is my favorite of any version I've tasted in either country. Swedish Meatballs are great as a hot smorgasbord item — but also make a fine main course with rice or noodles.

Yield: 36 meatballs

3 tablespoons butter
¼ cup finely chopped onion
½ cup plus 2 tablespoons fresh bread crumbs
½ cup milk
½ pound ground beef
¼ pound ground pork
¼ pound ground veal
1 large egg, beaten
½ teaspoon ground allspice
½ teaspoon ground nutmeg
¾ teaspoon kosher salt
¼ teaspoon ground pepper
3 tablespoons flour
2 cups beef stock
½ cup whipping cream
1 teaspoon chopped dill
¼ teaspoon lemon juice

I. In a small skillet, melt I tablespoon of the butter over low heat. Cook onion until soft-ened, about 5 minutes. Transfer to a small bowl to cool to room temperature.

2. In another bowl, combine bread crumbs and milk. Set aside for 5 minutes for bread to absorb milk.

3. In a large bowl, combine cooled onion, soaked bread crumbs, beef, pork, veal, egg, allspice, nutmeg, salt, and pepper. Mix with hands until just combined; do not overmix. Using wet hands, form into 1-inch meatballs (you will get about 36 meatballs).

4. In a large skillet, melt the remaining 2 tablespoons of butter. Over medium heat, sauté meatballs in batches until browned. Remove from skillet and drain on paper towels.

5. After meatballs are removed, add flour to the skillet; stir with a wooden spoon to form a paste. Cook over low heat until the raw flour smell is gone, about 3 minutes. Add beef stock, whisking until no lumps remain. Return meatballs to skillet and simmer until cooked through, about 5 minutes.

6. Add cream to skillet, return to a simmer, and add dill. Add lemon juice a few drops at a time, until you have a well-balanced sauce. Adjust seasoning and serve.

Mexican Food

Let's get the preliminaries out of the way: there is a wonderful, ancient, vibrant, varied cuisine in Mexico — rich in people's food, rich in fancy restaurant food, especially rich in regional variety.

We don't get to see much of it in the United States.

An amazing thing happened as Mexican food migrated northward. It was so liked by Americans living on or near the border with Mexico that they created a version of Mexican cuisine that fit in neatly with the kinds of ingredients that were available to them. So this meant no hoja santa, huitlacoche, or epazote; it meant instead a ton of tortillas and Monterey Jack, an ocean of hot sauce. Tex-Mex was born. And it didn't catch fire only along the border. For years, cities with large Mexican populations — such as Los Angeles, Houston, and Chicago — featured concentrations of Tex-Mex–type restaurants. Then, thanks to the ubiquitous influence of chain restaurants and a lot of American holiday trips to Mexico (where hotels and resorts catered to American taste), the American idea of Mex spread much farther still. Restaurants and home cooks all over the country became enchanted with Tex-Mex and made it a fairly regular part of the American dining experience.

To a degree not associated with other ethnic cuisines, Tex-Mex became kind of standardized in the United States — lacking dramatic variations in the preparations of certain dishes, and even lacking a wide repertoire of dishes. Oh, the original enchiladas, tacos, burritos, and tostadas widened out a bit at some point to include flautas and chimichangas and fajitas . . . but not much.

Is this all a bad thing? Well, if you make your Tex-Mex from a can and a box, it's not a good thing. But if you make the best Tex-Mex you can make, from fresh ingredients and with a loving touch — it can be a delicious thing. I know. I've tasted it prepared by great and serious cooks.

How does it vary from Mex?

For one thing, the tortilla — which is indisputably important in Mexico — becomes even more important in Tex-Mex. It moves from its perennial Mexican role as starch on the side and its occasional role as main-course participant — to its new role as the Tex-Mex ingredient that sits at the center of nearly every entrée. Moreover, it changes its physical state in America. It is the soft tortilla that rules south of the border — but in the land of Tex-Mex, where two of our favorite flavors are "fried" and "crunchy," a taco becomes a shatteringly crisp shell. And tortilla chips and nachos become national obsessions. Mexican food snobs turn up their noses at these crunchies — but tell the truth, aren't they addictive? And if they could exist in a world alongside soft, fresh corn tortillas made every day with fresh masa — as they do — why not? When Americans think of going out to their local Tex-Mex restaurants for dinner, many of them are undoubtedly already tasting in their mind's palate the juxtaposition of that taco crunch against the chill of a margarita. What's wrong with that? In Mexico, of course, it's only the Americans who are drinking margaritas — which means the Mexicans are missing out on one of the world's greatest cocktails. And if they just happen to go beautifully with crispy tortillas — once again, what's wrong with that?

Another feature of typical Tex-Mex cuisine is the muchness factor — the same factor that informs a certain type of Italian-American cooking. If a little sauce was good in the Old Country, a lot of sauce is good in America. And if a little cheese for melting was good in the Old Country — *ay Chihuahua*, do things get cheesy here. Once again, however — if a lot of bad sauce and bad cheese are on your plate just to cover up bad ingredients, that's bad all the way. But a lot of good, flavorful sauce, combined with lovely strings of flavorful cheese, playing with their partners in a dish to create oozy, melty comfort food of a high order? Along with a coupla-three margaritas? I really have no problem with that at all.

One more feature defines Tex-Mex, and this ain't necessarily a good one: its approach to chilies. *Macho* is a Spanish word, but sometimes it's a very American thing. Some versions of Tex-Mex food pile on the heat — to a degree that you would not see in Mexico. In fact, south of the border the food is usually relatively mild; it's the hot sauces on the tables that are used to spice things up. But that doesn't mean chilies are absent from real Mexican cooking. Great Mexican chefs know amazing things about chilies: the differences among them, when to use fresh and when to use dried, how to toast and soak dried chilies to extract their flavor, at what stages of cooking to add them to food, and so on. The chili sophistication that lies at the foundation of great Mexican cooking is just not a prominent feature of Tex-Mex.

But that chili sophistication is growing every day in the United States. So is the number of restaurants throughout our country offering good versions of Mexican regional cuisine: Oaxaca, Jalisco, and the food of the Yucatán Peninsula seem to get special attention. We also have more and more white-tablecloth Mexican restaurants in the United States, where the elegant side of Mexican dining — as in the many elegant restaurants of Mexico City — is on display. Of course, when you put our young bucks in the kitchen of one of those places, it's not long before the cuisine starts "evolving" — into creative realms of Mexican possibility never seen before.

Most intriguing, I think, is that we now have many restaurants in the United States that are hybrid Mexican restaurants: that is, all these strands come together under the same roof. One of these strands, believe it or not, is good old Tex-Mex — which means that even Tex-Mex is in transition! I have been served, in recent years, enchilada casseroles with delicious, subtle chili sauces taking the place of the bland tomato sauces I saw years ago.

Makes me want to order another margarita.

✯ Pickled Mexican Vegetables ✯

Pickled vegetables are most traditional in Mexico's Yucatán Peninsula — and in the upscale Mexican-American restaurants that want to serve you something as an opening nibble that's a little more distinguished than chips and salsa. The following recipe is crisp, vinegary, not very sweet — and a great accompaniment to chips, salsa, and margaritas!

Yield: 2 quarts

4 cups cauliflower florets (about half
    of a large head)
2½ cups peeled, diagonally sliced carrot
    (¼ inch thick)
1 cup sliced zucchini rounds
    (½ inch thick)
6 jalapeño peppers, sliced ¼ inch thick
1 cup white vinegar
2 cups cider vinegar
2 cups water
6 tablespoons sugar
2 tablespoons kosher salt
1 tablespoon dried oregano (Mexican
    oregano if possible)
1½ teaspoons black peppercorns
1 teaspoon coriander seeds
1 teaspoon dried thyme
3 bay leaves, crumbled
1 large onion, thinly sliced
6 garlic cloves, halved

1. Bring a large pot of salted water to a boil. Add cauliflower and carrot. When the water returns to a boil, boil 2 minutes, then drain and refresh the vegetables in cold water. Place cooked vegetables in a large bowl with raw zucchini and jalapeños; mix to combine. Place the vegetables in a heat-proof 2-quart glass jar (with a tight-fitting lid). Set aside.
2. In a large saucepan, combine the white and cider vinegars and the remaining ingredients. Bring to a boil and simmer 5 minutes to blend flavors. Immediately pour over vege-tables in jar. Let cool to room temperature, then close lid and refrigerate until cold. The pickled vegetables will keep at least several weeks in the refrigerator.

✩ Quesadillas with Spinach ✩ and Rajas Poblanos

Here's a Mexican dish, in its Tex-Mex version, that has really broken out in America. Lots of home cooks in the United States today don't even have to be thinking in the Tex-Mex box before they say, "Let's make the kids quesadillas for lunch!" Why not? These Latinized grilled cheese sandwiches are delicious, and they're simple — the simpler, the better, say I. I enjoy 'em with cheese alone — but two of the variations I've tasted and loved are cheese with spinach and cheese with strips of roasted poblano peppers ("strips," in Spanish, are *rajas*). I discovered, happily, that these two ingredients are also delicious together.

Yield: 2 large quesadillas, good for 12 wedges
    (12 servings as a party pass-around,
    2 servings as a lunch dish)

10 ounces fresh spinach leaves
4 large flour tortillas (each about 7 to 9 inches
    in diameter)
½ pound grated melting cheese (see Note,
    page 123)
½ pound poblano chilies, roasted, peeled,
    and seeded
2 tablespoons butter

1. Wash the spinach. Place it in a large pot with whatever water is clinging to it. Place over medium heat and cook, stirring, until the spinach has drastically reduced in volume (about 5 minutes). Empty pot into colander

and let the spinach rest until it's cool enough to handle (a few minutes). When it's cool, very lightly squeeze out the water in the spinach (don't completely dry out the spinach). Season to taste with salt.

2. Lay out 2 of the tortillas side by side on your counter, placing the browner side down. Place a quarter of the cheese on each of them, spreading the cheese out evenly just up to the edge of each tortilla. Scatter the drained spinach evenly over the cheese.

3. Cut the roasted poblano chilies into strips and divide the strips evenly between the 2 tortillas, laying them over the cheese. Season with salt. Top the poblano strips with the remaining cheese, dividing it evenly between the 2 tortillas. Top each tortilla with a second tortilla, browner side up.

4. Place 1 tablespoon of the butter in each of 2 nonstick sauté pans (each one must be wider than the diameter of the tortillas you've chosen.) Place the pans over medium-high heat. Press down on each of the tortilla packages, then, using a wide spatula, transfer each one to one of the pans. Cook for about 1 minute, pressing down with your spatula to cook the cheese as quickly as possible (the bottoms should be golden brown). Flip the quesadillas over and cook for about 1 minute on the other side. The outside of each quesadilla should be golden brown, and the cheese inside should be melted.

5. Remove quesadillas from pan. Cut each one into 6 wedges and serve immediately. Pass around, if desired, any of the salsas on pages 124 to 125.

✹ Queso Fundido ✹

A highly popular starter in Tex-Mex restaurants, particularly west of the Mississippi, queso fundido (melted cheese) is sometimes called chile con queso (chili with cheese). The best name would combine the two concepts: queso fundido con chile. It is a kind of Tex-Mex junk food, deconstructed nachos, south-of-the-border fondue, featuring the dipping of tortilla chips into a pot of melted cheese. You could make it with all kinds of authentic Mexican cheeses — but why bother? The supermarket lineup of cheeses in this recipe is what's usually used — and the result is smooth, runny, creamy, delicious. As you'll see — a roasted poblano has the power to turn Velveeta into something special. If you must, throw out the Velveeta box before company arrives.

Yield: 4 appetizer servings

¾ pound poblano chilies
3 large jalapeño peppers
1 tablespoon olive oil
1 small onion, finely chopped
2 garlic cloves, finely chopped
1 teaspoon ground cumin
½ cup half-and-half
¼ pound shredded pepper jack cheese
2 ounces Velveeta, cut into small cubes
   (one-fourth of an 8-ounce brick)
Tortilla chips, for serving

1. Over a gas burner or under a broiler, char poblano and jalapeño peppers on all sides until blackened. Place in a large plastic bag, seal, and let steam until cooled, about 20 minutes. Peel away charred skin from poblanos, seed, and chop into ½-inch pieces. Peel and seed jalapeños and chop very fine.

2. To a medium saucepan over medium heat, add olive oil, onion, and garlic. Cook until onion is softened, about 8 minutes. Add reserved chilies and cumin; cook until cumin is fragrant, about 30 seconds.

3. Add half-and-half and bring to a simmer. Add pepper jack and Velveeta, stirring constantly until cheese is melted. Do not let the mixture boil. Serve hot, with tortilla chips in a basket alongside.

☆ Guacamole with Grilled ☆ Onion and Roasted Garlic

The Mexican idea of chunking avocados, tossing them with lime juice and cilantro and chilies, and presenting the whole as guacamole is one of the most important authentic Mexican ideas in Mexican-American restaurants. Of course, despite the track record we have for serving pretty good Mexican guacamole, we Americans do sometimes take guacamole in all kinds of new directions. One of the worst ones is our tendency to mash it to death, turning it into avocado puree. Another bizarre twist is the propensity of upscale chefs to give it a key role in ensemble dishes: a base for fish, a topping for pork, and so on. Another guacamole liberty that's taken is sometimes good and sometimes bad, in my opinion: the addition of "stuff" to the basic guacamole building blocks. I don't mind it, if the stuff doesn't come from left field. I'm particularly fond of the following recipe, in which the add-ins only serve to reinforce the classic flavors.

Yield: About 4 cups

1 small head of garlic
2 tablespoons plus 2 teaspoons extra-virgin olive oil
1 large sweet onion, peeled
1 tablespoon white wine vinegar
1 teaspoon freshly ground black pepper
Juice of 1 lime
2 small jalapeño peppers, seeded and finely chopped
1 teaspoon ground cumin
1 teaspoon salt
1 cup seeded and diced fresh tomato
¼ cup finely chopped cilantro, plus additional leaves for garnish
4 ripe Hass avocados, each weighing about 8 ounces

1. Preheat oven to 350 degrees.

2. Slice off ½ inch from the pointier end of the head of garlic and discard. Place garlic, cut side up and root side down, on an 8-inch square of aluminum foil. Drizzle the 2 teaspoons of olive oil over the top of garlic; bring up the sides of the aluminum and seal tightly. Place in the oven and bake for 1 hour. Remove from oven and allow to cool.

3. Slice the onion in ½-inch slices. Combine the remaining 2 tablespoons of olive oil, the vinegar, and black pepper and brush on the slices of onion.

4. Heat a 12-inch skillet over medium-high heat. When the skillet is very hot add the slices of onion. Cook until the slices are fairly brown on one side, then turn over and brown the other side. The slices should be fairly soft. Remove to a bowl and allow to cool.

5. Squeeze garlic cloves, cut side down, over a large bowl. (Discard papery skins.) Mash

with a fork and mix together with the lime juice, jalapeño peppers, cumin, and salt.

6. Chop the cooled onion. Add the onion, tomato, and the ¼ cup cilantro to the bowl and lightly toss with the other ingredients.

7. Peel the avocados and discard the stones. Cut the flesh into coarse chunks or break it with your fingers. Toss avocado chunks very gently with the other ingredients. Garnish with additional cilantro. Taste for seasoning, adding salt and pepper as necessary.

8. The guacamole can be served immediately, or it can be covered with plastic wrap and placed in the refrigerator for 1 to 2 hours.

✷ Cheese Enchiladas ✷

They do serve enchiladas in Mexico, but enchiladas certainly don't have the centrality there that they have in the world of Tex-Mex cuisine. You might even say that enchiladas — tortillas, usually corn, stuffed and baked in a casserole with sauce — are the backbone of most Tex-Mex menus in the United States. What would the standard combination plate be without them? Another difference is in the enchiladas themselves: the American ones tend to be a lot saucier and a whole lot cheesier. In fact, when people criticize Tex-Mex as "melted cheese on everything" — which makes it a lot heavier than Mexican regional cuisine — it is often the cheese enchilada that takes the heat. Well, fine . . . if you eat nothing but cheese-packed Tex-Mex food, the criticism is valid. But if you hanker only every once in a while for a bubbly, gooey casserole with lots of delicious cheese mingling with a delicious chili sauce . . . why not satisfy your craving? When my hankering hits, I go all the way and make sure my enchilada is stuffed with cheese as well! Chicken and beef enchiladas are good, but nothing hits the comfort food spot like a cheese enchilada. To approximate Tex-Mex restaurant conditions, serve enchiladas with Tex-Mex Rice (page 128), Refried Beans (page 127), sour cream, and a variety of salsas (pages 124 to 125). A margarita wouldn't be such a bad idea, either.

Yield: 6 main-course servings

FOR THE CHILI SAUCE:

4 large ancho chilies (about 2 ounces altogether)

2 teaspoons cumin seeds

2 tablespoons olive oil

1 cup chopped onion

3 large garlic cloves, minced

1 cup tomato puree

2 cups chicken or vegetable stock

¾ teaspoon oregano (preferably Mexican)

FOR THE ASSEMBLY:

Vegetable oil for frying

12 corn tortillas

8 cups shredded cheese (see Note)

½ cup sliced scallions for garnish

Grated cotija cheese (optional)

1. Make the chili sauce: Rinse, stem, devein, and seed the chilies. (You may want to wear rubber gloves for this.) Cut them open. Heat a cast-iron skillet over medium-high heat. Toast the chilies in the skillet, holding them down with a pair of tongs to make sure the chilies lie flat. Cook, turning, until they are fragrant, a little blistered, and smoking

slightly. It will take about 2 to 3 minutes per side.

2. Meanwhile, bring 2½ cups of water to a boil. Place the toasted chilies in a bowl and pour in the boiling water to cover. Let soak for ½ hour, until chilies are soft, turning on occasion to ensure even soaking.

3. Toast the cumin seeds in a small skillet over medium-high heat for about 30 seconds, or until they're fragrant. Do not leave them on the heat too long or they will burn. Grind them until fine in a spice grinder or in a mortar with a pestle. Set aside.

4. Heat a skillet over medium heat; add I tablespoon of the olive oil. When hot, add the onion and cook until the onion begins to soften, about 4 to 5 minutes. Add the garlic. Cook onion and garlic together until soft and light brown, stirring often to prevent sticking, about 10 to 12 minutes total. (Add more oil if necessary.)

5. Drain the chilies, reserving the soaking liquid. Into a blender jar, put the chilies, ½ cup of the reserved soaking liquid, the tomato puree, chicken stock, and onion-garlic mixture. Puree until smooth. Strain sauce into a saucepan, pressing down on the solids to extract all the liquid. Add the toasted cumin and the oregano. Simmer for 15 to 20 minutes, stirring on occasion to prevent sticking. If too thick, add more stock or soaking liquid to thin out. Once you've reached the desired consistency, season to taste with salt and black pepper. Turn off heat and set aside. (Makes about 4 cups of sauce.)

6. Assemble the enchiladas: Preheat oven to 350 degrees.

7. Ladle a small amount of sauce into a 9 by 13-inch pan, just enough to film the bottom.

8. In a heavy skillet, heat ½ inch of vegetable oil until it ripples. Fry a tortilla in the oil for a few seconds on each side until limp. Do no let it get crisp. Drain and proceed with the rest of the tortillas.

9. Ladle a small amount of enchilada sauce onto a large plate. Dip a tortilla in the sauce on each side, then fill with ½ cup of the cheese. Roll up tortilla and place in the pan, seam side down. Repeat until all 12 are done. Pour any remaining sauce from the plate back into the saucepan, then top enchiladas in the pan with the remaining sauce and the final 2 cups of cheese. Bake in the oven for 20 to 25 minutes, until cheese is fully melted and everything is heated through. You may pass the pan under a broiler if you like the top to get a little brown.

10. Divide the enchiladas among six dinner plates, garnish with chopped scallions, and if desired, cotija cheese. Serve immediately.

NOTE: It's hard to find the blend of cheeses that gives just the right chew to enchiladas and quesadillas stuffing. I have found that a supermarket product — the 4-Cheese Mexican shredded cheese by Sargento (a blend of Monterey Jack, mild cheddar, queso quesadilla, and asadero cheeses) hits it just right. The product is distributed nationally . . . but if you can't find it, you can make your own combination of shredded cheeses using Monterey Jack, cheddar (I'd go with a sharper one), mozzarella, and so on. I did discover some years ago that Danish fontina also melts very nicely in Tex-Mex dishes.

✴ Salsa Madness ✴

Of all the Mexican ideas that have crept into American gastronomic life, none has had as much coast-to-coast impact as salsa. Why? Perhaps it has much to do with the fact that salsa can be adopted by any type of American lover of Mexican food. If all you want to do is eat chips with beer, good ole salsa's at hand. If your relationship with Mexican food runs to the Tex-Mex specialties of enchiladas and burritos, there's plenty of appropriate salsa to brighten your table. If you wish to delve into the authentic, regional cuisines of Mexico, there are salsa surprises south of the border at every turn. And if you're a creative sort, what could be more fun than chopping up something new (kiwi? cherimoya? prune?), combining it with cilantro, and creating a masterpiece? It's not for nothing that salsa replaced ketchup some years ago as America's most-purchased condiment. Here are five great, diverse ones to get you going.

★ Chipotle Salsa ★

Chipotle chilies are among the hottest chilies — popularity-wise! — on the American scene. They got that way because they really stand out from other chilies — owing to the fact that they're smoked and have a distinctive smoky flavor. (Usually a chipotle is a smoked jalapeño.) They come to the market two ways: dried (like many other chilies), or wet (in a can of tomato sauce called adobo sauce). If you're making salsa from them — and a great, distinctive salsa they make! — the latter version of chipotles is easier.

Yield: About 2 cups

2 pounds ripe tomatoes, halved and seeded
1 cup minced onion
1 tablespoon red wine vinegar
1 tablespoon olive oil
3 garlic cloves, finely minced
3 chipotles (from canned chipotle peppers in adobo sauce), minced

Chop tomatoes until a chunky puree is formed. Add onion, vinegar, olive oil, garlic, and chipotles. Blend well. Season to taste with salt and pepper.

★ Pico de Gallo ★

There is much debate about the origin of this salsa's name — "rooster's beak" — and even more debate in Mexico as to what constitutes a pico de gallo. In the United States, things are a lot simpler. When you see pico de gallo at a Mexican restaurant, you can assume it simply refers to the restaurant's basic chunky salsa. The following excellent version — a little more complex than most — tastes best if you prepare it just before serving.

Yield: About 1¼ cups

3 fresh plum (roma) tomatoes, peeled, chopped into ¼-inch pieces, and drained
6 tablespoons roasted, peeled, and chopped red bell pepper (or you may use pimientos)
2 fresh jalapeño peppers, veins and seeds removed, finely chopped
3 tablespoons chopped cilantro (about 10 sprigs)
½ garlic clove, minced
¼ cup finely chopped white onion
½ teaspoon freshly squeezed lime juice
1 tablespoon olive oil

Mix all the ingredients thoroughly, seasoning to taste with salt. If the salsa seems runny and wet, place in a colander and squeeze lightly to drain off excess liquid.

★ Fire-Roasted Tomato Salsa ★

Many Mexican restaurants in the United States will serve you a bowl of smooth salsa to go with your chips, something like a room-temperature tomato sauce. It is usually insipid. An old Mexican tradition — and the creativity of New American chefs — yields a roasted alternative with real flavor interest. It's as good with grilled meats as it is with chips.

1 pound plum tomatoes, cored (about 6 tomatoes)
1 (2-ounce) onion, peeled, ends trimmed,
*   and cut in 2 thick slices*
½ large red bell pepper
1 jalapeño pepper
2 teaspoons minced garlic
Finely minced cilantro leaves for garnish
*   (optional)*

1. Expose the tomatoes, onion slices, bell pepper, and jalapeño pepper to some kind of flame. A hot broiler works well, as does an outdoor grill. Cook the tomatoes and the onion slices until they're just browned on the outside; don't blacken them. Transfer the tomatoes and onion slices to the work bowl of a food processor.

2. Continue cooking the bell pepper and the jalapeño until they're charred on the outside. Place them in a paper bag and let rest for 15 minutes. Remove from bag and peel away the charred skin from both. Cut the peppers open and remove the ribs and seeds. Place the remaining flesh of the bell pepper and the jalapeño in the work bowl of the food processor. Add the garlic and process until a fairly smooth salsa is achieved. Season to taste with salt and pepper. Serve topped with finely minced cilantro leaves, if desired.

★ Creamy Tomatillo-Avocado ★ Salsa

Tomatillos, which are not unripe tomatoes, have a wonderful, mystical flavor all their own — something like earthy apples, with a little cucumber thrown in. That flavor is enhanced by the complementary flavors of avocado and cilantro. When you make a salsa that preserves the natural tartness of the tomatillo — as the following tingly one certainly does — you have a fantastic salsa with which to top any Mexican or Southwestern fish dish. I especially love a little of this salsa on raw oysters.

6 small tomatillos (about 6 ounces),
*   husked and rinsed*
1 ripe Hass avocado
2 teaspoons lime juice, plus extra for sprinkling
*   on avocado*
½ cup firmly packed minced cilantro leaves
2 large scallions, cleaned and finely minced
*   (white and green parts)*
1 tablespoon finely minced fresh jalapeño pepper
2 teaspoons very finely minced tomato
1 teaspoon very finely minced garlic

1. Core the tomatillos and cut them into small chunks. Place in a mixing bowl.

2. Cut the avocado in half, remove the pit, and remove the peel. Cut into small chunks. Sprinkle avocado with lime juice and a little salt. Add to mixing bowl with tomatillo.

3. Add the 2 teaspoons lime juice, the cilantro leaves, scallions, jalapeño, tomato, and garlic. Blend well. Season to taste with salt and pepper.

★ Simple Salsa Verde ★

It's amazing how much Mexican-style flavor is packed into this smooth and simple salsa verde. I like to place it in a sieve for about an hour, after which time it becomes pleasingly thick. Push on the contents of the sieve with a wooden spoon to speed things up a bit. Great stuff for melted-cheese-and-tortilla dishes.

½ pound tomatillos, husked, rinsed, and diced
⅔ cup tightly packed cilantro leaves
4 teaspoons Tabasco green pepper sauce

Place the tomatillos, cilantro, and green Tabasco sauce in the work bowl of a food processor. Process until a smooth puree is formed. Pour contents of work bowl into a sieve set over a bowl. Let drip until desired consistency is reached. Season to taste with salt.

★ Chilaquiles with Chicken ★ and Green Sauce

Happily, chilaquiles — the great Mexican next-day casserole of leftover corn tortillas — is finally finding its way onto menus in Mexican-American restaurants. It is my favorite Mexican comfort food, particularly when the wedges of tortilla are drenched in a green sauce made from tomatillos; all the ancient flavors of Mexico are on display here. In Mexico the dish is usually served for almuerzo, a kind of late breakfast; in the United States, I've seen it on menus as a lunchtime, even as a dinnertime, main course. The inclusion of shredded chicken helps the main-course strategy, but the dish is delicious as well with no protein enhancement.

Yield: 4 main-course servings

2 chipotle chilies plus 2 tablespoons
    adobo sauce (from canned chipotle
    chilies in adobo sauce)
¼ cup tomato sauce (canned is fine)
2 boneless, skinless chicken breast halves,
    flattened to ½ inch thick
2 small white onions, peeled
12 ounces tomatillos, husked and rinsed
3 large jalapeño peppers
5 garlic cloves, unpeeled
1 cup cilantro leaves
2 teaspoons sugar
½ teaspoon salt
¼ cup water
Canola oil for frying tortillas,
    plus 1 tablespoon extra
10 (6-inch) corn tortillas, each cut into
    8 wedges
1½ cups chicken stock
1 cup crumbled queso fresco cheese, for garnish

½ cup grated cotija cheese, for garnish
    (optional)
½ cup sour cream, thinned with 2 tablespoons
    milk, for garnish

1. Place the chipotles, the adobo sauce, and the tomato sauce in a blender. Puree. Place chicken breasts in a baking dish and pour the sauce over them, coating all sides of the chicken with the sauce. Cover and refrigerate for at least 4 hours or overnight.

2. Cut 1 of the onions into thick rings. Heat a large skillet, preferably cast-iron, over medium heat. Place the onion rings, tomatillos, jalapeño peppers, and garlic in the skillet. Blacken on all sides. As tomatillos char and soften, place in a blender. Once jalapeños are blackened on all sides, place in a plastic bag and seal. Once garlic is charred and softened, squeeze from skin into blender container. Once onion is charred on all sides, add to the blender as well. Once jalapeños are cooled, peel skin off, remove stems and discard. Add the jalapeño flesh to the blender.

3. To the blender, add ½ cup of the cilantro, the sugar, and the salt. Blend on medium speed until smooth (though there will still be seeds from the tomatillos). Add the water, blend again just to combine. Set sauce aside.

4. In a large saucepan, heat 2 inches of canola oil to 365 degrees. Fry tortilla wedges a few handfuls at a time until crispy and golden, about 2 minutes per batch. Drain on paper towels and season with salt.

5. Remove chicken from marinade and pat dry. Season with salt and pepper. In the same skillet used to char the tomatillos, heat 1 tablespoon canola oil over high heat. Cook chicken until browned and cooked through, about 2 minutes per side. Remove from skillet and set aside.

6. In the same skillet over medium-high heat, add reserved tomatillo sauce. Bring to a simmer and cook for 5 minutes. Add chicken stock and return to a simmer. Add fried tortillas and stir to combine with sauce. Simmer on low heat until tortillas are softened but still chewy in some places, about 5 minutes.

7. To serve, cut chicken into bite-size shreds. Chop the remaining 1 onion coarsely. Divide tortillas and sauce among four wide, shallow soup bowls (the kind of bowl you'd serve pasta in). Top chilaquiles with chicken, chopped onion, the remaining ½ cup of cilantro leaves, queso fresco, cotija, and sour cream. Serve immediately.

☆ Refried Beans ☆

This staple of the Mexican-American kitchen — and countless combination plates in Tex-Mex restaurants — actually has a mistranslated name. Did you ever wonder about the first frying, before the *re*frying? There is none! The name actually comes from the dish *frijoles refritos* — which means something like "well-fried beans." I'm glad they're fried at all, frankly, because the frying drives lots of extra flavor (such as porky lard!) into the beans. The following are the most flavorful re- or well-fried beans I've ever tasted — particularly with their unusual third cooking, a visit to the oven under a mantle of white Mexican cheese.

Yield: 8 servings

1 pound dried pinto beans
1 small ham hock
2 medium onions, peeled (1 onion quartered,
   1 onion finely chopped)
4 garlic cloves, peeled (2 cloves crushed,
   2 cloves finely chopped)
4 tablespoons lard
2 tablespoons chopped chipotle chile in adobo
   sauce
Pinch of sugar (optional)
2 tablespoons sour cream
½ cup crumbled queso fresco cheese
   (you can substitute dryish feta cheese)

1. Prepare beans: Rinse beans thoroughly; pick through for small stones. Place beans in a pot and add water to cover by about 2 inches (about 5 to 6 cups of water). Bring to a boil, then simmer for 1 minute. Remove from heat, cover, and let soak 1 hour.

2. Drain beans, rinse thoroughly and return to pot with ham hock, the quartered onion, the 2 crushed garlic cloves, 1 tablespoon of the lard, and 1 tablespoon of the chipotle. Add water to cover. Bring to a simmer, cover, and cook until beans are very tender, about 1½ hours. Check water level occasionally, adding more if water level goes below top of beans.

3. Prepare refried beans: In a large pot, melt the remaining 3 tablespoons of lard over low heat. Add the chopped onion and cook, stirring occasionally, until onion is well browned, about 15 minutes. A pinch of sugar can be added to help this process along. Add the

2 chopped garlic cloves. Continue to cook over low heat about 5 minutes to perfume the oil with the garlic flavor.

4. Remove ham hock. Using a slotted spoon or spider, add beans to the pot with the onions and garlic but reserve the bean liquid. Add about ½ cup of bean liquid to onion-bean pot. Mash with a potato masher. Once beans are partially mashed, they should be a little soupy but still thick, about the consistency of oatmeal. If not, add a bit more bean liquid. Place beans in a food processor (or use an immersion blender); process beans until almost smooth. Stir in the sour cream and the remaining 1 tablespoon chipotle. Season to taste with salt and pepper.

5. Preheat oven to 350 degrees. Place refried beans in a roasting pan that's approximately 16 inches long and 4 to 6 inches wide. Top with crumbled queso fresco. Place in oven, uncovered, and cook for 15 minutes.

✩ Tex-Mex Rice ✩

Every Tex-Mex restaurant in the United States serves rice and beans alongside most main courses. The rice is usually not exactly what you'd get in Mexico — it's tricked up with more flavors — but it is based on Mexican ideas and ingredients.

Yield: About 4 side dish servings

1 tablespoon canola oil or lard
½ cup finely minced onion
2 tablespoons finely minced red bell pepper
1 teaspoon finely minced garlic
1 small fresh green chili, seeded and finely
    minced (more or less, to taste)

½ cup long-grain white rice, washed
½ teaspoon chili powder
1 tablespoon tomato sauce
1 scant cup chicken stock

1. Place canola oil or lard in a saucepan with a tight-fitting lid over medium-high heat. Add the onion, red pepper, garlic, and chili. Cook for 5 minutes with the lid on, removing lid occasionally to stir; try to prevent browning.

2. Add rice to the pan, stirring well with a fork to coat the grains. Stir in chili powder and tomato sauce, blending well. Add chicken stock. Bring liquid to a boil, stirring occasionally with a fork.

3. When liquid comes to a boil, reduce heat so that liquid is simmering. Cover with lid and cook for approximately 15 minutes, or until the rice is cooked through and fluffy. Taste for seasoning. You may hold the rice in the saucepan for a few hours by placing a clean tea towel over the rice and topping with the lid. When ready to use, refluff rice with a fork.

Central and South American Food

The cuisine of Mexico has always gotten a lot more attention in the United States, quite naturally, than have the cuisines of the more distant Central American countries and the much more distant South American countries. In recent years, however, wonderful cooking ideas from those farther places have started to have an impact on what we eat here.

Several trends have contributed to this.

Most visible has been the trend toward fancy, creative food forged out of Central and South American culinary traditions. Loosely called Nuevo Latino and spearheaded by great chefs like Douglas Rodriguez, this has been a restaurant force in major cities for more than a decade now; though most Americans are not regularly dining "Nuevo Latino," the attention it gets has made many Americans think about the food from that part of the world.

At the same time, some Americans have been knocked out by a one-two punch of South American meat traditions. We started to hear about the quality of Argentine beef some years ago, and — despite its on-again, off-again approval by the bureaucrats in Washington — Argentine beef, or beef Argentine style, headlines at a number of Argentine-style steak houses that have sprung up and caused excitement all over the country. Arguably causing even more excitement is the rise of the Brazilian "churrascaria, rodizio style" — a place where you indulge in all-you-can-eat skewers of meat, many types of them, and refresh yourself between carnal riffs by making visits to salad bars that feature "lighter" Brazilian specialties. These salad bars have proved so popular that there has even been a surge in non-churrascaria Brazilian restaurants serving non–steak house Brazilian food, including the exciting food of Brazil's Bahia region.

Inspired by the popular Nuevo Latino, and by Argentine and Brazilian restaurants, many foodie Americans who live in big cities are now looking toward Central and South American neighborhoods to try to anticipate the next *grande* thing. There's more buzz today about nonfancy Nicaraguan, Salvadoran, Venezuelan, Colombian, and Peruvian restaurants than I've ever heard before.

Of course, one important thing that you discover when you visit those neighborhoods, aside from the cuisine, is the people — lots of them! According to the U.S. Census Bureau, by the year 2025 something like one-quarter of all Americans will have Hispanic roots. At that stage, we won't have to research the ways in which the south-of-the-border foods influence the cuisine of America; in an important sense, they will be the cuisine of America!

✶ Seared Shrimp Ceviche ✶ with Avocado Sauce and Crunchy Corn

The wonderful South American idea of "cooking" raw fish in a citrus juice marinade became hotter than hot in the United States with the rise in popularity of Nuevo Latino restaurants in the 1990s. One ceviche area that Americans seemed to especially appreciate was crustacean ceviche: shrimp, lobster, scallops. But many chefs in America followed the letter of the ceviche law, applying no heat to these shelled critters — whereas in Peru and Ecuador, the epicenter of ceviche, shellfish often get at least a partial cooking over heat before the lime juice dunk. This greatly intensifies their flavors and therefore improves the shellfish ceviche. The following recipe is a good example of a partially seared, New Wave shellfish ceviche — enhanced, if you wish, by the very Old Wave idea of tossing some toasted corn in with the fish. Believe it or not, the packaged, nationally available snack food called Corn Nuts works extremely well in this context. But if you'd rather make your own "corn nuts," an easy recipe follows this one.

Yield: 4 appetizer servings

1 cup freshly squeezed orange juice
½ cup freshly squeezed lime juice
1 small red onion, finely chopped
1 teaspoon minced garlic
1 jalapeño pepper, finely chopped
1 short, medium-hot red pepper,
　　finely chopped
3 tablespoons finely chopped cilantro
Vegetable oil
1 pound medium shrimp (about 25),
　　peeled and deveined
1 ripe Hass avocado
3 tablespoons olive oil
Tabasco sauce
8 leaves Bibb lettuce, washed and dried
12 to 15 corn nuts (either purchased or made
　　from the following recipe), crushed
　　into small pieces (optional)
8 cherry tomatoes, halved

1. Combine the orange juice and lime juice in a large, nonreactive bowl. Place bowl in the freezer for 15 minutes. Remove from the freezer and add the onion, garlic, jalapeño and red peppers, half the cilantro, a generous pinch of salt, and a few grindings of black pepper, mixing well to dissolve the salt.

2. Heat a large, heavy skillet over high heat until it smokes. Carefully add 1 tablespoon of vegetable oil to the skillet, then add one-third of the shrimp to the pan; sear them for no more than 20 to 30 seconds. The shrimp should remain uncooked in the center. As you sear them, sprinkle them with salt. As they finish searing, quickly transfer the shrimp to the bowl of marinade to cool and stop the cooking. Repeat two times, using more oil as needed, until all the shrimp are cooked. Immediately return the bowl of shrimp and marinade to the freezer for 25 to 30 minutes to marinate and cool further, tossing them occasionally.

3. Meanwhile, cut the avocado in half, discard the pit, and cut again into quarters. Peel each quarter and, using a paring knife, thinly slice 3 of the quarters lengthwise. Drizzle the 3 sliced quarters and the remaining quarter with a bit of the marinade or additional lime juice to prevent discoloration. Cover with plastic and reserve.

4. When the shrimp have finished chilling, strain the marinade into the jar of a blender and return the shrimp and vegetables to their bowl. Add the unsliced avocado quarter and the olive oil to the blender and process the mixture for about 30 seconds. Taste for salt, adding a bit if necessary, and season with 3 or 4 dashes of Tabasco sauce. Process for a few seconds more. The mixture should be a somewhat thin, slightly creamy sauce, with the flavor of the citrus juices predominating and the avocado flavor in the background. Process additionally with a slice or two of the reserved avocado or additional lime juice

if you feel it needs it. Add 6 tablespoons of the avocado-citrus sauce and the remaining cilantro to the bowl of shrimp and toss well to combine.

5. Divide the reserved avocado slices among four wide, shallow serving bowls or salad plates, fanning them attractively to one side. Place 2 of the lettuce leaves near the avocado, toward the center of the dish, forming a nest for the shrimp. Divide the shrimp mixture among the lettuce nests and drizzle each serving with an additional tablespoon of the avocado-citrus sauce (refrigerate the remainder for use as a salad dressing or a sauce for fish). Sprinkle each serving with crushed corn nuts, if using them. Garnish each with the cherry tomatoes and serve.

★ Fried Corn Nuts ★

Yield: 1 cup

Vegetable oil for frying
1 cup dried giant white corn kernels,
*   such as Goya brand*
*   (available where Latin*
*   American products are sold)*
Kosher salt
¼ teaspoon sweet paprika
Cayenne

Place 1 inch of vegetable oil in a medium saucepan and bring to 300 degrees over high heat. Reduce the heat to medium and fry the corn kernels in two or three batches until golden brown, about 2 to 3 minutes per batch. Transfer the fried kernels to a medium bowl lined with paper towels. When all the kernels are fried, discard the paper towels and toss the corn with a generous sprinkling of kosher salt, the paprika, and cayenne to taste. Serve as a snack or crush them to accompany the seared shrimp ceviche above.

✻ Street-Fair Arepas ✻ with Mozzarella Filling

The wonderful, golden, corn-and-cheese griddle cakes of Colombia — arepas — are becoming increasingly well known to American city dwellers. Not because it's a boom time for Colombian restaurants but because, along with Italian sausage-and-pepper heros and Greek shish kebabs, arepas are turning up as a staple dish at street fairs. The first time I heard about arepas, I was told about a mysterious woman who shows up at odd hours of the night, making them on street corners in Queens, New York. My friend, the wonderful food writer Anya von Bremzen, coaxed this Colombian lady into giving up her recipe and published it in a terrific book called *Fiesta! A Celebration of Latin Hospitality*. Recently, at the street fairs in my part of the city, I've been seeing two-tier arepas, with cheese melted between the arepa layers, which seems very much like an American extension of the dish. So I played around with Anya's recipe, revised it — and came up with a great version of what they're serving these days in Manhattan: a Colombian grilled cheese sandwich.

Yield: 4 filled arepas

1 cup whole milk
1 cup evaporated milk
5 tablespoons unsalted butter, cut into small
*   pieces, plus more for brushing*

☆☆

*1½ cups white or yellow arepa flour
    (called masarepa or arepaharina
    and available in Hispanic markets)*
1¼ teaspoons salt
5 teaspoons sugar
Pinch of nutmeg
*2 cups grated mozzarella cheese (use the
    supermarket stuff, not fresh Italian
    mozzarella)*
Corn oil, for the griddle
¼ cup finely grated pecorino Romano cheese

1. Combine the whole and evaporated milk. Place 1½ cups of the milk mixture in a small saucepan over high heat. Bring it to a boil. Pour into a bowl and add the 5 tablespoons of butter, stirring to blend. Reserve and keep warm.

2. Place the arepa flour, salt, sugar, nutmeg, and 1 cup of the mozzarella in a large bowl. Slowly pour in the hot milk mixture, stirring to blend. Continue pouring and blending until there are no lumps. Knead the mixture for 5 minutes; you may need some extra milk as you do this, and that's what the reserved ½ cup of mixed milk is for. After 5 minutes, you should have a smooth, sticky dough.

3. Roll the dough into a ⅓-inch-thick sheet between two pieces of waxed paper. With a cookie cutter or the rim of a glass, cut out 4-inch circles. Reroll the scraps into a ⅓-inch-thick sheet and cut out more circles. You should end up with 8 circles.

4. Lightly film a griddle or a large cast-iron skillet with corn oil and place over medium-low heat. Add as many arepas as you can fit in, making sure that they do not touch each other. Cook until arepas are lightly golden on the outside, about 2 minutes per side. Every 30 seconds or so, lift each arepa from the cooking surface with a metal spatula, then lay it back down (they threaten to stick). Remove when done.

5. When ready to serve, toss the remaining 1 cup of mozzarella with the pecorino Romano. Brush the arepas with a little butter on both sides. Place 4 arepas (if they fit) back on the griddle or skillet over medium heat. Divide the mozzarella-pecorino mixture evenly over the 4 arepas. Top each arepa with another arepa. Press down on the arepas with a spatula to help melt the cheese. Flip as necessary. Ideally, the cheese filling should melt just as the arepa sandwiches become golden brown on the outside and slightly crusty. Serve immediately.

✹ Beef Empanadas ✹

Half-moon pies, stuffed with meat (or other tasty fillings), baked in the oven, are ubiquitous in Central American and South American countries — and are now prime snack food in the communities that citizens of those nations have established in the United States. Sometimes here you find beef empanadas with raisins alongside the meat; sometimes you find empanadas with strong spicing inside. The best empanadas I've ever had have been in Argentina, where they endeavor to make beef itself the dominant flavor in the filling. The following recipe catches that quality and adds a marvelous, crumbly dough that tastes like comfort food from another era. You can now find empanadas like this as appetizers in the newly popular Argentine restaurants across the United States . . . but the following recipe is hard to top.

Yield: 12 empanadas (6 first-course servings)

3 extra-large eggs

2 cups plus 1 teaspoon self-rising flour

½ teaspoon kosher salt

½ cup plus 4 tablespoons lard, chilled

¼ cup margarine, chilled

6 tablespoons cool water

1 teaspoon all-purpose flour, plus extra for
    kneading and rolling dough

1 pound sirloin steak, diced into ¼-inch cubes

½ cup finely minced onion

3 garlic cloves, finely minced

1 tablespoon finely minced red bell pepper

1 tablespoon finely minced green bell pepper

¼ teaspoon ground cumin

¼ teaspoon paprika

⅛ teaspoon cayenne

1/16 teaspoon dried thyme

1/16 teaspoon dried basil

1/16 teaspoon dried oregano

⅓ cup beef broth

1. Hard-boil eggs. Place 2 of the eggs in a small saucepan. Cover them with water and boil for 10 minutes. As soon as you can handle them, peel the eggs and chop into small pieces. Reserve.

2. Combine the self-rising flour, kosher salt, the ½ cup of lard, and the margarine in the bowl of a food processor fitted with the chopping blade. Pulse the mixture until it resembles coarse bread crumbs. Continue to pulse, this time adding the water, 1 tablespoon at a time, until the flour mixture forms into one ball of dough. Do not overprocess. Remove the dough and place it on a lightly floured countertop. Gently knead the dough with lightly floured hands for 30 seconds. Wrap the dough in plastic wrap and place it in the refrigerator for 1 hour to chill.

3. Place the remaining 4 tablespoons of lard in a large heavy-bottomed sauté pan over medium-high heat. When the lard is very hot, add the sirloin steak, onion, garlic, red and green bell peppers, cumin, paprika, cayenne, thyme, basil, and oregano. Cook, stirring frequently to keep it from burning, until the steak is almost fully cooked (about 3 minutes). Bring the heat down to low and stir in the 1 teaspoon of all-purpose flour, blending it into the steak mixture. Add the beef broth to the pan and stir to incorporate. Quickly bring the mixture to a boil, then remove from the heat. Using a fork, stir in the chopped boiled eggs. Add salt and pepper to taste. Place the mixture in a small mixing bowl and refrigerate it until ready to use.

4. Place the chilled dough on a lightly floured countertop. Using a floured rolling pin, roll half the dough out to a thickness of ⅛ inch. When rolling out the dough, turn it frequently on the countertop, adding more flour under the dough, if necessary, to keep it from sticking to the countertop. Using a round cutter of 4½-inch diameter, cut each half of the dough into 6 circles, yielding 12 circles in all. Place them on a floured baking sheet and refrigerate for 15 minutes.

5. Preheat oven to 500 degrees. Break the remaining 1 egg into a small mixing bowl and, using a whisk, thoroughly combine the egg with ⅓ cup of water to make an egg wash.

6. Remove the empanada filling and empanada pastry circles from the refrigerator. Place

an empanada circle on a floured countertop and place a mounded tablespoon of filling at the center of the circle. Using a pastry brush, lightly wet the perimeter of the circle with egg wash (this makes the empanada stick together while baking). Fold the dough over the filling to make a pie in the shape of a half-moon. Using a fork, press down gently on the outer edge of the pie; the crimps will keep it from popping open while baking. Repeat this process until you have made 12 empanadas.

7. Place the empanadas on a nonstick baking sheet. Brush the tops of the empanadas with the egg wash. Bake them in the oven for 5 minutes. Turn the baking sheet 180 degrees in the oven and continue to bake the empanadas until they are golden brown and cooked throughout (another 5 to 7 minutes). Serve immediately (see Note).

NOTE: In Argentina no sauces are served along with empanadas; Argentineans love to savor the beefy taste all by itself. But there is one quaint serving custom you should be aware of. When they pick up an empanada, which is finger food, they shake it slightly to distribute the beefy juices throughout the pie. Then they wrap the bottom of the pie in a towel — paper will do just fine — to absorb the juices. They eat the empanadas while holding them in this towel wrapper. I lost quite a few shirts before I discovered the trick.

✴ Moqueca ✴

Regional Brazilian restaurants are still not hot, hot, hot in the United States — but the buffet bars at the fairly popular Brazilian barbecue places are giving lots of Americans a broader taste of Brazilian cuisine. The management of these restaurants, perhaps anticipating someone in the party who doesn't eat meat, often provides a fish stew on the buffet — and more often than not, it's a Bahian-style stew called moqueca. Bahia, a region far north of Rio de Janeiro (and therefore much more tropical), has a wild cuisine that combines Portuguese elements (such as dried shrimp) and African elements (such as dende oil — a rich orange oil that comes from the African palm). Moqueca, with its coconut-milk base and its profusion of fresh cilantro, is a wonderful, eye-opening, little-known stew that will someday be a world classic — and not just as a substitute for beef. Serve with white rice and a brace of caipirinhas, the great Brazilian cocktail.

Yield: 2 main-course servings

2 tablespoons vegetable oil
1 small onion, peeled and finely chopped
2 large garlic cloves, peeled and finely chopped
½ green bell pepper, seeded and finely chopped
1 jalapeño pepper, seeded and finely chopped
    (or more, to taste)
1 medium tomato, finely chopped
Leaves from 1 sprig thyme, chopped
    (or ¼ teaspoon dried thyme)
1 bay leaf
1 (13½-ounce) can unsweetened coconut milk
1 pound firm-fleshed fish, such as cod, boneless,
    cut into 1-inch cubes
1 tablespoon dende oil (see Note)
1 cup loosely packed roughly chopped
    cilantro leaves

1. Heat the vegetable oil in a medium skillet over medium-high heat and add the onion. Cook until onion is soft, about 7 to 8 minutes. Add the garlic, bell pepper, and jalapeño pepper and cook until the peppers are tender (about 5 minutes), stirring frequently so the garlic doesn't burn. Add the tomato,

thyme, and bay leaf; continue to cook until the mixture looks dry, about 10 minutes (stir occasionally to make sure the tomatoes don't stick).

2. Add the coconut milk, stirring to combine. Reduce heat to medium; continue to cook until the coconut milk is reduced by one-quarter and the sauce is slightly thickened, about 15 minutes. Season to taste with salt.

3. Add the fish to the simmering sauce and cook until the fish is just done, about 5 minutes. Gently stir in the dende oil and the cilantro leaves, reserving a few leaves for garnish. Serve immediately.

NOTE: Dende oil is available at stores selling either Brazilian or African products.

☆ Argentine Grilled Steak ☆ with Chimichurri Sauce

The Argentine steak house really heated up in the late 1990s when the U.S. government gave the green light to imports of beef from Argentina. However, the feds keep switching green-red-green-red — so the Argentine steak house in America isn't necessarily defined any longer by the presence of Argentine steak. It is defined by Argentine trappings — such as the wonderful Argentine condiment for steak called chimichurri. Intriguingly, chimichurri is getting less popular in Argentina, as steak lovers learn to savor the taste of steak alone. But its popularity here is soaring. By the way, one of the things that distinguish Argentine beef is its lean, grass-fed quality. If you wish to serve beef like that at home with your chimichurri — and if we're in a red-light period — you can contact

Olympian Foods in Beverly Hills, California, or Lasater Grasslands Beef in Matheson, Colorado; they're both producing lean, natural beef. You may have a more authentic Argentine experience. Me — I'd prefer to dribble my chimichurri on a good ole grain-fed American prime steak any day.

Yield: 8 hungry-gaucho servings

3 tablespoons kosher salt
1 cup warm water
8 strip steaks, each about 1½ inches thick
2 bunches flat-leaf parsley, leaves only
6 garlic cloves, peeled
1 cup extra-virgin olive oil
1 cup roasted red bell peppers, diced
2 tablespoons sweet paprika
2 tablespoons fresh oregano
2 tablespoons dried oregano
1 tablespoon crushed red pepper
1 teaspoon freshly ground black pepper
½ teaspoon ground cumin
½ cup white vinegar
2 tablespoons red wine vinegar

1. Whisk together the kosher salt and warm water; this is called the salmuera. Set aside to cool.

2. Prepare a hot charcoal fire.

3. When fire is ready, season steaks with salt and pepper. Place on the fire and cook, turning once, until crusty on the outside and rare on the inside (or whatever degree of doneness you prefer). Remove from grill and let rest for 5 to 10 minutes.

4. In the work bowl of a food processor, combine the parsley, garlic, and olive oil. Pulse several times. Now add all the other ingredients except the salmuera. Process until all is

well combined but the sauce is still somewhat chunky.

5. Transfer the sauce to a mixing bowl and whisk the cool salmuera into it. Divide the steaks among eight plates and pass the chimichurri. Chimichurri sauce, tightly covered, will stay fresh in your refrigerator for weeks.

✸ Feijoada Black Beans ✸

Brazil has an amazing national dish: a multiplatter production number known as feijoada, which shuts the country down every Saturday as Brazilians while away hours consuming this delight. You can now find feijoada at Brazilian restaurants in the United States, though Americans haven't really taken to it yet. At the heart of a feijoada is a delicious bowl of black beans, served alongside a platter of multifarious parts of the pig. The following recipe is a kind of abbreviated feijoada, in which smoked pork hocks mingle with bean juices — creating one of the best Latin black bean side dishes you've ever tasted. If you find the finished product a little soupy, you can either (1) savor the soupiness and pour the beans over steaming white rice, (2) puree some of the beans and blend them back into the pot (as the recipe instructs), or (3) simply strain the pot of beans.

Yield: 6 to 8 side dish servings

*1 pound black beans, soaked overnight
   (see Bean Note)
2 green bell peppers
2 bay leaves
2 smoked pork hocks, about 1½ pounds total
2 tablespoons olive oil
1 medium onion, chopped into
   ¼-inch dice*

*4 garlic cloves, minced
2 medium tomatoes, chopped
2 teaspoons ground cumin
1 tablespoon dried oregano leaves
Hot sauce (optional; see Hot sauce note)*

1. Drain beans. Place the soaked beans in a 6-quart pot and just cover with fresh water. Cut 1 of the bell peppers into quarters and remove its seeds. Add to the bean pot along with the bay leaves and pork hocks. Place over high heat and bring to a boil, stirring occasionally so the beans don't stick. Reduce the heat to low, cover, and cook until the beans are almost tender but still retain a little chew; this will take about 2 hours, depending on how old the beans are. Check from time to time and add more water if necessary.

2. Meanwhile, place the olive oil in a sauté pan over medium-high heat. Add the onion; cook until soft and beginning to brown, about 5 minutes. Remove the stem and seeds of the remaining 1 bell pepper, chop it finely, and add to the pan. Cook for 5 minutes, stirring occasionally, then add the garlic. Cook for 1 minute, then add the tomatoes. Turn the heat to low and cook until the moisture from the tomatoes has evaporated, an additional 5 minutes or so. Add the cumin and the oregano. Set this mixture aside.

3. When the beans are cooked, remove the pork hocks and set aside. Remove the bay leaves and the green pepper and discard. Add the onion-tomato mixture to the beans and continue to simmer, covered, for an additional 30 minutes. Add more water if necessary.

4. After 30 minutes the beans should be very tender. Scoop out 3 cups of beans and coarsely puree in a food processor or a blender. Return the puree to the beans and blend well. Remove the meat from the pork hocks, shred, and add to the beans. Add salt and pepper to taste. Make sure the beans are hot, and serve immediately. Pass hot sauce, if desired.

BEAN NOTE: Before soaking the beans, it's very important to pick them over, looking for stones and other foreign objects. Spill them onto a flat surface (a baking sheet is ideal) and sort out the impurities with your fingers.

HOT SAUCE NOTE: The Brazilians like to sprinkle their feijoada with vinegar in which very hot chilies, called malaguetas, have soaked. This bottled preparation of vinegar is now available in groceries in South American neighborhoods of the United States. But feel free to substitute the hot sauce of your choice.

☆ Saffron-Scented ☆ Quinoa Pilaf

One of the most revered "grains" of the Incas — a diet staple in Peru that goes back five thousand years, to when it had mystical status — finally got noticed in the U.S. of A. about twenty years ago, when a group of Colorado entrepreneurs decided to import it, even to grow it. Before you could say "bran muffins," quinoa (pronounced KEEN-wah) became one of the trendiest side dishes in restaurants of many kinds. It had more than good PR going for it; quinoa is an absolutely delicious side dish, nutty in flavor, light in texture, with a weird, luminous ring effect on each little kernel that makes visual sense of the mystic

connection. Additionally, the National Academy of Science calls it one of the best protein sources in the whole vegetable kingdom. Now any time an ingredient becomes trendy, you can be sure that trendy chefs will further trendify its preparation. Happily, quinoa takes well to other flavorings — as chefs have discovered in the Nuevo Latino restaurants that present upscale versions of Central and South American dishes. I love the old Spanish, even Arabic roots of the following newfangled quinoa variation.

Yield: 4 to 6 side dish servings

¼ teaspoon saffron threads
1⅔ cups chicken broth, hot
1 cup quinoa
1 tablespoon olive oil
1 cup minced onion
2 teaspoons minced garlic
1 teaspoon lightly toasted cumin seeds
½ cup diced roasted red bell pepper
1 bay leaf
3 tablespoons minced cilantro leaves
2 tablespoons unsalted butter, at room
    temperature (optional)

1. Place saffron threads in hot chicken broth. Let steep for 10 minutes.
2. Meanwhile, rinse quinoa under cold running water and drain well.
3. Place olive oil in saucepan over medium heat. Add minced onion and cook until the onion is softened (about 4 to 5 minutes). Add quinoa, garlic, and cumin seeds; cook, stirring, for 1 minute more. Add the saffron-broth mixture, red pepper, and bay leaf. Taste broth and season to taste with salt. Bring the liquid to a boil, reduce to a simmer, cover,

and cook for 15 minutes. Remove pan from heat and let stand, covered, for 5 minutes. Stir in cilantro and, if desired, butter. Serve immediately.

☆ Tres Leches ☆

Other than serving as inspiration for Häagen-Dazs Dulce de Leche ice cream, Latin desserts have not yet made a major mark in the United States. But some are sure to gain popularity soon. "Three milks" go into this one, an amazingly moist and succulent soaked cake that's a specialty of Nicaragua. It is also very popular in all the Central American communities of the United States and has even started making appearances (with creative spins, of course) on upscale non-Latin dessert menus across the country. I don't know how the original can be improved upon — unless you were to serve some fruit on the side, or top it with a rum-flavored whipped cream.

Yield: 12 servings

¾ cup (1½ sticks) plus 1 tablespoon
    unsalted butter
2½ cups plus 2 tablespoons cake flour
1¾ cups sugar
8 egg yolks
2 teaspoons baking powder
½ teaspoon kosher salt
1 cup whole milk
2 teaspoons vanilla extract
Whites of 6 large eggs
1 (12-ounce) can evaporated milk
1 (14-ounce) can condensed milk
1 cup whipping cream

1. Preheat oven to 350 degrees. Using the 1 tablespoon of butter, grease a 9 by 13-inch pan. Sprinkle the 2 tablespoons of flour over the butter, making sure to coat pan evenly. Set aside.

2. In the bowl of a stand mixer using the paddle attachment and medium speed, cream the remaining ¾ cup of butter until fluffy. Mix in 1 cup of the sugar and continue beating until mixture is light and creamy. Continue mixing, and add egg yolks one at a time, scraping down the sides of the bowl from time to time.

3. Sift the 2½ cups of cake flour with the baking powder and salt. Gradually add to butter-egg mixture in the bowl of the electric mixer, with the beater on low speed. Add the whole milk and the vanilla. When combined, turn mixer speed to medium-high and beat for 2 minutes.

4. In a separate bowl combine the egg whites with the remaining ¾ cup sugar and beat until whites are thick and glossy. Do not overbeat. Working slowly with a whisk, evenly mix one-third of the egg whites into the cake mixture. Then gently fold in the remaining egg whites with a rubber spatula.

5. Spread the cake in the prepared pan and bake for approximately 40 minutes, or until a skewer inserted in the center comes out clean. Set on a rack to cool for about 15 minutes.

6. When cake is cool, combine evaporated milk, condensed milk, and cream in a 2-quart saucepan. Bring to a boil, stirring to combine.

7. Prick cake with a fork and spoon hot milk

mixture over all, ½ cup at a time, waiting until each addition is absorbed before adding another. Serve at room temperature.

✱ Caipirinha Sorbet ✱

This amazing sorbet mimics the flavors of Brazil's brilliant cocktail, the caipirinha — currently one of the hottest cocktails in the United States. The sorbet is made, as the drink is, with cachaça, a sugarcane distillate, now available in liquor stores across the United States (the Pitu brand is particularly available). Why, I could even enjoy this tingly, refreshing stuff as an intermezzo!

Yield: About 1 pint

⅔ *cup sugar*
⅔ *cup water*
Finely grated zest of 4 limes
1 cup freshly squeezed lime juice
    (about 8–10 limes)
5 tablespoons cachaça (Brazilian
    sugarcane liquor)

1. Combine the sugar and water in a 1-quart saucepan. Bring to a boil over medium-high heat. Add the lime zest. Set the syrup aside to cool.
2. In a medium bowl, combine the cooled syrup with the lime juice. Strain the juice if you prefer a finer texture, or leave in the pulp. Stir in the cachaça. Cover with plastic wrap and cool in the refrigerator for 1 hour.
3. Freeze in ice cream machine according to manufacturer's directions.

Cuban and Caribbean Food

Of all the culinary cultures south of the border — other than Mexico's — it has been the culinary culture of Cuba, one could argue, that is most familiar to most Americans. Many of the reasons behind this, of course, are extraculinary. We simply have more specific images from Cuba than we do from other Latin places, a more concrete sense of the place. Cuban cigars. Cuban rum. Hemingway. Ricky Ricardo. Castro. Kennedy. The waterfront in Havana. The Bay of Pigs. Guantánamo. The Cuban missile crisis. The list goes on and on.

But I like to think that Cuban food has also earned its position in America by dint of its quality and distinctiveness. It is a lovely, even subtle, blend of Spanish foundations and Caribbean ideas — very far removed from some of the wilder, more chili-influenced cuisines around it.

Of course, the image of Cuban food in the United States has not been hurt by the concentrated presence of Cuban communities in several major cities and the restaurant enclaves that they have spawned. Most famous, of course, is Calle Ocho, in Miami — and based on images emanating from that sizzling city, eating black beans and rice with fried plantains on the side has come to seem almost glamorous to many Americans.

The cuisines of other Caribbean islands

have gotten less focus in the United States; in fact, no island other than Cuba has really broken out of the Caribbean category to be understood by Americans as a culture unto itself with a cuisine of its own. There are many, many restaurants in New York City serving delicious Puerto Rican food, but they're not usually thought of as Puerto Rican restaurants. Nevertheless, the dream of warm Caribbean winds, and a rum-based drink in a tall glass on a long beach, has caused the sporadic flare-up, over the last two decades, of Caribbean "sugar shack" type party places; the food may be only vaguely Caribbean, but the fantasy endures.

Americans don't know a lot yet about the cuisines of Trinidad, Tobago, Haiti, the Dominican Republic, or Jamaica — but they sure seem willing to learn.

✹ Callaloo ✹
(West Indian Vegetable and Crab Soup with Coconut Milk)

It was a friend from Trinidad who turned me on to this terrific soup — popular in the Caribbean, and now popular in Caribbean communities in the United States as well. The soup takes its name from callaloo leaves, which are the very popular leaves of the taro plant — and, of course, a main ingredient in the soup. Though callaloo leaves are occasionally available in the United States, most cooks here substitute spinach leaves, as the following recipe advises you to do. It can be served as a soup course — but if you include the pile of crabs called for in the recipe and serve the soup with hot white rice, it makes a great main course.

Yield: 4 main-course servings

10 ounces raw spinach
8 okra, cut into ½-inch rounds
4 ounces peeled pumpkin, cut into ½-inch dice
1 medium onion, coarsely chopped
4 scallions, sliced into ½-inch rounds
4 ounces salted pork (see Note)
2 cups unsweetened coconut milk
2 cups water
4 sprigs fresh thyme
2 whole cloves
1 Scotch bonnet, habanero, or other hot chili
3 pounds crab (either whole live crabs, well washed, or cooked crab claws, defrosted)
1 tablespoon unsalted butter

1. Remove any tough stems from spinach. Place in a 4-quart saucepan. Add okra, pumpkin, onion, scallions, pork, coconut milk, and 2 cups of water.
2. Place the thyme, cloves, and hot chili in a piece of wet cheesecloth. Tie securely and add to the saucepan. Bring to a boil over medium-high heat, then turn the heat to low and simmer, covered, until all the ingredients are soft (about 45 to 60 minutes).
3. Remove and discard the cheesecloth bag. Remove and discard the pork. Pour half of the remaining contents of the pot into a blender and puree them. Return puree to the pot and blend well.
4. Add the crab and cook for another 10 minutes.
5. Stir in the unsalted butter before serving. Taste for seasoning.

NOTE: The most accessible pork ingredients to use would be either salt pork or bacon. If using either, keep the pork in one chunk. A less accessible but more authentic option would be salted pig's tail, which you can obtain from a butcher in a Caribbean neighborhood; ask the butcher to cut a 4-ounce piece into 4 chunks. Whichever type of pork you're using, prepare it for the callaloo by placing it in a small saucepan, covering it with water, bringing the water to a boil, then draining the pork in a colander under running tap water.

☆ Cuban Black Bean Soup ☆

I want a bean soup to be . . . beany! This version is exactly that — especially if you make it one day in advance and hold it overnight in the refrigerator. This one is also a particularly light and clean-tasting version of the soup classic that's served at thousands of Cuban lunch counters across America; you could give it a heavier feel, if you want, by using chicken stock instead of water.

Yield: About 12 large bowls of soup

1 pound dried black beans
24 cups cold water
2 bay leaves
3 tablespoons extra-virgin olive oil
3 slices bacon, minced
2 small yellow onions, chopped
1 red bell pepper, diced
1 green bell pepper, diced
½ jalapeño pepper, minced
8 large garlic cloves, minced
2 teaspoons ground cumin
2 teaspoons ground coriander
2 teaspoons dried oregano
¼ teaspoon ground cloves

2 tablespoons lime juice
1 tablespoon chopped cilantro,
*   plus extra leaves for garnish*
Minced red onion for garnish
Sour cream for garnish

1. In a large soup pot, place the beans, water, and bay leaves and bring to a boil. Take off the heat and set aside, covered, for 1 hour.
2. Return the beans to a boil, lower the heat, and simmer, uncovered, for 2½ hours.
3. Place the olive oil in a large skillet over medium-high heat. Add the bacon and cook, stirring, until crispy, about 3 minutes. Remove bacon with a slotted spoon and reserve.
4. Add the onions, red and green bell peppers, and jalapeño to the bacon fat in the skillet and cook, stirring, until vegetables have softened, about 5 minutes. Add the garlic, cumin, coriander, oregano, and cloves and cook, stirring, until lightly browned and fragrant, about 4 minutes more.

Caribbean Black Bean Side Dish

The soup recipe on this page can also be the basis of a great Caribbean side dish of black beans. Follow the recipe through step 5. Then pour out most of the liquid from the pot, leaving behind just the moist beans. Season to taste with salt and pepper and serve. Another possible black bean side dish is the Brazilian Feijoada Black Beans, page 136.

5. Add the onion-pepper mixture to the beans. Simmer beans uncovered 1 hour more; they should be very tender, and the liquid should be medium thick. (The beans will crack open slightly and their starch will seep out, giving the soup the proper body and beany flavor.)

6. Stir in the lime juice and the 1 tablespoon chopped cilantro. Season with salt and pepper. Divide among soup bowls and garnish with the reserved bacon, extra cilantro leaves, red onion, and sour cream.

☆ Shrimp Asopao ☆

In the Hispanic countries of the Caribbean and Central America, there is a wonderful dish called asopao; it is, essentially, soupy rice with flavorings. I love the pressure it takes off the cook: the rice doesn't need to be light, fluffy, or dry, nor does it need to be perfectly creamy and al dente. It simply needs to be tender and to sit in a big bowl of broth, ready to be savored with a big spoon and a big smile. In Puerto Rico, and in the Puerto Rican restaurants of North America, it is the ultimate comfort food.

Yield: 4 main-course servings

7 tablespoons extra-virgin olive oil
1¼ pounds shrimp (about 24 jumbo),
   peeled and deveined, shells reserved
6 cups fish stock or chicken stock
15 good-quality green olives, pitted and chopped
   into ¼-inch pieces
2 teaspoons finely chopped fresh oregano,
   or 1 teaspoon dried oregano
3 tablespoons finely chopped cilantro

Grated zest of 1 lime, plus 4 lime wedges
   for garnish
3 large garlic cloves (mashed to a paste
   with 2 teaspoons of salt),
   plus 2 garlic cloves, minced
1 red bell pepper
1 medium onion, minced
2 jalapeño peppers, seeded and minced
2 ounces thinly sliced smoked ham,
   cut into shreds
1 (14-ounce) can tomatoes, drained and
   chopped (⅔ cup)
⅔ cup white rice (not instant)
1¼ cups butternut squash, cut into
   ½-inch cubes (a scant ¼ pound)
⅔ cup green beans cut into ⅓-inch lengths
   (about ¼ pound)

1. Add 1 tablespoon of the olive oil to a medium pot over high heat. Just as the oil begins to smoke, add the reserved shrimp shells and sear them for 1 minute. Reduce the heat to medium-high and continue searing them, stirring occasionally, until toasted and fragrant, about 2 to 3 minutes more. Carefully add the fish stock, or chicken stock, and bring to a boil. Reduce to a bare simmer and cook, partially covered, until reduced to 5 cups, about 20 minutes. Remove the pot from the heat and let the stock rest for 20 minutes more. Strain the stock into a clean bowl, pressing on the shells with a large spoon to extract their flavor (if you find you have less than 5 cups, you can add water to make up the difference). Set the stock aside. Discard shells.

2. Meanwhile, in a medium bowl, combine the green olives, oregano, cilantro, lime zest, the garlic-salt paste, a few grindings of black pepper, and 3 more tablespoons of the olive oil. Add the shrimp, tossing them thoroughly with the mixture. Cover and set aside at room temperature.

3. Place the bell pepper on the burner of a gas range over medium-high heat. Char and blacken one face of the pepper, rotating it when the exposed side just begins to look ashen. Repeat until blackened all over, about 10 minutes. (Alternatively, you can place the pepper under a broiler to char.) Place the pepper in a paper bag, close the bag, and allow the pepper to cool for at least 15 minutes. Gently scrape off the blackened skin and remove the seeds. Cut the pepper into strips about ¼ inch by 1 inch and reserve them for garnishing the finished dish.

4. Add the remaining 3 tablespoons of olive oil to a large stockpot over medium-high heat. When the oil slides easily in the pot, add the onion, the 2 cloves of minced garlic, and the jalapeños; cook, stirring occasionally, for 5 minutes. Reduce the heat if the mixture threatens to burn. Add the ham and cook for 1 minute. Add the tomato and cook for 3 minutes more. Add the reserved stock and bring to a boil.

5. Place the rice in a colander and run cold water over and through it until the water runs clear. Stir the rice into the hot stock, add salt to taste (you may need about a teaspoon). Gently simmer for 5 minutes, stirring occasionally. Stir in the squash and beans and continue to simmer until the rice is still firm but almost cooked through, 8 to 10 minutes more. Add the shrimp, scraping all the marinade ingredients into the pot, and cook, stirring occasionally. Make sure the shrimp are immersed in the broth. Cook until the shrimp are just cooked through, about 3 minutes. Ladle the asopao into wide bowls, garnish each with the reserved red pepper strips, and serve with lime wedges.

✱ Ajiaco ✱
(Cuban Root Vegetable Stew with Pork and Chorizo)

If you wander into the real Cuban restaurants of Miami (beyond the touristy ones), and order some of the real Cuban food (beyond the touristy dishes), you might find ajiaco, an amazing stew of tropical root vegetables (which are called viandas in Cuba) and meat. I found it at a wonderful hole-in-the-wall in Coral Gables called Islas Canarias. The stew is found in other parts of the Caribbean as well as Cuba — and in Colombia, where it has a more delicate character. But my fave is the Cuban ajiaco, a brilliant combination of Spanish roots and Caribbean root vegetables.

Yield: 8 generous main-course servings

4 pounds country-style pork spareribs
2 tablespoons salt
2 teaspoons freshly ground black pepper
8 garlic cloves, peeled
4½ quarts water
3 bay leaves
⅓ cup olive oil
3 cups finely chopped onion

1½ cups finely chopped green bell pepper

½ cup drained and chopped whole canned
   tomatoes

1½ teaspoons ground cumin

½ teaspoon paprika

½ teaspoon ground allspice

2 large peeled green plantains, cut into 2-inch
   rounds and tossed with 2 tablespoons
   lime juice; 1 large peeled green plantain,
   cut into 2-inch rounds and tossed with
   1 tablespoon lime juice

1 pound peeled yucca, cut into
   2-inch rounds

1 pound peeled large white sweet potato
   (boniato), cut into 2-inch chunks

1 pound peeled white taro (malanga),
   cut into 2-inch chunks

½ pound peeled tropical yam (name),
   cut into 2-inch chunks

2 tablespoons butter

1 pound peeled calabaza or
   butternut squash, cut into
   2-inch chunks

2 large ears of corn, husked and cut into
   2-inch rounds

½ pound cured chorizo,
   very thinly sliced

1. Rub pork ribs with some of the salt and pepper. Crush 6 of the garlic cloves with a mallet or the bottom of a small pot. Put pork, the 6 crushed garlic cloves, water, bay leaves, and the remaining salt and pepper into a 9-quart stockpot over high heat. Bring to a boil. Reduce heat immediately and maintain at a simmer for 1 hour. While the meat is cooking, occasionally skim and discard the foamy substance that appears on top of the water.

2. Finely chop the remaining 2 garlic cloves. Heat olive oil in a large skillet over medium heat for 1 minute. Add the garlic, onion, and bell pepper and reduce the heat to low. Cook for 10 minutes, stirring occasionally. Add the tomatoes, cumin, paprika, and allspice; continue to cook for an additional 5 minutes. Reserve this cooked mixture of vegetables (sofrito).

3. After the meat has simmered for 1 hour, remove pot from the heat. Allow the meat to remain in the broth for ½ hour. Remove meat from the pot and take the meat off the bones. Discard fat and bones. Chop meat into 1-inch cubes. Strain broth, discarding garlic and bay leaves. Pour 4 quarts of the strained liquid back into the stockpot and add the meat. Reserve any remaining broth.

4. Add the sofrito to the stockpot and bring to a boil. Add 1 of the plantains, yucca, boniato, malanga, and name. Maintain the stew at a simmer for 30 minutes. Do not allow to boil hard, or the vegetables will break up too much.

5. While the ajiaco is cooking, heat the butter in a skillet over medium heat until it just begins to brown. Add the remaining 2 plantains and sauté for 1 minute.

6. Add sautéed plantain, calabaza or butternut squash, corn, and chorizo to the stockpot. Simmer for an additional 20 minutes.

7. Remove from heat and let rest for 10 minutes. Reserved broth may be added if a thinner consistency is desired. Season to taste with salt and pepper.

☆ Picadillo ☆

A big favorite in the Cuban restaurants of Miami, New York, and New Jersey, picadillo is kind of like a sloppy joe without the bread but with a lot more flavor. In fact, the two dishes are actual relatives; a bar in Key West, Florida, called Sloppy Joe's served the Cuban dish picadillo, and the dish morphed there into what we now call sloppy joes. There are many, many recipes for picadillo; the following one, because it has more ingredients than most, has even more flavor than most. Of special interest are the hard-boiled eggs, which are sometimes added as a garnish; here they're incorporated. (Another great egg idea, this one traditional, is to place a fried egg on top of your picadillo serving.) Picadillo is either used as a stuffing for other dishes or served as a main course with white rice, black beans, and fried sweet plantains (see page 149). If you make it a few days in advance and hold it in the refrigerator, it will taste even better.

Yield: 4 to 6 servings

2 tablespoons olive oil
1 pound ground beef (chuck)
½ pound soft chorizo, removed from casing and finely chopped
1 large onion, chopped
½ cup chopped red bell pepper
2 garlic cloves, chopped
1 tablespoon ground cumin
2 teaspoons chili powder
1 teaspoon dried oregano
1 teaspoon sweet paprika
¼ teaspoon cayenne
¼ teaspoon ground cinnamon
1½ cups chopped canned tomatoes
¾ cup beef stock
1 tablespoon sugar
½ cup raisins
¼ cup chopped Spanish green olives with pimiento
2 tablespoons cider vinegar
1 tablespoon drained capers
⅓ cup toasted slivered almonds
2 hard-boiled eggs, peeled and coarsely chopped
1 tablespoon lime juice

1. Place olive oil in a Dutch oven over medium heat; add ground beef and chorizo. Cook, stirring, until well browned and crumbly, about 10 minutes.
2. Add onion and bell pepper to pot; cook until both are soft and onion is golden, about 10 minutes. Add garlic and spices; cook until fragrant, about 1 minute.
3. Add tomatoes, beef stock, and sugar. Cover and cook about 20 to 30 minutes, until onion and pepper are very soft and tomatoes have begun to dissolve.
4. Add raisins, olives, vinegar, and capers. Simmer uncovered about 5 minutes to blend flavors and plump raisins. Add almonds, eggs, and lime juice and season with salt and pepper to taste. Stir and simmer just to heat through. Serve with rice.

☆ Bistec Encebollado ☆
(Puerto Rican Steak with Onions)

Bistec Encebollado, I've been told, is the Puerto Rican "national dish"; you could surmise this from its presence on the menu of every restaurant near my house in New York that's run by Puerto Rican families. It is comfort food at its finest: steak and onions in gravy, with a Latin spin or two. It was prepared for me once by Wilo Benet, the chef of an upscale San Juan hotel called the Tanama Princess; his version was absolutely delicious, though he was tweakin' away on the classic. I thought his tower of steak, onions, haricots verts, and French fries was a little too much. However, I picked up a number of fabulous improvements from his recipe — and if you make it with French fries and string beans on the side, I'm sure it will raise your spirits higher than Benet's tower.

Yield: 2 modest
main-course servings

½ teaspoon ground cumin

½ teaspoon dried oregano, crumbled

½ teaspoon garlic powder

½ teaspoon onion powder

½ teaspoon salt

¼ teaspoon freshly ground pepper

1 (8-ounce) slab filet mignon

1 large garlic clove, peeled and mashed
    to a puree

2 tablespoons olive oil

1 (8-ounce) sweet onion, peeled and cut
    into ⅛-inch rings

¾ cup beef stock

2 teaspoons white vinegar

1 tablespoon unsalted butter at room
    temperature

¼ cup cilantro leaves

1. Blend together the cumin, oregano, garlic powder, onion powder, salt, and pepper; reserve.

2. Cut the filet mignon into 4 even chunks. Place the chunks between pieces of waxed paper and pound with a mallet (or the side of a heavy knife or the bottom of a heavy saucepan) until you have 4 wide and thin cutlets (each one about ¼ inch thick).

3. Evenly sprinkle both sides of each cutlet with the spice mixture. Evenly smear each side of each cutlet with the mashed garlic. Wrap cutlets well in plastic wrap and place them in refrigerator. Hold for 4 hours.

4. When ready to cook, place the olive oil in a wide skillet (wide enough to hold the 4 cutlets in a single layer) over high heat. When the oil is smoking, add the cutlets. Brown as quickly as you can, not more than a minute per side. Remove cutlets and reserve.

5. Turn the heat down to medium. Add the onion to the pan. Stir well. Cover and cook until the onion is medium brown and just starting to soften (about 5 minutes).

6. Remove cover. Add ½ cup of the beef stock to the pan. It will probably sizzle up and reduce significantly within 30 seconds. If so, add the remaining ¼ cup of beef stock. Add the vinegar and butter. Cook, swirling the butter, for a minute or so; the goal is a moderate amount of lightly thickened sauce. Immediately add the reserved beef cutlets. Combine with the sauce and onions, making sure every cutlet is coated with sauce. Don't allow the beef to remain in the pan for more than a minute.

7. Remove pan from heat and toss in the cilantro leaves. On each of two dinner plates, place a bed of onion, a cutlet, more onion, another cutlet, and top with more onion. Serve immediately.

☆☆☆

☆ Cuban-Style ☆ Roast Pork Shoulder

There are many wonderful Cuban roast pork traditions — and many Cuban restaurants and lunch
counters in the United States that prepare some version of them. Most popular back in Cuba is a whole
roast suckling pig, served on Christmas Day with a
mojo (sauce) made with bitter oranges and garlic.
More common here is the Cuban roast pork shoulder,
known as pernil, also delicious. The following recipe
for the home chef brings together many of the best
things about Cuban pork cookery — and more! You
get tender, long-cooked, well-marinated meat and a
sauce with an orange-lime dimension that approximates the taste of bitter oranges. The sauce even goes
beyond Cuba, incorporating some flavors from other
Caribbean countries. Most important, you get the
greatest thing of all about a whole roast suckling pig:
crunchy skin! The use of a cooking bag–enclosed
roast in the following recipe, and then the roast's
short stay in a hot oven without the cooking bag,
guarantees juicy meat and crisp skin. Don't fail to
serve this dish with black beans (see page 141) and
rice — and a great mojito (Hemingway's favorite rum
libation). It's a Caribbean festival.

Yield: 6 main-course servings

*1 (4- to 5-pound) pork shoulder
    with the skin on*
½ cup olive oil
¼ cup annatto seeds
1 head garlic, peeled and finely chopped
½ cup freshly squeezed orange juice
½ cup freshly squeezed lime juice
2 teaspoons ground cumin
1 teaspoon dried oregano
1 tablespoon ground pepper
1 teaspoon kosher salt

2 bay leaves
1 tablespoon onion powder
1 tablespoon sugar
*¼ teaspoon (1 individual package) Goya Sazón
    with Annatto (optional)*
3 tablespoons flour
1 tablespoon chopped fresh cilantro leaves
1 tablespoon chopped fresh oregano leaves

1. Using a sharp, serrated knife, carefully
score the skin of the pork shoulder in a criss-
cross pattern; the trick is to completely cut
through the skin but not to cut into the meat.
The crisscrossing should leave a pattern of
1-inch squares on the surface of the pork.

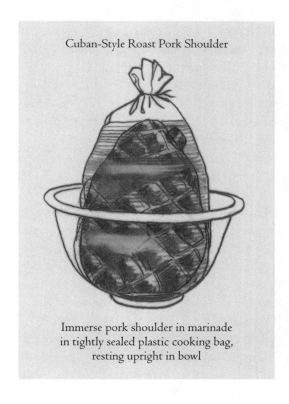

Cuban-Style Roast Pork Shoulder

Immerse pork shoulder in marinade
in tightly sealed plastic cooking bag,
resting upright in bowl

2. Add the olive oil and annatto seeds to a small sauté pan over low heat. Cook for 5 minutes, or until the oil turns very orange. Let the mixture cool slightly, then strain and discard the annatto seeds.

3. In a large bowl combine the garlic, orange juice, lime juice, cumin, oregano, pepper, salt, bay leaves, onion powder, sugar, and Goya Sazón. Whisk in the warm annatto oil mixture.

4. Open the cooking bag and place the flour inside; shake the bag to coat the inside with flour. Place the pork shoulder inside the bag, making sure that the fat end of the roast is at the bottom of the bag. Cover roast with the marinade mixture. Twist the bag to take all of the excess air out of the bag and then tie it with its accompanying tie. The bag should be tight around the pork shoulder; this keeps the entire pork roast immersed in the marinade. Place the tightly wrapped pork shoulder in its bag in a bowl and refrigerate overnight.

5. When ready to cook, preheat the oven to 350 degrees. Remove the pork roast bag from its bowl. Place the bag with the roast and marinade in a roasting pan. It should stand in the pan on the fat end of the roast, and the tie should be straight up in the air. Using scissors, trim off any excess of the bag that extends upward beyond the tie. At the very top of the bag, just below the tie, make 5 (½-inch) slits, which will allow some of the steam to escape. Place the roasting pan in the oven and bake pork shoulder for 3 hours.

6. Remove the roasting pan from the oven, and remove the shoulder from the cooking bag. Work carefully so as to retain all the juices from the bag. Reserve them.

7. Put the shoulder back in the roasting pan and return it to the oven. Bake for 20 minutes more, still at 350 degrees, to make the skin crispy.

8. Meanwhile, place the reserved pan juices in a small saucepan. Remove some fat, if desired. Stir in the fresh cilantro and oregano. Season to taste with salt and pepper.

9. Remove the roast from the oven and let it rest for 15 minutes. While it's resting, make sure the sauce is still warm; if not, heat it just a bit. Carve roast and serve immediately, spooning the sauce over the pork slices.

☆ Tostones ☆
(Deep-Fried Unripe Plantain Chips)

At many Cuban, Caribbean, Central American, and even Mexican restaurants in the United States, one is given "the plántano choice" these days: would you like unripe plántanos or ripe plántanos as a side dish? Plántanos, of course, or plantains, look almost exactly like large bananas, with thicker skins. But unlike bananas — the ripeness of which makes only a small difference — unripe plantains and ripe plantains are almost like two completely different items. Therefore, Caribbean chefs cook the two plántanos in two different ways. The green, unripe ones, which have practically no sweetness, are fried, smashed, fried again, and salted — which gives them a crispy, savory quality that's akin to fried potatoes. Incidentally, for the mashing of unripe plantains there is a specially designed hinged plantain masher, which you can get at stores with a Caribbean clientele. But you can also substitute a heavy pan or knife, as described below.

Yield: About 4 side dish servings

6 cups water
2 tablespoons table salt (not kosher),
    plus coarse salt for sprinkling
3 garlic cloves, peeled and smashed
4 green plantains
Canola oil for frying

1. In a large bowl, combine water, salt, and garlic. Stir until salt is dissolved.

2. To peel plantains, cut off ends, then cut crosswise into 3 sections. Cut 3 slits into the skin lengthwise down the entire length of each section. Peel sections as you would a banana. You may need to use a paring knife to trim any small pieces of peel that don't come right off. Slice plantains diagonally into ¾-inch slices; place in the water mixture and soak 1 hour.

3. Heat 2 inches of canola oil in a deep saucepan to 350 degrees. Drain and pat plantain slices with paper towels until very dry. Fry in several batches, 3 minutes per batch, turning once during frying. Plantains will cook but not take on any color in this stage. Drain on paper towels. Make sure oil returns to 350 degrees before frying the next batch.

4. Using a heavy skillet or a very wide and heavy cleaver, smash each plantain slice to ¼-inch thickness. You must smash them with a forward sliding motion, so that they get elongated as they are smashed; do not smash them directly down toward the counter.

5. Increase oil temperature to 375 degrees. Fry smashed plantains in several batches until golden and crisp, about 2 to 3 minutes per

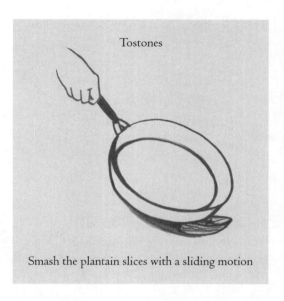

Tostones

Smash the plantain slices with a sliding motion

batch, turning once during frying. Drain on paper towels and season with coarse salt. Serve immediately. Make sure oil returns to 375 degrees before frying the next batch.

NOTE: This is the classic method for fried unripe plantains. However, should you wish to go upscale and creative a bit, you can lightly brush garlic oil on each chip just before serving; this adds a great flavor. To make the oil, heat ½ cup olive oil and 8 large cloves of garlic, minced, in a saucepan over low heat for 5 minutes. Place oil and garlic in a blender and puree.

☆ Plántanos Maduros ☆
(Fried Ripe and Sweet Plantains)

When the skin of the plantain turns brownish black, the Caribbean chef likes to complement the higher sugar content . . . by adding more sugar! The result is a skillet sauté, brown and slightly sticky, with great banana-like flavor. It too works very nicely as a side dish for Caribbean food; it's especially nice when the other food is spicy.

Yield: About 4 side dish servings

3 brown-black plantains
4 tablespoons butter
1 tablespoon vegetable oil
2 tablespoons light brown sugar
2 tablespoons dark rum
1 tablespoon lime juice
2 to 3 tablespoons water, as needed

1. To peel plaintains, cut off ends, then cut crosswise into 3 sections. Cut 3 slits into the skin lengthwise down the entire section. Peel off pieces of skin as you would a banana. The skin should come off easily; if not, the plantains are probably not ripe enough to make this recipe. Cut diagonally into ½-inch-thick slices.
2. In a large skillet, melt 2 tablespoons of the butter with half of the vegetable oil over medium heat. Cook the plantains in one layer until golden on both sides, about 4 to 5 minutes total. You will have to do this in two batches, using the remaining 2 tablespoons butter and the remaining oil for the second batch. As plantains are cooked, remove to a plate.
3. Once all the plantains are browned, add brown sugar, rum, and lime juice to the skillet over medium heat; stir until the mixture simmers and sugar dissolves. Add plantains back to pan and return mixture to a simmer. Sauce should cover the bottom of the pan; if not, add a tablespoon or more of water until there is enough sauce. Simmer plantains until they're softened and glazed, about 5 minutes.

Chinese Food

With Italian-American food, Chinese-American food has been, for at least seventy-five years, the "other option," the thing that you go out to eat (or order in to eat!) when you're bored with your everyday fare. The moment that says it all for me is the scene in *The Godfather* when, during a "business" meeting, the Corleone family is busy eating Chinese food out of the classic white take-out containers.

But the position of Chinese-American food in America has always differed from the position of Italian-American food in one key way: we don't cook Chinese food at home very much. Whereas lasagna and eggplant parmigiana have become as common in American kitchens as meat loaf and fried chicken, wonton soup and spareribs have remained things that someone else cooks for you. Yes, there have been outbursts of home activity over the years. In the 1950s La Choy penetrated the domestic scene pretty well with chicken chow mein and the other greatest hits of the day, in cans; such was the popularity of those dishes in contemporary restaurants that people actually bought this stuff. In the 1970s, a great boom decade for home gastronomic exploration, woks moved into the housewares departments of stores and into the burgeoning cookware shops; talk of "stir-frying" was constantly in the air, and it seemed as if we were headed toward a future of Chinese home cooking. But it never really happened on a large scale — which is a shame, since some areas of Chinese food are relatively easy to execute at home and vastly rewarding.

As for Chinese food in restaurants — well, describing its history in America is like going on an archaeological dig. There are layers and layers of food styles, going back to the middle of the nineteenth century. I like to think that our current Chinese restaurants are preserving the best of the strata — but it ain't always so.

The first layer was set down by the Chinese immigrants who came to America to work on the railroad in the West — or rather, who came to feed those who were working on the railroad. The cooks didn't have much to work with, but they imaginatively threw together little bits of meat and vegetables in their large pans and gave it a name: chop suey — which, according to John Mariani in the *Encyclopedia of American Food and Drink,* was a rough translation of *tsa tsui,* the Mandarin words for "a little of this and that."

Before long there were "chop suey parlors" in San Francisco, Chicago, New York, and other large cities. By the first half of the twentieth century, Chinese cooks had added chow mein to chop suey, along with egg rolls, fried rice, spareribs, pepper steak, and other dishes that had roots in Chinese cooking. But — because of ingredient limitations and the chefs' desires to please American patrons — these dishes would more properly be identified as Chinese-American food than as Chinese food. Many of the original workers and restaurant people came from Canton — so the base cuisine behind Chinese-American cooking has always been Cantonese.

As the twentieth century progressed, this Chinese-American cuisine moved into its golden era. In the 1950s and 1960s seriously delicious Cantonese-inspired food was being served to Americans at Chinese restaurants. The repertoire grew a bit, adding such then-exotic specialties as Lobster Cantonese and Moo Goo Gai Pan, a stir-fry of chicken breast with "Chinese" vegetables. Chinese restaurants were opening everywhere in the sprawling new suburbs, and Chinese-American cooking reached its apex at luxurious downtown restaurants, such as the House of Chan in New York's theater district. Some of it may have been a bit too gloppy and a bit too sweet — but at its best it combined porky tastes, garlicky tastes, and fried tastes in an absolutely irresistible manner.

By the 1970s, when Chinese restaurants were ensconced as a regular part of our lives and Americans across the country were in the habit of "ordering Chinese" once or twice a week, something new was happening again. It was the era when Americans turned on their boxed pasta; suddenly only freshly made pasta got any respect. And in Chinese restaurants, "one from column A and two from column B" took a nosedive in popularity. If you put crunchy noodles on your chow mein — if you ordered Chow Mein at all! — you were suddenly "irrelevant."

And that's exactly when the stage was set for the introduction and acceptance of the first Chinese regional cuisine in America to go beyond Cantonese. If you were a Chinese food maven in 1973, you were taking your friends to "Szechuan" restaurants. Imagine the wide-eyed thrill of discovering a whole new idea of Chinese cooking — this one shot through with chilies and peppercorns and a slew of ingredients we hadn't seen before. The movers and shakers of the Chinese-restaurant business were moving and shaking in a Szechuan direction — which was great for Szechuan food, but the old quasi-Cantonese restaurants across the country started to suffer. And they began a quality decline from which most have never really recovered.

Shockingly, Szechuan held pride of place for only a year or two — because another western Chinese regional cuisine came along immediately, nipping at its heels: Hunan food, from Hunan province. The food as represented in America didn't seem wildly different from Szechuan food, but two points of distinction were soon established. We were told that Szechuan food was "city" food and that Hunan food was "country" food — with more preserved things in the latter cuisine, and longer, more casual preparations ("Hunan ham" sounded duly country-like). But the other point of difference seemed at odds with the first: the early Hunan restaurants here were some of the most elegant Chinese restaurants ever seen in America, with some of the most careful, sophisticated cooking ever attempted here (such as Uncle Tai's Hunan Yuan in Manhat-

tan). The Szechuan restaurants fell a notch or two in esteem. And the old warhorse restaurants, with increasingly awful versions of Chinese-American food, were hopelessly outdated.

Over the last thirty years or so, the names Cantonese and Szechuan have remained strong, good-draw restaurant names. The Hunan palaces died off, and — though a few restaurants still include "Hunan" in their names — you chiefly see the designation "Hunan" today in restaurants that feature a conglomeration of things on their menus. Oddly enough, after the wonderful specificity of the early Szechuan and Hunan years, most Chinese restaurants today offer Cantonese, Szechuan, and a few Hunan-designated dishes all clumped together. And, sad to say, the quality is not high at a lot of them.

But it's not all doom and gloom. There have been wonderful developments in Chinese food in America over the past decade or two. The kind of very authentic Cantonese restaurant that features hanging ducks, soy sauce chicken, roast pork, and sides of roasted pig — in tandem with huge bowls of steaming noodles in broth — has spread beyond its Chinatown bases. Dim sum parlors, with wonderful dumplings and other delights, are booming in Chinatowns. A certain style of quasi-elegant Chinese dining, known as Hong Kong style, has spread through the Chinese eating neighborhoods; many restaurants now feature huge fish tanks brimming with superfresh critters that are quickly converted, Cantonese style, into your dinner. And other regional wrinkles — especially Shanghai, but also Fukien and what is known (in various spellings) as Chiu Chow — are now available both in and out of America's Chinatowns.

If you go today to either of San Francisco's Chinatowns (the old one downtown, the new one in the Richmond district) or to Monterey Park outside L.A. or to the surprisingly excellent Chinese restaurants in Houston or to New York City's old Chinatown (in Manhattan) or to one of its new Chinatowns (such as in Flushing, Queens) — you will likely be treated to some of the very best Chinese food that has ever been available in America.

But there's a double unhappiness. First of all, owing to the constant shifting from one style to another and the wholesale blending of styles and, perhaps, the fact that Chinese food has become so ordinary in our lives — there is very mediocre Chinese food these days in restaurants not in the primary Chinese areas. And though it seems no one but me is mourning its passing, the worst food of all these days is the old-fashioned Chinese-American food, which at its best was distinctive and good. Just as no self-respecting Italian-American chef these days would spend time on a meatball, so would no self-respecting Chinese-American chef spend time these days on an egg roll or a platter of chicken chow mein.

The following recipes treat all the layers of Chinese-American food with respect. I present here versions of the various dishes as they might have appeared at their "peak" periods in U.S. dining history — and encourage you to cook more Chinese food at home.

I guarantee it'll be better than what you find at your neighborhood takeout today.

☆ The Old-Fashioned ☆ Chinese-Restaurant Shrimp Roll

You might think there's no reason to make this deep-fried egg roll treat at home — until you realize that most high-quality Chinese restaurants today don't make it at all anymore. It's too retro-retro, too fifties without the irony. And if they do make it today, you can be reasonably certain that they're mucking it up with something trendy: black beans, Szechuan peppercorns, tree ears, whatever. The good old taste that I love was simplicity itself — and that's the first lesson in making an authentic-tasting egg roll at home. The second lesson concerns the cooking time of the filling: fast! The stuffing in the glorious old Chinese-American days was a quick-cooked thing. It also avoided all the Chinese seasoning temptations and emphasized something quite prosaic — black pepper, which was also quite delicious. All of these things are grandly easy to do at home, and the classic shrimp roll is within your grasp. But to finish it off right, two challenges arise for the home chef. The first is the quality of the egg roll skins; many sold today at even Asian grocery stores are inferior (see sidebar). And once you've got a great one, if you want to make a shrimp roll that recalls the golden House of Chan era, you've got to stuff it to the gills; the old-fashioned boys were fat, not like the long, skinny pretenders of today (probably inspired by the far trendier spring roll). Keep it simple, say I . . . and keep it fat.

Yield: 4 egg rolls

1 tablespoon peanut oil

3 cups firmly packed shredded napa cabbage,
leafy parts only

½ cup cooked tiny shrimp, or small pieces of
shrimp

½ cup mung bean sprouts

2 fresh water chestnuts, peeled and cut into
coarse dice

¼ teaspoon sugar

¼ teaspoon freshly ground pepper

¼ teaspoon MSG (optional)

Vegetable oil for deep-frying

4 egg roll skins

1. Place a large, heavy wok over high heat. After a minute, add the peanut oil. Then add the cabbage, shrimp, bean sprouts, water chestnuts, sugar, pepper, and MSG, tossing as you go. The mixture must cook for no more than 1 minute. Remove it from the wok and let it cool in the refrigerator for a few minutes. You should have about 4 cups of filling.

2. When ready to make shrimp rolls, place the vegetable oil in a deep fryer or a wide pan over medium heat. Heat the oil until it reaches 325 degrees on a deep-fry thermometer.

3. While the oil is heating, thoroughly dry the filling by dabbing it with paper towels. Spread out one egg roll skin and dab the perimeter with a little water. Place one-fourth of the filling mixture (about 1 cup) on the lower portion of the skin, about 1 inch up from the bottom. Make sure that you leave a margin to the left and right of the filling; there should be about ½ inch of white egg roll skin showing on each side of the filling. Now grab those left and right margins and fold them inward, toward the center of the skin, draping them over the left and right extremities of the filling. Make sure that the draping fold you've made extends from the bottom of the egg roll skin clear up

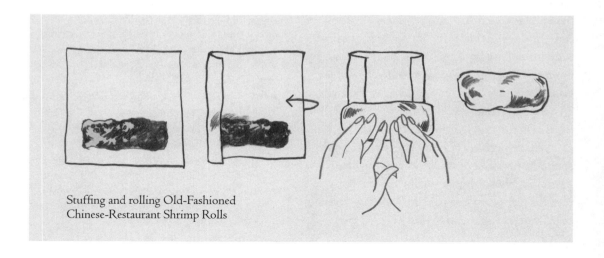

Stuffing and rolling Old-Fashioned
Chinese-Restaurant Shrimp Rolls

Beauty Is Only Egg Roll–Skin Deep

Believe it or not, there are many egg roll skins in the market today that don't have eggs as an ingredient. Many of them, after cooking, end up tasting dry, like sawdust. Other problems abound. Some skins in the market are too thin, some too thick, some don't bubble up on the outside or become crispy tender. The skin I've found that always works for me — and I love seeing "egg yolk" in the list of ingredients — is called Golden Dragon, manufactured by Nanka Seimen in Los Angeles. It is available in Asian markets nationwide.

to the top. Grab the bottom edge of the egg roll skin and move it upward, away from you, covering (or almost covering) the filling. Keep rolling away from you, making sure that the folded-in margins on the left and right sides of the skin remain folded in and straight. As you roll away from you, try to keep the emerging roll snug by tucking in filling whenever you can. Finally, when you're near the top, push the roll away from you once more, until you roll it right over the top margin of the egg roll skin. You should now have one fat, holding-together shrimp roll. Check the seam along the length of the roll; if it's not adhering, dab it with a little more water and make it stick. Continue with the rest of the skins until you've made 4 rolls. They can rest on the countertop on a damp cloth for a few minutes as the oil heats.

4. When the oil is ready, drop the shrimp rolls into it (if your fryer's not large, do only 1 or 2 at a time). Turn the rolls frequently in the oil. They should take about 4 to 5 minutes to turn golden brown; if you see a lot of browning after a minute or so, the oil's too hot — turn it down.

5. When the shrimp rolls are fried, remove them from the oil and drain on paper towels. They taste best after resting for 5 to 10 minutes.

✸ Chinese-Restaurant ✸ Spareribs

There's a certain taste in Chinese-American restaurant spareribs that is different from the taste of other ribs. Part of the secret is the marination (which is very simple); the other part of the secret — the perfect cooking on hooks in a roaster — is much harder for the home cook to emulate. Good news, however: the following recipe, specifically designed for the home cook, gets you very close to the Chinese-restaurant taste and texture. It does require you to steam two racks of ribs, which means you need a steamer large enough to accommodate them. If you have access to a Chinese housewares store, your problems are solved: they sell huge aluminum, double-deck steamers that are very inexpensive. The recipe also requires you to roast the ribs on a rack, or a slotted tray, over water. If you have a rack that can hold the ribs, and a roasting pan in which you can put that rack, simply pour an inch of water into the pan and you're all set. Another option is to place the ribs directly on the grate of your oven and to set pans of water under the ribs on a lower grate. It's all a lot easier than it sounds — and the results are worth the trouble!

Yield: 12 appetizer servings

1 cup dark soy sauce
½ cup water
1½ cups sugar
¼ cup hoisin sauce
8 large garlic cloves, smashed
2 racks of spareribs

1. Place the soy sauce in a roasting pan that's large enough and deep enough to hold the 2 racks of ribs. Whisk in the water, sugar, and hoisin sauce. Scatter about a third of the smashed garlic across the bottom of the pan. Add a rack of ribs to the pan. Top with another third of the garlic, scattered evenly. Top with the second rack of ribs, and top that with the remaining garlic. If the ribs are not covered by the marinade, spoon some of the marinade from the bottom of the pan over the ribs. Marinate, covered and refrigerated, for 24 hours, making sure to rotate ribs frequently (every few hours, except when you sleep) to make sure that the racks are evenly marinating.

2. When ready to cook ribs, remove them from the marinade and place them in the basket of a large steamer (two baskets would be even better). Reserve marinade. Steam ribs gently for 1 hour and 15 minutes. Remove ribs and dry with paper towels.

3. While ribs are steaming, preheat oven to 375 degrees.

4. After ribs have steamed, place each slab of ribs on a rack that has a pan of water under it. Brush all sides of the ribs with the marinade. Cook ribs in the oven for 1 hour. While the ribs are cooking, turn them every 15 min-

utes (a total of 3 times), and brush all sides of the ribs with the marinade when you turn.

5. When the ribs are done, remove them from the oven, brush the tops with marinade, and place the racks under a broiler, top side up, for 2 to 3 minutes, or until they sizzle a bit on top. Remove them from the broiler and let them rest for 5 minutes. Cut into individual ribs and serve immediately.

✫ Panfried Potstickers ✫ with Dipping Sauce

Pork-stuffed potstickers, also identified on many restaurant menus as "fried dumplings," initially became popular in Chinese-American restaurants as an appetizer option in the Early Post–Chop Suey Era. Then, with the later rise in popularity of dim sum, more-sophisticated versions of potstickers starting turning up in dim sum houses. The following recipe is in that latter style: the very coarse pork, and the inclusion of many vegetables, give the potstickers layers of flavor and texture. The cooking process itself is quite interesting: the dumplings are shallow fried in oil, then steamed in the same pan with chicken stock — threatening to literally become pot stickers. I think you'll have no trouble.

Yield: 30 to 35 potstickers

1 pound pork shoulder meat, closely trimmed
*   and cut into 2-inch chunks, chilled*
4 cups chopped napa cabbage
3 tablespoons kosher salt
¼ cup chopped, canned water chestnuts
*   (medium-size pieces)*
⅓ cup thinly sliced scallion
*   (including tender green tops)*

☆★☆

1 large egg, lightly beaten

3 tablespoons chopped coriander leaves

2 tablespoons minced red bell pepper

1 tablespoon minced gingerroot

1 tablespoon minced garlic

1½ tablespoons chili paste with garlic (see sidebar)

½ tablespoon dark sesame oil

2 teaspoons dark soy sauce

2 teaspoons light soy sauce

2 teaspoons Shao Xing (Chinese rice wine), or dry sherry

2 teaspoons oyster sauce

60 to 70 fresh or defrosted round gyoza wrappers (3 inches in diameter; see Note)

Peanut oil for panfrying

Chicken stock (canned is fine) for steaming

1. Place half of the chilled pork chunks in the work bowl of a food processor fitted with the chopping blade. Pulse the meat in the food processor until it is a little chunkier than store-bought ground pork, about 10 seconds. Remove ground pork. Repeat with the remaining half of the pork chunks. Refrigerate ground pork, covered, until ready for use.

2. Place the cabbage in a large colander set inside a large bowl. Mix the cabbage well with the salt. Let it stand for 25 minutes. Then, using your hands, squeeze as much liquid as possible from the cabbage. Remove squeezed cabbage to a bowl. Using a clean towel or several layers of cheesecloth, take a small batch of the cabbage, roll it up in the towel, and with a wringing action squeeze until all moisture is removed. Set aside. (*Note:*

Most of the salt will be eliminated along with the drained moisture.)

3. In a medium-size bowl, combine the water chestnuts, scallion, egg, coriander, red bell pepper, ginger, garlic, chili paste with garlic, sesame oil, dark soy sauce, light soy sauce, Shao Xing, and oyster sauce. Stir with a fork to combine. Mix in drained cabbage. Then blend this mixture into the ground pork; incorporate it well but be as gentle as possible. Avoid compressing and squeezing the meat. This is very important for the final texture of the cooked dumplings; think of the process as similar to folding ingredients into whipped egg whites for a soufflé. Refrigerate, covered, for ½ hour.

4. Scoop up a scant tablespoon of the mixture and shape it into a small ball. Then,

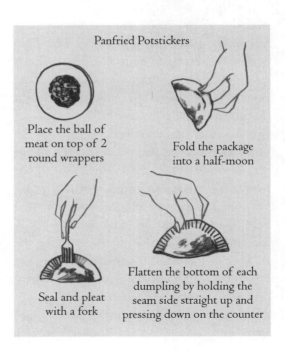

Panfried Potstickers

Place the ball of meat on top of 2 round wrappers

Fold the package into a half-moon

Seal and pleat with a fork

Flatten the bottom of each dumpling by holding the seam side straight up and pressing down on the counter using your fingers, lightly wet one whole rim of a potsticker wrapper with water and lay another wrapper on top of it. Press them so they stick to each other, creating a double wrapper. Wet the edges of the doubled wrapper and place the ball of meat on the center of the wrapper; fold the wrapper over the meat to seal the dumpling, creating a half-moon. Pleat the edge of the dumpling by pressing down on it with a fork. Set the dumpling on waxed paper. Repeat until all dumplings are made. Just prior to cooking, flatten each dumpling by holding the seam side straight up and pressing down on the dumpling bottom.

5. To fry the dumplings, choose a large, heavy nonstick skillet with a tight-fitting lid. You will need to use a number of skillets if you wish to cook all the dumplings simultaneously, or you could cook the dumplings in batches. Place the skillet(s) over medium heat. Add the peanut oil to each skillet or each batch; add enough to create a shallow pool. When the oil is hot, carefully set dumplings in the pan on their bottoms, seam side standing straight side up in the pan. Do not overcrowd the pan or let the dumplings touch. Cover the pan(s), and fry until the bottoms are crispy and deep golden brown.

6. Immediately add chicken stock to the pan(s), adding enough stock to measure ⅛ inch deep. Replace the cover and steam the dumplings for 8 to 10 minutes. Remove the lid and let all the liquid evaporate. Test a dumpling for doneness. If undercooked, add more chicken stock to pan and cover once again until dumplings are cooked through.

When the dumplings are cooked, rebrown the bottoms of the dumplings until they are very crisp. Serve immediately with Potsticker Dipping Sauce (recipe follows).

NOTE: Gyoza wrappers, also called jiao, jiao-zi, jiaozi pi, or ji pi, are sold fresh or frozen, in packages of varying weights. If you buy a one-pound package, you should have eighty to one hundred skins, enough to cover this recipe.

★ Potsticker Dipping Sauce ★

½ cup light soy sauce
¼ cup rice wine vinegar
⅛ cup thinly sliced scallion
1 teaspoon chili paste with garlic (see sidebar)
¼ teaspoon ground white pepper
½ teaspoon sesame oil
½ teaspoon toasted sesame seeds

Chili Paste with Garlic

One of my favorite products of all in the Chinese pantry has various names. I first came to know it as chili paste with garlic — but I've also seen it called chili garlic sauce, chili sauce with garlic, and so on. Different producers call it different things. Whatever the name, it's a pulpy puree made from pounded chilies, usually bright orange red, a little sweet and salty, loaded with garlic flavor, chili flavor, and heat. It is indispensable for Szechuan cooking, and many of the spicy recipes in this section call for it. My favorite one is made by a Hong Kong company called Lee Kum Kee. It is an invaluable addition to your Asian ingredient collection. Refrigerate after opening.

★☆

In a small bowl, using a small whisk, thoroughly combine the soy sauce, wine vinegar, scallion, chili paste with garlic, white pepper, sesame oil, and sesame seeds. Let the mixture sit for 20 minutes before serving.

☆ Shao-Mai with Pork, ☆ Shrimp, and Scallops

The rise of the dim sum parlor has brought shao-mai (usually pronounced shoo-MY) to many Americans. This delightful dumpling is distinctive for the fact that it is open topped. It is often a combination of pork and seafood and often has a chunky texture. The following version calls for hand-ground pork and minced shrimp, with a sliced-shrimp topping and a scallop-slice base. The inclusion of minced hard-boiled egg gives it a very dim sum—parlor flavor. It is much easier to shape in your hand than you'd expect; you simply place it in your palm and close your hand around it. Serve, if desired, on plates lined with lightly steamed cabbage leaves.

Yield: About 20 dumplings

⅔ cup peeled, deveined, finely minced shrimp, plus 10 whole medium shrimp, peeled and sliced in half lengthwise (buy 1 pound medium shrimp to be sure you have enough)
⅔ cup fatty pork loin, finely minced by hand
½ cup Chinese mushrooms, soaked for 30 minutes in hot water, squeezed dry, and minced
½ teaspoon cornstarch
½ teaspoon salt
⅔ teaspoon sugar
½ teaspoon sesame oil
¼ teaspoon ground white pepper
1 teaspoon finely minced garlic
1 teaspoon finely minced gingerroot
1½ tablespoons Thai fish sauce
1 tablespoon light soy sauce
1 hard-boiled egg, minced
20 fresh or defrosted round gyoza wrappers (3 inches in diameter; see Note on page 158)

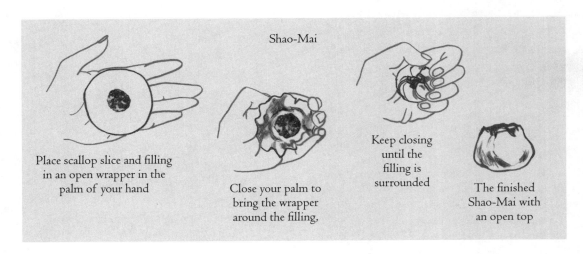

Shao-Mai

Place scallop slice and filling in an open wrapper in the palm of your hand

Close your palm to bring the wrapper around the filling,

Keep closing until the filling is surrounded

The finished Shao-Mai with an open top

20 slices of sea scallop, each slice ¼ inch thick
    and the diameter of a quarter (you may
    need 5 sea scallops, or more, depending
    on the size of the scallops)
1 cabbage leaf

1. In a large bowl combine the ⅔ cup minced shrimp, pork, mushrooms, cornstarch, salt, sugar, sesame oil, white pepper, garlic, ginger, fish sauce, soy sauce, and hard-boiled egg. Using a fork, but without mashing, thoroughly combine all the ingredients to make the dumpling filling.

2. Place an open wrapper on your open palm, then place a slice of scallop in the center of the wrapper. Place a rounded teaspoon of filling on top of the scallop. Close your palm to bring the wrapper up around the filling; using the fingers of your other hand, make the wrapper adhere to the filling all around the perimeter of the top. You will have an open-top dumpling. Place a slice of shrimp on top of each dumpling, pressing it lightly into the filling.

3. Arrange the dumplings, with a little space between them, in a bamboo steamer lined with a cabbage leaf and steam the dumplings over high heat for 10 minutes, or until cooked through. Serve immediately.

☆ Shanghai Soup Dumplings ☆

About ten years ago, just when Americans felt they knew the Chinese-dumpling scene — along came a hot new dumpling sensation from Shanghai, the curious and delectable "soup dumpling," called xiao lung bao, from which the first bite elicits a spurt of hot, gauzy, delicious broth. "How do they get the broth inside the dumpling?" everyone asked. The answer is simple: the broth is gelled in the refrigerator before a stiff square of it gets inserted in the dumpling. Then it melts inside the dumpling during steaming. It's a little tricky to ensure you have a firm seal on these dumplings, but practice will make you adept. I'd recommend, in fact, that you make a few dumplings and steam them before going on to make the whole recipe; you'll probably see some improvement that you can make in the seal. It is easiest to steam these dumplings in a wide steamer so that you can steam many at the same time. A steamer rack set in a wide wok is good. Even better is a multitiered steamer, possibly made out of bamboo. One other Chinese device nice to have on hand: wide and deep ceramic Chinese soup spoons, so that when you puncture the dumpling with your first bite, the "soup" will run into the spoon. Remember, these are served with no broth: all the broth is inside the dumpling.

Yield: 50 to 60 dumplings

GELLED SOUP FILLING:
6 cups Chinese double stock
    (page 166)
¼ teaspoon whole Szechuan peppercorns
1 whole star anise

PORK FILLING:
½ pound ground pork
1 small garlic clove, peeled and
    mashed to a paste with
    1 teaspoon kosher salt
1 teaspoon grated gingerroot
1 large scallion, minced
1 tablespoon finely chopped coriander leaves
⅛ teaspoon Szechuan peppercorns,
    finely ground
1 point of star anise, finely ground
1 tablespoon dark sesame oil

½ teaspoon Shao Xing (Chinese rice wine),
　　or dry sherry
1 large egg, beaten
60 medium-thick wonton wrappers
Vegetable oil for oiling tray
Soft lettuce leaves to line the steamer

1. Make soup filling: At least 8 hours before you plan to assemble the dumplings, place the stock, peppercorns, and anise in a saucepan and cook over high heat until reduced by two-thirds in volume (down to 2 cups). Pour the stock through a fine mesh strainer into a 9 by 12-inch baking dish and cool to room temperature. Cover the dish with plastic wrap and chill in the refrigerator at least 6 hours or overnight to allow the stock to gel. When it has gelled, use a paring knife to cut the

gelled stock (in its dish) into 60 pieces about 1½ inch square. Reserve, refrigerated, in the dish.

2. Make pork filling: Place the pork, garlic, ginger, scallion, coriander leaves, ground peppercorns, anise, sesame oil, and Shao Xing in a mixing bowl. Carefully pour half of the beaten egg into the bowl (you can do this by eye). Combine the ingredients in the mixing bowl thoroughly and reserve. Add 1 tablespoon of water to the remaining egg; whisk it with a fork and reserve.

3. To assemble the dumplings, have ready the wonton wrappers, the reserved pork filling, the reserved gelled stock, a half-teaspoon measuring spoon to measure the filling, the reserved egg-water mixture, a pastry brush, a kitchen towel to cover the stack of unfilled wrappers (to prevent them from drying out), a second towel to dry your work surface, and a large, lightly oiled tray to hold the finished dumplings. Begin by placing a wrapper on your work surface with the whiter, starched side facing up. Place 1 square of gelled stock in the center of the wrapper and place a generous ½ teaspoon of pork filling on top of the stock. Next, brush a very thin coating of the egg mixture around the outside margins of the wrapper. Lift an edge of the wrapper up and just over the center of the filling. Join to it another edge that you've lifted over the center. Keep working around the wrapper until all edges are lifted and joined in the center, forming a round, squat purse. There should be a small tail of dough at top center; working with your hands, mold it along with the joined edges into a sealing pleat, firmly

Shanghai Soup Dumplings

Place pork filling on gelled stock on wrapper

Lift one side of wrapper around filling

Keep lifting all sides of wrapper to envelop filling

The finished product, with sealing pleat on top

pinching the dough closed. Place it on the oiled tray and repeat with the remaining wrappers and filling, wiping away any moisture on your work surface and hands between wrappings. If not steaming the dumplings right away, place in the refrigerator, covered, for up to 3 hours. (Or freeze in an airtight container for up to a week. Frozen dumplings will take an additional minute or so to cook.)

4. Line a steamer tray with a layer of lettuce leaves and carefully transfer as many dumplings as will fit onto the tray, keeping ½ inch between each. Place the steamer tray over simmering water. Cover, and steam the dumplings until the wrappers are cooked through, about 6 to 7 minutes. Carefully transfer the dumplings to small plates and serve. A classic dipping sauce for this dumpling is Chinese black vinegar with a julienne of fresh gingerroot in it.

☆ Fiery Marinated ☆ Szechuan Cabbage

One of the great "improvements" that Szechuan and Hunan restaurants brought to the Chinese-American dining scene was the realization that the opening nibbles in a meal didn't have to be deep-fried, or even cooked; we learned that there really are cold and room-temperature Chinese appetizers. When Szechuan restaurants got hot in the 1970s, they started competing with each other by offering little giveaways to each table, appetite provokers for the diner to munch on while perusing the menu. One of the great ones was spicy cabbage — uncooked, but softened through a kind of quick pickling process. The following version of this palate-opening winner can be on your table in

as little as four hours — though it's better if you can make it in the morning and serve it at night. It also holds nicely for a couple of days.

Yield: Enough for 8 to 12 diners to nibble

1 (1¼-pound) green cabbage
1 tablespoon kosher salt
2 tablespoons finely minced gingerroot
2 large garlic cloves, finely minced
2 tablespoons plus 1 teaspoon sesame oil
1 to 4 small dried red chilies (depending on taste)
3 tablespoons rice vinegar
2 tablespoons sugar
1 to 3 tablespoons chili paste with garlic (depending on taste; see sidebar, page 158)

1. Remove the outer leaves of the cabbage and cut away and discard the core. Quarter the remaining cabbage, then cut it into strips that are about ½ inch wide. In a bowl, toss the cabbage strips with the kosher salt, blending well. Place a plate over the cabbage and a heavy weight on the plate. Let sit at room temperature for 4 hours.

2. Place the salted cabbage in a colander. Working over the sink or a large bowl, squeeze the cabbage firmly in your hands to extract liquid. Work it hard; the texture of the cabbage will soften as you do. Place cabbage back in the bowl and toss with the ginger and garlic. Reserve.

3. Place a wok over medium-high heat. Add the 2 tablespoons of sesame oil to the wok. Break the dried chilies into 4 pieces each and add the pieces to the oil in the wok. Stir-

fry them until they darken in color, about 1 minute. Add the vinegar and sugar; mix well. Pour mixture over the cabbage and toss. Add the chili paste with garlic to the cabbage and blend well.

4. The dish may be served at this point — but it's better if you let it sit at room temperature for another 4 hours. Just before serving, toss with the remaining 1 teaspoon of sesame oil.

☆ Wonton Soup ☆

Along with chow mein and egg rolls, wonton soup is one of the great iconic dishes of Chinese-American cooking. It actually has roots in real Chinese food. The words *wonton, huntun,* and *yuntun* all mean the same: "swallowing clouds," which indicates that the cloudlike dumplings are "swallowed" by soup. But the classic thin dumpling has undergone a transformation here — becoming much thicker, larger, heartier. If you make wonton soup at home using the usual store-bought wonton wrappers, which are thin, you'll end up with a limp wonton that doesn't resemble the typical restaurant versions. So I prefer to use a thicker Chinese dough for wontons: egg roll wrappers (see page 155 for recommendations), which you must cut down to wonton size (many wonton wrappers are three and one-half inches square, but the larger restaurant versions need wrappers that are five inches square). For the wonton broth, you may use either the single-stock or double-stock versions that follow this recipe. By the way, after playing around for years with wonton fillings, I finally discovered that adding a little Chinese sausage to the mix supplies just the right degree of funk that restaurant wonton fillings often have. If you can't acquire the sausage, simply add an extra two ounces of ground pork to the recipe.

Yield: 5 to 6 servings (makes about 25 wontons)

2 ounces Chinese-style cured sausage
    (see Note)
1 small dried shiitake mushroom,
    soaked in a small bowl of hot tap
    water until soft
¼ pound coarsely ground pork (see Note)
1 small garlic clove, peeled and mashed to a
    paste with ½ teaspoon kosher salt
¼ teaspoon MSG (optional)
¼ teaspoon kosher salt
Scant teaspoon of sugar
¼ teaspoon dark sesame oil
1 large egg, beaten
1 tablespoon cornstarch
1 package Chinese egg roll skins, cut with a
    knife into 5-inch squares (you'll need
    25, plus additional for practice)
Flour for the tray
6 cups single or double Chinese Meat Stock,
    lightly salted to taste (recipe follows)
Green leafy tops from 3 heads of
    baby bok choy
Slivers of roast pork for garnish, at room
    temperature (optional)

1. Cut the Chinese sausage into bite-size chunks and place them in the work bowl of a food processor. Lightly squeeze the excess moisture from the mushroom and add it to the work bowl. Process the sausage and mushroom until very finely chopped, about 3 to 5 minutes, pausing occasionally to scrape down the sides of the bowl. Transfer the mixture to a mixing bowl and add the ground pork, garlic paste, MSG, salt, sugar, and sesame oil. Carefully pour about one-third

of the beaten egg into the bowl (you can do this by eye) and discard the remainder. Combine the ingredients in the mixing bowl thoroughly. Sprinkle the cornstarch over the pork mixture and, using a large fork or wooden spoon, beat the mixture until the cornstarch is evenly distributed and the mixture is a bit fluffy, about 1 minute. Set the pork filling aside.

2. To assemble the wontons, have ready the pork filling, the egg roll skins, a tablespoon to measure the filling, a small cup of water for sealing the wontons, a kitchen towel to cover the stack of unfilled egg roll skins (to prevent them from drying out), a second towel to dry your work surface, and a floured tray to hold the finished wontons. Begin by placing an egg roll skin on your work surface with a straight edge parallel to you and with the whiter, starched side of the skin facing upward. Place a scant ½ tablespoon of the pork filling slightly above the center of the skin. Next, dip your fingertips in the water and run them just along the outside margins of the skin along all four edges. Fold the edge of the skin nearest you over the filling to meet the edge farthest from you (folding it in half, forming a rectangle). Before you fully seal the edges, place your index fingers on either side of the enclosed lump of filling and slide them gently outward a few times to remove any trapped air bubbles (they're especially likely to form closest to the filling itself). Gently press the edges together to seal the rectangle fully. Next, bring the edge farthest from you back over the lump of filling, folding toward you, forming a still nar-

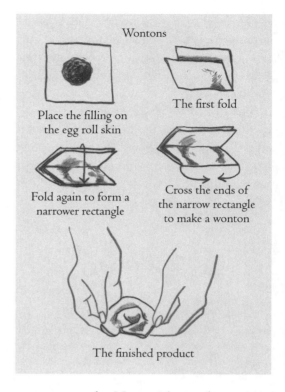

Wontons

Place the filling on the egg roll skin

The first fold

Fold again to form a narrower rectangle

Cross the ends of the narrow rectangle to make a wonton

The finished product

rower rectangle. Now pick up the wonton with the bottom (the side that's been resting on the work surface) facing you and, with the newly formed open edge pointing upward, fold each end (the tails) of the rectangle toward you, crossing them almost at right angles in an X pattern, crossing as close as you can to the lump of filling. Gently pinch the tails together where they cross, dabbing first with a bit of water. Place finished wonton on the floured tray; when sitting flat, the wonton will look something like an antique nurse's cap. Repeat with the remaining skins and filling, wiping away any water on your work surface between wrappings. Don't worry if your wontons are a bit irregular in shape;

the important thing is to try to make a compact and tightly wrapped package without internal air bubbles. Practice helps.

3. When ready to serve the soup, bring a large stockpot of generously salted water to a boil over high heat, and bring the Chinese meat stock to a simmer in another pot.

4. Place the bok choy tops in the boiling water and cook for 1 minute. Scoop them out with a skimmer/strainer and run them under cold water to stop the cooking. Place the greens on paper toweling, gently squeeze out the excess moisture, and set them aside.

5. Carefully place the wontons in the stockpot of water, allow it to return to a boil, then immediately reduce it to a simmer. The wontons will initially sink to the bottom of the pot. Once they float to the surface, they will cook through, depending on the size of your pot, in 3 to 4 minutes (test with a couple of wontons first; they are done when the pork is just cooked through). Remove, and divide the wontons among five to six soup bowls.

6. Place equal parts of the bok choy greens in each soup bowl. Divide the simmering stock among the bowls. If using the roast pork (see recipe on page 177, or use leftover Chinese-restaurant pork), drop 6 to 8 slivers in each soup bowl. Serve immediately.

NOTE: If you have access to a good Chinese grocery store, you'll be able to find cured and dried Chinese sausage. I found a brand that works perfectly in this dish, so you might want to look for it: it's the Kam Van Jan brand, made by January Company in Seattle, and it's the type that has liver added. Also on the subject of meat: ask your butcher to grind the pork for this dish coarsely — just once through the meat grinder will do the trick.

☆ Chinese Meat Stock ☆ (Single and Double) for Chinese Soups

Stock is hugely important in good Cantonese cooking, particularly in the preparation of such traditional dishes as wonton soup. I'll never forget the press release I once received from a famous, fancy restaurant in Hong Kong, which claimed that the secret of the chef's success was his magnificent "stork." When I inquired about this gastronomic rarity, I found out that someone had typed in an *r* where a *c* should have been! Chinese soup stocks often include esoteric ingredients (such as dried fish stomach) that would be difficult for most home cooks to acquire. But the following recipes, with very little esoterica involved, create delicious stocks not unlike the ones used in soups at Chinese-American restaurants. If you're in a relative hurry, the single-stock version is very, very good; if you've got another hour and a half and a few more bones to invest, I'd recommend the double-stock version.

★ Single Stock ★

Yield: About 2½ quarts

4 pounds chicken wings, chopped into 1- to 2-inch pieces (if you don't have a meat cleaver, have this done by your butcher)
2½ pounds pork spareribs, cut into individual ribs and chopped into 1- to 2-inch pieces
14 cups cold water
1 medium onion, peeled and quartered
3 large scallions, chopped
1 large carrot, peeled and chopped
1 celery stalk, chopped
3 long ¼-inch slices gingerroot
1 large garlic clove, peeled and sliced
6 sprigs coriander with long stems

1. Place the chicken and pork in a 12-quart stockpot and rinse under running water, swishing the meat around with your hands until the water runs clear. Drain, and add 12 of the cups of cold water.

2. Place the stockpot over medium-high heat and bring to a simmer, skimming off and discarding the foam that rises to the surface. Add the onion, scallions, carrot, celery, ginger, garlic, and coriander. Continue to simmer very gently for 3 hours, occasionally skimming the stock and pressing on the solids with a large spoon. After half of that cooking time (1½ hours), add the remaining 2 cups of water, return the stock to a simmer, and cook for the remaining 1½ hours.

3. Remove the pot from the heat and let it rest for 30 minutes. Strain the stock through a colander double lined with cheesecloth, pressing lightly on the solids. Discard the solids (see Note). Let the stock cool to room temperature and refrigerate or freeze in airtight containers, skimming additional fat if desired.

★ Double Stock ★

Yield: About 2 quarts

2 tablespoons vegetable oil
1 medium onion, chopped into
    ½-inch pieces
3 large scallions, cut into ½-inch lengths
1 carrot, peeled and chopped into
    ½-inch pieces
1 celery stalk, chopped into ½-inch pieces
2 tablespoons finely chopped fresh gingerroot
2 garlic cloves, peeled and finely chopped

4 pounds chicken wings, chopped into
    1- to 2-inch pieces (if you don't have a
    meat cleaver, have this done by your
    butcher)
2½ pounds pork spareribs, cut into individual
    ribs and chopped into 1- to 2-inch pieces
2½ quarts Chinese single stock
    (preceding recipe)
6 sprigs coriander with long stems

1. Heat the vegetable oil in a 12-quart stockpot over medium heat and add the onion, scallions, carrot, celery, ginger, and garlic. Reduce the heat to medium-low and cover, cooking very gently for 15 minutes.

2. Meanwhile, place the chicken and pork in a large bowl and rinse under running water, swishing the meat around with your hands until the water runs clear. Drain and reserve.

3. After the vegetables have cooked for 15 minutes, uncover the pot and add the reserved chicken and pork. Add the single stock, raise the heat to medium-high, and bring to a simmer, skimming off and discarding the foam that rises to the surface. Avoid removing the vegetables as you skim. Add the coriander and continue to simmer gently for 1½ hours, occasionally skimming and pressing on the solids with a large spoon.

4. Remove the pot from the heat and let it rest for 30 minutes. Strain the stock through a colander double lined with cheesecloth, pressing lightly on the solids (see Note). Let the stock cool to room temperature and refrigerate or freeze in airtight containers, skimming additional fat if desired.

NOTE: In either recipe — particularly the shorter-cooked double stock — any meat that you wish to retrieve from the pot can be saved and used for soups or stews.

✸ Quick and Easy ✸ Cantonese-Style All-Purpose Pork Stock

One of the things I loved about the Chinese-American food of the old days was the way in which the flavor of pork permeated so many of the dishes. It's easy to catch that flavor at home — by preparing the following simple recipe and keeping it on hand for when, say, a stir-fry needs a little backbone.

Yield: About 4 cups

6 cups water
2 teaspoons soy sauce
1 teaspoon sugar
3 garlic cloves, smashed
4 dried Chinese mushrooms
3 pounds meaty pork bones

Place the water, soy sauce, sugar, garlic, and dried mushrooms in a medium-size pot and stir together well. Add the pork bones. Place pot over high heat and bring to a boil. Skim off the foam and scum that appear on top of the liquid and discard. Reduce heat until the stock is simmering gently and cook for 1½ hours. Keep the pot partially covered, but skim the foam and scum occasionally. When the stock is done, season to taste with salt, strain, refrigerate, and use within a few days. Or you may freeze the stock for future use.

✸ Shrimp Egg Foo Yung ✸

Is there any dish, other than chop suey, that fell so hard from the top? In the 1950s you couldn't get through a meal at a Chinese-American restaurant without having this stuff! Maybe chop suey deserved its fall — but not egg foo yung! Egg foo yung is wonderful, nostalgic comfort food. Okay, it seems to have little connection to food in China — other than the name, which may come from a Cantonese word for "egg white" — but as some kind of nonspecific quasi-Asian omelette, it's delicious when cooked well. Its reputation has probably been harmed by the gloppy, tasteless sauce that usually accompanied it in the 1950s — but that's not the case here. One of my favorite elements in the following recipe is the steaming, at the end, of omelets and sauce together; the result so well reproduces the feel of the dish as it came out of those covered steel servers that Chinese restaurants used to use. Fortune cookies, anyone?

Yield: 4 servings
as part of a Chinese meal

FOR THE SAUCE:

1 tablespoon peanut oil
1 teaspoon minced garlic
2 tablespoons thinly sliced scallion
1 cup Quick and Easy Cantonese-Style
    All-Purpose Pork Stock (above),
    or chicken stock
2 tablespoons light soy sauce
1 tablespoon oyster sauce
Pinch of Chinese five-spice powder
4 teaspoons cornstarch stirred with
    2 tablespoons cold water

FOR THE OMELETS:

5 tablespoons rendered pork fat
    (see Note accompanying
    fried rice recipe, page 181),
    or vegetable oil

½ cup finely chopped onion
¼ cup finely sliced scallion
¼ cup finely sliced celery
1 tablespoon minced garlic
4 ounces medium shrimp, peeled, cleaned,
        and cut in half lengthwise
1 teaspoon sugar
1 teaspoon light soy sauce
1 cup mung bean sprouts
6 large eggs, lightly beaten

1. To make the sauce: Heat a medium-size wok over high heat. Pour the peanut oil down the sides of the wok and add the garlic and scallion. Stir for 1 minute. Stir in the pork stock, soy sauce, oyster sauce, and five-spice powder. As soon as the mixture comes to a boil, whisk in the dissolved cornstarch and cook until thick (just a moment or two). Taste for seasoning and add salt if necessary. Remove from heat and keep warm while you make the egg mixture.

2. To make the omelets: Place wok over high heat. Add 1 tablespoon of the rendered pork fat, swirling to coat sides. Add onion, scallion, and celery. Stir-fry until the vegetables begin to soften, about 2 minutes. Add garlic and stir-fry for 1 minute.

3. Add shrimp and stir-fry until just opaque. Add sugar and light soy sauce. Cook for 30 seconds more, then add bean sprouts. Remove from heat and keep warm.

4. Set up a steamer that's large enough to hold a plate of egg foo yung (see Note).

5. Wipe out the wok. Heat over high heat and swirl in 2 tablespoons of the remaining rendered pork fat. Return half the filling mixture to the pan. Pour in half of the beaten eggs, stir, reduce the heat to medium-high, and cook until the underside is brown (about 2 minutes). Flip the omelet and cook the other side until brown (about 2 minutes more). Keep omelet warm while you repeat the process to make a second omelet.

6. Slide the 2 omelets onto a large plate, overlapping each other. Cover with sauce and place in steamer over boiling water. Steam for 3 minutes and serve immediately on a platter. Cut the omelets in two at the table, serving each diner a half omelet.

NOTE: You can use a bamboo steamer or a metal steamer. Or you can improvise a steamer by pouring boiling water to a depth of one inch into a wok large enough to accommodate the plate; you simply set the plate on an empty can (such as a tuna can) that sits in the boiling water, making sure the plate is above the water.

☆ Shrimp with Lobster Sauce ☆

This dish with a confusing name is one of the great Chinese-American restaurant staples. The confusion stems from the fact that there's no lobster in the dish — but as the Chinese are quick to point out, it is so named because the sauce is one they use for lobster. And that sauce is the soul of this dish: a thickened, garlicky broth, shot through with clumps of tasty ground pork, exquisitely velvetized at the end by the addition of raw eggs that barely get stirred. Intriguingly, when the sauce does get used for lobster — as it often does in Chinese-American restaurants, in the dish called Lobster Cantonese (see page 171) — the

A Chinese-Inspired Breakfast Idea

Egg-White Omelet with Chinese Mushrooms, Scallions, and Sesame Seeds

(Umami Omelet)

I do love a good egg foo yung, but recently another type of Chinese omelet entirely caught my attention. One type of omelet I distinctly do *not* like is the wildly popular egg-white omelet. Thin people are ordering egg-white omelets all around me these days, but I've never been moved to do the same. Until now. The downfall of the egg-white omelet, to me, has been its insubstantiality and its usual lack of flavor. However, by dressing up the egg-white omelet with some lively Chinese flavors, you can turn it into a great taste experience. Intriguingly, this brand-new breakfast idea draws on the Japanese concept of *umami* — a "fifth" flavor description (after salty, sweet, sour, bitter) that is usually used for meaty-brown-salty things. This egg-white omelet is a *umami* festival!

Yield: 1 serving

Whites of 3 large eggs
¼ teaspoon thin soy sauce
1 teaspoon vegetable oil
  (or a generous amount
  of Pam cooking spray)
1 teaspoon sesame seeds
1 tablespoon finely minced scallion
  (white and green parts)
1 medium-size dried Chinese mushroom,
  soaked in hot water for 15 minutes,
  squeezed dry, and minced
½ teaspoon Chinese oyster sauce,
  room temperature

1. In a small bowl, beat together the egg whites and the soy sauce for 20 seconds. Reserve.
2. Place the oil in a small, 6-inch sauté pan over medium-high heat. Or spray the pan well with Pam and place over heat. Add the sesame seeds and spread them out evenly. As soon as they start to color (they'll turn golden in 30 to 60 seconds), add the scallion. Distribute evenly. Immediately add the mushroom. Distribute evenly. Pour the egg-white mixture over all, spreading it out evenly. Let the egg whites set for 30 seconds, then insert a spatula under the egg whites, all around the pan, to loosen them from the bottom and to make sure they're not sticking. Once they're loose, immediately swirl the pan so that any extra uncooked egg white on top of the omelet swirls out to the perimeter (this cooks the excess egg quickly). Turn the omelet over — either with a wide spatula or by flipping the pan or by inverting the omelet onto a plate, then sliding the omelet back into the pan. Cook on the second side for 10 seconds only. (The total cooking time of the eggs should be 1 to 2 minutes.) Then flip the omelet onto a plate, browned side up. Brush omelet with Chinese oyster sauce. Serve immediately.

sauce is usually darker and sometimes contains fermented black beans. The lobster sauce variation that's used for shrimp is usually whitish, and doesn't contain beans.

Yield: 2 to 3 servings as part
of a multicourse Chinese meal

½ pound medium shrimp
1 teaspoon salt
1¾ teaspoons sugar
1 small dried Chinese mushroom
¼ pound ground pork
¾ teaspoon Chinese sesame oil
7 large garlic cloves, peeled
3 large eggs
3½ tablespoons cornstarch
1⅓ cups stock (either the Cantonese-Style
    All-Purpose Pork Stock on page 167,
    or chicken stock)
1 tablespoon Shao Xing (Chinese rice wine),
    or dry sherry
Vegetable oil for deep-frying (such as canola)
3 scallions (green and white parts),
    finely minced
2 tablespoons grated gingerroot

1. Peel the shrimp, devein them, and butterfly them, keeping them just attached at the back. Toss in a bowl with ½ teaspoon of the salt and ½ teaspoon of the sugar. Reserve in refrigerator for at least 30 minutes.

2. Soak the Chinese mushroom in hot water until it's soft, about 20 minutes. Then cut away the stem and chop the rest until it's practically a paste. Place it in a bowl and add the ground pork, ¾ teaspoon of the remaining sugar, and ¼ teaspoon of the sesame oil. Blend well.

3. Smash one of the garlic cloves and sprinkle it with the remaining ½ teaspoon of salt; pound and mince until a paste is formed. Add to the pork mixture.

4. Break the eggs in a bowl and just break the yolks with a fork; they must not be beaten together. Pour about half an egg's worth of this mixture into the ground-pork bowl. Reserve the remaining eggs.

5. Add 1 tablespoon of the cornstarch to the ground-pork bowl. Beat the pork mixture with a fork until well blended and fluffy. Place in refrigerator.

6. In a bowl, blend together the pork or chicken stock, Shao Xing, the remaining ½ teaspoon of sesame oil, and the remaining ½ teaspoon of sugar. Season to taste with salt. Reserve. In a cup, beat together the remaining 2½ tablespoons of cornstarch with 3 tablespoons of cold water, until a creamy liquid is formed. Reserve.

7. When ready to prepare the dish, place vegetable oil in a wide saucepan to a depth of 2 inches. Heat oil to 350 degrees, or until drops of water splatter when tossed in the oil. Add the shrimp, all at once, and stir to prevent them from sticking to each other; cook until shrimp are just done (about 30 seconds). Remove shrimp and drain on paper towels.

8. Meanwhile, bring a quart or so of water to a boil. Drop the pork mixture into it in walnut-size clumps. Cook for 3 minutes. Remove with a slotted spoon and drain on paper towels. When pork is cool enough to handle, break it into pea-size clumps with your fingers.

9. Place a large wok over medium heat. Take a tablespoon of oil from the pot in which the

shrimp cooked and add it to the wok. Finely mince the remaining 6 garlic cloves and add them to the wok, along with the scallions and ginger. Stir-fry mixture for 2 minutes.

10. Add the stock mixture and turn heat to high; after the stock comes to a boil, boil for 1 minute. Stir the reserved cornstarch mixture in its cup, then whisk it into the boiling sauce in the wok; the sauce will become very thick. Immediately add the shrimp and the pork; stir well to blend.

11. Turn heat to low and pour the broken eggs on top of the shrimp dish. Very slightly stir them into the sauce. If you stir too much, you won't have a sauce that shows its egginess. If you stir too little, the eggs won't blend into the sauce. You want large, runny clumps of white and yolk to just blend with the cornstarch-thickened sauce. Turning the mass once or twice in the wok should do the trick; the whole process takes about 30 seconds.

12. Remove from heat, place on a platter, and serve immediately.

☆ Lobster Cantonese ☆

The big-bucks item at the local Chinese-American restaurant was always Lobster Cantonese. It's a splurge, to be sure . . . but the combo of lobster flavor with that eggy Cantonese sauce is exquisite. The dish's chief difference from Shrimp with Lobster Sauce is that the eggy Cantonese sauce is usually darker in color. If you prefer, you can leave out the soy sauce and the black beans in the following recipe, which would make this dish's sauce more like the light-colored sauce in Shrimp with Lobster Sauce (page 168). With actual lobster in the dish, however, I prefer the dark character.

Yield: 2 to 3 servings as part of a multicourse Chinese meal

1 small dried Chinese mushroom
¼ pound ground pork
1¼ teaspoons sugar
¾ teaspoon Chinese sesame oil
7 large garlic cloves, peeled
½ teaspoon salt
3 large eggs
3½ tablespoons cornstarch
1⅓ cups stock (either the Cantonese-Style All-Purpose Pork Stock on page 167, or chicken stock)
1 tablespoon Shao Xing (Chinese rice wine), or dry sherry
1 tablespoon thin soy sauce
1 tablespoon fermented black beans
8 meaty pieces lobster (see Note)
2 tablespoons vegetable oil (such as canola)
3 scallions (green and white parts), finely minced
2 tablespoons grated gingerroot

1. Soak the Chinese mushroom in hot water until it's soft, about 20 minutes. Then cut away the stem and chop the rest until it's practically a paste. Place it in a bowl and add the ground pork, ¾ teaspoon of the sugar, and ¼ teaspoon of the sesame oil. Blend well.

2. Smash one of the garlic cloves and sprinkle it with the salt; pound and mince until a paste is formed. Add to the pork mixture.

3. Break the eggs in a bowl and just break the yolks with a fork; they must not be beaten together. Pour about half an egg's worth of this mixture into the ground-pork bowl. Reserve the remaining eggs.

4. Add 1 tablespoon of the cornstarch to the ground-pork bowl. Beat the pork mixture with a fork until well blended and fluffy. Place in refrigerator.

5. In a bowl, blend together the pork or chicken stock, Shao Xing, and soy sauce. Crush the black beans with the flat side of a cleaver and add to the mixture. Blend in the remaining ½ teaspoon of sesame oil and the remaining ½ teaspoon of sugar. Reserve. In a cup, beat together the remaining 2½ tablespoons of cornstarch with 3 tablespoons of cold water until a creamy liquid is formed. Reserve.

6. When ready to prepare the dish, cook the lobster. How you cook it depends on what kind of lobster you have (whole lobster, tails, and so on) and what condition they're in (fresh, frozen, in the shell, out of the shell); you'll need to use your common sense. For most situations — including a cut-up, in-shell lobster in 8 pieces — all you'll need to do is stir-fry the lobster pieces in a medium-hot wok in 1 tablespoon of the vegetable oil; place the larger pieces in the wok first, smaller pieces later. Total cooking time shouldn't exceed 6 minutes or so. Remove lobster pieces when done and reserve on paper towels.

7. Meanwhile, bring a quart or so of water to a boil. Drop the pork mixture into it in walnut-size clumps. Cook for 3 minutes. Remove with a slotted spoon and drain on paper towels. When pork is cool enough to handle, break it into pea-size clumps with your fingers.

8. Place a large wok over medium heat. Add the remaining 1 tablespoon of vegetable oil. Finely mince the remaining 6 cloves of garlic and add them to the wok, along with the scallions and ginger. Stir-fry mixture for 2 minutes.

9. Add the stock mixture and turn heat to high; after the stock comes to a boil, boil for 1 minute. Stir the reserved cornstarch mixture in its cup, then whisk it into the boiling sauce in the wok; the sauce will become very thick. Immediately add the lobster and the pork; stir well to blend.

10. Turn heat to low and pour the broken eggs on top of the lobster dish. Very slightly stir them into the sauce. If you stir too much, you won't have an eggy sauce. If you stir too little, the eggs won't be part of the sauce. You want large, runny clumps of white and yolk to just blend with the cornstarch-thickened sauce. The whole process takes about 30 seconds.

11. Remove from heat, place on a platter, and serve immediately.

NOTE: When I make this dish, I buy a live lobster, about one and a quarter to one and a half pounds. I ask the fishmonger to kill it and cut it into eight pieces: four pieces of tail, two knuckles, and two claws. I ask for all the meat to remain in the shell. With a poultry shears, I like to cut an opening along the sides of the knuckles and along the sides of the claws; this enables those pieces to cook faster and for more of the sauce to seep in. But you could also make this dish with a pound or so of lobster tails, either fresh or frozen (defrost and cook accordingly). Or, if you had nothing but a half pound of cooked, shelled lobster meat — that could work too! You would simply warm the meat by tossing it briefly in the hot oil (step 6) and then proceed with the recipe. Follow your intuition; what you're looking for finally is just-cooked, not-toughened lobster meat.

☆ Old-Fashioned ☆ Chicken Chow Mein

There is almost nothing authentically Chinese about chow mein. But the dish that became emblematic of Chinese-American food in the 1950s — an almost stewy mass of celery, onions, and bean sprouts, with a very specific flavor — functions for me, and others, as powerful comfort food. My dad, for example, who traveled with me to China and became quite a sophisticated Chinese-food eater, insisted until the day he died that no one was making that "great chow mein" the way they used to do it at the House of Chan in New York City. Well, the following recipe is for him. When they were making chicken chow mein way back when, they would just pile some shredded slices of cooked chicken on top of the cooked vegetables. I think you get more flavor, and a better dish, if you cook the chicken with the vegetables (choice of white meat or dark meat is yours). When the chow mein is ready, you can eat it without the usual accompaniments, but I'm recommending that you go the whole retro route: the "mein" part means "noodles," and chow mein in America was traditionally served mixed with white rice and those crunchy, deep-fried noodles that always appeared on the tables of Chinese-American restaurants.

Yield: 4 servings

1 tablespoon vegetable oil
2 cups thinly sliced celery (sliced on the
    diagonal about ⅛ inch thick)
2 cups thinly sliced onion (about ⅛ inch thick)
1 teaspoon sugar
½ pound boneless, skinless chicken meat,
    cut into pieces about ½ inch wide
2 cups firmly packed shredded napa cabbage
    (pieces about ½ inch wide)
1½ cups fresh mung bean sprouts
1 tablespoon soy sauce

1 cup stock (preferably the Cantonese-Style
    All-Purpose Pork Stock on page 167,
    but chicken stock can be used)
About 5 teaspoons cornstarch
2 cups cooked white rice
1 cup chow mein noodles
    (crispy room-temperature ones)

1. Place a very large wok over high heat and let it sit for a minute. Add the vegetable oil, spilling it around the sides of the wok. When it's smoking, toss in the celery and onion. Sprinkle ½ teaspoon of the sugar over them and stir well. Stir-fry for 2 minutes, then push the celery-onion mixture to the side of the wok, leaving the center empty.

2. Season the chicken well with salt. If the empty space in the wok is dry, add a little more vegetable oil. Add the chicken to the center of the wok and stir-fry until the chicken browns slightly and loses its pinkish color (about 2 to 3 minutes). Toss with celery and onion, bringing the mass into the center of the wok.

3. Add the cabbage and bean sprouts to the wok, tossing with the other ingredients already in the wok. Add the remaining ½ teaspoon of sugar and toss again. Turn heat down to medium-high and let mixture cook for 5 minutes; the vegetables should start losing their distinctness, merging together.

4. Add the soy sauce and toss. Add the pork or chicken stock and toss. When the stock starts to boil, mix the cornstarch in a small bowl with a little water until a milky liquid is formed. Making sure the chow mein is boiling, add most of the cornstarch liquid to the

wok, stirring immediately. If you'd like the chow mein to be a little thicker, add more cornstarch mixture. Remove chow mein from heat.

5. Divide the rice among four plates or bowls, spreading rice out across the bottoms of the plates or bowls. Top each plate or bowl with a quarter of the chow mein mixture, then divide chow mein noodles over the tops of the four plates or bowls. Serve immediately.

☆ Moo Goo Gai Pan ☆ (with Velveted Chicken)

In American-Chinese restaurants, long before General Tso, aeons before Kung Pao . . . there was moo goo gai pan. If you wanted chicken in the 1950s and you were willing to venture beyond chicken chow mein, you ordered this stir-fry with a light-colored sauce and bright green vegetables. Today, you hardly ever see it on menus. But if you make it at home — combining the simple taste of old with the newly popular awareness of Chinese obsession with texture — you come up with something subtle and marvelous. The following version of moo goo gai pan features velveted chicken — a wonderful ingredient that emerges from marinating chicken in egg white and cornstarch, then barely poaching it in deep oil.

Yield: 2 to 3 servings as part
of a multicourse Chinese dinner

½ pound boneless, skinless chicken breast
1 egg white
2 teaspoons sesame oil
1 tablespoon cornstarch
½ teaspoon salt
½ cup small dried Chinese mushrooms
　　(about 8)
½ cup good chicken or pork stock
　　(see the Cantonese-Style Pork Stock on
　　page 167)
1 teaspoon Shao Xing (Chinese rice wine),
　　or dry sherry
½ teaspoon sugar
1 cup vegetable oil
⅓ cup thin julienne of gingerroot
6 large garlic cloves, coarsely chopped
¼ pound snow peas
⅓ cup sliced canned bamboo shoots

1. Cut the chicken breast into lengthwise slices that are about ¼ inch thick. (This will be easier if you chill the chicken in the freezer for an hour or so.) Place the egg white, 1 teaspoon of the sesame oil, 2 teaspoons of the cornstarch, and salt in a bowl; whisk together until there are no cornstarch lumps. Add the chicken to the mixture, coat it well, and reserve in the refrigerator for 30 minutes.

2. Cover the Chinese mushrooms with hot water in a bowl and let soak for 20 minutes. After soaking, cut away the stems and cut the mushrooms into thick slices. Reserve.

3. Blend together the chicken or pork stock, Shao Xing, and sugar. Reserve. Place the remaining 1 teaspoon of cornstarch in a small cup and mix with a little water until a smooth, creamy liquid is formed. Reserve.

4. When the chicken has rested in the refrigerator for almost 30 minutes, heat the vegetable oil in a wok until it's quite warm but not hot. Pluck the chicken pieces out of their marinade and place them, one by one, in the oil. Separate them just after they go in; they have a tendency to stick to each other or to

the wok. Cook until the pieces just turn white; this may take about 1 to 2 minutes, depending on the heat of your oil. They should look slightly undercooked. Remove each piece as it reaches this stage and reserve the pieces on a plate.

5. As soon as the chicken has come out of the wok, drain most of the oil (reserving for another use, if desired), leaving behind a tablespoon of oil in the wok. Place wok over high heat. Add the ginger and garlic; stir-fry until garlic starts to brown (1 to 2 minutes). Add snow peas, bamboo shoots, and reserved Chinese mushrooms; toss well with garlic and ginger. Add reserved stock mixture. As soon as the stock mixture comes to a boil, give cornstarch mixture a stir and pour it into the wok; stir rapidly. The sauce will thicken immediately. Add chicken pieces and stir for 30 seconds. Turn off heat. Stir in the remaining 1 teaspoon of sesame oil, taste for seasoning (you may want to add some salt), and serve immediately.

☆ Kung Pao Chicken ☆

Kung pao chicken is a wildly popular perennial on Szechuan menus in the United States — where the name is usually code for "spicy stir-fried diced-chicken dish with peanuts." To me the dish rises or falls — as do many Szechuan dishes — on the distinctiveness of the "spicy" part. The following recipe offers four types of heat, all of which end up in a lovely layering of spice sensations. Most important are the brown Szechuan peppercorns, which give the dish the wild, mouth-anesthetizing character of real Szechuan food. Black pepper adds a more familiar note to the Szechuan one; dried red chilies fried in the wok give a toasty character; and chili paste with garlic lends a fresh capsicum taste. If you use the full quantities suggested below, you will have a very hot dish (which makes it authentic). If you'd prefer a milder dish, scale back on the Fiery Four (but please try to leave in at least a little of each one).

Yield: 2 to 3 servings as part
of a multicourse Chinese dinner

½ pound white-meat chicken, cut into
⠀⠀½-inch cubes
1 tablespoon Shao Xing (Chinese rice wine),
⠀⠀or dry sherry
¼ teaspoon salt
¼ teaspoon freshly ground black pepper
2 teaspoons cornstarch
2 tablespoons hoisin sauce
1 to 3 teaspoons chili paste with garlic
⠀⠀(see page 158)
2 teaspoons thin soy sauce
2 tablespoons vegetable oil (canola, peanut,
⠀⠀or other)
1 tablespoon brown Szechuan peppercorns
1 to 2 dried red chilies
3 large scallions (white and green parts),
⠀⠀minced
8 garlic cloves, finely minced
1 tablespoon grated gingerroot
2 tablespoons diced water chestnuts
⠀⠀(about 3 peeled fresh ones)
⅓ cup dry-roasted peanuts (I like them salted)

1. Place the chicken cubes in a bowl. Mix well with Shao Xing, salt, and black pepper. Hold for 1 to 2 hours in refrigerator. Just before cooking, toss the chicken pieces with the cornstarch.

2. Make the sauce: Blend together the hoisin sauce, chili paste, and soy sauce. Reserve.

3. Place a large wok over medium heat. Add the vegetable oil and the Szechuan peppercorns. Let the peppercorns sizzle for about 5 minutes, making sure they don't burn. With a slotted spoon, remove the peppercorns (it's fine if a few remain behind). Break the dried chilies into a few pieces and add to the oil in the wok.

4. Add two-thirds of the minced scallions to the wok, along with the garlic and ginger. Stir-fry for 30 seconds.

5. Raise heat to high. Add the cornstarch-coated chicken to the wok, immediately tossing it with the scallions, garlic, and ginger. Let sit over high heat for 30 seconds, then start tossing the chicken — at the same time scraping up the brown, crusty bits in the bottom of the wok. Let sit, then toss, let sit, then toss. Repeat until the chicken cubes are just cooked through (perhaps 2 to 4 minutes). Add water chestnuts and toss.

6. Turn heat down to medium-low. Add the reserved sauce, stirring well to coat the chicken. Add the peanuts, stirring well to blend. Turn chicken onto serving platter and top with the remaining minced scallion.

☆ General Tso's Chicken ☆

Every Chinese restaurant with — or often without — "Hunan" in its hype offers some version of this dish. It's a best-seller all right, and even seems to be based on real Hunanese cooking — but the irony is that the name is not standard (General Tso's? General Tsao's? General Cho's? General Tang's?). Nor is the recipe. Suffice it to say that if you order a dish with a name something like this you'll probably get crispy, boneless pieces of deep-fried chicken in a reddish, spicy sauce. Is that a good thing? Not according to healthy-eating watchdog agencies, who have picked on this dish because they deplore the combination of greasy deep-frying and a gloppy sauce. Well, if my General Tso's Chicken came out that way, I'd deplore it too. The following recipe offers a light, crunchy, greaseless coating and a sauce that's both lighter than the usual in texture and lower in sugar. I love it. And if you make it at home rather than ordering it from takeout, your crunchy chicken won't spend a delivery ride getting uncrunchy in the sauce. One extra tip: If you'd like to go all the way in crunchiness, don't even blend the fried chicken in the wok with the sauce before serving. Simply place the chicken on a platter and pour the hot sauce over it.

Yield: 2 to 3 servings as part
of a multicourse Chinese dinner

3 tablespoons Chinese black vinegar
1 tablespoon soy sauce (dark soy,
*   if possible)*
2 teaspoons Shao Xing (Chinese rice wine),
*   or dry sherry*
1 teaspoon minced-to-a-paste garlic
1 tablespoon sugar
1½ teaspoons sesame oil
½ pound boneless, skinless chicken thighs
6 tablespoons all-purpose flour
¼ cup plus 1 teaspoon cornstarch
1 teaspoon baking powder
¾ teaspoon salt
½ cup club soda
1 tablespoon hoisin sauce
1 teaspoon chili paste with garlic
*   (see page 158)*
½ cup chicken stock

Vegetable oil for deep-frying
1 to 3 dried red chilies, broken into pieces
10 large garlic cloves, peeled and thinly sliced
1 tablespoon grated gingerroot
½ cup loosely packed coriander leaves

1. Make the marinade: In a bowl, mix together 1 tablespoon of the vinegar, the soy sauce, Shao Xing, garlic, 1 teaspoon of the sugar, and 1 teaspoon of the sesame oil. Cut the chicken into strips that are about 1 inch long and ½ inch wide. Mix together the chicken and the marinade. Reserve in refrigerator for 3 to 4 hours (you can use it immediately, but the chicken won't be as flavorful).

2. Prepare the batter: In a bowl, mix together the flour, the ¼ cup of cornstarch, the baking powder, and the ¾ teaspoon salt. With a fork, mix in the club soda, working the batter just until it's blended; it should be slushy. Blend in 1 tablespoon of the vinegar and let the mixture sit, covered, at room temperature for 30 minutes.

3. Make the sauce: In a bowl, blend together the remaining 1 tablespoon of vinegar, the remaining 2 teaspoons of sugar, the hoisin sauce, chili paste with garlic, and chicken stock. Reserve.

4. Place the remaining 1 teaspoon of cornstarch in a cup and mix with a little cold water until a creamy liquid is formed. Reserve.

5. When ready to cook, pour vegetable oil into a wide, heavy vessel to a depth of about 2 inches. Heat to 350 degrees. Remove chicken from marinating bowl, drain, and place in reserved batter. Coat well. When oil is ready, pick chicken pieces out of batter with a fork, letting each piece drip, then place pieces in oil. After adding pieces, make sure to stir through the oil with a long utensil such as a chopstick or wooden spoon to prevent the chicken pieces from sticking to each other. If they do stick, remove them, separate them, and put them back in the oil. Cook until chicken pieces are dark golden brown outside and just cooked through inside (about 3 to 4 minutes). Remove, place on paper towels, sprinkle with a little salt, and reserve.

6. While the chicken is cooking, remove a tablespoon of the deep-frying oil and place it in a large, heavy wok over medium heat. Add the chili pieces and stir-fry for 30 seconds. Add the garlic and ginger; stir-fry until the garlic is slightly brown, about 2 minutes. Add the reserved sauce mixture and turn heat to very high. When the sauce comes to a rapid boil, let it boil for 1 minute. Stir the reserved cornstarch mixture in its cup, then whisk it into the sauce, which will become medium-thick.

7. Turn the heat down to medium. Add the fried chicken pieces; blend well with the sauce. Turn heat off. Blend in the remaining ½ teaspoon of sesame oil. Turn the dish out onto a platter and top with the coriander leaves. Serve immediately.

☆ Chinese Roast Pork ☆

Char shiu — roast pork — was at the center of the Chinese-American restaurant kitchen; even if it wasn't the star player in a dish, little morsels of it, and juices from it, appeared in many, many other dishes. I'll never forget how the elegant restaurants of the day used to serve beautiful slices of it, on a sizzle platter, with juices — alongside, in some cases, white bread and mustard! Very un-Chinese, but mighty delicious. Those slices were usually cut from the tenderloin, to ensure the least amount of fat for American diners. When I make roast pork, I prefer the more heterogeneously textured loin, a larger piece with more chewing interest. The following recipe was done with the loin — but if you prefer to use the less fatty tenderloin, this marinade should cover three of them (they weigh about a pound each). You'll have to adjust the roasting time, because they will take less time — and should be cooked in high heat all the way. One of the things I like about the larger cut is that you can cook it slowly for a while, ensuring an insane amount of juiciness within — and then crust it up with a finishing blast of heat.

Yield: 8 appetizer servings, or enough pork
for 4 stir-fried roast-pork-with-vegetable dishes

*1 loin of pork, 8 to 9 inches long,
    about 5 inches wide, weighing about
    2½ pounds*
1½ cups water
1 cup thin soy sauce
¾ cup sugar
¼ cup hoisin sauce
3 tablespoons minced garlic
1 tablespoon grated gingerroot

1. Size the pork in a large bowl for marination: make sure that it fits snugly into the bowl you choose. Remove pork from bowl and puncture it 30 to 40 times with a fork.
2. In the same bowl, mix together the water, soy sauce, sugar, hoisin sauce, garlic, and ginger. Add the pork, making sure it's covered or mostly covered by the marinade. Cover the bowl with aluminum foil, place in the refrigerator, and marinate for 24 hours.

3. When ready to cook, preheat the oven to 250 degrees. Arrange a rack in the middle of the oven and place a roasting pan half filled with water under the rack.
4. Remove the pork from the marinade and dry it extremely well with paper towels. Place it right on the rack in the oven, over the pan of water. Roast until the meat reaches 115 to 120 degrees on a meat thermometer, about 45 minutes to 1 hour. Raise heat to 475 degrees and roast until the pork reaches 145 to 150 degrees on a meat thermometer (an additional 30 to 45 minutes). Remove from oven, let rest for 10 minutes, then serve. Or you may store the roast pork and use as an ingredient in other Chinese dishes.

☆ Cantonese-Style Broccoli ☆ with Roast Pork and Oyster Sauce

Every Cantonese restaurant brings together bright greens and oyster sauce. The closer to Chinatown you get, the more likely the greens are to be gai lan or choy sum; the farther away you are, the more likely the greens are to be broccoli. They are all delicious set against the shiny, dark, salty-sweet oyster sauce — which contains a tiny percentage of oyster extract. Roast pork plays in nicely as well. But you could substitute other meats, or seafood — or leave protein out entirely and make this a vegetarian dish.

Yield: 4 servings as part of a Chinese meal

½ pound broccoli stalks
½ cup oyster sauce
1 tablespoon peanut oil

8 large garlic cloves,
     smashed and peeled
6 ounces Chinese roast pork, cut in thin, broad
     slices (see Note)
1 teaspoon Chinese sesame oil

1. Put a large pot of water over high heat and bring to a boil.

2. Meanwhile, prepare broccoli stalks. Cut a small slice from the woody ends and discard. At the other end, cut off florets — about 2 inches below the spot where the florets grow out of the stalk. You now have florets and stalk. Cut the florets in pieces; each floret should be about the diameter of a large walnut. Cut the stalks in pieces, each about 3 inches long and ½ inch thick. For both florets and stalks, working with a small, sharp knife, remove the tough, shiny green peel of the broccoli (you will see a wetter green flesh just below it).

3. When the water is boiling, add the broccoli all at once. When the water comes back to a boil, cook broccoli for 1 minute more. Remove immediately and drain on paper towels.

4. Mix the oyster sauce in a bowl with 2 tablespoons of water.

5. Place a large wok over high heat. Pour the peanut oil into it, swirling the oil around. When it's smoking, add the drained broccoli pieces. Stir-fry for 30 seconds; the pieces should pick up a little browning. Add the garlic and stir-fry with the broccoli for 30 seconds more. Add the roast pork slices and stir-fry for 30 seconds more. Turn heat to low, and add the oyster sauce–water mixture. Cook just until the sauce heats up, about 30 seconds. Stir in the sesame oil and turn out onto a platter.

NOTE: You could make the roast pork needed for this dish by following the preceding recipe. Or you could use leftover roast pork from your last Chinese take-out meal.

✯ Hunan Crispy Beef ✯ with Ginger Sauce

Soon after the Szechuan craze hit the United States in the early 1970s, the Hunan revolution followed. At the beginning, the Hunan restaurants were more elegant than the Szechuan restaurants, with fancier cooking to match. Immediately noticeable was the attention paid to texture. I'll never forget the chew of the beef in about 1974 at Uncle Tai's Hunan Yuan in Manhattan; the chefs there marinated it briefly in baking soda, which tenderized it in a most intriguing way. The following recipe brings together a few New York Hunan ideas — but the miracle is that the cheap cut of beef you use in it ends up with a fantastic chew: crispy on the outside, velvety on the inside.

Yield: 4 servings as part of a Chinese meal

½ pound bottom round or top round beef
1 scant teaspoon baking soda
Vegetable oil for frying
1 tablespoon cornstarch
¼ cup hot bean sauce with garlic (see Note)
2 tablespoons beef stock
1 tablespoon dark soy sauce
1 tablespoon grated gingerroot
1½ teaspoons sugar
2 tablespoons finely minced scallion

1. Freeze the beef slightly so that it slices more easily. Cut it into strips that are approximately ⅛ inch thick, 3 inches long, and 1½ inches wide. In a bowl, mix together the baking soda with 2 teaspoons of water. Place the beef slices in the bowl, mixing well to make sure the baking soda mixture is evenly distributed. Reserve in refrigerator for 1 hour.
2. When ready to cook, heat 3 inches of vegetable oil to 380 degrees in a large pot or wok or deep fryer. With your hands, massage 2 tablespoons of water into the beef until it is absorbed. Sprinkle the cornstarch over beef in the bowl and mix until pieces are coated evenly.
3. Meanwhile, prepare the sauce. Mix together the hot bean sauce, beef stock, soy sauce, ginger, and sugar. Set aside.
4. When the oil is hot enough, lower beef into oil. Stand over the beef with a fork or chopsticks, making sure the pieces don't stick together. You may need to deep-fry the beef in several batches. The beef is done when it's fairly dark and crispy on the outside, anywhere from 45 seconds to 1 minute. Remove cooked pieces and drain on paper towels.
5. When all the pieces are cooked, place a clean wok over medium-high heat. Add the sauce mixture. Cook for 30 seconds. Add the cooked beef, stirring to coat evenly with sauce. Turn out onto platter and sprinkle with minced scallion. Serve immediately.

NOTE: I use a hot bean sauce with garlic from Taiwan, which comes in a glass jar. It is available at Chinese grocery stores. If you can't find it, you could make a substitute by combining two tablespoons of chili paste with garlic (which is more widely available; see page 158) and two tablespoons of hoisin sauce.

☆ Classic Fried Rice ☆

This dish was a bonanza for Chinese-American restaurants: they took their leftover white rice and converted it into an item that, in the fifties and sixties, all American patrons wanted alongside their main courses. But don't let its quaint history put you off: when it's made well, fried rice is a delicious accompaniment. The most important thing in getting it right is to give the rice its first cooking two days ahead, until it's completely dry, and then let it dry out further in the refrigerator. Another secret is to incorporate some pork fat into the dish, which really gives it the restaurant flavor; a good way to do this is to throw a chunk of pork fat (cut from a piece of raw pork) into a wok and let it sizzle for a few minutes until three tablespoons of fat are rendered. Of course, the following recipe would be ameliorated by the addition of little pieces of roast pork . . . or chicken or shrimp or duck or, as in Yung Chow Fried Rice, all of them!

Yield: 4 servings as part of a Chinese meal

3 tablespoons pork fat (see Note), or peanut oil
6 scallions cut diagonally into ¼-inch pieces
½ cup chopped onion
2 large garlic cloves, finely minced
1 teaspoon finely minced or grated gingerroot
2 cups cold, cooked-dry, long-grain white rice
1 tablespoon dark soy sauce
1 teaspoon light soy sauce
1 large egg, lightly beaten
1 cup loosely packed bean sprouts

1. Heat the fat or oil in a wok over high heat. Add scallions, onion, garlic, and ginger; stir-fry until the mixture is fragrant and starting to turn brown.
2. Add the rice and cook for 2 minutes, stirring, taking care it doesn't stick. Add the soy sauces and mix gently to combine.

3. Make a well in the center of the rice and pour in the egg. Let it set for 30 seconds, then stir to scramble. Just before it sets completely, mix it with the rice, breaking it into large clumps. Add the bean sprouts and season the fried rice to taste with salt and pepper. Serve immediately.

NOTE: There are lots of ways to get the pork fat you need to make this dish taste authentic. You could use supermarket lard (my least favorite option). You could skim the fat off the top of a cold pot of Quick and Easy Cantonese-Style All-Purpose Pork Stock (page 167). You could also buy a hunk of raw pork — such as a loin that you intend to cook — cut off a half cup or so of pork fat, and sizzle that fat in a wok until you have about three tablespoons of fat rendered. Then you discard the solid pork that's left and begin the fried rice recipe with the fat remaining in the wok.

Japanese Food

The recent history of Japanese restaurants in America is nothing short of startling — because the prior history of Japanese restaurants in America was just a little short of nonexistent.

Up to the 1970s or so, most Americans — the same Americans who were ordering Chinese food twice a week — knew very little about Japanese food. Big cities had a few Japanese restaurants, and our pockets of Japanese population — principally in California and Hawaii — could boast of a few more. But most Americans had their only exposure to Japanese food at Benihana restaurants — which offered lots of good showmanship but a very odd rendering of Japan's great and subtle cuisine.

A number of cuisines in America — such as Japanese and French — have had the same obstacle to overcome: if the essence of your cuisine is fresh and outstanding ingredients, and if you can't develop a "substitute" cuisine that can forge ahead without those ingredients — as the Italians and Chinese managed to do — you're not going to get far in America.

Intriguingly, however, everything turned around for the Japanese about thirty years ago. All that incredible raw fish that forms the ingredient backbone of sushi bars in Japan — fish that was simply unavailable here, or unavailable at an appropriate level of freshness, for most of our history — started becoming available to American sushi chefs. And why not? Some of it was coming from American waters. Today you've got fish buyers from Japan elbow to elbow with fish buyers from American restaurants on the docks of Boston and at the fish market in Honolulu, vying for the outstanding sushi-bound fish coming out of American waters.

And most of all: you've now got the midtown areas of our cities overrun with sushi bars, and the suburban areas not far behind. In my residential neighborhood, on the Upper West Side of Manhattan, I used to have to choose from among a dozen sushi bars within a ten-minute walk of my house. Things have changed in the last year — now I have to pick from nearly two dozen! There's no question that Italian restaurants still dominate the ethnic dining scene in America and that Chinese restaurants and Mexican restaurants come after that. But to select the next big ethnic player, I submit, you'd have to consider the tidal wave of sushi bars that have come out of nowhere in the last twenty years. And best of all: the sushi being made at these places is excellent. If one had to choose an ethnic restaurant cuisine in America that comes closest to that ethnic food on its home turf, sushi would be a leading candidate.

But we still have a long way to go. There's a lot more to Japanese dining than sushi — and, though sushi bars often serve other types of Japanese cuisine, and though there has been an increase in Japanese restaurants that focus on other Japanese foods (meat cooked in front of you has always been popular; noodle houses are getting more popular), it's the sushi that has put Japanese cuisine on our restaurant map.

How about on our home cookin' map? Japanese food is not there yet, not by a long shot. For one thing, the very type of Japanese food that has Americans excited — sushi — will probably never be something that Americans prepare at home. It looks simple, but looks can be deceiving; a great deal of training is required to turn out sushi that sparkles. Moreover, there are real health questions about eating raw fish — and it takes the trained eye of a sushi master to determine what's edible and what's dangerous. For both of these reasons, I'm not

including sushi recipes in the following section, nor am I expecting that anyone will miss them. Even in Japan, eating sushi means going to the sushi bar!

However, there are many other Japanese foods that are wonderful to make at home. We've already shown our willingness to consume Japanese-style noodles at home; almost every supermarket in America sells quick ramen noodles. From there it's a short step to the glories of soba. And many of the Japanese foods suggest great dinner parties: set up a deep fryer, master a tempura recipe (like the one on page 189), and give your Saturday-night guests something wonderful that they weren't expecting.

☆ Japanese Breakfast, ☆ with Salmon, Rice, Eggs, Soy, and Seaweed

One of the most surprising ways in which Japanese food is having an impact on American dining habits is at breakfast! Many American business travelers to Hawaii and California now open their breakfast menus at their hotels and see an item called Japanese Breakfast, usually priced at about twenty dollars. It is a wonderfully light and clean way to start the day, very far from the traditional American breakfast. Me, I'm out-and-out crazy about it: a bowl of rice tossed with raw egg and seaweed; a piece of grilled fish, usually salmon; a quivering, hot egg custard; a simple salad of lightly pickled cucumbers and octopus slices; a great bowl of miso soup with bean curd. The following recipes for all the components come from my favorite hotel in America for the Japanese breakfast (and just about my favorite spot anywhere to wake up in) — the remarkably serene and wonderful Halekulani in Honolulu.

Yield: Serve all the following six recipes together and you have breakfast for 4

★ Sunomono ★
with Cucumber and Octopus

Yield: 4 breakfast servings

6 ounces English cucumber, washed, sliced into
    paper-thin slices
1⅛ teaspoons salt
1 cup cool water
1½ tablespoons rice vinegar
2 teaspoons sugar
¼ teaspoon Japanese soy sauce
½ cup dried wakame (Japanese seaweed,
    see Seaweed note)
3 ounces cooked octopus, sliced paper-thin
    into rounds (see Octopus note)
1 tablespoon fresh gingerroot, peeled and
    cut into thin julienne

1. In a large mixing bowl combine the sliced cucumber, 1 teaspoon of the salt, and the cool water. Mix the cucumbers through the liquid with a spoon to thoroughly blend the salt and water. Let the mixture stand for 10 minutes, then drain off the liquid.
2. In a small bowl combine the remaining ⅛ teaspoon salt, rice vinegar, sugar, and soy sauce. Blend well.

3. Place the dried wakame in a small bowl and top it with 3 inches of very hot tap water. Let the seaweed hydrate for about 3 minutes before using.
4. In a small bowl, combine the salted cucumbers, the soy sauce mixture, the hydrated wakame, octopus, and ginger. Toss the mixture gently to combine thoroughly and let stand at room temperature for 30 minutes prior to serving.

SEAWEED NOTE: The dried wakame you want is black colored and in very tight, small curls; after you hydrate it, it should unfurl into surprisingly wide, dark green ribbons of seaweed.

OCTOPUS NOTE: Cooked octopus is a standard sushi-bar item. If you cannot find it at a Japanese grocery, you might want to ask your local sushi chef if he'll sell you some. If these plans fail, you could substitute about ½ cup of shrimp that have been boiled, peeled, deveined, and cut in half lengthwise.

★ Chawan-mushi ★

Yield: 4 breakfast servings

2 large eggs
1 cup prepared Dashi (Japanese soup stock),
    cooled (page 186; instant dashi is also
    acceptable)
¼ teaspoon salt
½ teaspoon Japanese soy sauce
1 teaspoon mirin (sweet rice wine)
1 tablespoon peanut oil (for oiling ramekins)

1. Preheat oven to 350 degrees and bring a teakettle-full of water to a boil.

2. Combine the eggs, dashi, salt, soy sauce, and mirin in a medium-size bowl and whisk them together. Strain the mixture through a fine strainer into a measuring cup with a pouring spout.

3. Place four oiled, 3-ounce ramekins or minisoufflé dishes on a baking pan that is about 9 by 9 by 2 inches. Carefully fill each of the ramekins about three quarters of the way with the egg mixture. Add the boiling water to the baking pan to form a water bath; fill the pan just halfway up the sides of the ramekins. Carefully place the pan in the oven and bake for 20 minutes, or until custards are set.

★ Boiled Rice with Egg ★ and Soy Sauce Dressing

The hot rice cooks the egg, which then acts as a sauce for the rice.

Yield: 4 breakfast servings

2 cups uncooked sushi rice (short-grained sticky rice)
2½ cups water for cooking, more for washing
2 large eggs
2 tablespoons Japanese soy sauce

1. Place the rice in a medium-size bowl. Run cool water into the bowl while agitating the

A perfectly arranged Japanese Breakfast for one, on a bamboo mat

rice with your hand for 1 minute. Run more water on the rice, letting it run off into the sink; do this until the water runs clear. This takes about 2 minutes.

2. Combine the rice with the 2½ cups water in a medium-size heavy-bottomed saucepan that has a tight-fitting lid. Rapidly bring it to a boil over high heat, then reduce the heat to low; cover, and cook the rice for 20 minutes. Do not lift the lid. Remove from heat and let the saucepan rest, covered, for 10 more minutes. It is very important that you serve the rice while it is piping hot.

3. Break the eggs in a small mixing bowl and whisk them together with the soy sauce. Divide raw egg mixture among 4 small, decorative bowls. Place bowls on serving table, along with 4 bowls of hot rice. Each diner pours the desired amount of raw egg mixture on his or her hot rice.

★ Miso Soup ★

The miso recipe on page 186 is great for breakfast and will make 4 breakfast portions.

★ Grilled or Broiled Salmon ★

Yield: 4 breakfast servings

4 fresh salmon fillets, 2 to 3 ounces each
2 tablespoons peanut oil

1. Preheat the oven broiler, an outdoor grill, or a grill pan.

2. Using a pasty brush, gently brush the fresh salmon fillets with the oil. Season them with salt and pepper to taste.

3. Broil or grill the salmon fillets, using high heat, for about 2 minutes per side. This will yield "medium-rare" salmon; cook a little further if desired. Serve immediately.

★ Strips of Nori ★

A great accompaniment to the Japanese breakfast is toasted seaweed strips to sprinkle over rice — or over other things, if you wish.

Yield: 4 breakfast servings

2 sheets of nori

1. Slightly toast the sheets of nori on all sides until they are crisp, by holding for about 30 seconds over a medium gas flame.

2. Using scissors, cut the sheets of nori into strips that are about ½ inch wide. Divide the strips into 4 portions and serve them to each diner on a small plate along with the Japanese breakfast.

NOTE: Another possibility for the dried-seaweed element in a Japanese breakfast is furikake — bits of nori that are mixed with bits of other flavors (dried fish, sesame seed) and marketed in jars. I call them Japanese sprinkles — and they are delicious!

☆ Edamame ☆

Suddenly, edamame (pronounced ed-a-MAH-may) — a variety of soybean harvested when green and immature — are everywhere at the start of Japanese restaurant meals. Almost completely absent from the Japanese-American dining scene as little as ten years ago, they are now either a giveaway before your meal or an à la carte option that many diners choose. They arrive at your table warm, in fuzzy, inedible green pods with salt sprinkled all over them. You liberate the beans from their pods with your teeth and pop 'em into your mouth; the subtle, almost lima bean flavor makes you want to keep popping. You can find them in Japanese stores, cooked and refrigerated, or frozen. You can even find them fresh, in season — which runs from June to October. I think that if you're going to the trouble of finding them, you might as well do it the Japanese way and cook them yourself in season — especially since the cooking's real easy. A great way to start a Japanese dinner party!

Yield: 3 to 4 premeal snack servings

3 quarts water
½ pound fresh edamame
1 tablespoon plus 1 teaspoon sea salt
2 quarts of cold water in a bowl
  with a large scoop of ice

1. Bring the 3 quarts of water to a boil in a large pot. Meanwhile, rub beans with the 1 tablespoon of salt. When water is boiling, add beans and boil over high heat for 6 to 10 minutes, or until beans are tender. To test, plunge a pod in ice water, pop out a bean, and taste.
2. When beans are cooked to taste, remove from boiling water with a large strainer. Add the 1 teaspoon of salt to the cold water. Submerge beans in ice bath for 30 seconds. Remove, drain, and sprinkle with additional sea salt if desired. Serve in small bowls.

☆ Dashi ☆

Before you move on to other Japanese dishes, you're going to need dashi. This seaweed-and-dried-fish stock is one of the fundamental elements of the Japanese kitchen; it is a building block for many, many dishes in the Japanese repertoire. Dashi is very simple

to make; finding the ingredients is a whole lot trickier. But any good Japanese grocery will carry dried bonito flakes and kelp, a type of dried seaweed. Ironically, if you have access to those ingredients, you probably have access to something else as well: instant dashi powder, which is certainly the most acceptable powdered "stock" or "bouillon" of any kind that I've ever tasted.

Yield: 2 quarts

2 quarts plus ¼ cup cold water
1½ ounces (45 grams) kombu
  (giant kelp)
2 ounces dried bonito flakes

1. Place the 2 quarts of water and the kombu in a large saucepan over medium heat and bring to just under a boil.
2. Remove the kombu and discard; add the ¼ cup of cold water and the bonito flakes. Again, bring the liquid to just under a boil. Then turn off the heat and let the mixture steep for 1 minute.
3. Pass the mixture through a fine mesh sieve. Dashi is best used right away but can be refrigerated for up to a week or frozen for about a month.

☆ Miso Soup with Tofu ☆

Almost every diner in every sushi bar in America today is given a choice: salad or miso soup? Because of this, miso soup, and miso, have become known to millions of Americans. But miso is actually a broad, complicated subject. It is always fermented soybean paste, but the way it's made can yield hundreds of different variations. The consumer in Japan has access to many,

many different styles and brands — and since the average Japanese consumer eats miso every day, he or she has lots of knowledge and opinions about the subject. It's much easier here. Japanese groceries, and some gourmet stores, now carry a few styles of miso, usually identified by color (lighter ones are less intense in flavor). If you wish to make miso soup at home — and you should, because it's easy and a dead ringer for what you get in restaurants — all you have to do is buy the miso and combine it with a few other ingredients. It is a wonderful soup any time — particularly in winter, when you might want to enrich your miso with pieces of fish, shellfish, and vegetables.

Yield: 4 first-course servings

⅛ cup aka miso (red)
1 teaspoon shiro miso (white)
2 cups hot Dashi (see preceding recipe;
    instant dashi is acceptable)
1 cup firm tofu, diced into ½-inch cubes
2 teaspoons dried wakame
    (Japanese seaweed)
2 scallions (green and white parts), washed and
    thinly sliced on a bias
½ cup enoki mushrooms (remove the bottom
    parts around the root area)

1. Place the aka miso and shiro miso in a 2-quart saucepan. Whisk in a few tablespoons of the hot dashi, making a smooth paste. Whisk in the rest of the dashi and place the saucepan over medium heat. Heat the miso until it's just below the boiling point.
2. Divide the tofu, dried wakame, scallions, and mushrooms among four bowls. Three minutes before serving, pour the hot miso broth over the garnishes. Let rest, covered if possible, for 3 minutes. Serve immediately.

☆ Cold Soba Noodles ☆ with Dipping Sauce
(Mori-Soba)

The consumption of soba noodles is practically a cult in Japan, with its own history, lore, rituals, and rules. We haven't reached that stage of connoisseurship in the United States — but soba is now widely available in Japanese restaurants here, and there are even a few restaurants, à la Tokyo, devoted exclusively to soba. The noodles are made from buckwheat flour, and this may be why they inspire such passion: they are firmer, more textured, more flavorful than most other noodles of the world. The noodles may be either freshly made (which is what soba restaurants do) or dried and sold in stores (this is the soba I recommend you use at home). There are two main ways of eating soba: cold (called mori-soba, which means "piled soba"), and hot (see following recipe for description of hot soba). The cold soba noodles, particularly popular in summer, are often served on bamboo screens, which allow excess moisture to drip off (feel free to simply serve your cold soba on a plate). Garnishes are presented, and the noodles are dipped quickly in a dipping sauce.

Yield: 4 first-course servings

½ pound dried soba noodles
1 (8 by 7-inch) sheet of nori (seaweed)
¼ cup finely minced scallion, rinsed and
    patted dry
2 teaspoons finely grated daikon radish, squeezed
    and drained of excess moisture
½ teaspoon prepared wasabi (green Japanese
    horseradish, usually available as a
    powder then mixed with water),
    or more to taste
1¼ cups Noodle Dipping Sauce
    (recipe follows)

1. Bring a large pot of generously salted water to a boil and add the soba, stirring well to separate the noodles. Return the water to a boil. Add 1 cup of cold water and return to a boil again. Repeat the process of adding cold water and returning to a boil 2 or 3 more times, until the noodles are just tender but still firm to the bite (see Note). Immediately drain the noodles and rinse under cold running water for a few minutes, massaging as you rinse, to release the surface starch. Drain the noodles well and set aside to cool.

2. Bring a gas flame on your range to medium and, holding the sheet of nori with kitchen tongs, pass it back and forth over the flame on one side only, until it is lightly toasted and crisp. Be careful not to burn it. Alternatively, you can toast the nori over an electric burner set on high. With a sharp knife or scissors, cut the nori into pieces 1 by ⅛ inch and reserve.

3. To serve: Divide the scallion, daikon, and wasabi among four small serving plates, each plate carrying a bit of the three ingredients. Divide the Noodle Dipping Sauce among four small bowls. Place equal portions of the soba attractively on four serving plates or in Japanese noodle baskets and top each portion with a quarter of the reserved nori. At the table, each diner can season his or her dipping sauce with the scallion, daikon, and wasabi, to taste. Then, picking up the noodles with chopsticks or a fork, each diner dips the noodles into the sauce before eating.

NOTE: The texture of the soba is the soul of this dish, so test the noodles frequently as they cook. There will come a point when they are almost limp but have the barest trace of a firmness at the core, an uncooked center you can actually see when you bite into it (the Italian notion of al dente). At this point they will need no more than another minute of cooking.

★ Noodle Dipping Sauce ★

Yield: 1¼ cups

1 cup Dashi (page 186)
3 tablespoons dark soy sauce
2 tablespoons mirin (sweet rice wine for cooking)
1 teaspoon sugar
½ ounce (15 grams) dried bonito flakes

Mix the dashi, soy sauce, mirin, and sugar in a small pot and bring to just under a boil. Remove from the heat and add the bonito flakes. Let the mixture steep for 10 to 20 seconds, pass it through a fine mesh strainer, and allow it to come to room temperature before serving.

✲ Hot Soba Noodles in Broth ✲
(Kake-Soba)

The other soba option is hot soba noodles served in a hot, flavorful broth. Classically speaking, you don't want too much broth — because an old Japanese tradition holds that the diner who eats too much broth with his soba doesn't appreciate the noodles themselves and is probably an unsophisticate from the sticks. Don't be afraid to slurp those noodles, however, which even the city slickers do — because slurping enables you to cool them as you eat them, which means you can eat them while they're still hot, which means they won't get soft in the broth as they sit waiting for you to deem them cool enough. Some Japanese diners like to add an egg to the soba experience; you can either break a raw one into each bowl of hot soba (stirring it in) or poach an egg for each bowl and float the egg on top of the noodles.

Yield: 4 main-course servings

1 pound dried soba
5½ cups Noodle Broth (recipe follows)
4 tablespoons minced scallion
Shichimi togarashi (Japanese seven-spice
mixture)

1. Bring a large stockpot of generously salted water to a boil and add the soba, stirring well to separate the noodles. Return the water to a boil. Add 1 cup of cold water and return to a boil again. Repeat the process of adding cold water and returning to a boil 2 or 3 more times, until the noodles are just tender but still firm to the bite. Place noodles in colander. Immediately rinse the noodles under cold running water for a few minutes, massaging as you rinse, to release the surface starch. Drain the noodles well.
2. Divide the noodles among four large soup bowls. Divide the noodle broth evenly among the bowls; garnish each with minced scallion and a few pinches of shichimi. Serve immediately, passing additional shichimi at the table.

★ Noodle Broth ★

Yield: 5½ cups

5¼ cups Dashi (page 186)
3 tablespoons plus 1 teaspoon dark soy sauce
1½ tablespoons mirin (sweet rice wine
for cooking)
1½ tablespoons sugar
1¼ teaspoons kosher salt

Combine all the ingredients in a medium saucepan and bring just to a boil, stirring once or twice to dissolve the sugar and salt. Serve hot with soba noodles.

☆ Tempura ☆

This remarkably light Japanese frying technique (which, apparently, Japanese cooks learned from the Portuguese) has become a mainstay at Japanese restaurants in America, even sushi bars. In Japan they don't like to mix cooking styles at the same meal — so there are many restaurants dedicated to tempura alone that don't serve other things. This is a great concept for an American party. On the kitchen counter, line up a deep fryer, the batter, and an array of different ingredients (mostly seafood and vegetables) to be dipped and fried. Dip and fry a few at a time, offer the morsels to guests as the food is cooked, make sure the wine or sake is flowing — and everyone will have a great tempura party! Of course, first you have to have a great tempura recipe — and, frankly, most of the quick-mix ice-water-and-flour recipes I see in Japanese cookbooks don't really do the job. I'm always looking for ultralight, lacy, crisp, golden tempura — and by throwing a few surprise ingredients into the following recipe, I think I've finally found it.

Yield: 4 servings

Seafood and vegetables for deep-frying
(see Note)
Vegetable oil for deep-frying
½ cup rice flour
½ cup Wondra (quick-mixing flour)
1 teaspoon baking powder
½ teaspoon salt
1 cup chilled club soda
Tempura Dipping Sauce (recipe follows)

★☆★

1. Before preparing batter, make sure all seafood and vegetable items are peeled and/or trimmed and ready to go.

2. In a large deep saucepan, place 4 inches of vegetable oil. When oil reaches about 300 degrees, make batter.

3. In a small bowl, sift together rice flour, Wondra, baking powder, and salt. Using chopsticks and working quickly, stir in club soda until just blended. Make sure the batter remains lumpy. Place batter bowl in another larger bowl filled with ice water while you fry.

4. When oil reaches 365 degrees, dip 5 or so pieces of seafood and/or vegetables in batter. Place morsels in oil, one at a time. Fry 2 to 3 minutes, or until crisp but not too dark; tempura should remain light in color. Remove the pieces and drain on paper towels. Pieces can be held in a warm oven for a few minutes while you fry more, but ideally they should be eaten as soon as possible. When oil returns to 365 degrees, repeat with additional pieces. Serve with dipping sauce.

NOTE: The exact roster of foods to be fried is up to you. I always like to include some shrimp and some vegetables. The amount of batter in this recipe will cover a half pound of medium shrimp — peeled, deveined, and scored three times — and any three of the following:

- ✪ 1 small sweet potato, peeled and cut into ¼-inch-thick slices
- ✪ 1 large carrot, peeled and cut into ¼-inch-thick slices
- ✪ 1 Japanese eggplant, peeled and cut into ¼-inch-thick slices
- ✪ 12 broccoli florets
- ✪ 12 green beans or snow peas, trimmed
- ✪ 12 small shiitake or other mushroom caps

You may use any vegetables you like, of course . . . but avoid wet ones, such as cucumber or tomato.

★ Tempura Dipping Sauce ★

It's best to make this sauce in advance and let it chill in the refrigerator for a few hours. If you can find daikon — Japanese white radish — you might want to grate some and add it to the sauce at the last minute; the Japanese believe it helps to digest oily foods. If you're feeling a little more ambitious, serve your tempura with Ponzu Sauce (recipe follows).

> *1 cup dashi (see Note)*
> *¼ cup mirin (sweet rice wine for cooking)*
> *¼ cup soy sauce*
> *1 teaspoon rice wine vinegar*
> *1 (1-inch piece) gingerroot, peeled and julienned*

Combine all ingredients.

NOTE: Dashi is Japanese soup stock, made from dried bonito flakes and dried kelp (see recipe on page 186). Happily, there's a wonderful product available at Japanese groceries that makes life easier for everybody: powdered dashi bouillon, the only powdered stock I've ever loved. If you don't make the dashi from scratch and can't get the powder, you can use fish stock or bottled clam juice instead.

☆ Ponzu Sauce ☆

Every once in a while a somewhat obscure element of a foreign cuisine gets pistol hot in the United States, takes on cachet, even breaks out of its ethnic confines. Such an element in the current American environment is ponzu sauce — a mixture of Japanese citrus juices, soy sauce, and other flavors, used in Japan as a dipping sauce. American sushi bars sometimes offer it as a dipping sauce — but multiculti fusion chefs across the land have swiped it from the sushi bar and given it a more prominent position in their creations. In Japan ponzu is made from a variety of sour citrus fruits, the most well known one being yuzu. Yuzu is quite rare in the United States, though good Japanese groceries carry yuzu juice. My favorite Japanese cookbook (*Japanese Cooking: A Simple Art,* by Shizuo Tsuji) gives a good lemon juice–lime juice substitute for yuzu. I think the substitute tastes even more like the real juice if you throw in some lime zest. Tsuji recommends storing the ponzu for three months to develop flavor. But I find that adding more bonito flakes today means you can enjoy the sauce tomorrow. Many chefs in America leave out the dried fish entirely, but I think the results are insipid. Enjoy it with anything Asian that could use a lively dip, particularly seafood and vegetables: steamed fish, grilled lobster, sautéed Chinese vegetables. Excellent with the preceding tempura as well.

Yield: About 2½ cups

½ cup lemon juice (about 8 lemons)

¼ cup lime juice (about 6 limes)

2 teaspoons grated lime zest

⅓ cup plus 3 tablespoons rice vinegar

¼ teaspoon salt

1 cup dark soy sauce

½ cup mirin (sweet rice wine for cooking)

¾ cup dried bonito flakes (a little less than an ounce)

1 (2-inch) square kombu (giant kelp)

1. Combine lemon juice, lime juice, lime zest, 2 teaspoons of the rice vinegar, and salt in a medium-size bowl. Stir to combine ingredients; let sit for 30 minutes so that the citrus mixture can absorb the flavor of the lime zest.

2. In a small bowl, combine the remaining rice vinegar with the soy sauce.

3. Pour mirin into a small saucepan. Bring to a boil over high heat and boil until the liquid has reduced by half, about 2 minutes. Pour hot liquid into a small bowl and let cool.

4. Strain the citrus mixture through a fine mesh strainer, removing the lime zest and any seeds. Add the strained citrus mixture to the vinegar-soy mixture. Whisk until well blended. Add the mirin, bonito flakes, and kombu, whisking until combined. Cover sauce with plastic wrap and let sit 24 hours before serving. Strain before serving.

☆ Salmon Teriyaki ☆

One of the few Japanese cooking words widely known to Americans is *teriyaki* — thanks to the spread of bottled sauces known as teriyaki sauce. Originally, however, teriyaki was more of a glaze for grilled food than a sauce. The following recipe follows the current practice of many Japanese restaurants in the United States: the "teriyaki" here is poised deliciously between a glaze and a sauce. The recipe also includes a wonderful Japanese technique for lightening oily fish such as salmon: after the initial cooking of the fish, boiled water is poured over it to wash away some of the heavy fish oil.

Yield: 4 main-course servings

¼ cup light soy sauce

3 tablespoons mirin (sweet rice wine for cooking)

2 tablespoons sake

2 tablespoons firmly packed brown sugar

1½ tablespoons finely chopped gingerroot

2 garlic cloves, peeled and crushed

4 (6-ounce) center-cut salmon fillets with skin

1 tablespoon canola oil

1 tablespoon toasted sesame seeds

2 scallions (green parts only), thinly sliced

1. In a small saucepan, combine soy sauce, mirin, sake, brown sugar, ginger, and garlic. Bring to a boil, reduce heat, and simmer 2 minutes to blend flavors. Remove sauce from heat and cool to room temperature.

2. When ready to serve, season salmon with freshly ground pepper to taste (you won't need salt, as the sauce is salty enough). Bring a kettle of water to a boil. Heat a large non-stick skillet over high heat and add canola oil. Place salmon fillets skin side down in pan and cook until skin is crispy, about 2 minutes.

3. Carefully remove salmon from pan. Place skin side down in a large colander and immediately pour boiling water over salmon. Return salmon to pan, flesh side down. Cook until brown, about 2 minutes longer. Flip fish, pour sauce into pan, and bring to a boil. Boil until sauce is reduced by half, brushing fish with sauce as it cooks, until fish is lightly glazed, about 2 minutes more. Divide the fish among four plates. Sprinkle fish with sesame seeds and scallions, dividing the seeds and scallions evenly among the 4 pieces of fish. Serve immediately.

✹ Tonkatsu ✹

Tonkatsu has become extraordinarily popular at Japanese restaurants in America. Let's face it: we love deep-fried food, and this is one of the world's great deep-fried dishes. But don't think tempura batter when you think tonkatsu — for this fried pork (or sometimes chicken) cutlet is coated instead in panko crumbs, those amazingly light, puffy, crispy Japanese creations. The dish, years ago, developed in Japan through the influence of Portuguese sailors — and even its sauce, today, has Western touches, with the inclusion of ketchup and Worcestershire sauce. Come to think of it . . . why doesn't someone open a chain of Japanese KFC shops: Kyoto Fried Chicken?

Yield: 4 main-course servings

Canola oil for frying
½ cup ketchup
2 tablespoons dark soy sauce
1 tablespoon rice vinegar
4 teaspoons sugar
1½ teaspoons Worcestershire sauce
1 teaspoon grated gingerroot
1 pound boneless pork loin, cut into
  8 slices
½ cup all-purpose flour
2 eggs beaten with 1 tablespoon water
3 cups panko crumbs
Finely sliced green cabbage for serving
Lemon wedges for garnish

1. In a large skillet, heat oil to 375 degrees.

2. In a small bowl, combine ketchup, soy sauce, vinegar, sugar, Worcestershire sauce, and ginger. Cover sauce and refrigerate until ready to serve.

3. Place a pork slice between 2 pieces of plastic wrap. Using a meat mallet, pound to about ½-inch thickness. Repeat with remaining pork. Season on both sides with salt and pepper.

4. In each of 3 shallow bowls, place flour, eggs, and panko crumbs. Season all with salt

and pepper. Dredge a pork slice in flour, tapping off the excess. Dip in eggs, then panko crumbs. Repeat with remaining pork.

5. Fry pork slices 2 at a time until golden and crispy, about 4 minutes total, turning once after 2 minutes. Drain on paper towels and keep warm in a 250-degree oven until all pork is cooked. Serve over finely shredded cabbage and garnish with lemon wedges. Serve the sauce in individual bowls on the side for dipping.

Korean Food

Of all the major Asian cuisines that have established a restaurant presence in the United States, Korean food has caused the fewest ripples in the gastronomic lake. To those who know and love Korean food, this is difficult to understand. It is a fascinating cuisine, with the kind of strong, direct flavors that Americans love.

I suspect that the trouble stems from the organization of the Korean menu. Other Asian cuisines on their home turfs are, like Korean cuisine, not decisive about exactly which dishes are appetizers, which are second courses, which are main courses; in some countries there are no course divisions at the table at all. But the menus of most other kinds of Asian restaurants in America cater to the hometown crowd — inventing, if necessary, a meal order that follows American expectations. The Korean restaurant owners, as yet, have not done this; I know people willing to experiment with Korean food who feel lost as soon as a Korean menu is placed in their hands.

Despite this roadblock, Korean food seems to be getting more press and more attention all the time. One of the measures of progress is the location of Korean restaurants; once confined to the Korean areas of major cities (Koreatown in Los Angeles, the area just south of Macy's in New York, "Shambodia" in Atlanta), Korean restaurants are now spreading into non-Korean areas. It remains to be seen whether these satellite establishments will stick to the wonderful authenticity demonstrated in the older restaurants. For Korean food in the United States, at least until now, has the classic mark of a late arrival: authentic ingredients were available from the beginning, and there hasn't been time for the cuisine to morph into anything else.

But morph it will, almost certainly, as Americans discover the joys of Korean food at home. And I think it's likely many more will make this discovery — for what's more Korean, or American, than a backyard beef barbecue, with all kinds of spicy marinades and condiments? The Koreans, like us Americans, are among the world's greatest beef mavens, and among the world's most avid grill-meisters. Some of the following recipes suggest a path that the Americanization of Korean food might take.

✸ Napa Cabbage Kimchi ✸

Americans have good reason to associate kimchi with napa cabbage; one of my Korean sources tells me that more than 75 percent of all kimchi made in Korea is made with choson paech'u, or napa cabbage. Delicious in taste, lovely in texture, this cabbage preserves extremely well, since about 90 percent of the cabbage's liquid is drawn out of it during the salting phase of kimchi making. The following napa cabbage kimchi will, in fact, keep well in your refrigerator longer than the cucumber kimchi that follows; I enjoy it for four to six weeks after I've made it. Koreans often put a little salted shrimp in their napa cabbage kimchi; the product they use is hard to find, so I've substituted Thai or Vietnamese fish sauce.

Kimchi Here, Kimchi There

Americans are starting to develop a genuine passion for kimchi — perhaps, in part, because it's a quick-to-eat, amazingly vivid bite that comes with very little caloric guilt.

But there are some broad misconceptions here about Korea's most famous dish.

Most important is the basic definition of kimchi. Because we in the United States so often see kimchi made from napa cabbage — in the Korean restaurants that are booming in major American cities, even in grocery stores and supermarkets — many people assume that that's what kimchi is: a kind of cabbage pickle made with salt, spices, and garlic. The pickle part is right, because the cabbage does ferment — but in Korea there are approximately two hundred kinds of kimchi, made from all manner of vegetables, herbs, fruits, even fish.

Sometimes, conversely, our misconception is too broad rather than too narrow. Americans who go to Korean restaurants love the amazing array of small dishes that are usually served "on the house" to go with meals. Sometimes these are all assumed to be kimchi — but they're not. These small side dishes are called panchan, and usually, of the dozen or so you're served, only three or four are the fermented wonders called kimchi.

In Korea, where kimchi goes back two thousand years, life is sometimes organized around this dish. Many Koreans live with their pots of fermenting kimchi; the traditional jahng dak, or kimchi pot, was typically stored on the roof of one's home or buried in one's garden or sequestered in parts of one's house. Today it is more common for a Korean home owner to have a special refrigerator set at forty degrees in which the kimchi can ferment perfectly over two to three months.

There is also a mass national ritual in Korea with the approach of winter — the kimchang ch'ol, or kimchi-making season, in which many, many people make and put up their kimchi supply for the cold weather. The type of kimchi made, broadly speaking, is kimjang kimchi, or winter kimchi — which is usually heartier kimchi with larger chunks of vegetables (such as whole heads of cabbage), sometimes made with complicated layering techniques.

It is not common in the United States to see these types of winter kimchi; our products much more closely resemble the cut-up, faster-to-ferment, simpler kimchis that the Koreans associate with summer. In fact, to make the kimchi recipes in this section, you don't have to worry about kimchi jars or even about carefully sterilized jars (though it's never a bad idea to sterilize). These kimchis can go in any old jars that have lids, and they are good right after you make them.

✩✩✩✩✩✩✩✩✩✩✩✩✩✩✩✩✩✩✩✩✩✩✩✩✩✩✩✩✩✩✩✩✩✩✩✩✩✩

7 tablespoons kosher salt

2 quarts cold water

1 (2½- to 3-pound) napa cabbage,
  split lengthwise

3 tablespoons minced garlic

1 tablespoon plus 1 teaspoon
  grated gingerroot

3 tablespoons ground dried red chili
  (more or less, to taste), or crushed
  red pepper

2 tablespoons sugar

4 tablespoons Thai or Vietnamese fish sauce

4 tablespoons hot water

8 large scallions, white and pale green parts
  minced, green tops split and cut into
  2-inch lengths

1 cup peeled and julienned daikon radish
  (cut in rounds ⅛ inch thick,
  then in julienne strips 3 inches long)

I. In a large mixing bowl, dissolve 3 tablespoons of the salt in the cold water and immerse the cabbage halves, spreading the leaves slightly to allow the water to reach all the surfaces. Weight the cabbage pieces with a plate to submerge them, and soak for 5 minutes. Remove the cabbage and thoroughly rinse under running water. Gently squeeze the cabbage to remove excess water, and place on paper towels for a few minutes to drain. Sprinkle and rub the remaining 4 tablespoons of salt between the leaves of cabbage, lifting each leaf with one hand while sprinkling and rubbing with the other, until all the surfaces have been coated. Place the cabbage halves in a glass or ceramic dish and set aside at room temperature for 3 hours.

2. Rinse, squeeze, and drain the cabbage as you did in the previous step. Chop the cabbage halves crosswise into 1½-inch pieces and reserve. In a large bowl, combine the garlic, ginger, ground chili, sugar, fish sauce, hot water, and the minced scallion, stirring well to dissolve the sugar. Add the cabbage, the split scallion tops, and the radish, mixing all the ingredients thoroughly with a rubber spatula. Serve immediately or pack the kimchi (and all the remaining liquid) into a jar with a screw top and allow the mixture to ripen in the refrigerator for up to a month.

✺ Cucumber Kimchi ✺

I love the refreshing quality of cucumber kimchi.

5 firm, fresh Kirby cucumbers (about 1 pound
  total), washed, ends trimmed, quartered
  lengthwise, and cut crosswise in half (in
  spears that are about 2½ inches long)

2 tablespoons kosher salt

½ small onion, very thinly sliced,
  slices cut in half

1 teaspoon minced garlic

1 teaspoon grated gingerroot

1 teaspoon ground dried red chili

1 tablespoon plus 1 teaspoon minced scallion
  (white and pale green parts only)

1 tablespoon plus 1 teaspoon sugar

2 tablespoons Thai or Vietnamese fish sauce

2 teaspoons hot water

1 tablespoon toasted sesame oil

2 teaspoons toasted sesame seeds

1. Place the cucumber spears in a large bowl, sprinkle evenly with the salt, and toss well to coat the pieces. Set aside at room temperature for 3 hours. Meanwhile, soak the onion slices in a small bowl of cold water for 30 minutes. Drain, blot dry, and reserve.

2. Drain the cucumber pieces and gently blot dry on paper towels. In a large bowl, combine the garlic, ginger, ground chili, scallion, sugar, fish sauce, and hot water, stirring to dissolve the sugar. Add the reserved cucumber and onion, tossing well to combine. Serve immediately or store for up to 1 week in the refrigerator. Just before serving, toss with the sesame oil and garnish with the sesame seeds.

✿ Bulgogi ✿
(Korean Barbecued Beef)

In Korea the most revered cut of beef for slicing and barbecuing is kalbi, or short ribs — and kalbi is indeed on the menus of all Korean barbecue houses in the United States. But when the menu says "bulgogi," you can be sure that the meat is not short ribs, since anything from tenderloin to round to sirloin may be used. The skirt steak called for in this recipe is absolutely delicious, and very Korean tasting, though it's not a traditional choice. But you must give it its traditional serving context. Slice it as it comes off the grill, then have your guests wrap the slices in lettuce leaves with their choice of soybean paste/toenjang (you may substitute brown miso), red pepper paste/kochujang (you may substitute Chinese chili paste with garlic; see page 158), steamed white rice (each roll-up needs a few tablespoons of rice), and raw slices of hot green chili. You should put scallions in the roll-up as well — preferably marinated scal-lions, as described in this recipe. And it is also traditional to include garlic in the roll-up. Koreans use either raw peeled garlic cloves (whole!) or peeled whole garlic cloves that have been cooked on the grill briefly. The following recipe gives you one extra garlic option, very American in spirit: you may skewer whole unpeeled garlic cloves, place the skewers on the grill, then serve the skewers with the bulgogi; your guests will squeeze the sweet, cooked garlic out of the cloves and onto their roll-ups.

Yield: 4 main-course servings

1½ pounds skirt steak
3 tablespoons plus 2 teaspoons soy sauce
3 tablespoons Shao Xing (Chinese rice wine),
*   or dry sherry*
1½ tablespoons plus 2 teaspoons
*   rice wine vinegar*
1 tablespoon plus 2 teaspoons sesame oil
2 whole star anise
1½ tablespoons dark brown sugar
1 tablespoon toasted sesame seeds,
*   ground in a spice grinder or*
*   with a mortar and pestle*
¼ teaspoon freshly ground black pepper
2 tablespoons finely chopped garlic
2 tablespoons finely chopped gingerroot
Vegetable oil for the grill
8 unpeeled whole garlic cloves threaded
*   on 2 soaked bamboo skewers*
*   (optional)*
2 cups lightly packed scallions (green part
*   only), cut into fine slivers*
⅛ teaspoon crushed red pepper
¼ teaspoon sesame seeds
1 head red leaf lettuce or green leaf lettuce,
*   leaves separated, rinsed, and dried*

All about Korean Barbecue and the Accompanying Barbecue Recipes

It is Korean grill food that has had the biggest impact on the American restaurant-goer. Though this fascinating cuisine has many, many kinds of main-course dishes — stews, soups, casseroles, broiled fish dishes, noodle dishes, and so on — when Americans think about going out for Korean food, they often say, "Let's go get Korean barbecue!"

Being great grillers ourselves and enthusiastic consumers of beef, it makes sense that the beef-oriented Korean grilling would appeal to us. But Korean barbecue is no simple throw-a-steak-on-the-fire operation; there is a ritual involved and a series of methods that add up to a very particular, very Asian taste.

For one thing, the fire in the Korean restaurant — unlike the fire in the steak house — is right in front of the diner; it is traditional for the diner to grill the meat right at his or her table.

Second, the platters of meat that come from the kitchen to the grill contain meat that has been sliced, usually quite thinly, in the kitchen; therefore, the tabletop cooking for each piece rarely takes more than a minute or two.

Third, the meat is only occasionally brought to the grill with no marinade; many of the Korean barbecue-destined meats receive either a light and simple marinade or a heavier, spicier one.

Lastly, the meat is rarely eaten right off the grill, just as it is; rather, in Korean-American res-taurants it usually forms the basis for elaborate roll-ups, kind of like Korean tacos, in which the wrappers are soft leaves of green lettuce. Here are some of the ingredients that typically go on the roll-up:

> soybean paste/toenjang (you may substi-
> tute brown miso)
> red pepper paste/kochujang (you may sub-
> stitute Chinese chili paste with garlic)
> steamed white rice
> cut scallions
> whole garlic cloves (either raw or grilled)
> slices of hot green chilies

The Korean barbecue recipe here, though authentic in taste, does, for practical reasons, diverge a bit from Korean-restaurant practice. I can certainly see many, many Americans (myself included) preparing Korean barbecue in their backyards and patios — what a great party it makes! But, since the grilling on our Webers is not, as in restaurants, tabletop (with every seated diner controlling his or her own precut slices of meat), the method that makes more sense in the backyard is one chef grilling large pieces of marinated meat. After cooking, the grill chef can slice the cooked meat and present it on a platter, along with the let-tuce leaves and all the other ingredients that go into the roll-ups. Each diner, then, can make his or her own roll-ups.

The other deviation from standard Korean res-taurant practice is in the cut of meat that is used; what I'm calling for is a little easier to find and works a little better when you're cooking meat pieces whole.

1. Lay skirt steak out flat on the counter. With the back edge of the blade of a heavy knife, pound the steak diagonally first in one direction and then in the other direction. Turn the meat over and repeat the process on the other side. After pounding, the steak should be no thicker than ¼ inch.

2. Combine the 3 tablespoons of soy sauce, the Shao Xing, the 1½ tablespoons of rice wine vinegar, the 1 tablespoon of sesame oil, the star anise, brown sugar, ground sesame seeds, black pepper, chopped garlic, and ginger in a rectangular 9 by 13 by 2-inch baking dish. Place the steak in the marinade. Turn the meat over and massage the marinade into it for about 1 minute. Turn it over again and repeat the process, making sure all the meat is covered with marinade. Cover and refrigerate for 1 hour.

3. To grill the beef, start the coals 30 minutes before cooking, or preheat a gas grill. Lightly brush the grilling rack with vegetable oil and place it about 4 inches from the heat source. If using garlic skewers, place them on the grill about 5 minutes before adding meat. Remove beef from the marinade and grill about 3 minutes per side or to the desired doneness. (To broil the beef, preheat the broiler. Brush a rack with vegetable oil and set it over a shallow baking pan. Place meat on rack and set it 5 inches from heat source. Broil about 2 minutes on each side or until done.)

4. Remove meat to a cutting board and slice diagonally into thin pieces.

5. Right before serving, toss scallions with the remaining 2 teaspoons of soy sauce, the remaining 2 teaspoons of rice wine vinegar, the remaining 2 teaspoons of sesame oil, the crushed red pepper, and sesame seeds. (If tossed too early, the scallions will wilt and lose their color.)

6. Serve meat on one platter, leaves of lettuce on another. Diners should each take a lettuce leaf, place a few slices of the meat on the lettuce, and place Korean barbecue condiments on the lettuce (see headnote). Roll up the leaf and eat immediately.

✳ Bibimbap ✳ with Vegetables and Beef

Well, it's usually pronounced bay-bim-bop, giving equal stress to each syllable — though I'm a little stressed about how to spell it exactly, because some Korean cookbooks say "pibimbap." What's considerably clearer is the deliciousness, and wide appeal, of this great rice dish. In Korea, it is the luncheon dish of choice in both restaurants and homes. It comes in many different forms, including the technically challenging variation in which the rice is sizzled in a stoneware bowl called a tolsot, forming a crunchy crust. I actually prefer it as it is in the following version: a wide bowl of various cooked and raw vegetables to which you add hot rice and a sauce, and blend everything together into a mass of warm yumminess. You have several options for that sauce. Most restaurants serve the incendiary Korean red pepper paste called kochujang. I prefer to use the Korean soybean paste called toenjang — or a mix of the two. If you have trouble finding them, you may substitute a hot bean sauce from China. If you can't find that, a blend of hoisin sauce and hot chili-and-garlic sauce would be a decent substitute. There are also lots of options concerning the service of bibimbap — but my favorite way is to give each diner a wide, shallow bowl with his or her own ingredients decoratively nestled side by side, pass bowls of hot rice, and put a bowl of sauce on the table; each diner is then asked to convert the elements into a customized, perfectly blended mass in his or her wide bowl. And one last variable: when do you serve it? It could be lunch, it could be a dinner main course — but my favorite moment is as an after-course, as soon as the Korean barbecue (see page 196) is finished.

Yield: 4 post-main-course servings

½ cup dried lily buds
8 dried shiitake mushrooms, medium-large
4 garlic cloves, minced
1 tablespoon Asian sesame oil
5 tablespoons light soy sauce
½ teaspoon grated gingerroot
3 tablespoon rice wine vinegar
½ teaspoon freshly ground black pepper
½ English cucumber (cut in half crosswise)
⅛ teaspoon sugar
Pinch of cayenne
Salt
¾ pound skirt steak, thinly sliced (about ⅛ inch thick) with the grain
Peanut oil, as needed (less than ½ cup overall)
1 cup bean sprouts
1 (10-ounce) package prewashed spinach, tough stems removed
1 tablespoon toasted sesame seeds
1 cup loosely packed julienned carrot
4 large eggs
½ cup thinly sliced scallion
2 cups hot, cooked sushi rice (see package instructions)
Kochujang (Korean red pepper paste) or toenjang (Korean bean paste) or Chinese hot bean sauce with garlic, to serve at the table (see headnote)

1. In 2 separate bowls, cover the lily buds and mushrooms with hot water. Set aside to soak for about 20 minutes. Once the lily buds are reconstituted, drain the liquid from the bowl and set the lily buds aside. Once the mushrooms are reconstituted, drain the liquid from them and slice them into ⅛-inch slices; set them aside in a small bowl.

2. Make the soy sauce mixture: Thoroughly blend the garlic, sesame oil, light soy sauce, ginger, 1 tablespoon of the rice wine vinegar, and black pepper. Set aside.

3. Peel the cucumber. Slice thinly on the diagonal (about ⅛ inch thick) and place slices in a bowl. Add the remaining 2 tablespoons rice vinegar, the sugar, and cayenne. Salt to taste. Set aside.

4. Mix the beef slices with 2 tablespoons of the soy sauce mixture. Place a wok over high heat; when the wok surface is very hot, drizzle 1 tablespoon peanut oil down the sides of the wok. Add the beef and stir-fry until it's cooked to your taste (medium-rare is good!). Don't overcook the meat; it will become tough if you do. Remove and set aside.

5. Don't clean out the wok. Add a scant tablespoon of peanut oil. Once it is hot, add the sliced mushrooms and 1 tablespoon of the soy sauce mixture. Stir-fry them over high heat for 1 minute. Remove and set aside.

6. Don't clean out the wok. Add another scant tablespoon of oil. Once it is hot, add the lily buds and 1 tablespoon of the soy sauce mixture. Stir-fry them over high heat for 1 minute. Remove and set aside.

7. Don't clean out the wok. Add another

scant tablespoon of oil. Once it is hot, add the bean sprouts and 1 tablespoon of the soy sauce mixture. Stir-fry them over high heat for 1 minute. Remove and set aside.

8. Don't clean out the wok. Add another scant tablespoon of oil. Once it is hot, add the spinach, 1 tablespoon of the soy sauce mixture, and the sesame seeds. Stir-fry them over high heat for 1 minute. Remove and set aside. Add the carrots to the wok, stir-fry for 1 minute, and set aside.

9. Place a large nonstick frying pan over medium heat; it should be large enough to fry 4 eggs simultaneously. Add a tablespoon of peanut oil; when it's hot, fry the eggs sunny side up, keeping them separate from each other. When cooked, they should be white around the edges, not brown and frizzled.

Bibimbap with Vegetables and Beef

The arranged plate, with egg at center

10. To make the individual servings, select four wide, shallow soup bowls. Use one quarter of each of the items that you have prepared per bowl. Place the items in the bowls next to each other in the following order: beef, spinach, lily buds, cucumber, mushrooms, bean sprouts, and carrot. The items should form a wheel around the inner rim of the bowls. Garnish each dish with a quarter of the sliced scallion. Place a fried egg in the center of each bowl, partially overlapping the other ingredients.

11. Serve immediately, along with the hot rice divided into four bowls. Each person should mix the rice with the other ingredients in his or her vegetable-beef bowl at the table using chop sticks; the Korean red pepper paste, or your condiment of choice, should be mixed in as well (quantity depends on the individual diner). When the mix is done, all ingredients, including the egg (which you break up with your chopsticks) should be blended together.

Southeast Asian Food

Once upon a time it was Chinese food, and Chinese food alone, that represented Asia on the American restaurant front. However, since the early 1970s there have been explosions here of one Southeast Asian cuisine after another — first Thai, then Vietnamese, then Malaysian. Today Southeast Asian food in general is an incredibly vibrant part of our American ethnic restaurant patchwork.

Most of these cuisines, especially Thai, have had a decade or two to adapt to American tastes — and that is why you sometimes get an American version of Southeast Asian food in these restaurants. Thai food, for example — that heroic collision of basic tastes on your palate, the implosion of salty, sour, sweet, and hot — is sweeter here than it is in Thailand and maybe a little less hot. It's also not as funky as it can be there, with a somewhat standardized set of dishes that only timidly wander into the intriguing regional cuisines of Thailand. One other touch marks most Thai-restaurant food in the United States: a borrowing of display from the royal Thai cuisine, which means that almost every dish gets garnished with carved melons, splayed scallions, chili curls, and so on; you can be sure that when the computer programmer comes home from work in Bangkok he or she doesn't start carving melons.

However, though I've enjoyed these Southeast Asian cuisines in their home countries, I don't complain about what we have here: it is extremely tasty food, celebratory and festive, that fully deserves more attention from American home cooks. Indeed, I see more and more Southeast Asian convenience products in American supermarkets these days — a good sign that we're actually taking these cuisines to heart. And that's a good thing; as you'll see below, for example, wonderful Thai curries can be made with Thai curry paste in that most American of packaging: cans.

☆ Vietnamese ☆
Summer Rolls with Crab

One of the classic Vietnamese dishes that get some attention and play in the United States is summer rolls — a wonderful appetizer, a kind of salad rolled up in a rice paper wrapper called banh trang. The cool thing is that — unlike Vietnamese and Chinese spring rolls — the summer roll does not get fried. It's a cold dish, light and clean, that Americans especially prize for its nutritional correctness.

Yield: 8 rolls, good for 8 light appetizer servings

3 tablespoons Vietnamese fish sauce
1 tablespoon sugar
¼ cup finely shredded fresh mint
½ pound lump or backfin crabmeat
8 sheets of banh trang, preferably square, about 8½ inches per side
1 cup shredded lettuce
½ cup mung bean sprouts
½ large carrot, very finely shredded
½ cup chives in 2-inch lengths
2 tablespoons smashed roasted peanuts
1 cup loosely packed coriander leaves
Dipping sauce (see Note)

1. In a large mixing bowl, blend together the fish sauce, sugar, and mint. Add the crabmeat and combine well. Reserve.
2. Prepare a large basin of warm water. Place a large, clean towel next to it. Pick up 1 sheet of banh trang and dip it into the water for 3 seconds. Try to dip the whole sheet at the same time. Remove sheet from water and place on the towel.
3. About 1 inch above the lower edge of the

sheet, evenly spread out ⅛ cup of lettuce into a rectangle that's about 5 inches long (from side to side) and 3 inches wide. There should be a 1½-inch gap between the left and right edges of the sheet and the lettuce.

4. Evenly top the lettuce with one-eighth of the carrot, one-eighth of the chives, one-eighth of the peanuts, and one-eighth of the coriander. Top that with one-eighth of the crabmeat.

5. Carefully pick up the left edge of the sheet and fold it toward the center of the filling, making a flap that covers a little of the filling on the left-hand side. Make sure that this flap goes from the bottom edge of the banh trang all the way up to the top edge and that the folded flap is even and uncreased. Repeat on the right-hand side, making another flap that goes from the bottom edge of the banh trang all the way up to the top edge. Now pick up the bottom edge of the banh trang and start rolling away from you, toward the top edge. Roll so that the filling is tightly packed inside. When you reach the top, roll the roll over. It should hold the seal nicely. Place seam side down on a tray and cover with a damp towel.

6. Repeat filling and rolling with the remaining 7 banh trang sheets.

7. When done, cut each roll in 3 diagonal pieces, arrange 3 pieces on each of eight plates, and serve with dipping sauce.

NOTE: I love summer rolls with a light dipping sauce. The Ponzu Sauce on page 190 is fantastic with them, and the Potsticker Dipping Sauce on page 158 is also very good. A typically Vietnamese dipping-sauce thing to do would be to mix together a few tablespoons of fish sauce, a few tablespoons of water, a tablespoon of lime juice, and two teaspoons of sugar. A little minced garlic and a little hot chili are optional.

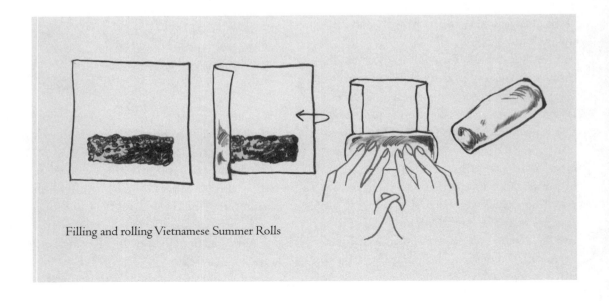

Filling and rolling Vietnamese Summer Rolls

✺ Spicy Thai Minced ✺ Chicken Salad with Peanuts and Celery Leaves

Among the most popular offerings at Thai restaurants in the United States are the wonderful, light, tingling, superflavorful salads. They can be pretty elaborate affairs, with all kinds of intricate garnishes. But I love the simplicity of the following recipe, which takes mere minutes to make — and gets any meal, Thai or otherwise, off to a rousing start.

Yield: 4 appetizer servings

Vegetable oil for deep-frying
1 pound skinless, boneless chicken breasts
  or thighs
½ teaspoon Thai chili powder or cayenne
4 teaspoons granulated sugar
½ cup lime juice
8 teaspoons Thai fish sauce
1 small, hot chili, seeded and minced
  (or more to taste)
4 teaspoons grated gingerroot
½ cup smashed roasted peanuts
¼ cup finely minced celery heart
½ cup firmly packed celery leaves
¼ cup firmly packed coriander leaves
¼ cup firmly packed shredded mint leaves
4 leaves green leaf lettuce

1. Place vegetable oil in a wide pot, several inches deep, and heat to 300 degrees.
2. Mince chicken coarsely. When oil has reached 300 degrees, lower the chicken, all at once, into the oil. Immediately swirl with a spoon to break up clumps. Cook until chicken just loses its pink; this may be as little as 10 seconds. Pour chicken immediately into a colander, discarding oil (or saving for another use). Let chicken drain for a moment.
3. Place chicken in a mixing bowl. Add the chili powder and mix well to color chicken evenly. Add the sugar, lime juice, fish sauce, minced chili, ginger, and peanuts; toss vigorously to blend. Add celery heart, celery leaves, coriander leaves, and mint leaves and toss gently (so as to keep the leaves fluffy).
4. Place the lettuce leaves on four serving plates and top each leaf with a quarter of the chicken mixture. Serve immediately.

✺ Lumpia ✺
(Philippine Egg Rolls, Shanghai Style)

There's not a whole lot of Philippine food in the United States — but many major cities have at least one Philippine restaurant, and most of those restaurants offer Lumpia, a Philippine version of the Chinese spring roll. It has become the one Philippine appetizer that non-Philippine Americans may have heard of. My Philippine-American friend tells me that there are several different kinds of lumpia prepared in the United States. One of the favorites is a long and narrow lumpia, as in the following recipe; it is always cut into three pieces after it's fried, and in many homes it is served with a thick and sweet ketchup-based sauce. This long roll is known as Shanghai-style Lumpia. The most important thing you can do to ensure its quality and authenticity is to find a source for Philippine lumpia wrappers, also known as poh-pia. They are made from flour, cornstarch, and egg and are very thin — leading to a crisp, crackling product that holds its crackle longer than most wrappers do after they're cooked.

Yield: 15 lumpia, which becomes 45 pieces,
enough for 15 people as a
pass-around party appetizer

2 tablespoons canola oil, plus more for
        deep-frying
1 shallot, minced
1 tablespoon minced garlic
2 tablespoons minced gingerroot
½ pound ground pork
½ pound shrimp, peeled and finely chopped
½ cup finely chopped canned
        water chestnuts
½ cup finely chopped scallion
1 large egg, beaten
1 tablespoon soy sauce
1 teaspoon salt
1 teaspoon freshly ground pepper
1 package Philippine lumpia wrappers
        (or Chinese spring roll wrappers)
Philippine Sweet-and-Sour Sauce
        (recipe follows)

1. Heat a large sauté pan and add the 2 tablespoons of canola oil. When hot, add the shallot, garlic, and ginger and sauté until starting to soften, about 3 minutes. Add the pork, shrimp, water chestnuts, scallion, egg, and soy sauce. Cook, stirring occasionally, until pork is cooked through, about 5 minutes. Season with salt and pepper, and reserve in a bowl.

2. Spread one lumpia wrapper out on a flat surface. Place 2 level tablespoons of filling in a straight horizontal line ½ inch from the bottom of the wrapper. Make sure that the line of filling is not flush with the left or right edges; there should be ½ inch of space between the edge and the filling on both sides. Begin rolling the wrapper away from you, making sure that it is tight and that the filling remains securely in the middle. When you reach the other end of the wrapper, seal with a little water by dabbing the wrapper with your wet fingertip. The ends remain unsealed. Let rest for a few minutes while you heat the oil for frying and while you make the other 14 lumpia.

3. Fill a deep, wide pan with approximately 2 inches of canola oil. Heat the oil to 325 degrees. Gently place the lumpia rolls in the oil, gently turning them with tongs until they become golden brown. Cook as many at one time as you can without crowding them. Drain on paper towels.

4. When they have cooled a bit, cut into thirds crosswise. Serve with sweet-and-sour sauce.

★ Philippine ★
Sweet-and-Sour Sauce

Yield: 2½ cups

2 cups water
½ cup ketchup
⅓ cup sugar
1 teaspoon salt
1 teaspoon hot sauce, or more to taste
2 tablespoons cornstarch, dissolved in
        3 tablespoons cool water

Mix all ingredients together in a saucepan. Bring to a boil, reduce heat, and simmer until thickened (just a few minutes). Serve warm.

★ Pho ★
(Vietnamese Beef Soup with Herbs)

A few decades ago, most Chinatowns in America broadened to include a smattering of Vietnamese restaurants. There wasn't much buzz about that food at first. Today not only are there lots of Vietnamese restaurants in Chinatowns, with lots of buzz, but they are about to have on their hands a breakout dish; I know this because in New York, in San Francisco, in Honolulu, I have heard people say, "Let's go down to Chinatown and get some pho." No dish is more deserving of a breakout, I'm telling you. Pho is a big bowl of beef stock and beef and rice noodles and fabulous Southeast Asian seasonings — into which, at the table, you add more Southeast Asian seasonings and a profusion of fresh herbs. It is a specialty of Hanoi, but there are many regional variations. Think of it as a Southeast Asian pot-au-feu — which is quite curious, since the pronunciation of the dish (fuh) is damned close to the French pronunciation of "feu," and we know that French colonials were around for quite some time. Linguists with whom I've spoken, by the way, deny the connection. I say, "Feh," and just grab another bowl.

Yield: 4 main-course servings

4 pounds meaty beef bones
5 quarts water
1 large onion, unpeeled
6 whole cloves
1 (2-inch) piece of gingerroot
4 large shallots, unpeeled
3 whole star anise
1 (3-inch) cinnamon stick (preferably Vietnamese)
8 ounces medium-size dried rice sticks, ¼ inch wide
8 ounces sirloin or filet mignon, very thinly sliced
1 cup mung bean sprouts
1 cup loosely packed coriander leaves
½ cup sliced scallion (each slice ¼ inch thick)
2 tablespoons Vietnamese fish sauce (nuoc mam), or to taste

ACCOMPANIMENTS:
2 cups loosely packed coriander leaves
1 cup loosely packed mint leaves
1 cup loosely packed Thai basil leaves (or other basil leaves)
1 cup mung bean sprouts
1 cup sliced scallions (each slice ¼ inch thick)
2 small hot red chilies (such as Thai bird peppers), thinly sliced
Vietnamese fish sauce (nuoc mam)
Hot sauce (such as sriracha sauce from Thailand)
2 limes, each cut into 4 wedges

1. Place the beef bones in an 8-quart stockpot, cover the bones with the water, and bring to a boil over medium heat. As soon as the broth comes to a boil, lower the heat, bring to a simmer, and cover.

2. Meanwhile, peel the loose outer skin from the onion but leave some skin on. Cut in half and stud each half with 3 of the cloves. Cut the ginger in half and cut the shallots in half. Place a heavy cast-iron skillet over high heat and moderately char the onion, ginger, and shallots. Add to the stockpot. Add the star anise and the cinnamon stick. Simmer the broth for 4 hours, occasionally skimming any impurities from the surface.

3. Strain the broth, clean out the pot, and return the broth to the cleaned pot. Let the

meat bones cool slightly, then take off the meat, shred, and set aside. Discard the bones and other solids.

4. Cook the broth, uncovered, over medium-high heat. Reduce until you have about 8 cups of liquid.

5. While broth is reducing, simmer the rice sticks in 2 quarts of boiling water until just cooked, about 4 minutes. Take care not to overcook them. Drain.

6. Divide the noodles among four large, deep soup bowls. Divide the thinly sliced sirloin or filet mignon meat and the reserved shredded meat equally among the bowls. Divide the bean sprouts, coriander, and scallion equally and arrange on top of the meats.

7. Bring the broth to a boil and add fish sauce to taste. Season with salt, if necessary. Pour a quarter of the broth into each bowl. Serve at once with accompaniments on the side.

✶ Chicken Satay ✶ with Peanut Sauce

Indonesia is a huge country, with many islands and many culinary regions — each with its own ideas about grilling meat or fish on skewers! We have not yet advanced to a widespread interest, in the United States, in regional Indonesian cuisine — but satays have certainly penetrated our culinary consciousness. You are likely these days to see satays on pan-Asian menus, at grill parties, and especially, on the menus of caterers (for whom they stand out as ideal, no-silver-ware, pass-around hors d'oeuvres). The chicken satay is particularly popular, as is a peanut sauce to accompany it.

Yield: About 24 skewers, 6 appetizer servings

2 teaspoons minced garlic
½ teaspoon minced gingerroot
1 tablespoon fresh lime juice
1 tablespoon peanut oil
2 teaspoons dark brown sugar
1 teaspoon fish sauce
½ teaspoon ground cumin
½ teaspoon ground coriander
½ teaspoon turmeric
½ teaspoon salt
1 pound boneless, skinless chicken thighs,
     cut into strips ¼ inch thick by
     3 inches long (you should have about
     72 strips)
Peanut Sauce for dipping (recipe follows)

1. Combine garlic, ginger, lime juice, peanut oil, brown sugar, fish sauce, cumin, coriander, turmeric, and salt in a bowl. Add the chicken pieces, blend well, cover, and refrigerate for at least an hour (and as long as 4 hours).

2. Choose 24 bamboo skewers, each one approximately 10 inches long (or a little less). About an hour before grilling, soak the skewers in water (this helps prevent burning).

3. Prepare a hot fire or turn on your broiler. Thread 3 strips of chicken on each skewer. Cover the exposed wood of the skewers with foil if desired.

4. Place skewers on the grill or under the broiler — in either case, about 3 inches from the heat. Cook until the chicken is lightly browned on one side; turn and grill the other side. Cook until the chicken is just cooked through (a total of 8 to 10 minutes). Serve satays immediately with peanut sauce.

★ Peanut Sauce ★

Yield: 1 cup, 6 servings

½ cup chunky peanut butter
2 tablespoons hot tea
½ hot green chili, seeded and minced
1 tablespoon grated gingerroot
2 garlic cloves, minced
1 teaspoon dark brown sugar
1 teaspoon fish sauce
1 teaspoon light soy sauce
1 teaspoon peanut oil
1 teaspoon fresh lime juice
Salt, if needed
Chopped coriander leaves for garnish

Combine peanut butter, tea, chili, ginger, garlic, brown sugar, fish sauce, soy sauce, peanut oil, and lime juice in a medium bowl. Stir well to mix. Season with salt, if necessary. Garnish with finely chopped coriander leaves and serve with chicken satay.

☆ Shrimp Satay ☆ with Spicy Dipping Sauce

Here's another very popular satay variation.

Yield: 6 skewers, 6 appetizer servings

2 tablespoons water
1 teaspoon salt
1 tablespoon sugar
1 tablespoon lime juice
1 small hot green chili, minced
½ red bell pepper, deveined, seeded, and finely minced
1 teaspoon fish sauce
2 garlic cloves, minced
1 tablespoon minced fresh coriander leaves
1 pound medium shrimp (about 30), shelled and deveined but tails left on
Spicy Dipping Sauce (recipe follows)

1. Make the marinade: In a bowl blend the water, salt, sugar, lime juice, chili, bell pepper, fish sauce, garlic, and coriander leaves. Reserve.
2. Thread the shrimp on 10-inch bamboo skewers, arranging 5 shrimp on each. Place the skewers in a wide pan.
3. Pour the marinade over the shrimp; refrigerate for 1 hour, turning frequently if the shrimp are not completely covered by the marinade.
4. Prepare a hot fire or turn on your broiler. Cover the exposed wood of the skewers with foil if desired.
5. Place skewers on the grill or under the broiler — in either case, about 4 inches from the heat. Cook until the shrimp are lightly browned on one side; turn and grill the other side. Cook until the shrimp are just cooked through (a total of 5 to 6 minutes). Serve satays immediately with dipping sauce.

★ Spicy Dipping Sauce ★

Yield: 6 servings

4 teaspoons peanut oil
4 teaspoons minced garlic
4 teaspoons minced gingerroot
2 to 6 small hot green chilies, minced

4 tablespoons thinly sliced scallion
4 teaspoons granulated sugar
Juice of 4 limes
¼ teaspoon grated lime zest

1. Place the peanut oil in a small saucepan over medium heat. Add garlic, ginger, and minced chilies and cook for about 1 minute. Take care not to color the garlic. Remove from heat.
2. Add scallion, sugar, lime juice, lime zest, and salt to taste. Mix well. Serve slightly chilled; stir well prior to serving.

☆ Thai Yellow Shrimp Curry ☆ with Red Pepper and Asparagus

Thai food, we Americans have discovered, features a fascinating range of "curries," each one made from a paste of a different color. Yellow curry paste in Thailand is often used in fish or chicken dishes. It is a medium-hot paste that gets its color from turmeric and a good deal of its flavor from curry powder — which imbues it with a relationship to the "curry" tastes of India. You could think of it as a Thai-Indian fusion paste — and the following recipe reflects the way it might be used in another fusion environment, an upscale Thai restaurant in the United States. This dish is very fresh tasting, and though it's not unusual to use vegetables in a yellow curry in Thailand, you're not likely to see asparagus. But the spears work beautifully in this dish — which, despite the vegetable transplant, is brimming with authentic Thai flavor.

Yield: 4 main-course servings

4 cups fish stock, preferably homemade
1 pound large shrimp (about 25), peeled and deveined, with shells reserved
6 tablespoons (about 4 ounces) Thai yellow curry paste (krung kaeng kari; see "Thai Curry in a Hurry" sidebar)
4 tablespoons finely chopped coriander leaves
Grated zest of 1 lime
3 tablespoons vegetable oil
1 large yellow onion, peeled and thinly sliced
2 tablespoons palm sugar (crushed if solid), or light brown sugar
3 tablespoons tamarind concentrate diluted with a bit of hot water (or you can make your own concentrate from a dried tamarind block; see "All about Tamarind" sidebar)
2 tablespoons Thai fish sauce (nam pla)
1 red bell pepper, washed, cored, seeded, and sliced about ⅜ inch thick
¼ cup plus 2 tablespoons Thai coconut milk
1 small bunch asparagus (about ½ pound), tough stalks trimmed, sliced on the bias ¼ inch thick

1. Bring the fish stock and the reserved shrimp shells to a boil in a medium saucepan. Reduce to a brisk simmer and cook, stirring occasionally, for 30 minutes. Remove the stock from the heat and allow it to cool for about 10 minutes. Pass the mixture through a fine mesh sieve or cheesecloth into a bowl, pressing hard on the solids to extract their flavor. Set stock aside.
2. Meanwhile, combine the shrimp with

2 tablespoons of the curry paste, 2 tablespoons of the coriander leaves, the lime zest, and a few grindings of black pepper. Toss thoroughly; cover with plastic wrap and set aside at room temperature.

3. Once the stock has been strained, heat the vegetable oil in a stockpot or large wok over medium heat and add the onion, stirring occasionally, until it's softened, about 4 minutes. Add the remaining 4 tablespoons of curry paste and cook, stirring regularly, for 3 minutes. Regulate the heat so the mixture doesn't burn. Add the palm sugar, tamarind paste, fish sauce, and the reserved stock and bring to a boil over high heat. Reduce to a brisk simmer over medium heat and cook for 20 minutes to combine and concentrate the flavors. If you've used good-quality fish stock, the mixture should at this point be thicker than water but not yet as thick as a sauce. If it still seems a bit watery, continue to simmer the mixture a little longer (it will thicken a bit further as the recipe proceeds). Stir in the bell pepper and cook until softened, about 10 minutes. Stir in the coconut milk, asparagus, and the reserved shrimp and cook, stirring regularly, until the shrimp are just cooked through but still a bit opaque at the center, about 3 minutes more. Serve immediately, garnished with the remaining 2 tablespoons of chopped coriander leaves.

All about Tamarind

Three of the four Thai curry recipes here require tamarind. The easiest way to use tamarind is in the form of runny tamarind concentrate, which you can buy in jars. My absolute favorite is Laxmi brand tamarind concentrate, available from www.hosindia.com. But if you have some of that do-it-yourself spirit . . . no, I don't suggest growing a tamarind tree. But you could buy blocks of dried tamarind pulp and work them up into a usable form. See directions in the Tamarind Chutney recipe on page 219.

☆ Thai Green Chicken Curry ☆ with Eggplant and Mixed Herbs

Just as green chilies can be the hottest capsicums, so can the Thai green curry be the hottest of its group — and this despite the fact that green curry paste is often blended with cooling coconut milk in the curries! You do get a lovely chili taste in addition to the heat in a green curry, along with a range of herbal tastes. The central character is usually meat: chicken, pork, or beef.

Yield: 4 main-course servings

2 pounds boneless, skinless chicken breast,
        cut into ¾-inch cubes
4 tablespoons finely chopped coriander leaves
4 tablespoons finely chopped basil
4 tablespoons finely minced scallions
Grated zest of 1 lime
3 tablespoons vegetable oil
1 large onion, peeled and thinly sliced
2 tablespoons minced garlic

3 teaspoons freshly grated gingerroot
6 tablespoons (about 4 ounces) Thai
    green curry paste (gaeng kiow wan;
    see "Thai Curry in a Hurry"
    sidebar)
½ teaspoon ground coriander
2 tablespoons Thai fish sauce (nam pla)
4 cups chicken broth, homemade or canned
2 cups Thai coconut milk (canned and
    unsweetened)
2 medium Japanese eggplants
    (about 12 ounces), sliced on the bias
    into ¼-inch-thick ovals
2 hot red chilies (such as Thai bird peppers),
    sliced on the bias into thin rings
1 tablespoon arrowroot or cornstarch
Lime wedges

1. Combine the chicken with a generous pinch of salt, the coriander leaves, basil, scallions, and lime zest. Toss thoroughly; cover with plastic wrap and set aside at room temperature.

2. Heat the vegetable oil in a stockpot or large wok over medium heat and add the onion and garlic. Cook gently, stirring occasionally, until they're slightly softened, about 4 minutes. Add the ginger, curry paste, and ground coriander and cook, stirring regularly, for 3 minutes. Regulate the heat so the mixture doesn't burn. Stir in the fish sauce and chicken broth, raise the heat to high, and bring to a boil. Reduce to a brisk simmer over medium heat and cook for 10 minutes to combine and concentrate the flavors. Stir in the coconut milk, return the pot to a bare simmer, and add the eggplant slices and chili

rings, stirring to immerse them in the liquid. Maintain a bare simmer and let the mixture cook, stirring occasionally, until the eggplant slices are nearly tender, about 10 minutes. Stir the reserved chicken and all the herb mari-

Thai Curry in a Hurry

One of the things that distinguishes Thai curries from Indian curries is the fact that the flavor in Thailand is imparted to stews through the use of pounded pastes, not through the use of unblended spices. Where do those Thai pastes come from? There is a long and noble tradition in Thailand of pounding various roots, spices, and dried fish into a spectrum of curry pastes — each with its traditional color, flavors, and uses.

As you might imagine, there is no such tradition in the United States. In fact, the process is a little too complicated for the busy lives of most of us. But Americans who like to cook Thai at home have discovered that canned pastes, made in Thailand, are quick and excellent substitutes for pounding your own. And they relieve the pressure of finding a lot of inaccessible fresh ingredients — such as lemon grass, kaffir limes, and galanga root — because those flavors are built into the pastes.

One brand I particularly like is Maesri, which markets perhaps a dozen different pastes. They come in four-ounce cans or resealable fourteen-ounce plastic containers. The different curries are very distinct from each other, and the flavors are very vivid. Maesri curry pastes — as well as a wealth of other Thai goodies — can be purchased by logging on to: www.ImportFood.com.

nade into the stockpot and cook at or below a simmer, stirring regularly, until the chicken is almost cooked through, about 5 minutes. Taste for seasoning.

3. Blend the arrowroot or cornstarch with a few tablespoons of cold water, making a milky slurry. Stir it into the simmering curry and heat until the chicken is just cooked through, 1 to 2 minutes more. Serve immediately with steamed rice and lime wedges on the side.

✴ Thai Massaman Beef Curry ✴ with Cabbage and Fresh Mint

Massaman curries — the only major Thai curries not named for a color — are a relief for those who can't take the blistering heat of other Thai curries. *Massaman* is the Thai transliteration of *Muslim* — and the Muslims who settled in southern Thailand brought with them a range of nonincendiary spices that appear in their curries (such as cinnamon and cardamom). These curries are regularly seen on Thai-American menus, but they get ordered a bit less than the "color" curries because of name confusion. That situation would change, I'm confident, if Americans could get a taste of the following warm, winning, sweetly spiced combination.

Yield: 4 main-course servings

1½ pounds beef flank steak or sirloin, trimmed of excess fat and sliced against the grain into ⅜-inch-thick slices, each about 2 inches long

9 tablespoons (a scant 7 ounces) Thai Massaman curry paste (krung kaeng Massaman; see "Thai Curry in a Hurry" sidebar on page 210)

3 tablespoons vegetable oil

1 large onion, peeled and thinly sliced

1 tablespoon minced garlic

6 green cardamom pods, barely cracked open with the broad side of a knife

1 stick cinnamon

2 bay leaves

1 tablespoon palm sugar (crushed if solid), or light brown sugar

1½ tablespoons tamarind concentrate diluted with a bit of hot water (or you can make your own concentrate from a dried tamarind block; see "All about Tamarind" sidebar on page 209)

2 tablespoons freshly squeezed lime juice

2 tablespoons Thai fish sauce (nam pla)

4 cups beef broth, homemade or canned

¾ pound napa cabbage, cut into 1-inch pieces

2 jalapeño peppers, thinly sliced into rings and seeded

½ cup loosely packed coarsely chopped fresh mint leaves, plus mint sprigs for garnish

3 cups hot cooked white rice

½ cup coarsely crushed unsalted peanuts

Lime wedges

1. Combine the beef with 4 tablespoons of the curry paste in a medium mixing bowl, thoroughly coating the meat. Set aside at room temperature.

2. Heat the vegetable oil in a stockpot or large wok over a medium flame and add the onion and garlic. Cook gently, stirring occasionally, until they're slightly softened, about 4 minutes. Stir in the remaining 5 tablespoons of curry paste, the cardamom pods, cinnamon, and bay leaves and cook, stirring

regularly, for 3 minutes; regulate the heat so the mixture doesn't burn. Add the palm sugar, tamarind concentrate, lime juice, fish sauce, and beef broth. Raise the heat to high and bring to a boil. Reduce to a brisk simmer over medium heat and cook for 15 minutes to combine and concentrate the flavors.

3. Stir in the cabbage and jalapeños and cook until slightly softened, about 3 minutes. Add the reserved beef and the mint leaves to the pot, stirring well a few times to expose the beef to liquid on all its sides. Cook, stirring occasionally, for 2 to 3 minutes, or until the meat is just medium-rare in the center. Taste broth for seasoning.

4. Divide rice among four wide, shallow soup bowls. Spread the rice out in each bowl, but make a well in the center of each. Immediately pour the curry into the center of each bowl. Garnish the curry in each bowl with 2 tablespoons of the peanuts and the mint sprigs. Serve immediately, with lime wedges on the side.

☆ Thai Red Pork Curry with ☆ Bamboo Shoots and Holy Basil

Red curry is normally just behind green curry in the fiery-hot sweepstakes, just as it is here. In addition to the lively spicing, the look of a red curry is particularly attractive, especially when it includes coconut milk. Keep in mind that the coconut milk in this recipe might threaten to "break" — which is never a problem for Thai chefs, for they are accustomed to serving curries in which you can see the milk solids separating. But it's more frowned on in the West — so that's one reason why I've advised you to do much of the cooking in this recipe at a bare simmer.

Yield: 4 main-course servings

1½ pounds loin end or rib end pork chops, trimmed of any bone and excess fat, cut into approximately ¾-inch cubes

10 tablespoons (about 7 ounces) Thai red curry paste (gaeng pet; see "Thai Curry in a Hurry" sidebar on page 210)

3 tablespoons vegetable oil

⅓ cup minced shallot

1 tablespoon plus 1 teaspoon minced garlic

2 teaspoons freshly grated gingerroot

2 tablespoons palm sugar (crushed if solid), or light brown sugar

2 tablespoons Thai fish sauce (nam pla)

2 tablespoons tamarind concentrate diluted with a bit of hot water (or you can make your own concentrate from a dried tamarind block; see "All about Tamarind" sidebar on page 209)

2½ cups Thai coconut milk (canned and unsweetened)

2 hot red chilies (such as Thai bird peppers), sliced on the bias into thin rings

16 ounces canned, sliced bamboo shoots, drained

¼ cup firmly packed washed and dried Thai holy basil leaves (or you can substitute regular basil)

1. Combine the pork with 2 tablespoons of the curry paste in a medium mixing bowl, thoroughly coating the meat. Set aside at room temperature.

2. Heat the vegetable oil in a medium stockpot or wok over medium heat and add the

shallot and garlic. Cook gently, stirring occasionally, until they're slightly softened, about 4 minutes. Add the remaining 8 tablespoons curry paste and the ginger and cook, stirring regularly, for 3 minutes. Regulate the heat so the mixture doesn't burn. Add the palm sugar, fish sauce, tamarind concentrate, coconut milk, and chilies, raise the heat to medium-high, and bring just to a bare simmer. Add the reserved pork and cook for 4 minutes, stirring regularly to help the meat cook evenly, and regulating the heat so that the mixture never exceeds a bare simmer. Add the bamboo shoots and holy basil and cook, stirring regularly, until the pork is just cooked through, about 2 minutes more. Taste the mixture for salt, and stir in a bit if you feel it needs it. Serve immediately with rice or thin rice noodles on the side.

✲ Chicken Adobo ✲

Though adobo is considered the national dish of the Philippines, it's very hard to get a handle on exactly what it is, since it takes so many forms in that multi-culti society (which is a blend of Asian and Hispanic cultures). But the name adobo — in addition to appearing on all Philippine menus in the United States — is also starting to crop up as a creative-restaurant buzz word here. So it's time to pay attention. Many adobos in the Philippines start with marinated meat (usually chicken or pork soaked in the fusionist pairing of soy sauce and wine vinegar), then involve the stewing of the meat. In some cases the stewed meat is served as a stew, in some cases the stewed meat is later fried and served dry. The following recipe has the best of both strategies: the chicken thighs, after marination and stewing, are broiled, then recombined with the reduced stewing liquid. The result is a crispy, wonderfully homey dish with a thin, flavor-packed sauce. I like to serve the chicken thighs in a wide, shallow soup bowl next to white rice — then pour the sauce around the thighs.

Yield: 4 servings

½ cup thin soy sauce
½ cup white wine vinegar
6 garlic cloves, crushed, plus 2 cloves garlic, chopped
2 bay leaves, crumbled
1 tablespoon crushed black peppercorns
1 tablespoon packed light brown sugar
8 bone-in, skin-on chicken thighs
1 tablespoon canola oil
1 medium onion, sliced
2 tablespoons gingerroot, chopped

1. In a large bowl, combine soy sauce, vinegar, crushed garlic, bay leaves, crushed peppercorns, and brown sugar. Add chicken and toss to coat well. Cover and marinate overnight in the refrigerator.
2. Strain chicken and reserve marinade; discard solids. In a large pot or Dutch oven, heat canola oil over medium heat. Add onion, the chopped garlic, and ginger; cook until softened, about 5 minutes. Return chicken and marinade to pot, bring to a boil, and simmer, covered, until chicken is tender, about 45 minutes.
3. Cool to room temperature. Remove chicken thighs and bone them, discarding bones. Reserve thighs, covered, in the refrigerator. Refrigerate sauce several hours until fat solidifies; remove fat and discard.
4. When ready to serve, preheat broiler. Place

defatted sauce in a small saucepan and boil until reduced by half. Pat chicken dry with paper towels. Place chicken skin side up on a sheet pan and broil until skin is crispy, about 2 minutes. Serve with sauce.

✿ Pad Thai ✿

The following is a wonderful recipe for pad thai, the great noodle dish that is one of the most popular dishes of any kind in Thai restaurants in America. But keep in mind that it's only a recipe: it is very much in the tradition of pad thai to improvise your ingredients. If you have leftovers you want to use — great! If you want to use chicken instead of shrimp — great! The one thing I'd love you to retain is the authentic Thai rice noodle, sen lek, that's used for this dish.

Yield: 4 servings as part of a Thai meal

*4 ounces sen lek, medium-wide Thai rice
    noodles, soaked in hot water for ½ hour*
2 tablespoons Thai fish sauce (nam pla)
2 tablespoons tomato ketchup
1½ tablespoons sugar
½ teaspoon chili garlic sauce (or to taste)
3 tablespoons peanut oil
½ cup thinly sliced onion
*6 medium scallions (white part plus about
    1 inch of the green stem), cut into
    ¼-inch slices*
½ cup finely sliced shallot
1 tablespoon finely minced garlic
½ cup shredded carrot
½ cup finely sliced cabbage
3 slices smoked bacon, cut into ¼-inch dice
*½ pound medium shrimp, peeled and deveined,
    with tail section left on*

2 large eggs, beaten
*1 cup mung bean sprouts, plus more for
    accompaniment*
½ cup minced coriander leaves
*¼ cup crushed roasted peanuts,
    plus more for accompaniment*
*1 tablespoon crushed dried shrimp
    (optional)*
2 limes, each cut into 4 wedges

1. Drain the noodles and set aside.
2. Stir together the fish sauce, ketchup, sugar, and chili garlic sauce in a small bowl. Set aside.
3. Place a wok or sturdy skillet over high heat. Pour in the peanut oil down the sides of the wok. Quickly add the onion, half of the scallions, and the shallot. Using a spatula, move the ingredients around the wok enough so they don't burn but not so much that they don't get a chance to brown a little. After the onion and shallot start to soften, add the garlic. Stir-fry for 1 minute more. Add the carrot and cabbage and stir-fry for another 2 minutes. Add the bacon and cook for 2 minutes. Stir in the shrimp and cook for 1 minute.
4. Using the spatula, push the ingredients to the side of the wok. Pour in the eggs and stir. When they become firm scrambled eggs, stir them into the other ingredients.
5. Stir in the noodles, then the fish sauce–ketchup mixture. Taste for seasoning. Stir in the bean sprouts.
6. Turn out onto a heated platter. Sprinkle the remaining scallions, the coriander leaves, peanuts, and dried shrimp over the pad thai.

Arrange the lime wedges around the dish and serve immediately. Pass extra bean sprouts and peanuts for mixing in.

Indian Food

The case of Indian food in America is a curious one. It has never been a very popular ethnic-restaurant option here (certainly not as popular as it has been in England) — but American home cooks have for many decades been, in a sense, cooking "Indian" food in their homes. That sense, of course, is a completely indirect one — for adding some curry powder to cream sauces, or even producing sweet chicken "curries" (see sidebar, page 222) shot through with apples, raisins, and desiccated coconut flakes, does not Indian cuisine make. Nevertheless, I can think of no other ethnic situation here in which some home awareness initially outstripped any restaurant awareness.

Through these years there were, of course, Indian restaurants in major American cities. But they were largely devoid of American diners. It's not that they weren't trying to please the American palate. Indeed, in some ways Indian food has followed the Italian-Chinese model in America: several decades of exposure in the American restaurant marketplace led to a new, American-influenced form of the original cuisine. And I for one — as I do with good Italian-American cuisine and good Chinese-American cuisine — absolutely love Indian-American cuisine. When I started going to Indian restaurants in the 1960s, there were always samosas (stuffed and fried pastries) as a first course, served with a spicy onion sambal. There were the same curries on the menu, over and over again, each available with any protein you wanted as headliner: Madras, korma, vindaloo. Along with the curry always came a big platter of fragrant rice, a thin version of dal (stewed Indian legumes), a side dish of yellow cabbage curry, and a small serving of mango chutney. The flavors did not diverge widely from dish to dish, as they do in the best Indian cooking — but those of us who loved Indian restaurants didn't care: the familiar flavors grew into comfort food. Of course, once again following the Italian-American and Chinese-American models, fine Indian-American chefs today wouldn't be caught dead re-creating those old flavors.

What do they create today? I'm happy to say that Indian cuisine in America is one of our healthiest, most vibrant restaurant cuisines. Chefs and restaurateurs are just starting to test the limits of authenticity that they can bring to the American table. And American diners — for the first time, I would say — are becoming truly excited about what they're eating in Indian restaurants, are loving the discovery of regional variety and Indian-style freshness. The phenomenon exists at every level of Indian dining — from the fancy palaces down to the inexpensive and informal places situated near universities.

One other trend is also upon us: Indian fusion, with elements of other Asian cuisines, and Western cuisines, added to the Indian bass line. I question the logic of this development: if an eating public, such as ours, is not really familiar yet with classic Indian cuisine, is it a good moment to create postmodern variations? Fusion usually works best, I find, when the diner is familiar with the cuisines being fused. I can only give you my personal response to Indian fusion food: after I eat it, I want to go out and eat some Indian food. Even chicken curry with cabbage and dal!

☆ Samosas ☆
with Ground Lamb Filling

In the old days, Indian samosas were to Indian restaurants in the United States what Chinese egg rolls were to Chinese restaurants: a must-have first course. This is no longer true, of course; both types of restaurant have developed a less predictable array of appetizer options. But that doesn't take away from the appeal of samosas — full-flavored, deep-fried triangles of pastry stuffed with spice-accented meat and/or vegetables. These days most Indian restaurants have "upgraded" the presentation by serving tamarind chutney (see page 219) and/or coriander sauce (see page 218) as accompaniments to samosas. The following recipe is made with keema, or ground meat — in this case, lamb. In India, where samosas are sold from pushcarts all over the country, a special pastry is used; I find that a good egg roll wrapper approximates it best (see discussion of wrappers on page 155). When you're filling that wrapper, don't be afraid to pile on the filling; the samosa tastes best when it is well stuffed. Make extras if you have the time: sealed, unfried samosas freeze well.

Yield: About 3 cups, enough for 16 samosas

1 tablespoon ghee (clarified butter, see page 227)
1 tablespoon vegetable oil, plus more for deep-frying
1 small onion, finely diced
2 large garlic cloves, minced
1 tablespoon grated gingerroot
2 teaspoons caraway seeds, lightly crushed
1½ teaspoons ground cumin
1 teaspoon ground cardamom
1 teaspoon ground coriander
1 teaspoon ground turmeric
½ teaspoon ground cinnamon
¼ teaspoon cayenne
1 bay leaf
1 medium-size fresh tomato, chopped into ¼-inch dice
1 small hot green chili, minced
1 pound ground lamb
½ cup frozen peas
2 cups loosely packed chopped coriander leaves
8 Chinese egg roll wrappers (Golden Dragon brand, if possible)

1. Place the ghee and the 1 tablespoon vegetable oil in a medium skillet over low heat. Add the onion, garlic, and ginger and cook until the onion is soft, about 10 to 12 minutes. Add the caraway seeds, cumin, cardamom, ground coriander, turmeric, cinnamon, cayenne, and bay leaf; cook, stirring, until the mixture becomes fragrant, about 3 minutes. Add the tomato and chili and cook until the juice from the tomato is absorbed, about 10 minutes. Check seasoning.

2. Raise heat to medium-high. Add the lamb

and brown on all sides. Add ½ cup of water and stir. Crumble lamb with a wooden spoon. Turn heat to low, cover, and cook for 40 minutes. Check from time to time; if the mixture looks dry, add a little more water. After 40 minutes of cooking, add the frozen peas and cook for 5 minutes more.

3. Turn off heat, remove and discard bay leaf, stir in the coriander leaves, and season to taste with salt and pepper. Let the lamb cool before stuffing the samosas.

4. Keep the egg roll wrappers covered with a damp paper towel as you work. Take out

I wrapper and cut it in half diagonally. Put half of it back under the towel. You will now have a triangular half wrapper on your counter. Fold it in half into a smaller triangle, then unfold it; this gives you a center seam to use as a guide. Place 2 tablespoons of the cooled lamb mixture on the left half of the triangle, to the left of the seam, using your seam as a visual reference to make sure the mixture is centered on the left side. Spread the lamb mixture out evenly across the left side of the wrapper, spreading it to within ¼ inch of the edges. Place another tablespoon of filling on top in the center of the spread-out meat; do not spread this tablespoon.

5. Using your fingers, dampen the edges of the wrapper with water. Bring the empty half of the triangle (on the right side of the seam) over the left side of the triangle. You now have a small, triangular packet. Seal the edges, pressing down hard with your fingers.

6. Heat 3 inches of vegetable oil to 375 degrees, either in a deep fryer or in a 3-quart saucepan. Fry the samosas a few at a time; cook for 1 minute on each side until golden. Drain on paper towels and serve while warm.

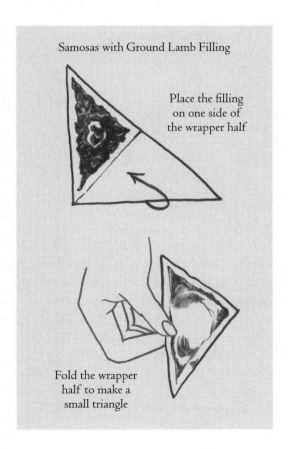

Samosas with Ground Lamb Filling

Place the filling on one side of the wrapper half

Fold the wrapper half to make a small triangle

☆ Onion Sambal ☆

One of my favorite side dishes in the old Indian-American menu was the onion sambal: bits of raw onion tossed with lemon juice, spices, and tomato paste. Long before anyone in the United States ever put tamarind chutney or coriander sauce next to the pappadams and samosas that open an Indian meal, restaurants were offering onion sambal next to those things. But there is no standard style of onion sambal in America; I've seen them go from very tomatoey and almost gritty with spices to very light and clean. The following sambal is my favorite; with its lemony blast and minimal tomato paste, it's in the light-and-clean school.

Yield: About 1 cup of onion sambal, a good accompaniment to an Indian meal for 4 diners

1½ cups finely minced onion
    (see Note)
3 tablespoons freshly squeezed
    lemon juice
1 teaspoon firmly packed grated
    lemon zest
5 teaspoons tomato paste
¼ teaspoon ground fenugreek
¼ teaspoon ground cumin
⅛ teaspoon cayenne (or more
    to taste)

1. Place the onion in a mixing bowl immediately after mincing it. Pour the lemon juice over the onion right away; toss to blend.
2. Add the lemon zest, tomato paste, fenugreek, cumin, and cayenne. Mix well, until the sambal has a uniform reddish color. Season to taste with salt and serve immediately.

NOTE: This dish is vastly improved if you use sweet onions to make it; the increased sugar and decreased harshness make the dish much more pleasant. These days, most American shoppers have a choice of sweet onions: Vidalia onions from Georgia or California (springtime), Texas Sweets (springtime), Walla Walla onions from Washington (July), and Maui onions from Hawaii (year-round). You'll need about one large one for the one and one-half cups of minced onion in this recipe.

☆ Indian-Restaurant ☆ Coriander Sauce

Just as the old Chinese restaurants in the United States used to automatically put the trinity of fried noodles, "duck" sauce, and hot mustard on the table — so do modern Indian restaurants usually offer diners the trinity of pappadams, coriander sauce, and tamarind chutney. The coriander sauce, a thinnish, bright green affair, is usually tangy and herbal, a little salty and sour. In addition to serving as a dip for pappadams, it's also delicious with Punjabi grill food, such as chicken tandoori.

Yield: About ¾ cup

1 cup tightly packed fresh coriander leaves
    (all stems removed)
¼ cup tightly packed fresh mint leaves
    (all stems removed)
⅔ cup cold water
1 teaspoon lime juice
2 teaspoons brown sugar
¼ teaspoon cumin
⅛ teaspoon salt
⅛ teaspoon red chili pepper
⅛ teaspoon garlic powder
3 tablespoons whole-milk yogurt

1. Plunge coriander leaves and mint leaves into a pot of boiling water. Using a strainer, remove leaves after 5 seconds. Submerge strainer with leaves into a bowl of ice water for another 5 seconds. Remove and drain.
2. Place coriander and mint, cold water, lime juice, brown sugar, cumin, salt, red chili pepper, and garlic powder in a blender. Process for about 10 seconds.
3. Add yogurt and process for a couple more seconds or until incorporated.

Completing the Trilogy: Coriander Sauce, Tamarind Chutney... and Pappadams

The recipes for coriander sauce (page 218) and tamarind chutney (this page) give you two-thirds of the great giveaway snack that most Indian restaurants offer today at the top of the meal. For the all-important "chip" to go with the "dips" ... you simply buy a package of pappadams, or bean wafers, at an Indian grocery store. They are dry and unchewable when you get them home. But if you dip them in deep, hot oil (about 365 degrees) for 3 seconds, they become gloriously crisp and delicious. Remember, as you purchase your pappadams, that some are mild and some are quite chili intense; check with the merchant. My favorite brand is the fairly mild Cumin Papads manufactured by Shri Mahila Griha Udyog Lijjat in Mumbai and available in most Indian groceries.

✳ Tamarind Chutney ✳

Chutney — a term apparently based on the word *chaat-na*, "to lick," but converted by English colonials in IN-juh — has come to describe a bewilderingly wide assortment of condiments, from very sweet to savory, from thick to thin. Most Americans think first of mango chutney, thanks to the wildly successful supermarket product called Major Grey mango chutney. Out of deference to that American familiarity, many Indian restaurants in the United States offer a side dish of mango chutney (almost always from a jar) for a small extra charge. Indian restaurants of more recent vintage, however, are making their own chutneys — and not always from mango, though the chutneys usually are thick and sweet. Tamarind chutney has become a fairly standard giveaway in good Indian American restaurants today — usually a sweet counterpart to the more tart coriander sauce that's served at the same time. A good one has the blend of sweet and sour that you find in a good balsamic vinegar. And that made me realize: un-Indian as it is, balsamic vinegar is a delicious, undetectable quick route to India in making this dish! Try it; no one will ever guess. I especially like this sauce as a dip for samosas.

Yield: About I cup

*4 ounces dried, compressed, block tamarind
(see "All about Tamarind" sidebar,
page 209)*
1¼ cups room-temperature water
1 tablespoon roasted garlic
2 tablespoons brown sugar
¼ teaspoon ground coriander
⅛ teaspoon salt
⅛ teaspoon red chili powder
⅛ teaspoon ground cardamom
⅛ teaspoon ground turmeric
⅛ teaspoon ground cinnamon
½ cup balsamic vinegar

I. Put tamarind and water in a small bowl, making sure the tamarind is covered with water. Set aside for I5 minutes.
2. With your hands, break up tamarind and continue to work it until the pulp has come away from the seeds and the mixture begins to look like a medium-thick sauce. Using a wooden spoon, press the tamarind mixture through a strainer over a bowl. Discard the seeds remaining in the strainer.

3. In another bowl, mash the roasted garlic, brown sugar, and spices together. Stir the garlic-spice mixture into the tamarind sauce.
4. Add balsamic vinegar and blend thoroughly.

✱ Sweet Tomato Chutney ✱

Tomato chutneys are very popular in India — and becoming more popular here at restaurants trying to push the Indian envelope. The following recipe yields a fairly sweet, thick chutney that is loaded with Indian flavor. Because sweet and hot go so well together, it's a lovely thing to have on the table during a particularly incendiary Indian meal. Once made, it can be enjoyed as soon as it cools. Or you can hold it in the refrigerator for a few days, during which time the spices will increasingly penetrate the tomato chunks. I prefer it a day or two after it's made.

Yield: About 1 cup of chutney,
a good accompaniment for an Indian meal for 4

1 pound fresh plum tomatoes (about 7)
1 tablespoon vegetable oil
¼ cup very finely minced onion
2 large garlic cloves, peeled and finely minced
2 teaspoons grated gingerroot
½ jalapeño (or more to taste), seeded
  and finely minced
1 tablespoon sugar
Seeds from 5 cardamom pods
½ teaspoon ground cumin
½ teaspoon ground coriander
½ teaspoon ground cinnamon
½ teaspoon ground turmeric
¼ teaspoon cayenne (or more to taste)
1 tablespoon white vinegar
2 tablespoons golden raisins
3 tablespoons coriander leaves, for garnish

1. Place the tomatoes in a large cast-iron skillet over high heat. Cook, turning, until the skins are blackened, about 10 minutes. Set aside to cool. When the tomatoes have cooled, remove and discard the skins. Cut away the tiny remnants of the stems. Slice each tomato in half lengthwise, then crosswise, creating 4 chunks for each tomato. Reserve juices.
2. Add the vegetable oil to a large saucepan over medium-low heat. Add the onion, garlic, ginger, and jalapeño. Cook, stirring occasionally, until the vegetables are very soft, about 10 minutes.
3. Working carefully with the tomatoes to keep the chunks whole, add them and their juices to the saucepan. Add the sugar, cardamom seeds, cumin, coriander, cinnamon, turmeric, cayenne, vinegar, and raisins. Stir gently. Allow mixture to come to the barest simmer. Simmer for 15 minutes, stirring occasionally very gently.
4. After 15 minutes, season to taste with salt. Remove chutney to a bowl or container and let cool to room temperature. You can eat the chutney right away or save it for 3 days in the refrigerator. When you do serve it, garnish the top with coriander leaves.

✱ Raita ✱
(Indian Yogurt and Cucumber Condiment)

As aficionados of hotter-than-hell food will tell you, the best way to cool off your mouth (and really enjoy that endorphin rush!) is with dairy products. Perhaps that's why cooling raita has a regular place on the Indian table — both in India and in Indian restaurants here. I've become particularly fond of the up-scale versions you find in better Indian restaurants — in which tomatoes and coriander leaves are added to the basic yogurt-cucumber mix.

Yield: About 1½ cups

1 medium cucumber
½ teaspoon salt
1 teaspoon cumin seeds (or ½ teaspoon
*   ground cumin)*
⅓ cup diced fresh tomato
2 tablespoons whole
*   coriander leaves*
2 teaspoons lemon juice
1½ cups plain yogurt

1. Peel the cucumber and cut in half length-wise. Scoop out the seeds with a spoon and discard. Grate the cucumber coarsely. Place cucumber flesh in a colander set in the sink, or over a bowl, and sprinkle with the ½ teaspoon salt. Let drain for 30 minutes, then squeeze excess water out with your hands.

2. Place a medium skillet over medium heat for 2 minutes. Add the cumin seeds and cook, stirring, for 30 seconds. Remove from skillet and set aside to cool. (This step can be omitted if using ground cumin.)

3. In a medium bowl, combine the drained cucumber, tomato, coriander leaves, lemon juice, and yogurt. Blend well.

4. Grind the cooled cumin seeds in a spice grinder and mix the cumin into the raita (or mix in the ½ teaspoon of already ground cumin). Season with salt and pepper. Store in the refrigerator for at least 3 hours (for flavors to meld).

✼ Mulligatawny Soup ✼

There's no separate soup course in an authentic Indian meal — but there it is nevertheless, on every Indian restaurant menu in the United States and Britain, the famous mulligatawny soup. We've got the Brits to thank for this; while colonizing the subcontinent, they took a shine to a thin, lentil-less, spicy, flavorful broth served in the south as an accompaniment to other dishes. They took the Tamil words for "pepper water" and converted them into English as "mulligatawny." They didn't, however, decree how to make it — and today you find a wide range of mulligatawny styles in Western restaurants serving Indian food, from thin to thick, from stock based to water based. The chief departure these days from the classic progenitor is that lentils are now usually involved; in fact, many versions of this soup are really soup versions of dal, the spiced legume dishes of India.

Yield: 6 servings

3 tablespoons vegetable oil
2 medium yellow onions, chopped
4 large garlic cloves, finely chopped
2 tablespoons finely chopped gingerroot
2 teaspoons ground coriander
1 teaspoon ground cumin
1 teaspoon ground turmeric
½ teaspoon Indian chili powder (or ¼ teaspoon
*   paprika and ¼ teaspoon cayenne)*
1½ cups split masoor dal (pink lentils;
*   see "All about Dal" sidebar, page 229)*
9 cups chicken broth
1 tablespoon plus 1 teaspoon lemon juice
2 tablespoons finely chopped coriander leaves

1. In a large saucepan over high heat, heat 2 tablespoons of the vegetable oil. Add the onions and cook, stirring, until well browned, about 5 minutes. Add the garlic and ginger

and cook, stirring, until soft and fragrant, about 45 seconds. Add the remaining 1 tablespoon oil and the ground coriander, cumin, turmeric, and chili powder. Cook, stirring, for 45 seconds more.

2. Add the dal and chicken broth and bring to a boil. Lower the heat and simmer, covered, stirring occasionally, until the dal has disintegrated into a puree, about 30 minutes.

3. Stir in the lemon juice and coriander leaves. Season to taste with salt and pepper. Divide among six soup bowls and serve immediately.

☆ Saag Paneer ☆

One of the dishes I order a lot in Indian restaurants in the United States is this one — a delicious blend of spinach (saag), spices, and chunks of the Indian fresh cheese called paneer. Paneer is now available at gourmet groceries — especially Indian ones — or you can make a terrific substitute for it out of ricotta (see following recipe). I especially like making this saag paneer recipe at home because the spinach ends up a little greener, brighter, and fresher than it normally does in the restaurant. Serve it as a vegetarian main course in an Indian dinner, or alongside other main-course dishes.

Yield: 4 main-course servings

2½ pounds fresh spinach leaves
¼ cup plus 2 tablespoons ghee (see page 227)
2 medium yellow onions, finely chopped
1 tablespoon plus 1 teaspoon ground coriander
2 teaspoons ground cumin
2 teaspoons ground turmeric
1 teaspoon sugar
¼ teaspoon cayenne

4 cardamom pods
1 cinnamon stick, broken in half
1¼ cups yogurt
Ricotta-Baked Paneer (recipe follows),
    about 16 chunks

1. Bring a large pot of salted water to a boil.

2. Add the spinach to the water in two batches. Cook each batch, stirring occasionally, until soft and dark green, about 3 minutes per batch. Using a slotted spoon, transfer to a colander. Let cool, then squeeze out any excess liquid. Roughly chop the spinach.

3. In a large skillet over medium-high heat, heat the ¼ cup of ghee. Add the onion and cook, stirring, until lightly browned, about 10 minutes. Add the remaining 2 tablespoons ghee. Stir in the coriander, cumin, turmeric, sugar, cayenne, cardamom pods, and cinnamon and cook, stirring frequently, until dark and fragrant, about 2 minutes. Stir in the spinach and cook, stirring, until coated and hot, about 2 minutes. Lower the heat to medium, stir in the yogurt, and cook, stirring, for about 2 minutes more. Remove from the heat and gently stir in the cheese. Season with salt and pepper. Serve immediately.

☆ Ricotta-Baked Paneer ☆

Fresh Indian cheese — paneer — is really quite simple to make; you just add lemon juice (or vinegar) to milk, let the liquid separate into curds and whey, place the curds in cheesecloth, hang them, weight them, and you're all set. But some home cooks, understandably, find cheese making to be intimidating. If you feel that way, you're going to love this simple method of making a very fine paneer substitute: you merely bake ricotta cheese in the oven! A little weighting — and paneer is here. The following instructions are for the small quantity I usually make. If you wish to increase quantities, just make sure to spread your ricotta out in an appropriate pan until it's about one inch deep — then follow the same heat and timing instructions.

Yield: About ½ cup of cheese chunks (16 pieces)

1 hefty cup smooth whole-milk ricotta
(about 12 ounces)

1. Preheat oven to 250 degrees.
2. Choose a round baking dish that's about 4 inches in diameter. Place the ricotta in the dish and smooth it out until it's about 1 inch deep all over. Cover tightly with foil and place in the oven. Cook for 2½ hours.
3. When the paneer is done, it should be quite firm, with a good deal of liquid oozing out. Pour off the liquid and cover again with foil. Place another baking dish of exactly the same size on top of the foil. Weight with heavy pans or cans. Let rest for 2 hours.
4. Remove weights and foil. Cut paneer out of baking dish and place on counter. Cut roughly into 4 long strips, each 1 inch across. Cut each strip into 4 pieces. You should now have about 16 pieces of paneer, each about 1 by 1 by ⅜ inch (the weighting really compresses it). You'll have a total of about ½ cup of chunks, which weigh 2 to 3 ounces. Use immediately, or refrigerate, tightly covered, for a few days.

Ricotta-Baked Paneer

Paneer in the bottom baking dish covered by foil, another baking dish of the same size, and a weight

☆ Chicken Tandoori ☆

Back in the 1960s, when Indian restaurants in the United States had few patrons indeed, there was no clamor for chicken tandoori. But go to an Indian restaurant in the United States today, and every two minutes, it seems, a platter of sizzling chicken tandoori, piled high with similarly noisy onions, is hissing past your ear to another table. Could it be that the rise of chicken tandoori instigated the rise of the Indian restaurant in the United States? It's a perfect dish for us: full of flavor, very colorful, with little caloric guilt. Surprisingly, not many Americans have been cooking it at home. Perhaps it seems a tad too exotic. Perhaps the knowledge of its name's meaning impedes us: chicken lowered into a tandoor, a deep clay oven, the likes of which only the most esoteric foodies own (you can buy them!). But perhaps the average backyard-grill cook doesn't realize that (1) it is tremendously easy to prepare a great chicken tandoori marinade, and (2) when you cook it on your barbecue or under your broiler, it's every bit as delicious as when the Indian chefs cook it in a tandoor.

Yield: 4 main-course servings

8 large boneless chicken thighs
1 cup plain yogurt
5 medium garlic cloves, peeled
¼ cup coarsely chopped gingerroot
1 teaspoon ground coriander
1 teaspoon garam masala (bottled spice blend)
½ teaspoon ground cumin
¼ teaspoon ground cinnamon
¼ teaspoon Indian chili powder, or cayenne
¼ teaspoon ground cardamom
¼ teaspoon ground fenugreek
⅛ teaspoon ground clove
Red food coloring (optional; see Note)
8 thick sweet onion slices for garnish
2 lemons, quartered, for garnish

1. Score the thighs across the skin, cutting no more than ¼ inch deep into the meat. Salt the chicken lightly and reserve.
2. Place the yogurt and all the spices in the work bowl of a food processor. Run machine until mixture is smooth. Place yogurt-spice mixture in a large bowl. If you wish to add food coloring, do it now. Add the chicken thighs, stirring well to coat them evenly. Cover and refrigerate for 24 hours.
3. When ready to cook, prepare a hot outdoor fire or turn on your indoor broiler.
4. Remove chicken thighs from marinade and dry well. Place the thighs either over the hot fire or under the hot broiler. Cook until just done: brown and sizzled on the outside, just past pink on the inside. While the chicken is cooking, place the onion slices either over or under the same fire. They should be browned but still slightly crunchy.
5. Divide the chicken tandoori among four dinner plates. Top chicken with sizzling onion slices and serve lemon wedges on the side.

NOTE: Indian cooks love to turn their chicken tandoori red or orange. It doesn't affect the flavor, but it does have a dramatic visual impact. If you wish to go this route, simply add enough red or orange food coloring to the yogurt marinade to turn it a deep, vivid color. Then add the chicken. If you have access to an Indian grocery, you might want to buy the red or orange powder they sell there for this purpose; about one teaspoon of red or orange powdered food coloring turns a cup of yogurt a gorgeous restaurant-tandoori red.

☆ Shrimp Madras ☆

The language of old-fashioned Indian menus in American restaurants was a kind of code. "Madras" this or "Madras" that didn't tell you that the dish in question was an authentic creation from that great Indian city; it told you that your "curry" would have tomatoes in it. The following recipe has 'em, and madras curry powder as well — for as our restaurants have demonstrated over and over again, though curry powder is not traditionally used, traditional is not a prerequisite for delicious.

Yield: 6 main-course servings

6 large garlic cloves, peeled
1 (2-inch) chunk peeled gingerroot
3½ cups plus ½ cup water
About 18 canned whole tomatoes in tomato puree
¼ cup ghee (see page 227)

The Curious Case of Curry

When Americans think of Indian food, the first thing they usually think of is curry — either curry powder or cooked dishes they refer to as curries. It usually comes as a surprise that the concept of curry is completely foreign to Indian cooks.

Take curry powder, that blend of Indian spices found in many an American cupboard and used as the main flavoring agent for many a "curry" in this country. Though Indian cooks do use a few specialized blends of spices (such as garam masala or sambar powder), for the most part they create new blends of spices for every dish they cook. This is the genius of Indian food and what enables it to be so endlessly varied. If you use a blend of dried herbs called "Italian seasoning" in every Italian dish you make, how exciting or authentic would that be? Italian chefs would never do that, and Indian cooks don't use curry powder. What they do do is select a group of spices for each dish — the long list of possibilities includes coriander seeds, cumin seeds, cinnamon, cloves, cardamom seeds, turmeric, asafetida, fennel seeds, fenugreek seeds, poppy seeds, and mustard seeds. Most often they will toast or roast whole spices in a pan before using them; sometimes they'll grind those toasted spices into a powder before using them. Every chef has his or her tricks and secrets for the timing of the addition of each spice. Before the onions? After? Early in the cooking? Late? It's perennially fascinating, and about as far from the concept of curry powder as you can get.

Then there's "curry" — what many Americans think of as a standard Indian dish, as in chicken curry, or shrimp curry. In India, however — except in hotel restaurants that cater to foreigners — there are no dishes called curry. Indian cuisine features a wide range of stews with gravies that have specific names: vindaloo, korma, dhansak, makhani, and so on. The English looked at this range of dishes and, probably because they wished to simplify this vastly varied cuisine so they could better understand it, pronounced all these dishes curries. Where did they get the name? There are many theories — but the one I buy involves the Tamil word *kaari*, which is used in the region around Madras. To the highest caste there, a kaari is a vegetable dish cooked with spices; the lower castes, who pronounce the word with a stress on the second syllable, use it to mean meat. If the meat is in gravy, they'd call it kaaree kolambu. I think the Brits looked at those vegetable stews and meat stews with more or less the same name and jumped all over *kaari*, turning it into *curry*.

In the Anglo-influenced world of Indian food in America, we've long tended to make the same mistakes. In my kitchen I like to customize my spices — though I do have high-quality curry powder on hand for occasional use.

½ teaspoon cumin seeds
¼ teaspoon fennel seeds
8 cardamom pods, crushed and seeds removed
4 whole cloves
1 cinnamon stick, broken in half
1 bay leaf
1 large yellow onion, thinly sliced

1 tablespoon Madras curry powder
1 tablespoon plus 1 teaspoon sugar
1 teaspoon ground turmeric
Pinch of cayenne
1 cup unsweetened coconut milk
1½ pounds peeled and deveined medium
    shrimp, tails removed

2 tablespoons unsalted butter
2 teaspoons lemon juice
1 tablespoon minced coriander leaves

1. In a blender, combine the garlic, ginger, and the ½ cup of water. Puree into a paste. Transfer to a small bowl and reserve.
2. In the blender, puree enough of the tomatoes to make 1 cup tomato puree. Reserve puree, along with the remaining tomatoes.
3. In a medium pot, over medium-high heat, heat the ghee. Add the cumin seeds, fennel seeds, cardamom seeds, cloves, cinnamon, and bay leaf and cook, stirring constantly, until fragrant, about 1 minute. Add the onion and cook, stirring, until well browned, about 5 minutes. Add the curry powder, sugar, turmeric, and cayenne and cook, stirring, until dark and fragrant, about 3 minutes. Add the garlic-ginger paste and cook, stirring, until most of the water has evaporated, about 2 minutes. Add the reserved tomato puree to the mixture and cook, stirring, until dark red, about 3 minutes.
4. Add the 3½ cups water and bring to a boil. Lower the heat and simmer, uncovered, stirring occasionally, until the liquid has thickened to a saucelike consistency, about 20 minutes.
5. Whisk in the coconut milk and bring to a boil. Add shrimp and remaining tomatoes and bring to a simmer. Cook until shrimp are just cooked through, about 3 minutes. Stir in the butter until incorporated. Stir in the lemon juice and coriander leaves and season with salt and pepper. Serve immediately.

☆ Chicken Korma ☆

In the code language of Indian-American restaurants, *korma* — though it has a different meaning in India — means "the curry that's not hot and comes with a creamy sauce." There are some insipid kormas out there, but there are also some rich, velvety, intensely flavored ones. The following recipe is one of the latter.

Yield: 4 servings as part of an Indian meal

2 tablespoons chopped garlic
1 tablespoon chopped gingerroot
½ teaspoon ground turmeric
6 saffron threads
½ cup hot water
1 pound boneless and skinless chicken thighs
½ teaspoon salt
½ teaspoon ground pepper
1 teaspoon ground coriander
2 teaspoons ground cardamom
3 green cardamom pods, lightly crushed
2 cinnamon sticks
2 whole cloves
2 tablespoons ghee (see page 227)
1 cup chopped onion
½ cup chicken broth
¼ cup whole-milk yogurt

1. Add garlic, ginger, turmeric, and saffron to hot water and set aside for 1 hour.
2. Cut each thigh into 3 pieces. Combine salt, pepper, coriander, and the ground cardamom; rub chicken with spice mixture and set aside.
3. Heat a 12-inch skillet over medium-high heat. Add the crushed cardamom pods, 1 of the cinnamon sticks, and cloves to skillet; sauté for 1 minute.

Ghee, or Clarified Butter

The use of ghee, or clarified butter, in Indian cooking is not as widespread in India as you might imagine; it's an expensive ingredient, and I'm told that the only people who use a lot of it are those who want to show off! Its use has a different spirit in America; we think of it as a basic Indian ingredient, and lots of our upscale restaurant chefs and avid home cooks use it. Of course, ghee performs the same vital role in Indian cooking as it does in Western cooking: if you want to fry something in butter, using clarified butter reduces the chance the butter will burn along the way. The following easy recipe can be used as ghee for Indian dishes or as clarified butter for other kinds of cooking.

Clarified Butter

Yield: ¾ cup

½ pound (2 sticks) unsalted butter

1. Cut the butter into 1-inch slices and place in a saucepan. Melt gently over medium heat, then immediately pour into a glass measuring jar.
2. Place jar in the refrigerator. After an hour or so the milk solids will sink to the bottom. There may also be some foam on top. Remove the foam and discard, then spoon off the clarified butter into a clean dish. Discard the solids at the bottom of the cup. Store the clarified butter in the refrigerator.

4. Add ghee and onion. Reduce heat to low and cook, stirring occasionally, for about 10 minutes. Do not let the onion brown.
5. Increase the heat to medium and add

chicken. Cook 4 minutes on each side. Strain the water containing the garlic, ginger, turmeric, and saffron into the skillet. Add remaining 1 cinnamon stick and chicken broth. Increase heat and bring to a boil. Reduce heat, cover, and maintain at a simmer for 15 to 20 minutes or until tender. Strain out broth and reserve
6. Stir in yogurt. Add back enough broth to make a creamy sauce. Heat for 1 minute. Serve immediately.

✭ Lamb Vindaloo ✭

Vindaloo is a specialty of Goa, the lovely, beachy area on India's west coast, today a fashionable resort. Portuguese sailors settled there centuries ago, and helped forge one of India's most distinctive regional cuisines. If you go to Goa, you'll be surprised to discover that the dish is not mind-blowingly hot. You'll be surprised, that is, if you're an aficionado of vindaloo in Indian restaurants in the United States — where the designation "vindaloo" has come to mean something like "our hottest dish." I love the subtle hot-sweet-sour balance of a vindaloo in Goa, almost always made from pork — but I must confess I also love the hotter-than-hell kick and the rich, brown, cooked-in goodness of a well-made "American-style" vindaloo. In our restaurants you almost never see pork vindaloo on menus; shrimp, chicken, and especially lamb are the usual choices. You also never get the typical Goan taste here. No matter. Try the following powerhouse American-restaurant-style version (the chili count is up to you) with a fluffy mound of rice pilaf (page 231) and some cooling raita (page 220).

Yield: 6 main-course servings

2 pounds boneless leg of lamb, cut into
1-inch pieces
1 cup white vinegar

16 whole garlic cloves, peeled

4 tablespoons ghee (see page 227)

16 to 24 dried red chilies,
   stems removed

1 tablespoon cumin seeds

1 teaspoon coriander seeds

¼ teaspoon ground clove

1 cinnamon stick, broken into pieces

1 large onion, coarsely chopped

1 (3-inch) piece peeled gingerroot,
   coarsely chopped

1 tablespoon dark molasses

2 cups beef stock

1 cup whole, peeled tomatoes packed
   in tomato puree

1. In a large bowl, combine the lamb, vinegar, and 16 garlic cloves. Store in the refrigerator for at least 3 hours and up to 6. Drain the lamb and reserve the vinegar and garlic.

2. In a medium Dutch oven with a tight-fitting lid, over medium-high heat, heat 2 tablespoons of the ghee. Add the chilies, cumin, coriander, clove, and cinnamon stick and cook, stirring until toasted and fragrant, about 2 minutes.

3. Transfer the toasted mixture to a blender or food processor and add the reserved vinegar and garlic. Add the onion, ginger, and molasses and puree into a loose paste.

4. In the Dutch oven, over medium-high heat, add the remaining 2 tablespoons of ghee. Dry the reserved lamb well, season generously with salt and pepper, and sauté in batches, if necessary, until the lamb starts to brown. Add the reserved paste and cook, stirring, until the paste is thick and bubbly,

about 4 minutes. Add the beef stock and tomatoes, with their puree, and bring to a boil. Lower the heat and simmer, covered, stirring occasionally, until the lamb is very tender, about 1½ hours.

5. Remove the lid and continue cooking, stirring occasionally, until the liquid has thickened to a rich sauce, about 5 to 10 minutes. Season with salt and pepper to taste and transfer to a serving bowl.

☆ Side Dish Dal ☆

Thirty years ago, dal — a spiced puree of legumes — was served with every main course in every Indian restaurant in the United States. Now that Indian restaurants have gotten a lot fancier, this practice has diminished. But here's the good news: the super-thin, tasteless dals that were once served have now modulated into à la carte side dishes with much more body and flavor. Here's a good example of latter-day restaurant dal — complete with the last-minute spice addition, or tadka, that authentic restaurants in the United States now employ.

Yield: 6 side dish servings

3 tablespoons unsalted butter

1 cup finely minced onion (about 2 medium
   onions)

6 tablespoons very finely minced garlic

2 tablespoons finely minced gingerroot

1 teaspoon finely minced seeded jalapeño
   (adjust to desired heat)

2 cups chana dal (see sidebar; you may
   substitute yellow split peas),
   checked for stones or impurities
   and washed

1 tablespoon ground coriander

1 tablespoon ground cumin

1 teaspoon celery seed

1½ teaspoons ground cinnamon

¼ teaspoon ground clove

6 cups chicken stock

½ teaspoon cardamom seeds, removed from husks

1. In a heavy-bottomed pot, melt 1 tablespoon of the butter over medium heat. Add the onion, 2 tablespoons of the garlic, the ginger, and jalapeño. Sauté for 2 minutes, stirring. Add the dal, 1 teaspoon of the coriander, 1 teaspoon of the cumin, the celery seed, ½ teaspoon of the cinnamon, and the clove. Mix well. Add the chicken stock,

All about Dal

We think of many things as typical Indian food . . . but not all of them are served everywhere in India. Dal, however, comes closer than anything else I can think of to being the Indian national dish.

The name itself has several meanings. First of all, think split peas, dried lentils, dried beans — and you've visualized dal. When dal producers take the pods of a pod-bearing vegetable (think pea pods or string beans), split them open, remove the seeds from the pods (the seeds are the peas, beans, or lentils inside the pods, also called legumes), and dry the peas, beans, or lentils, they've made dal. In America we don't tend to lump these products together terminologically; split peas are split peas, lentils are lentils, garbanzos are garbanzos, kidney beans are kidney beans, and so on. But in India they are all grouped together in the category known as dal, sometimes called pulses.

The naming situation is made more confusing by the fact that *dal* also refers to the dish that's made by cooking these pulses with liquid and spices. Sometimes it's a puree (something like thick split pea soup), and sometimes the pulses hold their individual shapes — but at all times the cooked preparation is called dal. If it's made right, it's a wonderfully satisfying dish — hearty, filling, brimming with exotic flavor, a fabulous opener for an Indian meal or a delicious accompaniment to other Indian dishes. Just as the flavor of lime-slaked corn in Mexico suggests something ancient and mystical, so does the flavor of cooked dal — from the other side of the world — pull you back into the mists of prehistory.

So, to summarize: you can walk into an Indian grocery and ask for dal, which will be a plastic bag of dried peas or lentils or beans, or you can order dal in a restaurant, which will be a cooked dish of dried peas or lentils or beans.

Unfortunately, the confusion doesn't stop there. For if you're serious about dal and wish to understand the vast array of dried peas, beans, and lentils that are out there just waiting for you to buy and use . . . then you really walk into a terminological minefield. Since India is a country with sixteen major languages and hundreds of dialects, and scores of pulses that are consumed everywhere, trying to identify in English what's for sale in Indian groceries can be nightmarish. But I urge you to work at this a little, since there's tremendous pleasure to be derived from the variety of Indian dals.

stir again, and bring to a boil. Turn heat down to low and simmer slowly, partially covered, for 30 to 60 minutes, or until dal is just soft.

2. When dal is almost ready, place the remaining 2 tablespoons of butter in a heavy sauté pan over medium-high heat. When it foams, add the remaining 4 tablespoons of garlic, the remaining 2 teaspoons of coriander, the remaining 2 teaspoons of cumin, the remaining teaspoon of cinnamon, and the cardamom seeds. Cook, stirring, for 2 minutes. Remove from heat.

3. With a wooden spoon, crush some of the dal against the side of the pot. Stir well. If the dal is too thick, add a little chicken stock. Season with salt and pepper to taste. Ladle the hot dal into six bowls. Swirl the hot spice mixture into each bowl. Serve immediately.

✫ Classic Indian-Restaurant ✫ Cabbage Curry

Another foundation dish of the classic 1960s Indian-American restaurant was the side dish of cabbage curry that came with all meat curries. Sometimes it was watery and insipid, but sometimes it showed how wonderful the mixture of cabbage and Indian spices can be. The following recipe is relentlessly yellow and very intense. I love to give it a Bengali character — especially when I can acquire good Bengali mustard oil, which makes a delightful drizzle at the end of cooking.

Yield: 4 side dish servings

3 tablespoons vegetable oil
1 medium-large onion (about ½ pound),
    peeled and thinly sliced
6 large garlic cloves, peeled and thinly sliced
¼ cup julienne strips of gingerroot
1 small cabbage (about 1½ pounds)
2 teaspoons yellow mustard seeds
3 whole cloves
1 teaspoon ground turmeric
1 teaspoon powdered fenugreek (or substitute
    a good curry powder)
½ teaspoon ground cumin
½ teaspoon ground coriander
¼ teaspoon ground cinnamon
1½ cups chicken stock (or water)
Drizzle of Bengali mustard oil (optional)

1. Place the vegetable oil in a Dutch oven over medium-high heat. Add the onion, garlic, and ginger. Sauté, stirring occasionally, until the onion and garlic have turned medium brown (about 10 minutes).

2. While the onion-garlic mixture is cooking, prepare the cabbage. Remove the tougher, greener outer leaves. Cut the cabbage in half through the core, then remove the tough core. Lay each cabbage half on the counter, cut side down, and cut each crosswise into long strips that are about half an inch wide. Reserve.

3. When the onion is brown, add the mustard seeds and cloves; stir, and cook for 1 minute more.

4. Reduce heat to medium-low. Add the turmeric, fenugreek, cumin, coriander, and cinnamon. Stir to blend. Sauté for 1 minute. Add the cabbage strips and stir well to blend. Add the chicken stock and stir well to blend. Bring heat up to medium, cover the pan (except for a small crack), and cook until the

cabbage is tender and the liquid is almost completely evaporated (about an hour). If the cabbage is tender and there's still more than 1 or 2 tablespoons of liquid left, uncover, turn heat to high, and evaporate the liquid. When the cabbage is ready, add salt to taste. If desired, stir in a drizzle of Bengali mustard oil just before serving. Serve immediately.

☆ Fragrant Indian Rice Pilaf ☆ with Saffron and Curry Leaves

One of the loveliest moments in Indian-American restaurants is when the waiter appears, wiping off your hot, empty dinner plates with a clean towel. They are placed on the table, and within seconds, usually, a steaming platter of fragrant, colorful rice appears. That's when my appetite really kicks into gear. You can know such Pavlovian bliss at home — and the even greater bliss of a great pilaf. It is extremely easy to reproduce the light and fluffy texture they achieve — if you use the best quality of basmati rice and if you follow the instructions below carefully (including the unconventional soaking of the rice, then using very little cooking liquid — which works like a charm!). If you can find fresh curry leaves at an Indian grocery — bright green, nutty-minerally-smelling leaves that have nothing whatsoever to do with curry — your pilaf will be more wonderfully fragrant still.

Yield: 4 side dish servings
(or 2 servings for rice fanatics)

*1 cup basmati rice, preferably Dehra Dun
    (a growing area northwest of Delhi)*
*1 generous tablespoon ghee (see page 227),
    or regular unsalted butter*
⅓ cup very finely minced onion

6 pods of cardamom, cracked slightly
5 whole cloves
*3 pieces of cinnamon stick, each about
    2 inches long*
½ teaspoon firmly packed saffron threads
6 fresh curry leaves (or 3 bay leaves)
*½ cup chicken stock mixed with
    ¾ cup water*

1. Pour 1½ cups of water into a measuring cup. Add the basmati rice to the water. Let stand for 30 minutes.

2. When ready to cook, put the ghee in a high-sided sauté pan with a tight-fitting lid (any vessel about 10 inches in diameter that holds 2 cups of rice will do). Place over medium-low heat. Add the onion and sauté, stirring occasionally, until the onion is very soft (about 10 minutes). Do not allow the onion to brown.

3. Drain the rice in a sieve and run the rice under cold water from the faucet for a minute or so. Shake off the excess liquid and add the rice to the cooked onion. Add the cardamom pods, cloves, cinnamon stick, and saffron. Stir together for a minute or so, coating the rice with the ghee. Turn heat to high and add the curry leaves, along with the stock-water mixture. When the liquid begins to boil, turn heat down to medium-low and taste the liquid carefully for salt. Add salt if necessary. Cover tightly and cook over medium-low heat until the rice is tender and fluffy, about 15 minutes. Set rice aside, covered, for 5 minutes, then transfer the rice to a platter with a fork, fluffing the rice as you go. Serve immediately.

Making the Pilaf Even More Festive

Most Indian restaurants in the United States give us a taste of (or a look at) the traditional celebratory red color that turns up in Indian food in India; the dyeing of chicken tandoori is a good example. But the most memorable use of the red color, for me, was at a place in New York called India Pavilion, where Oswald Stevens, the owner, would dye red some of the rice going into his rice pilaf. The result was really quite beautiful, and extremely festive. I've seen others use orange dye for the same process. If you'd like to try it, here's what you do:

1. Bring 1½ cups of salted water to a boil in a small saucepan. Add about 10 drops of red (or orange) food coloring.
2. With the water boiling, drop 3 tablespoons of basmati rice into the red water. Boil until the rice is tender, 12 to 15 minutes. Drain the rice in a sieve and reserve.
3. When you reach step 3 in the recipe for Fragrant Indian Rice Pilaf with Saffron and Curry Leaves, you're ready to incorporate the red rice. After the pilaf has cooked for 15 minutes, blend in the red rice with a fork, fluffing as you go. Set rice aside, covered, for 5 minutes . . . just as the recipe instructs. Transfer, fluff, and serve as you would the regular pilaf recipe.

☆ Indian Chapatis ☆

India is a fascinating bread country — and that fascination hasn't been lost on the American patrons of Indian restaurants, who regularly order bread with their Indian meals. Chapati is the most basic bread of India, and the most basic choice in our Indian restaurants. It is a form of roti and is traditionally eaten at all meals (even breakfast). A really great one is light, flaky, slightly nutty. All these qualities can be yours if you journey to an Indian grocery and purchase ata (or aata) flour — a lovely product that's stone-ground from a low-gluten wheat. It is very fine in texture and can't be easily replaced — but a combination of two-thirds all-purpose flour and one-third whole wheat flour will get you close.

Yield: 12 breads

2 cups ata flour (soft wheat flour available from Indian groceries), plus an extra ½ cup for rolling
2 cups warm water
¼ cup ghee (optional; see page 227)

1. If using the food processor, add the 2 cups flour and pulse once to aerate the flour. If making the chapatis by hand, sieve the flour.
2. Slowly add warm water to flour, either in the food processor or by hand. Add just until a sticky dough is formed (this may take less than 2 cups of water). The dough must not be dry, otherwise the chapatis will be tough. Cover sticky dough with plastic wrap and let it rest for 2 hours.
3. Break off pieces of dough and form into 1½-inch balls. Cover.
4. Heat an 8-inch nonstick skillet or a griddle until a drop of water sizzles on contact. Put the extra ½ cup ata flour in a bowl. Flatten the chapatis slightly and dip each side into the flour so they won't stick when you're rolling them. Roll each ball with a rolling pin into a 6-inch circle. Place as many chapatis on the griddle as you have space for. If bubbles form, press them down gently with a wadded up dishtowel.

5. After 20 seconds turn the chapatis over. Cook the other side for 10 seconds.

6. Using tongs, lift the chapatis, one by one, and, with tongs, hold them closely over the open flame on your range to finish cooking. Cook chapatis briefly, turning, just until crispy brown spots are formed. The chapatis will puff up. (They will deflate as they cool.) Continue until all 12 chapatis are cooked.

7. Brush chapatis with softened ghee and sprinkle with kosher salt to taste.

8. As the chapatis are cooked and seasoned, stack them and keep them covered — either in aluminum foil or in a dishtowel.

✺ Aloo or Keema Paratha ✺
(Flaky Indian Breads Stuffed with Potatoes or Ground Lamb)

Paratha, the great layered bread of India, is often served there — unstuffed — at the same time as all the other foods in a meal. In America it is the stuffed paratha that has really taken off in popularity. In Indian-American restaurants, where foods are divided into courses, the stuffed bread is often served with the main course — or, very commonly, as an appetizer before the main course (along with coriander sauce, tamarind chutney, and raita; see pages 218, 219, and 220).

★ Paratha ★

Yield: 6 parathas

2 cups ata flour (available from Indian grocers), or substitute 1 cup whole wheat flour and 1 cup all-purpose flour
1 teaspoon salt

¾ to 1 cup warm water for mixing
Ghee (see page 227) or melted butter for spreading
3 cups Aloo Filling or Keema Filling (recipes follow)

1. Place ata flour and salt in the bowl of a food processor or in a mixing bowl. If using the food processor, pulse, adding the water gradually through the feed tube until the dough forms a soft mass. Be careful not to add too much water. You want a soft, slightly sticky dough. If mixing by hand, make a well in the center of the flour and pour in the water gradually, mixing with a wooden spoon.

2. Turn the dough out onto a lightly floured surface and knead by hand until it forms a soft, smooth ball. This will take about 2 minutes.

3. Let the dough rest for several hours or overnight in the refrigerator.

4. When ready to use, roll the dough into a rope about 2 inches in diameter and divide into 6 equal pieces. Take 1 piece and, on a lightly floured surface, roll it into a circle about 7 inches in diameter and ⅛ inch thick. Brush with melted ghee or butter. Don't use too much, as you don't want the butter to leak through when the paratha is rolled again. As you work on one paratha, keep the remaining dough in the refrigerator — both the breads you've rolled and the dough you haven't rolled yet.

5. Fold the sides of the dough so they meet in the middle, then the top and the bottom so they meet in the middle, as if you were forming an envelope. Carefully roll the dough

Aloo or Keema Paratha

The 7-inch round of dough, brushed with ghee or butter

After the first folding: the left and right sides meet in the middle and, on top of that, the top and bottom sides meet in the middle

After rolling the dough into a 7-inch square, spread filling on dough

After the second folding: once again, the left and right sides meet in the middle and, on top of that, the top and bottom sides meet in the middle. Now roll again into a 7-inch square.

into a square about 7 inches on all sides and ⅛ inch thick.

6. Spread about ½ cup filling over the dough, coming within ½ inch or so of the borders. Gently repeat the folding process and roll out again to a 7-inch square. If a little of the filling pokes through the dough, that's all right — but you don't want gaping tears.

7. Have ready a hot, lightly greased griddle pan or sturdy skillet. Place the paratha on the hot surface. If bubbles form on the paratha, press them down lightly with a dry cloth or wadded paper towel. After 30 seconds, using a spatula, check the bottom of the paratha. It should look dry and flecked with brown spots. Turn, using the spatula, and cook the other side in the same way. Keep warm by stacking on a plate and covering with a towel, or in a 200-degree oven. Brush parathas with additional ghee or butter and serve warm.

★ Aloo Filling ★

Yield: 3 cups, enough for 6 parathas

1 pound russet potatoes, baked and peeled
1 tablespoon ghee (page 227) or butter
1 tablespoon vegetable oil
1 medium onion, minced
2 garlic cloves, minced
1 (1-inch) piece gingerroot, peeled and minced
1 tablespoon minced hot green chili (optional)
2 teaspoons good-quality curry powder
1 teaspoon ground cumin
1 teaspoon ground turmeric
2 cups loosely packed coarsely chopped
  coriander leaves

1. Cool the potatoes, then cut into roughly ¼-inch dice. Set aside.

2. In a medium skillet, melt the ghee or butter with the vegetable oil over medium-high heat. Add the onion and cook, stirring, until

it turns golden, about 5 minutes. Add the garlic, ginger, and chili. Cook for another 2 minutes, stirring. Add the curry powder, cumin, and turmeric. Cook, stirring, 1 minute more.

3. Stir in the reserved potatoes and mash down with a fork, mixing well with the onion-garlic mixture. The mixture should look like lumpy mashed potatoes. Remove from the heat and stir in the coriander leaves. Let the potato mixture cool before stuffing the parathas.

★ Keema Filling ★

Yield: 3 cups, enough for 6 parathas

1 tablespoon ghee
1 tablespoon vegetable oil
1 small onion, finely diced
2 large garlic cloves, minced
1 tablespoon grated gingerroot
2 teaspoons caraway seeds, lightly crushed
1½ teaspoons ground cumin
1 teaspoon ground cardamom
1 teaspoon ground coriander
1 teaspoon ground turmeric
½ teaspoon ground cinnamon
¼ teaspoon cayenne
1 bay leaf
1 medium-size fresh tomato, chopped into
    ¼-inch dice
1 small hot green chili, minced
1 pound ground lamb
½ cup finely minced coriander leaves

1. Place the ghee and vegetable oil in a medium skillet over low heat. Add the onion, garlic, and ginger and cook until the onion is soft, about 10 to 12 minutes. Add the caraway seeds, cumin, cardamom, ground coriander, turmeric, cinnamon, cayenne, and bay leaf; cook, stirring, until the mixture becomes fragrant, about 3 minutes. Add the tomato and the chili and cook until the juice from the tomato is absorbed, about 10 minutes. Check seasoning.

2. Raise heat to medium-high. Add the lamb and brown on all sides. Add ½ cup of water and stir. Mash lamb with wooden spoon to avoid clumps. Turn heat to low, cover, and cook for 40 minutes. Check from time to time; if the mixture looks dry, add a little more water. After 40 minutes of cooking, turn off heat, remove and discard bay leaf, stir in the coriander leaves, and season to taste with salt and pepper. Let the lamb mixture cool before stuffing the parathas.

Middle Eastern Food

Other than in a few ethnic areas — among Iranians in L.A., among Arabs in Detroit, among all kinds of Middle Easterners along Atlantic Avenue in Brooklyn — there is little Middle Eastern restaurant activity across America. And yet the wonderful food of the Middle East has broken out in our lives in some interesting ways. We are much more likely to encounter the region's great "dips" at a party than at a restaurant; hummus, the wonderful chickpea puree, often comes my way with a stack of toasted pita chips at pass-around hors d'oeuvre time. And some elements of Middle Eastern food have become street-food traditions in the United States — such as the terrific falafel being sold every day from carts in cities across America. There's no foreseeable boom in Middle Eastern food across the United States — but it's there, in the background, occasionally supplying spice and color to our gastronomic lives.

✿ Hummus ✿

This ingenious chickpea puree is one of the great dishes of the Arab world. A little bit of tahini (sesame paste), lemon juice, and garlic set the puree off just right, turning it into a wonderful dipping pool for pita or other bread. It is very popular in the United States, both in Middle Eastern restaurants and as a finger food option for home parties. It's terrific all by itself — but I like it even a little better when the hummus is drizzled with olive oil, topped with toasted cumin seeds, sprinkled with tart sumac powder, and garnished with cherry tomatoes.

Yield: Enough for 12 moderately hungry people

2 cups dried chickpeas, soaked in water
overnight
1 medium onion, peeled and quartered
4 garlic cloves, peeled and halved, plus
1½ teaspoons garlic mashed to a paste
2 sprigs thyme
8 tablespoons extra-virgin olive oil,
plus additional for drizzling
8 cups water, plus more as needed
2 teaspoons kosher salt

1 tablespoon plus 1 teaspoon tahini
(sesame paste)
2 to 3 tablespoons freshly squeezed lemon juice
1 to 3 tablespoons club soda
Cumin seeds for garnish, toasted in a pan until
fragrant (optional)
Sumac powder (optional; see headnote for
Sumac Onions on page 56)
Cherry tomatoes, halved (optional)
Pita Bread (page 59), warmed

1. Drain the soaked chickpeas. Place them in a large saucepan along with the onion, the 4 halved garlic cloves, thyme, 2 tablespoons of the olive oil, and the 8 cups of water. Set over high heat and bring to a boil. Reduce to a simmer and cook, stirring occasionally, until the chickpeas are tender, adding water to keep the level above the chickpeas. Depending on the age of the chickpeas, this could take as little as 1 hour or as long as 3 hours. Once they're tender, add the salt and continue to cook until the water has almost completely evaporated (watch carefully and stir frequently so they don't scorch).

2. Pass the chickpeas through a food mill or potato ricer into a bowl, leaving the skins and thyme stems behind.

3. Transfer the chickpeas to the bowl of a food processor and add the tahini, 2 tablespoons of the lemon juice, the 1½ teaspoons garlic paste, and the remaining 6 tablespoons of olive oil. Process the mixture until very smooth, with no grainy bits of chickpea remaining (6 to 8 minutes). Place the processor bowl with the hummus in the refrigerator and cool the mixture for 20 to 30 minutes.

4. Return the bowl to the machine, taste the hummus, and process with additional lemon juice if necessary (it should be just slightly lemony), and salt if necessary. Process with 1 tablespoon of the club soda to thin and lighten the mixture. The hummus should be just firm enough to stand without running but not at all dry or chalky. Process with small additions of club soda as needed.

5. To serve, spread a generous amount of hummus in a circle, covering most of a plate. Drizzle with additional olive oil, sprinkle with a pinch of toasted cumin seed, if desired, sprinkle with sumac powder, if desired, and garnish with cherry tomatoes, if desired. Serve with warmed pita bread.

✴ Baba Ghanouj ✴

I love this grilled eggplant dip from the Middle East; what I love most is the "grilled" (which translates into smoky flavors) and the eggplant. That's why you don't see too much sesame paste or other distractions in the following version. To emphasize the eggplant still further, I recommend that you chop it coarsely — not beat it into a puree, as chefs sometimes do. It's terrific as one of many little courses as a prelude to a Middle Eastern dinner — or even a Greek one.

Yield: About 6 servings

1 large, firm eggplant
4 tablespoons lemon juice
2 tablespoons tahini (sesame paste)
2 garlic cloves, chopped
2 tablespoons olive oil
1 teaspoon honey

1. Preheat a grill or broiler. Pierce whole eggplant several times with a fork. Grill or broil over medium heat about 15 minutes, turning occasionally, or until eggplant collapses. Cool.

2. Scoop pulp from eggplant, discard skin, place pulp on a cutting board, and chop it coarsely. Place in a bowl and mix well with remaining ingredients. Serve at room temperature.

✴ Falafel ✴

These wonderful deep-fried chickpea patties, staples of the Middle Eastern street . . . have become staples of the New York street as well! There are stands all over midtown Manhattan selling thousands of them at lunch every day. Sometimes they can be dry and pebbly or under- or overspiced, but the following recipe gives you wonderfully moist falafel with a perfect balance of spice and chickpea flavors. You can eat them plain, with a fork . . . or you can place them inside pita, along with slices of onion and tomato, fronds of flat-leaf parsley, and a sauce of garlic-spiked yogurt. At the New York stands, the falafeliers also, on demand, drizzle hot sauce on these great sandwiches.

Yield: About 24 falafel
(good for 8 sandwiches or so)

1 tablespoon ground cumin
2 teaspoons ground coriander
1 pound dried chickpeas,
*   soaked in water overnight*
*   and drained*
1 medium onion, chopped
2 garlic cloves, coarsely chopped

½ cup chopped flat-leaf parsley

⅓ cup chopped coriander leaves

3 green onions (white and green part), chopped

1½ teaspoons salt

2 tablespoons water

2 tablespoons olive oil

1 egg

1 tablespoon lemon juice

1 teaspoon baking soda

1 teaspoon hot pepper sauce

Vegetable oil for deep-frying

1. In a small skillet, toast cumin and ground coriander over medium heat until fragrant, about 1 minute. Set aside.

2. In a food processor, combine drained chickpeas, onion, garlic, parsley, coriander leaves, green onions, salt, and the toasted spices. In a small bowl, stir together the water, olive oil, egg, lemon juice, baking soda, and hot pepper sauce. Add to food processor. Process mixture until almost smooth; this may take 2 to 3 minutes. If your food processor is small, you may have to do it in two batches. Refrigerate mixture until chilled, about ½ hour.

3. In a large saucepan, heat 3 inches of vegetable oil to 365 degrees. Form chickpea mixture into patties about 2 to 3 inches in diameter, ½ to 1 inch thick. Drop into hot oil, 3 or 4 patties at a time. Deep-fry about 3 minutes total, turning halfway through cooking time. Drain on paper towels. Repeat with remaining patties, keeping the fried patties warm in a 250-degree oven until serving time.

★ Fattoush ★

The great bread salad of the Middle East — similar to Tuscany's panzanella in concept — is not as popular in Middle Eastern restaurants here as are the restaurant staples baba ghanouj, hummus, and tabbouleh. But as Americans get to know its charms, fattoush is becoming more popular all the time. Because it's made in homes all over Syria and Lebanon and elsewhere, there are thousands of recipes for it. In the Middle East, most recipes are likely to include two ingredients that are exotic to us: purslane and sumac. The former is a fleshy green that's hard to find across the United States — so I've left it out, substituting the more common arugula. I've left the sumac in, because you have a much better chance of finding it (see the headnote for Sumac Onions on page 56). The bread used in fattoush is pita, the wonderful flat bread of the Middle East. However, because fresh pita is hard to find — and, especially, since the pocket pita is thin and gets crisped up in the broiler, making it perfect for this recipe — I'm calling here for good ole supermarket pocket pita.

Yield: 4 servings

4 ripe plum tomatoes, seeded and diced

1 cup peeled and seeded English cucumber, cut into ¼-inch dice

1 cup arugula, stems removed, washed, and torn into bite-size pieces

1 cup firmly packed chopped flat-leaf parsley leaves

½ cup sliced scallion (white and tender green parts)

½ cup firmly packed chopped mint leaves

¼ teaspoon sugar

8 tablespoons olive oil

3 tablespoons lemon juice

☆☆

1 tablespoon red wine vinegar
1 garlic clove, crushed
1 teaspoon ground sumac (see headnote for
   Sumac Onions on page 56)
3 pita breads with pockets, slightly stale

1. Preheat broiler. In a serving bowl, combine tomatoes, cucumber, arugula, parsley, scallion, mint, and sugar. Season with salt and pepper to taste. Set aside to let flavors mingle.

2. In a small bowl, whisk together 6 tablespoons of the olive oil, the lemon juice, and vinegar; add garlic and sumac. Set aside.

3. Separate pitas so that you have 6 rounds. Tear into small uneven pieces (about ½ to ¾ inches); place in a large bowl. Toss with the remaining 2 tablespoons olive oil. Place on a sheet pan and place under broiler about 4 inches from the heat. Broil about 1 minute, or until they begin to brown, then toss with tongs and return to broiler. Broil 1 to 2 minutes more, until crisp and golden. Season with salt and pepper; let cool.

4. Strain garlic from dressing and season dressing with salt and pepper. Pour dressing over tomato-cucumber mixture and toss to coat. Add pita pieces to salad; toss until dressing coats all the pita. Season again with salt and pepper; serve immediately.

✸ Tabbouleh ✸

This bright Middle Eastern parsley-and-bulgur salad has become a staple of American delis, take-out salad bars, health food restaurants — not to mention Middle Eastern restaurants. Unfortunately, most of the time I sample it, I find it way too bulgur heavy; good tabbouleh is a green thing, with emphasis on its delicious chopped parsley.

Yield: 4 servings

½ cup medium-grind bulgur (cracked wheat)
½ cup boiling water
¼ teaspoon salt
¼ cup extra-virgin olive oil
4 tablespoons lemon juice
Finely grated zest of 1 lemon
1 teaspoon honey
3 cups flat-leaf parsley leaves, washed, dried
   very well, and chopped
1½ cup mint leaves, washed, dried very well,
   and chopped
½ cup finely diced plum tomato
½ cup finely sliced scallion
Small romaine lettuce leaves for serving
   (optional)

1. In a medium bowl, combine bulgur, boiling water, and salt. Cover tightly with plastic wrap; let stand 30 minutes. Remove plastic and fluff with a fork.

2. While bulgur is steaming, in a small bowl whisk together olive oil, lemon juice, lemon zest, honey, and salt and pepper to taste. Pour half of the dressing over the bulgur; toss well. Refrigerate until ready to serve (at least 30 minutes).

3. Place dressed bulgur, parsley, mint, tomato, and scallion in a serving bowl. Pour remaining dressing over; toss well. Season with additional salt and pepper if necessary. Serve cold or let come to room temperature before serving. Serve surrounded with romaine lettuce leaves for scooping, if desired.

✷ Raw Kibbeh ✷

Virtually the national dish of Syria and Lebanon — and very popular in Middle Eastern restaurants in the United States — kibbeh is the combination of pounded meat (usually lamb) and bulgur. It is used in a multitude of ways, forming the base of many different dishes. The following variation uses the kibbeh paste raw; it is a kind of Middle Eastern lamb tartare. When you drizzle good olive oil over it and scoop it up with warm pita, it becomes a magnificent appetizer.

Yield: 8 first-course servings

½ cup fine bulgur (see Note)
2 teaspoons salt
½ teaspoon freshly ground pepper
¼ teaspoon ground cinnamon
⅛ teaspoon ground allspice
1 large onion, grated
½ pound boneless lamb, preferably from the leg, very lean
2 scallions, very finely sliced
2 teaspoons finely chopped parsley
2 teaspoons extra-virgin olive oil
Pita bread for scooping (see recipe on page 59)

1. Put bulgur into a fine mesh strainer and rinse under cold water. Drain thoroughly and sprinkle with the salt. Stir. Place strainer over a bowl. Place in refrigerator for ½ hour.
2. Add pepper, cinnamon, and allspice to the grated onion and mix together in a bowl.
3. Chop the lamb by hand as finely as you can, making sure to remove any visible fat or sinew.
4. Put chopped lamb into the work bowl of a food processor and pulse on and off for 10 seconds, or until the lamb is finely ground. Add bulgur to the work bowl. Add the onion-spice mixture. Pulse on and off until all the ingredients have blended together completely.
5. Turn out onto a platter and flatten to about ½-inch thickness, spreading mixture with your fingers. Spread chopped scallions around the outside edges of kibbeh. Sprinkle with parsley and drizzle with olive oil. Serve immediately, or keep refrigerated until serving. Serve with pita bread.

NOTE: Bulgur is specially processed wheat that is ground fine, medium, or coarse. Sometimes it is packaged and labeled no. 1 (fine), no. 2 (medium), or no. 3 (coarse). You want fine bulgur for this recipe, so look for no. 1.

✷ Kibbeh Stuffed ✷ with Pine Nuts

Raw kibbeh, as in the preceding recipe, is typical — but kibbeh is even more often shaped and cooked. In fact, its very name comes from the shaping; *kibbeh* comes from an Arabic verb that means "to form into a round shape." The following recipe, sometimes called mihshiyyi, yields delicious baked lamb patties, subtly spiced, stuffed with pine nuts, in the shape of small footballs (some books say "torpedoes," but they look a lot more like footballs). Crunchy without, buttery-juicy within, these stuffed kibbeh make a wonderful pass-around party starter.

Yield: 24 kibbeh patties

1 cup fine bulgur (see Note above)
2 large onions, plus ½ cup finely chopped onion
3 teaspoons salt
1¼ teaspoons freshly ground pepper

½ teaspoon ground allspice
½ teaspoon ground cinnamon
¼ teaspoon ground cumin
1 pound lean ground lamb
2 round-bone lamb chops, about ½ pound each
    (cut from the shoulder; 1 pound of chops
    will yield about 8 ounces lean meat)
1 tablespoon butter
½ cup pine nuts
4 tablespoons olive oil

1. Place bulgur in a medium-size bowl and cover with cold water. Let rest for 15 minutes. Drain water from bulgur through a fine mesh strainer. Set aside.

2. Peel and finely grate the large onions. Transfer to a medium-size bowl. Add 2 teaspoons of the salt, 1 teaspoon of the pepper, ¼ teaspoon of the allspice, ¼ teaspoon of the cinnamon, and the cumin. Mix together well.

3. Add bulgur and ground lamb to onion-spice mixture using your hands. Transfer half of the mixture to the bowl of a food processor and process for 5 seconds. Repeat with other half. Return to bowl, cover, and refrigerate.

4. Remove meat from bone of shoulder lamb chops with a sharp knife. Remove fat from the meat and discard. Chop meat finely by hand.

5. To make the stuffing, melt butter in a medium skillet over medium heat. Add pine nuts to skillet and cook until golden brown. Add the ½ cup of chopped onion and cook for 5 minutes. Add the meat from the lamb chops and the remaining 1 teaspoon salt, ¼ teaspoon pepper, ¼ teaspoon allspice,

and ¼ teaspoon cinnamon. Sauté meat for 5 to 8 minutes or until browned. Remove from the heat and cool.

6. Preheat oven to 375 degrees.

7. Remove lamb-bulgur mixture from the refrigerator. Place a heaping tablespoon in the palm of your hand and roll it into a ball. With your forefinger, poke a hole in the ball; expand the hole by rotating your finger and pressing the kibbeh against the palm of your hand until the shell around the hole is approximately ¼ inch thick. Place a heaping teaspoon of stuffing into the shell. Carefully close, manipulating the pattie until it is in the shape of a small football. Dabbing your hands with cold water throughout the shaping makes things easier.

Shaping Kibbeh Stuffed with Pine Nuts

8. Coat two 13 by 9 by 2-inch pans with the olive oil. Arrange kibbeh patties in the pan and bake for 20 to 25 minutes, turning occasionally until browned. Allow to cool long enough so that they can be picked up, as they are usually eaten with the fingers.

Moroccan Food

Moroccan food is stunning in Morocco, particularly in the homes of great cooks. It is an intriguing blend of northern African ideas, Mediterranean ideas, Moroccan Atlantic Coast ideas, Arabic ideas — whirled into a colorful cuisine with the sophistication of Europe and the spicing of India (though much more subtle).

In Morocco, though, it also has a wildly funky side: whole pigeons in pies, cheesy old butter with outrageous aroma, an oil made from nuts that have purportedly passed through the . . . uh . . . systems of animals.

These elements, of course, have been bowdlerized from Moroccan cuisine in America. Even so, Americans have not embraced this great cuisine, certainly not to the extent that the French have. One of the chief alternatives to French restaurant food in Paris is Moroccan restaurant food; in the United States, only southern California has any concentration of Moroccan restaurants.

Happily, ingredients (other than the outré ones) are available to Moroccan chefs here, and the chefs have not been under commercial pressure to transform their cuisine. So when you do find Moroccan food in the United States, it's a pretty faithful representation of what you see in Marrakesh. And there's no reason why more home cooks in America shouldn't be making delicious couscous and tagines at home.

☆ Moroccan Carrot Salad ☆ with Orange Blossom Water

Moroccan meals in Morocco, and in Moroccan-American restaurants here, often start with an array of lovely, lightly scented "salads" — usually arrangements of cooked vegetables. The following one is a classic and provides a good sense of the subtlety of Moroccan spicing.

Yield: 4 appetizer servings

½ clove garlic, mashed into a paste
½ teaspoon ground cinnamon
1 teaspoon ground cumin
Pinch of cayenne
A few grindings of black pepper
1 scant teaspoon sugar
2 teaspoons lemon juice
3 tablespoons extra-virgin olive oil
1 tablespoon orange blossom water
*1 pound carrots, peeled and sliced on a sharp
    bias ⅛ inch thick (about 4 cups)*
1 tablespoon finely chopped parsley

1. Bring a large pot of generously salted water to a boil over high heat.
2. Meanwhile, in a medium-size mixing bowl,

stir together the garlic, cinnamon, cumin, cayenne, black pepper, sugar, lemon juice, olive oil, and 1 teaspoon of the orange blossom water. Set aside. Clear a space in your freezer to accommodate the mixing bowl.

3. When the water is boiling, add the carrots and cook until tender but still a bit crisp, tasting occasionally as they cook. When the carrots are done, drain and immediately transfer them to the mixing bowl, tossing them thoroughly with the dressing. Place them in the freezer to chill for 15 to 20 minutes, tossing them once or twice. Remove from the freezer and toss once more with the remaining 2 teaspoons of orange blossom water. Taste for salt and add if needed. Serve slightly chilled, or at room temperature, sprinkled with parsley.

☆ Fez-Style Couscous with ☆ Chicken and Seven Vegetables

Couscous can refer to little pebbles of pasta, made from semolina wheat (there's even confusion in this; some mistakenly believe that couscous is a grain), or the classic northern Africa dish — in which the pebbles of pasta are steamed over a fragrant stew, then served together with the stew on a platter. Couscous (in the first meaning) has become quite popular in the United States as a side dish, instead of rice or potatoes; people like its lightness and fluffiness. The second kind of couscous is the centerpiece dish of Moroccan restaurants in the United States. Couscous can have some fiery heat to it, as is the custom in Tunisia — or it can be sweet and mild, as is the custom in Fez, Morocco, where seven vegetables, and

raisins, are traditionally part of the stew. The following big-deal couscous includes some unorthodox techniques, such as marinating and browning. But I think it's the most flavorful couscous I've ever had — and it still ends up tasting traditional! The rich broth that accompanies it is all the sauce you need. But there is the option, for additional excitement, of serving either Moroccan preserved lemons or harissa (the Tunisian chili sauce commercially available here) on the side. In Morocco, believe it or not, this hearty dish is usually served after the main course, just to make sure everyone's filled up — preferably at Friday lunch.

Yield: 6 to 8 main-course servings

1½ teaspoons ground cinnamon
1½ teaspoons ground turmeric
1½ teaspoons ground ginger
1 teaspoon ground black pepper
½ teaspoon freshly grated nutmeg
⅛ teaspoon cayenne
2 large pinches saffron threads,
	briefly toasted in a pan and crumbled
2 garlic cloves, peeled and mashed into a paste
1½ tablespoons kosher salt
¼ cup plus 3 tablespoons extra-virgin olive oil,
	plus a little extra for handling couscous
8 chicken thighs (about 2½ pounds altogether)
2 small onions, peeled and quartered
1 pound butternut squash, peeled and cut into
	spears 1 inch square by 3 inches long
	(pick a squash about 1¾ pounds and
	use just its solid neck)
3 medium carrots, peeled and cut on the bias
	into 3-inch lengths
4 medium parsnips, peeled and cut as for
	carrots, above (if the top sections are
	very wide, cut them into ⅜-inch disks
	instead)

3 small zucchini, washed, quartered
lengthwise, and cut crosswise into
8 pieces each
¾ cup dried chickpeas (see Chickpea note)
6 tablespoons unsalted butter
¾ cup blanched whole almonds
1 (14-ounce) can tomatoes, drained, tomatoes
cut in half
5 sprigs coriander, plus 3 tablespoons
finely chopped for garnish
5 sprigs parsley
4 cups (about 27 ounces) couscous
(see Couscous note)
¾ cup golden raisins
4 tablespoons butter, cut into 4 pieces
(optional; see Butter note)

1. In a large glass or ceramic bowl, mix together the cinnamon, turmeric, ginger, black pepper, nutmeg, cayenne, and toasted saffron threads. Remove half of the spice mixture to a small dish, cover with plastic wrap and set aside. To the other half of the spice mixture add the garlic paste, the 1½ tablespoons of kosher salt, and the ¼ cup of olive oil. Mix well. Add the chicken and coat well with the mixture. Add the onions, squash, carrots, parsnips, and zucchini and gently toss to coat. Cover with plastic wrap and allow the chicken and vegetables to marinate for 2 hours at room temperature.

2. Meanwhile, prepare the dried chickpeas. In a medium pot, cover the chickpeas with water by 3 inches and bring to a boil. Reduce to a simmer and partially cook for 1 hour. Drain the chickpeas, return them to the pot, and cover with cold water. Loosen their skins by firmly rubbing small handfuls of chick peas between your palms, allowing them to fall back into the pot. Repeat this procedure a few times and then pour off the water along with the skins that have risen to the top, leaving the peas behind. Refill the pot with fresh water and repeat until all the skins have been removed. Set the chickpeas aside.

3. Melt 2 tablespoons of the unsalted butter in a small sauté pan over medium heat. Add the almonds and cook, tossing them regularly, until they are golden brown, about 5 to 7 minutes. Make sure they don't burn. Scoop the almonds from the pan, place them on paper towels, and allow them to cool. Chop them into pieces roughly ⅛ inch and set aside.

4. Prepare a jerry-rigged couscous steamer: Choose a stockpot and a colander that fit together well. The colander must be wrapped around the outside of its circular upper edge with 2 damp kitchen towels, and the towel-wrapped colander must rest snugly, by its

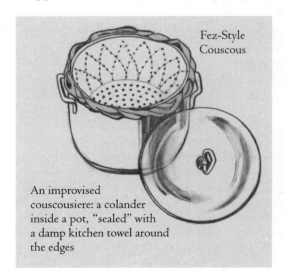

Fez-Style
Couscous

An improvised
couscousiere: a colander
inside a pot, "sealed" with
a damp kitchen towel around
the edges

The Traditional Couscous Pot

In northern Africa, and in northern-African restaurants in the United States — and in a tiny number of American homes — grains of couscous are steamed over a simmering stew in a two-tiered vessel with a lid called a couscousiere. Its design allows the vapors of the stew beneath to gently steam the couscous above, keeping the tiny pasta grains light, fluffy, and separate while flavoring them subtly. The goal for would-be couscous cooks without a couscousiere is to replicate its benefits. This involves jerry-rigging some combination of your largest, heaviest stockpot (in which to cook the stew) and a large colander or strainer resting on top of it (to steam the couscous). The stockpot needs only to be able to accommodate all the chicken and vegetables and broth comfortably. The colander or strainer, however, needs to do three things: (1) its basket must be slightly smaller than the stockpot so that it fits inside the pot; (2) it must support itself on the edge of the stockpot with its handles (found on many metal colanders) or with its rim (found on many plastic versions) so that the bottom does not touch the simmering stew beneath (you want the couscous to steam, not soak), and to prevent the colander from falling in the stew; and (3) it needs to be rigged so that when the colander is placed in the pot (and the couscous is then placed in the colander), all the steam that rises from the stew goes directly up into the couscous and does not seep out between the edges of the colander and the stockpot (the grains will not steam properly if it does). This means that you have to create a kind of gasket to fill this gap. This is done best with a couple of damp kitchen towels folded lengthwise once or twice and wrapped around the edge of the colander, or draped over the edges of colander and stockpot, or both. Fold them, tie them, tuck them; do whatever works best with your combination of pot and colander to prevent the steam from escaping as described. If couscous becomes a part of your life, however — as I suspect it might, after you try this recipe — you may want to invest in a couscousiere.

handles, on the rim of the stockpot. There must be no room for steam to escape between the towel-wrapped edge of the colander and the rim of the stockpot. Also, the stockpot you choose needs a lid that covers all. Finally, you must be sure that the stockpot is deep enough so that when you fill it with 4 cups of liquid, 8 pieces of chicken, and assorted vegetables, the level of the stew in the pot is below the bottom of the colander that sits over the stew; you don't want liquid to lap the bottom of the colander later on (this is a job for your eyeballs). (See also the sidebar on this page.) Once you've chosen your equipment, set the towel-wrapped colander and the lid aside to use later.

5. Place the stockpot by itself over medium-high heat and add the remaining 3 tablespoons of olive oil. Extract the chicken from its marinade with the vegetables, pat it dry, and sprinkle chicken with a little additional salt on each side. Add the chicken pieces to the stockpot skin side down and cook until

deeply golden brown, about 8 to 10 minutes. Turn chicken pieces over and cook 5 minutes more. Remove the chicken to a plate and set aside. Pour the oil out of the pot and discard.

6. Reduce the heat under the stockpot to medium-low; add the remaining 4 tablespoons of unsalted butter and the reserved spice mixture, cooking for 1 minute, scraping up any browned bits on the bottom of the pot. Add the chicken, skin side up, along with any juices on the chicken plate. Extract the onions from the spice-marinated vegetables and add them to the stockpot along with the tomatoes. Bundle together the coriander sprigs and parsley sprigs with kitchen string; add them to the stockpot. Add 4 cups of water to the stockpot and bring to a boil over high heat. Reduce to a bare simmer; cover the pot with the lid and cook, stirring occasionally, for 1 hour. Check occasionally to make sure that the simmer remains gentle.

7. During that hour in which the chicken cooks in the stockpot, you'll be carrying out the first handling of the couscous. Place the couscous in a large bowl. Cover the grains with a few inches of cold water and swish them around with your hands for 10 seconds. Drain well and evenly spread the couscous onto a large rimmed baking sheet and allow it to dry for 15 minutes. Next, pick up a handful of couscous and firmly massage the grains between your palms, breaking up any lumps that may have formed and letting the couscous fall back onto the baking sheet. Repeat this process with all the couscous,

until the grains appear to be separate and free of lumps.

8. Uncover the stockpot and make sure the liquid is bubbling gently and releasing steam. Set the towel-rimmed colander on the pot, over the simmering chicken. Pour the couscous into a pile in the center of the colander and distribute it across the bottom without compacting the grains. Adjust the toweling so that all the steam is coming up through the colander, not around it. Allow the couscous to steam, uncovered, for 25 minutes. Remove the colander and return the cover to the pot. Return the couscous to the rimmed baking sheet, spreading it out evenly. Sprinkle it with a few pinches of salt and about ⅓ cup of water. Moisten your hands with a bit of olive oil and massage the couscous as in the previous step. The grains should be just barely damp and free of lumps. If they feel dry, sprinkle a bit more water and massage again. Allow them to dry again for 15 minutes, massaging them thoroughly once more. Cover with a damp cloth and set aside.

9. By now the chicken will have had its 1-hour simmer. Add the reserved chickpeas and the squash, nestling them between the chicken pieces and underneath the liquid. Cover the pot and continue simmering for 10 minutes. Add the carrots and parsnips, positioning them as you did the chickpeas and squash, and simmer for 10 more minutes, covered. Add the zucchini and the raisins in the same fashion and return the towel-rimmed colander to the pot. Add the couscous as in the previous step, making sure that no steam is escaping around the colander. Cover the pot

and colander with the lid and continue to simmer the stew for 20 minutes, finishing the stew and couscous simultaneously.

10. While the stew is having its final 20-minute simmer, preheat your oven to 150 degrees (just warm).

11. After the 20 minutes of simmering, lift the cover and toss the couscous with the 4 tablespoons of butter, until the butter melts. Season with salt and pepper to taste. Spoon the couscous onto a warmed serving platter and make a large well in the center. With a slotted spoon, place the chicken and vegetables attractively in the well, and place the platter in the warmed oven. Taste the broth in the pot; if you feel it could be a bit more concentrated in flavor, boil it, uncovered, for an additional few minutes. Add salt if you feel it needs it. You may also skim off some fat, if desired. Pour one-third of the broth into a sauceboat, remove the platter from the oven and spoon the remainder of the broth over the entire dish. Garnish with the reserved almonds and the 3 tablespoons chopped coriander and serve, passing the sauceboat of broth at the table.

CHICKPEA NOTE: If you'd prefer to use canned chickpeas (a whole lot easier), simply skip the procedures for dried chickpeas in step 2 and add the canned chickpeas to the stew in step 9.

COUSCOUS NOTE: All the couscous available today in boxes in American stores is, essentially, "instant" couscous; whether the package says "instant" or not, the stuff inside can be steamed to an edible stage in five minutes or so. However, this five-minute simple steaming is far from ideal. For one thing, the finished grains of couscous will be quite heavy. But if you treat your five-minute couscous in the traditional way —

moistening, drying, first steaming, second drying, second steaming (as in the accompanying recipe) — the finished couscous will be light, fluffy, and almost dry, as it's supposed to be (see also sidebar on page 245). Moreover — according to Moroccan food authority and culinary goddess Paula Wolfert — the fully handled couscous will be much easier to digest. That five-minute stuff, she says, continues its cooking in your stomach, expanding and making you feel unexpectedly bloated.

BUTTER NOTE: In Morocco they like to use an aged butter called smen, which has a cheesy flavor. If you'd like to replicate that acquired taste, use a butter that has been sitting out of the refrigerator for a few weeks.

☆ Lamb Tagine ☆ with Butternut Squash, Dried Apricots, and Almonds

One of the primary main-course options at Moroccan restaurants in the United States — as at Moroccan restaurants in Morocco — is a long-cooked stew known as a tagine. The name comes from the conical terra-cotta pot in which it's cooked — also known as a tagine, and available at American kitchenware stores. But please, if you don't have a tagine, by all means make the following tagine in any pot you do have. Tagines often (though not always) feature something sweet and something starchy along with the meat — and our California dried apricots, along with our butternut squash, are beautifully up to the assignment. This dish is really wonderful nestled on a bowl of steamed couscous — but buttered orzo or rice would also hit the spot.

Yield: 4 main-course servings

4 tablespoons vegetable oil
3 pounds boneless lamb shoulder, trimmed of excess fat and cut into 1¼-inch cubes
6 tablespoons unsalted butter

¼ teaspoon saffron threads, crushed in your
   fingers
½ teaspoon ground cinnamon
½ teaspoon freshly ground black pepper
½ teaspoon ground turmeric
⅛ teaspoon cayenne
1½ teaspoons grated gingerroot
1 small yellow onion, minced (about ⅔ cup)
1½ teaspoons kosher salt
5 cups water
5 sprigs coriander, plus extra leaves
   for garnish
1 medium sweet onion (such as Vidalia),
   peeled, cut in half, and sliced
   ⅜ inch thick
½ cup blanched, roasted almonds
1 (2-pound) butternut squash (see Note)
3 tablespoons honey
16 dried apricots, soaked in warm water
   until soft, and cut in half

1. Place a large stockpot over medium-high heat and add 2 tablespoons of the vegetable oil. When it begins to smoke, add half the lamb and lightly brown the meat on all sides, regulating the heat if the meat threatens to burn. Set meat aside in a bowl. Repeat with the remaining lamb.

2. Remove the pot from the heat and let it cool slightly. Return it to medium-low heat. Add 4 tablespoons of the butter and let it melt. Add the saffron, cinnamon, black pepper, turmeric, cayenne, ginger, and minced yellow onion, scraping the bottom of the pot to loosen any browned bits. Let the mixture cook gently for 4 minutes. Add the reserved lamb and any accumulated juices along with the 1½ teaspoons salt, stirring to coat the lamb with the spice mixture. Stir in the water, raise the heat to high, and bring just to a simmer. With kitchen string, tie together the 5 coriander sprigs and add to pot. Let the mixture cook, uncovered, at a bare simmer — the bubbles should be lazy — for 1 hour 45 minutes, stirring occasionally.

3. Add the sliced sweet onion and the almonds and simmer for 30 minutes more. Taste the tagine and add salt if you feel it needs it. Remove the coriander bundle and discard. Turn off the heat and allow the tagine to rest at least 30 minutes and up to 2 hours at room temperature (if you're serving the tagine beyond this time, cover and refrigerate until ready to reheat and serve).

4. While the tagine is simmering or at rest, prepare the squash: Heat a large skillet over medium-high heat and add the remaining 2 tablespoons of vegetable oil. When the oil slides easily in the skillet, and working in batches if necessary, sauté the squash pieces on both sides — lightly salting each side as you go — until just tender and golden brown at the edges, about 5 minutes per side. Regulate the heat if the squash threatens to burn. Toward the end of cooking, and while the squash pieces are still a bit firm, add the remaining 2 tablespoons of butter and drizzle the honey over the squash. Swirl the pan to blend the ingredients, and gently toss the squash to coat. Turn off the heat and reserve in the skillet.

5. When ready to serve, gently reheat the lamb and stir in about two-thirds of the squash pieces. Combine the apricots with the remaining squash in the skillet, cover and reheat gently, swirling to coat the pieces. Divide the lamb mixture among four wide, shallow bowls. Drizzle with some of the juices. Distribute the apricots and remaining squash attractively over the lamb. Drizzle any liquid remaining in the squash/apricot skillet over each serving. Garnish with fresh coriander leaves. Pass the remaining lamb juices in a sauceboat at the table.

NOTE: For this recipe, you need only the seedless neck (one to one and a quarter pounds) from the squash. Peel and halve the neck lengthwise, then cut it into three-eighths-inch-thick half-moons. Reserve the remaining squash for another use.

Part Two

Regional America

D̲oes America have a vital "regional cuisine" tradition?

Many would say no.

I, emphatically, say, "Yes."

There is an unfortunate but widely shared feeling that to speak of "American regional cuisine" is to force the issue, to give a grand name to something that's not so grand at all. Oh, people may maintain that technically we have a regional cuisine, that certain elements of New England food, Cajun food, and California food are distinctive; however, there's usually a "Yeah, but . . ." tacked on to the argument, or an implicit understanding that American regional cuisine is just a sketchbook compared with the virtual encyclopedia of regional cuisine in a country like Italy.

And this may have been so some decades ago. But have you been to Italy lately? A friend was telling me recently that the best risotto she ever had — risotto! the starchy mainstay of the north! — was in Sicily. And I can tell you for a fact that the best garlicky, oily tomato sauces I've had in Italy — the ones always associated with the sunny south — have been served in the supposedly butter-drenched north. And yet we cling to the mistaken notion that every twenty miles in Italy brings a new cuisine and every two hundred miles in America brings only more McDonalds. Just because we in America have similar things across the country — as they do everywhere! — doesn't mean that we have no true regional cuisine.

The misperception has been sorely exacerbated by the types of dishes we usually choose to discuss when the conversation turns to American regional cuisine. For the most part, the dishes that supposedly demonstrate "regionality" are showcase dishes only — antiques and relics at worst, restaurant dishes at best, country-fair dishes, dishes from folk-dancing events. Part of the reason we look with suspicion at American regional cuisine is that we all know in our souls that people in Wisconsin aren't having a Door County fish boil every night and that New England clam bakes are actually quite few and far between. On any given night, any Wisconsin or New England resident is about a million times more likely to have a hamburger.

But here's what we usually miss: what types of condiments will go on that hamburger? I'll never forget walking up to Havens Brothers, a famous all-night hamburger stand in Providence, Rhode Island, ordering a burger, getting asked "Regular?" saying "Sure!" . . . and being handed a warm bun enclosing a grilled ground beef patty with a lot of mustard, alongside pickles, onions, relish, and a little ketchup. It was the first time I'd ever heard of a burger served with that particular configuration of condiments, and — belittle the burger as you will — it was evidence of a genuine regional consciousness that is in the gastronomic lives of the residents there every day.

When you travel throughout the United States, you find that there really are things people make and eat in their regions that are not made and eaten elsewhere. Like Chile Relleno Casserole in New Mexico. Like the amazing hot dogs of Chicago. Like the great Cuban Sandwich of Florida. Like poke and lomi-lomi salmon — wonderful raw fish treats — in Hawaii. Like the way some Californians have of preparing their hamburgers — cooking them on rye bread, in a pan, like a grilled cheese sandwich, with lots of oozing Swiss cheese inside (the Patty Melt!).

If it's not foie gras, if it's not some esoteric farinaceous specialty, if it's not chorizo, if it's not a spice blend from the cardamom fields, if it's not from the imperial court of China, if it's not a peasant's corn creation under a Mexican volcano — can't it still be regional cuisine? Of course it can. And the things that Americans eat every day in their regions — either as local versions of national dishes or as completely idiosyncratic local dishes — really don't get the attention they deserve. These things may not seem important enough to us to add up to regional cuisine — but to the foreign eye, they are just as exotic as the regional cuisine of Indonesia is to American eyes.

American regional cuisine is not a collection of rarely enjoyed curiosities. It is a real, vital, living cuisine, and it exists right under our upturned noses.

You will see a good deal of it in the following pages: what people really eat in their regions.

But you will notice two great areas of American regional cuisine that are missing from this chapter.

One area that I've excluded, for the most part — for logistical reasons only — has to do with the incredible products in America today that rarely get shipped beyond their regions. There is a true cuisine developing in all parts of the United States that is based on regional bounty. But since the reader of this book probably cannot find the singing scallops of the Pacific Northwest or the walleyed pike of the upper Midwest or the Hatch chilies of New Mexico or the limpets that cling to sea rocks in Hawaii, I've not included recipes for them.

Another excluded area is the "regional cuisine" that chefs are attempting to forge across the country today. Why? Because, in my judgment, this "new" regionalism is still too new. Mustard on a burger in Providence, Rhode Island, is truly regional to me; we'll have to wait and see whether "Nage of Narragansett Top Necks with Fiddlehead Ferns, Confit of Linguiça, and a Portuguese Bread Pudding" really has anything to do with that region. In other words: the big-deal restaurant food that most loudly gets trumpeted these days as regional cuisine may turn out to be nothing of the sort.

I was in Denver recently — a good eating town — where I read in a local magazine about a "regional" dish at a local upscale restaurant. The chef, the article said, "layers three toast tips brushed with olive oil with very thinly sliced roasted tomatoes, shaved pickled red onion, and one fine layer of de-boned, house-smoked white trout. The dish is garnished with basil-infused olive oil." Mediterranean? New American? No. Coloradan. "It's a dish that reminds me so much of Colorado," proudly proclaims the chef. Which part, I wonder — the basil or the olive oil? Clearly, this is Rocky Mountain Hype; the chef's been smoking too much trout. Okay, okay — maybe the trout came from a local stream. But once you start infusing this and that, shaving that and this, layering, swirling, towering, globalizing, giving the dish a primary character that comes from somewhere else — do you have regional cuisine? And by repeating the *regional cuisine* mantra without really thinking about it, are you not preventing yourself from really forging a regional cuisine?

How many restaurants have you been to lately that squawk "regional cuisine," then proceed to serve you the same clichés that everyone else is serving all over the planet — except here they're made with local tomatoes and local goat cheese. Now, I might be able to pick out Tuscan olive oil in a blind tasting, or Spanish ham — but I'll be damned if I could tell you the difference between a Georgia tomato, a Kansas tomato, and a Colorado tomato. Just because some of your ingredients are local — admirable as that may be — doesn't mean you're creating a local cuisine!

It takes a lot more than that. It takes real imagination to apprehend the essence of a region's gastronomic character. And it takes real creativity to transmogrify that into something dynamic that people want to eat in restaurants today.

It will come, I'm sure. Within a decade or two, as chefs become more confident of who they are and where they're from, we are likely, I'm convinced, to see the growth of genuine regional cuisine.

For now, I'm sticking with all the things that people in our regions really do eat . . . and particularly, with all the delicious and truly regional things that will be easy for you to reproduce in your kitchen.

New England

Call me Ishmael, but I'm convinced that the great informing influence of New England cuisine is the sea. I daresay that no other American region — with the exception of Hawaii — has been so powerfully shaped by the proximity of water. When one thinks of food from New England, one immediately envisions clams, lobsters, scallops, cod, bluefish, and scores of other piscine delights. No other gastronomic image comes as powerfully to mind.

Of course, there is more in New England. There's a hearty, inland Yankee cuisine, a thing of maple syrup and heavy meats. There are ethnic influences — particularly the Portuguese influence, which is strong along the coast of Rhode Island and Massachusetts, and the Italian influence, in Boston's North End. But the ethnic character that has really stamped the region as a whole, it seems to me, is that pre-Revolution English puritan spirit. Nothing is banned in Boston anymore — but there's an austerity, a directness, an absence of flourish at the heart of New England cuisine that seems particularly appealing today.

Especially when applied to seafood.

✻ New England Steamers ✻

Steamed clams are served around the country, but the Yankees of New England have a definite advantage in this delicacy — for New England is soft-shell clam country, and soft-shell clams make the best steamed clams in the world. Their main advantage is that they don't get tough or rubbery when you steam them open — and the fact that they're also extremely sweet and clammy tasting doesn't hurt either. You will know them in fish stores (they are increasingly available outside New England) by their white, brittle shells and by the curious-looking tube that protrudes from one end (often referred to as the pisser). Enjoying them is simplicity itself. Follow the easy recipe below, then serve piles of the clams. Each diner removes the clam belly, peels off the brown skin around the attached "pisser," breaks open the rim of the belly (in case it contains sand) and dips it in clam broth, then dips the belly, just before eating, in melted butter. The following recipe yields a particularly strong-flavored broth — because I like to use it as the base for New England Clam Chowder (following recipe).

Yield: 2 hearty first-course servings

4 cups water
4 large celery stalks with leaves
1 firmly packed cup of coarsely chopped parsley leaves and stems
4 pounds steamers (soft-shell clams)
¼ pound (1 stick) unsalted butter, melted

1. Place the water, celery, and parsley in a large pot with a tight-fitting lid. Bring to a boil. Add the steamers, close the lid, and shake the pot. Cook over medium-high heat for 5 to 10 minutes, or until all the clams have swung wide open.
2. Divide the clams among two large serving

bowls. Pour the clam broth (leaving celery, parsley, and sediment behind) into two large mugs. Divide the melted butter between two small bowls. Serve immediately, with a large bowl on the table for discarding empty clamshells.

☆ New England ☆ Clam Chowder

Everyone knows about the clam chowder wars: New Englanders like creamy clam chowder, Manhattanites like tomatoey clam chowder. But even within New England there's a good deal of chowder controversy. What kind of clams? What kind of dairy product? What degree of thickening? I like my New England Clam Chowder to be very basic. The most important thing, to me, is the taste of clams — something often missing in "clam" chowder, because home cooks often use canned clams in this dish. Other cooks use hard-shell clams, a better choice. But I submit that soft-shell clams — steamers! — are really the ones that bring clammy sweetness to the chowder. Thickness? I'm leaving that up to you. The following recipe yields a pretty thick chowder; if you like yours to be thinner, I recommend thinning it out with milk, broth, and canned corn juice — which adds a flavor to the soup nostalgically reminiscent of good diner chowdah!

Yield: Makes 4 soup servings

1 recipe New England Steamers (page 254)
4 ounces fatty, nonsmoky bacon, coarsely chopped
½ cup very finely chopped celery
½ cup very finely chopped onion
4 tablespoons butter
6 tablespoons flour

½ pound waxy potatoes, peeled and finely diced
½ teaspoon dried thyme leaves
½ cup liquid from a can of corn niblets (plus more, if desired)
¼ cup whole milk (plus more, if desired)
Finely chopped parsley for garnish

1. Prepare New England Steamers through step 1 (page 254).
2. When clams have swung open, remove them from the hot liquid. As soon as the clams are cool enough to handle, pluck the bellies from the shells. Peel back the brown skin around the "pisser" and discard skin. Chop the bellies into coarse chunks and reserve. Discard shells. Strain liquid and reserve. Wipe out pot.
3. Return pot to stove over medium-low heat. Add bacon. Cook, stirring occasionally, until the bacon is soft and transparent; do not let it brown. Add the celery and onion to the bacon and bacon fat. Sauté, stirring occasionally, until vegetables are soft (about 10 minutes).
4. Add butter to pot. When it has melted, add the flour, stirring vigorously. Cook the roux for 2 minutes. Turn heat up to medium, then pour 4 cups of the hot clam liquid into the saucepan. Whisk until thickened and smooth. Add the potatoes, reserved clams, and half of the dried thyme. Season to taste with black pepper. Cover and simmer gently for 20 minutes.
5. When the soup has simmered, thin it out a bit by adding corn juice and milk. Add a little more of these if a thinner broth is

New England: Paradise for Scallop Lovers

Two of the world's greatest scallop varieties come from the waters of New England. The bad news is that they're not easy to find in stores. The good news is that if you find 'em, it's a cinch to cook 'em.

Over the last decade, restaurant chefs around the country have increasingly had access to the large sea scallop harvested off the coast of Maine. What makes this scallop so special is that the divers bring the scallops back to port that day, rather than holding them on the boat; this guarantees freshness and sweetness. The thing to look for is Maine Day-Boat Diver Scallops. The thing to do with them is simply open them up with a clam knife, discard one shell, cut the scallop muscle and its delicious orange roe away from the half shell to which it clings, sprinkle the scallop and roe with salt and pepper, drizzle with a little melted butter, and put this scallop on the half shell under a broiler until it's just cooked, about 2 to 5 minutes, depending on your broiler. Six of them make an awesome Maine course.

Even greater — but even rarer — are the incredible bay scallops that get harvested from the ponds and pools of Nantucket Island, Massachusetts. The season extends only from October through March, and the scallops are in incredibly high demand during that period. Why? Because you've never tasted a sweeter lump of seafood in your life. These sugary little scallops are sold without the shell and require you merely to melt a few tablespoons of butter in a pan over medium-high heat, season the scallops, toss them in the hot butter, and sauté for 2 to 3 minutes. No sauce; no lemon; no garnish. No need.

desired — as well as any leftover clam broth. Add remaining ¼ teaspoon of dried thyme leaves. Season to taste with salt and pepper. Divide among 4 soup bowls and serve immediately, each bowl topped with a little parsley.

NOTE: Some New Englanders recommend cooling the chowder and letting it "age," or "ripen," in the refrigerator before serving. I think they're right — and that 2 to 3 days in the fridge brings out just the right clammy flavor. Beyond that — well, things get a little too ripe.

☆ The Lobster Roll ☆

Nobody knows exactly where or when the lobster roll was invented, but rumor has it that this divinely simple treat has been served on the New England coast for close to a hundred years. It has also, starting in the 1960s, become associated with the eastern end of Long Island. Well, the origins are unimportant. It strikes me as a quintessentially American dish: one of the country's greatest shellfish delights (Maine lobster) tossed with one of America's greatest condiments (Hellmann's mayonnaise), and served on a buttered, griddled hot dog bun without pretension or fuss. I'm almost ashamed to admit that I've introduced a few new ingredients here — but I've done it only because (a) I really like them and (b) you can easily omit them (the lemon zest and dill) if you wish.

Yield: 4 lobster rolls,
enough for 4 light lunch servings

¼ cup mayonnaise (preferably Hellmann's)
    or more, according to taste
⅛ teaspoon firmly packed grated lemon zest
⅛ teaspoon firmly packed finely chopped
    fresh dill
Sweet paprika

1 pound cooked lobster meat, cut into coarse
chunks (approximately 2 cups)
¼ cup celery, cut into ½-inch dice
Butter for greasing the griddle and the buns
4 special lobster roll buns or hot dog buns
(see Note)

1. Place the mayonnaise in a mixing bowl, and with a wire whisk blend in the lemon zest and dill. Season well with salt and pepper, and whisk in a pinch of paprika. Using a spoon, gently fold the lobster meat and celery into the mayonnaise dressing. Add more mayo if desired. Refrigerate until mixture is very cold.

2. Grease a griddle or a cast-iron skillet over moderate heat with a little butter. Open the buns (without separating the two halves). Smear a little butter on the outside of each bun, then place on the hot griddle or in the hot skillet, spread open, exterior side down. Place a weight on the buns (a heavy pan will do). Cook until the exteriors are golden, about 1 minute. Remove buns.

3. Fill each bun with one quarter of the lobster mixture, sprinkle with paprika, and serve immediately.

The ideal bun for the Lobster Roll

NOTE: Supermarkets now carry the type of bread that is uniquely suited to this dish. It looks like a cross between a hot dog bun and a piece of white bread; the key is that the sides of this bun are crustless and look like a slice of white bread.

☆ New England Boiled Dinner ☆

This New England dish is probably a descendant of an Old England dish. The meat originally used in this Yankee dish (which was first named in print in the 1890s) was salt beef; today, corned beef (quite similar) is the meat of choice. I love the following version, which instructs you to cook the vegetables separately (and I've used more vegetables here than you'll find in most recipes) — leading to a pretty, colorful array of perfectly cooked veggies surrounding the boiled meat. The wonderful broth is sweet and clean, so I choose to use a bit of it (one-half cup per customer) as a moistener for the starred players — and that is why I prefer serving this boiled dinner in individual bowls rather than on a communal platter.

Yield: 8 servings

1 (3½-pound) corned beef brisket (if you wish
to make your own, see Home-Cured
Corned Beef, page 268)
2 bay leaves
2½ teaspoons whole black peppercorns
4 whole cloves
4 whole allspice berries
1½ teaspoons brown mustard seeds
½ medium onion, with skin
2 garlic cloves, crushed
12 cups cold water
2 medium beets (about ½ pound)
1 small cabbage, outer leaves removed,
cut through the stem into 8 wedges
¾ pound rutabaga, peeled and cut into
1-inch chunks

2 medium turnips (about ¾ pound),
    peeled and cut into 1-inch chunks
2 medium parsnips (about ½ pound),
    peeled and cut into 1-inch chunks
2 medium carrots (about ½ pound),
    peeled and cut into 1-inch chunks
6 small white onions, peeled but left whole,
    root end trimmed
1 pound russet potatoes, peeled and cut
    into 1-inch chunks
1 tablespoon chopped parsley, for garnish
1 tablespoon chopped chives, for garnish
Horseradish as accompaniment
Grainy mustard as accompaniment

1. Trim all but ¼-inch fat from the corned beef. Place in a large pot and add water to cover. Bring to a simmer and simmer 5 minutes. Drain and rinse the corned beef. Return to the pot and add bay leaves, peppercorns, cloves, allspice, mustard seeds, onion, and garlic. Add cold water. Bring to a simmer and cook gently, partially covered, for 3 to 4 hours, until corned beef is tender but not falling apart. Add more water as necessary to keep the brisket submerged.

2. Preheat oven to 400 degrees. Wrap beets in foil and roast until tender, about 1 hour. Cool, peel, and cut into wedges. Keep warm for serving.

3. Remove corned beef from the pot and strain cooking liquid. Wrap corned beef in foil and keep warm in low oven. Return liquid to a simmer and cook the vegetables until tender in the following groupings and for the following approximate times:
    cabbage: 20 minutes

    rutabaga and turnips: 18 minutes
    parsnips, carrots, and onions: 15 minutes
    potatoes: 10 minutes

As vegetables cook, set them aside and add the next batch, or cook them in stages in the same pot.

4. To serve, return all vegetables to the pot with the cooking liquid (if cooked separately). Slice warm corned beef thinly against the grain. Serve corned beef in shallow soup bowls with vegetables strewn around the bowl. Ladle hot stock over all, about ½ cup per bowl. Garnish with parsley and chives and serve immediately, with horseradish and mustard on the side.

☆ Succotash ☆

No one is quite sure what, other than corn, is in a classic succotash . . . or even where the center of succotash classicism is! There is a place called Succotash Point on Narragansett Bay, in Rhode Island, and the Narragansett Indians who lived there did use the word *msíckquatash*, which meant "boiled whole kernels of corn." Today, however, succotash is even more popular in the South than in New England . . . and lima beans are likely to be part of the mix. The following superb version is upscaled just a bit with the inclusion of cream, butter, and a few Mediterranean herbs.

Yield: 6 side dish servings

2 cups frozen baby lima beans, thawed
2 cups frozen supersweet corn niblets, thawed,
    or 2 cups fresh uncooked corn niblets
2 tablespoons butter
1 teaspoon chopped fresh thyme
1 teaspoon sugar

⋆⋆⋆

⅛ teaspoon cayenne
1 cup whipping cream
½ teaspoon lemon juice
1 tablespoon chopped parsley for garnish
1 tablespoon chopped chives for garnish

1. Bring a large saucepan of salted water to a boil. Add limas and simmer until almost tender, about 5 minutes. Drain immediately and refresh in a colander under cold water for a minute. Put about one quarter of the limas in a small bowl and mash with a fork.

2. Bring another saucepan of water to a boil. Add corn, boil 1 minute. Drain immediately and refresh under cold water. Set aside.

3. Meanwhile, in a large skillet, melt 1 tablespoon of the butter over medium heat. Add thyme, sugar, and cayenne. Cook 1 minute, then pour in cream. Increase heat, bring to a boil, and boil until cream is reduced by half.

4. Add mashed limas, whole limas, corn, and the remaining 1 tablespoon of butter and bring to a boil, stirring until vegetables are coated in cream. Add lemon juice and season with salt and pepper. Serve immediately, garnished with parsley and chives.

☆ Boston Baked Beans ☆ with Smoky Bacon and Molasses

The canned product has perhaps dimmed the reputation of this brown and luscious New England classic. Please try the real thing at home; you'll find much deeper flavor and a much better bean texture. I love it in winter with a hearty main course, such as the New England Boiled Dinner on page 257. Serve with Boston Brown Bread (page 260) for a real Saturday-night-in-Boston touch.

Yield: 6 servings

1 pound dried Great Northern beans,
    or other dried white beans
½ pound smoky bacon, thinly sliced and
    coarsely chopped
1 medium yellow onion, chopped
½ cup molasses
¼ cup dark brown sugar
¼ cup ketchup
1 tablespoon dry mustard
2 teaspoons kosher salt
⅛ teaspoon ground cloves

1. Place the beans in a large bowl or container and cover with cold water by 4 inches. Let soak for at least 12 hours. Drain the beans and discard the liquid.

2. Place the beans in a large pot and cover with cold water by 5 inches. Bring to a boil, lower the heat, and simmer, uncovered, until tender, about 40 minutes. Drain the beans; reserve them and the cooking liquid.

3. Preheat the oven to 250 degrees. Heat a large Dutch oven with a tight-fitting lid over medium-high heat. Add the bacon and cook, stirring, until crispy, about 6 minutes. Add the onion and cook, stirring, until lightly browned, about 5 minutes. Add the reserved beans and stir in 4 cups reserved cooking liquid. Stir in the molasses, brown sugar, ketchup, mustard, salt, and cloves. Season with pepper to taste. Bring to a boil on top of the stove, then bake in the oven, covered, until thick and fragrant, about 3 hours. If the beans

seem too thick, stir in a little of the reserved cooking liquid.

4. Remove the beans from the oven and serve.

☆ Boston Brown Bread ☆

I love this odd, yeastless "bread" from New England, made with rye flour and molasses since the early nineteenth century. It steams in the oven, leading to a mildly sweet, extremely soft and moist product. The following recipe has a little bit more of a "bread" texture than most — which I like — and a great taste of the grains in the bread. Absolutely terrific with Boston Baked Beans (see page 259) and/or New England Boiled Dinner (page 257).

Yield: I loaf

½ cup stone-ground cornmeal
½ cup graham flour (coarse stone-ground wheat flour)
½ cup rye flour
1 teaspoon baking soda
½ teaspoon salt
1½ teaspoons ground ginger
¼ cup canola oil
⅓ cup molasses
1 cup buttermilk
2 tablespoons applesauce
1 egg, lightly beaten
½ cup raisins

1. Preheat oven to 350 degrees. Grease and flour an empty 1-pound coffee can. Put a kettle of water on to boil.

2. Combine cornmeal, graham flour, rye flour, baking soda, salt, and ginger in a bowl.

In a separate bowl, combine canola oil, molasses, buttermilk, applesauce, and egg. Stir to combine.

3. Add wet ingredients to dry, stirring until just combined. Stir in raisins and pour batter into coffee can. Cover the top of the can with buttered foil and place in an ovenproof pot. Add boiling water to pot to come halfway up the sides of the can. Steam bread in oven until a skewer inserted in the center comes out with just a few crumbs, about 1¼ hours. Cool on a rack for about 15 minutes, then unmold.

New York

New York — and especially New York City — is notable for nothing so much as its dizzying diversity. The neighborhoods of New York City have teemed for centuries with successive waves of immigrant groups — and foods from every one of them, transformed, are available today in New York's restaurants. Some of what was invented there went on to become national food, in a sense: the great Italian-American cuisine of Little Italy and the "exotic" Chinese-American cuisine of Chinatown. But some of what was invented there never moved much beyond New York — such as the cuisine of the European Jews who once populated Manhattan's Lower East Side in great numbers and left such a strong culinary legacy. Indeed, if a first-time visitor arrives in New York today and wants to taste something truly "New York" — I send him or her right away to a New York deli.

But New York state's diversity is not merely a question of the city's melting pot, of cohabitating ethnic groups; New York is also the place where some of the country's earliest restaurant luxury food was created, as well as the place where Buffalo Chicken Wings and Nathan's Hot Dogs and potato chips first saw the light of day. "New York food" will always be thought of as rich, sophisticated, cutting-edge restaurant food — as well as the kind of food you can snack on crazily to your heart's content or your cardiologist's alarm.

☆ Scrambled Eggs ☆ with Cheddar Cheese and Horseradish from Barney Greengrass

The Upper West Side of Manhattan is a great breakfast area — for here, many of the traditions of the old Jewish immigrants to New York are preserved. The "temple" of this cooking is Barney Greengrass, founded in 1908, where you can get an amazing array of smoked fish, bagels, bialys, and egg dishes on a Sunday morning (or any morning!). My favorite egg dish there is a startling, eye-opening concoction made with a horseradish–cheddar cheese spread that is manufactured in Wisconsin. You must try the following unusual combo of creamy, eggy, cheesy . . . and pungently hot!

Yield: A large portion
for one hungry person

3 tablespoons unsalted butter
3 extra-large eggs, beaten well
½ cup Old-Fashioned Foods Extra Hot
    Horseradish Cheese Spread
    (see Note)

Melt the butter over medium-high heat in a heavy skillet. Add the eggs and the cheese spread; working with a large metal spoon, immediately start mashing down the cheese. Over the course of the next 1 to 2 minutes, keep the eggs and the cheese in almost constant motion: swirling, scrambling, mashing cheese — until you have a pan full of soft scrambled eggs with large flaps, and with some discrete veins of cheese spread showing. Try not to brown the eggs; golden and creamy is the ideal.

NOTE: You can easily acquire the horseradish cheese spread used by Barney Greengrass through the mail. It costs just a few dollars for a one-pound tub and comes from:

Old Fashioned Foods
650 Furnace Street
P.O. Box 111
Mayville, WI 53050
920-387-4444
800-346-0154 (toll-free)
920-387-7929 (fax)

You can also make your own version using WisPride Sharp Cheddar Cheese Spread, available in supermarkets everywhere, and prepared horseradish; your version won't have the pungency of the original (Old Fashioned Foods uses horseradish oil), but you may prefer that! The recipe follows.

★ Horseradish Cheese Spread ★

½ cup WisPride Sharp Cheddar Cheese Spread
Scant 3 tablespoons prepared extra-hot
horseradish

Mix ingredients together. Let sit for 30 minutes for flavor to develop.

✼ Salami and Eggs ✼

One of the great traditional breakfast dishes of New York City — or anyplace in America where Jewish immigrants congregate — is the salami omelet known as salami and eggs, made with the exquisitely garlicky kosher salami. Believe it or not, there are many little choices to be made in preparing this dish. The most important choice is: thick-cut salami or thin-cut salami? Most home cooks use the narrow kosher salamis they buy in the supermarket and cut them into thick slices. I far prefer going to a deli and buying ultrathin slices of the wider kosher salamis sold there. For one thing, those deli salamis taste better than the supermarket ones. For another, the texture of the finished dish, when it's made with thin salami, is infinitely superior, to my taste: salami and eggs become an almost light and lacy treat. By the way, the dish is traditionally enjoyed with knife and fork — but you could do worse than serving the warm eggs on two slices of fresh, soft white bread for a salami-and-egg sandwich. Try it with an Egg Cream! (See page 271.)

Yield: 1 serving

1 tablespoon unsalted butter
5 very thin slices kosher salami, barely
⅛ pound, cut from a salami that's
4 inches in diameter
2 jumbo eggs, beaten well with a pinch of salt

1. Place the butter in an 8-inch nonstick sauté pan over medium-high heat. After the butter has melted, and the foam has subsided, add the slices of salami. They should completely cover the bottom of the pan; to do this, you'll need to overlap them somewhat.
2. Cook the salami slices until they bubble up and turn slightly brown on the undersides (about 1 to 2 minutes). Do not turn them.
3. Add the eggs to the pan. Pour them over the salami slices, making sure the eggs are evenly distributed. Let them set for 30 seconds, then insert a spatula under the eggs, all around the pan, to loosen the eggs from the bottom and make sure they're not sticking. Once they're loose, immediately swirl the pan so that any extra uncooked egg on top of the omelet swirls out to the perimeter (this cooks the excess egg quickly). Cook very briefly, just until the egg on the perimeter firms up. Overall, the eggs should cook a total of 1 to 2 minutes.
4. Fold the salami and eggs in half, making a half circle. Flip it over once (either with a spatula or with a jerk of the wrist on the pan handle). Slide salami and eggs onto a plate and serve. They taste best after cooling for 3 to 4 minutes.

✼ Smoked-Salmon Eggs ✼ Benedict with Fresh Dill

Eggs Benedict was invented in New York. Today, lots of upscale breakfast restaurants are now getting fancy with their eggs Benedict . . . and you should too! This combo of smoked salmon and cream cheese (New York's favorite bagel toppings) with the usual Benedict players is devastatingly good — better, perhaps, than the original.

Yield: 6 servings

4 cups water
½ cup distilled white vinegar
½ teaspoon kosher salt
12 large eggs
6 English muffins
12 tablespoons cream cheese (about 6 ounces),
    at room temperature
6 ounces thinly sliced smoked salmon
1½ cups Hollandaise Sauce (see sidebar,
    page 407)
Chopped dill for garnish

1. Preheat the broiler.
2. In a large skillet, pour in the water, vinegar, and salt and bring to a simmer.
3. Meanwhile, carefully crack 4 of the eggs into separate small cups. One at a time, carefully pour the eggs into the water against the side of the skillet and cook until firm, about 3 minutes. Remove poached eggs, drain on a kitchen towel, and cover with another towel that has been soaked in hot water and squeezed dry, to keep warm. Repeat with the remaining eggs. If the cooked eggs' whites have any ragged edges, you may trim them with kitchen shears.
4. While the eggs are poaching, make a small slit on the side of each English muffin and gently pull each muffin into two halves. Transfer the muffins to a baking sheet and toast under the broiler, turning once, until crispy, about 2 minutes per side. Spread each muffin half with 1 tablespoon of the cream cheese and divide the muffins among six plates.

5. Place some of the smoked salmon on each muffin half and top each with an egg. Spoon about 2 tablespoons of hollandaise sauce over each egg (if the hollandaise is too thick, thin it with warm water). Sprinkle with dill and serve immediately.

☆ Pickled "Lox" ☆ with Cream Sauce and Onion

Oy vey. What does *lox* mean? Once upon a time, in New York in the 1920s, before Scottish smoked salmon — or any smoked salmon — became a big thing, barrels of fresh, unsmoked salmon in brine would be shipped from Alaska to the big metropolitan center. There, the owners of delis would remove the "lox" from the barrels (the name is taken from *Lachs,* the German word for salmon), soak it in water for a few days to remove the extreme salty sting, and sell it. Jewish customers loved to slice their lox and put it on bagels with cream cheese. Some years later, a new idea from Nova Scotia was introduced to New York: cured salmon (just a tiny bit salty) that had been cold-smoked. To some this was an improvement — and salty, brine-cured, unsmoked "true" lox began to fade away. Over time, "lox" and "Nova" became more and more alike — and to make things more confusing still, Nova stopped coming exclusively from Nova Scotia. The following recipe is a throwback to the days when lox was brined salmon; this one isn't quite as salty as lox used to be, so I prefer to call it pickled lox. I have added a bunch of seasonings that were not used back then, but I have resurrected the old idea of serving the pickled lox in a sour cream–based sauce. Have you ever been tempted by herring in cream sauce but didn't like the idea of herring? Try this fabulous old-time dish — fresher tasting, less fishy than herring but brimming with the flavor of old New York.

Yield: 4 to 6 first-course servings

4 cups water

1 cup white distilled vinegar

1 cup sugar

¼ cup kosher salt

6 bay leaves

2 teaspoons coriander seeds

2 teaspoons mustard seeds

1 teaspoon whole black peppercorns

½ teaspoon whole allspice berries

½ teaspoon dried dill

½ teaspoon celery seeds

½ teaspoon crushed red pepper

1 pound skin-on salmon fillet

1 large onion, peeled and thinly sliced

1 cup sour cream

1. In a large saucepan, combine water, vinegar, sugar, salt, bay leaves, and spices, including pepper flakes; bring to a boil. Simmer 5 minutes to blend flavors, remove from heat, and cool to room temperature.

2. Place salmon and onion in a nonreactive container (plastic or glass). Pour cooled brine over all. Cover and refrigerate for 4 days.

3. To serve, remove salmon from the marinade. Remove skin from the salmon and cut the salmon into ¼-inch slices (my preference) or into 1-inch cubes. Place the salmon in a bowl and toss it with 1 cup of the onion slices from the marinade (try to leave seeds behind). Mix sour cream with 8 teaspoons of the marinade. Season with salt and pepper to taste. Blend the salmon and onion in the bowl with the sour cream sauce. Divide among four to six appetizer plates and serve immediately.

SERVING NOTE: The pickled lox is extremely versatile. You could, for example, leave out the cream sauce; simply slice the lox and put it on a bagel with cream cheese. You could also put the creamless lox slices on blini (page 105) with melted butter and sour cream. Or you could toss pieces of the lox in some sort of old-fangled/new-fangled salad (I vote for beets in the mix!). Once you add the cream sauce, there are still many news ways to go. I love this dish as is — but the inclusion of such things as capers and/or parsley would be great. How about thin slices of Granny Smith apple?

✵ Vichyssoise ✵ with White Truffle Oil

Here's a good example of the kind of fancy-dan, luxuriant, Frenchified food that was being invented in New York City restaurants at the dawn of the twentieth century. Louis Diat, a chef at the Ritz-Carlton Hotel in New York, had memories of potage parmentier, a hot potato-and-leek soup, from his childhood in France. In New York, somewhere around 1910, he turned it into a cold soup and gave it the elegant name vichyssoise (properly pronounced "VEE-shee-swaz"). The following great version is extremely simple to make, intensely potato flavored, and lighter than most. I have, however, combined the early 1900s and the early 2000s: a New York chef today couldn't resist tweaking this old classic. My tweak: a drizzle of truffle oil, the earthy flavor of which goes superbly with potatoes.

Yield: 4 soup servings

2 cups peeled and diced russet potatoes
    (about 10 ounces of potato)

2½ cups sliced and cleaned leeks, white part
    only (about 4 large leeks)

2 cups water

1 cup chicken stock
1 teaspoon salt
⅓ cup whipping cream
1 to 3 teaspoons white truffle oil

1. Place potatoes, leeks, water, and stock in a saucepan. Bring to a boil. Add salt, lower heat and simmer until potatoes and leeks are tender, about 10 to 15 minutes. Let cool for a few minutes.

2. Puree potato-leek mixture in a blender, or use an immersion blender. If using a standing blender, return soup to pot.

3. In a separate saucepan, bring cream just to a boil. Add cream to soup and bring to a simmer. Season with salt and pepper to taste. Chill soup.

4. When ready to serve, whisk truffle oil to taste into cold soup. Adjust seasoning. Ladle soup into chilled bowls and serve.

☆ New York City Pushcart ☆ Onions for Hot Dogs

You have yer cherce at a New York hot dog pushcart: warm sauerkraut? or warm onions in a tomatoey sauce? I grew up on sauerkraut, but in recent years I'm lovin' the onion thing. The onions are saucy, orange red, slightly gloppy, with low-key flavor — perfect as a complement to the beefy, garlicky New York hot dog. Now you can make this treat at home — just boil up some dogs (Sabrett, Nathan's, and Hebrew National are good brands in the right style), place dogs on hot dog buns, dribble a few tablespoons of the following recipe on top of each dog, and, if you wish (I do), squirt some mustard over all. In fact, I think it's better if you make this at home — since the steam table stuff on the street is usually diluted and usually overcooked from standing around. If you like that street quality, by all means add water to the following recipe and cook it longer — but I like my onions just a tad fresher and tastier than they are on the street.

Yield: Enough sauce for 12 to 16 hot dogs

1 tablespoon vegetable oil
4 firmly packed cups of thinly sliced onion
    (about 2 large or 4 medium onions)
2 teaspoons minced garlic (about 2 medium
    cloves)
1 tablespoon flour
8 ounces canned, smooth tomato sauce
1 cup water
2 tablespoons light corn syrup
2 teaspoons white vinegar
2 bay leaves
½ teaspoon dry mustard
Pinch of cayenne
Pinch of ground cloves

1. Place the vegetable oil in a heavy saucepan over medium-low heat. Add the onion and the garlic. Cover and cook for 20 minutes, stirring occasionally. After 20 minutes the onion should be softened but not browned.

2. Add the flour and stir well to distribute evenly among the onion slices. Cook for 1 minute, stirring to make sure the flour doesn't burn. Add the tomato sauce, water, corn syrup, vinegar, bay leaves, mustard, cayenne, and cloves. Stir well to blend. Season to taste with salt and pepper. Cover and cook very slowly over low heat for 45 minutes. If the mixture has become too thick, add a little water. Serve on New York–style hot dogs.

✳ Rochester White Hots ✳

This is a grand local tradition that very few people outside upstate New York know about. "White hots" — bratwurstlike hot dogs — are served on buns with a few required condiments and, most required of all, a thin, pebbly, spicy meat sauce that is a unique local creation. The sauce, frankly, is not a work of gastronomic art — but it all comes together in an extremely comforting way when sauce meets dog meets condiments.

Yield: 8 hot dogs

½ pound ground beef, crumbled
1 tablespoon minced onion,
*   plus extra for garnishing dogs*
½ teaspoon paprika
½ teaspoon black pepper
¼ teaspoon chili powder
¼ teaspoon cayenne
¼ teaspoon ground cinnamon
¼ teaspoon salt
Pinch of crushed thyme leaves
1¼ cups water
8 "white" hot dogs (see Note)
8 buns
Mustard

1. Place the beef, the 1 tablespoon of onion, the paprika, pepper, chili powder, cayenne, cinnamon, salt, and thyme in a small saucepan. Pour the water over all and mix well. Place saucepan over low heat, cover, and cook for 1½ hours; the mixture should be very slowly simmering during that time.

2. Remove cover from saucepan. Simmer very slowly for another 1½ hours. When the time is up, the meat sauce should be the consistency of a thin gravy, a little watery, not dried out.

3. "Butterfly" the hot dogs, then grill or griddle them. Place them on buns, smear them with mustard, and top each with a few tablespoons of the meat sauce. Sprinkle with raw minced onion and serve immediately.

NOTE: White hots are bratwurst-style sausages in a hot dog size. You can use any brats you like to make this dish — or you can order white hots from Rochester by contacting

Zweigle's
651 Plymouth Avenue
North Rochester, NY 14608
716-546-1740
www.zweigles.com

𝒯he Garbage Plate

The Rochester white hot meat sauce is one of the building blocks of Rochester's most famous dish: the Garbage Plate, as served at either of the Nick Tahou's locations. This is great late-night comfort food: a plate of macaroni salad, baked beans, and French fries is topped with a white hot or two, and then the meat sauce is poured over all. Bread is served on the side to soak up the drippings that the paper plate doesn't absorb. Add ketchup and consume lustily.

✰ Buffalo Chicken Wings ✰

Frank and Theresa Bellismo, owners of the Anchor Bar in Buffalo, were essentially raiding the depleted refrigerator on an off night when they came up with this wacky dish, in which deep-fried chicken wings get tossed in a mix of butter and hot sauce. Today you see many "improvements" on the original recipe — which mostly involve not frying the wings. But an oven can't give you the crunchy crispness that a deep-fryer can. If you're going to improve — as I've tried to do here — you must leave the frying in. My touch-ups include a quick brining of the chicken, which makes it juicier still; a coating of the wings with spices, which makes them more flavorful still; and a blend of butter and margarine in the dunk, which to my palate yields a more harmonious taste in the dish than either butter or margarine alone. By all means, retain the original garnishes, which at first seem arbitrary: but without celery sticks and blue cheese dressing on the side, the dish just wouldn't be the same (sometimes I dip the celery in the blue cheese, sometimes I dip the wings!). Most important of all: do not disdain this dish just because it's familiar. It is a truly American, truly delicious combination of elements.

Yield: 48 wing pieces,
about 6 to 8 first-course servings

24 chicken wings (about 4½ pounds)
2 tablespoons coarse salt
1 tablespoon sugar
6 cups cold water
1½ tablespoons paprika
2 teaspoons cayenne
2 teaspoons freshly ground black pepper
1 tablespoon garlic powder
1 tablespoon onion powder
4 tablespoons unsalted butter

4 tablespoons margarine
½ cup red hot sauce (the original was Frank's)
1 quart vegetable oil
Celery sticks
Blue Cheese Dressing (page 422)

1. Cut off and discard the small wing tip from each wing. Then cut the remainder of the wing into two pieces.
2. Mix salt, sugar, and water in a large bowl and submerge wings for 20 minutes.
3. Remove wings from the water, rinse, and dry thoroughly with paper towels.
4. Combine paprika, cayenne, black pepper, garlic powder, and onion powder and put in a large bowl. Add wings and turn them, using a large spoon, thoroughly coating them with the spices.
5. Melt butter and margarine in a small saucepan. Add hot sauce and bring to a simmer. Turn off heat and set aside.
6. Heat oil to 375 degrees. Fry all the pieces that resemble small drumsticks together for about 11 minutes (in batches, if necessary). These pieces take slightly longer to cook than the remaining flatter-looking pieces — which will take about 10 minutes to fry to a golden brown.
7. Remove wings and drain on paper towels.
8. Place all the wings together in a bowl and pour butter mixture over them. Turn the wings in the sauce. Remove wings to a serving platter and serve immediately with celery sticks and Blue Cheese Dressing.

☆ Home-Cured Corned Beef, ☆ New York Deli Style

One of the greatest things about New York City, gastronomically speaking, is the delicatessen, or "deli," tradition. At the heart of every deli are sandwiches — warm piles of cured meat (almost always beef, since pork's not kosher) stacked on seeded rye and other breads, served with tangy deli mustard. And at the center of interest in the world of deli meat is corned beef — usually a huge hunk of brisket that has sat in brine for a couple of weeks, then melted to tenderness in hot water, before being thinly sliced and served on a sandwich. Unless you go to a New York–style deli in other cities (L.A., for example, has several great ones), it's not easy to find a New York–style sandwich outside New York. Good news: you will not believe how easy it is to cure your own corned beef — and how much the result of the following recipe tastes like corned beef from a New York deli! The hardest part is finding space in your refrigerator for a big container of beef in brine. This fabulous corned beef is well worth the space it takes. The name corned beef, by the way, does not indicate the presence of corn in the dish. The "corn" part apparently comes from an old English term for any small granule — for example, a grain of salt is a corn.

Yield: 8 to 10 servings

1 gallon water
1 cup kosher salt
2 teaspoons Prague powder, optional
    (see Note)
½ cup sugar
1 tablespoon whole yellow
    mustard seeds
2 teaspoons whole black
    peppercorns
2 teaspoons whole coriander seeds
2 teaspoons whole dill seeds
5 bay leaves
5 pounds whole beef brisket (preferably
    second-cut; see page 441 for
    explanation of brisket cuts)

1. In a medium-size nonreactive pot over medium-high heat, combine the water, salt, Prague powder, sugar, mustard seeds, peppercorns, coriander seeds, dill seeds, and bay leaves. Boil, uncovered, until the sugar and salt are dissolved; this will take about 1 minute. Transfer the brine to a nonreactive container with a tight-fitting lid (a large pot will do); the container should just be large enough to hold the brisket and brine. Refrigerate the brine, uncovered, until it is cool.

2. Add the brisket to the chilled brine, making sure it is completely submerged. Cover the container tightly. If needed, weight the brisket down with a heavy object to keep it submerged in the brine. Keep covered and refrigerated for 14 days, turning the brisket over in the brining liquid every 2 days throughout the process; this will ensure even curing throughout the brisket. After 14 days, the corned beef is ready to be cooked (see Cooked Corned Beef, page 269).

NOTE: Prague powder is mostly salt with some sodium nitrate added. If you use it in your cure, the sodium nitrate will ensure that your corned beef will have the pretty pinkish red color that the deli corned beef has; if you prefer to omit the powder, the corned beef will still taste great, but its color will be a much less attractive brown gray. I use Prague powder in my cure, but some people feel that the consumption of

☆☆

sodium nitrate is risky business. If you happily eat ham, salami, hot dogs, and so on — all "pinkened" by sodium nitrate — there's no reason to leave it out of this recipe.

It is, however, tricky to acquire; it's not sold at the supermarket. Happily, I do have a great mail-order source for Prague powder:

The Mandeville Company
2800 Washington Avenue N.
Minneapolis, MN 55411
800-328-8490 (toll-free)
612-521-3671
612-521-3673 (fax)
www.mandevillecompany.com
mandevilleco@aol.com

Catalog: The Mandeville Company will mail customers a free catalog. Just contact them by e-mail or phone or request it when you make an order.

Prague powder from the Mandeville Company is very inexpensive; it's only about $1.50 a pound . . . and the more you buy the lower the price!

☆ Cooked Corned Beef ☆

After corned beef is cured, it needs to be cooked for several hours. Most home cooks do the cooking in plain water — but I've found that the subtle flavors of corned beef are perfectly nurtured by the following broth. Use this broth and cooking method either for Home-Cured Corned Beef or for one you've bought at the supermarket.

Yield: 8 to 10 servings

12 cups water
3 bay leaves
1 head of garlic, peeled and smashed
1 teaspoon whole yellow mustard seeds
2 teaspoons whole black peppercorns
1 teaspoon whole coriander seeds
2 allspice berries
2 onions, peeled
½ teaspoon dill seeds
1 corned beef brisket, preferably
   home-cured (page 268),
   about 5 pounds

1. In a large nonreactive pot over medium-high heat, combine water, bay leaves, smashed garlic cloves, mustard seeds, peppercorns, coriander seeds, allspice berries, onions, and dill seeds to make the cooking liquid.

2. If using Home-Cured Corned Beef, remove the beef from the brining liquid; if using store-bought corned beef, remove the beef from its package. Place the beef in the pot with the seasoned cooking liquid.

3. Bring the brisket cooking liquid just to a boil and then lower the heat to a very low simmer. Cook the corned beef, covered, turning every 30 minutes or so, for 3 to 4 hours, or until it is tender. The best way to tell if the corned beef is tender is by piercing it with a thin-bladed knife such as a sharp boning knife. Begin testing to see if the brisket is done after about 2 hours of cooking time, and then about every 20 minutes throughout the remaining cooking time. When the brisket is fully cooked, there will be little resistance when inserting the boning knife.

4. Remove the brisket from the cooking liquid and, if desired, serve immediately, thinly sliced. The cooking liquid can also be used to cook potatoes, cabbage, carrots, or any

New York State Wine

The nation's second-largest wine industry just doesn't get the respect it deserves. New York State wines are still having difficulty shaking off the reputation they earned a century ago: sweet, simple wines, lacking European elegance and style.

It was a deserved reputation, once upon a time. The industry, clustered around Hammondsport, New York, in the Finger Lakes, was based on a hardy species of North American vine called *Vitis labrusca*. Grapes from these vines (such as Concord and Niagara), and wines from these grapes, tasted extremely grapey, like Welch's grape juice, a taste the pros disparagingly call foxy.

Later, twentieth-century scientists began crossing grapes from *Vitis labrusca* with grapes from the European vine, *Vitis vinifera*. They came up with what was called French-American hybrid grapes, such as Seyval Blanc and Baco Noir. Wines from these grapes are more European in style but — despite the fact that they're still being made today — don't really help to expunge the bad old reputation.

It took a Russian émigré named Konstantin Frank to demonstrate that *Vitis vinifera* itself could be grown in the Finger Lakes — and, by extension, in all of New York State. In the wake of his experiments, things really picked up in the 1970s — and today four regions of New York State are producing wines from *Vitis vinifera* grapes that are absolutely worthy of world attention.

It is white wine that leads the way, with excellent German-style Riesling (both dry and sweet) being produced in the Finger Lakes and crisp, surprisingly delicious Chardonnay (that goes better with food than most Chardonnays do!) being produced in the Hudson Valley and Long Island.

Long Island, in fact — just ninety miles from New York City and planted to vines only in the 1970s — has been the wine groupie's hottest New York spot. The region, mostly on the north fork of eastern Long Island, has attracted tremendous attention and investment. Surprises are endless. Some of the best dry Gewürztraminer in the world is being made there. There is Long Island sparkling wine in a Champagne style that rivals wine from Champagne. The greatest hope of all for the future lies in something a bit unusual for New York State: red wine. Merlot, in particular, a grape made famous in Bordeaux, has caused a stir on Long Island. But most insiders say that the greatest grape of all in the region will someday be a red grape used only modestly in Bordeaux: Cabernet Franc.

I think New Yorkers would be foolish indeed to continue to ignore Long Island and Hudson Valley Chardonnay with their bluepoint oysters, Long Island Cabernet Franc and Merlot with their New York steak, and Finger Lakes Riesling with their apple tarts and pies. New York City should be to New York's wines as Bordeaux is to the wines of Bordeaux, as San Francisco is to the wines of Napa and Sonoma: a place where everybody is very happy to drink local.

vegetable you'd like to serve with the corned beef. Alternatively, you could cool the cooked corned beef to room temperature and refrigerate it, wrapped in foil, for a few weeks. It can be eaten cold or hot or used for other dishes (such as Corned Beef Hash, page 408). If you wish to reheat the corned beef, the cooking liquid can be saved and used.

★ The Reubenized New York ★ Deli Corned Beef Sandwich

One of the reasons a corned beef sandwich is so terrific in New York delis is that the corned beef is served warm. Sometimes even the bread (usually Jewish-style rye) is warm. So: if you want to make a great corned beef sandwich at home, simply place 6 to 8 ounces of corned beef slices in a steamer for 3 to 4 minutes. Then surround the corned beef with rye bread, making a corned beef sandwich, and steam for 1 minute more. But I like to take it one step further. One of the greatest sandwiches ever invented is the Reuben sandwich — a combo of corned beef, sauerkraut, Swiss cheese, and Russian dressing on rye. There are multiple claims of ownership (including a claim that Reuben Kalofsky of Nebraska invented it in Omaha in 1922), but most corned beef historians believe that the sandwich was invented in New York at Reuben's, in 1914, by Arnold Reuben. Many people find the Reuben — which is sautéed in butter, like a grilled cheese sandwich — to be a little too heavy and greasy. I have created the Reubenized New York Corned Beef Sandwich, in which the Reuben is steamed rather than fried. It is magnificent! If you wish to make it the traditional way, be my guest. But I suspect that if you try it this way, you'll never go back.

Yield: 1 sandwich

6 ounces thinly sliced cooked corned beef, cold or warm
2 slices Jewish-style rye bread with seeds, each about 5½ inches by 3½ inches
½ cup sauerkraut
2 ounces thinly sliced Swiss cheese
2 tablespoons Russian Dressing (page 420)

1. Place the corned beef slices on one slice of rye bread. Mold them so that they fit evenly on top of the bread slice. Then transfer the corned beef slices to the top of your counter, making sure to preserve the shape you created. Top the slices evenly with the sauerkraut. Top the sauerkraut with the cheese so that the cheese lies evenly across the top of the package.

2. Heat water in the base of a steamer. When the water comes to a boil, using a spatula, transfer the meat-and-cheese package to the steamer basket. Cover and steam until cheese has melted (about 3 to 4 minutes).

3. While cheese is melting, spread each slice of bread with 1 tablespoon of the Russian dressing. After the cheese has melted, using a spatula, transfer meat-and-cheese package to one slice of the bread, placing it on top of the Russian dressing. Top with the other slice of bread, dressing side down. Transfer the package with your spatula to the steamer. Cover. Steam until the bread is just warm and soft, about 1 minute. Remove sandwich with spatula, cut in half, and serve immediately.

★ Egg Cream ★

The egg cream, a drink that was the emblem of Jewish immigrant life on New York's Lower East Side in the early twentieth century, famously has neither egg nor cream in it. This paradox almost captures the spirit of Talmudic disputation: "What . . . you want eggs and cream, too?" But there is logic in the name, for the collar of the drink resembles creamy egg whites. The egg cream was created by a Jewish immigrant in the 1890s, who made his own chocolate syrup. A New York company called Fox's created a facsimile around 1920, and to this day, Fox's U-Bet is still the chocolate syrup of choice for an egg cream. The egg cream is an extremely refreshing and delicious drink, just lightly sweet, a good way to end a traditional Lower East Side meal (lots of seltzer water was used down there, to cut through the fat-heavy food, like corned beef).

Yield: 1 drink

¾ *cup very cold milk*
Very cold seltzer
¼ *cup Fox's U-Bet or other chocolate-flavored*
   syrup

1. Pour milk into a chilled 16-ounce glass with a wide mouth.
2. Add seltzer to milk while stirring vigorously with a long spoon. Fill to 1 inch below the rim of the glass.
3. Drizzle in syrup, stirring vigorously with small wrist motions. This will leave a glass that's practically filled with a brown chocolate drink, with a creamy white top that's about 1 inch high.

☆ New York Cheesecake ☆

The ancient Romans appear to have made some form of cheesecake, the English had a glorious cheesecake period, and the Germans, most of all, were famous for perfecting the kind of cheesecake that finally morphed into New York Cheesecake. Even within the genre of New York Cheesecake there are myriad variations (crust or no crust? what kind of crust? airy or dense texture? to bake or not to bake?). Many American home cooks, particularly in the fifties and sixties, chose not to bake, using instead a gelatinized filling that sets up just by chilling. The following recipe is "bake" all the way — following the great Lindy's tradition (a New York restaurant) in most of its particu-

lars. To me the most important thing of all in a cheesecake is: Does the cake give you that euphoric dairy afterglow, a golden sensation all over your tasting apparatus that makes you forget your worries? This one does. Make sure you have a nine-inch springform pan for making this great cake. *Note:* This cheesecake does nothing but get better in the refrigerator for about a week — if you can keep your hands off it.

Yield: 1 cake (9 inches), 6 to 8 servings

4 *tablespoons (½ stick) unsalted butter*
¼ *cup graham cracker crumbs*
1½ *cups plus 2 teaspoons sugar*
¼ *teaspoon plus a pinch of salt*
2½ *pounds cream cheese, at room temperature*
¾ *cup sour cream*
5 *whole eggs plus 2 extra egg yolks*
1 *cup whipping cream*
⅓ *cup milk*
Pinch of lemon zest
Pinch of orange zest
1 *teaspoon vanilla extract*
¼ *teaspoon lemon juice*

1. Preheat the oven to 250 degrees.
2. Melt 1 tablespoon of the butter in a small bowl in the microwave. Place the melted butter, graham cracker crumbs, the 2 teaspoons of sugar, and a pinch of salt in a small bowl and combine with a fork to make the crust crumb mixture.
3. Use the remaining 3 tablespoons of butter to grease a nine-inch springform pan evenly.
4. Place the crumb mixture in the pan. Using your hands, evenly dust the sides and bottom of the pan with the crumbs.
5. Lay a 20-inch-long piece of plastic wrap

across your countertop from left to right. Lay a second 20-inch-long piece of plastic wrap on top of the first so that it is perpendicular to it; position it directly at the center of the first piece. You will have a very even cross on your counter. Place the pan with the crumbs directly on the center of the crossed plastic wraps. Lift all sides of the plastic, fold them upward, and completely encase the outside of the pan, bottom and sides, with tight-fitting plastic wrap. You will have to improvise as you go, but your goal is a completely tight, waterproof seal around the outside and bottom of the pan. This will prevent any water from the water bath from seeping into the cheesecake batter.

New York Cheesecake

Place the plastic-wrapped pan on a cross of aluminum foil pieces. Now encase the pan with the foil, improvising as you go, to make a waterproof seal.

6. Repeat this process with two 20-inch-long pieces of aluminum foil that cover the plastic wrap. The foil will keep the plastic wrap from burning while the cake bakes.

7. Combine the remaining 1½ cups of sugar, the remaining ¼ teaspoon salt, the cream cheese, sour cream, the eggs and extra egg yolks, the whipping cream, milk, lemon zest, orange zest, vanilla extract, and lemon juice in a food processor bowl. Process the mixture for 20 seconds, then stop and scrape down the sides of the food processor bowl. Process again until the mixture is smooth, about 10 seconds.

8. Pour the prepared cheesecake mixture into the dusted cheesecake pan. Set the pan in a larger baking pan. Carefully pour very hot water into the larger pan until it rises 1½ inches up the sides of the cheesecake pan.

9. Carefully place the pan with the cheesecake on the center rack of the oven. Bake until cheesecake is golden brown, about 2 hours. After 1 hour of baking, when the cheesecake is half done, gently rotate it 180 degrees.

10. When cake is done, remove from water bath and place onto wire rack to cool. When the cheesecake has cooled to approximately room temperature, place it in the refrigerator, still in the cake pan. Refrigerate overnight.

11. The next day, remove the cheesecake from the refrigerator and remove the tinfoil and plastic wrap. Dip a cake knife in warm water and run it around the inner circumference of the pan, loosening the cake from the sides. Unlock the springform and remove its sides. The cheesecake will be sitting on the bottom of the springform pan. Place on a platter and let the cheesecake come to room temperature before serving. *Note:* If you worry about scratching the base of your springform pan when cutting the cake, you'll have to move the cake from the base onto another surface. I don't worry; I just cut gently.

Philadelphia

Philadelphia is a city with a fascinating culinary past. More than just the largest city in revolutionary America, Philly was actually the cultural center of the brand-new United States. Old British culinary ideas in the city got transformed through contact with new African and West Indian slaves, who brought all kinds of exotic foods and food ideas through the ports. The Pennsylvania Dutch — whose wonderful cuisine is still interwoven today with Philadelphia's — contributed delicious Germanic ideas to the party, including many soups, stews, and sausage dishes. Not least, an influx of French expats right after the French Revolution put a patina of elegance and refinement on the local cuisine.

All these influences dwindled with time; in the mid–twentieth century, W. C. Fields apparently wasn't excited about the prospect of eating in Philadelphia. And when foodies today think of Philadelphia, they most likely think not of the past but of the vital, creative restaurant scene that has emerged in the past two decades.

However, to go to modern Philadelphia looking only for modern, fancy food would be to miss something grand. For the one ethnic influence that has truly merged into the local culinary culture is that of the Italians in South Philly — and in particular, their influence on sandwiches. Make no mistake about it: Philadelphia is the greatest sandwich city in the United States.

★ Scrapple ★

I am really excited about this scrapple recipe — because it has greatly enhanced flavor over the normally boring commercial product. Scrapple has a fascinating history. Some say the Pennsylvania Dutch brought it from Germany; some say it's a Philadelphia dish, with roots in northeastern Holland. Some say the Amish taught it to the Philadelphians. In any event, it's an atavistic dish, harking back to the medieval days when pig slaughtering meant a busy kitchen; lots of pig parts, including the pig's blood, were used in the making of this dish. Though today the dish is thought of as a kind of rustic breakfast sausage, it is more closely related to the charcuterie (especially the pâtés) of northern Europe. That's the quality I tried to emphasize in the following recipe — making this, after all, one of the most interesting breakfast sausages you'll ever taste. When cut in slices, browned in bacon fat, and served next to a couple of fried or poached eggs, this scrapple is guaranteed to take the chill off any winter day. It takes a little work, but it's worth it.

Yield: 2 loaves, about 6 to 8 servings each

4½ pounds pork ribs (country style),
*   or any pork stew meat with bones*
1 ham hock (about ½ pound)
1 pig's foot (have the butcher split it and
*   cut it into 2-inch pieces)*
1 medium onion, peeled and cut into 4 pieces
1 medium carrot, peeled and cut into large
*   chunks*
2 stalks celery, cut into large chunks
1 garlic clove
1 sprig thyme, plus 2 teaspoons chopped
*   fresh thyme*
1 sprig parsley
1 bay leaf
1 pound breakfast sausage, removed from casings

¼ cup lard
2½ cups fine yellow cornmeal
1½ teaspoons salt
1 teaspoon dried sage
¼ teaspoon freshly ground pepper
Bacon fat (or vegetable oil or butter)
Wondra (quick-mixing flour) for dredging
    scrapple slices (optional)

1. The day before you plan to serve the scrapple, in a large pot place pork, ham hock, pig's foot pieces, onion, carrot, celery, garlic, thyme sprig, parsley, and bay leaf. Add cold water to cover. Bring to a boil, then simmer over very low heat until meat falls from the bones, about 1½ to 2 hours. Strain broth. Refrigerate broth and meat separately. Discard vegetables.

2. Once the broth is cool, scrape and reserve the fat that forms on top (you should have about ½ cup fat). Over high heat, reduce the broth until you have 6 cups. Reserve. Pull the meat from the bones of the ribs, hock, and foot, discarding skin and bones. Chop the meat coarsely and reserve. You should have about 6½ cups of meat.

3. In a large saucepan, brown breakfast sausage until cooked through, breaking up into small chunks with a wooden spoon. Add lard, reserved pork fat, and reserved chopped meat. Cook, breaking up the meat chunks with a wooden spoon, until meat is soft and very shredded.

4. Bring reserved stock to a simmer. Add cornmeal in a slow stream, whisking constantly. Add salt, chopped thyme, sage, and pepper. Simmer over very low heat, with just an occasional bubble popping the surface, for 30 minutes or until mixture is thick, like polenta, and begins to pull from the sides of the pan. Stir in meat mixture. Pour into 2 small loaf pans lined with plastic wrap, tapping the pans on the counter to release any air bubbles. Pull sides of plastic up to cover top and cool slightly, then refrigerate until set, about 3 to 4 hours or overnight.

5. To serve, peel off plastic wrap and cut into ½-inch-thick slices. In a large skillet, melt enough fat (bacon, vegetable oil, or butter) to cover the bottom of the pan. Lightly dredge scrapple slices in Wondra, tapping off excess, if desired, for a crisper crust. Over medium heat, cook scrapple until golden on both sides and heated through. Serve immediately.

✸ Philly Cheesesteak ✸

There is no Philadelphia specialty with greater fame than the Philly Cheesesteak. Though the story has been challenged, Philly Cheesesteak was purportedly invented by an Italian, Pat Olivieri, in 1930, who sold hot dogs and other fast treats to taxi drivers at his roadside stand. One day serendipity led to this improvisation — griddled slices of beef with melted cheese on an Italian roll. If you've never tasted one in Philadelphia, you might wonder what all the fuss is about; this is a dish that just doesn't travel well. Almost any Philadelphian will tell you that the bread's the thing: the almost insipid fluffiness of the center, combined with the light crackle of the crust, is the perfect medium for the greasy, gooey filling. A bakery called Amoroso's supplies many of the Philadelphia shops with the bread — but similar bread in the rest of America is not to be found. Another factor that goes against good Philly Cheesesteak elsewhere is its name. Cooks in other places, hearing the monicker, mistakenly set out to make a steak. Diners in other places anticipate something having to do with steak, then get disappointed. Well, there is beef in the thing — but what's good about it has nothing whatsoever to do with steak. The meat must be griddled so that it's gray and soft, not brown and crispy. It must be dripping with grease. And the finished taste is far more like the taste of a good greasy burger with onions than like any steak I've ever had. Speaking of onions . . . if you want 'em, along with your cheese, you step up to the counter and say, "Cheese wit'." They're essential, to my taste. And when you say "cheese wit'," the cheese you'll get wit' the onions is going to be Cheez Whiz. You have other cheesy options, but I must tell you that they bring the classic dish in another, not better, direction entirely. Controversy swirls around every other condiment choice as well. In addition to bread, meat, onions, and Cheez Whiz, the only thing I like on my Philly Cheesesteak . . . is ketchup.

Yield: 4 sandwiches

3 tablespoons vegetable oil, or more
2 medium onions, peeled and sliced
1 cup Cheez Whiz
1½ pounds boneless rib eye steak,
    sliced paper thin (for best results,
    ask your butcher to slice the steak
    on a meat slicer for you)
4 Philadelphia cheesesteak loaves (page 277)
    or 4 Italian hero breads,
    each about 8 inches long (see Note)

1. Heat 1 tablespoon of the oil in a medium-size skillet over medium heat. Add onions and cook over medium heat until onion is softened and golden, about 15 minutes. Set aside but keep warm.

2. Place Cheez Whiz in a small nonmetal bowl, cover loosely with plastic wrap, and microwave until bubbly. Keep warm and covered.

3. Heat one or more large cast-iron skillets over lowest heat. Season steak with salt and pepper. Add a tablespoon of vegetable oil to each skillet and add the beef slices in a single layer. Cook, flattening with a metal spatula, about 5 minutes, flipping once or twice with the spatula. Meat should turn gray, not brown, and remain soft, not crusty. When one quarter of the beef is ready, approximately 6 ounces, you're ready to make a sandwich. (Continue cooking remaining meat in one or more skillets, adding a tablespoon of vegetable oil each time before adding meat, until all meat is cooked.)

4. To make one sandwich, cut a bread loaf down the middle but do not cut through completely. Stuff with 6 ounces of the meat, then one-fourth of the onions, then drizzle with one-fourth of the Cheez Whiz. Serve immediately. Continue until 4 sandwiches are made.

NOTE: As discussed above, having a loaf of Amoroso's bread on hand is your best guarantee of making an authentic cheesesteak. They do ship — but when the bread arrives from Philadelphia a few days later, it's not in its best condition. Remember that fluffiness at the center is ultraimportant — so a good, insipid Italian loaf from the supermarket is probably your best local shopping bet. Crisp it in the oven a bit (at 350 degrees) to emulate the crackling exterior of Amoroso's bread. Of course, if you wish to take the time, your best shot at the right bread outside Philadelphia would be to make the Philadelphia Cheesesteak Loaf below. If you bake it, and if you follow the recipe instructions above, you will have in your household on that day possibly the only authentic Philly Cheesesteak in the country outside of Philadelphia.

✶ Philadelphia ✶ Cheesesteak Loaf

You hear it again and again: "You cannot make a Philly Cheesesteak outside Philly, because you cannot get the bread." Indeed, the Italian-hero-type bread baked in Philadelphia for this sandwich specialty (most famously at Amoroso's) does not exist elsewhere. Local residents claim it's the local water that makes the difference ("dirty," they joke). But I think it's just a question of know-how. What makes the loaf so distinct, so perfect for the oozy filling, is that the crust is crunchy and the inside is soft and tender. Yet the crunchy crust is not as thick or crunchy as the crust of a great Italian loaf, and the tender inside is not as tender as the inside of a supermarket loaf. It's a compromise of great beauty. With the recipe below, you can now create your own cheesesteak loaf at home. What do you do with it after you've baked it? You immediately make the preceding recipe.

Yield: About 8 rolls

5¾ cups all-purpose flour (preferably bleached), plus extra for handling dough
1 cup minus 1 tablespoon water
1 tablespoon rapid-rise (instant) yeast
2 tablespoons sugar
1 tablespoon kosher salt
2 tablespoons olive oil, plus extra for greasing bowl
Cornmeal for dusting
Handful of ice cubes

1. Place the 5¾ cups flour, water, yeast, sugar, salt, and the 2 tablespoons olive oil in the large bowl of a stand mixer fitted with a dough hook attachment.

2. Mix the ingredients on very low speed until they are well combined. Increase the mixer speed to medium-high and mix the dough until thoroughly kneaded, about 8 minutes more.

3. Lightly grease a large bowl with olive oil. Remove the ball of dough from the mixer and place in oiled bowl. Cover the bowl and place it in a warm spot until the dough ball has doubled in size, about 1 hour.

4. Lightly flour a rolling pin and a countertop with extra flour. Remove the risen dough to the counter. Using the rolling pin, flatten the dough to expel all the gases that have developed inside.

5. Using a knife, divide the large dough ball into smaller dough pieces that are each a little larger than a baseball. You should have about 8 pieces total. Place the pieces on the countertop so that they are not touching each other. Cover them with a damp cloth and let them rest for 15 minutes.

6. Sprinkle another section of the countertop with flour. Dust your hands with flour and roll your palms over the pieces of dough with a back-and-forth motion to shape the dough pieces into 6-inch-long cylinders. Continue until all the rolls are shaped. Place the shaped rolls on a cornmeal-dusted baking sheet, separated by several inches of space, and cover with plastic wrap. Allow the rolls to double in size, about 1½ hours.

7. Place a baking stone in the oven on the center rack. Place an ovenproof baking pan

on the bottom of the oven. Preheat oven to 425 degrees.

8. Dust a pizza peel with cornmeal. Place 4 of the rolls on the pizza peel at a time. Using a razor blade or a serrated knife, score each roll in a straight line down the center lengthwise, cutting them approximately ½ inch deep. Spray the loaves with water using a spray bottle. Carefully toss some of the ice cubes into the ovenproof pan at the bottom of the oven. Slide the loaves onto the baking stone from the peel and immediately close the oven door. Repeat these steps until all the rolls are in the oven.

9. Bake until the rolls are a light golden brown and completely cooked on the inside (200 degrees internal temperature). Use the pizza peel to remove the bread from the oven. Allow rolls to cool completely.

✯ Philadelphia-Style Hot ✯ Roast Pork and Roasted Green Pepper Sandwich

Don't dare tell a Philadelphian that Philadelphia's a one-sandwich town! Philadelphia goes far beyond Philly Cheesesteak to offer a wide range of delicious possibilities. Most of the sandwiches are made with Italian bread and draw inspiration from Italian food (as well as from the Italian community of South Philly). One of the best themes is the hot-roast-pork-with-greens sandwich. You can get a magnificent Pork and Broccoli Rabe Sandwich at the eater's paradise Tony Luke's and at other locations. Or you can find the Tommy Dinic stand in the bustling Reading Terminal Market, where a mouthwatering Roast Pork

Sandwich is served — if you ask for it "loaded" — with roasted green peppers and "aged" provolone cheese. If you want the middle of the bread taken out, ask for "an operation." One of the best parts of their sandwich is the hot pan juices that go on it; if you really like your sandwich dripping, make sure to ask for it "wet." The following recipe is based on Dinic's delight.

Yield: 4 sandwiches

3 tablespoons plus 1½ teaspoons kosher salt
¼ cup sugar
16 large garlic cloves
3 bay leaves
2 tablespoons plus ½ teaspoon cracked black pepper
2 teaspoons dried rosemary
2 teaspoons dried oregano
1 teaspoon dried thyme
1 teaspoon dried basil
1 (5-pound) boneless pork loin, with fat
5 tablespoons olive oil
1 cup finely chopped onion
6 parsley stems with leaves, washed
2 cups water
4 green bell peppers, cored, seeded, and cut into thirds
½ teaspoon crushed red pepper
4 Philadelphia Cheesesteak Loaves (see Note on page 277) or 4 Italian hero breads, each about 8 inches long
6 ounces thinly sliced, aged provolone cheese (about 12 slices)

1. Place a quart of cold water in a medium-size nonreactive mixing bowl. Add the 3 tablespoons of kosher salt, the sugar, 6 of the garlic cloves, smashed, the bay leaves, the

2 tablespoons of the black pepper, I teaspoon of the rosemary, I teaspoon of the oregano, the thyme, and the basil. Using a whisk, stir the mixture until the salt and sugar are dissolved. Add the pork loin, cover bowl with plastic wrap, and refrigerate overnight.

2. Preheat oven to 475 degrees. Remove the pork loin from the brine mixture, dry it, and place it in a 9 by 13 by 2-inch baking pan. Finely mince 6 of the garlic cloves and rub them onto the roast with your hands, along with the remaining ½ teaspoon of black pepper, the remaining I teaspoon of rosemary, the remaining I teaspoon of oregano, I teaspoon of the remaining salt, and 3 tablespoons of the olive oil.

3. Roast the pork loin for 10 minutes at 475 degrees. Remove pan from oven and add the onion, parsley stems, and water. Lower the heat to 375 degrees and roast the pork until the internal temperature of the roast is 140 degrees (about 40 minutes more). Let the roast rest for 10 minutes before slicing thinly. Then place the sliced meat back into the baking pan to soak up the flavors of the pan gravy. Serve hot.

4. While the pork is roasting, prepare the green peppers. Place the pepper pieces on a baking sheet in a single layer. Chop the remaining 4 garlic cloves. Sprinkle the peppers with the garlic, red pepper, the remaining 2 tablespoons of olive oil, and the remaining ½ teaspoon of salt. Cover the pan with aluminum foil and bake peppers for 25 minutes at 375 degrees (alongside the pork).

5. Remove the pepper pan from the oven, carefully uncover, and drain and discard any excess juice from the pan. Place the pan back in the oven and bake the peppers uncovered for an additional 15 minutes. Serve hot.

6. To assemble: Carefully slice open the bread loaves the long way, using a serrated knife, being careful not to cut all the way through the bread. Spoon 2 tablespoons of the pork pan gravy evenly onto each loaf, then on each roll place 3 slices of provolone, add one-fourth of the thinly sliced pork loin, and add 3 pieces of roasted green pepper. Make sure cheese, pork, and peppers are evenly spread out in each sandwich. Serve immediately. Pass extra pan juices, so people can make the sandwiches wetter if they'd like.

☆ Special Italian Hoagie ☆ with Cheese, Peppers, and Five Meats

It's the spectacular hot sandwiches of Philadelphia that get all the buzz, but do not underestimate for a minute that city's seriously delicious cold sandwiches, which are known as hoagies. Everywhere you turn in Philly, someone is slapping something — usually meat, usually Italian in spirit — on a hero bread. The best sandwich makers realize that terrific ingredients make terrific sandwiches. For starters, there's the bread. Unlike the fluffy stuff from Amoroso's that works so well in Philly Cheesesteaks, it's the crunchy, chewy hero breads from Sarcone's Bakery that make Philly's best hoagies. And if you go to a top sandwich shop — like Cileone's or Rocco's — you'll also be dazzled by the quality of what's inside the bread. So to make the following hoagie — inspired by something called the Italian Special with Prosciutto at Rocco's — be sure to get the best of everything at a good Italian deli.

Yield: 1 hoagie, enough for 2 persons
with normal appetites

1 hero bread, about 8 inches long and 3½
inches wide (see Bread note)
4 teaspoons good quality olive oil
1 teaspoon red wine vinegar
⅓ cup shredded iceberg lettuce
1 ripe, medium tomato, very thinly sliced
2 ounces thin-sliced boiled ham
1 ounce thin-sliced soppresata (a dried salami)
2 ounces thin-sliced provolone
1 ounce thin-sliced prosciutto
1 ounce thin-sliced Genoa salami
2 ounces thin-sliced cappicola (a spicy ham)
¼ cup marinated peppers (see Pepper note)
¼ cup thinly sliced purple onion

1. Cut the bread in half lengthwise. Open it on the counter. Pull out some of the interior. Sprinkle the oil and vinegar over the cut side of each half, distributing evenly.
2. Lay the lettuce on one of the halves, spreading it out evenly. Top with 2 thin layers of tomato slices. Reserve remaining tomato. Season with salt and pepper.
3. Begin layering meat and cheese, making sure each layer is distributed evenly along the length and width of the bread half: the ham, the soppresata, 1 ounce of the provolone, the prosciutto, the remaining ounce of provolone, the Genoa salami, and the cappicola.
4. Top meats with the peppers and onion, spreading them out evenly. Top that with 2 final layers of thin tomato slices. Season tomato with salt and pepper. Lay the second half of bread on top of the hoagie, cut in half crosswise, and serve.

BREAD NOTE: You could use the Philadelphia Cheesesteak Loaf on page 277 to make this sandwich, but they wouldn't do that at a good shop in Philly. It's much better to buy a great Italian bread that's about three and one-half inches wide; the length doesn't matter, just as long as you can cut it into eight-inch sections (most long Italian breads will yield two sections for two sandwiches). The crust of the bread should be very crunchy, and the interior should have a lot more chew than the interior of the Philadelphia Cheesesteak Loaf.

PEPPER NOTE: There's a wide range of pepper products available — even at your supermarket! — that could be used in this sandwich. Store shelves contain many bottled variations of pickled peppers, roasted peppers, sweet peppers, hot peppers, and so on. You're on your own in choosing your fave. The supermarket product in a jar that I prefer on this sandwich is called Mancini Fried Peppers (red and green together), made with onions, in Zolfo Springs, Florida, and nationally distributed.

✫ Soft Pretzels, ✫ Philadelphia Style

Philly has one other great form of street food: warm, soft, German-style pretzels, a Pennsylvania Dutch specialty that hit it big in the big city. Today, the pretzels on Philly streets are utterly seductive, quite unlike the tougher, chewier pretzels that you find on New York streets. Serve the pretzels warm and buttery for the peak experience.

Yield: 18 pretzels

4 cups all-purpose flour, plus extra for rolling
pretzels
1 package active dry yeast
2 teaspoons kosher salt, plus extra for sprinkling
1 tablespoon molasses
¾ cup milk
¾ cup water

Oil for greasing bowl
2 teaspoons baking soda dissolved in 1 cup water
1 cup melted butter

1. In the bowl of a food processor, pulse 4 cups of flour, yeast, and the 2 teaspoons salt just to mix them together (about 30 seconds).
2. Add the molasses and milk. While pulsing, gradually add the water until a soft ball forms. This will take about a minute. (Depending on the dryness of the flour, you may not need this much water — or you may need more. If more liquid is needed, add a mixture of half milk and half water gradually.)
3. Once the soft ball has formed, continue to mix the dough for 3 more minutes. Turn onto a floured board and knead by hand until the dough feels smooth (about 2 minutes). Form into a ball and set in a lightly greased bowl; cover and leave in a warm place until doubled in size. This will take about an hour, depending on the temperature of the room. (Don't be tempted to set the bowl too close to a heat source, as the dough might start to harden on the bottom.)
4. Lightly flour a work surface. Keeping the dough covered, break off a walnut-size piece — one-eighteenth of the dough — and roll into a rope about 18 inches long. Form an upside down U with the opening pointing toward you. Cross the two ends, leaving about 2½ inches of dough beyond the point of intersection. Still grasping the two ends of the dough rope, cross again, so that the dough intertwines at the intersection point. There will be a teardrop shape above two intertwined ends. Now hold the top of the teardrop and fold it down, toward yourself. The final shape will be pretzel-like: a circle overall, that has inside it two open

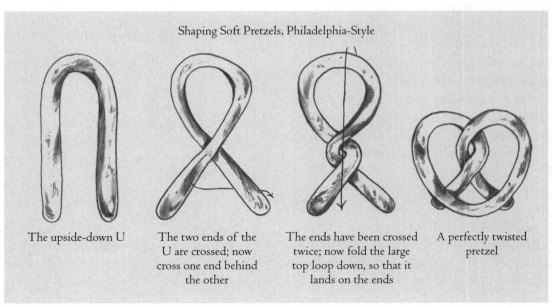

Shaping Soft Pretzels, Philadelphia-Style

The upside-down U | The two ends of the U are crossed; now cross one end behind the other | The ends have been crossed twice; now fold the large top loop down, so that it lands on the ends | A perfectly twisted pretzel

loops at the top, and one open loop at the bottom. Set each pretzel onto a lightly greased cookie sheet. Repeat 17 times.

5. When all the pretzels are shaped, cover lightly with a towel and let rise again until doubled, about 40 minutes.

6. Preheat oven to 375 degrees.

7. Brush each pretzel lightly on top with baking soda mixture. Bake until golden, crusty on the outside but still soft inside, about 12 to 15 minutes.

8. As soon as the pretzels are done, brush them liberally with melted butter. Sprinkle with kosher salt to taste. Best when served warm.

sects who had faced religious persecution in the Rhineland: Mennonites, Amish, and Moravians. William Penn had invited anyone being persecuted anywhere to find a haven in the lush fields of Pennsylvania — and the Pennsylvania Dutch accepted his offer, soon turning those fields into some of the best farmland in young America.

All of this is apparent in the food. It features the heartiness of a people rooted in northern Europe, the bounty of an agrarian society with access to wonderful products, and the solidity of a culture with a distaste for radical change. Pennsylvania Dutch foods always taste to me as if they were prepared by a cook who loves to spend time in the kitchen and also loves to sustain others.

Pennsylvania Dutch

If you had to make a short list of regions in the United States where regional food is actually consumed on a daily basis, the land of the Pennsylvania Dutch — in and around Lancaster County, Pennsylvania — would be at or near the top of that list. Of course, this standing has much to do with the fact that Pennsylvania Dutch country remains an isolated cultural enclave in many ways, not just culinary ones.

The main gastronomic influence here is German — since the original Pennsylvania Dutch were not Dutch at all but Deutsch, or German. They were a collection of itinerant

☆ Pennsylvania Dutch ☆ Chicken Corn Soup

The Pennsylvania Dutch love soups and make lots of wonderful ones; this is one of my favorites. One of the ingredients is egg noodles — for which the Pennsylvania Dutch happen to be famous, since the airwaves used to be bombarded with advertisements for "Pennsylvania Dutch Egg Noodles"! Well, you can buy that product for inclusion in this soup — or better still, you can follow this recipe and make your own. Don't be surprised by the saffron addition; this is no modern creative intrusion. Saffron has been cultivated in the Pennsylvania Dutch country since the War of 1812 and remains a favorite of the locals in their cooking.

★☆☆

Yield: 6 servings as a main-course soup

FOR CHICKEN STOCK:

1 (4-pound) roasting chicken, cut into pieces
    and skin removed
2 pounds chicken backs and necks
1 medium onion, peeled and cut into 4 pieces
1 medium carrot, scraped and roughly chopped
1 stalk celery, roughly chopped
1 sprig thyme
1 sprig parsley
1 bay leaf
¼ teaspoon whole black peppercorns
4 corncobs, cut in half lengthwise
    (from corn used for soup, below)

FOR EGG NOODLES:

2 eggs
1 egg yolk
½ teaspoon salt
1¼ cups all-purpose flour, plus extra for dusting
Cornmeal for dusting

FOR THE SOUP:

8 cups chicken stock (from above)
½ teaspoon saffron threads
1 cup carrot, cut into ½-inch dice
1 cup celery, cut into ½-inch dice
2 cups uncooked corn kernels, removed from the
    cob (reserve cobs for chicken stock, above)
2 to 3 cups cubed cooked chicken
    (from chicken used for stock, above)
2 tablespoons chopped parsley
1 recipe egg noodles (above) or 2 cups wide,
    dried egg noodles

I. To make stock, place all ingredients for stock in a large pot and add water to cover. Bring to a boil, then simmer until chicken is tender, about 1½ hours. Skim foam that accumulates during simmering and discard.

2. Remove chicken pieces and cool, but simmer stock (with backs and necks still in it) for another hour. Cut chicken meat into ½-inch cubes and reserve. Discard bones. After the additional hour, strain stock and discard the rest of the solids. You should have about 8 cups stock.

3. Make noodle dough: In a medium bowl, beat eggs and egg yolk with salt. Add 1 cup of the flour and stir with a fork to combine. Add additional flour, 1 tablespoon at a time, until you have a dough that comes together and is no longer wet and sticky. Turn onto a floured surface and knead for only 1 to 2 minutes, until the dough is no longer lumpy. Wrap in plastic and let rest in refrigerator for at least a half hour.

4. Roll noodles: Divide noodle dough into 4 pieces. Using a rolling pin, roll dough out as thin as you can on a well-floured surface. Cut dough into noodles that are 2 inches long by ⅓ inch wide. Place noodles on a sheet pan dusted with cornmeal and dry, uncovered, for an hour. While still pliable, twist each noodle once at the center and return to sheet pan. Dry, uncovered, in the refrigerator, until ready to use.

5. Make soup: Bring stock to a simmer. Add saffron, carrot, and celery and simmer until vegetables are tender, about 15 minutes. Add corn, chicken, parsley, and noodles. Continue to simmer until noodles are cooked, about 5 minutes (longer for dried noodles). Season with salt and pepper to taste. Serve hot.

★★

✩ Amish Chicken Pot Pie ✩

The name of this dish is a complete surprise — because when the Pennsylvania Dutch say "pot pie," they're not talking about a baked pie with golden pastry on top! They are talking about a wonderful meat stew that includes large, slippery noodles called pot pie squares. The Amish might use any number of meats in this dish — but I'm partial to the following chicken pot pie recipe given to me by an Amish friend. Amish Chicken Pot Pie can be served either as a side dish or as a main course.

Yield: 8 to 10 servings as a side dish,
4 to 6 servings as a main course

1 whole chicken, about 3½ pounds
1 celery stalk roughly chopped, plus 4 celery
stalks, cut into ½-inch chunks
½ medium onion, peeled and cut into
large chunks
1 medium carrot, scraped and cut into
large chunks
1 sprig parsley
1 sprig thyme
1 bay leaf
½ teaspoon whole black peppercorns
1 teaspoon salt
3 cups flour, plus flour for dusting

1. Place the chicken, the 1 chopped celery stalk, the onion, carrot, parsley, thyme, bay leaf, and peppercorns in a large saucepan or Dutch oven. Cover amply with water. Bring to a boil, then lower heat and skim off any foam that accumulates on top. Simmer until chicken is very tender, about 1 to 1½ hours.
2. Strain the stock. Cool, then refrigerate stock and whole chicken separately. Discard vegetables.

3. When chicken is cool enough to handle, remove meat, discarding skin and bones. Cut or shred meat into bite-size chunks; cover and refrigerate.
4. When stock is cool, skim congealed fat from the top and discard.
5. Bring 1 cup of the defatted chicken stock to a boil, then place in a large bowl. Stir in salt to dissolve. Add 2 cups of the flour, stirring to make a dough. Add remaining flour, ¼ cup at a time, until you have a dough that is still slightly sticky but that can be rolled out.
6. Dump dough out onto a floured surface and knead just until it comes together, no more. Wrap dough in plastic and refrigerate for 30 minutes.
7. Cut dough into 4 pieces. On a floured surface, roll out one piece at a time to a ¼-inch thickness. With a knife, cut into 1- to 1½-inch squares. As you cut the squares, place them on a floured baking sheet in one layer. They can be made several hours ahead of time and left to dry, loosely covered, in the refrigerator.
8. In a large saucepan or Dutch oven, bring remaining defatted chicken broth to a simmer. Add the remaining celery chunks, simmer for 5 minutes, then add enough pot pie squares to make one layer across the surface of the pot. Once the broth bubbles over the dough and the dough sinks to the bottom, add the next layer, continuing until you have used all the squares. (It's done this way so the squares don't stick together.) Simmer for about 10 minutes, until pot pie squares are tender. Add chicken meat and heat through. Serve immediately in individual bowls.

✻ Pennsylvania Dutch ✻ Potato Filling on the Side with Saffron

This version of the great Pennsylvania Dutch potato-and-bread filling is very wet; it's almost custardy before baking and can't be used to stuff a bird. However, it is magnificent when cooked separately alongside a bird or any other roast: the finished product is light, airy, loose, unique.

Yield: 8 side dish servings

½ cup butter
½ cup finely chopped celery
½ cup finely chopped onion
1 teaspoon paprika
1 teaspoon chopped fresh thyme
1 teaspoon dried sage
½ teaspoon saffron threads
½ cup chicken stock
4 cups stale white bread cubes (from firm
    bread, such as Pepperidge Farm)
2 cups cooked, mashed potatoes
    (see recipes on pages 448 and 449)
2 cups milk
3 large eggs, beaten
1 tablespoon chopped fresh parsley
1 teaspoon salt

1. Preheat oven to 350 degrees. Grease an 8-inch round soufflé dish (see Note). Melt butter in a medium skillet over low heat. Add celery, onion, paprika, thyme, and sage and cook until the vegetables are softened, about 8 minutes.
2. Meanwhile, place saffron threads in chicken stock in a saucepan over medium-high heat. Bring to a boil, then turn off heat. Let sit for 10 minutes.
3. Place celery-onion mixture in a large mixing bowl with bread cubes. Pour in saffron stock and toss to coat. Let cool to room temperature.
4. In another bowl, whisk together potatoes, milk, eggs, parsley, salt, and pepper (to taste). Pour over cooled bread mixture and mix well. Pour into soufflé dish and bake until puffed and golden, about 45 minutes.

NOTE: This stuffing can also be made in a standard 9 by 13-inch baking dish, although it will not puff up as much. If using the standard dish, reduce baking time by 5 to 10 minutes.

✻ Amish Dried-Corn Pudding ✻

An amazing Amish specialty is dried corn — that's dried and toasted sweet corn, the stuff that tastes so great in August, not the feed corn that's usually used for drying. It looks a bit like granola but has the most intense corn taste you can imagine, with an almost caramel-like sweetness making things even more interesting. It's crunchy, and I can't stop eating it as a snack right out of the container. But the Amish use it to make a wonderful custardlike dish that's terrific alongside many main courses (such as fried chicken). There are two basic variations on this dish: baked or stovetop (the following is baked). Either can be made with just milk (not cream) . . . but cream makes it infinitely better, in my opinion. Flour is sometimes used as a thickener, but it makes things a little pasty; I prefer the result when cracker crumbs are used.

Yield: 6 servings

1 cup dried toasted sweet corn (see sidebar)
2 cups milk
3 large eggs

1 cup heavy cream
1 tablespoon sugar
1 teaspoon salt
3 tablespoons cracker crumbs
4 tablespoons butter

1. Combine corn and 1 cup of the milk. Refrigerate overnight.
2. Preheat oven to 350 degrees. Whisk together eggs, the remaining cup of milk, cream, sugar, and salt. Add a little black pepper. Whisk in cracker crumbs and soaked corn mixture. Pour into a greased baking dish. Dot with butter.
3. Bake until top is golden and custard is set, about 30 to 40 minutes.

☆ Apple Butter ☆

This eighteenth-century Amish dish is not really a butter at all; it is, instead, a thick reduction of apples and spices that ends up being as smooth as butter. Sweetness, and therefore use, can vary. Very sweet ones are good on bread, with real butter, as a breakfast

Buying Dried Toasted Sweet Corn

The most consistent source for dried toasted sweet corn is an old company called John Cope's Foods. You can reach them two ways:

800-745-8211 (toll-free)
www.copefoods.com

Either way, they will sell you three seven-ounce boxes of the corn for $14.45 (shipping included). Alternatively, you can buy the same Cope's product (in person or by mail order) from a wonderful little store in New York City called Kitchen Market, at $2.75 for an eight-ounce plastic bag. That's cheaper than Cope's if you buy the corn right at Kitchen Market's store. But for a little more, you can also get it mail order. Here are the details:

Kitchen Market
218 Eighth Avenue
New York, NY 10011
212-243-4433
212-243-4735 (fax)

One more note: the best version of this product I ever tasted was marketed by a company called Amish Acres, in Indiana. However, I subsequently discovered that the very dark, very caramel-like batch they sold me was an anomaly: "It's not usually that dark," the salesperson said. Darn! Dark was good! Unfortunately, I didn't like the light stuff they also sent me nearly as much. If you want to try your luck with them, here are the details:

Amish Acres
1600 West Market Street
Nappanee, IN 46550
800-800-4942 (toll-free)
http://store.yahoo.com/
    amish/driedcorn.html

Remember: No matter where you buy this stuff, always try to get the darkest batch available. Color varies widely! If what you buy is light and not sweet, you might want to try adding a little sugar and toasting it in a 350-degree oven.

thing; tarter, less sweet ones have applications at tables beyond breakfast. The following recipe is definitely in the tart camp but still delicious on pancakes, biscuits, even scrapple (see recipe on page 274). But I also like it as a condiment on a plate of roast pork at dinnertime.

NOTE: Refer to "General Preserving Guidelines" on page 324.

Yield: 4 half-pints

7 pounds apples, peeled, cored, and coarsely
chopped (tart varieties work best, such as
Granny Smith and Macoun)
1 cup apple cider vinegar
2 cups dark brown sugar, packed
2 tablespoons lemon juice
1½ teaspoons grated lemon zest (from
1 large lemon)
1 tablespoon plus 1 teaspoon ground cinnamon
1¼ teaspoons ground clove
1¼ teaspoons ground ginger
½ teaspoon ground allspice
½ teaspoon salt

1. Wash 4 half-pint canning jars with lids and bands in hot soapy water. Rinse well. Sterilize canning jars in boiling water for 10 minutes. Keep jars and caps in hot but not boiling water until ready to use.
2. In a large nonreactive pot, combine apples and vinegar. Cover and cook until apples fall apart, about 30 minutes. Run through a food mill on the coarse disk or press through a strainer and return to pot.
3. Add remaining ingredients and cook on a very low simmer for about 1½ hours. Watch carefully; you don't want the butter to scorch. The butter is done when it is very thick. Test

it by putting a dollop on a plate; if the butter no longer leaks a liquid ring, it is ready.
4. Ladle apple butter into each jar, tapping the jars on the counter to release any air bubbles. Leave a ½-inch headspace in each jar, then wipe the rims with a clean damp towel. Seal with lids and bands and return to boiling water, placing jars upside down. Once the water returns to a boil, cook for 10 minutes.
5. Remove pot from heat; let jars cool slightly before removing from pot. Jars may not all be sealed at this point but will seal as they cool and a vacuum is created. Cool completely, upside down, on kitchen towels.
6. Refrigerate any jars that did not seal and use those first. Store sealed jars in a cool, dark place for at least 2 weeks before serving. Refrigerate after opening.

Chesapeake Bay

There are all kinds of interesting footnotes concerning the cuisine of the states that surround Chesapeake Bay. A few hundred years ago, as in the deeper South, wealthy English settlers established a grand style of living and entertaining in this region; later, former slaves ran the kitchens of those estates, mixing their Caribbean love of spices with the great Chesapeake Bay seafood. Later still, in the 1920s, egg farmers on the Delmarva Peninsula — a spit of land that includes territory from three states — *Dela*ware, *Maryland* and *Virginia* — began to market the chickens that yielded those eggs. Today something like fifty million chickens a month are raised there — and though no defining Delmarva chicken recipes have emerged, there are many quasi-Southern ideas in the area that make it a great place to eat chicken.

Above all, however — way above all — the Chesapeake Bay region, particularly Maryland, is one helluva great place to eat crab. James Beard once noted that crab is the most American of shellfish; no European culture adores crab as we do. And in my opinion, though there are lots of great crab species all over North America, the finest eating of all comes from the Maryland blue crab, or *Callinectes sapidus.* It's not much of a leap from there to the perception that Maryland is the crab capital of the world. Happily, the most famous local product is not just for shipping, export, or tourists; Marylanders love their crab, both in restaurants and at home, and have devised, over the years, scores of wonderful ways in which to prepare the "beautiful swimmer."

☆ Tomatoey ☆
Maryland Crab Soup

When you reach crab heaven — which to me is a crab house in Maryland — you will have a choice of appetizers before the main event (crabs!) is served. Ubiquitous on the menus of these places is a tomatoey Maryland crab soup — that by all rights should be a great soup. It's usually not. It usually tastes like canned Campbell's vegetable soup with a microscopic por-

tion of crabmeat tossed in. The following version — inauthentic, in that it's better than any soup I've ever tasted in a crab house — puts this soup on the plateau it deserves. I've preserved the tomatoey vegetable soup quality — but the megadose of good crabmeat makes everything better. I advise you to turn off the heat for 10 minutes after warming the crab so that the crab flavors can permeate the rest of the soup, without the lumps of crabmeat breaking down.

Yield: 4 to 6 soup servings

2 tablespoons butter
½ cup chopped onion
½ cup diced celery (¼-inch dice)
½ cup diced carrot (¼-inch dice)
½ cup baby lima beans, frozen
2½ cups crushed tomatoes in puree
3⅔ cups chicken or vegetable stock
½ cup diced green beans (¼-inch dice)
½ cup fresh corn niblets (from about
    2 ears of corn)
2 bay leaves
4 teaspoons Old Bay seasoning
½ cup peas, frozen
1 pound lump crabmeat, picked over for shell
    bits and cartilage
2½ teaspoons Worcestershire sauce
2 tablespoons chopped parsley, for garnish

1. Melt the butter in a large stockpot over medium-low heat. Add the onion, celery, and carrot. Cook until vegetables begin to soften, about 5 minutes. Stir occasionally to prevent sticking or browning.
2. Meanwhile, rinse the lima beans under water in a small strainer for 10 seconds. Drain. Add the lima beans, tomatoes, stock, green beans, corn, bay leaves, and Old Bay seasoning to the onion-celery mixture and

bring to a simmer. Gently simmer until the vegetables are tender, about 35 to 40 minutes.
3. Rinse the peas under water in a small strainer for 10 seconds. Add the peas, crab, and Worcestershire sauce to the soup and cook very gently until warmed through, about 5 minutes. Turn off the heat and let sit for 10 minutes. Reheat gently, season to taste, and serve, garnished with chopped parsley.

☆ Maryland Crab Cakes ☆

One of the truly great American dishes is Maryland Crab Cakes, a culinary result of the abundance of crabmeat that has always been harvested from the Chesapeake Bay. It is not a hard dish to make, but it is an easy dish to mess up — if you add too much other stuff, either as filler or as seasoning, and don't let the wonderful crabmeat speak for itself. The following recipe contains just a little bit of a few things, just enough to hold the crab cake together and to provoke its essential flavor. When chefs in restaurants across the country serve crab cakes as appetizers these days, they usually add some chefy creativity to them in the form of sauces, condiments, and garnishes. I prefer to take my crab cakes as a main course, and in classic Maryland style: nothing but French fries (page 444) and Coleslaw (page 418) on the side. Pitcher of cold beer, please.

Yield: 8 crab cakes, for 8 appetizer servings
or 4 main-course servings

1 pound lump crabmeat
2 tablespoons plus 1 teaspoon mayonnaise
1 teaspoon lemon juice
2 teaspoons finely minced onion
1 egg, lightly beaten
½ teaspoon Worcestershire sauce
½ teaspoon dry mustard
¾ teaspoon Old Bay seasoning
¼ teaspoon cayenne
⅓ cup crushed salted soda crackers
1 tablespoon melted butter, plus at least 3 tablespoons butter for frying
3 tablespoons or more of vegetable oil for frying
Lemon wedges for garnish

1. Pick over the crabmeat to remove any bits of shell or cartilage in the meat. Try not to shred the crabmeat while picking it over; you want big lumps of crab in your crab cakes.
2. In a large mixing bowl, combine the mayonnaise, lemon juice, onion, egg, Worcestershire sauce, mustard, Old Bay seasoning, and cayenne. Using a fork, thoroughly combine until mixture is smooth.
3. Using your hands, very gently fold in the cracker crumbs, the 1 tablespoon butter, and the crabmeat. Gently shape the crab cake mixture into 8 fat patties that are about 3 inches in diameter and 1½ inches thick.
4. Place a medium-size nonstick skillet over medium heat. Add 3 tablespoons of butter and 3 tablespoons of vegetable oil. When the butter has melted and is foaming, add the crab cakes. (You can fry them all at once in a large pan, fry them all at once in multiple pans, or fry them in the same pan in batches. For the last two options, you'll need extra butter and vegetable oil.) Fry them for 2 to 3 minutes per side, or until they are golden brown on the outside and hot throughout. Remove the crab cakes from the pan and place them on paper towels. Let them rest for 5 minutes before serving. If needed, hold them in a low-temperature oven to keep them warm. Serve hot with lemon wedges.

Staging a Maryland Crab Feast

It is easy to reproduce a Maryland crab feast right in your home — or better yet, in your backyard or on your patio!

Simply prepare the Steamed Crab recipe on page 294. Figure at least six crabs per diner . . . and the recipe can easily be divided or multiplied.

Cover your table with several layers of newspaper or wide brown paper from a roll. Make sure the table holds plenty of the following: wooden crab mallets (for cracking the claws), serrated knives (for cutting open the bodies and helping with the picking), rolls of paper towels (this is one messy event). Don't worry about the discarded shells; they simply get piled up on the newspaper, which you roll up afterward for an easy cleanup.

Do you need garnishes or condiments? In Maryland's crab houses they aren't served — but you could consider lemon wedges, melted butter, and saucers of Crabhouse Spice Blend (page 293).

Side dishes? Once again, crab eating in Maryland is a fairly austere affair, with the crabs themselves getting the focus. But if you're up for it, accompanying platters of cole slaw, potato salad, French fries, steaming corn on the cob, and fresh sliced summertime tomatoes would be great. And don't forget icy pitchers of beer!

The hardest part of the Maryland crab feast for beginners is getting at the crabmeat; the sweet lumps inside cooked blue crabs are the most delicious crab pickin's in the world, but small as those nuggets are, and tucked away as they are, they are devilishly difficult to get at.

For starters, pull off all the crab's little legs; if the crabs are sizeable, it's good to run the legs through your teeth, extracting sweet bits of meat.

Then pull off the two large claws. To eat them, you pound them lightly with your mallet — don't crush them, or the meat and shell will be crushed together. Just break the shell, then, working with a knife, a fork, a pick, or your fingers, extract the meat.

Now comes the main event. Pick up your legless, clawless crab and stand it on its bottom edge, so that the white underbelly is facing you. The design on the underbelly that looks like a baseball catcher's chest protector should have an arrow-shaped flap on it that's pointing downward. With your fingers, grab that arrow, force it out of its groove, then, pulling upward, rip back and remove the whole "chest protector," a triangular piece of soft shell. You're ready to go in.

Keep the crab standing on the same bottom edge. Planting one thumb at the top of the crab on the underbelly side and another thumb on the top of the crab on the red top-shell side, pry the crab open by moving your thumbs in opposite directions. Push hard if you must. Suddenly the crab will pop open and you'll have two pieces: the nearly empty top shell and the white underbelly shell, filled with cartilage and crabmeat.

I like to start with the nearly empty red shell. I describe it as "nearly" empty because it may have in it some roe (reddish orange, absolutely delicious) and some tomalley. The latter, to the crab connoisseur, is also absolutely delicious — though I've seen crab neophytes quake at this soft mass of yellow-green material. For my money, it has more flavor than any other part of the crab. I sometimes take a spoon and eat it by itself or along with the roe or as a kind of sauce to spread on the pieces of crabmeat that I extract later. Use your spoon to probe every corner of the "empty" red shell, looking for tomalley.

When it comes to the meat-stuffed underbelly

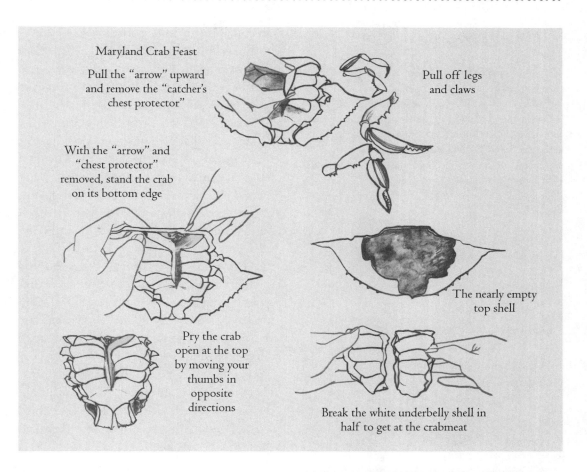

Maryland Crab Feast

Pull the "arrow" upward and remove the "catcher's chest protector"

Pull off legs and claws

With the "arrow" and "chest protector" removed, stand the crab on its bottom edge

The nearly empty top shell

Pry the crab open at the top by moving your thumbs in opposite directions

Break the white underbelly shell in half to get at the crabmeat

shell, there are literally scores of techniques that Marylanders employ to get at the meat. I like to start by breaking the body in half; grip the left-hand side firmly in one hand, the right-hand side firmly in the other, and snap the body open. Each half is identical and requires the same technique. Basically, each half is filled with what I think of as hard chambers, and the chambers contain the meat. The largest chamber, on each half, is near the part of the body where the large claw once was; you can recognize the area by the large hole you made when removing the claw. A good way to get at this chamber, and all chambers, is to gently saw it open with a serrated knife (some like to pick it open with their fingers; others prefer to crack it open with their teeth). Extract the meat and enjoy! Keep going until you've worked your way around all the chambers of both halves . . . then, your lips atingle, reach for another crab and start over again!

✦ Baltimore Crab Fluffs ✦

Though Maryland Crab Cakes have made it onto menus across the United States, another crabhouse appetizer option, very popular in Baltimore, has not hit the national menu: Crab Fluffs. In Maryland they love to present all kinds of options based on basic crab cake mix, and this is one of the best ones. You simply take your prepared crab cake mixture, dip balls of it in batter, and deep-fry to a crunchy gold. This is a great pass-around for the start of a dinner party.

Yield: About 16 crab fluffs, good for 8 appetizer portions

Maryland Crab Cakes (page 289), unformed
Yolks of 3 large eggs, beaten
½ cup ice-cold seltzer
⅓ cup plus 2 tablespoons cold milk
½ teaspoon lemon juice
¼ teaspoon dry mustard
1½ teaspoons Old Bay seasoning
½ teaspoon salt
1¼ cups all-purpose flour, plus more
     for dredging
3 teaspoons baking powder
Vegetable oil for frying
Lemon wedges for garnish (optional)

1. Using your hands, gently shape the crab cake mixture into 16 round crab balls that are each about 1½ inches in diameter, or just a little smaller than a Ping-Pong ball.
2. In a medium-size bowl, using a fork, mix together the egg yolks, seltzer, milk, lemon juice, mustard, Old Bay seasoning, and salt. Sift together the flour and baking powder, then slowly add them to the liquid ingredients, using a fork to combine them just until a lumpy batter is formed. Do not overmix.

3. Pour the oil into a medium-size heavy-bottomed pot to a depth of 4 inches. Place the pot over medium heat. Bring the oil to 345 degrees and maintain this temperature while frying the crab fluffs.
4. Gently lower a crab ball into the batter, making sure that the entire outside surface of the crab ball gets evenly coated with batter. Place a slotted spoon under the ball and remove the ball from the batter. Using your fingers, transfer the batter-enrobed crab ball onto a clean fork, then gently drop it into the oil. Repeat this step, frying about 4 or 5 crab fluffs at a time. When frying the crab fluffs in the hot oil, make sure to turn them frequently while they are cooking. Cook them until they are evenly golden brown and are warmed throughout (about 4 to 5 minutes). After removing the crab fluffs from the oil, drain them on paper towels. Let them rest for 5 minutes before serving. If needed, hold them in a low-temperature oven to keep them warm. If desired, serve lemon wedges next to the fluffs.

✦ Crab Imperial ✦

Another great first-course possibility in Maryland is a hot serving of crabmeat held together in a creamy sauce, and gratinéed under the broiler. Sometimes it is mayonnaise that supplies the cohesion, sometimes it's a sherry-scented white sauce. The dish gets enhanced with different ingredients depending on who's cooking (though capers and pimientos usually figure in) and gets different names depending on who's writing the menu (though Crab Imperial is the most common name by far).

★☆★

Yield: 4 first-course servings

1 pound backfin crabmeat
⅓ cup melted, clarified butter
    (page 227)
2 teaspoons lemon juice
½ cup plus ⅓ cup mayonnaise
2½ teaspoons Dijon mustard
½ teaspoon Worcestershire sauce
⅛ teaspoon Tabasco sauce
2 tablespoons chopped pimiento
½ teaspoon capers, finely chopped
1 extra-large egg, beaten
½ teaspoon Old Bay seasoning
1 tablespoon finely chopped parsley

1. Preheat oven to 375 degrees.
2. Pick through crabmeat with your fingers to ensure that all shells and cartilage have been removed.
3. Pour butter into a medium-size bowl and stir in 1 teaspoon of the lemon juice. Add the crabmeat to the bowl and coat the crabmeat with the butter mixture by tossing gently.
4. In a small bowl mix together the ½ cup mayonnaise, 2 teaspoons of the Dijon mustard, the Worcestershire sauce, Tabasco, pimiento, and capers. Add mixture to the crabmeat and again toss gently until the mayonnaise mixture is completely incorporated. Season to taste with salt and pepper.
5. Spoon the mixture into four 6-inch gratin dishes. Place them on a baking sheet and bake in the oven for 15 minutes, or just until the mixture begins to bubble.
6. While the crabmeat is baking, prepare the topping by mixing together the egg, the remaining ⅓ cup of mayonnaise, the remaining 1 teaspoon of lemon juice, the remaining ½ teaspoon of Dijon mustard, the Old Bay seasoning, and the parsley.
7. After removing the crabmeat dishes from the oven, heat the broiler. Divide topping equally among the four dishes. Place them under the broiler for 2 minutes, or until nicely browned. Serve immediately.

☆ Crabhouse Spice Blend ☆

The real joy of the Maryland crab houses, of course, is spiced and steamed crabs. There was a time when crabs from Chesapeake Bay were served without hot spices. But the influx of slaves to Maryland plantations from the Caribbean islands brought an influx of spice as well — which soon worked its way onto the most revered local product. One of the pleasures of touring the modern crab houses is discovering the different spice blends used by different restaurants; many of them make their own blends . . . and are damned proud of them! Now, with the following recipe, you can make your own blend to be proud of. As you'll notice, there is in it a good deal of Maryland's most famous seasoning, Old Bay — but that's because Old Bay is used as a base for many a restaurant blend.

Yield: Enough to spice 24 crabs

1 cup Old Bay seasoning
½ cup kosher salt
2 tablespoons ground ginger
2 tablespoon ground black pepper
2 tablespoons garlic powder
1 tablespoon dry mustard
1 tablespoon yellow mustard seeds
1 tablespoon dried thyme
1 tablespoon onion powder
1 tablespoon cayenne

Place all the ingredients in a small mixing bowl. Use a fork to combine them into a homogeneous spice blend. Use immediately or store, well covered, for 6 months.

☆ Spiced and Steamed ☆ Crabhouse Crabs, Maryland Style

One of America's greatest gastronomic traditions is the merry consumption of crabs in Maryland's great crab houses. The vivid blends of spices the restaurants use (for a great homemade one of your own, see page 293) are caked onto the live crabs, which then get steamed for 20 minutes or so before being strewn across your table. If you're used to eating crabs without spice, you might at first find the fiery Maryland tradition odd — because the spices may seem to hide the subtle crab flavor. But the more you eat, the more that worry slips away; the sweet, insistent crab flavor mounts in your mouth, finally rising above the flavor of spices. The following recipe, which yields crabs that have the exact crabhouse taste, is very flexible; it can be halved or doubled or tripled, depending on the size of your steamer(s) and the size of the crowd you're expecting. Steam crabs fight a lot in the steamer basket, which often leads to claws falling off. By dipping the live crabs in an ice bath, you slow down their activity in the steamer and retain many more crabs with claws attached.

Yield: 4 servings for moderately hungry novice pickers (6 crabs each); 2 servings for very hungry blue crab pros (12 crabs each)

3 cups beer
2 cups white vinegar
1½ cups water
10 bay leaves
3 gallons water
1 gallon ice cubes
2 dozen live blue crabs, preferably large ones
Crabhouse Spice Blend (page 293)

1. Select a large pot that has a steamer basket and a tight-fitting lid. Place the pot on the stovetop and place the beer, vinegar, water, and bay leaves in the pot. Cover the pot and bring the mixture to a boil (you will need to maintain the boil throughout the steaming process).
2. Fill another large pot with 3 gallons of cold water and add 1 gallon of ice cubes. Using long-handled tongs, place the live crabs in the ice-cold water. Leave the crabs in the water for 3 minutes.
3. Place the steamer basket on the counter. Using tongs and working quickly, remove the crabs one at a time from the ice-water bath and place them blue shell side up in the steamer basket. Sprinkle each crab with a scant tablespoon of the Crabhouse Spice Blend. Repeat this process until all the crabs are loaded into the steamer basket.
4. Remove the lid from the steamer pot and place the steamer basket in the pot. Place the lid back on the pot, sealing it well, and steam the crabs for 17 to 25 minutes, depending on the size of the crabs. Medium-size crabs should steam for about 17 to 20 minutes; larger crabs should steam for about 20 to 25 minutes. To test if the crabs are done, take a single crab out of the pot toward the end of the cooking time and check to see that it is completely cooked. The meat should be firm, juicy, white, and relatively easy to

extract from the crab body. Once the crabs are completely cooked, remove them from the steamer basket and place them on a serving platter. Alternatively, you could simply spill the hot crabs onto the dining table, crabhouse style, with brown paper or newspaper covering the table. Serve immediately.

☆ Grilled Soft-Shell Crab ☆ Sandwich with Crabhouse Spices

The soft-shell crab is one of the jewels of American waters. Crabs shed their shells everywhere in the world, but only in the Chesapeake area and the southeast United States is there a massive industry set up to bring the just-molted crabs to market. And that's why most foreign visitors who come to the United States, even from Europe, go gaga over this specialty, which they've never seen before. Soft-shell crabs are delicious, of course, and so much easier to eat than their hard-shell cousins. However, there's always an inherent cooking problem, which, unfortunately, many chefs do not overcome. The crabs turn themselves watery to slip out of their shells — and many of the conventional cooking techniques, such as sautéeing, lead to a watery result. One of the great ways to avoid this is rarely done: throw the crabs on a hot fire, which, while cooking the crabs, helps evaporate the liquid. Season 'em correctly, toss 'em on sandwich bread with some grilled onions and tartar sauce — and you've actually got an easy-to-eat sandwich version of the crabhouse experience.

Yield: 4 sandwiches

4 large or jumbo soft-shell crabs, cleaned
    (you can have your fishmonger do this),
    rinsed, and patted dry

1 large red onion, peeled and sliced
    in ¼-inch-thick rounds
¼ cup vegetable oil
2 teaspoons Crabhouse Spice Blend (page 293)
8 slices firm white sandwich bread
    (purchase upmarket white breads
    such as Arnold or Pepperidge Farm)
½ cup Crabhouse Tartar Sauce
    (recipe follows)

1. Make a hot gas or charcoal fire.
2. Brush both sides of the crabs and onion slices lightly with oil. Sprinkle a small amount of the spice blend on each side of the crabs.
3. When the fire is ready, place the crabs, top side down, on the grill and surround them with the onion slices. Grill the crabs and onion for 3 to 4 minutes per side; the crabs should be reddish brown, a bit crispy, and just firm to the touch; the onion should be just tender.
4. Toward the end of the cooking time, grill the bread on both sides (if your grill isn't large enough to hold everything, you can grill the bread before starting the crabs). Spread 1 tablespoon of tartar sauce on each slice of bread. Sandwich the crabs and a few rounds of onion between the slices of bread and serve immediately.

☆ Crabhouse Tartar Sauce ☆

Yield: About ½ cup

1 tablespoon minced shallot
¼ teaspoon minced garlic
1 tablespoon finely chopped celery

1 tablespoon finely chopped cornichons
  (sour French pickles)
1 tablespoon minced parsley
1 tablespoon minced tarragon
1 teaspoon Old Bay seasoning
½ cup mayonnaise
1 tablespoon water
Lemon juice, as needed

Thoroughly mix all the ingredients (except the lemon juice) in a small bowl. Taste the mixture and blend in a little lemon juice if it seems a bit sweet (some brands of mayonnaise are sweeter or more tart than others). Refrigerate for at least 1 hour before serving.

Low Country

The cuisine of the Low Country — an indefinite area of coastal marshes and swamps that is usually mapped out as southeastern South Carolina and northeastern Georgia — is an intriguing composite. Some of the great shellfish species of the more-famous Chesapeake Bay are also found in these waters, and have always inspired Low Country cooks. Ideas that seem Southern are very much woven through the cuisine — as are ideas that seem Creole, reminiscent of New Orleans. Most important of all, perhaps, is the influence that has been exerted over the centuries by the region's two most important cities: Charleston, South Car-

olina, and Savannah, Georgia — both of them great port cities that received exotic shipments from all over the world, both of them hubs of sophistication where the level of culinary skill was high.

✹ She-Crab Soup ✹

The creamy crab soup of Maryland — which appears on every crabhouse menu there — can't hold a candle to the creamy crab soup of Charleston and Savannah. In the Low Country they specify that the soup be made from female crabs — which means that all that wonderful crabby orange roe becomes a taste and texture element in the soup. The ideal way to make this soup, then, is with female crabs; though they're almost never seen in crab houses, they are abundantly available in fish stores in Chinese neighborhoods. Ask the fishmonger for females. If you can't find 'em and are forced to use "jimmies," or male crabs, a traditional substitute for the roe is minced hard-boiled egg added to the top of the soup just before serving. In the following recipe, I was looking for one thing above all: sheer crab flavor. That's why the soup starts with live crabs and their shells and uses no stock or water. The result is startlingly intense and rich — so much so that you might want to consider serving only small portions of it in, say, espresso cups, as a kind of elegant *"amuse-bouche"* at the start of a fancy dinner party (on the verandah, of course).

Yield: 12 to 16 servings as a small-soup taste;
6 to 8 servings as a soup course

12 large, live blue crabs, female if possible
6 tablespoons butter
1 cup coarsely chopped onion
1 cup coarsely chopped celery
1 teaspoon dried thyme
Parsley stems from 1 large bunch, about ½ cup

6 cups whipping cream
4 cups milk
1 tablespoon dry sherry
Cayenne
Tabasco sauce
Paprika

1. Plunge the crabs into a large pot of boiling salted water. Cover, and cook for 8 minutes. Place crabs in a colander and run under cold water to stop cooking.

2. When crabs are cool enough to handle, pick out the crabmeat, tomalley, and roe, reserving the shells. (See crab-pickin' description on pages 290 to 291.) You should have about 1½ cups crabmeat and 1 cup of roe. Pick through the meat to make sure you've removed all the cartilage. Refrigerate the crabmeat and roe until needed.

3. Rinse the shells of any sand and crush them with a mallet, the side of a cleaver, or the bottom of a heavy pot. Set aside.

4. Melt the butter in a large, heavy stockpot over medium-high heat. Add the crab shells and cook, stirring on occasion, for 10 minutes. Add the onion, celery, thyme, and parsley stems. Cook for another 10 minutes, stirring every now and then to prevent sticking.

5. Add the cream and milk. Bring to a boil. Immediately lower the heat and cook at a low simmer for 1½ hours, stirring on occasion to keep from scorching.

6. Strain the mixture through a fine sieve into a large pot. Bring to a simmer. Add the crabmeat, roe, and sherry. Season to taste with salt, pepper, and cayenne. Simmer for 5 minutes, then serve immediately. Place the cayenne, Tabasco, and paprika on the table for diners to add to the soup.

NOTE: If you'd like the soup to be even more crab intense, put it in the refrigerator at the end of step 5, before straining. Hold the shells in the liquid overnight. Then strain the next day, proceeding with step 6.

☆ Country Captain ☆

Savannah, Georgia, has long been a port of international exchange — so it's little surprise that this "exotic" chicken stew, brimming with "foreign" spices, developed there at the dawn of America. No one is sure how Country Captain got its name . . . but the leading theory concerns a British army officer who had been stationed in India, then brought some of what he learned at the table there to Georgia. In today's gastronomic world, delicious as Country Captain is, it seems comparatively unexotic. But you can certainly love it if you think of it in this nostalgic way: Indian food for ladies who lunch, wonderfully rich and sweet (with chutney in the sauce), and ever-so-slightly naughty.

Yield: 4 main-course servings

1 tablespoon butter
⅓ pound slab bacon, cut into ½-inch chunks
½ cup all-purpose flour
1 chicken (about 3 to 4 pounds),
      cut into 8 serving pieces
1 large onion, chopped (about 2 cups)
1 medium red bell pepper, chopped
      (about 1 cup)
1 medium green bell pepper, chopped
      (about 1 cup)
2 garlic cloves, chopped

2 tablespoons curry powder

1 teaspoon chopped gingerroot

½ teaspoon dried thyme

½ teaspoon paprika

¼ teaspoon ground allspice

¼ teaspoon ground cinnamon

¼ teaspoon mustard seeds

2 (14½-ounce) cans chopped tomatoes,
    undrained

¾ cup chicken stock

¼ cup mango chutney

1 tablespoon light brown sugar

2 teaspoons lemon juice

¾ cup golden raisins

Cooked white rice, for serving

¼ cup toasted sliced almonds, for garnish

1. Melt the butter in a large Dutch oven over medium heat. Add bacon and fry over medium heat until crisp, then drain on paper towels. Reserve.

2. Place flour on a plate and season with salt and pepper. Season chicken with salt and pepper. Dredge chicken in flour and place pieces skin side down in bacon fat, over medium-high heat, without crowding (you may have to cook the chicken in two or three batches, which will require more butter and bacon fat). Cook chicken until browned on all sides, about 8 minutes per batch. Place chicken pieces on a plate.

3. Pour off all but 2 tablespoons of the fat in the pot (even if you've used extra butter and bacon fat, you'll still need only 2 tablespoons fat at this point). Add onion and bell peppers and cook until softened, about 5 minutes. Add garlic, curry powder, ginger,

thyme, paprika, allspice, cinnamon, and mustard seeds. Cook, stirring, until curry is fragrant, about 1 minute. Add reserved bacon, tomatoes, chicken stock, chutney, brown sugar, and lemon juice. Bring to a simmer, scraping the bottom of the pot to loosen any browned bits.

4. Return chicken to pot, immersing it in the sauce. Cover and cook over low heat until chicken is tender, about 45 minutes. Add raisins and cook 5 minutes more. Serve over rice, garnished with almonds.

☆ Red Rice ☆

This side dish from Charleston and Savannah is not as well known as Louisiana's Dirty Rice. But a dish remarkably similar to Red Rice — namely, the completely inaccurately named Spanish Rice — used to be a home and cafeteria staple all over the country. I love the great, dense, tomatoey mouthful of tender rice that this Red Rice recipe yields.

Yield: 6 to 8 side dish servings

¼ pound bacon slices

1½ cups chopped onion

½ cup chopped green bell pepper

½ cup chopped red bell pepper

2 cups long-grain white rice

½ teaspoon chopped fresh thyme (or 1 teaspoon
    dried)

¼ teaspoon cayenne

1 (28-ounce) can crushed tomatoes

1 teaspoon sugar

¾ teaspoon salt

Hot sauce for serving

1. Preheat oven to 350 degrees.

2. In a large ovenproof saucepan with a lid, fry bacon over medium heat until crisp. Drain on paper towels; crumble and set aside. Remove and discard all but 2 tablespoons bacon fat from pan. Over medium heat, cook onion and bell peppers until softened, about 5 to 7 minutes.

3. Add rice, thyme, and cayenne. Stir well to coat rice with bacon fat, about 2 minutes. Add tomatoes, sugar, and salt. Bring to a simmer, cover, and bake in oven 1 hour. Remove from oven, top with crumbled bacon, and serve with hot sauce to taste.

✩ Benne Seed Wafers ✩

Sesame seeds — called benne seeds by the slaves who brought them to the United States from Africa — became very important in Southern cooking. Nowhere were they more important than in the great city of Charleston, South Carolina, where one of America's greatest cookies developed: the benne seed wafer. At their best, these wafers are remarkably light, thin, crisp, delicate; it took me many go-throughs to develop a recipe that measures up to what I've tasted in Charleston! One secret is flattening each cookie until it's really thin — a laborious process but worth every second of trouble. You can serve these great cookies anytime someone wants a snack. Or you can treat them as if they were America's answer to the tuile and serve them after the main course of a fancy American dinner, just before the main dessert.

Yield: 5 dozen

1 cup white sesame seeds (see Note)
¼ pound (1 stick) unsalted butter, softened,
*   plus extra for greasing cookie sheet*

1 cup granulated sugar
½ cup light brown sugar
1 teaspoon dark (Asian) sesame oil
½ teaspoon vanilla extract
1 egg, beaten
1¾ cups flour, plus extra for flattening cookies
1 teaspoon fine salt
2 teaspoons baking powder
½ teaspoon baking soda

1. Preheat oven to 325 degrees. Spread sesame seeds on a sheet pan and toast in the oven on the middle rack until light golden and fragrant (about 5 to 7 minutes). Remove from oven and cool completely.

2. In a mixer with paddle attachment, cream the 1 stick of butter, the granulated sugar, and brown sugar until light and fluffy, about 2 minutes. Add sesame oil, vanilla extract and egg, and mix to combine.

3. Combine the 1¾ cups flour, salt, baking powder, and baking soda. Sift. Add to mixer, mixing with paddle just to blend. Remove bowl from mixer and stir in sesame seeds by hand.

4. Chill dough for at least ½ hour so it is easier to work with. Pinch off pieces of dough and roll into balls about the size of a hazelnut. Place pieces on a well-greased cookie sheet, about 2 inches apart. Dip the bottom of a drinking glass in the extra flour and flatten each cookie as thinly as possible, re-dipping the glass in flour if the cookies stick when pressed. You should be able to get the cookies less than ⅛ inch thick — or even thinner if you are meticulous. Bake in the preheated oven — rotating the cookie sheet once

halfway through baking — for about 9 minutes, or until cookies are light golden.

5. Remove from oven and cool on the cookie sheet until slightly firm, only a minute or two. Remove from sheet with a spatula and cool on a rack.

NOTE: Most people buy sesame seeds in the supermarket, from little spice jars; this is an exceedingly expensive way to buy them. Instead, go to an ethnic grocery store or a health food store and purchase raw sesame seeds in bulk (especially if you love this recipe!) at a huge saving.

Dixie

The prodigious history of Southern food really starts with the Native American tribes of the area — who generally get much less credit for their contributions in this region than they do in places like the American Southwest. But it was those original inhabitants who taught a trick or two — such as the use of corn, which led to Southern corn bread and Southern grits — to the arriving English. The English gentry, busy establishing estates and plantations, were wise enough to incorporate Native American ideas into the essentially English cooking tradition they had brought over with them.

Later on, though they weren't wise enough to free the slaves they held, they were wise enough to pay attention to the culinary ideas that came from Africa. With time, African ingredients such as yams, okra, and peanuts (which originated in Peru, then came to North America from Africa) became prominent in traditional Southern cooking. The food that the slaves ate had another powerful influence on Southern cuisine. Because the plantation owners ate "high on the hog," it was the more humble cuts of pork that went to the back of the house. The cooks recognized how tasty those humble cuts could be — and, today, porky dishes such as Collard Greens with Ham Hocks owe their existence to the contempt of the masters and the frugality of the slaves.

Building on the Native American/English/African base, Southern food has evolved in these lip-smacking directions:

✪ Wealthier types held on to large amounts of land . . . which meant vegetable gardens, which meant a great respect in the South (still alive today) for seasonal produce.

✪ Poorer types had to make do with whatever ingredients were at hand. Unable to go to the store to buy bread, some Southerners learned to convert the wheat and cornmeal they had on hand into quick and delicious biscuits and corn bread.

✪ Simplicity and plainness ruled, then and now. Southern cuisine has always been highly ingredient focused, with basic ingredients often receiving the support of nothing more than salt and pepper.

✪ A love of sweets emerged — which is manifest in the addition of sugar to savory items, in sweet condiments that accompany meals, in the ubiquitous mealtime beverage of sweet tea, and, of course, in a range of very sweet desserts.

✪ Deep-frying has been a much-beloved, mainstream technique in the South for centuries. Fried chicken is just the tip of the lardberg.

✪ Most important of all, perhaps — the South is the homeland of barbecue, meats cooked long and slow over indirect, smoky heat. The invention of barbecue may be the single most important contribution of the United States to world gastronomy — and the profusion of barbecue styles, ideas, dishes, and cultures all across the South is truly American and truly thrilling.

✫ Redeye Gravy ✫

This Southern classic always sounds so rural and romantic: after you've sizzled your country ham in a cast-iron skillet, you throw some coffee into the pan, scrape up the brown bits, and you've got gravy. The reality, however, is that if this is all you do, your redeye gravy will taste pretty awful. Southerners who actually make this thing like to cut the coffee with another liquid. Reasoning that many modern Southerners actually drink Coca-Cola rather than coffee in the morning — and having heard the legends of Coke going into the pan, though I've never seen a recipe for it — I decided to try a Coca-Cola/coffee mix. The outcome: if you soften it all with a little butter, the resulting gravy is startlingly delicious, with coffee and caramel and buttery notes in lovely proportion. Use it in all the classic ways. For example, prepare the biscuits on page 303, cut them in half, top with sizzled slices of ham (see sidebar), and pour Redeye Gravy over all. Or serve Redeye Gravy over the Baked Southern Cheese Grits on page 303.

You could make Redeye Gravy in the pan that cooked any breakfast meat: bacon, sausages, regular ham. But the classic application, of course, is to make it in the pan that has sizzled slices of that little-known Southern specialty, country ham. This is an amazing cured product — epicenter: Kentucky — that is America's rustic answer to prosciutto. It's saltier than prosciutto and drier than prosciutto, never mimicking prosciutto's velvety texture. But the advantages are (1) the depth of flavor, and (2) the fact that slices of prosciutto get ruined when sizzled in a pan, whereas slices of country ham taste great when treated that way.

American country ham is sometimes called "an acquired taste," and it's true that many of the hams available are too salty for most tastes. But there is one producer in Bremen, Kentucky, who ships absolutely delicious country ham that almost anyone will love at first tasting: Gatton Farms, whose ham is marketed as Father's Country Hams.

They are available by logging on to *www.fatherscountryhams.com* or by calling either 270-525-3554 or 877-525-HAMS (toll-free).

When you have your slices of ham (they should be cut thin, less than ⅛ inch), place a cast-iron skillet over high heat. When it's hot, add the ham. Cook for 1 minute per side, remove, and prepare Redeye Gravy in pan.

A full-blown, blowout Southern breakfast would include country ham, Redeye Gravy, cream gravy (I love the Southern Sausage Cream Gravy on page 302), biscuits, grits, and eggs (probably scrambled).

Yield: Enough for 2 servings

½ cup strong but not bitter black coffee
(espresso's not a good idea)
6 tablespoons Coca-Cola Classic
2 tablespoons unsalted butter, cut into
2 pieces

After sizzling meat in a pan, removing it (see sidebar), and draining fat, turn heat to high and add coffee and Coca-Cola. Scrape the bottom of the pan with a wooden spoon as the liquid comes to a boil. When it does, let it boil for 30 seconds, then toss the butter into the pan. Whisk the sauce just until the butter melts and thickens it, about 30 seconds. Serve immediately.

✵ Southern Sausage ✵ Cream Gravy

Now, to me, this is a great gravy. In the South, an old-fashioned breakfast option is to take warm, freshly made biscuits, split them in half, and smother them with this incredible sausage-studded elixir. The biscuits with Sausage Cream Gravy become the main course, the centerpiece of the breakfast.

Yield: 6 servings

1 pound crumbled pork breakfast sausage
(see Note)
2 tablespoons Crisco
¼ cup all-purpose flour
3 cups cool milk
6 warm biscuits

1. Place the sausage meat in a large, straight-sided sauté pan over medium heat. As the sausage is cooking, crumble it into small pieces using a fork. Once all of the sausage crumbles are lightly browned and fully cooked, remove them with their pan juices from the pan and place them in a small bowl. Reserve.

2. Add the shortening to the hot pan. Once it has melted, add the flour, stirring it in slowly with a whisk. Stir the mixture constantly to brown the flour evenly. Cook the mixture until the flour is slightly browned (about 3 to 4 minutes). The mixture should smell nutty, not burned. Then add the milk to the pan, stirring the mixture constantly with a whisk until the gravy comes to a boil. Lower the heat to medium-low and simmer gently for 15 minutes.

3. Using a spoon, add the reserved sausage meat and the pan juices to the gravy. Mix well with a wooden spoon, seasoning to taste with salt and pepper. The gravy should be a medium-thick sauce; if necessary, the gravy can be thinned by adding warm milk.

4. Using your hands, split the biscuits in half. Place two halves, split side up, on each of six plates. Cover each half generously with warm gravy. Serve immediately.

NOTE: For the sausage in this recipe, you can use either bulk breakfast sausage or sausage links; if you use the latter, take the meat out of the casings and discard the casings. But the type of sausage you use is important. Southern brands of sausage, like Jimmy Dean, have lots of seasoning; Northern brands can be blander. If you are using a bland one, simply blend some powdered sage, cayenne, and freshly ground black pepper into the meat to taste.

☆ Southern Breakfast Biscuits ☆ with Cheddar Cheese

Light, fluffy hot biscuits are practically synonymous with Southern cooking. But most people are not aware that the modern Southern biscuit — dating only from 1825 or so — was probably served chiefly as a breakfast treat. It makes sense. The quick-acting leavenings meant that you didn't have to wait for the bread to rise — so breakfast cooks could serve fresh baked goods at 9 A.M. that they started making only at 8 A.M.! Helps extend that beauty sleep. The recipe here is based on great breakfast biscuits I've had in the South made with cheese — which adds flavor interest but does not weigh down the miraculous lightness. The very best way to attain that miracle, incidentally, is to make the biscuits with flour from the South's own "soft" wheat, or "winter" wheat. The most famous brand is White Lily.

Yield: About 12 biscuits

*2¼ cups White Lily flour (or 2 cups
    all-purpose flour), plus a little extra
    for the cookie cutter*
2½ teaspoons baking powder
½ teaspoon baking soda
2 teaspoons sugar
¾ teaspoon salt
*6 tablespoons butter, cut into small pieces and
    chilled well*
*1 cup grated extra-sharp cheddar cheese, chilled
    (grate on smallest holes of grater)*
2 tablespoons grated Parmesan cheese
⅔ cup chilled buttermilk
2 tablespoons melted butter

1. Preheat oven to 425 degrees and adjust oven rack to the middle setting. Sift together flour, baking powder, baking soda, sugar, and salt. Add cold butter and cut together with two knives, or a pastry blender, until the flour resembles coarse meal. This can also be done in a food processor, with about 10 to 15 quick pulses.

2. Add cheeses to flour mixture in a bowl and toss lightly with a fork to separate cheese strands and coat with flour.

3. Add buttermilk all at once and toss with a fork until just combined. Don't overwork! Dump dough onto a lightly floured surface and knead 2 or 3 times until it just comes together. Pat or roll out to a ½-inch thickness. Dip a 2¼-inch cookie cutter into some flour and shake off excess. Cut biscuits and place about ½ inch apart on an ungreased sheet pan. Gather scraps together and pat out again to cut additional biscuits (though these won't be as light and fluffy).

4. Brush biscuit tops with melted butter and bake for 15 minutes, rotating the sheet pan halfway through baking time, until browned on bottom. Cool biscuits on a wire rack for a few minutes before serving, to allow internal steam to finish cooking biscuits. Serve very warm, slathered with butter!

☆ Baked Southern ☆ Cheese Grits

Nothing divides the North and the South like grits; Yankees never eat 'em, Southerners can't live without 'em. What are they exactly? They are made from hominy, which is a Native American phenomenon that inspired the Mexican kitchen. To make hominy, those early cooks took large kernels of dried corn and soaked them in an alkaline solution (sometimes lye); after this the tough hull was slipped off, and the remaining soft center had a new taste — exactly like the taste of Mexican corn tortillas. Now, if you don't grind this treated corn, you have whole hominy, big kernels of corn. If you crack the hominy, you have cracked hominy. If you grind it pretty finely, you, at long last, have grits (sometimes called hominy grits). The name probably comes from Old English — either from *greot*, which means "ground," or *grytt*, which means "bran." Grits, when added to hot liquid (traditionally water), thicken up into a kind of porridge with a superhigh comfort-food factor. You can't have a real Southern breakfast without grits, served with eggs, ham, sausages, redeye gravy, and so on. My favorite way to have them at breakfast is cooked with cheese — a very common pairing in the South.

Yield: 6 servings

1 tablespoon finely minced garlic
1 tablespoon finely minced onion
4 tablespoons butter (½ stick)
2 cups water
2 cups milk
1 teaspoon salt
1 cup yellow stone-ground grits (not instant)
½ cup cream cheese, softened at room
    temperature
1¼ cups grated cheddar cheese
3 tablespoons chopped fresh chives

1. Preheat the oven to 450 degrees. In a large saucepan over medium heat sweat the garlic and onion with 3 tablespoons of the butter for 2 minutes, making sure they don't brown or burn. Add the water, milk, and salt and bring to a boil. Then reduce the heat to moderate so the liquid comes down to a simmer.
2. Pour in the grits by the handful in a thin stream very slowly, stirring constantly with a whisk to prevent lumps. Once they're all in, keep the mixture at a bare simmer and stir constantly with a wooden spoon. Cook the grits, stirring and crushing any lumps that might form against the side of the pan, for 15 minutes. (The grits will thicken considerably while cooking.)
3. Remove the pan from the heat and stir in the cream cheese, ¾ cup of the cheddar cheese, and 2 tablespoons of the chives. Season to taste with salt and pepper. Smear the remaining butter evenly into a small baking dish that just holds the grits. Place the grits in the buttered dish and top with the remaining ½ cup of cheddar cheese. Place the grits on the center rack of the oven for 10 minutes. Remove and sprinkle with the remaining 1 tablespoon of chives.

✸ Boiled Raw Peanuts ✸

One of the great roadside treats in South Carolina, Georgia, Alabama, and Mississippi is a huge cauldron of peanuts boiling away for nine, ten, eleven, or twelve hours; the boiled nuts are served warm, and the shells are thrown on the ground. The taste and texture are completely different from the taste and texture Northerners know from supermarket peanuts; the latter come to us industrially toasted by someone else. In the Southern tradition, raw, untoasted peanuts are thrown into boiling water at home or at roadside stands. But the very happy news is this: a great South Carolina–based company has now made it possible for eaters everywhere to receive a shipment of these raw peanuts for boiling (see Note). When you receive your package from Lee Brothers, you will receive a set of cooking instructions for a big pot. These are good instructions, but I prefer to cook the raw peanuts in a

★★★

The Peanut Test

If you're not sure what your taste in boiled peanuts is, the first time you make this recipe consider it an experiment. Starting with the seventh hour of cooking, remove and reserve a peanut from the Crock-Pot at hourly intervals. After twelve hours, you'll have six peanuts at six different degrees of doneness. Taste them all, side by side, to see which cooking time you like best. When you boil peanuts again, you'll know exactly how long to cook them.

Crock-Pot, which is easier and safer and requires much less baby-sitting. The following recipe tells you exactly how to do it.

Yield: 4 to 6 servings as a snack

1 pound raw peanuts for boiling (see Note)
Water to cover peanuts
½ cup kosher salt

1. Place the raw peanuts in a Crock-Pot and cover them with water; add the salt.
2. Place the lid on the Crock-Pot. Set the cooking temperature to high. Every 2 hours, while the peanuts are cooking, give them a stir, and add some additional water if necessary. The water should always be at about the same level as the peanuts. Except for your spot checks, keep the Crock-Pot covered throughout the cooking process.
3. Once the peanuts have cooked for about 6 hours, taste them. If they are too salty for your taste, remove some of the salty water and replace it with fresh water. If they are not salty enough for your taste, add more salt.
4. Continue cooking for at least a few hours more. Every hour after the initial 6 hours of cooking, remove a peanut, let it cool down, and taste it for doneness. The final product, once the peanut is removed from its shell, should be tender yet firm and should be salty and earthy in taste. The peanuts can take up to 12 hours to reach this point. The proper cooking time is a very subjective thing; cook the peanuts to your taste. When they've arrived, drain the peanuts and serve them warm. They can be stored in their shells, in a sealed container, refrigerated, for up to 1 week; reheat before serving.

NOTE: Raw peanuts can be ordered from

The Lee Brothers Boil-Your-Own Peanuts Kit
62 Broad Street
Charleston, SC 29401
843-720-8890
www.boiledpeanuts.com

☆ Calabash-Style ☆ Seafood Fry

Calabash-style seafood is a specialty from the "fish camps" alongside the Calabash River in eastern North Carolina. In the town of Calabash itself, there are about thirty fish camps — seasonal fried seafood restaurants — and, oh, about three hundred residents. The fish camps, obviously, are there for travelers — including many families headed to the nearby summer vacation hotspot, Myrtle Beach, South Carolina. Now the Calabash fish camp concept has spread throughout North Carolina and South Carolina. Many of these fish camps fill up on Friday and

Saturday nights with people wanting to load up on mounds of all-you-can-eat fried seafood, served alongside French fries, cole slaw, and hush puppies, not to mention ice-cold glasses of sweet tea. It would all sound pretty heavy — were it not for the delicate, miraculously light and flavorful coating that goes on the fried seafood.

Yield: 4 main-course servings

Vegetable oil for frying
1½ cups simple beer, such as Budweiser
1½ cups milk
4 teaspoons salt
4 teaspoons pepper
3½ tablespoons cornstarch
1 teaspoon baking powder
1 teaspoon baking soda
¼ cup white cornmeal
⅔ cup Wondra (quick-mixing flour)
1 pound baby shrimp, scallops, catfish pieces,
*   or trout (or a mix of them all)*

1. Pour oil into a medium-size heavy-bottomed pot until the oil comes halfway up the sides of the pot. Place it over medium-high heat and bring the oil to 370 degrees. Maintain this temperature by adjusting the heat throughout the cooking process.
2. In a medium-size bowl, whisk together the beer, milk, 2 teaspoons of the salt, and 2 teaspoons of the pepper.
3. In a pie pan, combine the remaining 2 teaspoons salt, the remaining 2 teaspoons pepper, the cornstarch, baking powder, baking soda, cornmeal, and Wondra. Blend them together with a fork.
4. Fry the seafood in batches, depending on the size of your pot. Begin by placing some of the seafood in the beer and milk solution and soak for about 1 minute. Remove the seafood using a slotted spoon. Let the excess moisture drip off the spoon. Then place the seafood immediately into the coating in the pie pan and roll it around to coat evenly. Place the seafood in a wire strainer, place it over the pie plate, and tap the side of the strainer to remove any excess coating from the seafood.
5. Immediately transfer the seafood to a large slotted spoon (what chefs call a spider is best), and lower the seafood into the hot oil. Cook for about 1 minute, or until the seafood is golden brown and cooked throughout. Remove the seafood from the oil using the slotted spoon or spider and let it drain on paper towels. Don't overcook the seafood. Repeat until all seafood is cooked. Serve immediately.

☆ Louisville Hot Brown ☆

This delicious gratinéed sandwich — amazing comfort food, whether you had it in childhood or not — is a good example of the kinds of little-known but wonderful food traditions that exist across the United States. In the early 1920s, the Brown Hotel in Louisville, Kentucky, drew a swank late-night crowd every evening — and these people needed to be fed! The hotel's chef, Fred Schmidt, got bored with the bill of fare he prepared midnight after midnight — so he got creative in 1923 and came up with an open-face sandwich in a gratin dish, made with some variation of chicken, turkey, ham, and bacon, topped with tomatoes and Mornay sauce, and passed under the broiler. You can still find it today in Louisville — or in your kitchen. No need to wait for midnight; it's a great dish for lunch, brunch, or a light supper.

☆☆

Yield: 2 servings

2 tablespoons unsalted butter
2 tablespoons flour
1½ cups whole milk
Pinch of freshly grated nutmeg
1 egg yolk
½ cup loosely packed grated Gruyère cheese
3 slices good-quality white bread
     (or as a variation, brioche)
6 ounces thinly sliced roast turkey breast
     (leftovers are good; turkey roll is not)
6 slices crisp-cooked, thinly sliced bacon
4 slices ripe tomato, cut ¼ inch thick
2 tablespoons grated Parmesan cheese

1. Make the Mornay sauce. Melt butter in a saucepan. Add flour, stirring with a wooden spoon to make a smooth roux. Cook over medium-low heat, until the mixture smells nutty (about 2 to 3 minutes). Do not allow the roux to color.

2. Whisk in the milk. Use the wooden spoon to get lumps out of corners. Whisk until mixture is free of lumps. Bring to a simmer and add nutmeg. Simmer white sauce for 5 minutes to thicken.

3. Place yolk in a mixing bowl and slowly add white sauce, whisking constantly, to temper the yolk. Return mixture to pan and cook over low heat for another 2 to 3 minutes to thicken slightly. Add Gruyère and continue cooking until cheese is melted and Mornay sauce is smooth.

4. Preheat broiler. Place about 2 tablespoons of Mornay sauce in the bottom of each of two gratin dishes. Lightly toast the bread, then cut each slice on a diagonal into two tri-angles. Place 3 bread triangles in each gratin dish, overlapping slightly.

5. Cover the bread slices with the remaining ingredients in the following order: turkey, bacon, tomato slices. Make sure to divide these ingredients evenly between the two gratin dishes. Cover with remaining Mornay sauce; each sandwich will get about ½ cup of the sauce or a little more. Sprinkle each dish with 1 tablespoon of the grated Parmesan.

6. Place dishes under broiler and cook until the sauce is browned and bubbly. Serve immediately.

☆ Southern Chicken ☆ and Dumplings

All across the South, chicken and dumplings hits the same therapeutic, comfort-food spot that chicken soup with matzo balls hits in New York. Therefore, the following recipe — straight out of the home kitchen of a friend in North Carolina — has plenty of cookin' comfort built into it. So what if you use a little canned cream of chicken soup? The first time I tasted this amazing dish — with its large, soft, fluffy, pillowy dumplings — I had no idea that Campbell's had anything to do with it. Cold night? Touch of flu? Feeling blue? Y'all try some of this.

Yield: 4 main-dish servings

1 large chicken (about 5 pounds), cut into quarters
1 teaspoon freshly ground pepper,
     plus extra for the dumplings
1 (10¾-ounce) can low-sodium chicken broth
     or an equal amount of homemade broth
     (and possibly a little extra)
1 (10¾-ounce) can Campbell's cream
     of chicken soup

2 cups all-purpose flour
1 tablespoon baking powder
1 teaspoon salt
⅓ cup solid vegetable shortening (such as Crisco)
1½ cups milk

1. Place the chicken pieces, pepper, and chicken broth in a large, heavy-bottomed pot. Add enough water to completely cover the chicken, turn heat to medium-high, and bring liquid to a boil. Immediately reduce the heat to medium, cover the pot, and cook until the chicken is completely cooked (it should be almost falling off the bone). This takes about 1 hour.

2. When the chicken is fully cooked, remove the pot from the heat. Remove the chicken from the pot using a pair of tongs and reserve it in a large bowl.

3. Measure the broth that remains in the pot. Make sure you have at least 5 cups of broth. If you have less, try to make up the difference with any liquid that the reserved chicken in the bowl has given off. If there's still not enough, add a little extra canned chicken broth. If you have more than 5 cups of broth, reserve extra broth for another use. Whisk the canned cream of chicken soup into the broth in the pot. Reserve.

4. Make the dumpling dough. Place the flour, baking powder, and salt in a medium-size mixing bowl. Stir the mixture with a fork to blend all the dry ingredients together. Then add the shortening. With a fork, draw the shortening and flour together up against the side of the bowl to blend them. Keep going until the entire mass is crumbly, with little pieces of shortening (the size of oatmeal flakes) well distributed throughout. Slowly stir the milk into the dough mixture until it is just blended. Don't overmix it. Let the dough rest for 7 minutes.

5. While the dough is resting, pick all the meat from the chicken bones. The chicken should be torn into pieces that are a little larger than bite size. Reserve.

6. When the dumpling dough has rested, bring the enriched chicken broth in the pot back to a medium boil. Dip a large spoon into the boiling broth, then use it to scoop up a spoonful of dumpling dough (about ¼ cup) and gently place it into the broth. Repeat until all the dough is used. Sprinkle the tops of the dumplings with pepper. Cover the pot and lower the heat to medium-low (the liquid should be at a lazy bubble). Cook the dumplings for 15 minutes. Remove the lid and, using a large spoon, gently flip the dumplings over. Place the reserved chicken on top of the dumplings. Cover again and cook for another 15 minutes. With a knife, split open a dumpling to make sure the center is completely cooked. Taste broth and adjust the seasoning. Serve hot in bowls with some freshly ground pepper.

✩ Southern Fried Chicken ✩

Great Southern fried chicken is a thing of beauty. When the chicken is done right, the pieces have a crazy, crispy, crackling, curly coating, light and flavorful at the same time. The chicken within is juicy and deeply chickeny. It is a simple dish that can approach sublimity in the hands of a gifted great Southern cook; unfortunately, what passes for Southern Fried Chicken in much of the country doesn't even come close. The biggest fried chicken sin is the failure to capture the wild joy of a perfect coating; most coatings I see either form a hard, helmet-like casing around the chicken or cling tentatively to the chicken, yielding something more like fried skin than fried chicken. There are many keys to getting this thing just right — but three of them are especially important. For one thing, in most recipes, the flour doesn't adhere well enough and much of it falls off once the chicken hits the fat. In the following recipe, based on advice from a Southern friend — untraditional as it sounds — you are asked to dip the chicken in an egg-and-oil mixture before coating it with flour. Second, the shallow frying that most cookbooks advise leads to chicken pieces sitting flat on the bottom of the pot — which leads to chicken pieces with a flat surface, not a curly one. I advise cooking the chicken in deep fat, not shallow fat, and placing it on a rack while it's cooking. Lastly, most cookbooks recommend cooking the chicken in Crisco, with the advice that this is what old-fashioned Southern cooks use. *Really* old-fashioned cooks used lard! If you put a piece of Crisco-cooked chicken and a piece of lard-cooked chicken side by side, you will not believe the difference in depth of flavor. Come on, folks, this is fried chicken; you're gonna pick up a few calories anyway.

Yield: 8 pieces, enough for 2 hungry diners or 4 dabblers

FOR THE CHICKEN:
2 pounds lard
1 frying chicken, cut into 8 parts

FOR THE FLOUR MIXTURE:
2 cups all-purpose flour
1½ tablespoons salt
1 tablespoon ground black pepper
2 teaspoons garlic powder
1 teaspoon onion powder
1 teaspoon paprika
½ teaspoon cayenne

FOR THE EGG MIXTURE:
2 eggs, beaten
¼ cup canola oil
1 teaspoon paprika
1 teaspoon garlic powder
1 teaspoon onion powder
1 teaspoon ground black pepper
½ teaspoon salt

1. Place a rack in the bottom of a fairly deep, heavy-bottomed pot (the pot should ideally be about 4 inches deep and 8 inches wide, and the rack should be no taller than an inch or so). If you don't have a rack that fits, you can improvise one from aluminum foil. Tear off a sheet of aluminum foil that's about 3 feet long. Extend it from left to right on the counter, then roll the foil away from you into a foil snake that's about 3 feet long. Coil the snake into a spiral that just fits into your pot; this is your rack. Remove rack from pot and reserve.

2. Place lard in pot. Bring it to 375 degrees; check temperature with a thermometer.

3. While lard is heating, in a large plastic bag combine all the ingredients for flour mixture. Shake to blend.

4. In a wide, shallow bowl or pan, combine all the ingredients for egg mixture. Beat with a fork to blend.

5. Dip a chicken piece into the egg mixture, remove, hold it over the egg mixture for

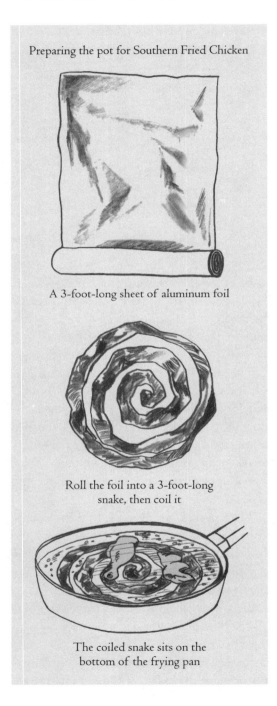

Preparing the pot for Southern Fried Chicken

A 3-foot-long sheet of aluminum foil

Roll the foil into a 3-foot-long
snake, then coil it

The coiled snake sits on the
bottom of the frying pan

a moment to let excess egg drip off, then immediately toss the egg-coated chicken piece into the flour bag. Shake briskly for 10 seconds. Make sure the flour is coating the entire piece. As you remove the piece from the bag, using your hands, press the flour onto the chicken so it adheres to the skin. Place the floured piece on a wire rack (not the rack for the pot) to rest for 5 minutes. Repeat procedure with the other 7 chicken pieces.

6. When the lard has reached 375 degrees, lower the pot rack or improvised pot rack into the pot. Working in batches (4 pieces at a time is perfect), gently place the chicken in the lard, on top of the rack. The temperature should reduce immediately to 325 degrees. Watching your thermometer, adjust the flame or heat to maintain 325 degrees for the rest of the time the chicken is cooking. Be sure not to crowd the pieces or the lard temperature will drop below 325 degrees and the chicken will absorb too much fat.

7. Using tongs, occasionally turn the pieces until a uniform golden brown crispness appears and the internal temperature of the chicken is about 160 degrees. This will take about 20 minutes.

8. Carefully remove the chicken and drain on paper towels. To keep it warm while finishing your remaining batch(es), you may place the fried chicken on a sheet pan with a wire rack in a 200-degree oven. Don't let it sit too long in the oven because it will dry out. To fry the remaining batch(es), make sure to bring the lard back to 375 degrees before adding the chicken.

☆ Brunswick Stew ☆

You can't get much more American than this — a big old stew pot with assorted meats, corn, tomatoes, beans, and hot sauce. But you also can't get too specific, because Brunswick stew means different things to different people. Two places called Brunswick in the United States claim the dish as their own: Brunswick County, Virginia, and Brunswick, Georgia (historians usually side with the Virginians, who apparently started making a stew like this in the early 1800s). Then . . . what's in the pot? Originally the dish was made with squirrel. Over the years, squirrel morphed into rabbit. But many cooks today in the Brunswicks and beyond make Brunswick stew with just pork and chicken (as I do). Next controversy: Is the meat in big chunks or shredded? Well, that all depends on your response to the next, and last, controversy: Is Brunswick stew a main course or a side dish? Throughout the South today, you may be offered Brunswick stew with shredded meat as a side dish to your barbecue; in the following recipe, the meat is shredded for side dish duty. If you wish to make this more of a main-course affair, simply cut your chicken and pork pieces into large chunks.

Yield: 12 side dish servings;
8 main-course servings

½ pound lean slab bacon, cut into ½-inch cubes
1 tablespoon vegetable oil (such as canola)
2 pounds pork butt, cut into 2-inch chunks
1 roasting chicken (about 4 pounds),
　　　cut into serving pieces,
　　　skin removed
3 cups chopped onion
1 cup carrot, cut into ¼-inch dice
1 cup celery, cut into ¼-inch dice
1 tablespoon fresh thyme
¾ teaspoon cayenne
1 meaty ham hock

2 cups fresh corn, cut from the cob
　　　(about 4 ears), cobs reserved
1 bay leaf
3 cups chopped tomato, canned or fresh
　　　(peeled and seeded, if fresh)
2 tablespoons Worcestershire sauce, plus extra
　　　for seasoning at the table
2 tablespoons sugar
2 cups baby lima beans
2 cups toasted white bread crumbs
　　　(see recipe on page 9)
Chopped parsley for garnish
Chopped scallion for garnish
Hot sauce for seasoning at the table

1. In a large Dutch oven, render and brown the bacon in the vegetable oil. When crisp, remove bacon, drain on paper towels, and reserve.
2. Season pork and chicken with salt and black pepper. Sauté in batches over medium-high heat in bacon fat until brown on all sides.
3. Remove meat from pot and reserve. Add onion, carrot, celery, thyme, and cayenne. Sauté until soft, over medium heat, about 10 to 15 minutes. Return chicken and pork to pan. Add ham hock, reserved corncobs, bay leaf, and enough water to cover (about 12 cups). Simmer uncovered until meat is very tender, about 1½ hours.
4. Remove corncobs and discard. Remove meat from liquid and cool slightly. Remove meat from bones and cut or shred into ½-inch pieces. Add meat back to pot, along with reserved bacon, tomato, Worcestershire sauce, and sugar. Simmer for 30 minutes to blend flavors.

5. Add lima beans and bread crumbs. Simmer for an additional 15 minutes. Finally, add the corn and simmer 5 minutes, so that corn retains a slight crunch. Serve hot, garnished with parsley and scallion, with hot sauce and Worcestershire on the table to be added as desired.

☆ Carolina Pulled Pork ☆ Shoulder Barbecue with Two Sauces

Cooking a hog shoulder long and slow in proximity to wood smoke . . . then pulling it apart, piling it on soft bread, slathering it with barbecue sauce, is one of the glories of the Carolina table. This kind of barbecue is usually not done at home, because most home cooks don't have the smoking pit that it takes to do the dish just right. But the following recipe combines a short visit to your Weber with a long stay in a Crock-Pot to create a startlingly accurate facsimile of Carolina 'cue. Don't have a Crock-Pot? They cost about ten bucks — and if you're a barbecue aficionado, I'm sure you'll agree it's money well spent. The pork recipe below is followed by two recipes for warm barbecue sauce that accompanies the meat — one in the mustardy South Carolina style, one in the vinegary eastern North Carolina style. Both are especially delicious because they're flavor-boosted by cooking juices from the pork.

Yield: 6 servings

5-pound bone-in pork shoulder, sawed into
    4 pieces by the butcher
1 tablespoon salt
1 tablespoon black pepper
¼ teaspoon cumin
½ teaspoon paprika
½ teaspoon chili powder
½ teaspoon cayenne
1 tablespoon sugar
3 tablespoons vegetable oil
1 large onion, peeled and sliced into
    1-inch-wide rings

SPECIAL EQUIPMENT:
Lump charcoal
2 cups hickory wood chips, soaked in water
    for 20 minutes

1. Make sure the chunks of pork shoulder are well chilled. Place pieces in a large bowl. Toss them with the salt, black pepper, cumin, paprika, chili powder, cayenne, sugar, and vegetable oil. Let the pork marinate at room temperature for 30 minutes.

2. Prepare the grill: Make a hot fire with the lump charcoal. Add the hickory wood chips. Immediately add the pork chunks to the grill with the onion rings alongside. Grill, covered, for 15 minutes, turning pork pieces and onion slices frequently. Remove pork and onion.

3. Finely chop the grilled slices of onion. Place the pork chunks, chopped onion, and 1 cup of water in a Crock-Pot (you will need at least a 2-quart size Crock-Pot). Cover and cook on the low setting for 8 hours or until the pork is falling off the bone.

4. Remove the pork chunks from the Crock-Pot and place them in a 9 by 12 by 2½-inch baking pan. Set 1½ cups of the pork juice aside for use in South Carolina Mustard Barbecue Sauce, 1 cup for use in Eastern North Carolina Vinegar Barbecue Sauce (see page 314). Pour the remaining juice over the

About the Barbecue Strategies in This Book

The amazing barbecue tradition of the South has become . . . well, let's face it . . . restaurant food. The cool part about this is that the restaurants are cheap and plentiful, and everyone in the South goes all the time to enjoy this supreme regional specialty. But the bad news is that those of us outside the South, where authentic barbecue restaurants are practically nonexistent, rarely get to eat barbecue, because we don't usually get the opportunity to reproduce this food at home.

Why not? Well, it's not just a question of equipment. You could buy a smoking pit, if you were truly dedicated to the proposition. It's just that the way in which real barbecue is cooked poses problems for the nonprofessional. To wit: The temperature under the 'cue must remain fairly constant (usually 200 to 225 degrees), which means the smoky fuel must be replenished regularly, both to maintain the temperature and to consistently impart smoky flavor. This would not be a problem for anyone if barbecue cooked for an hour or two. But the reality is that the fuel-and-smoke vigil must be maintained for three hours, six hours, or in some cases, eighteen hours. It's the dead opposite of a TV dinner . . . and it's the rare American who has time for it.

Now, I'm not pretending that the recipes in this book solve all your barbecue-preparation problems. Oh, the results are absolutely delicious; that problem is just about solved. But there is

some fuss required to get it right. Not as much fuss as there'd be at a barbecue restaurant, mind you — and incidentally, no expensive equipment at all. But you do have to have your day and your mind clear for some barbecue action.

All the barbecue recipes herein are different from each other . . . but the basic strategy employed is to smoke the meat outside on your Weber, or whatever grill you have, over fuel that has been scattered with wood chips. Then, when this smoking part is done — which takes far less time than it would to completely cook the meat in a smoking pit — the meat comes inside to be finished in your kitchen.

The Carolina Pulled Pork Shoulder Barbecue is the easiest to accomplish; the meat cooks for just fifteen minutes outside on the smoky grill, then spends an unwatched eight hours in a Crock-Pot. The Owensboro-Style Lamb Barbecue is almost as easy: twenty-five minutes on the grill, then five to six hours in the oven does the trick. Most laborious are the Memphis-Style Dry-Rub Ribs; to really get this specialty right, you have to nurse them for six hours over indirect smoky heat on your grill. But you don't have to worry about them when the company arrives, for they finish cooking in your oven for one and one-half hours.

If you like these barbecue shortcuts, don't fail to try the similar strategy for Texas-Style Barbecued Brisket on page 362.

All the barbecue recipes are much, much easier than true barbecue cooking — and all give you dazzling, south-of-the-Mason-Dixon-line results.

---

pork chunks, cover with foil, and hold them in a very low oven until ready to serve.

5. Just before serving, shred the pork into bite-size pieces with your fingers. Discard the

bones. Serve the pulled pork on steamed hamburger buns or on white bread. Top generously with barbecue sauce. Pass extra sauce on the side.

★ South Carolina ★
Mustard Barbecue Sauce

Yield: About 4 cups

1 tablespoon butter
1 cup apple cider vinegar
¾ cup French's mustard
1 tablespoon ketchup
¼ cup light brown sugar
1 tablespoon molasses
1 tablespoon Worcestershire sauce
⅛ teaspoon cayenne
1½ cups cooking liquid from pork shoulder

Combine the butter, vinegar, mustard, ketchup, brown sugar, molasses, Worcestershire, cayenne, and the cooking liquid from the pork shoulder in a small saucepan over medium-low heat. Cook the mixture for 3 minutes, stirring frequently with a wire whisk. Season to taste with salt and pepper. Serve immediately.

★ Eastern North Carolina ★
Vinegar Barbecue Sauce

Yield: About 2 cups

½ cup apple cider vinegar
⅓ cup white vinegar
2 tablespoons light brown sugar
2 teaspoons salt
½ teaspoon hot red pepper flakes
1 cup cooking liquid from pork shoulder

Combine all the ingredients in a small saucepan over medium-low heat. Cook the mixture for 3 minutes, stirring frequently with a wire whisk. Serve immediately.

✳ Memphis-Style ✳
Dry-Rub Ribs

To a hard-core group of Southern rib aficionados, barbecue sauce is something for Northerners, for people who don't have access to ribs that are extraordinary all by themselves. They season their ribs, of course — but are scrupulous in avoiding any wet stuff as the ribs come out of the pit. The epicenter of this phenomenon — known as dry-rub ribs — is Memphis, Tennessee, where a restaurant called Charlie Vergos' Rendezvous produces the best damned ribs you've ever tasted. The following recipe is a strategy for the home cook to create a delicious facsimile at home. It takes a lot of words to describe what you must do — but once you get the hang of it, it's a whole lot easier than it sounds. This particular recipe, by the way, calls for a last addition of dry rub about one and one-half hours before the ribs are done; some cooks in Memphis like to sprinkle their ribs with dry rub just before serving them. If you'd like to try that, double the proportions of spices in step 2 and save the extra for the hot, ready-to-serve ribs. Sprinkle on both sides before slicing. If you also want to serve your favorite barbecue sauce on the side, the Memphis food police probably won't be watching.

Yield: Enough for 6
modest portions

3 meaty slabs of spareribs,
    approximately 2½ to 3 pounds each
    (see Note)
1 teaspoon rubbed sage
4 tablespoons sweet paprika
3 tablespoons Old Bay seasoning
1 tablespoon salt
1 teaspoon ground thyme
4 teaspoons chili powder
5 tablespoons brown sugar
1 tablespoon black pepper

1 tablespoon garlic powder
1 tablespoon onion powder
1 teaspoon cayenne
3 tablespoons white vinegar
3 tablespoons water

SPECIAL EQUIPMENT:
6 cups of wood chips (oak, mesquite, hickory,
*   or the like)*
1 large bag lump hardwood charcoal

1. Using a sharp knife, slice notches in the edge of the rib rack that contains the fatty flap; these notches must be between the ribs at the "top" of the rack, not between the thinner ends of the bones. Starting at the "top" side, make cuts between each rib that go about 2 inches down toward the middle of the ribs. This helps the rib meat to cook a little more evenly.

2. In a medium-size mixing bowl, mix together the sage, paprika, Old Bay seasoning, salt, thyme, chili powder, brown sugar, black pepper, garlic powder, onion powder, and cayenne. Rub half of the rub mixture all over the ribs. Reserve the other half of the mixture. Place the ribs on a baking sheet and refrigerate them overnight (up to 24 hours). Remove the ribs from the refrigerator an hour prior to smoking.

3. To smoke the ribs, use a charcoal grill (such as a Weber) that has a lid, adjustable air vents, and an internal temperature thermometer. If the grill is not equipped with a thermometer, stick a frying thermometer or meat thermometer into one of the air vents and contrive a way of holding it there (for instance, with tape).

4. Submerge the wood chips in a bowl of water.

5. Fill a throwaway aluminum bread loaf pan half full of water and place it on one side of the base of the grill (preferably not the side of the grill with the air vent, because it is best to put the charcoal on that side). On the air-vent side of the base of the grill, start the fire by igniting 1 gallon (about 35 pieces) of the lump charcoal. (I prefer to use a chimney starter to ignite the charcoal, but use any method you wish.) The fire is ready when about half of the charcoal is burning well and has turned gray and the other half is still black (about 15 minutes).

6. Carefully lay a piece of heavy-duty foil over the exposed hot charcoal. This will keep drippings from falling off the ribs onto the coals and starting a flare-up. Close the cover on the grill. Adjust all the air vents on the grill so that they are barely open; this will keep the temperature low, ideally around 235 degrees. Adjust your air vents throughout the cooking process to maintain this cooking temperature. Once you have the grill temperature regulated to 235 degrees, about 15 minutes, lift up the piece of tinfoil and place a handful of drained wood chips on top of the fiery charcoal, then put the foil back in place, pulling some back to leave one corner of the charcoal exposed (about 4 by 4 inches).

7. Place the grate on the grill and lay the slabs of ribs on the grate. Do not place them over the charcoal; place them over the water pan. Cover the grill immediately to prevent flare-ups. Cook the ribs, covered, maintaining

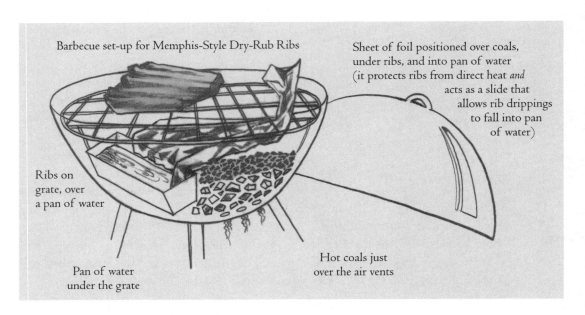

Barbecue set-up for Memphis-Style Dry-Rub Ribs

Sheet of foil positioned over coals, under ribs, and into pan of water (it protects ribs from direct heat *and* acts as a slide that allows rib drippings to fall into pan of water)

Ribs on grate, over a pan of water

Pan of water under the grate

Hot coals just over the air vents

the 235-degree temperature for about 1 hour by periodically adjusting your air vents.

8. After 1 hour, drop a handful of drained chips onto the top of the exposed part of the charcoal. Flip the ribs over and continue cooking them, covered, for 1 more hour. Repeat this process — more chips, flip over — one more time, for a total cooking time of 3 hours. At this point you will probably need to add some additional charcoal if the grill temperature has dropped below 200 degrees. If so, remove the ribs and start the process of igniting coals over again. Return the ribs, positioning them just as you did for the first 3-hour cooking. Now cook for 3 hours more, turning ribs and adding chips every hour, just as you did in the first 3 hours of cooking.

9. Remove the ribs from the grill after they've smoked for 6 hours. Place them on a baking sheet.

10. Preheat oven to 200 degrees.

11. In a small bowl, using a spoon, combine the reserved rib rub, the vinegar, and 3 tablespoons of water. Using a pastry brush, evenly coat the ribs all over with the vinegar mixture and then wrap them completely in foil.

12. Place the wrapped ribs in the oven and cook the ribs at 200 degrees for 1½ hours. At that time, check to see if they are fully cooked: stick a thin-bladed knife through the meat between the bones at the fattiest part of the rib. If it gives a lot of resistance, then continue cooking them for a little longer. You don't want them falling off the bone; they should have a nice chew but not be too tough. The best test is to cut a single rib off one of the slabs and taste it. When the ribs are ready, remove them from the oven, unwrap, and using a sharp knife, carve the slabs of ribs into individual ribs. Serve immediately.

★☆★

NOTE: This recipe was calibrated for the type of ribs I found at my local supermarket. Each rack was really half a rack; the butcher had cut it so that the entire piece had the good, meaty-fatty flap that is attached to a rack of ribs at its thickest end. The half-racks I bought had about six ribs per slab. You can use any rack, or portion of rack, you wish — but to keep the proportions of this recipe you should have about eighteen ribs, approximately seven to nine pounds altogether.

☆ Owensboro-Style ☆ Lamb Barbecue

A real curiosity in the world of barbecue is the barbecue that's made in and around Owensboro, Kentucky. The technique there is similar to other barbecue techniques — long and slow smoking over indirect heat — but what's being barbecued is completely different. For though they'll make some pork and beef and chicken in Owensboro for tourists, the real 'cue freak in Owensboro eats barbecued lamb. And not just lamb; we're talkin' mutton, old lamb, which has an even deeper, lambier flavor. If you've never tried it — and chances are you haven't if you haven't been to Owensboro — you must give the following recipe a try, which is a fine facsimile of what the Kentucky smoking pits yield. If you're looking for an interesting and authentic side dish, make the Brunswick Stew on page 311, which is very much like the burgoo that's typically served at an Owensboro barbecue pig-out . . . I mean sheep-out.

Yield: 5 to 6 servings

FOR RUBBING THE LAMB:
¼ cup coarsely ground pepper (freshly ground, if possible)
2 teaspoons garlic powder
2 teaspoons onion powder
½ teaspoon ground allspice

2 tightly packed tablespoons dark brown sugar
1 tablespoon kosher salt
3 tablespoons Worcestershire sauce
2 tablespoons vegetable oil
1 (4-pound) piece of bone-in lamb shoulder, cut into 2 pieces, each about 2½ inches thick, by your butcher (see Lamb note)

FOR THE OWENSBORO BLACK SAUCE:
½ cup Worcestershire sauce
½ cup white vinegar
2 tablespoons freshly squeezed lemon juice
1 teaspoon minced garlic
2 teaspoons freshly ground pepper
¾ teaspoon ground allspice
¼ cup tightly packed dark brown sugar

FOR ASSEMBLY:
Soft hamburger buns
Sour pickle slices
Sweet onion slices

1. To make the rub: In a small bowl, thoroughly combine all the rub ingredients except the lamb. Using your hands, smear the paste all over the lamb, coating each piece completely. Place the lamb in a glass or ceramic dish, cover tightly with plastic, and marinate in the refrigerator overnight. Let the meat come to room temperature before you proceed.

2. To make the sauce: Combine all the ingredients for the black sauce in a small saucepan and set aside.

3. Take two 30-inch lengths of aluminum foil and join them together with a few folds to form one large, double-width 30-inch sheet. Make sure the folds are tight, as these

sheets will later form the airtight braising pouch for the lamb and sauce. Place the sheet shiny side down on your work surface. Join together two more 30-inch sheets and place, shiny side down, on top of the first double sheet. Repeat the process so that you have two sets of two double-width foil sheets. Set them aside.

4. Make a hot outdoor fire (preferably with charcoal). Do not build it in the center of your unit; build it toward the edge. When the fire is ready, place the grate on the grill and close the cover, to preheat the grate for a few minutes. Uncover, and place hickory chips (see Hickory note) on the coals. They should begin to sizzle and smoke. Place the lamb pieces on the grate — not directly over the fire! — and cover the grill. Let the lamb smoke and sear for 15 minutes on the first side, checking it after 8 minutes to be sure it's not burning (a little blackening adds flavor — just don't let it scorch). If the fire

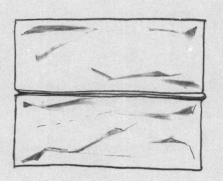

Owensboro-Style Lamb BBQ

Join 2 30-inch pieces of foil along the long edges to make a double-width 30-inch piece of foil. You will need 4 of these.

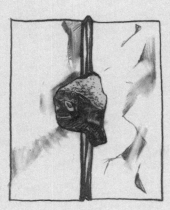

Place the grilled lamb on top of 2 stacked double-width pieces of foil. You will need to prepare another stack with lamb just like this one.

Ladle the black sauce over the lamb in each of the 2 "stork's pouches"

seems too hot, spray or sprinkle it with a bit of water. Turn the lamb over, return the cover, and smoke for another 10 minutes. The goal is to expose the meat to as much smoke as possible while cooking it as little as possible. Remove the meat to a dish and return to the kitchen.

5. Preheat the oven to 200 degrees, using an oven thermometer to help you maintain an even temperature.

6. Arrange one pair of the foil sheets on your work surface, with a short edge nearest you. Place one piece of the lamb in the middle of the foil and bring up the near and far edges and fold them together so as to form a large open-ended "stork's pouch" joined over the meat. Next, seal one of the two ends of the pouch, leaving one end still open. Repeat this with the second pair of foil sheets and lamb and reserve.

7. Place the saucepan with the black sauce over high heat and bring just to a boil, stirring occasionally to dissolve the sugar. Remove from the heat. Ladle the black sauce equally over the lamb in the open-ended pouches and seal the last side of each pouch. Each pouch should be very well sealed. Transfer the pouches to a baking sheet and cook in the oven for 5 to 6 hours or until the meat is extremely tender. Monitor the temperature occasionally and maintain, as best you can, a steady 200 degrees.

8. Remove the baking sheet from the oven and allow the chunks of lamb to rest in their pouches for 2 hours. Carefully open one end of each pouch and pour the black sauce into a bowl. Reserve. Using your fingers, pull the lamb meat from the bones and shred it into bite-size pieces. Place the meat in a glass or ceramic dish and toss with a few tablespoons of the reserved black sauce. Reheat it, uncovered, in a microwave, or covered in a 350-degree oven. Serve the lamb on the hamburger buns with pickle and onion slices. Pass a warm bowl of the remaining black sauce on the side.

LAMB NOTE: Whole lamb shoulder is commonly available from your butcher, but if it's not on display, it may be available in the walk-in cooler. Ask. If not, have the butcher order it. Usually a whole bone-in lamb shoulder weighs about seven or eight pounds and tapers a bit in shape: there's the fatter shoulder end and the skinnier rib end. For this recipe, you'll need to have the butcher first saw off a piece from the rib end (usually three to four pounds, which the butcher will keep), leaving you with a four-pound piece from the shoulder end. Next you want to have the butcher saw this four-pound piece crosswise into two two-and-one-half-inch-thick slabs, resembling fat steaks. This is what you'll take home.

HICKORY NOTE: You'll need about five cups of chips to make this recipe. Hickory would be my first choice, but other types of wood will also do well. Thirty minutes before putting the chips on the fire, soak them in water to cover. When ready to place them on the fire, simply drain the chips before using.

☆ Collard Greens ☆ with Ham Hocks

Say "greens" in the South and you're opening up a big subject: horticultural (which kinds of greens? turnip greens? mustard greens? kale? collard greens?) as well as cultural (because a mess of winter greens with "pot likker" wasn't proper fare for the upper class until it became mandatory fare during the widespread post–Civil War poverty). But most people in the South today eat their greens, and most people around the country, when they think "Southern," think first of collard greens (a variety of kale) cooked with ham hocks. *Collard* comes from the old English word *colewort* and was first in print here in the mid–eighteenth century. I love it as a side dish with something recognizably "Southern" — such as fried chicken or pork chops. And I love it when there's a delicious, smoky broth all around — though, in our twenty-first-century refinement, you're more likely to see that broth spelled "pot liquor" today. Make sure to choose collard greens at the market with snappable stems, not bendable ones. The finished dish keeps well for four to five days.

Yield: 6 side dish servings

2 smoked ham hocks (as meaty as you can find)
3 pounds collard greens
2 tablespoons vegetable oil (such as canola)
1 large Spanish onion, thinly sliced
3 garlic cloves, chopped
½ teaspoon red pepper flakes
2 tablespoons molasses
Cider vinegar
Hot sauce

1. Place ham hocks in a pot and cover with water (about 6 cups). Bring to a boil and simmer for about 1 hour, or until ham hocks begin to get tender. As it simmers, skim foam that accumulates on top and discard.
2. Remove large ribs and stems from collard greens. Wash well, then spin dry in a salad spinner. Roll several leaves at a time, lengthwise, into cigar shapes and cut crosswise into shreds about 1 inch wide.
3. Place a large saucepan over medium heat

and add vegetable oil and onion. Sauté until onion slices are a light gold, about 15 minutes. Add garlic and sauté for another minute. Add collards a few handfuls at a time and wilt before adding the next batch. When all are wilted, add red pepper flakes and molasses. Pour ham hock stock over all and add ham hock. Cover and simmer 1 hour more; collards should be tender. Remove ham hock, cool slightly, and shred meat. Discard skin and bone; add shredded meat back to the pot. Make sure the collards are hot.
4. Season with salt and pepper to taste (you may not need additional salt, as the ham hock is salty). Serve with vinegar and hot sauce at the table.

NOTE: There has been one more modern change in this dish. Lots of people today, even in the South — in the interest of "lightening up" — are making collard greens with smoked turkey wings. Well, I suppose there's a little less fat in it that way. But that sure seems less in the spirit of things than the original hog jowls (of which ham hocks themselves are a refinement).

☆ Hush Puppies ☆

There are lots of wild stories about the naming of this Southern classic — most of them involving small canines being told to stop making noise. The important thing is this: When they're deep-fried perfectly, golden hush puppies are absolutely irresistible, small balls of flavored cornmeal that would keep anyone quiet. Just as the mention of hamburgers across the country brings thoughts of French fries, so does the mention of fried fish in the South bring thoughts

☆☆☆☆☆☆☆☆☆☆☆☆☆☆☆☆☆☆☆☆☆☆☆☆☆☆☆☆☆☆☆☆☆☆☆☆☆☆☆

of accompanying hush puppies. They are now so popular — apparently they don't go back more than one hundred years or so — that they are being paired these days with all kinds of foods across the South. So why not in your kitchen? The following recipe will bring you frilly, phenomenally light ones.

Yield: About 4 dozen

Vegetable oil for deep-frying,
        plus 1 tablespoon vegetable oil
¾ cup yellow cornmeal
6 tablespoons all-purpose flour
1 teaspoon baking powder
½ teaspoon baking soda
1 teaspoon sugar
½ teaspoon salt
¼ teaspoon cayenne
1 large egg
½ cup buttermilk
¼ cup very finely chopped onion

1. In a medium pot or large saucepan, heat frying oil (at least 2 inches deep) to 365 degrees.
2. While oil is heating, make the batter. In a large bowl, combine cornmeal, flour, baking powder, baking soda, sugar, salt, and cayenne.
3. In another bowl, whisk together egg, buttermilk, and the 1 tablespoon of oil. Pour wet ingredients into dry and mix until just combined. Stir in onion.
4. Drop batter by heaping teaspoonfuls into the hot oil; fry about 8 hush puppies at a time. Cook about 3 minutes, turning occasionally, or until the hush puppies are golden brown all over. Drain on paper towels and repeat with remaining batter.

☆ Mustard Slaw ☆

Coleslaw is extremely popular in the South, as it is elsewhere in the United States — but one variation of this great dish that I think of as especially Southern is slaw doused with bright yellow mustard. This recipe came to me from a friend in Alabama, and it's the best thing imaginable with ribs or barbecue of any kind. If you thought French's mustard was just for kids or ballpark franks, open a jar, try this recipe, and open your mind. Believe me . . . Dijon mustard would never cut it here.

Yield: 12 to 16 servings

1 (4-pound) head of cabbage
1 large green bell pepper, seeded, stemmed,
        and very finely minced (about 1⅓ cups)
2 medium onions, very finely minced
        (about 2 cups)
2 medium carrots, peeled, shredded,
        and finely minced (about 1 cup)
4 teaspoons celery seeds
2 teaspoons salt (or more, to taste)
2 teaspoons freshly ground pepper (or more,
        to taste)
½ cup freshly squeezed lemon juice
24 ounces French's yellow mustard
1½ cups sugar
¾ cup cider vinegar
Hot sauce (try about ¼ cup of Frank's Red Hot)

1. Core the cabbage. Cut into broad, round slices about ⅓ inch thick, then chop crosswise so that you end up with a pile of chopped cabbage, each piece roughly the size of a corn niblet.
2. Place chopped cabbage in a large bowl and add the green pepper, onions, carrots, celery

seeds, salt, and pepper. Toss everything with the lemon juice and reserve.

3. Add the mustard to another bowl and blend in the sugar and the vinegar. Add the mustard mixture to the cabbage mixture and blend well. Add hot sauce to taste. Adjust seasoning. Serve immediately, or hold in the refrigerator for as long as a week.

☆ Real Southern Corn Bread ☆

Corn bread south of the Mason-Dixon is not what residents north of the Mason-Dixon always think it is. For one thing, there's a predilection for white cornmeal in the South, even though there's not much flavor difference between white and yellow; Northern corn bread is usually yellow. More important: despite the famous Southern taste for sugar, Southerners like their corn bread unsweetened! This, of course, is completely at odds with the sugary quality that so many Northern corn breads have. The following recipe will give you a technique-accurate, ingredient-accurate taste of the real thing. Southerners think of it as an essential side dish — either slathered with butter or crumbled into other side dishes, like beans.

Yield: 4 to 6 servings as a side dish

⅓ cup corn oil
½ cup all-purpose flour
1½ cups stone-ground white cornmeal
1 tablespoon plus 2 teaspoons baking powder
1½ teaspoons baking soda
1½ teaspoons salt
1 large egg, beaten
1 tablespoon mayonnaise
1½ cups buttermilk

1. Place the corn oil in a 9-inch cast-iron skillet and place the skillet in the oven on the center rack. Set oven to 415 degrees.

2. In a large mixing bowl, combine flour, cornmeal, baking powder, baking soda, and salt. Use a fork to mix all the dry ingredients together until they are completely combined.

3. Add the egg, mayonnaise, and buttermilk to the bowl of dry ingredients. Use a fork to mix the dry and wet ingredients. The mixture should be a little lumpy; do not overmix the batter.

4. Carefully remove the hot, oiled pan from the oven. Pour the batter into the hot oil and spread the batter evenly in the pan. Return the pan to the oven and bake the corn bread for 20 to 25 minutes or until it is completely cooked. Remove the corn bread from the oven. Check to see if the corn bread is done by inserting a cake tester or toothpick; if it comes out clean, the corn bread is done. Let it rest in the pan for 5 minutes.

5. Run a knife completely around the edge of the pan to make sure that the corn bread is not sticking to the side of the pan. Invert the cake of corn bread onto a plate. Serve immediately, while the corn bread is still warm.

☆ Big Fat Yeast Rolls ☆

These are wonderful soft rolls without a name — so I've called them exactly what they are. You will find them all over the South, particularly at buffet restaurants, where they're placed on your table. This is done, presumably, to fill you up — but I sure don't mind getting filled up with these puffy clouds. They are traditionally served with an individual crock of honey butter for each diner so that each person may dip his or her own puffy roll in fluffy sweet butter. If you prefer to go savory (as I do), you might want to brush the rolls with melted butter just before serving. However you serve them — and they are a great accompaniment to any homey dinner — make sure you serve them warm, and eat them quickly; they're not very good the next day.

Yield: About 12 rolls

2½ cups all-purpose flour, plus extra for dusting
2½ cups cake flour
½ cup sugar
⅓ cup warm water
1½ cups lukewarm whole milk
1 tablespoon plus 1½ teaspoons rapid-rise
    (instant) yeast
1 teaspoon salt
3 large egg yolks
⅓ cup vegetable shortening
1 teaspoon vanilla extract
Olive oil for greasing the bowl

1. Place the 2½ cups all-purpose flour, cake flour, sugar, water, milk, yeast, salt, egg yolks, shortening, and vanilla in the large bowl of a stand mixer fitted with a dough hook attachment.

2. Mix the ingredients on very low speed until they are well blended. Increase the mixer speed to medium-high and mix the dough for 3 minutes more to knead it.

3. Lightly grease a large bowl with the olive oil. Remove the ball of dough from the mixer and place in the oiled bowl. Cover and place in a warm area until the dough ball has doubled in size, about 1 hour.

4. Lightly flour a rolling pin and a countertop with extra all-purpose flour. Remove the risen dough to the counter. Using the rolling pin, flatten the dough to expel all the gases that have developed inside.

5. Using a knife, divide the large dough ball into smaller dough pieces that are each the approximate size of a baseball. You should have about 12 pieces. Place the pieces on the countertop so that they are not touching each other. Cover them with a damp cloth and let them rest for 10 minutes.

6. Sprinkle another part of the countertop with flour. Dust your hands with flour as well. Shape a dough piece into a ball rolling it in a circular motion on the countertop. Continue until all the rolls are shaped. Place the shaped rolls on a baking sheet, cover them with plastic wrap, and allow them to double in size.

7. Preheat oven to 425 degrees.

8. Place the baking sheet with rolls on the center oven rack and bake until golden brown, about 10 minutes. The internal temperature should be 200 degrees. Remove the pan from the oven and allow the rolls to cool a bit on a wire rack. Serve while still warm, with honey butter if desired (see following recipe).

✦ Honey Butter ✦

Yield: 6 to 8 servings

1 (12-ounce) container of salted whipped
    butter, at room temperature
Honey to taste (about 3 to 4 tablespoons)

Place the butter in a small mixing bowl. Using a small whisk slowly add the honey to the whipped butter 1 tablespoon at a time, to taste.

General Preserving Guidelines

One of the most old-fashioned American regional practices is preserving. It's particularly strong in the South, where a wide range of chutneys, pickled fruits and vegetables, and jams and jellies have been lovingly prepared for centuries.

I wouldn't say, however, that it's an endeavor that's gaining new devotees every year. In an age when young households across the country are avoiding the daily chore of preparing dinner — and picking up the phone instead to order Chinese takeout — is it likely that time will be taken for preserving? Unfortunately — as with many traditions — I think not.

But the ritual of preserving is even more challenged than other cooking traditions because many people perceive preserving as a difficult process, fraught with uncertainty. And this is exacerbated by health fears: many a would-be preserver simply buys Mrs. Fanning's Bread and Butter Pickles in the supermarket for fear that home preserving will end in error, botulism, and illness.

These fears are all unfounded. Preserving is easy, not to mention tremendously rewarding. And if you follow the simple guidelines below, you can rest assured that the contents of your jars will be as safe as they are delicious. If you've never had the thrill of executing this very special kitchen task — now's the time!

First of all, the equipment: for putting up eight jars of preserves, you'll need

✪ eight glass jars for preserving, eight ounces each
✪ two-piece caps for each jar: eight rubber-lined flat lids and eight bands that screw on over the lids
✪ a large, wide, heavy-bottomed pot that will hold the eight jars comfortably (I recommend a pot that's about twelve inches wide and eight inches deep, with a thirteen-quart capacity)
✪ a funnel for liquid preserves, a ladle for chunky preserves (or . . . there is a funnel available with an extra-wide opening at the bottom that can be used for all preserving purposes)
✪ a clean, damp cloth for wiping jars
✪ clean and dry kitchen towels
✪ a jar lifter (a hinged affair with handles that comes in handy when removing hot jars from the pot)

And now, the technique:

1. To begin, wash the jars and two-piece caps in hot, soapy water in the sink. Then rinse with hot water only and dry everything with clean towels.

2. To sterilize the jars, bring a large pot of water to a simmer and add the jars. They should be completely covered by the water. Cook at a slightly bubbling simmer for 10 minutes. After 10 minutes, turn off the flame, add the caps to the pot, and hold everything in the hot water as you start to work. As you're ready to use a jar and its lid and band, simply lift (with tongs) out of the pot. Let the rest of the jars and caps remain in the water until you get to them. *Note:* Jars and bands can be reused many times, if there are no cracks or chips in the jars, but you must use new lids each time you preserve something, as the lids tend to warp.

3. If you're making a preserve that has been cooked before going into the jar, bring that mixture to a boil. If you're making a preserve that is uncooked, bring it to room temperature.

4. Using a ladle or funnel, pour the item to be preserved directly into each jar. Work with one jar at a time, just out of the hot water. Fill hot jars to within ¼ inch of the top for smoother things like jams and jellies or to ½ inch of the top for

chunkier items like pickles and relish. Grip jars with a towel and tap them firmly, several times, on the counter to release any air bubbles. Run a clean chopstick or skewer around the inside of the jar, also to release bubbles. Wipe the rims with a clean, damp towel to remove any spilled liquid. Place the rubber lined lids on each jar, then seal tightly with the screw-on bands.

5. When all the jars have been filled, bring the pot of water used to sterilize the jars back to a simmer. Add the sealed jars to the water upside down, so that the part that needs to seal (the lids) gets the hottest. The water should cover the jars by about 2 inches. Bring to a rolling boil and boil for 10 minutes. Turn the heat off and let the jars cool in the water slightly (15 minutes or so — just so they are a bit easier to handle). Remove the jars with tongs and place them on kitchen towels (once again, upside down) to cool. All the jars may not be sealed when you remove them from the water, but they will generally seal as they cool, creating a vacuum. You can tell if they're sealed by pushing down on the center of the lid. If the center yields to your finger and makes a little popping sound, it's not sealed yet. If the center is firm and does not pop, the jar is sealed.

6. Refrigerate any jars that don't seal and use those first, within a few weeks. The sealed jars should be stored in a cool, dark place (such as a pantry). Refrigerate them only after opening. Wait at least two or three weeks before opening the sealed jars to allow flavors to penetrate. Sealed and preserved items will keep about a year (depending on the recipe). Note: You will definitely know if something has gone "bad" in the jar: the seal will be broken, or the contents will have an "off" smell or color. When in doubt, don't use it!

☆ Vidalia Onion Relish ☆

Relishes are very popular in the South; an array of them may be served at any one meal. Technically, they are chopped-up vegetables, preserved with something acidic, balanced with something sweet. Chowchow and piccalilli are two well-known ones (their names are used interchangeably today). I'm most fond of the following relish, made principally from onions. It's great to give it the real Southern touch by using the country's most famous onions, Vidalias, which originated in Georgia.

Yield: 5 half-pints, if preserved

2 tablespoons canola oil
14 cups chopped Vidalia or other sweet onion
    (about 5 pounds of onions)
2 tablespoons chopped garlic
¾ cup bourbon
1½ cups plum tomatoes, peeled, seeded,
    and chopped
1 cup golden raisins
½ cup cider vinegar
½ cup white sugar
½ cup dark brown sugar
1 teaspoon turmeric
1 teaspoon dry mustard
2 teaspoons mustard seeds
1 teaspoon red pepper flakes
½ teaspoon ground black pepper
1½ teaspoons salt

1. Heat oil in a large Dutch oven and add onions. Cook over low heat, stirring occasionally, until onions begin to caramelize; this will take about 45 minutes. Add garlic, then deglaze with bourbon, stirring well to scrape up browned bits from bottom of pan.
2. Add all the remaining ingredients and simmer until relish is very thick, about another 15 minutes. Cool and place in a nonreactive container. Use within a week or two. You can also preserve this relish for longer shelf life; refer to "General Preserving Guidelines" on page 324 for complete canning instructions.

To Preserve or Not to Preserve?

All items that are preservable can also be consumed without being preserved. In other words, you can choose to go through the preserving procedure with, say, Vidalia Onion Relish — or you can simply put the relish in a bowl, or a nonsterilized jar, in your refrigerator. Which is better? Usually there's a trade-off. The preserved item will last longer, of course — much longer. During that time, its flavors will meld and deepen. The nonpreserved item will never reach the same depth of flavor — but when consumed soon after it's made (as you must do), its flavors will be fresher tasting, and its texture will probably be a little crunchier and fresher. The recipes for preserves in this book indicate my preferences — whether I think the item is better preserved or not preserved.

✽ Pickled Okra ✽

I buy lots of pickled okra from the South at supermarkets, and I love it! But I love it even more when I make it myself at home. To do so, make sure to find fresh okra that feel tender on the sides, not firm and spiky. The following recipe keeps very well in jars, but it's also delicious should you choose not to go the whole sealing route. Simply pack the okra in glass jars (or any other nonreactive container, even bowls), pour the hot pickling liquid over them, cool them to room temperature, and refrigerate. The flavor of the vinegar solution will not penetrate as deeply, and the pickles must be eaten within a few weeks. But they'll be delicious!

NOTE: Refer to "General Preserving Guidelines" on page 324.

Yield: 6 pints

2½ pounds medium to small okra pods
    (4 inches or less), tender, not spiky
6 medium garlic cloves, thinly sliced (about
    3 tablespoons)
1½ teaspoons red pepper flakes (or more,
    to taste)
24 sprigs dill, washed and dried
2 tablespoons brown mustard seeds
2 tablespoons cumin seeds, slightly crushed
4 cups cider vinegar (5% acidity)
4 cups water
¼ cup kosher salt
3 tablespoons sugar

1. Wash and trim okra, removing stems but not caps.
2. Wash 6 pint-size canning jars with lids and bands in hot soapy water. Rinse well. Sterilize canning jars in boiling water for 10 minutes. Keep jars and caps in hot but not boiling

water until ready to use. Dry jars and arrange on several kitchen towels.

3. Into each jar, place evenly divided amounts of the garlic (I sliced clove per jar), red pepper flakes (¼ teaspoon per jar), dill (4 sprigs per jar), mustard seeds (I teaspoon per jar), and cumin seeds (I teaspoon per jar). Arrange okra in each jar, alternating tops and bottoms facing up, packing tightly.

4. Combine vinegar, water, salt, and sugar in a nonreactive saucepan and bring to a boil. Simmer until sugar and salt are completely dissolved. Ladle hot liquid into jars, covering okra completely and leaving a ½-inch headspace at the tops of the jars. Tap jars lightly on the counter until bubbles stop rising to the surface, thus eliminating air bubbles.

5. Top with lids, screw bands on tightly, and return jars to boiling water, upside down. Boil for I5 minutes to process. Remove pot from heat; let jars cool slightly before removing. Jars may not all be sealed at this point but should seal as they cool and a vacuum is created. Cool completely, upside down, on kitchen towels.

6. Refrigerate any jars that did not seal and use those first. Store sealed jars in a cool, dark place for at least 2 weeks before serving. Refrigerate after opening.

☆ Spiced Pickled Peaches ☆

It was the Spanish who first introduced peaches to the New World, and the Native Americans who first took to them — but it was the preservation-happy Southerners who started turning peaches into a pickled treat you could store all winter. I love the following recipe; the white vinegar preserves the peach taste, and these pickles end up tasting very peachy and very fresh. I also like one part of the technique: because whole peaches would leave gaps in the quart-size jars, some half peaches are used to fill in those gaps. Think of these fruits as a relish, a condiment, to go alongside meats and savory dishes at a festive Southern-style meal.

NOTE: Refer to "General Preserving Guidelines" on page 324.

Yield: 2 quarts

> 2 lemons
> 3 to 4 pounds firm but ripe medium-size freestone peaches (about 1 to 2 days away from eating)
> 3 cups white vinegar
> 3 cups sugar
> 1½ teaspoons whole allspice berries
> ¾ teaspoon whole cloves
> ½ teaspoon whole black peppercorns
> 2 cinnamon sticks

I. Fill a large bowl with ice water and juice the lemons into the water. To peel peaches, cut an X in the bottom of each peach and drop (a few at a time) into a pot of boiling water. Boil until skin begins to loosen (about 20 seconds, depending on ripeness), then immediately remove peaches and drop into ice water. Skin should peel off easily. Discard skin and keep peaches in ice water until ready to use. Leave the 6 nicest peaches whole; halve and pit the others.

2. Wash 2 quart-size canning jars with their lids and bands in hot soapy water. Rinse well. Sterilize canning jars in boiling water for I0 minutes. Keep jars and caps in hot but not boiling water until ready to use.

3. Combine the rest of the ingredients and simmer for 10 minutes to blend flavors. Add peaches and cook for 2 to 4 minutes (add whole peaches first, add halves 1 or 2 minutes later), until peaches are easily pierced with a toothpick.

4. Pack peaches in hot canning jars (alternating wholes and halves for tightest fit), adding one of the cinnamon sticks from the cooking liquid to each jar. Ladle liquid into each jar, tapping the jars on the counter to release any air bubbles. Leave a ½-inch headspace in each jar, then wipe the rims with a clean damp towel. Seal with lids and bands and return to boiling water, placing jars upside down. Once the water returns to a boil, cook for 10 minutes.

5. Remove pot from heat; let jars cool slightly before removing from pot. Jars may not all be sealed at this point but should seal as they cool and a vacuum is created. Cool completely, upside down, on kitchen towels.

6. Refrigerate any jars that did not seal and use those first. Store sealed jars in a cool, dark place for at least 3 weeks before serving. Refrigerate after opening.

☆ Watermelon Rind Pickle ☆

This spicy pickle is, admittedly, quite a bit of trouble to make. But I'm telling you, it's worth the five-day labor — particularly because these pickles are hard to find. A real old-fashioned flavor.

NOTE: Refer to "General Preserving Guidelines" on page 324.

Yield: About 5 half-pints

1 large watermelon (about 15 pounds)
1 gallon water
¼ cup kosher salt
6 cups sugar
3 cups cider vinegar
1 (2-inch) piece of fresh gingerroot, peeled and thinly sliced
2 lemons, thinly sliced
2 teaspoons whole cloves
1 teaspoon mustard seeds
1 teaspoon whole allspice berries
2 cinnamon sticks, broken

1. Remove watermelon flesh from rind and reserve flesh for other uses. Using a vegetable peeler, remove green rind until you have only the white rind remaining. Cut rind into 1-inch pieces. Note that it is important to use a *whole* watermelon for this recipe rather than purchasing cut sections; to ensure that all of your pickles have the same texture, the rind should all come from the same watermelon. In total, you should have about 8 to 9 cups of white rind.

2. In a large pot or bowl, combine the water and salt, stirring to dissolve salt. Add rind and refrigerate overnight.

3. Drain rind and rinse well. In a large pot, add rind and fresh water to cover. Simmer until almost tender, about 20 minutes. Drain.

4. Meanwhile, in another large pot, combine the sugar and vinegar; bring to a boil and simmer to dissolve sugar. Tie the ginger, lemon slices, cloves, mustard seeds, allspice, and cinnamon in cheesecloth and add to hot

syrup. Simmer 5 minutes to blend flavors. Remove pot from heat and add drained rind. Cool to room temperature and refrigerate overnight.

5. The next day, drain rind, reserving syrup. Place rind back in bowl, bring syrup to a full boil, then pour over rind. Cool, then refrigerate overnight. On the next day, repeat this procedure once again.

6. On the day after that, prepare your canning jars. Wash 5 half-pint canning jars with their lids and bands in hot soapy water. Rinse well. Sterilize canning jars in boiling water for 10 minutes. Keep jars and caps in hot but not boiling water until ready to use. Bring rind and syrup to a boil, simmer until rind is easily pierced with a knife, about 8 to 10 minutes. Discard spice bag.

7. Pack rind into hot jars. Ladle syrup into each jar, tapping the jars on the counter to release any air bubbles. Leave a ½-inch headspace in each jar, then wipe the rims with a clean damp towel. Seal with lids and bands and return to boiling water, placing jars upside down. Once the water returns to a boil, cook for 10 minutes.

8. Remove pot from heat; let jars cool slightly before removing from pot. Jars may not all be sealed at this point but should seal as they cool and a vacuum is created. Cool completely, upside down, on kitchen towels.

9. Refrigerate any jars that did not seal and use those first. Store sealed jars in a cool, dark place for at least 2 weeks before serving. Refrigerate after opening.

✹ Southern Banana Pudding ✹

For its amazingly high pleasure-to-work ratio, this dessert has most others beat. It is a totally unfashionable vestige of the old South, the kind of dessert you might find at those wonderful cafeterias: banana slices layered with a vanilla custard, vanilla wafers, and meringue. The way these ingredients fall together into a dreamy, creamy, utterly seductive whole is simply astonishing. Now, you could work a lot harder on this thing — by making your own custard, even making your own vanilla wafers. But the following recipe — given to me by a friend from the South whose family makes it all the time and calls it nanner pudding — beats any hard-work "gourmet" version I've ever tried. So break out the Nabisco wafers and the Jell-O — and remember that cooks should be judged only by how good their cooking tastes.

Yield: 6 servings

1 (12-ounce) box Nabisco Nilla wafers
2 boxes Jell-O vanilla pudding (not instant)
4 cups milk
Pinch of freshly grated nutmeg
*4 very ripe bananas (make sure they have
  brown specks on the skin)*
*½ cup plus ⅛ cup raw, unbeaten egg whites
  (from about half a dozen eggs),
  room temperature*
2 tablespoons sugar
½ teaspoon vanilla extract
¾ teaspoon fresh lemon juice

1. Line the bottom and the sides of an 8 by 8 by 2-inch baking dish (about 2-quart capacity) — oven safe and nonreactive — with a layer of the vanilla wafers. They should just cover the bottom of the dish.

2. Prepare the vanilla pudding according to the pudding directions on the package (you will need the 4 cups of milk to do this). While the pudding is still hot, stir in the nutmeg; set the pudding aside to cool for 5 minutes (but no longer).

3. Preheat oven to 500 degrees.

4. Peel 2 of the bananas and slice them into rounds that are ⅜ inch thick. Top the layer of cookies in the bottom of the dish with the banana slices. Top the banana slices with a second layer of vanilla wafers. Peel the remaining 2 bananas, slice them into rounds that are ⅜ inch thick, and distribute them evenly on top of the second cookie layer. For the final layer, top those bananas with another layer of cookies.

5. Pour the still-warm pudding over all. Shake the dish carefully, and tap it on the counter, to remove any air holes within the layers.

6. Make the meringue. Add the egg whites, sugar, vanilla extract, and lemon juice to the medium-size bowl of a standard kitchen mixer with the whisk attachment. Whisk the mixture on medium speed until it just holds a peak. It should be light and fluffy; do not overmix it.

7. Using a rubber spatula, top the entire surface of the pudding evenly with the meringue. Dip a spoon into the surface of the meringue and pull it out quickly to create little peaks all over the top of the pudding.

8. Place the pudding on the top rack of the oven. Bake just until it is nicely browned on top, about 3 minutes. (It can burn very easily, so watch it carefully.) Remove the pudding from the oven and let it cool down for 1 hour on the countertop. Then place in refrigerator and chill for at least 3 hours, but not more than 5 hours.

✱ Bourbon, Chocolate, ✱ and Walnut Pecan Pie

What's more southern, and what's more classic, than pecan pie? Now, some folks don't like to mess with a classic — and if that describes you when it comes to pecan pie, by all means skip this recipe. But my personal pecan pie life changed a few years ago when an editor from *Southern Living* magazine demonstrated, during an interview I was conducting on TV, a pecan pie variation made with bourbon, chocolate, and walnuts. It was not only the greatest pecan pie I'd ever tasted, it was also one of the greatest pies of any kind in my tasting experience. Here's my version of the recipe. If you make it, I'm sure that you, too, will merrily ignore that little purist voice inside your head — especially if you top your slice with whipped cream.

Yield: 1 pie (9½ inches),
6 to 8 servings

½ the dough from 1 recipe for Superflaky
  Piecrust (page 458)
½ cup roughly chopped pecans
½ cup roughly chopped walnuts
4 large eggs
½ cup light corn syrup
¼ cup honey
⅓ cup granulated sugar
⅓ cup light brown sugar, firmly packed
6 tablespoons (¾ stick) unsalted butter, melted
3 tablespoons bourbon

1 tablespoon all-purpose flour
1 tablespoon vanilla extract
Pinch of ground nutmeg
Pinch of ground cinnamon
½ pound high-quality bittersweet chocolate,
    broken into ½-inch-square chunks

1. Preheat oven to 350 degrees.

2. Roll out half of the dough from the Superflaky Piecrust recipe to ⅛-inch thickness, 1 inch larger than the pie plate. Drape the crust over the rolling pin and carefully fit into the pie plate. Trim the edges to ½ inch wider than the rim of the pie plate. Fold excess under the rim, on the outside of the plate, and crimp, pinching the dough between your thumb and forefinger at 1-inch intervals.

3. Toast the chopped pecans and chopped walnuts in a small sauté pan placed over medium-high heat, stirring often with a wooden spoon, until they are evenly toasted and crisp, about 4 minutes.

4. In a medium bowl whisk together the eggs, light corn syrup, honey, granulated sugar, light brown sugar, melted butter, bourbon, all-purpose flour, vanilla extract, nutmeg, and cinnamon and blend until the mixture is smooth. Stir in the toasted pecans, toasted walnuts, and chunks of chocolate. Pour the mixture into the piecrust.

5. Bake the pie on the center oven rack until it is set, about 40 to 50 minutes. A cake tester inserted into the center of the pie should come out clean (unless you hit a chocolatey spot). Serve slightly warm or at room temperature.

Florida

The cuisine of Florida has more wrinkles in it than you might expect. The northern part of the state is akin to the rest of the southern United States, gastronomically speaking — with a little Low Country and a little Creole influence thrown into the mix. But as you get down to south Florida, particularly around Miami, everything changes — for here, Miami's claim as the gateway to Latin America really rings true, particularly if there's a kitchen just beyond the gate. The Cuban influence is especially strong, but the rest of the Caribbean also has powerful impact here. A lot of this food is available in simple, everyday restaurants and in people's homes — but happily, Miami also boasts one of the most focused regional-cuisine upscale-restaurant movements in the country, with a cadre of chefs forging something interesting out of Latino and south Florida motifs.

And everywhere across the peninsula, no matter what the style of cooking, is great seafood — from either the Gulf side or the Atlantic side. Some food historians say that the U.S. shrimping industry was developed at Fernandina Beach, in northeast Florida. Stone crabs are a Florida phenomenon. Conch, used widely in chowders and fritters, is found in Florida's coral reefs, particularly in the Florida Keys. And fin fish, such as pompano and mahimahi, are delicious from Florida's waters.

☆ Stone Crab Claws ☆ with Florida Mayonnaise

Stone crabs are a great Florida treat in the winter-time — and now, because of modern shipping, a great treat around the country during the stone crab season (October 15 to May 15). The only part of the stone crab that's eaten is the black-tipped large claw; this works out extremely well, since the rest of the still-living crab is tossed back into the water by the crabbers, and within eighteen months it grows a new claw. Stone crab is easy to eat; the very hard shell gets slightly cracked (best to do just before eating), and the sweet meat is very accessible in large lumps. The larger the claw, the deeper the satisfaction; "jumbos," which weigh more than six ounces each, are the most sought after. At the wildly popular Joe's Stone Crab, a mustard mayo is served with the crab that tastes as much of Worcestershire sauce as it does of mayo. The full-flavored recipe below adds a little curry powder to the blend, a surprisingly congruent flavor comple-ment to Worcestershire.

Yield: 4 first-course servings

½ cup mayonnaise
1 tablespoon Dijon mustard
1 teaspoon Worcestershire sauce
½ teaspoon ketchup
½ teaspoon sugar
¼ teaspoon curry powder
12 cooked, uncracked jumbo stone crab claws
(see Note)

I. Blend together the mayonnaise, mustard, Worcestershire sauce, ketchup, sugar, and curry powder. Season to taste with salt and pepper (though the sauce will probably need none). Reserve.

2. Remove claws from refrigerator about 15 minutes before serving them. Place them, one by one, inside a folded dish towel. One by one, crack them lightly with a mallet to just split the shells of each joint. Serve claws cracked, 3 to a diner, with Florida mayon-naise on the side.

NOTE: Cooked Florida stone crab claws are now avail-able in many seafood markets around the country. If, however, they're not available where you live, you can always order them in season from

Billy's Stone Crab Restaurant
400 North Ocean Drive
Hollywood, FL 33019
954-923-2300
www.stone-crabs.com

☆ The Cubano ☆ (The Cuban Sandwich)

There is some confusion as to where the original "Cubano" was made; some say it was in Havana, but others make a strong case for Ybor City, a Cuban neighborhood in the Tampa Bay metropolitan area in Florida. No matter where it started, two things are clear: (1) Miami, today, is the epicenter of Cubano making (with amazing places like the Latin American Cafeteria), and (2) no matter where you make a Cu-bano, if you make it right, it is a deliriously delicious creation. It belongs in the same family, curiously, as Italian panini — those wonderful sandwiches that also get squooshed on a hot sandwich press (which makes the outside crisp and the inside warm). But the seemingly arbitrary fillings inside the Cubano are quite different from anything in Italy — and add up to one of those American creations, like Buffalo chicken wings, and Chicago hot dogs, that take on their own irrefutable logic once you taste them.

☆☆☆

Yield: 1 sandwich

1 tablespoon mayonnaise
1 tablespoon prepared yellow mustard
1 Cuban Sandwich Loaf (recipe follows)
    or any French or Italian hero bread
    that's about 8 inches long (see Note)
4 thin slices Swiss cheese
4 thin slices boiled ham (preferably a ham
    known as bolo, but any good-quality
    boiled ham will do)
2 slices dill pickle (lengthwise slices)
4 ounces thinly sliced roast pork
    (page 334)
1½ tablespoons softened butter

1. In a small bowl, combine mayonnaise and mustard. Set aside.

2. Cut the ends from the bread, then split lengthwise into two halves. Layer fillings on one half as follows: half the mayonnaise/mustard, 2 slices of the cheese, the ham, pickles, and roast pork, and the remaining 2 slices of cheese; spread the remaining mayonnaise/mustard on the other half of the bread. Close the sandwich.

3. Heat a large cast-iron skillet over medium heat. Brush outside of sandwich on both sides with butter. Place sandwich flat side down in skillet. Using another heavy skillet, press straight down on the sandwich to flatten it. Place a folded kitchen towel in the top skillet while pressing if it gets too hot. Press until toasted, about 2 minutes. Flip and press the other side to toast, about another 2 minutes. Remove. Cut at the center but on an angle. Serve immediately.

NOTE: The most important thing in getting the Cuban sandwich right is the kind of bread you choose. If you're willing to bake your own bread, the recipe on this page comes damned close to what you'll find in Florida. If you'd rather buy the bread, make sure to avoid "serious" hero breads that are dense and structured. The classic Cuban sandwich bread is kind of fluffy inside, with a little crackle in the thin crust. That means that mass-market-style "Italian" breads at the supermarket will make a better Cuban sandwich than artisanal, authentically European-style loaves will. For whichever bread you choose: if it's not fresh baked, it is best to recrisp it in a 350-degree oven for two to three minutes before making the sandwiches.

☆ Cuban Sandwich Loaf ☆

The great Cubano sandwich of southern Florida (page 332) has the same problem as the Philly cheesesteak: you need a special kind of loaf to make the sandwich perfect. Intriguingly, the Cubano loaf is very much like the Philadelphia cheesesteak loaf, except that its interior is a little bit denser.

Yield: About 8 rolls

5¾ cups bread flour, plus extra
    for handling dough
1 cup minus 1 tablespoon water
1 tablespoon rapid-rise (instant) yeast
2 tablespoons sugar
1 tablespoon kosher salt
2 tablespoons olive oil, plus extra for greasing
    bowl and pans
Cornmeal for dusting
Handful of ice cubes

1. Place the 5¾ cups flour, the water, yeast, sugar, salt, and the 2 tablespoons of olive oil in the large bowl of a standard mixer fitted with a dough hook attachment.

Pork Roast for the Cubano

You have a wide choice of porcine possibilities for your Cuban sandwich. Often it is made with very innocuous-looking roast pork, almost something like a deli roll, with white meat and no evident skin or crackle on the outside. Some delis sell meat like this; deli-counter "fresh ham" would be perfect. Sometimes things go wildly in the other direction: a hunk of meat from a pork roast is used — skin, crust, and all. If you like this idea, you can use leftovers from the Cuban-Style Roast Pork Shoulder on page 147. The middle ground would be a nice home-roasted pork loin — cooked either expressly for this sandwich or cooked for dinner one night, its leftovers ennobling Cubanos the next day. The brined pork loin used for a great Philadelphia sandwich would be ideal for this recipe, minus the Philly/Italian spin. So here's an altered version of that recipe that would be excellent for dinner as is and wonderful in cold slices for your Cuban sandwich.

3 tablespoons plus 1 teaspoon kosher salt
¼ cup sugar
12 large garlic cloves
3 bay leaves
2 tablespoons plus ½ teaspoon cracked black pepper
2 teaspoons dried oregano

1 (5-pound) boneless pork loin, with fat
3 tablespoons olive oil
1 cup onion, finely chopped
6 parsley stems with leaves, washed
2 cups water

1. Place a quart of cold water in a medium-size, nonreactive mixing bowl. Add the 3 tablespoons of salt, the sugar, 6 of the garlic cloves, smashed, the bay leaves, 2 tablespoons of the black pepper, and 1 teaspoon of the oregano. Using a whisk, stir the mixture until the salt and sugar are dissolved. Add the pork loin, cover bowl with plastic wrap, and refrigerate overnight.

2. Preheat oven to 475 degrees. Remove the pork loin from the brine mixture, dry it, and place it on a 9 by 13 by 2-inch baking pan. Finely mince the remaining 6 cloves of garlic and rub them onto the roast with your hands, along with the ½ teaspoon of black pepper, the remaining 1 teaspoon of oregano, the 1 teaspoon of salt, and the olive oil.

3. Roast the pork loin for 10 minutes at 475 degrees. Remove pan from oven and add the onion, parsley stems, and water. Lower the heat to 375 degrees and roast the pork until the internal temperature of the roast is 140 degrees (about 40 minutes more). If eating hot, let the roast rest for 10 minutes before slicing. If using for Cuban sandwiches (page 332), refrigerate the roast until cold, then slice it thinly.

2. Mix the ingredients on very low speed until they are well combined. Increase the mixer speed to medium-high and mix the dough until thoroughly kneaded, about 8 minutes.

3. Lightly grease a large bowl with olive oil. Remove the ball of dough from mixer bowl to the oiled bowl. Cover the bowl and place it in a warm spot until the dough ball has doubled in size, about 1 hour.

4. Lightly flour a rolling pin and a countertop with extra flour. Remove the risen dough to the counter. Using the rolling pin, flatten the dough to expel all the gases that have developed inside.

5. Using a knife, divide the large dough ball into smaller dough pieces so that each is a little larger than a baseball. You should have about 8 pieces. Place the pieces on the countertop so that they are not touching each other. Cover them with a damp cloth and let them rest for 15 minutes.

6. Sprinkle another part of the countertop with flour and lightly flour your hands. Roll your palms over the pieces of dough and move them in a back-and-forth motion to shape the dough pieces into 6-inch-long cylinders. Continue until all the rolls are shaped. Place the shaped rolls on a cornmeal-dusted baking sheet, about 2 inches apart. Cover the rolls with plastic wrap and let them sit until doubled in size, about 1½ hours.

7. Place a baking stone on the center oven rack. Place an ovenproof baking pan on the bottom of the oven. Preheat oven to 425 degrees.

8. Dust a pizza peel with cornmeal. Place 4 of the rolls on the pizza peel at a time. Use a razor blade or a serrated knife to score the top of each loaf lengthwise in a straight line down the center, cutting them approximately ½ inch deep. Spray the loaves with water using a spray bottle. Carefully toss some of the ice cubes into the ovenproof pan in the bottom of the oven. Use the peel to slide the loaves onto the baking stone and immediately close the oven door. Repeat these steps again until all of the rolls are in the oven.

9. Bake the rolls for 15 minutes, or until they are light golden brown (they should have an internal temperature of about 200 degrees).

Using the pizza peel, remove the loaves from the oven and allow to cool completely before serving.

☆ Key Lime Pie ☆

There was a time when the Florida Keys were fairly isolated from the mainland and did not have access to a regular supply of fresh milk and cream — tough on bakers! What they did have was an abundance of supertart key limes, good supplies of condensed milk in cans, and plenty of eggs. Thus was the Key Lime Pie born. Today it sparks scads of controversies and variants. I stick to the "traditional" in one way only: I definitely prefer an uncooked filling made with key limes. The crust you see most often these days is made with graham crackers, but I like a real piecrust underneath my citrus. And the traditional topping — based on the former lack of cream in the Keys — is a meringue. However, now that cream is available to us all — even the residents of Key West — it is much easier, and I think more delicious, to top the lime filling with a whipped cream topping. Here's one great serving tip, advocated by Rose Levy Beranbaum in *The Pie and Pastry Bible:* the pie is best when served partially frozen.

Yield: 1 pie (9½ inches), 6 to 8 servings

Basic Piecrust (recipe follows)
Yolks of 6 large eggs
2 cups condensed milk
1 cup lime juice, preferably key lime juice
      (available at some upscale produce stores,
      see Note)
3 teaspoons finely grated lime zest,
      preferably from key limes
1 egg white, beaten to soft peaks
1 cup whipping cream

1. Preheat oven to 350 degrees.

2. Choose a 9½-inch deep-dish pie plate. Roll out piecrust dough to ⅛-inch thickness, making sure its diameter is 3 inches larger than the diameter of the pie plate. (You will probably need to cut away some dough and save for another use.) Drape the crust over the rolling pin and carefully fit it into the pie plate. Trim the edges to ½ inch wider than the rim of the pie plate. Fold excess under and crimp, pinching the dough between your thumb and forefinger at 1-inch intervals.

3. Cover base of piecrust with tinfoil and fill the pan with either beans or rice. Bake the crust until it begins to color, about 20 minutes. Remove from oven and remove the beans or rice and tinfoil. (The beans or rice may be used again as a weight.)

4. Return crust to the oven and cook until firm and golden brown, about 10 minutes. Cool on a rack.

5. In a bowl, lightly whisk egg yolks, then whisk in condensed milk, lime juice, and zest. Fold in beaten egg white.

6. Pour the filling into the baked and cooled pie shell. Use a spatula to smooth the top, then cover with plastic wrap and let stand in the refrigerator overnight.

7. When getting ready to serve, place pie in the freezer for an hour or so. Just before serving, whip the cream until soft peaks form, and spread whipped cream onto the lime filling. Serve immediately.

NOTE: If you're using key limes, it will take about twenty-four (they're small) to yield one cup of key lime juice.

✺ Basic Piecrust ✺

Here's an easy, wonderful crust that will work for all kinds of pies. It is a sturdy crust — necessary for runny fillings but dandy as well for thick or chunky fillings.

Yield: Enough for 3 (9-inch) piecrusts
or 2 (9½-inch) deep-dish piecrusts

3 cups all-purpose flour
1 teaspoon salt
½ cup unsalted butter, cut into
*   1-inch cubes*
2 tablespoons vegetable shortening,
*   chilled*
2 tablespoons ice water, plus extra
*   as needed*

1. Pour flour and salt into the bowl of a food processor. Pulse a couple of times to mix thoroughly. While the motor runs, drop the butter and the shortening down the feed tube. Continue processing until the fat is cut in and the mixture resembles fine bread crumbs.

2. Slowly pour chilled water down the feed tube, beginning with the 2 tablespoons and then adding water drop by drop until the mixture in the processor forms a ball. Stop the food processor immediately.

3. If making 9-inch piecrusts, divide the dough into 3 pieces; if making the large crusts, divide it into 2 pieces. Flatten each piece into a disk, cover with plastic wrap, and store in the refrigerator.

NOTE: If using the same day, let the dough rest for at least an hour before rolling out. The dough can be kept in the refrigerator for up to four days and in the freezer for up to six weeks.

Cajun/Creole

Louisiana cooking is indisputably the jewel in the crown of American regional cuisine. But it's not just the hundreds of great local specialties and recipes that make it so or the fact that local residents frequently consume them. It's not the profusion of great restaurants, and great home cooks, across the state that make it so. It is the passion that makes it so — the way that food, particularly in New Orleans and Cajun country, works its way into everyone's spirit, has become a part of the fabric of everyday life, and is as likely to be a topic of conversation as parish politics. There is obsession like this in France, in Italy, in Spain — but Louisiana, clearly, has more of it than any other place in the United States.

One likely reason behind this fact is the truly amazing collision of cultures that occurred in the Crescent City: New Orleans. American food history is always a story of fused cuisines — but here the cuisines are particularly multifarious and distinct. And the early arrival of the French, in the early 1700s, weaving it all together, didn't hurt either. They married their fastidiousness and passion to ideas from the native Choctaw Indians (such as the use of bark from the sassafras tree as thickener); to ingredients that African slaves brought (such as okra); to new notions (such as love of rice) from the Spanish, who took over the region in 1762; to the funky style of those new French arrivals, the Cajuns, who came down from French Canada and fell in love with the crawfish and shrimp of the bayous; to the influx of spicy ideas from the Caribbean, sent New Orleans way by slave revolts in French-speaking Haiti and Martinique.

Many streams of cuisine developed from this bubbling cauldron of cooking possibilities. But here's a handy way to simplify one's thinking about it all: think Creole and Cajun.

Creole, of course, is a troubled word, one that has meant different things to different people at different times. But the original meaning helps us make some gastronomic sense. The French were the "society" of early New Orleans. When the Spanish took over in the late eighteenth century, they began to marry with members of French families — and thereby gained high social standing. The name Creole comes from a Spanish word meaning "to create" — and the children of those French-Spanish marriages helped "create" a new element in society, the Creoles.

Today when people speak of Creole cuisine in Louisiana, they are referring to a stylish, elegant, high-end kind of restaurant food that is as likely to include French sauces as highly seasoned Spanish elements. Creole cuisine is alive and well at fancy restaurants in New Orleans such as Arnaud's, Antoine's, and Galatoire's. The recipe for Oysters Bienville in this section is a perfect example of Creole food.

The rougher side of the Louisiana experience — whether or not the dish really has anything to do with the descendants of the French Canadian "Acadians" who moved into the bayous — is usually described as Cajun. A big, messy shrimp boil is definitely not Creole, nor is a heap of fried oysters on a sandwich with a spicy dressing. If you think of Creole as city food and Cajun as country food, a complicated situation becomes a little easier to understand.

Of course, one more element also helps to make New Orleans and Louisiana an eater's paradise: the fabulous presence of modern chefs who draw on all the Louisiana history and transmogrify it into an exciting new cuisine — a cuisine that is one of the front-runners in the quest for authentic, modern, evolved, truly regional American cuisine.

✳ Mother's Debris ✳ and Roast Beef Hero

New Orleans is such a colorful place; everywhere you turn there's another wacky story, tradition, or legend, connected to food. Most cities have bustling lunch places; New Orleans has Mother's, located for decades on the edge of the French Quarter. Mother's has long lines, a wide range of well-cooked Cajun/Creole specialties . . . and debris. Don't call it de-BREE, as you were taught in school. In N'Awlins, boy, it's DEB-bree. What is it? The burned bits that fall off the roast beef they cook up at Mother's for their famous roast beef sandwiches. The sandwich is basically room temp — but a little warm debris topping turns it into Mother's Ferdi Special, something wonderful, a way of adding to a roast beef sandwich the crispy roast beef crust that usually gets left off. The following recipe requires you to cook up some debris, because there's no other way to get it. If you don't feel like cooking up your own debris — well,

even without it this is as tasty a version of a roast beef hero as you're likely to find.

Yield: 2 servings

1 (8-inch) loaf or section of good, crusty hero bread (ideally 3½ inches across)
½ tablespoon Creole mustard (see Mustard note)
3 heaping tablespoons mayonnaise
6 ounces thinly sliced rare roast beef, room temperature
½ cup debris (see Debris note)
A few tablespoons of stock (beef or chicken)
Tabasco sauce
¼ cup thinly sliced sour dill pickles
½ cup finely shredded raw cabbage
½ tablespoon prepared yellow mustard

1. Cut the hero in half. On the bottom half, spread the Creole mustard and 1 heaping tablespoon of the mayonnaise evenly. Season the roast beef slices with salt and pepper and place them on the bread. Top with a second heaping tablespoon of mayonnaise, spread evenly.

2. Warm the debris in a small saucepan briefly with enough stock just to moisten it. Top the roast beef with the warm debris. Sprinkle the debris with Tabasco to taste. Top with a layer of pickles, then a layer of cabbage.

3. Evenly spread the top half of the hero with the mustard and the remaining heaping tablespoon of mayonnaise. Close the sandwich, cut in half, and serve immediately.

MUSTARD NOTE: Creole mustard is a brown mustard with seeds in it and a mildly vinegary flavor. If you can't find it, substitute a similar mustard or any brown mustard you can find.

DEBRIS NOTE: Debris can be acquired only by cooking your own beef at home. Mother's says the "debris" is from roast beef — the charred outer bits that fall off as you slice cooked beef. So if you're making a roast beef — save the debris! I'll tell you a secret though. To me, the debris at Mother's actually tastes more like the browned bits that fall off pot roast or brisket. So . . . when I prepared this recipe, I used the "debris" from the Texas-Style Barbecued Brisket on page 362 — and it was everything you could want, in New Orleans, Texas, or Kalamazoo.

☆ Muffaletta Sandwich ☆

The Central Grocery in New Orleans, located right near the bustling French Market, invented this thick, Italian-theme sandwich in 1906. Today, *le tout* Nouvelle Orleans eats it and makes it — pronouncing it, oddly enough, "muff-uh-LAH-tuh." What gives the sandwich its distinctiveness, other than the round bread on which it's made, is a heavy dose of an oily, garlicky olive salad. The muffaletta tastes exactly as if a New Orleans chef wanted to add a lagniappe to a basic Italian hero — and succeeded wildly.

Yield: 2 large sandwiches,
enough for 4 lunch servings

⅔ cup coarsely chopped pitted green olives
⅔ cup coarsely chopped pitted black olives
    (preferably kalamata)
½ cup coarsely chopped pimiento
¼ cup finely chopped celery
¼ cup finely chopped carrot
¼ cup finely chopped scallion
6 tablespoons finely chopped garlic
2 tablespoons capers
½ cup finely chopped fresh parsley leaves
2 teaspoons finely chopped fresh oregano
3 tablespoons lemon juice
1¼ cups extra-virgin olive oil
6 tablespoons red wine vinegar
2 tablespoons balsamic vinegar
¼ teaspoon freshly ground pepper
2 loaves of fresh-baked Muffaletta Loaf
    (page 340; see Note for alternatives)
1 pound thinly sliced Italian salami
1 pound thinly sliced provolone cheese
1 pound thinly sliced boiled ham

I. In a medium-size nonreactive mixing bowl, thoroughly combine the green olives, black olives, pimiento, celery, carrot, scallion, 3 tablespoons of the garlic, the capers, parsley, oregano, lemon juice, olive oil, red wine vinegar, balsamic vinegar, and pepper. Cover mixture and refrigerate for 12 to 24 hours before using. (It will keep under refrigeration for several days.) Bring to room temperature before using. When ready to use, stir very well with a spoon.

2. Using a sharp serrated knife, evenly slice the muffaletta loaves in half horizontally. In a small bowl, combine the remaining 3 tablespoons of garlic with 2 tablespoons of juice from the olive mixture. Using a spoon, spread each of the interior sides of the bread with one-fourth of the garlic–olive juice mixture. On the bottom part of each sandwich, using a spoon, evenly spread about ⅔ cup of the well-stirred olive mixture. Then evenly spread out a layer of half the sliced salami, then half the sliced cheese, and then half the sliced ham on each of the sandwiches. Top the final layer on each sandwich with about ⅔ cup of the well-stirred olive mixture. Place the tops on the sandwiches.

3. Wrap the sandwiches in plastic wrap and refrigerate them for at least 1 hour, or up to 6 hours before serving. Place a weight (such as a liquid-filled teakettle or a heavy skillet) on top of the sandwiches while refrigerating them.

4. Remove the sandwiches from the refrigerator. Warm, if desired. Slice each sandwich into 4 wedges and serve immediately.

NOTE: The classic muffaletta loaf is completely round, like a huge hamburger bun — but it has the texture of Italian bread, including a crunchy crust. It is seven to eight inches in diameter, and about one and one-half inches high. Your options: make the Muffaletta Loaf below (relatively easy) or try to buy a loaf like it (extremely hard outside New Orleans) — or make the sandwich on any good loaf of Italian bread, round or not. The result may not look like the Central Grocery's, but it'll taste just as good.

☆ Muffaletta Loaf ☆

One of the factors that make the famous muffaletta sandwich of New Orleans taste so good is the large, round, Italian-type loaf of bread on which it's made. It is just about impossible to find this loaf outside New Orleans. So here's a recipe for an authentic version of the loaf that will really make an event of the Muffaletta Sandwich recipe on page 339.

Yield: 2 (8-inch) round loaves

4¾ cups all-purpose flour, plus extra
    for handling dough and dusting pans
1½ cups plus 1 tablespoon water
1 tablespoon plus 1½ teaspoons kosher salt
1 tablespoon sugar
2 tablespoons olive oil, plus extra for greasing
    bowls and pans
2 teaspoons rapid-rise (instant) yeast
4 tablespoons sesame seeds
Handful of ice cubes

1. Place the 4¾ cups flour, water, salt, sugar, the 2 tablespoons olive oil, and the yeast in the large bowl of a standard mixer fitted with the dough hook attachment.

2. Mix the ingredients on a very slow speed until all the ingredients are just blended together. Increase the mixer speed to medium-high and continue to mix the dough for 8 minutes more. It should be a little sticky.

3. Using extra olive oil, lightly oil a large bowl. Remove the dough from the mixer bowl and place in oiled bowl. Cover and place in a warm area until the dough ball has doubled in size, about 1½ hours.

4. Lightly flour your hands and a countertop. Remove the risen dough from the bowl to the counter. Using your hands, flatten the dough to expel all the gases that have developed inside. Using a knife, divide the dough into 2 equal pieces. Grab the opposite edges of 1 dough piece and pull them beneath the center of the dough so that the edges meet underneath. Repeat with the second pair of opposite edges so that all 4 edges meet beneath the center, forming a rough ball. Repeat with second dough piece.

5. Take 1 of the dough pieces and, keeping both hands light and firm on the ball at all times, roll the ball in a circular motion on the countertop, away from you and back and then around again. Think of the countertop

as a third hand in this process, relying on its pressure to push the ball of bread up as you move it around. The three points of pressure created by your hands and the counter will add to the surface tension of the bread, creating a firm, plump ball. As you move the ball, pressure from the countertop will also seal the bottom edges of the dough. Stop rolling when the ball feels tight and smooth. Repeat with second dough piece. Cover and let rest 15 minutes.

6. Lightly oil two 8-inch round cake pans and dust thoroughly with a thin layer of flour. Reserve the pans.

7. Using your hands, flatten the rounds of dough. Lightly flour a rolling pin and roll each flattened dough into a disk, 8 inches in diameter. Place each dough disk in a prepared pan. With a fork, randomly dock (punch holes in) each loaf about 8 to 10 times. Cover loaves with a damp cloth and place into a warm area until they have doubled in size, about 1 to 1½ hours.

8. Arrange a single rack in the center of the oven and place an ovenproof baking pan on the bottom of the oven. Preheat oven to 450 degrees.

9. Just before loading the bread into the oven, spray the loaves with water using a spray bottle and dust the loaves with the sesame seeds. Carefully toss a handful of ice cubes into the ovenproof pan in the bottom of the oven. Place the loaves in the oven and immediately close the oven door.

10. Bake the bread until golden, about 22 to 25 minutes. The internal temperature should be 200 degrees. Remove the bread from the oven and allow it to cool completely in the pans on a wire rack before serving.

✴ Oysters Rockefeller ✴

Most oyster lovers prefer their beloved bivalves raw, uncooked, ripped out of nature. But most oyster lovers who have been to New Orleans agree: those chefs can cook oysters for us anytime! I think the reason is a combination of the oysters they use — rich Gulf ones, which actually taste better to me when they're cooked — and that amazing Creole/Cajun creativity. This dish, the most famous of the cooked Louisiana oyster dishes, was created at the famous Creole restaurant Antoine's, around 1900. Many chefs around the country today make it with spinach. Surprisingly, however, the original recipe — and this one — contains no spinach. Why are the oysters named after Rockefeller? The traditional explanation is that they're "rich" — but I think the color of money has a lot to do with it too.

Yield: 4 first-course servings

3 pounds rock salt or other coarse salt
24 oysters in the shell
½ pound (2 sticks) unsalted butter
1 medium celery stalk, finely chopped
(about ⅓ cup)
½ small fennel bulb, finely chopped
(about ⅓ cup)
1 bunch scallions, ends trimmed, chopped
(about ⅓ cup)
1 small garlic clove, minced
1 small bunch parsley, tough stems removed
(about 2 cups loosely packed), coarsely
chopped
1 bunch watercress, tough stems removed
(about 2 cups loosely packed)

Leaves of 3 or 4 sprigs of thyme
Pinch of kosher salt
2 tablespoons Louisiana hot sauce
2 tablespoons Pernod
½ cup unseasoned bread crumbs
Lemon wedges for garnish

1. Divide half the rock salt between four dinner plates, each large enough to hold 6 oysters. Distribute the salt evenly on each plate. This is simply to provide an attractive base on which the curved oyster shells can evenly rest. Test with an oyster, placing the more deeply curved shell side down. If you need more salt to support the shells, add it. Set the plates aside. Now divide the remaining salt between two roasting pans, each large enough to hold a dozen oysters in one layer. Distribute the salt as you did for the plates (if you run out of salt, you can also use dried beans or lightly crumpled foil in the pans).

2. Open the top, flat side of each oyster (the deeply curved shell should be on the bottom). Retain in each shell as much of the oyster liquor as possible. Discard the top shell and free each oyster from its muscle. Transfer each oyster in its bottom shell to the salt-lined roasting pans.

3. Arrange the oven racks to accommodate both roasting pans and preheat the oven to 400 degrees.

4. In a large frying pan, melt the butter over medium heat. When the foam begins to subside, add the celery, fennel, scallions, garlic, parsley, watercress, thyme, and a large pinch of kosher salt. Cook the mixture for 2 minutes, stirring to incorporate the ingredients.

Remove the pan from the heat and transfer the mixture to a blender. Add the hot sauce, Pernod, a few grindings of pepper, and the bread crumbs. Puree the mixture for 2 minutes, or until it is uniformly green in color and the texture of a thick milkshake. Transfer the mixture to a small bowl.

5. Place 2 teaspoons of the mixture on top of each oyster if they are medium-size (a bit more if they are larger, a bit less if they are smaller). The mixture should almost, but not quite, cover the meat of the oyster. Place the roasting pans with the oysters in the oven and cook until there is a lively bubbling at the edges of the oysters, about 20 minutes. If your oven has hot spots, rotate the pans 180 degrees after 10 minutes. (And if your two roasting pans are on different levels, after 10 minutes carefully reverse the bottom and top pans to ensure even cooking.) When the oysters are done, allow them to cool for 2 minutes, then, wearing rubber gloves or with the help of a large spoon, carefully transfer 6 oysters to each of the salt-lined dinner plates. Garnish each plate with a lemon wedge and serve immediately.

NOTE: I love this and the following New Orleans oyster dishes cooked in the oven; the flavors become remarkably integrated. You do, however, sacrifice the integrity of the oyster. For a fresher, more lively oyster taste, either dish can also be broiled. To do so, follow the steps in both recipes, but preheat the broiler rather than the oven. Place one pan under the broiler (most home broilers will not accommodate more than one roasting pan at a time) until the oysters are bubbling on top, between three and five minutes. You may have to rotate the pan 180 degrees to ensure even cooking if the oysters are not evenly centered under the broiler. Repeat with second pan. Once this second pan has been removed, pass the first pan under the broiler again for thirty seconds. The two pans of oysters should now be at about the same temperature and are ready to be transferred to the dinner plates and served.

✳ Oysters Bienville ✳

In the 1920s, oyster lovers in New Orleans loved their oysters so much that they would go on progressive dinners around town — progressing on the same night from the cooked oysters at one restaurant, to the next, to the next, ad infinitum. Certainly on their rounds they had their fill of Oysters Bienville, named after the founder of New Orleans, Jean-Baptiste Le Moyne, sieur de Bienville. The dish is not as well known as Oysters Rockefeller, but with its creamy, cheesy, capsicum-scented topping, it is at least as delicious. The following recipe is pure time travel, taking you back to the genteel, white-tablecloth restaurants of another era that served "American" food. The following recipe is an adaptation of the recipe from Antoine's, the great New Orleans restaurant that claims to have invented the dish.

Yield: 4 first-course servings

2 cups milk
6 tablespoons unsalted butter
2 tablespoons flour
Pinch of nutmeg
1 medium green bell pepper, minced
    (about 1½ cups)
1 bunch scallions, minced (about ½ cup)
1 large garlic clove, minced
⅓ cup dry white wine
1 (7-ounce) jar pimientos, drained and
    cut into ¼-inch dice (about ⅓ cup)
3 ounces white American cheese, shredded
    (about ½ cup)
⅛ cup unseasoned bread crumbs
⅛ teaspoon cayenne
3 pounds rock salt or other coarse salt
24 oysters in the shell
Lemon wedges for garnish

1. Make the béchamel sauce base: In a small saucepan, warm the milk over medium heat and bring almost to a boil, watching it carefully so that it doesn't boil over. Remove from the heat and reserve. Meanwhile, place another small saucepan over medium heat and add 2 tablespoons of the butter. When it has melted and the foam begins to subside, sprinkle in the flour, stir the mixture to blend, and immediately turn the heat down to medium-low. Continue stirring while the mixture bubbles for two minutes. Gradually whisk in the reserved warm milk, raise the heat to medium-high, and bring to a boil, whisking continuously. Reduce to a bare simmer and add a pinch of nutmeg and a generous pinch of salt and cook, stirring regularly, for 15 minutes. The sauce should be very thick but still pourable. Whisk in a small quantity of milk if you think it needs thinning. Pass the mixture through a fine-mesh sieve into a small bowl and set the béchamel sauce aside. Place plastic wrap directly on sauce to keep a skin from forming.

2. Melt the remaining 4 tablespoons of butter in a large sauté pan over medium heat. Add the green pepper, scallions, and garlic and cook gently for 5 minutes. Do not let the vegetables brown. Add the wine, raise the heat to medium-high, and allow it to reduce by half. Add the pimientos, cheese, bread

crumbs, cayenne, a few grindings of black pepper, a pinch of salt, and the reserved béchamel sauce, stirring to incorporate the mixture well. Reduce the heat to medium-low and let the sauce gently simmer for 10 minutes, stirring occasionally. When finished, it should be almost, but not quite, the consistency of mayonnaise. Taste the sauce for salt. Transfer the sauce to a small bowl and set aside. The sauce can be made up to 2 days ahead and stored in an airtight container in the refrigerator.

3. Divide half the rock salt between four dinner plates, each large enough to hold 6 oysters. Distribute the salt evenly on each plate. This is simply to provide an attractive base on which the curved oyster shells can evenly rest. Test with an oyster, placing the more deeply curved shell side down. If you need more salt to support the shells, add it. Set the plates aside. Now divide the remaining salt between two roasting pans, each large enough to hold a dozen oysters in one layer. Distribute the salt as you did for the plates (if you run out of salt, you can also use dried beans or lightly crumpled foil on the pans).

4. Open the top, flat side of each oyster (the deeply curved shell should be on the bottom). Retain in each shell as much of the oyster liquor as possible. Discard the top shell and free each oyster from its muscle. Transfer each oyster in its bottom shell to the salt-lined roasting pans.

5. Arrange the oven racks to accommodate both pans and preheat the oven to 400 degrees.

6. Place 2 teaspoons of the sauce on top of each oyster if they are medium-size (a bit more if they are larger, a bit less if they are smaller). The mixture should almost, but not quite, cover the meat of the oyster. Place the pans with the oysters in the oven and cook until there is a lively bubbling at the edges of the oysters, about 20 minutes. If your oven has hot spots, rotate the pans 180 degrees after 10 minutes. (And if your two roasting pans are on different levels, after 10 minutes carefully reverse the bottom and top pans to ensure even cooking.) When the oysters are done, allow them to cool for 2 minutes, then, wearing rubber gloves or with the help of a large spoon, carefully transfer 6 oysters to each of the salt-lined dinner plates. Garnish each plate with a lemon wedge and serve immediately.

✮ Dirty Down-Home ✮ Cajun Shrimp Boil

One of the funky backwater delights of Cajun country is a huge pot of shrimp (and other crustaceans, if desired — see Note) boiled along with potatoes and corn in a ton of spicy seasonings, spilled onto a table (platters are optional), dunked in dipping sauce, and devoured with pitchers of ice-cold beer. Sometimes the boil gets a little "cleaned up," and the spices are enclosed in cheesecloth before going into the pot. I far prefer it the way it is in the following recipe — where the shrimp ends up littered with all kinds of tasty seeds and peppers.

Yield: 6 servings for hungry diners

6 quarts water
3 cups beer
4 tablespoons whole black peppercorns

4 tablespoons dried parsley

¼ cup yellow mustard seeds

2 tablespoons celery seeds

15 bay leaves

¼ cup cayenne

5 tablespoons coriander seeds

3 tablespoons dill seeds

2 tablespoons whole cloves

1 tablespoon ground allspice

1 tablespoon crushed red pepper

5 tablespoons Worcestershire sauce

5 teaspoons Tabasco sauce

⅔ cup Season-All (seasoned salt)

⅓ cup table salt

6 large garlic cloves, smashed

3 lemons, quartered

2 large jalapeño peppers, quartered

2 large onions, quartered

18 new potatoes, or 6 medium potatoes
    cut in thirds

6 ears of fresh corn, shucked and broken in half

3 pounds large shrimp, shell on (see Note)

Susan's Favorite Dipping Sauce
    (recipe follows), or Po'boy Dressing
    (see page 349)

1. Bring water and beer to a boil in a very large and heavy stockpot. While it's heating up, add to the pot: peppercorns, parsley, mustard seeds, celery seeds, bay leaves, cayenne, coriander seeds, dill seeds, cloves, allspice, red pepper, Worcestershire sauce, Tabasco, Season-All, table salt, garlic cloves, lemons, jalapeños, and onions. Boil rapidly for 15 minutes.

2. Add potatoes and boil for 5 minutes.

3. Add corn and boil for 10 minutes.

4. Add shrimp and immediately turn off heat. Let pot stand, covered, until shrimp are just cooked (about 3 to 5 minutes).

5. Pour the contents of the pot into a huge colander (or two colanders). Let liquid drain away. Remove lemons and reserve. Pour the contents of the colander(s) onto a serving platter or platters — or spill contents all over brown paper on a large table. Grab the reserved lemons in a towel and squeeze some of their juice over all. Serve hot with Susan's Favorite Dipping Sauce.

NOTE: This recipe is delicious as a Shrimp Boil alone — but if you've got the ingredients, don't hesitate to make it a Dirty Mixed Boil by throwing some crawfish and/or crabs into the pot! The crawfish, depending on size, will take ten to twelve minutes to cook, and the crabs, depending on size, will take seventeen to twenty-five minutes. The liquid called for in this recipe will accommodate, in addition to what's already in the pot, a few pounds of crawfish and a dozen large crabs.

★ Susan's Favorite ★
Dipping Sauce

My friend from Cajun country has been enjoying this very flavorful sauce for years along with the shrimp boils in her neck of the woods.

Yield: About ½ cup

3 tablespoons ketchup

1 tablespoon mayonnaise

2 teaspoons prepared horseradish

2 teaspoons Heinz chili sauce

1 teaspoon Worcestershire sauce

1 teaspoon Tabasco sauce

1 teaspoon brown mustard

1 teaspoon lemon juice

Mix all ingredients together in a bowl.

☆ Seafood and Okra Gumbo ☆

Arguably, gumbo is the most famous dish of Louisiana cooking. Beyond that, there's lots more to argue about: which ingredients? which texture? which thickening? I often like to include okra in my gumbo recipes, as in this one — first of all, because I love the way its mucilaginous texture thickens the soup, and second, because the very word *gumbo* came from an African word for okra (*gômbo* in Bantu). The following recipe, which I got from a Louisiana friend who's a great cook, tastes exactly like something you might find in Cajun country — where the okra doesn't appear in firm pieces but melts into the soup. It's green-brown, medium thick, with tons of soulful country flavor. One of the reasons I think it tastes so authentic, believe it or not, is the amount of prepared seasonings in it; try to use them all if you can (see "New Orleans Seasoning" sidebar). Serve with rice (see Note).

Yield: 6 to 8 servings

1½ pounds okra
½ cup plus 2 tablespoons vegetable oil
1 cup flour
1 medium onion, finely chopped
½ medium green bell pepper,
*   finely chopped*
1 celery stalk, finely chopped
2 large garlic cloves, finely minced
1 cup white wine
8 cups cold water
1 tablespoon Mrs. Dash seasoning
2 teaspoons Zatarain's liquid crab boil,
*   optional (see "New Orleans*
*   Seasoning" sidebar)*
1 pound small shrimp, peeled and deveined
2 dozen oysters, shucked
1 tablespoon Worcestershire sauce

1 tablespoon Tony Chachere's seasoning
*   (see "New Orleans Seasoning" sidebar)*
1 pound lump crabmeat, picked over
*   to remove cartilage*
¼ cup chopped parsley
3 scallions, green and white parts,
*   finely chopped*

1. Wash the okra and cut off the tough stem end. Cut okra into round slices about ½ inch thick. Place the 2 tablespoons of vegetable oil in a large sauté pan or Dutch oven over medium heat. Add the okra slices and cook, uncovered, stirring often, until the okra is soft and no longer sticky (about 30 minutes). Reserve.

2. Make a dark roux. Place the remaining ½ cup of oil in a large heavy stockpot over medium heat. Add the flour all at once; stir well with a wooden spoon to blend. Cook, stirring constantly, until the roux becomes the color of dark chocolate (20 to 30 minutes).

3. When the roux is ready, add onion, bell pepper, celery, and garlic and cook uncovered over medium-low heat, stirring occasionally, until the vegetables have softened (about 10 minutes). Add wine, water, and Mrs. Dash seasoning and bring to a boil. Reduce heat to a simmer and cook for 1 hour, partially covered, stirring occasionally.

4. After 1 hour add the reserved okra and, if using, the liquid crab boil; simmer the gumbo for another 30 minutes, partially covered, stirring occasionally.

5. Combine shrimp and oysters in a bowl. Sprinkle them with Worcestershire sauce,

New Orleans Seasoning

A number of the Louisiana recipes here rely on prepared blends of seasonings; that's one reason these recipes taste so authentic. Using blended spices is very much in the local spirit; think of how many jars of Paul Prudhomme's Cajun Magic get sold and used!

Here are two products that come up quite frequently in local recipes . . . and what you can do about them.

ZATARAIN'S LIQUID CRAB BOIL

This is a great Louisiana product that can be acquired by logging on to: *www.cajungrocer.com.* If you can't get it, I'd advise simply leaving it out of the recipes herein; it's hard to reproduce its flavor.

TONY CHACHERE'S SEASONING

This product can be obtained by logging on to: *www.cajunspice.com.* But here's some great news: if you can't get it, you can make your own substitute.

Cajun Spice Blend
(A Substitute for Tony Chachere's Seasoning)

> 4 tablespoons salt
> 4 tablespoons garlic powder
> 2 tablespoons cayenne
> 1 tablespoon sweet paprika
> A few grinds of black pepper

Blend all ingredients. Store in tightly stoppered container.

Tony Chachere's seasoning (or your homemade substitute), and desired amount of salt and pepper. Add to gumbo, along with crabmeat, parsley, and scallions. Simmer, partially covered, until shrimp and oysters are cooked (about 10 minutes). Serve over rice (see Note).

SERVING LOUISIANA RICE NOTE: I love the way they serve gumbos, étouffées, and other soupy-stewy dishes in Louisiana. They fill a teacup with hot white rice and invert it in the center of a wide, shallow soup bowl. Then the cup is removed, leaving a perfect dome of steaming rice. To finish, the gumbo or stew is ladled all around the dome. It makes a very pretty picture.

☆ Chicken and ☆ Sausage Gumbo

Here's gumbo in another mood: this one is red and spicy, with the wonderful thickening agent called filé powder sprinkled on at the last minute. The gumbo also features a very dark roux, which makes its nutty flavor known. If you can, make this dish with the great Louisiana sausage called andouille; if you can't get it, a spicy smoked sausage would be a fine substitute.

Yield: 6 to 8 servings

> 1 cup flour
> ½ cup vegetable oil
> 1 medium onion, peeled and finely chopped
> ½ medium green bell pepper, finely chopped
> 1 celery stalk, finely chopped
> 2 large garlic cloves, peeled and finely minced
> 1 cup dry white wine
> 8 cups chicken broth

★☆

1 (16-ounce) can whole peeled tomatoes,
*   undrained*
1 (10-ounce) can diced tomatoes with green
*   chilies, undrained (see Note)*
1 tablespoon Mrs. Dash seasoning
6 large chicken thighs, skinned, boned, and cut
*   into 4 pieces each*
2 tablespoons Worcestershire sauce
1 tablespoon Tony Chachere's seasoning
*   (see "New Orleans Seasoning" sidebar,*
*   page 347)*
½ pound smoked sausage (cut in half
*   lengthwise, then in ¼-inch slices)*
¼ cup chopped parsley
3 chopped scallions
Cayenne (optional)
Filé powder for garnish (optional,
*   see Note)*

1. Make a dark roux: Combine the flour and oil in a large heavy stockpot over medium heat. Cook, stirring constantly, until the mixture reaches a dark chocolate color (this should take about 20 to 30 minutes).

2. Add onion, bell pepper, celery, and garlic to the roux. Cook, uncovered, over medium heat, stirring occasionally, until vegetables have softened (about 10 minutes). Add wine, broth, whole tomatoes, diced tomatoes, and Mrs. Dash seasoning. Bring to a boil. Reduce heat to a simmer and cook, partially covered, for 1½ hours, stirring occasionally.

3. Season chicken with Worcestershire sauce, Tony's Chachere's seasoning, and salt and black pepper to taste. Add chicken to gumbo, along with sausage, and bring gumbo just to

a boil. Reduce heat and simmer, partially covered, until chicken is very tender (about 1 hour), stirring occasionally. Add parsley, scallions, and, if desired, cayenne during the last 10 minutes. Just before serving, swirl in a teaspoon or two of filé powder, if desired. Serve over rice (see Serving Louisiana rice note, page 347).

NOTE: There are some interesting Southern ingredients called for in this recipe:

❂ Canned diced tomatoes with green chilies are ubiquitous throughout the South. If you can't find 'em, simply add some coarsely chopped green chili to any canned diced tomatoes and cook together for ten minutes or so.
❂ See sidebar on page 347 for advice concerning Tony Chachere's seasoning.
❂ Filé powder is traditionally sprinkled on a gumbo at serving time. When swirled in, it turns a little stringy, thickening the gumbo — and it adds a wild sagelike taste to the dish (it is an old Choctaw Indian ingredient, made from sassafras bark). Filé is widely available today in specialty grocery stores or from Cajun Web sites. If you can't find it — though you'll lose this authentic note — this gumbo will still be delicious.

☆ Oyster Po'boy ☆

There are many po'boys in New Orleans — hero sandwiches made with a variety of fillings. But the one that I think is the most distinctive — particularly because New Orleans is such a great oyster town — is the oyster po'boy, once known as the oyster loaf. I'm not always partial to cornmeal coatings on deep-fried foods, but in the following recipe the firm crunch works beautifully against the soft bread, the saladlike ingredients, and the creamy dressing. I've left the amount of that dressing up to you — but you'll be a poor boy indeed if you don't put on at least a few tablespoons of this vivid dressing. "Fully dressed," in the local lingo, is what you want.

Yield: 2 sandwiches

2 dozen oysters, shucked
1 tablespoon Worcestershire sauce
½ teaspoon Tabasco sauce
1 cup coarsely ground cornmeal
½ cup flour
2 teaspoons garlic powder
2 teaspoons onion powder
1 teaspoon cayenne
1 teaspoon freshly ground black pepper
1 teaspoon salt
Vegetable oil for deep-frying
2 hero breads, each about 6 inches in length
        (if you want to make it yourself, you
        can use the Cuban Sandwich Loaf on
        page 333)
Po'boy Dressing (recipe follows)
Shredded lettuce
Sliced tomato
Thinly sliced red onion

1. Toss oysters with Worcestershire and Tabasco sauces. Set aside.
2. Mix cornmeal and flour in a shallow dish or in a bag, then add garlic powder, onion powder, cayenne, black pepper, and salt. Stir or shake to blend seasonings into flour mixture.
3. Dredge oysters, one at a time, in the cornmeal-flour mixture, making sure that oysters are completely coated. Drop into a saucepan with a few inches of hot oil (365 degrees) and fry until coating is brown and crunchy, about 3 minutes. Remove from oil and drain well on paper towels.
4. Cut one of the breads in half lengthwise; scoop out some of the middle part of the bread from both halves. Lay the two halves cut side up on the counter. Spread desired amount of Po'boy Dressing on both sides of bread. Cover the sauce on each half with 6 oysters (12 oysters per sandwich). Top the oysters on one half with lettuce, tomato, and red onion. Flip second half on top of sandwich, holding the oysters in place as you go. Serve immediately, with extra dressing on the side. Repeat with second loaf of bread.

☆ Po'boy Dressing ☆

This is a great all-purpose dressing for many Cajun/Creole possibilities in addition to Oyster Po'boys — very like the Shrimp Boil dressing on page 344. Use your imagination to find a place for it on all manner of sandwiches, salads, and fried foods.

Yield: 1½ cups

9 tablespoons ketchup
6 tablespoons mayonnaise
2 tablespoons prepared horseradish
2 tablespoons chili sauce (such as Heinz)
1 tablespoon Worcestershire sauce
1 tablespoon prepared mustard
1 tablespoon lemon juice
2 teaspoons Tabasco sauce
3 small dill pickles, finely chopped

Combine ingredients well in a mixing bowl. Keeps well in the refrigerator, covered, for a few weeks.

★☆★

✳ Blackened Redfish ✳

When Cajun cuisine roared out of New Orleans in the 1980s and onto menus everywhere across the country, the dish that was probably copied most was blackened redfish — a simple sear of spice-coated fish fillets in a very hot pan. Ironically, it was a creative, upscale dish that, according to most Cajuns, wasn't really part of their gastronomic world. But Americans took to the spice and the dramatic extremity of blackening. (I had a friend back then who used to say, "The only things chefs aren't blackening these days is soup.") The original dish was done with redfish — common in Louisiana but difficult to find elsewhere. No worries; other firm fillets do just as well. I particularly like to use skin-on red snapper, because of the color. Whichever fish you choose, do ask the fishmonger for fillets that are a uniform one-half inch thick, so they cook evenly. And be sure to open your windows so you don't get "blackened kitchen" as well. I love this spicy, lively dish with Rice Dressing (page 353) and Crawfish Corn Bread (page 355).

Yield: 2 hearty main-course servings

½ cup clarified butter (page 227), plus extra
  for drizzling over the cooked fish
2 teaspoons sweet paprika
1¼ teaspoons garlic powder
1 teaspoon sea salt, or more to taste
1 teaspoon dried thyme
½ teaspoon dried oregano
½ teaspoon cayenne, or more, to taste
½ teaspoon freshly ground black pepper
¼ teaspoon ground cumin
4 (6-ounce) red snapper fillets (or firm fish of
  choice), cut ½ inch thick, skin on or off

I. Heat a cast-iron skillet (large enough to hold all 4 fillets) until the pan is smoking and starting to turn white with the heat (about 5 minutes).

2. In a small saucepan, melt the butter and pour into a large, shallow dish.

3. Place the paprika, garlic powder, and salt in a small bowl. Add the thyme and oregano, crushing the leaves with your fingers. Add the cayenne, black pepper, and cumin. Mix well.

4. When the pan is ready, dip the fillets into the butter. Sprinkle one side of each fillet evenly with the spice mixture, patting it down lightly with your hand. Gently place the fillets, spice-coated side down, into the pan. While the first side is cooking, sprinkle spice evenly over the top side of each fillet. Cook for 2½ minutes. Turn and cook the other side for the same amount of time. The fish should be just done (cook another 1 to 2 minutes if it's not). Remove cooked fillets from pan and drizzle with a little clarified butter. Serve immediately.

✳ Shrimp Sauce Piquant ✳

This dish has achieved some fame around the country as shrimp Creole — the name that cooks everywhere give to shrimp in a spicy, Louisiana-accented tomato sauce. In Cajun country, however, they call it shrimp sauce piquant — and it's best when made with a dark brown roux. Serve in a wide soup bowl with a dome of hot rice at the center, and pass a bottle of hot sauce on the side.

Yield: 4 main-course servings

1 large onion, finely chopped
½ green bell pepper, finely chopped
1 celery stalk, finely chopped

4 garlic cloves, finely minced
4 tablespoons vegetable oil
2 tablespoons flour
¾ cup dry red wine
1 (10-ounce) can diced tomatoes with green
    chilies (see Note page 348)
1 (8-ounce) can tomato sauce
1 (14½-ounce) can whole peeled tomatoes
1 cup water
1 teaspoon brown sugar
1 bay leaf
1 teaspoon dried basil
⅛ teaspoon paprika
1½ pounds shrimp, peeled and deveined
1 tablespoon Worcestershire sauce
¼ teaspoon cayenne
1 teaspoon freshly ground black pepper
Dash of ground cloves
5 chopped scallions

1. Sauté onion, green pepper, celery, and garlic in 2 tablespoons of the oil over medium-high heat in a large nonstick stockpot, uncovered, until soft (about 15 minutes).
2. Make a roux by combining the flour and the remaining 2 tablespoons of oil in a small skillet; cook over medium heat, stirring constantly, until roux turns dark brown (about 20 minutes). Do not allow to burn. Add roux to sautéed vegetables and stir until vegetables are coated.
3. Add wine, diced tomatoes, tomato sauce, whole tomatoes, water, brown sugar, bay leaf, basil, and paprika. Stir well. Simmer for 1 hour, covered, stirring occasionally.
4. Toss shrimp with Worcestershire sauce, cayenne, and black pepper. Add to simmering sauce, along with a dash of ground cloves. Cook just until shrimp are cooked through, no more than just a few minutes. Add scallions at the last minute and serve hot over cooked rice.

☆ Crawfish Étouffée ☆

The term *étouffée* appears to be of twentieth-century origin in Cajun cooking — but its roots go back to classic French cuisine, where "étouffée" refers to a braised dish. In Cajun country it's a little less precise; it means something like a stew or a dish cooked in liquid. Some sources say that it also indicates that the pot is covered during the cooking process. Whatever its precise meaning, rest assured that when you come across a good one — like the one below — you will encounter true Cajun magic. Usually made with shellfish — crawfish is the biggie, but shrimp are sometimes used — the combo of the sweet meat and the Cajun spices in a rich sauce is irresistible. Some versions I came across do not use roux to thicken the sauce — and that's the case with the following cornstarch-thickened version, given to me by a great Louisiana home cook. Despite its simplicity, it's the best étouffée I've ever tasted — a beautiful, velvety orange sauce, laden with crawfish flavor. Serve with rice (see Serving Louisiana rice note on page 347) and pass hot sauce at the table, if desired.

Yield: 6 main-course servings

½ cup unsalted butter
1 celery stalk, finely chopped
1 medium onion, finely chopped
½ medium green bell pepper, finely chopped
4 large garlic cloves, finely minced
2 pounds shelled crawfish tails (see "Findin'
    Crawfish" sidebar)
½ cup white wine

★★★

1¼ cups cold water
Tony Chachere's seasoning (see homemade
    substitute in sidebar on page 347)
2 tablespoons cornstarch
½ cup chopped green scallions
1 tablespoon chopped parsley
Louisiana hot sauce (optional)

1. Place butter in a large heavy skillet over medium heat. Sauté celery, onion, bell pepper, and garlic, uncovered, until they are very soft (about 15 minutes).

2. Add crawfish, wine, and 1 cup of the water. Bring to a boil, then reduce heat to a simmer. Add the Tony Chachere's seasoning (or homemade substitute) and cook for 30 minutes, partially covered.

3. In a small bowl or cup, mix the remaining ¼ cup of water with cornstarch to make a creamy slurry. Add slurry to pot, along with scallions and parsley. Stir well and simmer, uncovered, for another 10 minutes. Serve immediately over rice. Pass Louisiana hot sauce.

Findin' Crawfish

Crawfish is one of the glories of Louisiana cuisine. It's easy to get into a fight in New Orleans; just suggest that better crawfish come from somewhere else! (The market is flooded these days with Chinese crawfish, for example.) Once upon a time, people in most other parts of the United States could only dream about these Louisiana critters, or buy a ticket to New Orleans. Happily, those days are over. Great crawfish from Louisiana are now just a mail order away — and are available in many forms (such as live, cooked in the shell, cooked and removed from the shell). The easiest form to deal with is the latter: cooked, peeled crawfish tails, which come in a plastic bag chockablock with orange crawfish fat that's unbelievably delicious. You can order this treat by logging on to any of the following Web sites:

www.crawfish.cc
www.crawfishguy.com
www.lacrawfish.com
www.tonyseafood.com

Small shrimp can be substituted for crawfish tails in any recipe in this book.

✩ Red Beans and Rice ✩

This innocuous-sounding dish is nothing of the sort; it is one of the great dishes of American cuisine, too often raising nothing more than a yawn among those who have never really tried it. It has a colorful tradition in New Orleans. Sunday was always baked ham day, so on Monday ham bone would be left over in the fridge. Monday was also laundry day, so the New Orleans housekeeper would put up a pot of beans with ham bone in the morning, expecting it to be ready many, many hours later when the washing and drying were done. To this day, households serve red beans with rice on Monday, and New Orleans restaurants offer it on that day — usually with "side dishes" of meat, like sausages or veal cutlets. Despite its African-American roots, the dish became a Cajun favorite — and the following exquisite recipe comes straight from the bayou. It may lack some of the more esoteric Louisiana ingredients — such as the small Louisiana red bean, and pickled pork — but it is exactly how red beans and rice is made in most homes today.

Yield: 4 main-course servings

1 pound dry red kidney beans
1 large onion, finely chopped
1 small green bell pepper, finely chopped
2 celery stalks, finely chopped
3 large garlic cloves, finely chopped
1 fresh jalapeño, seeded and finely chopped
1 tablespoon vegetable oil
1 (10½ ounce) can chicken broth
1 cup dry red wine
3 cups water
1 bay leaf
1 pound smoked ham hocks
½ teaspoon cayenne
1 teaspoon freshly ground black pepper
2 cups hot white rice
Chopped scallions for garnish

1. Wash beans well and sort through them, removing any pebbles or impurities. Place beans in a pot, cover with water, and soak overnight.
2. When ready to cook, drain beans and set aside.
3. Sauté onion, green pepper, celery, garlic, and jalapeño in oil in a large stockpot over medium-high heat, uncovered, until soft (about 10 minutes).
4. Add beans to the pot, along with chicken broth, wine, water, bay leaf, ham hocks, cayenne, and black pepper. Bring to a boil. Reduce heat to a simmer and cook, covered, for 2 hours, stirring frequently. Taste and adjust seasoning.
5. Remove ham hocks after 2 hours. Continue to simmer beans for another 30 minutes, or until the liquid in the beans has a thick, creamy consistency. As soon as the ham

hocks are cool enough to handle, remove all meat from the bones and shred it. Return meat to the beans.
6. Divide the hot rice among four wide, shallow serving bowls. Pour 1½ cups of the bean mixture over the rice in each bowl; you'll have a little bean mixture left over. Garnish with scallions and serve immediately.

✸ Rice Dressing ✸

We non-Louisianans hear a great deal about "dirty rice" — one of those Cajun dishes that captured the national imagination in the 1980s. A Cajun friend who grew up near Lafayette, in the heart of Cajun country, tells me that she's never seen or heard of dirty rice in her circle of eaters. "What we do serve," she said, "is what we call rice dressing." And this amazing dish — with its slightly muddy look, due to the inclusion of chicken livers and giblets — is better than any dirty rice I've ever tasted. The liver and seasonings melt down into a flavor that is so comforting, so nostalgic, you can't help but pile some more on your plate. And that's exactly what you do with it: this "dressing" is never used to stuff anything. The following recipe is utterly traditional, except for the sage, which my friend and I discovered adds a great undercurrent of flavor. I, for one, love the old-fashioned way it looks on my plate — but if you'd like to freshen it up a bit, don't hesitate to top it with a little minced parsley.

Yield: 6 to 8 servings

2 tablespoons vegetable oil
2 medium onions, finely chopped
½ green bell pepper, finely chopped
1 celery stalk, finely chopped
2 large garlic cloves, finely minced
1 pound ground pork

½ pound ground beef
1 pound finely chopped chicken giblets
    (heart, gizzard, and liver; see Note)
2 tablespoons flour
1 (14½-ounce) can chicken broth
1 tablespoon Worcestershire sauce
2 teaspoons cayenne
1 teaspoon ground sage
½ teaspoon paprika
3½ cups cooked rice
1 cup finely chopped scallions

1. Place 1 tablespoon of the vegetable oil in a large, heavy pot over medium heat. Add onions, green pepper, celery, and garlic; sauté until vegetables are tender, about 10 minutes. Add pork, beef, and giblets to pot and cook, uncovered, over medium-high heat, stirring occasionally, until the meats are brown and crumbly.

2. While the meats are browning, make a roux by blending the remaining 1 tablespoon of oil with the flour in a small, heavy pan. Cook uncovered over medium heat, stirring constantly, until the roux is dark brown (about 20 minutes). Do not allow to burn. Set roux aside.

3. When the meat is completely browned, add roux, chicken broth, Worcestershire sauce, cayenne, sage, and paprika. Cover pot and simmer gently for 1 hour, stirring often.

4. Stir in rice and scallions. Mix well. Season to taste with salt and pepper. Serve hot.

NOTE: If you wish, you can use as "giblets" all the chicken parts that usually come wrapped in a bag inside the cavity when you buy a whole chicken. Some may have bones or hard spots — and you can use those too, as long as your diners don't mind the funkiness of a little bone in their rice. A "cleaner" option, however — and I prefer its flavor — is simply to use a pound of chopped chicken livers in the dish.

☆ Maque Choux ☆
(Louisiana Corn Stew)

This is a terrific country Cajun side dish, made with fresh corn and peppers, that is very popular in the bayou but has not had a national breakout. It should, given how delicious it is. Perhaps its beyond-the-bayou prospects have been hampered by confusion over its weird name (and the fact that, confusingly, it also goes by the name of maquechou). Food historians theorize that the *maque* part may come from a word for corn (notice the first two letters of *maize*) . . . or may come from the word *mock*, as in false . . . or may come from a French word for thin. The *choux* part is similarly unclear: does it come from a word for child? From a diminutive? From the French word for cabbage (as in "mock cabbage")? We'll never know. What I do know is that if you make the following recipe (in which the corn stays crisp, despite the long cooking), spoon it over rice, and serve it alongside a roast (as they do in Cajun country), there'll be nothing mock about your delight.

Yield: 6 to 8 side dish servings

12 ears fresh corn
4 tablespoons unsalted butter
1 tablespoon Crisco shortening
1 medium onion, finely chopped
½ large green bell pepper, finely chopped
2 garlic cloves, finely chopped
1 fresh jalapeño pepper, seeded and finely
    chopped
1 banana pepper, finely chopped
    (or any long, nonspicy chili)

2 large fresh tomatoes, peeled and chopped
½ cup dry white wine
½ cup half-and-half
1 teaspoon freshly ground black pepper
¼ teaspoon cayenne
1 tablespoon chopped fresh basil

1. Remove husks and silk from corn, wash ears thoroughly, and dry with paper towels. Using a sharp knife, cut the corn kernels off the cob into a large bowl, scraping the cob to extract any milk left on the cob. Set aside.

2. Melt butter and shortening in a large nonstick stockpot over medium-high heat. Sauté onion, bell pepper, garlic, jalapeño pepper, and banana pepper until soft, approximately 15 minutes.

3. Add tomatoes and wine, bring to a simmer, and cook, covered, for 10 minutes, stirring occasionally.

4. Add reserved corn, half-and-half, black pepper, and cayenne. Adjust seasoning with salt. Bring to a simmer over medium heat, then reduce heat to medium-low and cook, covered, for 1 hour, stirring often. Add fresh basil to corn during last 5 minutes of cooking time. Serve immediately.

☆ Crawfish Corn Bread ☆

When a Cajun friend mentioned this wonderful but little-known dish to me, I had the wrong idea — for this is not a "bread" at all. It's more like a gratin or a soufflé. It's really most like a killer casserole that's crispy on top, soft and warm and sweet within. It's an amazing side dish in a Louisiana meal, particularly with fish, chicken, and sausage dishes.

Yield: 8 to 12 side dish servings

1 cup yellow cornmeal
½ teaspoon salt
½ teaspoon baking soda
2 extra-large eggs, beaten
½ cup vegetable oil
½ pound cheddar cheese, grated
1 medium onion, peeled and finely chopped
2 to 3 jalapeño peppers (depending on taste),
       seeded and finely chopped
1 (8-ounce) can corn niblets, drained
1 (8-ounce) can cream-style corn
1 pound cooked and peeled crawfish tails
       (see "Findin' Crawfish" sidebar on page
       352), or substitute 1 pound small
       shrimp, peeled and boiled
1 cup whole milk

1. Preheat oven to 375 degrees.

2. Mix all ingredients well in a large bowl. Pour mixture into a 9 by 13-inch glass pan, making sure it's spread out evenly. Bake in oven until the top is brown and puffy, about 45 minutes. Cut into squares and serve hot.

☆ Bread Pudding ☆ with Bourbon Sauce

No dessert is as firmly associated with New Orleans as bread pudding. This fabulous way of using leftover bread was probably an English idea originally; I've seen recipes going back as far as the 1600s. But the Brits must have popularized it in the American South, because it has been a dessert staple there for centuries. Currently it is a wildly trendy creative dish, with American chefs everywhere making their statements in bread pudding (everything from White Chocolate Bread Pudding, to Bread Pudding with Cherimoya). I especially love it when it's made with the eggy Jewish bread challah. If you can't find a loaf, brioche — or plain old white bread — may be substituted.

Yield: 12 to 15 servings

1 loaf challah, about 1 pound
8 large eggs
1 cup sugar
8 cups whole milk
2 teaspoons ground cinnamon
½ teaspoon ground nutmeg
2 teaspoons vanilla extract
1 tablespoon unsalted butter
1 cup dark raisins
Bourbon Sauce (recipe follows)

1. Preheat oven to 350 degrees.
2. Cut challah into ½-inch cubes (don't remove crusts). Spread cubes in one layer on an ungreased cookie sheet and bake until crisp and lightly browned, about 15 minutes. Remove from oven and set aside to cool. (This step can be done ahead.)
3. In a large bowl, beat eggs and sugar together until well combined. Gradually add milk. Add cinnamon, nutmeg, and vanilla.
4. Add bread cubes to milk mixture. Mix well.
5. Grease a 9 by 13-inch baking pan with the butter. Carefully pour milk-bread mixture into prepared pan and sprinkle raisins over the top. Press down lightly until the bread is submerged in the milk. Let sit for at least 1 hour (or refrigerate overnight) so the bread can absorb most of the milk. To help this along, cover pan with plastic wrap and use 3 one-pound cans to weigh down bread.

6. If the oven is not already hot, preheat to 350 degrees. Bake the pudding on the middle shelf of the oven for 40 minutes, or until a skewer inserted in the center comes out clean. Be careful not to overbake. Remove from oven and place pan on a cooling rack for about 15 minutes.
7. Prick pudding with a fork and spoon about ½ cup hot bourbon sauce over the top. Wait until the sauce is absorbed and then repeat until the pudding seems saturated and can't absorb any more. Any leftover sauce can be served along with the pudding or used as a topping for ice cream. It's best when warm — so serve within an hour, or reheat if served later.

★ Bourbon Sauce ★

Yield: About 3 cups

½ pound (2 sticks) unsalted butter
1 cup sugar
2 cups whipping cream
½ cup bourbon

1. Melt butter with sugar in a 2-quart saucepan over medium heat. Stir constantly. Continue to cook over medium-high heat, stirring, until the mixture turns into a rich, golden-colored caramel.
2. While the butter and sugar are cooking, heat the cream in another saucepan until small bubbles appear around the edges. When the sugar and butter reach the caramel stage, slowly whisk in the cream. If the mixture hardens, just continue to whisk over medium-high heat until it becomes smooth again.

3. Remove from heat, add bourbon, and pour over pudding while the sauce is still hot.

NOTE: This sauce reheats well in the microwave. Additional sauce may be served alongside the pudding. The sauce will harden when refrigerated — just reheat in microwave or on the stovetop, adding more cream if necessary to thin it down.

Texas

The huge state of Texas contains an interesting amalgam of culinary activities — just as it contains an interesting amalgam of cultures.

East Texas and north Texas — including the city of Dallas — have a character that could easily be described as Southern; think of this as the most westward extension of American Southern culture. There are specialties here — such as chicken-fried steak and pecan pie — that one would expect to see in Mississippi and Georgia as well; the great Texas cafeterias, such as Luby's, serve up a ton of this comfort food every day. And the amazing barbecue traditions of the American South find a Texas expression as well in mouth-watering beef barbecue.

But Texas, especially as you go south and west, reflects the habits of another important contiguous culture: Mexico. It is along the Mexican border, of course, that the cuisine known as Tex-Mex (which can be delicious!) was born. But there are many other, more subtle ways in which the flavors and ideas of Mexican cuisine permeate Texas kitchens.

As you arrive in far western Texas, of course, you're truly in the American West. We can thank the cowboys of this area for Texas's obsession with beef and for rustic old West dishes such as chili, jerky, and smoky beans. It is here, out near El Paso, that the food of Texas shades off into the food of the American Southwest.

✦ Texas Shellfish Cocktail ✦ with Tomato, Orange Juice, and Cilantro, Border Style

Have you ever noticed, when traveling in southern Texas, that "shrimp cocktail" on a menu can mean something other than the usual? What it can mean, deliciously so, is a version of the tomato-chile-lime-shellfish cocktail made in Campeche, in Mexico's Yucatan Peninsula. In America the dish is usually a little sweeter and chunkier — and puts convenience products to great use. I like to make it with shrimp, crabmeat, and raw clams. The latter addition is for real seafood lovers. If you like your cocktail with a milder taste, eliminate the clams and use any three-cup combo of cold, cooked shellfish you like for this utterly beguiling starter. Serve it in a parfait glass, or a margarita glass as they do in San Antonio.

Yield: 6 to 8 first-course servings

1 cup large chunks of peeled, cooked shrimp
(about 12 medium shrimp)
1 cup lump crabmeat, picked over for bits of
cartilage and shell
1 cup raw clam bellies, cut in half
(from about 18 cherrystones)

3 tablespoons minced raw tomato

3 tablespoons minced cilantro,
    plus a few extra leaves for garnish

4 teaspoons minced green olive

½ teaspoon minced fresh jalapeño, or more,
    to taste

1 cup ketchup

¼ cup orange juice

3 tablespoons freshly squeezed lime juice

½ teaspoon Worcestershire sauce

½ teaspoon Tabasco garlic pepper sauce,
    plus extra for garnish

Lettuce for serving

1. In a large bowl, mix together the shellfish, tomato, cilantro, olive, and jalapeño.

2. In another bowl, prepare the sauce: Mix together the ketchup, orange juice, lime juice, Worcestershire sauce, and garlic pepper sauce. Blend well.

3. Add most of the ketchup-orange sauce to the shellfish mixture, reserving a little for garnish. Serve immediately, or refrigerate for several hours. Just before serving, top each cocktail with a little extra garlic pepper sauce, some of the reserved ketchup-orange sauce, and a few cilantro leaves. Serve on a lettuce leaf in parfait dishes or wide margarita glasses, or on flat plates.

☆ Fajitas ☆

Every once in a while a local specialty catches fire around the country — and this is certainly the case with the fajita, a skirt-steak-in-tortilla sandwich, which appears to have been a very local Texas tradition until the 1980s. The name *fajita* — which means "girdle" in Spanish and describes the look of a skirt steak — was not even widely used in Texas until several operations commercialized the name in the 1970s. One decade later, Tex-Mex restaurants all over the country were offering fajitas on their menus as if they'd been there forever. Unfortunately, what they were offering — and what they're still offering — is not usually so good. It has become a restaurant tradition to serve the meat for fajitas to the diner on a sizzling platter, with a group of wan vegetables standing by, usually grilled onions and grilled peppers, to "add color." I like my fajitas brown and tan. I like them when they show their tacos al carbón roots — which is to say, simply great pieces of freshly grilled meat tucked into good tortillas without a lot of fuss. This makes it real easy on the backyard chef, too. By the way, "fajita" has come to mean just about anything grilled that gets wrapped in a soft tortilla. One of my favorite alternatives to skirt steak is pork tenderloin; simply substitute pork tenderloin in the following recipe and cook it until it's medium.

Yield: 8 fajitas

4 tablespoons olive oil

4 tablespoons fresh lime juice

2 tablespoons finely minced garlic

2 teaspoons dried oregano, crumbled

1 teaspoon ground cumin

1 teaspoon paprika

1 teaspoon salt

¼ teaspoon cayenne

1½ pounds skirt steak, preferably thick

8 large flour tortillas

Garnishes, if desired
    (see "Fancy Fajitas" sidebar)

1. In a bowl just large enough to hold the steak, mix together the olive oil, lime juice, garlic, oregano, cumin, paprika, salt, and cayenne. Place the steak in the marinade, coat-

ing it thoroughly on all sides. Cover and refrigerate for 24 hours.

2. When ready to cook, prepare a very hot fire (preferably charcoal) on your grill.

3. Remove steak from bowl and dry well with paper towels. Place meat on hot fire and cook quickly, until the meat is charred crusty brown on the outside and cooked medium-rare inside (you can cook it longer, if you wish). Remove to cutting board and let steak rest for 5 minutes.

4. Meanwhile, warm the tortillas by either steaming them, placing them in a hot pan (one by one), or placing them quickly over the hot fire.

5. When ready to serve, cut meat on the diagonal into broad, thin slices, reserving juices. Divide sliced steak among the 8 tor-

tillas, drizzle with reserved meat juice, fold tortillas, and serve immediately. Garnish if desired.

☆ Real Texas Chili ☆

To a chili purist, the modern additions of tomatoes and beans to a chili — and the common practice of grinding the beef, not cutting it into small cubes — are abhorrent, and ample evidence of the failure of modern civilization. The chili purist is in love with the romantic notion of the cowboy on the range — who rustled up a stew made only with water, dried chilies, and meat. This was chili con carne! Forget the chili con carne and frijoles, the chili con everything else! Of course, the meat that idealized cowboy probably used was pemmican, or preserved bison, which he had tucked under his saddle near his rifle. I don't hear the purists clamoring for pemmican . . . so I guess it's okay to accept a few modern adjustments. The following fabulous recipe, despite quite a few adjustments, does show you why the purist has a point: the end result is a rich, chili-laden "bowl o' red," with tender morsels of beef and deep, beefy flavor throughout. No bells or whistles are evident — but this Real Texas Chili has nevertheless become my favorite chili of all.

Yield: 4 to 6 main-course servings

2 ounces dried red chilies (see Note)
1½ teaspoons cumin seeds, toasted in a pan
        until fragrant, then ground
¼ teaspoon freshly ground pepper
⅓ pound beef suet, diced, or ⅓ cup vegetable oil
2½ pounds boneless beef chuck, trimmed
        of excess fat and cut into ¾-inch cubes
        (about 2 pounds after trimming)
¼ cup finely chopped onion
1 tablespoon minced garlic

Fancy Fajitas

If you want to serve garnishes on your fajitas, there's no dearth of ideas out there. Here's a short list of possibilities. If there's a recipe for that garnish in this book, you'll also find the page number.

grilled green or red bell pepper strips
grilled chilies
grilled onion slices
cilantro leaves
salsas (pages 124 through 125)
sour cream
guacamole (page 121)
Refried Beans (page 127)
Tex-Mex Rice (page 128)

2 cups unsalted beef broth (homemade
    or canned)
2 cups water
2 tablespoons masa harina
1 tablespoon firmly packed dark brown sugar
1 tablespoon plus 1 teaspoon distilled
    white vinegar
Sour cream for topping (optional)

1. In a large skillet over medium-low heat, gently toast the chilies until they're fragrant, about 2 to 3 minutes per side. Do not allow them to blacken, or they will turn bitter. Place the chilies in a bowl and cover them with very hot (but not boiling) water, and let them soak until they're soft, about 30 minutes.

2. When the chilies are soft, drain them and remove the stems and seeds. Place them in the bowl of a blender and add the cumin, pepper, and a few pinches of salt (if you're using salted broth, don't add any salt just yet — you may not need it). Puree the mixture with small additions of water until an almost fluid, smooth paste forms (you want to eliminate all but the smallest bits of chili skin in the puree). You should have about ¾ cup. Set the chili paste aside.

3. Meanwhile, if using beef suet, place it in a small skillet with ½ cup of water and bring to a boil over high heat. Let the water boil away, reduce the heat to medium, and allow the suet to render its fat and to brown lightly. This may take as long as 30 minutes. Strain the contents of the skillet, discard the solids (or sprinkle with salt and eat!), and reserve ⅓ cup of the rendered beef fat.

4. Add 2 tablespoons of the reserved beef fat, or of the vegetable oil, to a large, heavy skillet over medium-high heat. When the fat is just smoking, add half the diced beef and lightly brown it on all sides, about 5 to 6 minutes. Reduce the heat if the meat threatens to burn. Transfer the contents of the skillet to a bowl. Repeat with 2 more tablespoons of beef fat or oil and the remaining beef, transferring the browned beef to the bowl; reserve.

5. Let the skillet cool slightly and place it over medium-low heat. Add the remaining beef fat or oil, the onion, and garlic, and cook gently for 4 to 5 minutes, stirring occasionally. Stir in the beef broth, the 2 cups water, masa harina, and the reserved chili paste; with a wooden spatula, scrape the bottom of the skillet to loosen any browned bits.

6. Add the reserved beef, raise the heat to medium-high, and bring the mixture just to a boil. Immediately reduce to a bare simmer and cook, very gently, uncovered, for about 2 hours, stirring occasionally. During the last 10 minutes of cooking, stir in the brown sugar, vinegar, and salt to taste. At this point the meat should be surrounded by 1½ to 2 cups of thickened but still liquid sauce. It may look like there is still too much liquid. Turn off the heat and let the chili stand for at least 30 minutes, during which time the meat will absorb about half the remaining liquid in the skillet, leaving the meat bathed in a thick, barely fluid chili sauce. Stir in additional broth or water if the mixture seems too dry. Conversely, if the mixture seems a bit loose and wet, allow it to simmer a bit more, thickening it with small amounts of extra masa harina only if necessary. Adjust the bal-

ance of flavors with a bit of additional salt, pepper, cumin, and vinegar, to your taste. But remember: It's about beef and chilies! Reheat gently in the skillet and serve in individual bowls topped with sour cream, if you like.

NOTE: It's important to use good, fresh, flavorful dried red chilies for this dish — because it's all about the chilies. I've made it with a mixture of New Mexican and pasilla chilies, which is good — and I've made it with 100 percent guajillo chilies, which is even better. Don't be afraid to find the chili, or combination of chilies, that you like best.

✷ Chicken-Fried Steak ✷

Northerners are often confused by the name of this dish. Just remember: As in shrimp with lobster sauce, which has no lobster, chicken-fried steak has no chicken. It is steak (thin steak) fried in a pan in the manner used for frying chicken. "Steak fried like chicken" would be a more accurate but much clumsier name. You find chicken-fried steak all across the South, and no one knows exactly where it started. But Texans like to claim it as their own, and given the Texan predilection for beef, I'm inclined to go along. If it is Texan, of course, it's one of those Texas dishes that lean east toward Dixie — but I like to Westernize it a bit by adding some cumin to the creamy sauce that goes on top of the steak. I've tried it all kinds of ways — including with a more tender cut of beef, such as filet mignon! — but the following simple, low-cost recipe is my favorite. For authenticity's sake, just make sure the gravy gets to moisten some mashed potatoes as well as the fried meat.

Yield: 2 main-course portions

2 pieces of round steak, each about 8 ounces,
    each about ½ inch thick
1 cup plus 2 tablespoons flour
2 eggs, beaten

1 cup milk
Tabasco sauce
2 cups cracker meal
4 tablespoons lard
½ cup finely minced onion
½ cup chicken stock
½ teaspoon ground cumin
Worcestershire sauce
Cayenne

1. Place steaks on counter. Pound steaks evenly with the kind of mallet that has pointy projections for tenderizing beef. Pound until the steaks are about ¼ inch thick. Reserve.
2. Place the 1 cup of flour on a wide, flat plate. Place the eggs in a wide, shallow bowl and beat in ¼ cup of the milk plus 4 to 6 dashes of Tabasco. Place the cracker meal on a wide, flat plate.
3. Heat the lard in a large, heavy pan over medium heat.
4. While lard is heating, season the steaks with salt and black pepper. Dip each one in the flour to lightly coat, then in the egg mixture, then in the cracker meal. Press cracker meal onto steaks to make sure it adheres.
5. Place steaks in hot pan. Cook until golden brown on the outside, medium on the inside — about 2 to 3 minutes per side. When steaks are cooked, hold them on a paper towel–lined baking sheet in a 200-degree oven.
6. Pour off all but 2 tablespoons of the drippings in the pan. Place the pan over medium-high heat. Add the onion and cook for 1 minute. Stir. Add the remaining 2 tablespoons of flour and cook, stirring, for 2 minutes. Add the remaining ¾ cup of milk, the

chicken stock, and the cumin. Whisk until the sauce thickens (1 to 2 minutes). Add Worcestershire, cayenne, and salt to taste.

7. Place the chicken-fried steaks on two dinner plates and pour sauce over and around them.

✭ Texas-Style ✭ Barbecued Brisket

There's no doubt which dish reigns as the king of Texas barbecue: it is brisket, sometimes cooked as long as eighteen hours in the smoking pit, until the gray meat picks up a red ring under the surface (called a smoke ring) and the collagen of the meat collapses into an impossibly tender chew. It is pure Texas, a state that worships beef over pork as the 'cue of choice. It is a notoriously difficult dish to duplicate at home — but if you're willing to spend only four hours near your outdoor grill, and four to five more hours with the meat in your oven, the following recipe will bring you the magic of Texas at home. The great no-no in Texas brisket is dryness — it should be moist and tender — so the best cut of brisket to choose is the fattier "second cut"; the "first cut," if you must choose it, also survives the following recipe to become surprisingly moist and tender. Either cut should be moist enough so that if you wanted to be pure, austere Texan about it, you wouldn't need any barbecue sauce at all (please see brisket discussion on page 441). If you want to loosen up a bit, you could serve the sliced brisket, either on plates or on white-bread sandwiches, with the juices that collect in the brisket's foil bag. If you really want to sauce it up — and I, frankly, prefer it this way — use those foil-bag juices to build a great Texas-style tomatoey barbecue sauce. Then slather the sauce either on plated brisket slices or on that good ole white-bread and brisket sandwich. Mustard Slaw (page 321) and a side of Individual Jalapeño Corn Bread Loaves (page 380) would be ideal accompaniments.

Yield: 4 main-course servings or 8 sandwiches

2 teaspoons ground thyme
2 teaspoons commercial chili powder
4 tablespoons brown sugar
2 teaspoons ground black pepper
2 teaspoons ground cumin
1 teaspoon garlic powder
1 teaspoon cayenne
1 teaspoon onion powder
1 (4-pound) chunk of beef brisket
    (preferably the second cut)
1 tablespoon coarse salt
1½ teaspoons Worcestershire sauce
2 teaspoons Dijon mustard
1 cup ketchup
2 teaspoons red wine vinegar
⅓ cup pan juices (may need to add water and
    deglaze pan to get this amount of liquid)

SPECIAL EQUIPMENT:
4 cups wood chips (oak, mesquite, hickory,
    or the like)
1 large bag lump hardwood charcoal

1. In a medium-size mixing bowl mix together the thyme, chili powder, brown sugar, black pepper, cumin, garlic powder, cayenne, and onion powder. Rub the brisket all over with the salt and half the spice mixture. Reserve the other half of the seasoning rub. Place the brisket on a platter and refrigerate overnight, or up to 24 hours. Remove the brisket from the refrigerator 1 hour prior to smoking.

2. To smoke the brisket, use a charcoal grill (such as a Weber) that has a lid, adjustable air vents, and an internal temperature thermometer. If the grill is not equipped with a thermometer, stick a frying thermometer or

meat thermometer into one of the air vents, and contrive a way of holding it there (for instance, with tape).

3. Submerge the wood chips in a bowl of water.

4. Fill a disposable aluminum bread loaf pan half full of water and place it on one side of the base of the grill (preferably not the side of the grill with the air vent, because it is best to put the charcoal on that side). On the air-vent side of the base of the grill, start the fire by igniting 1 gallon (around 35 pieces) of the lump charcoal. (I prefer to use a chimney starter to ignite the charcoal, but use any method you wish.) The fire is ready when about half the charcoal is burning well and has turned gray and the other half is still black (about 15 minutes).

5. Carefully lay a piece of heavy-duty foil over the exposed hot charcoal. This will keep drippings from falling off the brisket onto the coals and starting a flare-up. Close the cover on the grill. Adjust all the air vents on the grill so that they are barely open; this will keep the temperature low, ideally around 235 degrees. Adjust your air vents throughout the cooking process to maintain this cooking temperature. Once you have the grill temperature regulated, about 15 minutes, lift up the piece of foil and place a handful of drained wood chips on top of the fiery charcoal, then put the foil back in place, pulling some back to leave one corner of the charcoal exposed (about 4 by 4 inches).

6. Place the grate on the grill and lay the brisket on the grate. Do not place it over the charcoal; place it over the water pan. Cover the grill immediately to prevent flare-ups. Cook the brisket, covered, maintaining the 235-degree temperature for about 1 hour by periodically adjusting your air vents.

7. After 1 hour, drop a handful of drained chips onto the top of the exposed part of the charcoal. Flip the brisket over and continue cooking it, covered, for another hour. Repeat this process — more chips, flip over — two more times, for a total cooking time of 4 hours. From time to time you will need to add more charcoal.

8. Preheat oven to 250 degrees.

9. Remove the brisket from the grill and completely wrap it in several layers of heavy duty foil. Crimp it so the closure is on top; you want to seal it completely so that the juice rendered by the brisket stays inside the foil.

10. Place brisket packet in a roasting pan, and place pan in the oven. Cook the brisket for 4 to 5 hours, or until it is tender. To see if it is tender, carefully open the foil packet and stick a thin-bladed knife through the meat in the fattiest part of the brisket. If it gives a lot of resistance, then continue cooking for a little longer . . . but you don't want it falling apart. It should have a nice chew but not be too tough. To test, cut a small piece off the brisket and taste it for tenderness.

11. When ready to eat the brisket, remove it from the oven and carefully unwrap, saving the juices. Let the brisket rest for a few minutes. If the juices have spilled out and dried up, you may need to deglaze the pan with a brimming ⅓ cup of water to yield ⅓ cup of cooking juices.

12. Prepare the barbecue sauce: Combine the

remaining brisket seasoning rub, the Worcestershire sauce, mustard, ketchup, vinegar, and reserved foil/pan juices in a small saucepan. Cook over low heat for 5 minutes.

13. Using a long, sharp knife and cutting against the grain, carve the slab of brisket into ¼-inch slices. Serve immediately on plates with barbecue sauce or on sandwiches with barbecue sauce.

✳ Smoky Texan ✳ Barbecue Sauce

Barbecue sauce is a much-abused condiment; the chief abuse is that many cooks use it for marination and cooking. But because barbecue sauce almost always contains sugar, this practice leads to flare-ups on the grill and burned spots on the meat. The name should be taken more seriously: barbecue sauce is *sauce* — meaning a tasty, runny liquid placed on meat after it's cooked. They know this well in Texas, where the sauce is something you apply at the table, if at all. And that application usually comes in small quantities . . . unless you've made the following smoky and addictive sauce, which proves that liquid smoke can sometimes be a very good thing. This sauce can be refrigerated in an airtight container for up to two weeks, while your barbecue really slow cooks. Incidentally, I prefer to serve this smoky sauce as an instant smoke-me-up with meats that haven't already been smoked; smoke on smoke is like secondhand smoke, not a good thing. Notice that the preceding smoky barbecued brisket recipe advises you to use another, nonsmoky barbecue sauce.

Yield: About 1 cup

1 teaspoon red wine vinegar
½ teaspoon minced dried onion
½ teaspoon minced dried garlic

¾ teaspoon chili powder
2 tablespoons plus 1 teaspoon Worcestershire sauce
1 tablespoon horseradish mustard
2 tablespoons plus 1 teaspoon liquid smoke
½ cup ketchup
¼ cup brown sugar
¾ teaspoon salt
½ teaspoon ground pepper

1. Combine all ingredients in a small saucepan and gently boil for five minutes, stirring constantly.

2. Remove sauce from heat, and let it stand for one hour to let flavors come together.

✳ Jalapeño Jelly ✳

One Texas cookbook says the different jalapeño jellies in Texas these days "probably outnumber bluebonnets." In Texas they like to spread it on cream cheese and crackers or slather it on corn muffins or serve it alongside a roast. But there is a great trick to making this kind of jelly that not everyone knows. Pectin is essential to jelly making. Many fruits already have it, but to make jelly out of peppers you have to add a great deal of it. To make that pectin gel, you have to add a great deal of sugar — and that much sugar masks the taste of the peppers. There is a solution at hand. There is a powerful product called Pomona's Universal Pectin, made from 100 percent pure citrus pectin and available in health food stores, that can gel your jelly. Because you're using less pectin, you can use less sugar. So the following recipe — which requires Pomona's product — is a better-tasting, more capsicum-intense, less sticky-sweet jelly. If you can't find Pomona's near you, just call them at 413-772-6816 to order.

NOTE: Refer to "General Preserving Guidelines" on page 324.

Yield: 3 half-pints

1 cup seeded and finely chopped red bell pepper
1 cup seeded and finely chopped yellow bell pepper
½ cup seeded and chopped jalapeño
1 tablespoon chili paste with garlic
⅔ cup cider vinegar
⅔ cup white distilled vinegar
2 teaspoons calcium water (see Note)
2½ cups sugar
1½ teaspoons Pomona pectin powder

1. Wash 3 half-pint canning jars with lids and bands in hot soapy water and rinse well. Sterilize canning jars in boiling water for 10 minutes. Keep jars and caps in hot but not boiling water until ready to use.

2. In a large saucepan, combine bell peppers, jalapeño, chili paste, vinegars, and calcium water. Bring to a simmer, and simmer for 5 minutes.

3. Meanwhile, combine ½ cup of the sugar and the pectin powder. Once peppers have simmered for 5 minutes, bring to a rapid boil and whisk in sugar-pectin mixture. Whisk and boil vigorously for 2 minutes to completely dissolve pectin. Add remaining 2 cups sugar and boil, whisking to dissolve sugar.

4. Ladle jelly into each jar, tapping the jars on the counter to release any air bubbles. Leave a ½-inch headspace in each jar, then wipe the rims with a clean damp towel. Seal with lids and caps and return to boiling water, placing jars upside down. Once the water returns to a boil, cook for 10 minutes.

5. Remove pot from heat. Let jars cool slightly before removing from water. Jars may not all be sealed at this point but should seal as they cool and a vacuum is created. Cool completely, upside down, on kitchen towels.

6. Refrigerate any jars that did not seal and use those first. Store sealed jars in a cool, dark place for at least 2 weeks before serving. Refrigerate after opening.

NOTE: When you purchase Pomona's Universal Pectin, you will receive a packet of monocalcium phosphate, or calcium powder. Follow Pomona's directions for mixing the powder with water — which will yield the calcium water called for in this recipe. Using it is a great way to help your pectin gel.

Midwest

The food of the Midwest, America's "heartland," conjures up images of home, Mom, purity. In fact, the food of the American Midwest is less homogeneous than that; it is as historically complicated as the food of any other American region.

Once again, the Native Americans were there at the beginning, sharing their secrets; I'm not sure you can claim corn dogs as Native American in origin, but you can certainly make that claim for the wild rice of Minnesota, one of the Native Americans' specialties. Later, immigrant groups arrived; what gives Midwestern food its most basic character is the fact that these groups tended to come from Germany, Scandinavia, and other northern European locales. Many of those immigrants built an amazing dairy industry in the Midwest, supplying milk, cream, butter, and cheese for the nation; others helped to make the Midwest the sausage (and hot dog) capital of the United States.

In the twentieth century, the ethnic picture broadened considerably — and today one is likely to find great Italian, Greek, Middle Eastern, and Mexican food throughout the Midwest, particularly in the large urban centers.

✷ Minnesota Wild Rice ✷ and Turkey Soup

Wild rice from Minnesota — now actually harvested in other states as well — turns up on the tables of many Americans at holiday time. There it is often joined by a big roast turkey. Later on, the leftover turkey meat and bones, and the rice left over in the box, face an uncertain future together. This is precisely why many Americans have taken command of the situation and — on the day after Thanksgiving or Christmas — are making wild rice and turkey soup. The flavors go wonderfully well together, with the wild rice — which is really a marsh grass native to the Midwest — contributing a deliciously nutty note.

Yield: 6 servings

2 quarts water
4 tablespoons salt
1 cup wild rice
5 tablespoons butter
7 to 8 cups turkey stock (recipe follows)
1 medium onion, finely chopped
2 large carrots, peeled and finely diced
2 celery stalks, finely diced
1 teaspoon minced fresh thyme
1 teaspoon minced fresh rosemary
1 large russet potato, peeled and finely diced
1 cup leftover turkey meat, cut into 1-inch cubes

1. Preheat oven to 350 degrees.
2. Boil the water and the 4 tablespoons of salt in a heavy ovenproof casserole dish with lid on top of the stove. Add the wild rice and let boil, uncovered, for 5 minutes. Drain the wild rice thoroughly in a sieve, discarding the water. Return rice to casserole dish and toss with 1 tablespoon of the butter to coat. Add 1 cup of the turkey stock and bring to a boil on top of the stove. Add a little salt and pepper to taste. Cover with lid and place in oven for 35 to 40 minutes, or until all liquid is absorbed and rice is tender.
3. While rice is cooking, melt the remaining 4 tablespoons of butter in a heavy stockpot over medium heat. Add the onion and sweat until translucent (about 10 minutes). Add the carrots, celery, and minced herbs and sweat 10 more minutes.
4. Add the potato and the remaining 6 to 7 cups of stock (or enough to cover vegetables by 2 inches). Simmer on medium heat until potatoes are tender, about 10 minutes.
5. Add turkey meat and cooked wild rice. Let simmer 5 more minutes, or until meat and rice are warmed through. Season to taste with salt and pepper and serve immediately.

★ Turkey Stock ★

This stock can be made either with fresh-bought, uncooked turkey wings or with a few pounds of leftover cooked turkey carcass and bones.

Yield: 7 to 8 cups

2 large turkey wings, separated at joints
2 large carrots, peeled and roughly chopped
2 celery stalks, roughly chopped

2 large onions, roughly chopped
2 garlic cloves, smashed and peeled
1 large leek, light part only, split in half lengthwise
1 bay leaf
2 sprigs fresh thyme
½ teaspoon black peppercorns
2 whole cloves

1. Place all ingredients in a large stockpot. Fill with cold water to cover by 3 to 4 inches. Bring to a boil, uncovered, over high heat. Reduce heat and simmer, partially covered, for 2 to 2½ hours, or until flavor seems fully developed.

2. Remove turkey parts with tongs and reserve. Strain stock through a medium sieve. Discard vegetables. Defat stock by skimming a ladle over the surface.

3. Remove meat from reserved turkey parts and use in Minnesota Wild Rice and Turkey Soup, or save for another use.

☆ Corn Dogs ☆

When you think of a beautiful early evening in July at a state fair in the Midwest, is there a dish that more readily comes to mind than the corn dog? You can get this specialty in many places — Texas and California are big corn dog states — but with those cornfields in Iowa and those sausage makers in Wisconsin, I always think Midwest. Of course, this hot dog on a stick, coated in batter, then deep-fried, has a tendency to draw scorn from city slickers. But if you love hot dogs and deep-frying and cornmeal batters, you'll be amazed how well those elements come together in this dish. I say: For your next outdoor party, bring the electric deep fryer outside and, while waiting for the main course to come off the grill, give your guests a delicious Midwestern surprise. The following corn dog is lighter than most, not greasy, almost fluffy; it is not the belly-bomber that you may sometimes find on the midway.

Yield: 6 corn dogs

1 quart vegetable oil, plus 1 additional tablespoon
¾ cup fine yellow cornmeal
½ cup all-purpose flour, plus additional
        for dredging hot dogs
2 tablespoons sugar
1 teaspoon dry mustard
1 teaspoon baking powder
½ teaspoon salt
½ cup milk
1 large egg
6 hot dogs
Ketchup and ballpark mustard, preferably
        in squeeze bottles, for serving

SPECIAL EQUIPMENT:
6 sticks (see Note)

1. In a medium saucepan (it must be wide enough to accommodate several hot dogs frying at once) heat the 1 quart oil to 375 degrees.

2. Meanwhile, in a large bowl, combine cornmeal, the ½ cup flour, sugar, dry mustard, baking powder, and salt. In another bowl, whisk together milk, egg, and the remaining 1 tablespoon of vegetable oil. Whisk wet ingredients into dry, whisking only until lumps are gone.

3. Pat hot dogs dry with paper towels. Place flour for dredging on a plate. Roll a hot dog in the flour, tapping off excess. Using a fork or tongs, dip floured hot dog in batter. Drop into hot oil. Fry about 3 minutes, turning to

brown evenly. Remove from oil and drain on paper towels. You can fry 2 or 3 at once, but let the oil return to 375 degrees between batches. While still hot, skewer each dog with a stick, pushing the stick about halfway up into dog. Serve immediately with ketchup and mustard.

NOTE: Your corn dog stick has to be solid enough to support the dog without bending or breaking. Bamboo skewers, for example, may not be sturdy enough. I have found the perfect corn dog stick right in my kitchen drawer: the chopstick. The one you choose should be a few inches longer than the hot dog and should have a pointy end to facilitate pushing the stick into the hot dog.

☆ Chicago Hot Dogs ☆

This is pure genius at play, an absolutely wonderful conglomeration of ingredients that at first seems random . . . and then, once you get used to it, seems ordained by the gods. It's a classic example of seemingly commercial American ingredients coalescing into something world-class (if you open your mind and let it happen). And here's the best news: You can come pretty close to making a dog at home that's almost identical to what you'd get in the Windy City. Choose a hot dog made mostly from beef, with a little garlicky character (like the Vienna Beef product used in Chicago). Follow the rest of the directions scrupulously. Before you know it, you'll find yourself inexplicably rooting for the Bears and the Cubs.

Yield: 4 hot dogs

4 hot dogs
4 hot dog buns (see Note)
Prepared yellow mustard
Bright green sweet relish
Thin tomato slices

Green pickled peppers (see Note)
Chopped onion
4 long, thin cucumber spears, peeled
4 long, thin slices of dill pickle
Celery salt

1. Steam or grill the hot dogs. Steam the buns. Place the dogs on the buns and slather with mustard.
2. Top dogs with relish, tomatoes, peppers, onion, cucumbers, and pickle. (Some ingredients fit best alongside the dog.) Sprinkle with celery salt. Serve immediately.

NOTE: The two trickiest ingredients to reproduce at home are the buns and the peppers.

The proper bun is a standard hot dog bun, but it has poppy seeds on the outside. You can make a facsimile at home by steaming the bun and, while it's still warm, sprinkling poppy seeds on the exterior.

The peppers are known in Chicago as sport peppers. They are dark green, pickled, and quite hot — all qualities easy to find in a bottled pepper. But they are also short and narrow, which means that in Chicago you can toss a few of them on your bun. It won't be exactly the same, but in a pinch, you could put strips of pickled jalapeño on your Chicago hot dog.

☆ Chicago Deep-Dish Pizza ☆

The pizza world saw something new in 1943: a thick-crust, deeply filled pizza in a round pan with high sides. It was invented by Ike Sewell and Ric Riccardo at Pizzeria Uno in Chicago, and today about one quarter of all pizza orders across the country are for pizza in this style. Most home cooks do not own the round pan that is used in restaurants for deep-dish pizza — but a ten-inch cast-iron skillet works perfectly! The following recipe yields a delicious, gooey pizza that tastes very accurately "heartland": the crust is a little cakey, a touch sweet, and authentically yellow (it's the cornmeal that does that). One great trick is to prebake that crust before the filling goes in; this helps to prevent gumminess. This pizza is worlds away from the grilled pizza on page 34, or from any authentically Italian pizza — but is absolutely winning in its own good-natured right.

Yield: 4 main-course servings

1 tablespoon active dry yeast
1 cup warm water (about 100 degrees)
1 teaspoon sugar
3 cups all-purpose flour
½ cup fine yellow cornmeal
1 teaspoon salt
¼ cup vegetable oil, plus a little more
       for greasing the bowl
3 tablespoons olive oil
2 garlic cloves, finely chopped
1 tablespoon chopped fresh basil
1 teaspoon dried oregano
2 (14½-ounce) cans chopped tomatoes, drained
8 ounces shredded mozzarella cheese
2 ounces sliced pepperoni
2 tablespoons grated Parmesan cheese

1. Dissolve yeast in warm water; add sugar, stir, and set aside. In the bowl of a stand mixer, combine flour, cornmeal, and salt. Add yeast mixture and the ¼ cup vegetable oil. Using the mixer's paddle attachment, beat to combine; switch to the dough hook and knead on medium-low speed until a smooth, elastic dough is formed, about 7 to 8 minutes. 2. Oil a large bowl with vegetable oil and place the dough in it, coating it on all sides with the oil. Cover with a towel, place in a warm spot, and let rise until doubled in size, about 1 hour.

3. Meanwhile, in a large skillet, heat 1 tablespoon of the olive oil over medium heat. Add garlic, basil, and oregano; cook until garlic is fragrant, about 1 minute. Add tomatoes; bring to a simmer and cook until excess liquid evaporates and mixture has thickened, about 15 to 20 minutes. Set sauce aside.
4. Preheat oven to 425 degrees. When dough has risen, punch down. Brush a 10-inch cast-iron skillet with ½ tablespoon of the olive oil. Flatten dough on the counter to a 12-inch round. Place in pan, pressing dough up the sides about 1 to 1½ inch. Prick all over with a fork. Place in the oven on the middle rack and bake 5 minutes. Remove from oven. Brush with ½ tablespoon of the olive oil; top with about three-fourths of the mozzarella, the cooked tomatoes, the rest of the mozzarella, the pepperoni, and Parmesan. Drizzle with remaining 1 tablespoon olive oil. Place in the oven on the middle rack. Bake 20 to 25 minutes or until cheese is browned and bubbly. (Check pizza after the first 10 minutes in the oven — if the bottom is getting too brown, switch to the top rack for the remaining 10 to 15 minutes of baking time.) Serve immediately.

✹ Wisconsin Reuben Rolls ✹

One of the great food categories in the upper Midwest, particularly in communities with Germanic roots, is sauerkraut seasoned with American ingenuity (see Sauerkraut Balls on page 90). I discovered this incredibly delicious treat — the ingredients of a Reuben sandwich encased in an egg roll skin and deep-fried — at a German restaurant in Milwaukee, where it's offered as an appetizer. I think you should take their cue and offer it as a pass-around starter at your next dinner party. This is fusion food I can love!

Yield: 8 rolls, good for
8 pass-around servings
or 4 starter servings

8 egg roll skins, each about 6½ by 6½ inches
(see page 155 for recommendation)
½ pound thinly sliced cooked corned beef,
homemade (see page 268) or
store-bought
½ cup sauerkraut
¼ pound thinly sliced Swiss cheese
Vegetable oil for deep-frying
Russian Dressing (page 420) for dipping

1. Lay an egg roll skin out on the counter. Take one-eighth of the corned beef and mold it into a little square at the center of the egg roll that's about 2 by 2 inches. Top it with a tablespoon of sauerkraut. Top that with one-eighth of the Swiss cheese, molded to fit evenly over the 2 by 2-inch package.

2. Dab all of the edges of the egg roll skin with water. Fold the left-hand side of the egg roll skin toward the middle, partially covering the egg roll package. Do the same with the right-hand side of the egg roll skin. Now grasp the bottom edge of the egg roll skin (the edge closest to you) and fold it upward toward the center of the skin; the package should now be covered. To finish, grasp the upper edge of the egg roll skin (the edge farthest from you) and fold it downward toward the center, over the other egg roll skin edges already at the center. You should now have a neat, stuffed square. With your fingers, press all the edges of the square, pinching layers of egg roll skin together. If desired, crimp edges with a fork to make a decorative pattern. Repeat until 8 Reuben rolls are made. Reserve.

3. Pour oil in large saucepan, or frying vessel, to a depth of about 2 inches. Heat oil to 350 degrees. When it's hot, drop Reuben rolls into the oil — working in batches if your frying vessel won't accommodate all eight at once. Cook each roll until golden brown on the outside, turning a few times (about 3 to 4 minutes). Remove rolls and place on paper towels. Serve immediately, with Russian dressing on the side.

✪ Cincinnati Five-Way Chili ✪

This dish sounds wacky when you read about it — but when you're sitting at a Skyline Chili restaurant in Cincinnati, it all makes delicious sense. The usual sensational headlines about "Cincinnati chili" tell only part of the story: "They use cinnamon in the chili . . . and they put it on top of spaghetti . . . and they throw other stuff on it!" Actually, the dish was invented in 1922 by a northern Greek immigrant who wanted to bring all kinds of Old Country spices into chili. Then he decided to layer his creation — with the approval of the customer, of course — with a series of cumulative options. One-way chili is the spiced chili alone; two-way chili is the chili on top of spaghetti; in three-way chili, cheese is added; four-way chili introduces chopped raw onions; and the famous five-way chili puts beans on top of it all. It is my favorite way to eat this dish — and if you're not going by way of Cincinnati anytime soon, you must give the following recipe a try. It's a slightly spicy, wonderfully fresh-tasting version of the original.

★☆★

Yield: 8 servings

1 tablespoon chili powder

2 teaspoons ground cumin

2 teaspoons ground cinnamon

1 teaspoon ground coriander

1 teaspoon sweet paprika

¼ teaspoon cayenne

¼ teaspoon ground cloves

¼ teaspoon freshly grated nutmeg

¼ teaspoon mustard seeds

1 tablespoon canola oil

2 pounds ground beef

1 medium onion, finely chopped

1 garlic clove, finely chopped

2½ cups tomato sauce

1½ cups water

½ cup commercial barbecue sauce
     (a sweet, nonsmoky variety)

2 tablespoons ketchup

1 tablespoon packed brown sugar

1 tablespoon red wine vinegar

1 (1-ounce) square unsweetened chocolate

2 bay leaves

1 pound thick spaghetti, cooked

GARNISHES:

2 cups shredded cheddar cheese
     (about 8 ounces)

1 cup finely chopped onion

1 (16-ounce) can kidney beans,
     drained and warmed

1. In a small bowl, combine chili powder, cumin, cinnamon, coriander, paprika, cayenne, cloves, nutmeg, and mustard seeds. Set aside.

2. In a large Dutch oven, heat oil over medium-high heat. Add beef and brown, breaking up into small crumbles with a wooden spoon. When beef is browned, add onion, garlic, and reserved spice mix, cooking 1 minute longer. Add tomato sauce, water, barbecue sauce, ketchup, brown sugar, vinegar, chocolate, and bay leaves. Bring to a simmer, stirring occasionally. Simmer uncovered for 1 hour; it should look more like a thick sauce than the chili most people are used to. Remove bay leaves before serving.

3. To go all the way (five ways): Divide the spaghetti among eight serving bowls. Divide the chili mixture among them, topping the spaghetti. Top the chili in each bowl with cheddar cheese, onion, and kidney beans, sprinkling the ingredients over all. Serve immediately.

☆ Pork Wiener Schnitzel ☆

Many Midwesterners have recollections of thin, fried veal cutlets from Vienna — the classic Wiener schnitzel — consumed either in the Old Country or in, say, a grandparent's kitchen in Milwaukee. But the Midwest has never had the veal tradition that central Europe had. What the Midwest does have is pork — wonderful pork, some of the best in America. And because of this, and pork's availability and low cost, many families began making fried veal cutlets . . . with pork cutlets instead! Because pork has more intrinsic flavor, the dish strikes many diners as even better. The following recipe adds yet another wrinkle to the old schnitzel: though you may use classic bread crumbs for schnitzel, using the fabulously light and airy Japanese crumbs called panko crumbs makes the dish better still. It's a long ride from Vienna, admittedly, but one thing that's both Viennese and Midwestern about this dish is the size of the cutlet: thin and very large. I love this dish with the warm German potato salad on page 98 and a big stein of cold lager.

Yield: 4 servings

4 boneless center-cut pork loin chops,
    cut ½ inch thick (about 3 pounds)
¾ cup all-purpose flour
1 tablespoon salt
2 extra-large eggs
1 tablespoon water
2 cups panko bread crumbs
¼ cup unsalted butter
¼ cup canola oil or corn oil

1. Pound cutlets between two sheets of waxed paper with a mallet until approximately ¼ inch thick. Season with pepper on both sides.
2. Mix flour and salt together in a large plastic bag.
3. In a pie plate, beat eggs lightly with water.
4. Place bread crumbs on a large dish.
5. Toss cutlets, one at a time, in flour mixture. Dip cutlets in the egg mixture, and then in the bread crumbs. Press bread crumbs into the meat with a fork, making sure it is coated well. Set cutlets aside to rest for a few minutes.
6. Melt butter over low heat in a 12-inch skillet. Raise heat to medium-high and add oil. When the butter-oil mixture is very hot, add as many cutlets as you can fit in a single layer. (You may want to cook this in batches, or in several pans simultaneously.) Cook until golden brown, about 1 minute. Turn and cook on the other side until golden brown, about another minute. Drain briefly on paper towels. Serve immediately.

Southwest

The American Southwest, a dazzling place for adventurous gastronomes, features the most serious penetration of meso-American, pre-Colombian culinary ideas into the mainstream dining habits of any American region. Sure, it's the term *Tex-Mex* that is widely used across the country for the fusion of American food and Mexican food — but Texans consume a whole lot of other foods as well; there's much more "Mex" in the diet of the average Arizonan or New Mexican.

Arizona has a border with Mexico too — and though outside the region you don't often hear the phrase "Arizonan-Mexican," inside the region you hear it and taste it a lot. Arizona-Mex is not unlike Tex-Mex — but in many Arizona restaurants it hasn't fallen into cliché territory. There's a brightness and liveliness to the tacos and tostadas here — perhaps reflecting the influence of the nearby Sonoran culture in Mexico, or the greater proximity of freshness-obsessed California.

New Mexico, in particular, has made something truly local out of Mexican culinary ideas. This fact goes hand in hand with the astonishing wealth of chilies that are grown in New Mexico; it is without question our most exciting capsicum state. Both green ones and red ones are roasted and eaten whole (particularly the green Hatch chilies) or go into a range of exciting meat stews or are dried and used to season a whole host of indigenous New Mexican dishes. Such homey ideas as chile relleno casserole and carne adovado (a pork and red-chili stew) are found nowhere else in America but are consumed every day in New Mexico.

Were all this not exciting enough, modern chefs, in Santa Fe and elsewhere, found this already-established New Mexican cuisine to be an ideal base for a new New Mexican cuisine: complex restaurant food that, along with the new food of Louisianan and Hawaiian restaurants, stands at the forefront of recently invented American regional cuisine. Almost without question, some of the new ideas being hatched by these regional chefs will merge into the general culinary mix of this region within a generation.

Simply stated: The region as a whole is heaven for anyone who loves chilies, beans, corn, cilantro — and the colorful permutations that can be spun from them.

☆ Three-Egg Western Omelet ☆ with Fresh Jalapeños

The Southwest is home to a number of great breakfast ideas — like the Western Omelet, which long ago found its way onto diner menus across the country. Also called a Denver omelet, particularly in Utah (don't ask me why!), this dish always makes me feel like a cowboy on the prairie waking up to good eggs and a tin percolator of coffee. One key to a great Western Omelet, I think, is finely minced vegetables that are cooked just enough to soften and sweeten them but not enough to make their crunch entirely disappear. Another key, for me, is pulling the omelet off the heat while the eggs are still a bit creamy. I like to serve it browned side down, so you can see all the colors. You could also serve it as a sandwich on white bread, in which case you'd simply call it a western. Either as breadless omelet or as sandwich, it gets a great kick from a little hot sauce; Tabasco's chipotle pepper sauce is just perfect. I have calibrated the following recipe for a small, nonstick sauté pan that is about six inches across on the bottom.

Yield: 1 omelet, good for one hungry cowboy

1½ tablespoons unsalted butter
2 tablespoons finely minced sweet onion
1 tablespoon finely minced jalapeño
1 tablespoon finely minced red bell pepper
3 extra-large eggs
¼ cup coarsely chopped thin-sliced boiled ham
Tabasco chipotle pepper sauce (optional)

Chile Today, Hot Tamale

One of my favorite companies that ship all kinds of Southwestern dried chilies and dried chili products nationally is Chile Today, Hot Tamale, located in Dover, New Jersey. You can reach them by phoning 800-468-7377, by faxing 973-537-2917, or by e-mailing: sales@ chiletoday.com.

1. Place butter in pan over medium heat. It will foam; when the foam starts to subside, add the onion. Sauté for 1 minute.

2. Add the jalapeño and the red bell pepper. Mix well with the onion and sauté for 1 minute more.

3. Meanwhile, beat the eggs for 30 seconds in a small bowl with a pinch of salt and a grind of pepper. Pour egg mixture over the sautéed onion and pepper. Scatter the ham evenly across the top.

4. After a minute or so, lift the pan and slowly start swirling and tilting so that the runny egg in the center of the omelet adheres to the hot sides of the pan. Let rest; repeat. Let rest; repeat. After the eggs have been over the fire for a total of 3 to 4 minutes, the center should be solid enough for you to turn the omelet over.

5. Flip the omelet onto its unbrowned side. Cook for 20 to 30 seconds, just to firm up the remaining runny egg most of the way. Flip onto a plate, browned side down, and serve immediately. Pass Tabasco chipotle pepper sauce, if desired.

☆ Southwestern Frittata ☆ with Potato, Chorizo, and Pico de Gallo

The frittata is an Italian idea — a kind of super-loaded omelet you cut into wedges — that appeals mightily to the American sense of muchness. These days you see the frittata on all kinds of breakfast and brunch menus — and in all kinds of ethnic guises.

The flavors of the American Southwest work particularly well with this dish, as do the flavors of Spain. The recipe below yields a delicious creation that's somewhere between a creative, new-fangled American frittata and a tortilla español (the great potato-and-egg dish of Spain). I even love nibbling it hours later as a leftover, long after breakfast.

Yield: 4 servings

4 tablespoons unsalted butter, cut into 4 pieces
3 ounces fresh chorizo sausage, removed from the casing and crumbled
⅓ cup chopped white onion
1 small russet potato, peeled and sliced ⅛ inch thick
5 large eggs
⅔ cup grated Monterey Jack cheese (about 3 ounces)
Pico de Gallo (page 124)

1. Add 1 tablespoon of the butter to a non-stick ovenproof pan (ideally 8- or 9-inch diameter) over medium-high heat. When the foam subsides, add the chorizo and cook, stirring occasionally, until it's lightly browned and cooked through, about 3 to 4 minutes. As it cooks, use a wooden spoon to break up the chorizo into the smallest possible pieces. Transfer the chorizo to a paper towel, wipe out the pan, and return it to the stove.

2. Reduce the heat to medium-low and add the remaining 3 tablespoons of butter. When it melts, add the onion and potato slices; toss gently to coat the potatoes with the butter. Evenly sprinkle a generous pinch of salt over the potatoes and allow them to cook gently, uncovered. After 8 minutes, carefully turn the potatoes over to finish cooking, uncovered.

They should cook a total of 12 to 14 minutes altogether, until they are tender but not browned.

3. Meanwhile, beat the eggs thoroughly in a medium bowl, add a pinch of salt, and stir in the chorizo. Preheat the broiler. When the potatoes are tender, turn up the heat to medium and add the egg mixture, gently stirring and swirling the pan to move the eggs between and around the potato slices. After 20 seconds, reduce the heat slightly and allow the eggs to cook slowly for 3 to 4 minutes; they should be just congealed, but the top of the frittata should still be somewhat runny. Carefully slide a rubber spatula around and under the frittata to free it from the sides and bottom of the pan. Evenly distribute the cheese over the top of the frittata and place the pan under the broiler; cook until the cheese melts and the egg is just cooked through but still soft. Depending on your broiler, this could take as little as 30 seconds; watch it carefully. Remove from the broiler and carefully slide the frittata onto a cutting board and cut into wedges. Serve hot or at room temperature with Pico de Gallo.

☆ Taco Salad ☆

My, how things evolve in the United States. A taco in Mexico is usually a warm, soft tortilla rolled around shredded or chopped meat. In the United States, *taco*, for a very long time, has usually referred to a crisp, hard, prefolded shell that gets stuffed (usually with something like chili con carne topped with saladlike things). But the American taco evolved even further — into something very non-Mexican called the taco salad, extremely popular in restaurants throughout the Southwest. It indulges the American passion for big; there's no teeny tortilla involved here! A large flour tortilla is fried in such a way that it forms a bowl for the salad. Then, the bowl gets filled with the taco toppings, including cooked ground beef. As you work your way through, collapsing the bowl with your knife and fork, you'll probably have to agree that this evolved concept is actually a delicious thing! The following recipe is a little lighter and fresher than some, leaving out beans, and leaving out a thick sauce around the meat.

Yield: 4 main-course salads

1 tablespoon vegetable oil, plus extra
    for deep-frying
1 pound lean ground beef
3 garlic cloves, minced, plus 1 teaspoon
    finely minced garlic
1 tablespoon ground cumin seeds
    (freshly toasted and ground, if possible)
1 tablespoon Mexican oregano
    (you may substitute regular oregano)
4 good-quality 10-inch flour tortillas
    (see Note)
3 tablespoons freshly squeezed lime juice
⅓ cup extra-virgin olive oil
½ teaspoon cayenne (or to taste)
4 cups shredded iceberg lettuce
1 cup diced fresh tomatoes (¼-inch dice)
1 medium green bell pepper, cut into
    ¼-inch dice
1 serrano chili, minced
¾ cup diced red onion (¼-inch dice)
2 cups grated jalapeño Monterey Jack cheese
1 cup loosely packed roughly chopped cilantro
1 cup guacamole (optional; see Guacamole
    with Grilled Onion and Roasted Garlic
    on page 121)

Forming the tortilla for Taco Salad

Plunge a can into a tortilla in oil

The deep-fried, bowl-shaped tortilla

1. Heat vegetable oil in a large skillet over medium-high heat. Add beef, crushing with a fork to crumble. Add the 3 minced garlic cloves, 2 teaspoons of the ground cumin, and 2 teaspoons of the oregano. Cook until the meat is browned, about 10 minutes.

2. Pour extra vegetable oil to a depth of 3 inches in a pan wide enough to hold a 10-inch tortilla. Heat to 350 degrees.

3. Using tongs, hold a tortilla over the oil. Working quickly, lower it until submerged, then immediately plunge a fryer basket or other implement, such as a one-pound can with top and bottom removed, into the center of the tortilla to form a bowl. The tortilla will automatically curl around the basket or implement. Remove from oil when golden, and gently pry the basket or implement loose. Repeat process with remaining tortillas. They will resemble bowls. Drain tortillas upside down on paper towels.

4. Make the dressing: Pour the lime juice into a medium bowl. Add the 1 teaspoon minced garlic clove. Add the olive oil gradually, whisking as you go. Whisk in the remaining teaspoon of cumin, the remaining teaspoon of the oregano, and the cayenne. Taste for seasoning.

5. To assemble: Set a fried tortilla bowl on a plate. Spread the inside evenly with one-fourth of the ground-beef mixture. Top with one-fourth each of the lettuce, tomatoes, green pepper, chili, onion, cheese, and cilantro, layering each addition evenly and gently. Avoid exerting pressure on the components.

6. Drizzle dressing over salad. If desired, top each salad with a dollop of guacamole.

NOTE: Another delicious "bowl" for this salad is the Native American Fry Bread found on page 385. Simply fry it in the same way that you would fry the tortilla in the recipe above.

☆ A Modern Southwestern Thanksgiving ☆

Why must New England steal the thunder every November? Some historians say that the first Thanksgiving-like meal — a harvest-time event attended by settlers and Native Americans — may well have taken place in the American Southwest. As luck would have it, the flavors of that blessed gastronomic region play extremely well with the Thanksgiving staples. And since the brilliant chefs of the Southwest are busy evolving a truly regional cuisine based on their novel ideas, it seems appropriate to support them in November — or anytime! — with this creative menu.

☆ Two-Stage Roast Turkey ☆ with Southwestern Honey-Pepper Rub

This new recipe includes a technique I've been using for years: roasting the turkey in two stages. I do this because of the Big Turkey Problem: while you're waiting for the turkey's dark meat to cook (which takes longer), the white breast meat dries out. My solution: cook the bird until the breast is still juicy, remove the bird from the oven, and carve off the two sides of the breast. Put the bird back in the oven — and while the dark meat's finishing, serve a white-meat first course. Twenty minutes

later, you can serve a dark-meat second course. And you get to drink two wines with this main course: I always like to serve a white wine with the white-meat course and a red wine with the dark-meat course. For this Southwestern meal, I've taken the two-course concept a step further: recipes for a sauce to go with the white meat and a sauce to go with the dark meat follow the turkey recipe. By the way: the honey-pepper rub burnishes the big bird beautifully.

Yield: At least 12 servings

3 sticks unsalted butter
2 tablespoons freshly ground pepper
½ cup ground cumin
4 tablespoons dried oregano
1 tablespoon chili powder
1 tablespoon garlic powder
1 tablespoon ground cinnamon
Pinch of ground clove
2 teaspoons salt
¼ cup honey
1 (14-pound) turkey, well chilled

1. Preheat oven to 425 degrees.
2. Prepare the rub: Melt the butter in a small saucepan. Pour butter into a large mixing bowl. Add pepper, cumin, oregano (pulverizing it with your fingers), chili powder, garlic powder, cinnamon, clove, and salt, mixing well. Drizzle in the honey and blend well.
3. Rub mixture all over the cold turkey — both on and under the skin, as evenly as possible. Place the turkey on a rack in a roasting pan in the lower portion of the oven, legs toward the back. Roast until

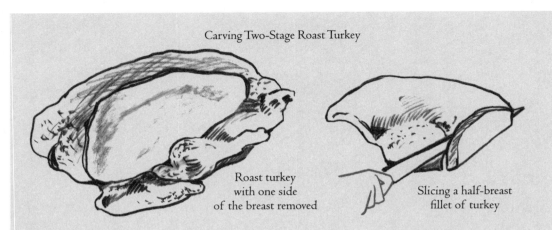

Carving Two-Stage Roast Turkey

Roast turkey
with one side
of the breast removed

Slicing a half-breast
fillet of turkey

the turkey starts to turn golden, about 15 to 20 minutes. Reduce the heat to 325 degrees and roast the turkey for about 1½ hours, basting with the pan juices every 20 minutes or so. (The white meat is done when a quick-read thermometer reaches 150 degrees.)

4. Remove turkey from oven and (at table, if desired), remove the large breast fillet from each side of the turkey. Let the fillets rest a few minutes before carving into slices. Serve white meat with Cilantro-Poblano Cream Sauce (recipe follows).

5. Meanwhile, return the rest of the bird to the 325-degree oven. Cook until the dark meat reaches 175 degrees, about 20 minutes more. Remove, let rest a few minutes, and serve the dark meat with Smoky Chipotle-Mushroom Gravy (page 379).

✳ Cilantro-Poblano ✳ Cream Sauce

Here's an ideal sauce for the white meat, brimming with the sophisticated tastes of the modern Southwest. It's also delicious on chicken, veal, even fish.

Yield: Enough for 12 diners

½ pound (2 sticks) plus 2 tablespoons unsalted
    butter (18 tablespoons altogether)
3 cups coarsely chopped leeks (about 2 large leeks)
3 cups coarsely chopped celery (about 3 ribs)
12 poblano chilies, seeded and coarsely chopped
    (about 3 pounds altogether; you may
    substitute green bell peppers)
3 cups cilantro roots and stems, coarsely chopped
    (cut from about 6 bunches of cilantro),
    plus ¼ cup finely minced cilantro leaves
1 cup plus 2 tablespoons flour
12 cups chicken stock
Pinch of nutmeg
Tabasco green pepper sauce (optional)

1. Melt the butter in a large, heavy-bottomed pot over medium-low heat. Add the chopped leeks and celery. Sauté for 5 minutes. Add the poblanos and the chopped cilantro roots and stems. Sauté for 5 minutes. Add the flour, stirring well to coat the vegetables. If the pot seems dry, add a little more butter. Sauté the roux for 2 minutes.

2. Add the chicken stock, stirring vigorously to blend well. Raise heat, bring mixture to a boil, then let simmer for 30 minutes. The sauce should be a medium-thick consistency.

3. Strain the solids out of the sauce, reserve them, and return sauce to saucepan. Finely mince some of the solids until you have ¾ cup. Return those to the sauce and add the minced cilantro leaves. Stir well to blend. Add the nutmeg and, if desired, a little Tabasco green pepper sauce. Taste for seasoning and serve.

☆ Smoky ☆ Chipotle-Mushroom Gravy

I love this deep, smoky sauce with the dark-meat turkey — but it's also terrific with other long-cooked meats. If you had, say, some leftover pot roast in the fridge — a second-day reheat with this sauce will probably be better than what you ate the first day.

Yield: Enough for 12 diners and one turkey

2 ounces dried mushrooms
½ pound bacon, minced
4 medium garlic cloves, minced
8 canned tomatoes
1 cup canned chipotles in adobo sauce
     (see "Finding the Gravy
     Ingredients" sidebar)
¼ cup smoky barbecue sauce (preferably
     Show-Me BBQ Sauce from Missouri;
     see "Finding the Gravy Ingredients"
     sidebar)
6 tablespoons butter

1. Submerge the dried mushrooms in 2 cups of hot water. Weight them so they stay immersed. After 20 minutes, strain the soaked mushrooms out. Reserve both mushrooms and liquid.
2. Meanwhile, place the bacon in a large pot over medium-high heat. Sauté for 2 minutes, stirring. Turn heat down to medium and add the garlic.

Finding the Gravy Ingredients

Chipotles are pretty easy to find. They are smoked chilies, usually jalapeños, and they usually come in cans in a kind of tomato sauce called adobo. Most gourmet stores carry them, particularly those with an interest in products of the American Southwest.

As for the Show-Me BBQ Sauce — you can order it from its creator, Harry Berrier, in Columbia, Missouri: 573-442-5309.

Sauté for 1 minute, stirring. Over sink, squeeze the tomatoes in your hands into a strainer until most of the juice has run out. Chop the tomatoes and add to the pot. Add the chipotles in adobo sauce, making sure the chipotles are cut into small pieces (some cans may contain whole chipotles, some may contain chopped chipotles). Add the barbecue sauce, the reserved mushrooms, and the reserved soaking liquid. Bring to a boil, then lower heat and simmer for 10 minutes.
3. When ready to serve, turn heat off and whisk in the butter to velvetize the sauce.

☆ Tortilla Stuffing ☆ with Sausage and Sage

I love this stuffing! It's warm, moist, soft, meaty, profound in flavor — all the good things. Who knew that taco shells could crumble up to make such a great dish? I do like to cook it outside the turkey, instead of inside the bird, to better control its cooking time. If you want a better flavor mingle between stuffing and bird, don't hesitate to dribble some turkey pan juices over the stuffing.

Yield: 12 servings

1½ pounds fresh Italian sausage (sweet or hot)
9 crispy corn taco shells
6 large eggs, beaten
Scant 1 cup bread crumbs
1½ teaspoons rubbed sage
¾ teaspoon pepper
Dash of nutmeg
1 tablespoon butter

1. Preheat the oven to 325 degrees.
2. Remove the sausage meat from the casings. Discard casings. Break the meat into chunks and sauté them in a skillet for about 10 minutes over medium-high heat, or until the chunks are golden brown. Remove the sausage chunks and place in a mixing bowl.
3. Break up the taco shells with your fingers until they resemble oatmeal. Add the flakes to the sausage meat. Add eggs, bread crumbs, sage, pepper, and nutmeg. Mix thoroughly with your hands to form a slightly wet mass that holds its shape well.
4. Butter a casserole dish that just holds the stuffing in a fairly thick layer. Place the mixture in the dish, cover tightly with aluminum foil, and bake in the oven for 45 minutes. Serve hot.

☆ Cranberry-Citrus Relish ☆ with Pomegranate and Tequila

I gotta confess: I find this sprightly, tingly mixture ever so much more interesting than cranberry goop out of the can.

Yield: 12 servings

2 limes
6 oranges
1 pound fresh cranberries
¼ cup tequila
6 tablespoons sugar
2 pomegranates

1. Remove or grate peel from the limes and from 2 of the oranges, making sure to leave the white pith behind. Very finely mince the peels. Reserve.
2. Squeeze out the juice from the limes and the 2 peeled oranges. Reserve.
3. In a medium-size saucepan combine the minced peels, lime juice, orange juice, cranberries, tequila, and sugar. Cover the saucepan with a lid, place over heat, bring to a boil, and let boil rapidly for 8 minutes. Place mixture in mixing bowl and let cool to room temperature.
4. Peel the 4 remaining oranges and separate them into segments. Remove as much membrane and pith as possible. Cut the segments in half. Add segments to the cooled cranberry mixture.
5. Cut the pomegranates in half and remove the seeds with a spoon. Try not to crush the seeds while separating them from the white membrane. Make sure to leave any membrane or white part behind. Using a rubber spatula, combine seeds gently with the cranberry mixture. Chill and serve.

NOTE: This relish can be made the day before serving.

☆ Individual Jalapeño ☆ Corn Bread Loaves

It is worth acquiring individual loaf tins just to make this recipe; everyone loves getting his or her own corn bread loaf at the Thanksgiving meal. However, the recipe can also be made in any single loaf pan — just as long as the uncooked batter fills the pan somewhere between halfway and two-thirds of the way to the top. The baking will, of course, take longer.

✫✫

Yield: 12 miniloaves

1¾ cups yellow cornmeal
2 cups sifted flour
⅔ cup sugar
1¾ teaspoons salt
1 tablespoon plus ¾ teaspoon baking powder
1¼ teaspoons baking soda
¼ pound (1 stick) plus 2 tablespoons butter, melted,
     plus extra butter for greasing pans
1¾ cups buttermilk
½ cup plus 2 tablespoons milk
2 jumbo eggs, beaten
6 ounces warm corn kernels
4 ounces cheddar cheese, grated
     (about 1¼ loosely packed cups)
6 tablespoons chopped scallions

Minced fresh jalapeño peppers to taste (¼ to
    ½ cup), seeded
3 tablespoons chopped cilantro

1. Preheat the oven to 425 degrees.
2. In a bowl combine the cornmeal, flour, sugar, salt, baking powder, and baking soda.
3. In another bowl whisk together the melted butter, buttermilk, milk, and beaten eggs. Add the dry ingredients, and just combine. Then fold in the corn kernels, cheddar cheese, scallions, jalapeño, and cilantro.
4. Pour the mixture into buttered loaf pans 1½ by 1½ by 3 inches, filling them two-thirds full. Bake for 20 minutes or until the bread is golden brown and a skewer inserted in the center comes out clean. Serve warm or at room temperature.

✪ Chile Relleno Casserole ✪

One of the great Tex-Mex dishes is chiles rellenos — luscious poblano chilies stuffed with cheese or meat, dipped in batter, and deep-fried. In New Mexico, home cooks don't usually go to all that trouble. Why should they? They have an alternative that may be even more delicious, and is certainly easier to prepare. Roll-ups of roasted poblano chilies, stuffed with meat, get covered with cheese and a batterlike mixture in a casserole. You pop it in the oven . . . and forty-five minutes later you have an incredible Southwestern spin on comfort food.

Yield: 6 main-course servings

6 large poblano chilies
1 to 2 tablespoons canola oil
½ cup chopped onion
2 cloves garlic, minced
1 pound ground beef
1 cup tomato puree

2 teaspoons ground cumin
1 teaspoon oregano, preferably Mexican
¼ teaspoon commercial chili powder
2¾ cups shredded cheese (see Cheese note)
1 cup milk
1 cup all-purpose flour
2 extra-large eggs, beaten
Tabasco sauce
Cotija cheese (optional)
Chili sauce (warm) for topping (optional;
    see Sauce note)

1. Blacken the poblano chilies: Stick a fork in the stem end of each chili, then place the chilies directly over the gas flame on your range. Turn frequently and roast until the chilies are charred on all sides (it will take 5 to 8 minutes). If you don't use gas, you can alternatively put them (minus the forks) under a broiler; turn occasionally with tongs

Chile Relleno Casserole

Place the filling on one spread-out poblano chili

Roll the chili into an open-ended cylinder

Place the stuffed chili cylinders in an oiled casserole, seam sides down

until they're charred. When chilies are done, place in a paper bag or in a large bowl covered in plastic wrap and let sit for 15 to 20 minutes.

2. When cool enough to handle, peel the chilies carefully with your fingers. Cut a little off the top and bottom of each chili. Make one slit up the side of each chili and spread each chili out (each one becomes a large rectangular piece). Devein and seed the chilies. Set aside.

3. Heat a large skillet over medium-high heat. Add 1 tablespoon of oil. When the pan is hot, add the onion. Cook for 2 minutes, then add the garlic. Cook for another 2 minutes, stirring often. Next add the beef, and more oil if necessary. Cook until lightly browned, about 8 to 10 minutes. Add the tomato puree, cumin, oregano, and chili powder. Salt and pepper to taste. Cook until most of the liquid is gone, stirring often. Check again for seasoning and set aside to cool.

4. Preheat oven to 350 degrees. Lightly oil an 8 by 8-inch casserole dish.

5. When the beef has cooled, add 1¾ cups of the shredded cheese. Stir to combine. Lay chilies flat on counter and top with beef mixture. Each chili, depending on size, should take about 5 to 6 tablespoons of filling (about ⅓ cup). Mound the filling into an oval toward one edge of each chili. Then roll the flesh of the chili over the meat, toward the other edge, until you have a neatly stuffed cylinder. Carefully place them in the oiled casserole, seam side down.

6. In a large bowl, whisk together the milk, flour, and eggs. Season with salt, pepper, and Tabasco sauce to taste. Sprinkle the stuffed chilies with ½ cup of the shredded cheese. Pour the batter over everything and sprinkle the final ½ cup of shredded cheese on top. Bake in the oven for 40 to 45 minutes, or until golden. Sprinkle with cotija cheese (if desired), and serve with chili sauce on the side (if desired).

CHEESE NOTE: You can use the same supermarket product for this dish that I call for in Cheese Enchiladas: the 4-Cheese Mexican Shredded Cheese by Sargento (a blend of Monterey Jack, mild cheddar, queso quesadilla, and asadero cheeses) hits it just right. If you can't find it, a homemade blend of grated cheddar and Monterey Jack will work well.

SAUCE NOTE: This casserole is delicious without any sauce — but a warm red chili sauce really sends it into orbit. If you follow steps 1 through 5 of the Cheese Enchiladas recipe on page 122, you'll have the perfect sauce for this dish.

✶ New Mexican Chile Verde ✶

Pork stews in New Mexico take on sublime flavors when poblano chilies — which look a bit like very dark green bell peppers but have so much more flavor — are in the stew pot. Do remember that poblanos can fool you: sometimes they're mild, sometimes they're medium hot. I love 'em either way.

Yield: 6 main-course servings

2 pounds poblano chilies (about 8)
2 tablespoons vegetable oil
2 pounds boneless trimmed pork shoulder,
    cut into 1-inch cubes
2 pounds onions, peeled and coarsely chopped
4 tablespoons minced garlic
2 jalapeños, seeded and minced
1 cup loosely packed cilantro leaves,
    plus extra for garnish
1 tablespoon ground cumin
1 tablespoon dried oregano (Mexican if possible)
6 cups chicken stock
A few teaspoons masa harina

1. Blacken the poblano chilies: Stick a fork in the stem end of each chili, then place the chilies directly over the gas flame on your range. Turn frequently and roast until the chilies are charred on all sides (it will take 5 to 8 minutes). If you don't use gas, you can alternatively put them (minus the forks) under a broiler; turn occasionally with tongs until they're charred. When chilies are done, place in a paper bag or in a large bowl covered in plastic wrap and let sit for 15 to 20 minutes.

2. After 20 minutes, peel off the blackened skin of the chilies. Cut the chilies in half; remove and discard seeds and veins. Chop the chilies finely. Set aside.

3. Heat a 6-quart Dutch oven over medium-high heat. Pour in the oil, then brown the pork cubes on all sides, seasoning with salt and pepper as you go. It may be necessary to work in batches; you want the pork to get a nice crust. When finished, return all the browned pork cubes to the pan.

4. Add the onions to the pan over medium-high heat. Cook, stirring the meat and onions occasionally, until the onions start to brown, about 5 minutes. Add the garlic and keep stirring for another 2 minutes. Add the jalapeños, the 1 cup of cilantro, and the peeled, chopped poblanos. Cook, stirring, for another 2 minutes.

5. Add the cumin, oregano, and chicken stock. Simmer the mixture gently over low to medium-low heat, covered, for 1 hour. The pork should be fork tender. If at any time during cooking the stew seems to need more liquid, add a little additional chicken stock. The likelier possibility is that the chile verde, after cooking, will be a little too runny. If

this is the case: Just before serving, and over medium-high heat, sprinkle the chile verde with a little masa harina to tighten it up. Stir well and cook for 1 minute. Season to taste. Serve immediately, garnished with minced cilantro leaves.

☆ Carne Adovado ☆
(New Mexican Red Pork and Chili Stew)

This is one of the grand dishes of New Mexican cuisine, but it's practically unknown outside the region. It began as a necessity; the red chilies were used as a way of preserving the pork. Today necessity has yielded to pure aesthetics; the dish is popular because it's delicious. It makes especial sense in New Mexico, where there's a wide variety of wonderful dried red chilies and dried red chili powders to choose from. You'll sense this if you travel there in the fall, when strings of drying chilies called *ristras* hang everywhere. My favorite New Mexico red chili — which I've seen only in New Mexico — is the Chimayo; it's deep and rich in flavor. But use whatever you can find for the chili powders in the recipe below; you can even use the standard supermarket chili powder blend. It would be best, of course — since this dish is really about the flavor of red chili — to acquire some special, single-chili chili powders to make Carne Adovado. A great source for these is Kitchen Market, 218 Eighth Avenue, New York, NY; 212-243-4433.

Yield: 6 main-course servings

2 tablespoons mild red chili powder
  (such as ancho chili powder)
2 tablespoons hot red chili powder (such as
  pequin or de arbol chili powder)
3 tablespoons cumin seeds, toasted,
  then ground
2 tablespoons Mexican oregano (you may
  substitute regular oregano)
6 garlic cloves, peeled
1 tablespoon liquid from canned chipotle
  in adobo sauce
1 tablespoon cider vinegar
2 cups chicken stock
3 pounds boneless pork shoulder,
  cut into 4 pieces
Steamed tortillas

1. Place everything except the pork and tortillas in the container of an electric blender. Blend until thick.
2. Place the pork in a large plastic storage bag and pour the marinade over. Place the bag in a bowl and let sit in the refrigerator for several hours or overnight, turning the bag from time to time so all sides of the pork are evenly coated.
3. When ready to cook, preheat the oven to 350 degrees. Pour the pork and the marinade into a baking dish. Bake for 2 to 2½ hours, covered, or until the pork is tender when pierced with a knife.
4. Uncover and bake for another 45 minutes to reduce the cooking liquid into a sauce.
5. Remove the pork from the sauce. When cool enough to handle, shred coarsely. Return pork to sauce; heat together, if necessary. Serve pork with sauce in a large serving bowl, with tortillas on the side.

NOTE: If you wish to reduce the fat in this dish: After shredding the pork in step 5, keep the pork, tightly wrapped, and the sauce separate overnight in the refrigerator. The next day, skim the accumulated fat from the sauce, then reunite pork and sauce.

☆ Native American Fry Bread ☆

Corn is the grain we associate with the Native Americans of the Southwest — but this traditional, addictive fried bread is made with wheat flour. The bread comes out of the deep oil puffy and warm, a great accompaniment to Southwestern dishes. The Navajo and Hopi like to drizzle something sweet over the bread, in much the same way that honey is drizzled over the deep-fried dough pillows called sopaipillas in Southwestern Mexican restaurants. My favorite use for Native American fry bread is as a base for Taco Salad (page 375).

Yield: 8 fry breads,
enough for 8 people

3 cups all-purpose flour, plus extra for
kneading and rolling dough
½ cup nonfat dry milk powder
1½ tablespoons baking powder
2 teaspoons salt
1½ tablespoons sugar
3 tablespoons lard or Crisco,
refrigerated for 5 minutes
1½ cups warm water
Oil for frying

1. In the bowl of a food processor combine the flour, dry milk, baking powder, salt, and sugar. Pulse the mixture to just combine, about 30 seconds.
2. Add the lard (or Crisco) and pulse for 20 seconds.
3. Turn the motor on and slowly add the water through the feed tube. As soon as the mixture forms a dough ball, turn the motor off.
4. Remove the ball of dough from the food processor. Place it on a lightly floured surface and gently knead the ball of dough until it becomes smooth, about 1 to 2 minutes. Wrap the dough ball in plastic wrap and refrigerate for 40 minutes.
5. When ready to fry, divide the large dough ball evenly into 8 pieces. On a lightly floured work surface, using a flour-dusted rolling pin, roll out each piece of dough to a thickness that is a little less than ¼ inch. Each disk should be about 7 to 8 inches in diameter. Using a small, pointy knife, poke a hole through the center of each disk of dough, cutting right through to the other side. To hold the rolled-out dough disks, dust them with flour and place plastic wrap between each of them to keep them from sticking to each other.
6. Fry one at a time in hot oil at 365 degrees, turning once and, using tongs, keeping the dough submerged in the oil throughout the frying. The fry bread is done when it is lightly browned all over, about 3 minutes. Drain the cooked breads on paper towels. Serve immediately with butter, jam, powdered sugar, honey, Honey Butter (page 323) — or use the Native American fry bread as the bottom layer of a taco salad (page 375).

California

California is one more state that shares a border with Mexico — and, predictably, this means that lots of Mexican elements have historically been woven into the cuisine of California. Unpredictably, Cal-Mex has taken idiosyncratic turns: it can be ultraheavy in the north (where the San Francisco burrito tips the scales) and ultralight in the south (where, around San Diego, fresh-tasting fish tacos are ubiquitous). Most important in understanding the "Mex" of California is the realization that it plays a smaller role in the big picture than does the "Mex" of the Southwest, or the "Mex" of Texas.

For California cuisine has long had other elements vying for dominance. Mexican culture here has, for centuries, been in a kind of friendly competition with Asian culture for the status of California's leading ethnicity; today many of the country's best Asian restaurants are in California, and aspects of Chinese and Japanese cooking, along with aspects of Mexican cooking, have worked their way into California home kitchens.

But the California food scene is not really defined by its ethnic components. Rather, the California food scene is shaped by those elements of California living that are familiar around the globe: glamour and health.

Let's face it: movie stars need to be svelte. And a good way to attain sveltehood is to eat a lot of vegetables, a lot of salads. In style-conscious, media-saturated California, this means a lot more than just what a few starlets are consuming: the way they eat has real impact on the way others eat. The Hollywood set discovered Caesar salad in the 1920s, for example, and look where that led. California, of course, has long been the unofficial salad bowl of America, with tons and tons of lettuces — as well as every other imaginable vegetable — coming out of California's soil.

This really got going in the 1920s and 1930s, when the first major California aqueducts were built; irrigation helped farms to spring up in places that theretofore had been able to grow only cactus. In recent decades, a new agricultural salad-and-vegetable subculture has developed: baby vegetables, exotic lettuces, super-high-quality goods, and, of course, organic produce.

Much of this was helped along by the great work of California's chefs — most notably, in this context, Alice Waters of Chez Panisse in Berkeley, who famously championed the primacy of garden-fresh organic vegetables and helped elevate such places as Chino Farm, outside San Diego, to star status. But for several decades chefs throughout the state have lived by these ideas and, along with Alice, have created a high-profile, high-influence restaurant industry that sometimes seems to have the glamour and reach of California's most famous industry. Certainly, the cutting-edge notions coming out of California's kitchens are among the very most talked-about and copied in the United States (think designer pizza, think Pacific Rim fusion, think grilled everything).

It is important to remember, however, that despite these high-minded culinary ideals, California is also the birthplace of the fast-food hamburger. And this is no historical quirk. Californians love their burgers, fast and slow, as well as a wide range of deliciously decadent simple foods. I always remind people that no visit to Los Angeles is gastronomically complete without making the rounds of the Spago restaurants, the tacquerias, the sushi bars . . . and the amazing hamburger and hot dog stands of the world's most glamorous city.

✦ Crunchy Oven-Roasted ✦ Homemade Granola

Okay . . . granola's not exclusively Californian. But it is a good symbol of the health consciousness of the classic Californian. Of course, "granola" means more than food; not since milk toast has there been a food so widely used to define a type of person. Starting in the 1980s, to be called "crunchy" by someone in his or her twenties was the kiss of death for someone in his or her forties; it meant "You're part of that antiquated, now-quaint California granola-eating crowd from the 1960s." But you really can't confine granola to that group alone; a wide range of Americans now think of granola — that cereal-like mix of sweetened nuts, seeds, and grains — as a healthy breakfast alternative. The irony is: nutritionists often eschew granola these days, citing the high amounts of oil and sugar. My opinion? Food's not medicine. When something tastes good, it makes you happy. And the following homemade granola, so filled with fresh and varied flavor, makes me happier than any I've ever tasted. And, yes, it's very, very crunchy.

Yield: 10 cups of granola

1 cup unsalted butter, melted
½ cup packed dark brown sugar
2 tablespoons finely minced orange zest
1 teaspoon ground cinnamon
½ teaspoon ground nutmeg
½ cup nonfat dry milk
⅓ cup maple syrup
⅓ cup honey
1 tablespoon vanilla extract
½ teaspoon salt

1 large egg, beaten
4 cups raw old-fashioned rolled oats
    (not instant)
1 cup slivered almonds
1 cup chopped pecans
½ cup white sesame seeds
½ cup wheat germ
½ cup raw sunflower seeds
1 cup sweetened, flaked coconut
1 cup dried blueberries

1. Preheat oven to 350 degrees. In a medium-size saucepan over medium heat, whisk together the butter, brown sugar, orange zest, cinnamon, nutmeg, dry milk, maple syrup, honey, vanilla, and salt. Cook the mixture until it almost comes to a boil (about 3 minutes). Remove from heat and let cool for 10 minutes. Whisk in the beaten egg. The ingredients should be thoroughly blended and the mixture should be smooth, like a sauce. Reserve.

2. In a large mixing bowl thoroughly blend together the oats, almonds, pecans, sesame seeds, wheat germ, and sunflower seeds.

3. Pour the reserved butter mixture into the large mixing bowl with the dry ingredients. Mix all the ingredients together until fully blended.

4. Spread the mixture evenly on two large roasting pans and place them in the oven on the middle rack. To get an evenly toasted granola, and to keep the mixture from burning, the granola must be stirred thoroughly every 5 minutes while it is baking; a heat-proof rubber spatula is useful for this. Bake the mixture for 30 minutes or until it is

evenly golden brown and pleasantly roasted. (Toward the end of the cooking time, take a small spoonful of granola mixture out of the pan. Place the granola on the counter to cool briefly, and then taste it: the granola should be crisp and have a nice roasted flavor, not a burned flavor. Burning happens fast in this recipe, so be careful.)

5. Right after removing the pans from the oven, divide the coconut and blueberries between the two pans. Mix in evenly. Place the pans of finished granola on a rack to cool to room temperature. Place the granola in an airtight container and keep at room temperature for up to one month.

☆ Caesar Salad ☆

To be perfectly accurate, the Caesar Salad is Mexican food . . . sort of. It was invented in Tijuana, Mexico, just south of San Diego, by one Caesar Cardini, restaurant owner, who created it on the Fourth of July weekend in 1924 at one of his restaurants frequented by southern Californians. Before you could say, "I'm ready for my close-up, Mr. DeMille," movie stars were eating Caesar Salad at all the fashionable Hollywood restaurants . . . and despite its Mexican birth and its Italian inventor, the Caesar became an emblematic California dish. Of all the California Caesars, the best one I've ever tasted is in the north, in San Francisco, at the fabulous Zuni Café. I'd say that in any history of Caesar Salad, the name of Judy Rodgers, Zuni's chef-owner, should go right up there with the name Cardini. He had the classic traditional; she has the classic modern — which is to say, a much fuller-flavored version. Cardini stressed subtlety; most diners are unaware that there were no anchovies in the original recipe. Judy stresses flavor: don't hold the anchovies,

blast away with the garlic and Parmigiano-Reggiano, and most of all, shower it with tingly lemon. This latter touch makes it light and powerful at the same time. The following recipe was lovingly put together out of taste memories from Zuni and the advice of a friend who worked in the kitchen there.

Yield: 4 appetizer servings

4 cups of ½-inch cubes of dense country-style bread (such as ciabatta)
2 garlic cloves, finely minced
3 tablespoons extra-virgin olive oil
3 small heads romaine lettuce (see Note)

FOR THE DRESSING:
1 large egg
3 garlic cloves, finely minced
4 anchovy fillets, finely minced
1 tablespoon red wine vinegar
3 tablespoons lemon juice
6 tablespoons extra-virgin olive oil
2 teaspoons finely grated lemon zest
½ cup grated Parmigiano-Reggiano

1. Preheat oven to 350 degrees.
2. In a medium bowl, toss the bread with the 2 cloves of garlic and 3 tablespoons of the olive oil. Spread cubes on a baking sheet in a single layer and bake in the preheated oven until toasted and beginning to brown around the edges (about 12 minutes). Set aside.
3. Wash the romaine, discarding the tough outer leaves and using the more tender leaves in the core. Depending on how you want to arrange the salad, trim the leaves to 6 inches or cut crosswise into 1-inch pieces.
4. Make the dressing: In a 1-quart saucepan, bring a pint of water to a boil over high heat. Carefully lower in the egg and cook for

1 minute. Remove and immediately plunge into cold water to stop the cooking.

5. Break the egg into a bowl and whisk in the 3 cloves of garlic and the anchovies. Add the vinegar and lemon juice.

6. Gradually whisk in the olive oil. Add the lemon zest and most of the Parmigiano-Reggiano, reserving 2 tablespoons.

7. Place the lettuce and bread cubes in a large bowl. Pour the dressing over them and toss to coat well, preferably using your hands. Season to taste with salt and pepper.

8. Arrange the salad on one large plate or on individual plates. Make sure some of the croutons lie on top. Sprinkle with the reserved Parmigiano-Reggiano and serve immediately.

NOTE: One of the things that make this recipe so good is the use of only light green inner leaves of romaine lettuce. In most supermarkets, you will find bags of romaine that are packed three smallish heads to the bag, with a high percentage of light green inner leaves. These are great to use. If you can't find them, use three regular heads of romaine — but to make the best possible Caesar, you'll have to pass on many of the tougher, greener outer leaves. Save them for another kind of salad tomorrow.

☆ Cobb Salad ☆

Arguably the world's most famous chopped salad — and arguably the best thing to order from room service in a California hotel — the Cobb Salad was invented by Bob Cobb, manager of the legendary Brown Derby restaurant in Hollywood in the 1920s. The story goes that he threw it together out of leftovers in the restaurant's fridge when Jack Warner and his buddies wandered in. The original recipe calls for French dressing — though I'm not sure if that meant vinaigrette or the orange stuff that was popular back then. If you want to serve it with vinaigrette, one tailored for this dish is in the recipe below. If you want to serve it with the orange stuff, see the great French Dressing recipe on page 422. I sometimes enjoy Cobb Salad with Blue Cheese Dressing; if you'd like to try it, see page 422. However you dress it, make sure that the rows of ingredients that sit on top of the lettuce base are neat and orderly; it sounds silly, but the visual effect is really quite beautiful.

Yield: 8 main-course luncheon servings

2 large whole chicken breasts
1 pound sliced bacon
4 large Hass avocados
1 lemon, cut in halves, 1 half squeezed
1½ teaspoons salt, plus extra for the avocados
1½ teaspoons freshly ground pepper,
    plus extra for the avocados
1 head romaine lettuce, washed, dried,
    and trimmed
1 head iceberg lettuce, washed, dried,
    and trimmed
1 bunch watercress, washed, dried,
    and trimmed
1 bunch chicory, washed, dried, and trimmed
½ cup red wine vinegar
½ cup water
½ teaspoon sugar
1½ teaspoons Worcestershire sauce
1½ teaspoons dry English mustard
1 garlic clove, minced
½ cup olive oil
1½ cups vegetable oil
2 cups finely crumbled blue cheese,
    preferably Roquefort
4 large tomatoes, cut into small cubes
6 hard-boiled eggs, cut into small cubes

1. Place chicken breasts in a large saucepan and just cover with cold water. Place pan over medium-high heat, bring to a gentle simmer, and adjust flame to keep liquid at a gentle simmer. Poach chicken until just cooked (the meat should be pure white with no pink showing); this will take 20 to 25 minutes.

2. When chicken is done, remove it from the hot water and immediately place it in the refrigerator. When cool enough to handle, remove skin and bones; discard. Chop the meat into small cubes and reserve in refrigerator.

3. Cook the bacon in a sauté pan (or pans) until it is fairly crisp. Drain on paper towels. When it is cool enough to handle, chop the bacon roughly. If the bacon pieces are sticking together, place them on a baking sheet into a 200-degree oven until they dry out a bit and separate. Reserve bacon.

4. Peel and stone the avocados, making sure to rub the exposed flesh with the unsqueezed lemon half as you work. Cut avocado flesh into small cubes; squeeze the remaining juice from the rubbing lemon and toss avocado cubes with the juice, salt, and pepper. Reserve, covered.

5. Chop romaine, iceberg, watercress, and chicory into small bits. Toss together. Reserve in the refrigerator, covered with a damp paper towel.

6. Prepare the dressing: Place the vinegar, water, sugar, the 1½ teaspoons salt, the 1½ teaspoons pepper, Worcestershire sauce, mustard, garlic, and the juice of the squeezed lemon half in the work bowl of a food processor. Blend for 10 seconds. Then, with the motor running, add the oils in a thin stream. When the dressing is done, adjust seasoning with salt and pepper. Place in a jar and reserve in refrigerator.

7. Choose an enormous salad bowl or a very large platter. Add the chopped greens to it; spread them across the bottom of the bowl or platter, forming an even base. Remove dressing jar from refrigerator, shake it, and pour enough dressing over the greens to moisten them well. Reserve extra dressing.

8. Arrange symmetrical, even, vertical rows of six ingredients — chicken, bacon, avocado, blue cheese, tomatoes, and eggs — on the lettuce base. The six rows should lie next to each other, touching each other, from one side of the bowl or platter to the other.

9. Provide eight dinner plates and serve the bowl or platter along with extra dressing.

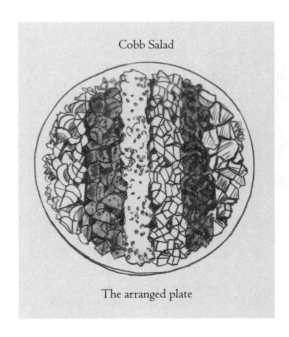

Cobb Salad

The arranged plate

Each diner helps himself or herself to a portion of the Cobb Salad. Diners may top salad with extra dressing, if desired.

☆ Green Goddess Dressing ☆

This American restaurant classic — a creamy, bright green friend for your salads, bursting with the flavor of fresh herbs — was invented in San Francisco in the 1920s. An actor named George Arliss, staying at the Palace Hotel, was appearing locally in a play named *The Green Goddess,* and the hotel chef created this dressing to honor the actor and the play. Good PR, even then! The following version has a little modern California in it: I think the lower quantity of mayonnaise and the addition of yogurt make Green Goddess even more celestial. It works best on hearty lettuces such as romaine; in one old tradition, a wooden salad bowl is rubbed with cut garlic, and the dressing is tossed therein with romaine, Boston lettuce, and chicory. Green Goddess is also heavenly with cold fish and shellfish.

Yield: Enough for 6
medium-size salads

¼ cup white vinegar
Juice of ½ lemon
1 garlic clove, peeled
1 shallot, peeled
5 anchovy fillets
1 cup parsley leaves, loosely packed
¼ cup tarragon leaves
¼ cup dill leaves
¼ cup chopped chives
1 scallion, white and green parts, chopped
¾ cup mayonnaise
½ cup plain yogurt

I. In a blender combine the vinegar, lemon juice, garlic, shallot, and anchovies. Blend until you have a puree.

2. If the herbs are at all sandy or gritty, wash them thoroughly and dry on paper towels or in a salad spinner. Add the parsley, tarragon, dill, chives, and scallion to the blender and puree until the mixture becomes bright green. Add the mayonnaise and yogurt and puree until smooth. Season to taste with salt and pepper.

☆ Crab Louis ☆

First-course arrangements of lump crabmeat are popular in restaurants across the country — but Crab Louis (pronounced Looey) is the most famous codified arrangement. There's a little controversy as to its origins, but most people agree that it was invented in San Francisco at the beginning of the twentieth century. It is simplicity itself — a kind of Russian dressing cloaks crab and lettuce, with hard-boiled eggs playing a secondary role. Other garnishes may be added.

Yield: 4 first-course servings

½ cup mayonnaise
2 teaspoons lemon juice
¼ teaspoon grated lemon zest
2 tablespoons sour cream
4 drops Tabasco sauce
4 tablespoons Heinz chili sauce
2 tablespoons finely diced green bell pepper
2 tablespoons thinly sliced scallion
1 teaspoon finely minced parsley
¼ teaspoon finely minced fresh dill
1 head iceberg lettuce, rinsed, cored, and dried,
    then torn into bite-size pieces
1 pound cooked lump crabmeat, picked over
    to remove any shells or cartilage

2 medium tomatoes, each cut into 6 wedges
2 hard-cooked eggs, each cut into 6 wedges
1 tablespoon capers in brine, rinsed in cold
    water to remove some of the salt
16 black olives, pitted

1. In a small mixing bowl whisk together the mayonnaise, lemon juice, lemon zest, sour cream, Tabasco, chili sauce, bell pepper, scallion, parsley, and dill. Cover and refrigerate at least 1 hour to let the flavors blend. Season to taste.

2. Place one-fourth of the torn lettuce leaves on each of four plates. Place about 1½ tablespoons of the dressing over the lettuce on each plate. Arrange one-fourth of the crabmeat evenly over the top of the lettuce on each plate. Spoon about 1 tablespoon of dressing over the crabmeat on each plate. Garnish each plate decoratively with tomato wedges, egg wedges, capers, and olives. Serve remaining dressing separately.

✩ Cod Steaks Poached ✩ in Olive Oil and Herbs

For some years, California has led the country in the discovery of new cooking techniques. And despite the usual fear of fat on the part of American restaurant patrons, the idea of poaching fish in something richer than water has become extremely trendy, in California and elsewhere. Many chefs are imitating the idea spawned by Tom Keller, of the French Laundry in the Napa Valley, of poaching lobster in butter. Olive oil poaches are equally trendy. Of course, if the fish ended up tasting oily, it never would have caught on. It doesn't. Instead, the fish, which does not absorb the oil, ends up beautifully moist and tender. Some chefs like to cook the fish with lemon slices in the pan, but I find that that takes away from the taste of the fish. If you can't find cod, another good fish to use for this method is halibut. The finished dish is fabulous with boiled yellow potatoes (with extra olive oil, of course!).

Yield: 4 main-course servings

1 small bunch of flat-leaf parsley
About 30 stems of fresh herbs (I use a mixture
    of marjoram, oregano, and thyme)
4 cod steaks, each about 1 inch thick
    (or you could use cod fillets, each
    about ½ pound and 1 inch thick)
1 teaspoon salt
¾ teaspoon freshly ground pepper
8 garlic cloves, peeled
2 to 3 cups inexpensive extra-virgin olive oil
    (see Note)
1 cup kalamata olives
2 lemons, quartered, for garnish
High-quality extra-virgin olive oil for garnish

1. Preheat oven to 250 degrees.
2. Rinse and dry the parsley and the other herbs. Pick half the leaves from each bunch of herbs, including the parsley, and reserve the leaves. Place the remaining stems (with half their leaves still attached) in a heavy baking pan (the one I use is 8 by 8 by 2 inches; just make sure the pieces of fish will fit in one layer and that the pan will contain all the oil).
3. Sprinkle the top and bottom of each piece of cod evenly with the salt and pepper. Place the fish in the pan on top of the herbs, strew the garlic evenly, and cover all with the inexpensive olive oil. Place the pan in the oven, uncovered, and cook for 50 minutes. The fish

should flake easily. Remove fish from oven and let the pan cool for about 10 minutes.

4. Meanwhile, while the fish is poaching, chop the reserved herb leaves for garnish, pit and halve the olives, and quarter the lemons.

5. When ready to serve, place a generous portion of olives on each plate. Carefully remove the fish and garlic and place on top of the olives, scatter with the reserved fresh herb leaves, and drizzle with a small amount of the high-quality extra-virgin olive oil. Serve each diner a few lemon quarters, which they may squeeze over the fish.

NOTE: It is wasteful to poach the fish in a large quantity of high-quality olive oil; it costs a bundle, and the oil characteristics you paid so much for will be lost in the long cooking. However, a flavorful, less-expensive extra-virgin olive oil is perfect; I like to make this recipe with Pompeian brand.

☆ Tuna Burgers with ☆ Lemon-Shallot Mayonnaise

With the growing popularity of raw or slightly cooked tuna — fed, of course, by America's sushi obsession — and with the ever present desire of some diners to avoid meat and eat more lightly . . . is it any wonder that the tuna burger became a hugely popular item at the kind of upscale but casual lunch places where fashionable people eat? And is it any wonder that California — a great burger state but a healthy one — has led the way? Of course, in the Golden State you'd be most likely to see tuna burgers on the grill. I choose to sauté the burgers in the following recipe because I love the browned butter from the pan licking them. But if you're with the fashionable crowds counting calories, these burgers are also delicious over a gas or charcoal fire. And the bacon, of course — which turns this into a kind of high-end BLT — is optional (but not for me!).

Yield: 4 main-course servings

1 pound yellowfin tuna that has been cleaned
    of dark spots and sinew (that's 1 pound
    total of usable fish)
2 tablespoons plus 2 teaspoons Lemon-Shallot
    Mayonnaise (recipe follows),
    plus additional for topping burgers
2 teaspoons kosher salt
¼ cup extra-virgin olive oil
3 tablespoons unsalted butter, cut into 3 pieces
4 kaiser rolls with sesame seeds
    (or other high-quality soft rolls), toasted
1 small red onion, peeled and sliced into very
    thin rounds
1 large ripe tomato, sliced into thin rounds
1 large bunch of arugula, tough stems removed,
    well washed and dried
8 slices of bacon, cooked as you like it

1. Using a very sharp chef's knife, cut the tuna into tiny cubes less than ¼ inch per side.

2. In a medium mixing bowl, combine the tuna with the mayonnaise, salt, and a few generous grindings of pepper. Mix thoroughly. Divide the mixture evenly into 4 parts and toss each gently back and forth between your hands, forming 4 balls. Shape each ball into patties about 1¼ inch thick. Place the burgers on a plate, cover with plastic wrap, and put in the refrigerator for 30 minutes to help firm them up (handle tuna burgers more gently than hamburgers; they are more fragile).

3. Place a frying pan, large enough to hold the patties without crowding, over high heat and add the olive oil. Just as it begins to smoke, quickly and carefully add the burgers, cooking them for about 30 seconds and then

reducing the heat to medium-high. Cook 2 to 3 minutes per side for medium-rare (they will be light golden on the outside), and about 4 minutes per side if you prefer them cooked all the way through. After you have carefully flipped them, add the butter and allow it just to melt, and begin basting the burgers with the help of a soupspoon. Continue basting every 30 seconds or so until they are cooked to your liking. Remove the burgers and blot briefly on paper towels.

4. While the burgers are cooking, place each of the toasted buns open-face on a dinner plate and spread a small amount of mayonnaise on the face of each bun. Lay slices of onion and tomato, some arugula leaves, and two slices of bacon on the bun tops. Transfer the cooked tuna burgers to the bun bottoms and serve immediately, with additional lemon-shallot mayonnaise on the side.

★ Lemon-Shallot Mayonnaise ★

Yield: About 1¾ cups

2 medium lemons, washed
2 medium shallots, peeled and finely chopped
    (about 2 tablespoons)
Yolks of 3 large eggs, at room temperature
1 teaspoon kosher salt
¾ cup high-quality extra-virgin olive oil
¾ cup vegetable oil (canola, corn, or grape seed
    oil work well)

1. Squeeze the juice of 1 of the lemons into a small nonreactive cup or bowl; add the shallots and allow them to soak for 5 minutes. Drain, discarding the liquid, and set shallots aside. Meanwhile, using the smallest holes on a box grater (or better still, one of the newer "microplane" graters), remove the zest of the second lemon, avoiding the white pith beneath, and reserve. Squeeze the juice of the second lemon into another small cup or bowl and reserve.

2. In a very clean, dry, medium-size ceramic or glass bowl, whisk together the egg yolks, salt, soaked shallots, the reserved lemon zest, and 1 teaspoon of the reserved lemon juice. Continue whisking and begin adding the olive oil, a drop at a time, until the mixture thickens considerably. Once the emulsion forms, add the remaining olive oil in small amounts, whisking continuously during each addition, to incorporate fully. Continue adding the vegetable oil in the same fashion. You should now have a thick, creamy mayonnaise. Whisk in 1 tablespoon of the reserved lemon juice and taste. It should taste strongly of lemon. If you feel it could be more lemony (I often do), whisk in additional juice to your taste.

NOTE: The mayonnaise could also be made in a food processor.

✴ San Diego Fish Tacos ✴

Tacos on the street in Mexico are one of that country's great gastronomic delights. Most typically, each taco is made from two soft and warm corn tortillas, folded together, filled with a little meat and salsa. A little farther north, in the world of Cal-Mex, predictably, things change. The tacos are stuffed a little fuller, they're less greasy and more saladlike. And in and around San Diego, you're most likely to see tacos that have no meat at all — for this is the home of the fish taco, a breezy, delicious treat. The fish that will stuff it can be either fried or grilled — but to make the following recipe as Californian as possible, I'm recommending the grill.

Yield: 2 tacos

2 (4-ounce) fillets of any fairly firm-fleshed
    fish (red snapper, tilapia, or the like),
    each fillet about 5 inches long and
    2 inches wide
1 teaspoon olive oil
½ teaspoon chili powder
Scant ½ teaspoon salt
¼ teaspoon pepper
Pinch of ground allspice
½ teaspoon very finely minced garlic
1 teaspoon grated lime rind
4 (6-inch) soft corn tortillas
¼ cup Creamy Tomatillo-Avocado Salsa
    (page 125)
4 teaspoons sour cream
2 tablespoons shredded cheese
    (such as Monterey Jack)
¼ cup shredded cabbage
¼ cup thinly sliced onion
1 plum tomato, cut in long, thin slices
2 tablespoons cilantro leaves
Hot sauce (optional)

1. In a bowl, coat the fish fillets with olive oil. Sprinkle on the chili powder, salt, pepper, and allspice; working with your hands, distribute the spices evenly. Rub each fillet with the minced garlic and the lime rind. Cover and refrigerate for 4 to 8 hours. (You can use it right away, but the fish won't have as much flavor.)

2. When ready to prepare the tacos, turn on a broiler or make a charcoal fire. Cook fish by either method until it's just done, about 3 to 4 minutes. Reserve.

3. Place the tortillas on a griddle, or steam them until they're soft and warm. Lay them out on the counter, making two stacks of two tortillas each. Divide the salsa between the two stacks, centering a few tablespoons on the top tortilla of each stack. Top salsa with sour cream, dividing it evenly. Top the sour cream on each stack with a cooked fish fillet. Divide the rest of the ingredients between the two stacks, resting them on the fish fillets: cheese, cabbage, onion, tomato, and cilantro leaves. Fold each stack of two tortillas once and serve immediately. Pass hot sauce if desired.

☆ Baja California ☆ Lobster Tacos

There is a town in Baja California just south of Tijuana, Mexico — and not too far from San Diego — called Puerto Nuevo. American tourists years ago discovered that local fishermen were catching lobsters in the sea there, which eventually led to an explosion of tourist-oriented lobster restaurants in Puerto Nuevo. The specialty of each restaurant was the same: a flour tortilla stuffed with rice, beans, spice-fried lobster, and most important — for this was made for American lobster eaters — melted butter! This collision of Mexican food and American lobster house is as startling as it is delicious. Today the Baja lobster taco can be found on both sides of the border. In fact, there's

★☆

no special reason to eat it in Puerto Nuevo any longer — since, I'm told, the lobster is now shipped in from other places! In deference to the *nuevo* reality in Puerto Nuevo, the following recipe calls for a frozen lobster tail — which crunches up fabulously well in deep oil.

Yield: 2 tacos

1 frozen ½-pound lobster tail
1 teaspoon chili powder
¼ teaspoon garlic powder
Vegetable oil for deep-frying
2 flour tortillas, each about 7 inches
*   in diameter*
4 teaspoons unsalted butter, melted
2 tablespoons warm Refried Beans
*   (page 127) or warmed-up canned*
*   refried beans*
2 tablespoons warm Tex-Mex Rice
*   (page 128)*
2 tablespoons cilantro leaves
½ lime

1. Defrost the lobster tail. Using scissors, cut through the shell on both sides of the meat, then slip the lobster meat out. Discard shell. Cut the meat of the lobster tail in half the long way.
2. Season the 2 pieces of lobster meat well with salt and pepper. Sprinkle with chili powder and garlic powder, distributing the powders evenly. Hold lobster in refrigerator.
3. Heat the oil in a saucepan (the oil should be an inch deep or so) until it reaches 350 degrees. Immerse the lobster meat in the oil, turning once or twice. Cook until crunchy on the outside, just done on the inside (about 3 minutes). The lobster will curl up in the oil; cut it into manageable chunks when it has cooled a bit.
4. Place the tortillas on a griddle or steam them until they're soft and warm. Lay them out on the counter. Drizzle 1 teaspoon of the warm melted butter over each one. Place a tablespoon of refried beans and a tablespoon of rice on the center of each one. Top the beans and rice with lobster chunks. Drizzle an additional teaspoon of melted butter over the lobster in each tortilla. Scatter the cilantro leaves over the lobster in each tortilla. Squeeze a quarter of a lime over the lobster in each tortilla. Roll up tortillas and serve immediately.

☆ San Francisco–Style ☆ Burritos with Grilled Chicken Breast

The stuffed and folded tortilla called a burrito — Spanish for "little donkey" — is far more popular in the United States than in Mexico. Particularly notable is the very un-Mexican but wildly popular California-style burrito — which finds its apotheosis in the funky burrito shops of Mission Street in San Francisco. There, all manner of unusual meats (such as tongue and blood sausage) are added to rice, beans, salsas, salad ingredients, and other things, then rolled into massive torpedoes that are usually too much for any one person to eat. The following burrito, though exactly in this style, is a slightly smaller version and includes a meat (grilled chicken) that anyone could love. Do feel free, of course, to substitute other meats: leftovers of chicken, roast pork, roast lamb, chorizo, and so on would be great.

Yield: 2 large burritos (good for 2 hungry people)

2 (6-ounce) chicken breast fillets, skin on

1 tablespoon olive oil

1 teaspoon finely minced garlic plus 3 whole
    garlic cloves, smashed

1 teaspoon dried oregano, crumbled

½ teaspoon ground cumin

½ teaspoon paprika

½ teaspoon salt, plus extra for the burrito

⅛ teaspoon cayenne

1 tablespoon lard or vegetable oil

2 large flour tortillas (preferably at least
    10 inches in diameter)

½ cup warm Refried Beans (page 127) or
    warmed-up canned refried beans

½ cup warm Tex-Mex Rice (page 128)

¼ cup guacamole (see guacamole recipe on
    page 121)

2 tablespoons sour cream

6 tablespoons shredded cheese (such as
    Monterey Jack)

Hot sauce

6 tablespoons Pico de Gallo (page 124)

½ cup thinly sliced sweet onion

½ cup cilantro leaves

½ cup shredded lettuce

1. Marinate the chicken: Place the breasts in a wide mixing bowl. Pour the oil over them and toss the breasts in the oil. Add the minced garlic, oregano, cumin, paprika, the ½ teaspoon salt, and cayenne. Use your hands to mix well, making sure the breasts are evenly coated with the marinade. Cover and refrigerate for 4 to 8 hours.

2. When ready to prepare the burritos, remove chicken from marinade and grill for 5 to 6 minutes, just until the chicken is cooked through (it should also be crispy brown on the outside). Cut into diagonal slices and reserve.

3. Place lard in a small sauté pan over medium-high heat. Add the smashed garlic and sauté, stirring, for 5 minutes. Turn off heat. Reserve.

4. Either heat the tortillas on a griddle or steam them to make them warm and soft. Lay them on the counter. Brush each with some of the garlic-flavored lard. Divide the refried beans among them, creating a rectangular block of the beans at the center of each tortilla. Top the block with the rice, dividing it between the tortillas. Continue to build on the block, dividing the ingredients: guacamole, sour cream, chicken slices, shredded cheese, hot sauce to taste, pico de gallo, onion, cilantro, and lettuce. Sprinkle with salt and pepper. Roll up the burritos, enclosing the filling. Serve immediately. Pass extra hot sauce, if desired.

☆ Patty Melt ☆

The Patty Melt is a California creation — a big, juicy cheeseburger, cooked in a pan inside bread, like a grilled cheese sandwich. The only other element that defines it, in my opinion, is rye bread — though you see the Patty Melt at diners across the country now, sometimes with rye bread, sometimes without. The following version includes Swiss cheese (which I love on it) and fried onions. The cooking of the whole package in butter makes the homemade Patty Melt taste more like a diner burger than any other burger you're likely to make at home. Ketchup? Of course. French fries and pickles too.

Yield: 4 big burgers

6 tablespoons butter at room temperature
2 large onions, peeled and
    thinly sliced
8 slices rye bread
1½ pounds ground beef chuck
8 slices Swiss cheese

1. Melt 3 tablespoons of the butter in a large skillet, preferably cast-iron, over medium heat. Add onions and cook, stirring occasionally, until caramelized, about 20 minutes. Remove onions from pan and set aside.

2. Lay rye bread flat on waxed paper on a baking sheet. Butter each slice of bread on

California Wine

Here's what I love about the California wine industry, our nation's largest: they have turned California into a wine-drinking state, a wine culture, the only place in the country where you walk into a restaurant and are likely to discover bottles of wine on most diners' tables. Bravo!

And it has happened in California for all the right reasons. They've been able to create a romance, a mystique about the places that grow the grapes; wine drinkers in California realize that wine is an agricultural product that comes from somewhere — and if that somewhere is in the next county, so much the better!

Furthermore, just as wine makers have done for centuries in Europe, California wine makers have created a style of wine that goes with a lot of the local food: rich, slightly sweet whites to go with the many slightly sweet foods of the Golden State; tannic reds that stand up well to California grill food; full-flavored wines everywhere that match all those full-flavored ethnic elements in California cooking. In addition to all this, the industry has been able to teach a very European lesson: wine is just something that goes with your meal. You've got your bread on the table, your butter, your vegetables, your fish or meat, your cheese,

and your wine. Same thing. The table's naked without any of them.

California has a long grape-growing history, and today the state is dotted with vineyards — from lonely northern viticultural outposts to crowded areas not far from teeming Los Angeles, from cool, windswept coastal vineyards in the west to hot, arid, desertlike vineyards in the center and east.

Here are some of the modern California wines I especially enjoy:

Mendocino sparkling wine, Anderson Valley
Mendocino Gewürztraminer, Anderson Valley
Sonoma sparkling wine, Green Valley
Sonoma Pinot Noir, Russian River Valley
Sonoma Zinfandel, Dry Creek Valley
Napa Valley Cabernet Sauvignon
    and Bordeaux varieties
Napa Valley Zinfandel
Dunnigan Hills Rhone varieties
Livermore Sauvignon Blanc
Santa Cruz Cabernet Sauvignon
Monterey Chardonnay
Monterey Cabernet Sauvignon
Sierra Foothills Zinfandel
Paso Robles Cabernet Sauvignon
Paso Robles Zinfandel
Santa Barbara Chardonnay
Santa Barbara Pinot Noir

the top side, dividing 1 tablespoon of the remaining butter among the 8 slices. Flip them over and butter the other sides of the 8 slices, once again dividing 1 tablespoon of butter among them.

3. Reheat the skillet that cooked the onions over medium heat. Toast bread on both sides in the skillet, until the bread is light gold, about 1 minute per side. Set aside.

4. Divide beef into 4 evenly sized pieces. Shape each piece into an oval patty about ½ inch thick. Season both sides of the patties with salt and pepper. In the same skillet as above, over medium-high heat, cook patties about 2½ to 3 minutes per side for medium-rare doneness. Remove from skillet and assemble sandwiches.

5. Lay out 4 slices of the toasted bread. Top each with one-fourth of the onion mixture, then a slice of cheese, a beef patty, and a second slice of cheese. Top with the remaining 4 toast slices.

6. Melt the remaining 1 tablespoon butter in pan. Toast sandwiches on both sides, about 1 minute per side, until bread is toasty brown and cheese is melted. Serve immediately.

☆ Strawberries Romanoff ☆

California is the home of many legendary movie star desserts. Of course, there are those who claim that this recipe goes back to the royal Romanovs in Russia at the beginning of the nineteenth century. Others place it with Auguste Escoffier, when he ruled the kitchen at the Carlton Hotel in London. But one thing is abundantly clear: high-spirited twentieth-century restaurateur Mike Romanoff, of the legendary Romanoff's restaurant in Los Angeles, grabbed the American franchise for himself when he popularized the dish in the 1940s at his Hollywood celebrity haunt. The part about his descent from Russian royalty may have been press agentry; the part that's significant is the way he changed the dish. For Escoffier, Strawberries Romanoff was a question of marinated strawberries and whipped cream. For Mike Romanoff, the whipped cream was folded into . . . ice cream! How wonderfully, flamboyantly American! If there's an eight-year-old somewhere deep inside you, you can't fail to love the following version of his creation.

Yield: 4 servings

1 pint strawberries
¼ cup sugar
2 tablespoons freshly squeezed
 orange juice
2 tablespoons triple sec (orange-flavored
 liqueur)
1 teaspoon finely grated orange zest
½ cup whipping cream
½ pint vanilla ice cream, softened

1. Wash and stem the strawberries. Cut into quarters, reserving 4 small, whole strawberries for garnish.

2. In a medium bowl mix the strawberries with the sugar, orange juice, triple sec, and orange zest. Let stand, covered, in the refrigerator for at least 2 hours.

3. When ready to serve, remove the berries from the refrigerator. Whip the cream to soft peaks, then gently fold into the softened ice cream. Gently fold strawberries into the ice cream mixture.

4. Serve in martini or wine glasses. Garnish with reserved strawberries.

Hawaii

In a way, there's a typical regional American food story here: twenty years ago, no one thought there was any regional food in Hawaii. Today people who have visited know that there is.

The Hawaiian specifics are a little different from most, however. There has actually been "regional" food in Hawaii for centuries — the foods of the native Hawaiians, such as mashed taro root, and seaweed. But this food got lost in the shuffle because — unlike the "native" foods of other American regions — it never got blended with the foods of arriving Europeans and failed to build a base for modern Hawaiian food. Oh, there are some old, old specialties in Hawaii — but with only a few thousand pure native Hawaiians left, and with few people outside that group clamoring for poi, it's not a vital cuisine any longer.

To make matters more complicated, twenty years ago those on the mainland who thought about Hawaiian food thought they understood it: Hawaiian food is a lot of expensive stuff that gets shipped from the mainland, yes? And ends up on "continental" buffet tables at fancy hotels? In other words, no one thought there was Hawaiian food.

But they were wrong, even then. Hawaii, for several centuries, has been an amazing crossroads of cultures: seafarers from all over the world — Russians, Japanese, Portuguese, English, among many others — have brought their culinary traditions to the Hawaiian Islands. In the twentieth century, a kind of people's fusion cuisine developed, conflating Eastern and Western elements into such everyday dishes as loco moco, chicken long rice, huli huli chicken, and pulehu ribs; some of these dishes are served (almost never to tourists) as part of a plate lunch that consists of an entrée, "two-scoop rice," and salad; just to round out the carbohydrates, the salad is usually macaroni salad, potato salad, or a mix of the two. To everyone except those who live in Hawaii, it is a virtually invisible cuisine.

But there are efforts under way to create a Hawaiian cuisine that's highly visible — and in the hands of top chefs like Alan Wong in Honolulu, the efforts are succeeding. Wong, in particular, takes that "invisible" food he grew up with and spins it into ravishing, upscale, big-deal restaurant food — some of the most successful newly minted regional cuisine in the country.

Of course, the big-deal chefs in Hawaii have a new advantage that they never had before: the islands have become product happy, spawning scores of cottage industries that produce wonderful raw ingredients. Forget about coconuts, pineapples, and macadamia nuts; these days you've got everything in the islands from goat cheese to venison to beef (including the largest cattle ranch in the United States) to sweet onions to chocolate to passion fruit.

But most important by far in the product department — aeons ago and now — is fish. Hawaii's waters yield the most impressive fish in the United States — from the awesome headlining tuna they call ahi to fish (such as swordfish) usually associated with other places to a wide range of spectacular indigenous fish (such as ulua and moi, both of which are more exciting than the better-known, ubiquitous pink Hawaiian snapper called opakapaka).

Oh, there's food in Hawaii — really great food — most of it undiscovered.

✭ Lomi-Lomi Salmon ✭ with Crushed Macadamia Nuts

Attend any luau in the state of Hawaii today and you're sure to encounter a curious side dish called lomi-lomi salmon. The name comes from the Hawaiian word *lomi*, which means "to work with the fingers"; indeed, you can get a lomi-lomi massage at your spa in the afternoon and have lomi-lomi salmon for dinner! It was made in Hawaii, historically, with salted salmon, which was brought to the islands in the nineteenth century by Russian sailors en route from Alaska. The Hawaiians would soak the salty salmon, then "massage" it with their fingers, adding tomato and onion as they went. Since it's not easy to find salted salmon anymore, I like to "massage" the dish in the other direction — that is, to rub some salt into raw salmon. Also, as a kind of throwback to ancient Hawaiian practice — centuries ago they added waxy candlenuts to raw fish — I like to sprinkle crushed macadamia nuts over the lomi-lomi salmon, which adds a little crunch. I think the dish is absolutely at its best when it's made at the very last minute. If you're a sashimi maven, you're going to love it. I would, however, advise avoiding the "side dish" concept; it works great as a light, refreshing starter.

Yield: 4 appetizer servings

1 pound raw salmon fillet, cut into cubes,
    about ¾ inch all around
1 teaspoon kosher salt
¾ pound large cherry tomatoes
1 tablespoon finely minced scallion,
    white and green part
2 tablespoons finely crushed roasted and salted
    macadamia nuts

1. Place the salmon in a mixing bowl and, working with your hands, rub the salt into it, distributing the salt evenly. Season to taste with pepper.

2. Drop the cherry tomatoes into boiling water until their skins split, about 30 seconds. Remove tomatoes. Remove skins and discard. Slice tomatoes in half and scoop out the seeds and pulp of each half. Discard. Finely chop remaining flesh and add to salmon, along with minced scallion. Rub the salmon with your hands, distributing the tomatoes and scallion evenly.

3. Divide among four appetizer plates. Top the lomi-lomi on each one with one-fourth of the macadamia nuts. Serve immediately.

✭ Basic Ahi Poke ✭

This is one of the great treats of the Hawaiian Islands; can it be long before it becomes a craze on the mainland too? *Poke* (pronounced POE-kay) in Hawaiian means "to cut up" or "slice" — and that's exactly what the ancient Hawaiians did to fish in making the first poke, combining it with seaweed, ground candlenuts, and Hawaiian salt. The dish, however, faded away with time — until it was revived in the 1970s by a great fish store in Honolulu. Tamashiro's was having a problem with surplus tuna at the end of each working day and decided to make a modern poke of it: tuna cubes mixed with Japanese ingredients, a kind of chunky Hawaiian sashimi. It was a huge hit, and poke today is everywhere in Hawaii. Of course, their basic poke benefits from the Hawaiian tuna, some of the world's greatest (if it's locally caught and the tuna is bigeye or yellowfin, it's called ahi). But there's probably great tuna near you, too; just make sure to get it superfresh from a reputable fish store, preferably one with a Japanese clientele.

Yield: 4 appetizer portions

¾ pound raw tuna, cut into cubes, each
    approximately ⅜ inch all around
2 tablespoons good-quality thin soy sauce
½ tablespoon Japanese sesame oil
3 tablespoons minced scallions, greenish parts

Place the tuna cubes in a mixing bowl. Add the soy sauce and sesame oil, mixing well. Add the scallions and mix once again. Serve immediately. (Though this poke is best right away, you can refrigerate it for up to 4 hours.)

☆ Spicy Poke ☆

Today if you walk into Tamashiro's Fish Market in Honolulu, you will be confronted by the poke bar — at least a dozen different varieties of poke to take home. If you go to the Big Island in September, you can attend Sam Choy's Poke Festival — one of Hawaii's best and most famous chefs paying homage to a great Hawaiian dish. And if you go to almost any restaurant in Hawaii, you will see endless poke variations. Fish other than tuna. All varieties of Asian influences (Korean-style poke, Thai-style Poke, and so on). Even all varieties of cooking — for it is quite popular today to heat the fish in some way, as in Sam

Choy's fried poke. The following version is very popular — a combination of Asian ideas yielding a delicious, incendiary mouthful. This doesn't taste like a sushi bar anymore.

Yield: 4 appetizer portions

¾ pound raw tuna (see Note), cut into cubes
    approximately ⅜ inch all around
1 tablespoon sugar
2 tablespoons good-quality thin soy sauce
1 tablespoon grated fresh gingerroot
1 teaspoon very finely minced garlic
1 tablespoon chili paste with garlic
6 tablespoons small-dice daikon
2 tablespoons finely minced cilantro leaves
1 tablespoon water (optional)

Place the tuna in a mixing bowl and sprinkle it with the sugar. Toss well. Add the soy sauce,

A Triple Hawaiian Appetizer

An absolutely thrilling starter for a Hawaiian meal — or almost any meal! — would be a service of all three Hawaiian seafood dishes in this section. Line first-course plates with soft lettuce — or, even better, with a banana leaf. Mound the three dishes next to each other, leaving a little space between them. I would advise diners to tackle the Lomi-Lomi Salmon first (it's the most delicate and subtle), then the Basic Ahi Poke, then the Spicy Poke (and for variety's sake it would be ideal to make the latter recipe with squid or octopus or shrimp). Add mai tais, leis, Hawaiian slide guitars — and you can practically see the sun setting off Waikiki.

ginger, garlic, chili paste, daikon, and cilan-tro leaves. Toss well to blend evenly. Place in refrigerator, covered, and allow flavors to blend for 30 to 60 minutes. When ready to serve, thin out with a little water, if desired.

NOTE: You might consider using other kinds of fish in this poke, especially if you're serving it in tandem with Basic Ahi Poke. Any rich-textured raw fish from the sushi bar will do — but cooked shellfish is also a strong possibility. One of the most popular spicy pokes in Hawaii today is tako poke — cut-up pieces of cooked octopus mixed with spicy seasonings. Use three-fourths of a pound of it — or cooked squid or cooked shrimp — to make the recipe above.

☆ Malasadas ☆
(Portuguese-Hawaiian Doughnuts)

One of America's greatest breakfast treats is completely unknown outside its home turf. The malasada — a doughnut brought to the Hawaiian Islands by Portuguese immigrants from another island group, the Azores — is a breakfast standard across our fiftieth state. The line forms every morning at Leonard's in Honolulu, an establishment that gets my personal vote for doughnut heaven on earth. What makes malasadas different? The high proportion of egg in the yeasty dough, which leads to a particularly rich and golden product. Malasadas are made in several different shapes; the following recipe yields square ones. Make sure to serve them warm!

Yield: About 24 doughnuts

4 large eggs, at room temperature
1¼ cups sugar
¼ cup warm water, at 115 degrees
¾ cup milk, at room temperature
½ cup whipping cream, at room temperature
1 envelope (¼ ounce) instant (rapid-rise)
*   dry yeast*

4 tablespoons unsalted butter, melted
2 teaspoons vanilla extract
¼ teaspoon ground nutmeg
¼ teaspoon salt
4½ cups bleached all-purpose flour
*   (approximate), plus extra for dusting*
Vegetable oil for deep-frying
¼ teaspoon ground cinnamon

1. Using an electric mixer equipped with the paddle attachment, beat the eggs and ¼ cup of the sugar until the mixture becomes thick, foamy, and pale yellow in color (about 5 minutes).

2. In a large vessel with a pouring lip (such as a large measuring cup), combine the water, milk, cream, yeast, butter, 1 teaspoon of the vanilla, and nutmeg.

3. Change the mixer attachment to a dough hook. With the machine on low speed, add the previously combined liquids and the salt to the egg mixture. When adding the liquids, scrape the pouring vessel clean with a rubber spatula, making sure to get all the yeast that may have stuck to the bottom. Start adding the flour, 1 cup at a time, and mix until a soft ball forms that leaves the side of the bowl and starts to climb up the dough hook. Remove the dough, place it in a lightly oiled bowl, and rotate the dough to pick up a little of the oil on all sides. Cover the bowl with plastic wrap and set the bowl in a warm, draft-free place until the dough doubles in size (about 1 hour).

4. Once the dough has risen, turn it out onto a floured work surface. Dust it very lightly with a little flour. Then, using a flour-dusted rolling pin, roll out the dough into a square

that is about 10 by 10 inches and ½ inch thick. Using a very sharp knife, cut the dough into 3 by 3-inch squares; you should have about 24. Immediately place them on a lightly flour-dusted baking sheet.

5. Cover the dough squares with a lightly oiled piece of plastic wrap. Put the dough in a warm, draft-free place and let the squares rise until they are almost doubled in size; this takes about 30 minutes.

6. Heat 5 inches of oil in a deep, heavy-bottomed pot, or an electric deep fryer, to 350 degrees. In a pie plate combine the remaining 1 cup of sugar, the remaining 1 teaspoon of vanilla extract, and the cinnamon.

7. Fry the squares, 2 to 3 at a time, until they are golden brown, or for about 3 to 4 minutes, turning them halfway through their cooking to get even browning. Place them on paper towels. Roll the malasadas in the pie plate to coat them with the flavored sugar, and serve warm.

❋ Malasadas Filled ❋ with Coconut Cream

As with all other products, modern malasadas have been upscaled! You can now walk into a bakery and choose from a plethora of different malasada "flavors." One of my favorites — and, of course, one that says "Hawaii" — is the malasada filled with a coconut cream.

Yield: About 24 doughnuts

1½ cups coconut milk
¾ cup milk
¾ cup whipping cream
¾ cup sugar
½ cup all-purpose flour
1 large egg
1 teaspoon vanilla extract
½ teaspoon salt
¾ cup sweetened shredded coconut
Malasadas (preceding recipe)

1. Heat coconut milk, milk, and cream in a 3-quart saucepan over medium-high heat until bubbles form around the edge. Cut heat.

2. Meanwhile, stir together the sugar, flour, egg, vanilla, salt, and shredded coconut.

3. Slowly pour the hot milk mixture into the coconut mixture and stir until blended.

4. Return mixture to saucepan, bring to a boil over medium-high heat, about 1 minute, then turn heat to low and simmer for 2 minutes, stirring constantly.

5. Cool filling, covering with plastic wrap resting on the surface so a skin doesn't form.

6. Fit a pastry bag with a medium-size tip, then fill the bag with the chilled coconut cream filling.

7. As soon as you have made the regular malasadas, slit a ½-inch-long hole in the side of each one with a sharp paring knife; the hole should penetrate about 1 inch into the malasada.

8. Insert the tip of the pastry bag about ½ inch into each malasada and gently begin to squeeze the bag. Each malasada will take 2 to 3 tablespoons of filling; be careful not to pop the malasadas by overfilling them. Use the tip of a knife to scrape off any excess coconut cream from the side of the malasada. If necessary, sprinkle the malasada with a little of the flavored sugar if a lot of it was lost in the filling process. Serve immediately.

Part Three

Classic America

Because we are a nation of so many regional and ethnic influences, much of what Americans cook at home has already been covered in the regional and ethnic chapters of this book. But the dishes described there are not necessarily national ones, made everywhere across the country. Oh, you'll see some of those Italian recipes cooked across the United States — but not as much as in the Italian enclaves of the Northeast. You'll see some of the Mexican dishes cooked across the United States — but not as much as in the Southwest. And you'll see some of the Asian dishes cooked in homes across the United States — but not as much as in California and Hawaii.

There is, however, a core American home food — a group of dishes that virtually all Americans, in all parts of America, prepare in their own kitchens.

It is mostly simple food — simple in its appeal, simple to cook. Ingredients for it are widely accessible; a good supermarket is just about all you need. And much of it doesn't take a great deal of time to prepare. Yes, there was an era in the American past when Mom had plenty of time to stand at the stove and cook dinner — but that day, in many households, is obviously gone. Things go faster today — and it may be Dad who's cooking the food!

Because of all these factors (except the Dad part), this type of American cooking attracts lots of criticism — both from those at a distance who don't know it at all and those who eat it every day and love it (but would never admit it in public).

It is important to remember that as a food culture evolves over time, the dishes that endure, ultimately constituting a nation's "cuisine," are almost always good dishes if cooked well. It does happen at some points in some nations' histories that, for various reasons, a cuisine is treated with indifference in its homeland. That can make it seem "bad." But if you approach any style of food with respect, you can always turn it into something delicious.

Is there anyone prepared to say that a great example of a burger, that a perfect meat loaf, that an impeccable macaroni and cheese . . . is not delicious?

Improvements and new techniques are being devised all the time to make all the foods of the world better still — from stir-fried Chinese dishes to classic French cuisine.

So I ask: Why not shrimp cocktail?

Breakfast Across America

☆ Classic Eggs Benedict ☆

Legend has it that this dish was invented in the 1890s at Delmonico's restaurant in New York City, to resuscitate the permanently bored palate of an upper-crust customer named Mrs. Legrand Benedict. It worked! Eggs Benedict is one of the great all-time breakfast indulgences, a surefire cure for the Sunday brunch blahs. Oh, people squawk about it continually — too much fat, too many calories — but if chefs ever took it off the buffet at Sunday brunches, there'd be a riot. I have a way to create another kind of riot: make the following version at home, where you can see how great a really fresh one tastes. I pretty much stick to the classic, with the exception of one Canadian bacon innovation. Normally a thickish slab of bacon gets used. I say that if you can get the deli counter folks or butcher to carve you very thin slices of Canadian bacon, and if you pleat a few of them on each English muffin, the final effect is much more pleasing. The following recipe enables you to serve six warm individual portions to six lucky people simultaneously.

Yield: 6 servings

4 cups water
½ cup distilled white vinegar
½ teaspoon kosher salt
12 large eggs
6 English muffins
6 ounces Canadian bacon, sliced as thinly as
    possible at your deli
Hollandaise Sauce (see sidebar)

1. Preheat the broiler.

2. In a large skillet, pour in the water, vinegar, and salt and bring to a simmer.

3. Meanwhile, carefully crack 4 of the eggs into separate small cups. One at a time, carefully pour the eggs into the water against the side of the skillet and cook until the whites are firm, the yolks still runny, about 3 minutes. Remove poached eggs, drain on a kitchen towel, and cover with another towel that has been soaked in hot water and squeezed dry, to keep warm. Repeat with the remaining eggs. If the cooked eggs' whites have any ragged edges, you may trim them with kitchen shears.

4. While the eggs are poaching, make a small slit on the side of each English muffin and gently pull each muffin into two halves (pulling English muffins apart, instead of slicing, creates pleasing "nooks and crannies"). Transfer the muffins to a baking sheet and toast under the broiler, turning once, until crispy, about 2 minutes per side. Divide the muffins among six plates.

5. Place the bacon on the baking sheet and heat under the broiler until just warmed through, about 1 minute.

6. Place some of the bacon in "ruffles" on each muffin half and top each with an egg. Spoon about 2 tablespoons of hollandaise sauce over each egg (if the hollandaise is too thick, thin it with warm water). Serve immediately.

Hollandaise Sauce

Many chefs have taken a stab at Hollandaise Sauce. Restaurant chefs often make this sauce with clarified butter — because whole butter has water in it and creates a thinner sauce than one made with clarified butter. Chefs normally want the sauce to be thicker because they're usually fond of adding lemon juice to taste at the end, and they like adding it to a thicker sauce that can stand to be diluted. Try it both ways; see which way you prefer. The following recipe is made, restaurant style, in a stainless steel bowl over simmering water; you may make it instead in a double boiler.

Yield: About 1½ cups

1¼ cups unsalted butter or clarified butter (page 227)
Yolks of 4 large eggs
2 teaspoons cold water
1 tablespoon plus 2 teaspoons lemon juice, or to taste
Tabasco sauce

1. In a medium saucepan, over low heat, melt the butter or warm the clarified butter. Set aside, covered, to keep warm.
2. Pour water to a depth of 1 inch into a large saucepan and bring to a simmer.
3. Place the egg yolks and the 2 teaspoons cold water in a large stainless steel bowl and whisk until frothy. Place the bowl over the simmering saucepan of water (make sure the water doesn't reach a boil). The water must not touch the bottom of the bowl. Whisk the yolks rapidly and constantly, until very thick, about 2½ minutes.
4. Remove the bowl and saucepan from the heat. While rapidly whisking the thickened yolks, slowly drizzle in a small amount of the melted butter; continue whisking until fully incorporated. Continue with the remaining butter until a thickened sauce is formed (if the yolks become too thick, add a little warm water). Whisk in the lemon juice and add Tabasco, to taste. Season with salt and pepper. Cover with plastic wrap and set aside in a warm place until ready to use.

☆ Mama's Deep-Dish ☆ Boiled Eggs with Shards of Buttered Toast

There's a great morning dish made in homes across America — but rarely seen in restaurants, cookbooks, or other countries. It is, plainly put, a couple of hot boiled eggs tossed in a bowl with pieces of buttered toast. Now, not everyone's mom made this — and if yours didn't, you must discover one of the easiest, and the most American, paths to breakfast bliss. I still tingle every time I taste it — but I can't tell anymore if that's nostalgia or just plain satisfaction.

Yield: 2 servings

2 slices well-browned white-bread toast, buttered well
4 extra-large eggs, medium-boiled

Tear each hot, buttered piece of toast into a dozen pieces. Place 12 pieces in one warmed bowl, 12 pieces in another. Cool the eggs slightly under running water so you can handle them. Cut each one open at the center with a serrated knife and, with a spoon, scoop the white and runny yolk out of the two halves of each one, dividing the cooked egg evenly between the toast in the two bowls.

Toss toast and egg together. Season to taste with salt and pepper. Let sit for a minute so toast can soften. Serve immediately.

✵ Homemade Breakfast ✵ Sausage Patties

There is an alchemy that turns meat loaf into pâté and ground meat into sausage. In most cases, the alchemical agent is properly added fat. In the following recipe, another basic element is at work: a little bit of water, which vastly improves the texture. Why should you go to the trouble of making homemade breakfast sausage? First, it's not that much trouble in this recipe; no sausage casings are involved. Second, it's a joy to offer something to family and friends that people don't usually make at home. Third, this may be the best breakfast sausage you've ever tasted; unlike the commercial types, in which the amount of sage usually blocks out all other tastes, this one uses sage as only one element in a wider, more complex range of flavors.

Yield: 6 servings

1 pound ground pork, fairly fatty
1¼ teaspoons salt
Generous ¼ teaspoon black pepper
Pinch of cayenne
Pinch of paprika
½ teaspoon ground sage
¼ teaspoon crushed fennel seeds
¼ teaspoon dried thyme leaves
¼ teaspoon garlic powder
1 tablespoon cold water
¼ cup vegetable oil

1. In a large bowl combine all ingredients except the oil and mix until fully blended. The mixture should be cohesive and feel a little sticky.

2. On a work surface, lay out a sheet of plastic wrap and place the pork mixture in the center. Fold the closest edge of the wrap over the mixture and roll forward into a thick, even log about 2½ inches in diameter. There should be an inch or so of plastic extending beyond the meat at each end. Tightly twist those ends of plastic wrap, making a sausage shape. Store the sausage in the refrigerator, with the twisted ends of plastic wrap tucked under the log, for at least 6 hours and up to 3 days.

3. Remove the pork log from the refrigerator and transfer to a cutting board. Unwrap and, using a sharp knife, cut the log into ¼-inch slices.

4. Heat 2 tablespoons of the oil in a large skillet over medium-high heat. When it's hot, add half the pork slices. Cook them until they're well browned and just cooked through, about 1 minute per side. Transfer slices to a paper towel–lined plate. Repeat with the remaining pork slices and oil. Serve immediately.

NOTE: This sausage is fairly tame in the fat category; you can eat it with only a modicum of guilt. But if you want to venture further into the realm of really juicy, really fatty sausage — I do! I do! — have the butcher coarsely grind ¼ pound of soft pork fat, and add it to the sausage mixture before rolling in plastic.

✵ Corned Beef Hash ✵

This is ultimate diner food — but it's usually even better at home, since lots of diners use canned corned beef hash. At home you can use really good corned beef — either leftovers from a store-purchased corned beef that you've cooked, or corned beef that you buy at a deli. (If you really want to go all the way, see Home-Cured Corned Beef on page 268.) I love corned beef hash with a pair of sunny-side up fried eggs on top of the portion — though poached eggs are also popular as hash toppers. Ketchup is totally permissible.

Yield: 4 generous servings

6 tablespoons unsalted butter
2 cups diced onion
3 tablespoons flour
2 cups diced, peeled, cooked potato
3 cups diced, leftover corned beef (see Home-Cured Corned Beef, page 268)

1. Preheat oven to 375 degrees.
2. Melt butter in a 10½-inch cast-iron skillet (or a skillet with an ovenproof handle) over low heat. Add onion to skillet and cook, stirring occasionally with a wooden spoon, until onion is transparent (about 8 minutes).
3. Sprinkle flour over onion and stir to blend well. Cook for 2 minutes more, stirring occasionally. Increase heat to medium. Add potato and corned beef. Season to taste with salt and pepper. Continue to cook for another minute, stirring constantly. Cover skillet and place in preheated oven. Bake for 30 minutes.

☆ Home Fries ☆

Home fries, ironically, usually taste best away from home, at diners. But that's because diner cooks know the secret: cooking the potatoes in advance, before crisping them up on a griddle. The following recipe gives you everything you need to make diner-worthy home fries at home. I would strongly advise cooking and peeling the potatoes the night before using them so they can dry out; if the potatoes are still moist, they won't develop the same crunchy browned exterior. If you can get them, use yellow Yukon Gold potatoes. Home fries are usually diced or cut in slices — your choice.

Yield: 4 servings

1 pound Yukon Gold potatoes
2 tablespoons vegetable oil or the fat rendered from 4 slices of bacon
1 small onion (4 ounces), thinly sliced lengthwise
Kosher salt

1. Scrub potatoes to remove any dirt, then cook — bake or boil — in their jackets until just tender. Peel potatoes while they are still warm (it's easier). Set aside to cool.
2. When ready to cook, heat the oil or bacon fat in a medium skillet over medium heat. Add the onion and cook until soft, about 7 to 8 minutes.
3. Meanwhile, cut the potatoes in ¼-inch slices or ½-inch dice. Raise heat to medium-high and add potatoes to onion. Brown them on one side (about 3 to 5 minutes), then turn them over. Cook until the other side is crisp and brown (another 3 to 5 minutes or so). They should be just crisp on the outside, hot and soft on the inside. Sliced potatoes will take about 6 minutes altogether, diced potatoes about 10 minutes. Season with kosher salt and pepper to taste and serve.

NOTE: To render bacon fat, cook the bacon over medium-high heat until the bacon is crisp and the fat is cooked out. The bacon can be served as part of the breakfast by itself or crumbled and served in an omelet or saved to sprinkle over baked potatoes or salad with blue cheese dressing.

☆ Hash Browns ☆

America's other great breakfast potato dish features less distinct pieces of potato — that's why it's a hash! The semimashing of the potatoes enables you to get a better crust on hash browns than you can on home fries. As with home fries, it's best to cook and peel the potatoes ahead — like the night before — so they can dry out a bit. I sure love hash browns with my fried eggs and breakfast sausage — but I also love them at dinner with a thick steak!

Yield: 4 servings

1 pound Yukon Gold potatoes
3 tablespoons clarified butter (page 227)
1 small onion, peeled and finely chopped
¼ large green bell pepper, cut into ¼-inch dice

1. Cook the potatoes (boil or bake) in their jackets until tender. Let cool slightly, then peel. Just before you're ready to use them, cut them into ¼-inch dice and set aside.
2. Melt 1 tablespoon of the clarified butter in a nonstick 8-inch skillet over medium-high heat. Add the onion and pepper and sauté until soft (about 7 to 8 minutes). In a small bowl, gently mix the pepper and onion with the potatoes. Season with salt and pepper.
3. Wipe out the skillet with a paper towel. Over high heat add the remaining 2 tablespoons of clarified butter. When the butter is sizzling, add the potato mixture. Using a fork, mash the mixture down until the surface of the skillet is covered. Turn heat down to medium-high.
4. After 5 minutes check to see if a crust has formed. When the bottom of the potato cake has browned, turn it over with a spatula to brown the other side. Don't worry if you can't turn it over in one piece; if you can't, just flip over the largest pieces possible, then mash the hash together again with your fork. Try not to break up the crust that formed on the first side. (If you have a good broiler, you don't need to turn the hash over — just brown the top under the broiler.)
5. When both sides are brown, serve immediately.

☆ Best Buttermilk Pancakes ☆

These are not only the best buttermilk pancakes but the best anything pancakes you can make at home! The interaction of the buttermilk with the baking soda gives the pancakes a particularly light texture and a delicious taste. Serve pancakes hot with butter and maple syrup in the traditional manner, by all means — or consider some of the more elaborate serving suggestions in the sidebar. If you choose an idea that includes butter melting on them, serve these pancakes piping hot; otherwise, you might want to let them sit for 2 to 3 minutes, during which time the texture improves slightly.

Yield: About a dozen pancakes

2½ cups cake flour
2 heaping teaspoons baking powder
2 teaspoons baking soda
Big pinch of salt
2 eggs, beaten
2½ cups buttermilk, at room temperature
½ cup sugar
¼ teaspoon vanilla extract
½ cup melted butter, at room temperature,
*   plus extra for griddle*

Brunch Ideas: A Cornucopia of Pancake Options

The Best Buttermilk Pancakes recipe produces a great-tasting, cakey, and hearty pancake — which means it's also a great basic pancake to do things to.

If it's fruit you crave, adding blueberries, blackberries, raspberries, thinly sliced strawberries, or thinly sliced bananas to the basic recipe makes a wonderful fruit-filled pancake. These are very simple to produce: simply place the batter on the griddle as if you were making a plain pancake, but as soon as possible, drop some fruit onto the surface of the cooking pancake batter. Flip the pancake over, being careful as usual. If you wish, serve the pancakes with fresh fruit piled on top of them. For an extra bit of fruitiness, layer macerated fresh fruits, or jam, between the pancakes when serving. To take this fruit craziness even a step further, place fresh berries in a blender with equal parts of simple syrup or maple syrup and puree them; strain through a fine mesh strainer and serve alongside the pancakes as a flavored syrup.

To take it all to the next level of pancake madness — maybe for a formal brunch — prepare flavored butters to accompany your guests' stacks of pancakes. Simply combine room-temperature unsalted butter and the desired amount of flavoring in a mixing bowl; flavorings could include molasses, honey, chocolate syrup, citrus zest, Grand Marnier (or other liqueurs), spices (such as cinnamon, nutmeg, or mace), vanilla extract, freshly chopped fruit, or freshly chopped herbs. Whip them together with a whisk until the butter is fluffy and the flavoring is completely incorporated. To serve the butter, scoop it on top of the stacked pancakes just prior to serving them. The most efficient way to do this is by using a small ice-cream scoop. To get a little more high-tech, use a pastry bag and tip, and pipe the flavored butter into rosettes on a waxed paper–lined baking sheet, then chill the individual rosettes and serve them on top of the pancakes.

If you're truly pancake obsessed, you can also spice things up by making a spice-scented powdered sugar. To do this, simply sift together confectioners' sugar and a small amount of spice (such as cinnamon, nutmeg, or allspice to taste). Sprinkle sugar over whichever pancake option you've chosen.

1. Sift together the cake flour, baking powder, baking soda, and salt into a medium-size mixing bowl. Whisk together the flour mixture, beaten eggs, buttermilk, sugar, vanilla, and melted butter until they are very smooth. Let the batter sit for 5 minutes before using it.

2. Preheat an electric griddle to 375 degrees, or place a nonstick griddle or large nonstick skillet over medium heat. Just before cooking the pancakes, coat the cooking surface with melted butter using a pastry brush.

3. Scoop up batter in a half-cup measuring cup, filling it to the top. Pour batter onto hot griddle, letting it spread by itself into a circle that's about 5 inches in diameter. Repeat with remaining batter (possibly in batches) until a dozen pancakes or so are formed.

4. Flip the pancakes when their edges appear to be hardening a little; there should also be many small holes opening up on the surface of the pancakes. This should take about 2 minutes. Cook the pancakes on the other

side for about 2 minutes more, or until the pancakes are golden brown and cooked through.

NOTE: When cooking the pancakes in batches, hold them in a warm oven covered with a damp cloth. Also, remember to reheat and butter the griddle after each round of pancake cooking.

✸ Fluffy Lemon Ricotta ✸ Pancakes

Pancake variations have gone through the roof at brunchy or fancy breakfast venues. Here's a creative spin that I particularly love.

Yield: About 12 pancakes, 4 servings

4 large eggs, separated into yolks and whites
1⅓ cups ricotta cheese
1½ tablespoons sugar
1 tablespoon grated lemon zest
½ cup all-purpose flour
¼ teaspoon salt
Melted butter for brushing the griddle

1. In a medium-size bowl, mix together the egg yolks, ricotta, sugar, and lemon zest. Add the flour and stir mixture until it is just combined.
2. Beat egg whites with salt (using either a large whisk, a stand mixer, or a handheld electric mixer) until the whites hold soft peaks. Stir one-third of the egg whites into the ricotta mixture, then fold in remaining egg whites gently.
3. Brush a hot griddle (375 degrees), or a nonstick skillet over medium-high heat, with

melted butter. Scoop up batter in a quarter-cup measuring cup, filling it to the top. Pour batter onto griddle or skillet, letting it spread by itself into a circle that's about 3 inches in diameter. Cook for 1 to 2 minutes on each side, or until the pancake is golden. Repeat with remaining batter (possibly in batches) until a dozen pancakes or so are formed. Serve warm.

✸ Sour Cream Waffles ✸

Waffles are big American favorites: waffle irons are inexpensive, and once you've got one, waffles are a snap to make. Waffles got their biggest boost in this country at the 1964 World's Fair in New York, when the contingent from Belgium introduced the world to Belgian waffles — in which the golden waffles are topped with strawberries and whipped cream and served as a snack. We haven't, however, really taken to the concept of the snack waffle, or the nonbreakfast waffle; we continue to eat them most often at breakfast, with butter and maple syrup, or just with confectioners' sugar. We have also created a waffle variation that is now popular across America: the sour cream waffle. The following one, with its combo of sour cream and beaten egg whites, is so light it's almost like a combination of a soufflé and a waffle.

Yield: About 10 waffles

2 cups all-purpose flour
¼ cup plus 2 tablespoons sugar
2 teaspoons baking powder
¾ teaspoon baking soda
¾ teaspoon salt
4 large eggs, separated
1½ cups milk

1 cup sour cream
¼ pound (1 stick) butter, melted and
    cooled slightly
1½ teaspoons vanilla extract
Vegetable oil for brushing waffle iron

1. Preheat waffle iron. Sift together flour, the ¼ cup sugar, the baking powder, baking soda, and salt. Set aside.

2. In a large bowl, whisk together egg yolks, milk, sour cream, butter, and vanilla. In another bowl, using an electric mixer, beat egg whites on low speed until foamy. Increase speed to medium, add the remaining 2 tablespoons sugar, and beat until soft peaks form.

3. Add flour mixture to egg yolk mixture, mixing just to combine. Fold in egg whites. Lightly brush waffle iron with oil. Pour about 1 cup batter into waffle iron and close. Cook about 4 to 5 minutes, or until steam no longer escapes from the sides of the waffle iron. The waffles should be deep golden brown and crispy. Keep warm in a 225-degree oven while you prepare remaining waffles.

☆ Blueberry-Corn Muffins ☆

Not as popular as the regular blueberry muffin, the blueberry-corn muffin nevertheless brings some real excitement to the party — such as a wonderful, crumbly texture and an earthy corn flavor. You may use either two 6-muffin tins or one 12-muffin tin.

Yield: 12 standard-size muffins

5 tablespoons vegetable oil, such as canola
1½ cups all-purpose flour
½ cup yellow cornmeal
¾ cup plus 1 tablespoon sugar
1 teaspoon kosher salt
4 teaspoons baking powder
¾ teaspoon ground cinnamon
2 large eggs
⅔ cup whole milk
1 cup fresh or frozen blueberries (if using
    frozen, don't thaw completely)

1. Preheat oven to 400 degrees.

2. Grease the muffin tin(s) with 1 tablespoon of the vegetable oil. Set aside.

3. In a medium-size bowl, sift together flour, cornmeal, the ¾ cup of sugar, salt, baking powder, and ½ teaspoon of the cinnamon.

3. In a separate bowl, beat eggs until well combined. Add milk and remaining 4 tablespoons of vegetable oil, stirring until mixed together.

4. Make a well in the center of the flour mixture and add the egg mixture. Don't overmix. Gently fold in the blueberries until just combined. Spoon batter into muffin tin(s), filling them two-thirds full. Mix together the remaining 1 tablespoon of sugar with the remaining ¼ teaspoon of cinnamon and sprinkle the mixture evenly on top of the muffins.

5. Bake until a skewer inserted in the center of a muffin comes out clean, about 20 to 25 minutes. When muffins are done, remove pan from oven and wait 5 minutes. Then remove muffins from tin(s) and turn out onto a rack to cool.

6. The muffins taste best served warm from the oven. If they aren't going to be eaten right away, wrap them individually and freeze.

☆ Perfect Cinnamon Rolls ☆

Cinnamon rolls — particularly with the rise of a cinnamon roll chain that's in shopping malls across the United States — have become one of America's favorite sweet pastries in the morning. There is some lingering confusion about cinnamon "rolls" versus cinnamon "buns" — but just remember that if your pastry is coiled, as is the pastry in the following recipe, it's a roll. A proper roll should also be glazed; a proper bun should not. Probably the most important goal in making a cinnamon roll, to me, is height, fluffiness — and that's why I use yeast in my recipe and call for a pan that will force the rolls to bump together as they bake (this pushes them up instead of allowing them to flatten out). The following rolls are good when they're warm and good at room temperature — but they're insanely good when they're hot, just a few minutes out of the oven.

Yield: 16 cinnamon rolls

SWEET DOUGH:

2 packages active dry yeast (5 teaspoons)
¾ cup warm water
¾ cup sugar
½ cup vegetable shortening (such as Crisco), melted
¼ cup plus 6 tablespoons unsalted butter, melted, plus extra butter at room temperature for the bowl and pan
3 eggs
1½ cups milk
6 to 7 cups bread flour
1 teaspoon salt

FILLING:

½ cup granulated sugar
¼ cup brown sugar
1 tablespoon powdered cinnamon

GLAZE:

¾ cup confectioners' sugar
1 teaspoon vanilla extract
Milk

1. Make the sweet dough: In a bowl, dissolve yeast in warm water. Make sure that the mixture bubbles after a few minutes (if not, your yeast is not fresh and you'll need to start over with a fresher package of yeast).

2. Combine the sugar, shortening, the ¼ cup melted butter, eggs, and milk in the work bowl of a Kitchen Aid stand mixer. Blend together quickly, using the paddle attachment. Add yeasted water and blend together quickly. In another bowl, stir the flour and salt together. Add the dough hook attachment to the mixer, then add flour a cup at a time to the liquid ingredients. Mix until thoroughly blended and the dough starts to pull away from the sides of the bowl. Remove dough from bowl, place on counter, and knead until it's almost smooth (5 minutes or so). Transfer dough to a buttered bowl, cover with plastic wrap, and place in a warm spot to rise for 1 hour.

3. Make the filling: In a bowl combine the granulated sugar, brown sugar, and cinnamon.

4. Preheat oven to 400 degrees.

5. After the dough has risen, roll it out in a rectangle (approximately 24 by 10 inches) with a thickness of ¼ inch. Brush dough with the remaining 6 tablespoons of melted butter. Sprinkle cinnamon filling over melted butter, covering all the dough. Roll the dough up like a jelly roll, starting at one of the rectangle's long sides. After you've rolled

it, the ends will be a little irregular — so trim them off. Slice roll into 1½-inch rounds; you should have 16 of them. Arrange them on one or more large, buttered sheet pans, or in two or more large, buttered cast-iron frying pans. Leave approximately 1 inch of space between the slices. Bake cinnamon rolls until golden and puffed up (approximately 20 minutes).

6. Meanwhile, make the glaze: In a bowl whisk together the confectioners' sugar, vanilla, and milk — a little milk if you like a thick glaze, more if you like a thinner glaze. Cover and set aside.

7. The rolls will emerge from the oven stuck together. Cool for 5 minutes and drizzle with glaze. Cut into individual rolls. Serve them hot if possible.

☆ Toasted Oatmeal with ☆ Cranberries and Maple Syrup

A simple bowl of oatmeal — with butter, sugar, and milk — is one of the most common winter breakfasts across America and has been for a long time. But since breakfast became an event, there are a lot of upscale oatmeal dishes out there in "creative" breakfast spots. As long as the cooks don't get too creative (I hesitate to even suggest what form that might take), I'm all for it. Try this wonderful little spin on a favorite comfort food.

Yield: 4 servings

 4 tablespoons unsalted butter
 1 teaspoon orange zest, chopped
 ½ teaspoon vanilla extract
 ¼ teaspoon ground cinnamon
 ⅛ teaspoon ground nutmeg
 ½ cup dried cranberries
 ⅓ cup maple syrup
 ⅛ cup brandy
 1 cup whipping cream, at room temperature
 ⅓ cup slivered almonds, with skins on
 2 cups old-fashioned rolled oats
   (5-minute cooking time)
 3 cups water
 ¼ cup brown sugar
 ¼ teaspoon salt

1. In a small saucepan over medium-low heat, combine the butter, orange zest, vanilla, cinnamon, nutmeg, cranberries, maple syrup, brandy, and ¼ cup of the cream. Stir to blend. Raise heat and bring the mixture to a boil. Lower heat and simmer for 4 minutes. While cooking, the mixture should thicken somewhat. Keep warm.

2. Place the slivered almonds in a large sauté pan over medium-high heat; stir constantly until they're lightly toasted, about 2 minutes. Remove them from the pan and reserve. Place the rolled oats in the same pan; stir constantly until they're toasted, about 3 minutes. Remove oats from pan and reserve.

3. Place ½ cup of the remaining cream, the water, brown sugar, and salt in a saucepan over medium-high heat. Bring to a boil. Once the mixture is boiling, remove from heat and stir in the oats. Return to medium-high heat and cook, stirring occasionally, for 7 minutes. Remove from heat and let sit for 3 minutes before serving.

4. Place 1 cup of the cooked oats in each of four wide bowls. Top each with 3 tablespoons

of the cranberry-brandy mixture and I tablespoon of the remaining cream, and sprinkle each with one quarter of the toasted almonds.

✳ Banana Bread with ✳ Cinnamon Crumble Topping

This is my favorite banana bread, by far. One of its virtues is that it has very concentrated banana flavor — owing to the number of bananas in it and the fact that they're roasted before going into the dough. Another great feature is the texture. Banana "bread" usually seems more like banana "cake" — but this one has the chew of a light, airy, moist bread. I also love the crunchy topping. I think this bread is best while it's still warm, twenty minutes or so after it has come out of the oven. But it holds extremely well — particularly if you wrap it in plastic wrap and keep it in the fridge. A nice breakfast idea is to toast slices of it, then slather them with butter (and/or jam).

Yield: 1 loaf (12 servings)

5 medium bananas, quite ripe
13 tablespoons (1 stick plus 5 tablespoons)
*   unsalted butter (at room temperature)*
1 cup sugar
¼ teaspoon powdered cinnamon
1½ cups plus ⅓ cup all-purpose flour
¼ cup sour cream
1 teaspoon baking soda
¼ teaspoon salt
2 extra-large eggs
1 teaspoon vanilla extract

1. Preheat the oven to 450 degrees.
2. Peel the bananas and cut them in half lengthwise. Using a tablespoon or so of the butter, lightly butter a baking pan and place the bananas cut side down in the pan. Roast them in the oven for 10 minutes.
3. Assemble the crumble topping: Melt 3 tablespoons of the butter and add it to a medium mixing bowl. Add ¼ cup of the sugar, the cinnamon, and the ⅓ cup of flour. Combine well and let the mixture rest for a few minutes, or until the butter cools slightly. Then, working with your fingers, crumble into pea-size pieces. Reserve.
4. Remove the bananas from the oven and allow them to cool. Lower the oven temperature to 350 degrees.
5. In a small bowl mix the sour cream with the baking soda and salt. In another small bowl lightly beat the eggs with the vanilla. Place 1 stick of butter and the remaining ¾ cup of sugar in a large bowl and, working with a handheld mixer, cream the butter and sugar together for 2 minutes. Add 4 of the roasted bananas (reserving 1), along with any of the liquid in the banana roasting pan. Cream the bananas, butter, and sugar until you have a smooth puree. Next, add the sour cream mixture and the egg mixture to the large bowl with the banana mixture; work it with the handheld mixer until the additions are thoroughly incorporated, about 1 minute. Add the 1½ cups of flour and mix until smooth with the handheld mixer, about 2 minutes. Cut the reserved roasted banana into small dice and, working with a rubber spatula, fold it into the banana mixture.
6. Butter a 5 by 9 by 3-inch loaf pan with the remaining tablespoon or so of butter. Place the banana mixture in the loaf pan and

sprinkle evenly with the crumble topping. Place the loaf pan in the oven on the center rack and bake for 45 minutes. Test for doneness by poking a toothpick into the center of the bread; if it comes out clean, the bread is done, but if the toothpick is sticky, put the loaf back in the oven for another 5 minutes or so. When the loaf is done, remove it from the oven and cool in the pan for 10 minutes. Then, with a butter knife, gently separate the bread from the sides of the pan. Holding the loaf pan upside down, let the bread fall gently onto the counter. Then place it, crumble side up, on a baking rack to cool.

Appetizers, Salads, and Salad Dressings

☆ Boiled Shrimp ☆ for Shrimp Cocktail

Here's a new discovery: when you cook shrimp quickly in a salt-and-sugar-water bath, then let them sit for a few hours in the cooled-down bath, you end up with the juiciest imaginable cocktail shrimps, which also happen to be beautifully seasoned. Start this great recipe about three to four hours before dinnertime and you'll be all set.

Yield: 8 first-course servings

8 cups water
4 teaspoons sugar
4 teaspoons coarse salt
2 pounds large shrimp (about 48), unpeeled

1. Place the water in a large saucepan over high heat. Swirl in the sugar and salt. Bring to a boil.

2. Add the shrimp, all at once. Remove saucepan from heat. Let stand until shrimp are cooked. The time will vary depending on many factors, but usually it takes no more than 2 minutes. Keep testing until shrimp are cooked as you like them (I prefer just-cooked-through shrimp that are springy in texture).

3. Drain shrimp, reserving both the shrimp and the broth. Run shrimp under fresh cold water and place in bowl in refrigerator. Place the broth in another bowl in the freezer to cool quickly.

4. When the broth has cooled, pour it over

Favorite Sauces for Shrimp Cocktail

I go with the American flow here: my all-time favorite shrimp cocktail sauce is the spicy, red ketchup-horseradish one. To make it, just mix together ¾ cup of ketchup, 3 tablespoons of prepared horseradish, 1 tablespoon of freshly squeezed lemon juice, and a few drops of Tabasco sauce (if desired). Some people prefer a pink sauce; I like it too. Mix together ¾ cup of mayonnaise and 3 tablespoons of ketchup — and serve both sauces, letting your guests make their own choices. For another type of shrimp cocktail, see the Texas Shellfish Cocktail with Tomato, Orange Juice, and Cilantro, Border Style on page 357.

the shrimp in their bowl in the refrigerator. Make sure the shrimp are covered with the broth. Hold in refrigerator for 2 to 3 hours.

5. Remove shrimp from broth and serve with favorite sauce. You may either serve the shrimp unpeeled (each diner peels his or her own) or peel them and serve.

★ Deviled Eggs with Crabmeat ★

Many a dinner party in America gets under way with a platter of deviled eggs: hard-boiled eggs that have been split in half, their yolks removed and mixed with cayenne, mayonnaise, and other seasonings, this mixture then stuffed back into the hard-boiled whites. I think the popularity of this dish can be explained by the fact that the eggs are easy to make, delicious, and very festive looking. The following new variation, with its alluring chunks of crabmeat — shellfish being a wonderfully sympathetic flavor in this ensemble — is even more cause for festivity. And no harder to make!

Yield: 16 egg halves

8 hard-boiled eggs
½ cup Hellmann's mayonnaise
1 teaspoon Dijon mustard
¼ teaspoon Worcestershire sauce
¼ teaspoon cayenne (or more to taste)
¼ teaspoon dry sherry
½ pound backfin crabmeat,
    picked over for shells and cartilage
Paprika for garnish

1. Cut the eggs in half lengthwise. Carefully remove the hard yolks from the eggs, making sure not to break the 16 halves of hard-boiled whites that remain. Place the yolks in a mixing bowl.

2. Mash the yolks with a fork. Add the mayonnaise, mustard, Worcestershire sauce, cayenne, and sherry. Blend well until the mixture is smooth. Fold in the crabmeat, trying to keep the crab pieces as intact as possible. Season with salt and black pepper to taste.

3. Divide the crabmeat mixture among the 16 halves of hard-boiled egg whites, placing the mixture in the cavity where the yolks used to be. Sprinkle decoratively with paprika and serve.

★ Coleslaw ★

Taken from the Dutch words for "cabbage salad," coleslaw has been with us in America for a very, very long time. Today it is as popular in diners and informal restaurants as it is at home barbecues and picnics. But there's a lot of indifference in coleslaw making — and rarely is this crisp salad as good as it can be. At most restaurants it's too old when it's served — and no matter where it's served, it's often wet and sugary. The following recipe, if served within an hour of so of being made, will startle you with its lively freshness. And most important, you'll discover a new quality in coleslaw: delicacy. For I find that if you don't take the time to shred the cabbage very, very thinly — you're not getting coleslaw at its best.

Yield: 6 side dish servings

¾ cup Hellmann's mayonnaise
5 tablespoons apple cider vinegar
2 tablespoons sugar
1 teaspoon celery seeds
6 cups firmly packed very thinly sliced cabbage
    (see Note)

In a large bowl, combine mayonnaise, vinegar, sugar, and celery seeds. Add cabbage and blend well. Season to taste with salt and freshly ground pepper (I like a lot of black pepper in coleslaw). Hold in refrigerator for about an hour for flavors to blend.

NOTE: There are several things to keep in mind if you're looking for very thin shreds of cabbage. First of all, small cabbages tend to have fewer thick folds of cabbage inside than large cabbages do — so buy a small head when making coleslaw. Second, savoy cabbages have more-delicate leaves — so they, too, are better for fine-shred slaw. The most important factor of all is the way you cut the cabbage. I like to slice each cabbage in half through the length of the core, then in half again into quarters. Take I quarter and cut out the thick core. Look at the strata of cabbage leaves remaining; most leaves will be thin. But inside your cabbage quarter you'll see a few thick layers of cabbage leaves. Cut them out or pull them out by

hand. Discard. Now you're ready to take a long, sharp knife and start shredding the cabbage quarter, shaving it into very, very fine shreds. Repeat with the remaining 3 quarters.

☆ Home-Style Potato Salad ☆

Well, I guess when home cooks have a taste for potato salad these days, they usually buy it at the deli or the supermarket. But it is so easy to make at home . . . and lots less expensive . . . and it can be so much better! There are, of course, a million ways to make potato salad. I like mine just a little less sweet than some deli versions. What sugar there is in the following recipe comes in the form of sweet juice from a pickle or relish jar, which adds great old-fashioned American flavor as well. I think you'll also love the velvety creaminess of this version. If you want to make the salad even more elegant, leave the potatoes in whole slices. I prefer them cut up. It takes at least 8 hours of refrigeration for the flavors in this potato salad to start to come together — but, frankly, it's at its best a few days after you make it.

Yield: 6 side dish servings

2 pounds new potatoes (preferably about 5 to the pound)
1 cup Hellmann's mayonnaise
6 tablespoons juice from a jar of sweet pickles or a jar of sweet pickle relish
¼ cup finely minced onion
¼ cup whipping cream
2 teaspoons cider vinegar
2 teaspoons celery seeds

I. Bring a large pot of salted water to the boil. Add the potatoes to the water. Boil until the potatoes are fairly tender when pierced with a knife (about 20 to 25 minutes, if your

Coleslaw

The knife points out one of the thick layers of cabbage (you can see two more). They must be removed before slicing cabbage for coleslaw.

potatoes are 5 to the pound). Remove potatoes and let them cool. As soon as they are cool enough to handle, slip off peels and discard them. Continue to cool potatoes. The potatoes should sit on the counter for a total of 30 minutes after they've come out of the water (that includes the unpeeled time and the peeled time).

2. In a large bowl, mix together the mayonnaise, pickle juice, onion, cream, vinegar, and celery seeds.

3. Slice the potatoes into rounds that are ¼ inch thick, then cut each round into 4 pieces. Spread the pieces out on the counter and salt them lightly. Add the potatoes to the bowl that has the dressing in it. Mix potatoes with the dressing until they are evenly coated; don't be afraid to handle the potatoes roughly, as a little breaking up is par for the course. Season to taste with salt and pepper. Chill in the refrigerator for at least 8 hours. Will keep, refrigerated, for several days.

✰ Chopped Salad ✰

For most of the twentieth century, for most Americans, *salad* usually meant a plate of large lettuce leaves, sometimes tossed with large chunks of other vegetables (such as tomatoes or cucumbers). Starting in the 1980s or so — and with antecedents in California salad ideas — upscale but informal eateries across the United States started offering the chopped salad. It is exactly what the name indicates: typical salad ingredients that are chopped rather than left in large pieces. It doesn't sound like much of a change — but the chew is wildly different, as is the number of tastes that you can experience simultane-

ously. Chopped salads are good with just a little oil and vinegar — but, frankly, their retro feel always inspires me to use one of the "retro" dressings below. I particularly love the following chopped salad with the French Dressing, 1890 Style on page 422.

Yield: 4 servings

3 cups chopped hearts of iceberg lettuce
1 cup chopped cucumber, unpeeled
1 cup chopped plum tomato
½ cup chopped celery heart
¼ cup chopped radish
¼ cup chopped green bell pepper, seeded
¼ cup chopped peeled carrot
¾ cup salad dressing
(preferably the French Dressing, 1890 Style on page 422)

1. Make sure that all the vegetables are chopped into pieces of equal size: cubes of about ¼ inch on all sides. Toss them together in a large bowl.

2. Toss with half of the salad dressing. Adjust seasoning with salt and pepper, if necessary. Divide salad among four large plates and drizzle the rest of the dressing over the salads, dividing it evenly among the four plates. Serve immediately.

✰ Thousand Island Dressing/ ✰ Russian Dressing

Though I'm sure each of these classic dressings entered the world as a distinct entity, the two have become so hopelessly intertwined that it is impossible today to predict what the name of either one on a menu will mean. Each is a blend of mayonnaise and ketchup, making each one pink and creamy. Russian, supposedly, originally contained caviar; we sure don't see that around these days. Thousand Island, supposedly, was originally so lumpy that the chef's wife said it reminded her of the Saint Lawrence River's Thousand Islands. However, I've seen plenty of Russian dressings that are just as lumpy with relish, bell pepper, onion, chopped egg, and capers as the "classic" Thousand Island is. Therefore . . . the following very simple version, perfectly balanced, can really be positioned as either. The main thing you need to know is this: If you're using the dressing as a sandwich spread (as in the Reuben sandwich on page 271), keep this recipe as is; if you're using it as a salad dressing, you may want to thin it out with a little water.

Yield: ¼ cup

3 tablespoons mayonnaise
1 tablespoon ketchup
1 teaspoon sweet pickle relish
½ teaspoon chopped onion
½ teaspoon prepared horseradish

Mix ingredients together. Hold in refrigerator for at least 30 minutes. Serve as is, or thin out with a little water.

☆ Ranch Dressing ☆

Americans are unique, I think, in pouring lots of white, creamy dressings over their salads. And why shouldn't we do so? Crunchy greens, raw vegetables, slices of tomato, are delicious with rich white sauces. One of the uniquely American salad dressings is ranch, though no two people agree as to precisely what ranch dressing is. To me a classic ranch must

include buttermilk (despite the fact that commercial nonbuttermilk ranch dressings do exist). The original ranch — which was marketed after World War II by the Henson family of Hidden Valley Ranch in California — did include buttermilk. The following recipe does too; see the Note for a way to make your dressing even more buttermilk intensive.

Yield: About 1¼ cups

½ cup Hellmann's mayonnaise
½ cup buttermilk (see Note)
¼ cup sour cream
1 tablespoon chopped parsley
1 tablespoon chopped celery leaves
2 teaspoons chopped chives
1 teaspoon chopped dill
1 teaspoon cider vinegar
1 teaspoon Dijon-style mustard
¾ teaspoon onion powder
⅛ teaspoon very finely minced garlic
⅛ teaspoon sugar

In a medium bowl, whisk together mayonnaise, buttermilk, and sour cream until smooth. Add remaining ingredients and stir to combine. Cover tightly and refrigerate for at least several hours to blend flavors.

NOTE: If you'd like this dressing to be even thicker and more buttermilky tasting, a great solution is at hand. A product exists that's called buttermilk powder — dried buttermilk, in essence. When you whisk it into the dressing, the dressing gets richer in body and deeper in flavor. Add as much as you like, tasting as you go. One widely distributed supermarket brand is Saco. You can also acquire buttermilk powder by logging on to the Web site of King Arthur Flour: *www.bakerscatalogue.com.*

⭑ Classic Salad Bar ⭑
Blue Cheese Dressing

I love the basic, old-fashioned blue cheese dressing that you get in salad bars — but I love it even more when I make it fresh at home. To preserve its blue-collar spirit, I'm calling for no Roquefort or Stilton; plain old supermarket blue (I use Danish) does just fine. And don't hold the store-bought mayo, the sugar, or the garlic powder; these convenient foods come together just right in this great version of the classic.

Yield: Enough dressing
for 6 to 8 salads

½ pound blue cheese
¾ cup Hellmann's mayonnaise
¾ cup buttermilk
2 teaspoons water
1 teaspoon sugar
½ teaspoon garlic powder

Place blue cheese in a bowl and mash with a fork until a fairly smooth paste is formed (leave a few chunks if you prefer a chunkier dressing). Blend in the mayonnaise until cheese and mayonnaise are well mixed together. Stir in the buttermilk and water, blending well. Add sugar, garlic powder, and salt and pepper to taste. For best results, serve immediately.

NOTE: You may hold the dressing in the refrigerator, which has the advantage of deepening the flavor. But it also turns this white dressing in a blue direction and yields a thicker result. If your refrigerated blue cheese dressing is too thick, simply thin it out with a little water.

⭑ French Dressing, ⭑
1890 Style

When the word got out in the 1970s and 1980s that there's nothing whatsoever French about French dressing — salads in France are typically dressed with a vinaigrette — the fortunes of this all-American classic began to decline. The days when the waiter automatically asked you if you wanted "Italian, Russian, or French" on your salad now seem prehistoric. Nevertheless, for many years this fairly thick, fairly sweet, red orange tomato-based dressing was a staple of the American table. In the aftermath of the crisis of faith, not only did this stuff disappear from many menus and homes — but the name got changed; what I call French dressing is now referred to as Catalina dressing by younger people, if they know it at all. The following recipe, presented completely without embarrassment, is an attempt to return to the glory days of . . . French — there! I said it! — dressing. A staple in my house was a now-extinct bottled brand called 1890 French Dressing — and this recipe, so good on wedges of iceberg lettuce, is a loving re-creation.

Yield: ¾ cup

1 teaspoon tomato paste
3 tablespoons ketchup
¼ cup cider vinegar
4 tablespoons sugar
¼ cup canola oil
½ teaspoon Worcestershire sauce
½ teaspoon garlic powder
¼ teaspoon celery salt

Whisk together tomato paste, ketchup, vinegar, sugar, canola oil, Worcestershire sauce, garlic powder, and celery salt in a mixing bowl. Season to taste with salt and pepper.

Sandwiches

✦ Egg Salad ✦
for Egg Salad Sandwiches

Nothing could be simpler — or more satisfying — than a fresh, creamy egg salad sandwich. Hard-boiled eggs and mayonnaise (which is also eggy) have a crazy-good synergy. Just remember to "toss" this "salad" lightly; it tastes better if it's not compressed. And keep in mind that seasoning egg salad is a tricky business; what seems like too much salt right after you've made egg salad somehow turns into too little salt after the salad has spent a night in the refrigerator. Similarly, what seems really creamy today will seem short on mayo tomorrow. In other words . . . if you're saving the salad in the fridge, consider adding a little more salt and mayo to it the next day.

Yield: Enough for 4 sandwiches

6 jumbo eggs, hard-boiled and peeled
6 tablespoons Hellmann's mayonnaise
¼ teaspoon salt

1. Place the cooked and peeled eggs in a large mixing bowl. Press down on each one with the underside of the tines of a fork; your goal is to break the eggs into medium-size, fairly uniform chunks.
2. Place the mayonnaise on top of the egg chunks. Sprinkle with salt. Working with a fork, toss mayo and eggs together very lightly. Toss just enough to blend the eggs and mayonnaise. Serve immediately, or hold in the refrigerator for several days.

Egg Salad Sandwich Suggestions

✪ Egg salad is excellent just as it is on plain white bread — toasted or untoasted.
✪ It's great on a fresh seeded roll or an onion roll with sliced tomato.
✪ My favorite variation: egg salad on lightly toasted seeded rye, with a mound of sweet, very thinly shaved onion.

✦ Chicken Salad ✦
for Chicken Salad Sandwiches

What makes a great chicken salad? It should be made from freshly home-boiled chicken (don't even think about chicken roll!). Good-quality chicken with mayonnaise alone is good enough — but I think chicken salad really comes alive when it's well seasoned, when it has a bit of crunch (as in celery), and when a little sweet-and-sour action is added (as in a small dose of sugar and good vinegar).

Yield: Enough for 4 sandwiches

2 cups well-seasoned boiled chicken
    (no skin or bones), in bite-size pieces,
    cold or at room temperature
3 tablespoons very finely sliced celery
    (see Note)
6 tablespoons Hellmann's mayonnaise
1 tablespoon sugar
2 tablespoons good-quality white wine vinegar
    or cider vinegar

1. Place the chicken in a large mixing bowl and taste for seasoning. Add salt and pepper if necessary. Toss with the celery slices.

2. In another bowl, combine the mayonnaise, sugar, and vinegar. Stir well to blend.

3. Add the mayonnaise mixture to the chicken and celery. Combine thoroughly. Mash slightly with a fork to give part of the salad a pasty quality, but leave lots of whole chicken chunks. Taste for seasoning. Serve immediately, or hold for several days in the refrigerator.

NOTE: It is best to use the more tender, lighter green celery stalks near the heart for this recipe. Lay a stalk from left to right and, starting at the narrower end, make paper-thin slices.

Chicken Salad Sandwich Suggestions

✪ Chicken salad is excellent as it is on plain white bread. You don't even need any lettuce.

✪ It's also wonderful on soft, seeded rye bread. I particularly like chicken salad on rye with a few slices of cooked bacon, a green leaf lettuce leaf, and a little extra mayo on the bread.

✪ Chicken salad also takes well to the "hoagie" treatment. Build a hero on Italian bread with chicken salad, thin slices of tomato, shredded lettuce, and thin slices of dill pickle.

✪ Historical oddity: At one time in Philadelphia (as elsewhere) oysters were cheap and chicken was expensive. So, to stretch a chicken salad sandwich . . . they would put a lot of fried oysters on a roll on top of a little chicken salad! It's actually pretty darned delicious, even though the market prices have flip-flopped.

✸ Tuna Salad Sandwich ✸

Is there a better sandwich at home than a good old-fashioned tuna salad sandwich? It's far from complex — but the simple combo of canned tuna, mayo, and white bread is devastatingly good. It's not as easy for me to produce a great one as it was for my mom. For starters, the quality of tuna in cans, I'm certain, has declined precipitously over the years; the smooth, luxuriant tuna salad of yore has yielded to the gritty, bumpy tuna salad of today. The supermarket product that brings me closest to the old tuna is Progresso tuna in olive oil (and the olive oil, by the way, does not affect the tuna salad taste). Then there are all the modern, complicating, add-in temptations: pickles or red peppers or avocado or kiwis or whatever. I've tried most of them, and they never provide the nostalgia hit that the plain tuna does. The only ingredient other than mayonnaise that I ever allow into my tuna salad is celery — but it has to be the heart of celery, chopped fine. Some like their tuna salad chunky, which is their privilege. For me, however, it has got to be beaten to a pulp. The old delis used to serve tuna salad that almost looked like a smooth tuna pâté. Then, of course, comes the bread issue: whole wheat, sourdough, focaccia, tortilla wraps — breads ad infinitum are now used to support tuna salad. And the results can be fine. But what I want to eat, when I return to America from a foreign trip, is plain tuna salad on supermarket white bread — preferably wrapped in foil and stored for a few hours so as to simulate the conditions of the sandwich that I carried to school in my lunch box.

Yield: 2 sandwiches on white bread

1 (6-ounce) can tuna (see Note)
2 to 3 tablespoons (or more) Hellmann's
    mayonnaise
1 tablespoon very finely chopped heart
    of celery (optional)
4 slices white bread

1. Open tuna can over sink, cutting it with the can opener most of the way — so that the lid is still connected to the can by a small hinge. Press down on the lid and turn it over, pressing hard, so that most of the water or oil spills out of the can and into the sink. Turn right side up again, twist off the lid and discard, and scoop the remaining tuna into a small mixing bowl.

2. Mash tuna with a fork for 2 to 3 minutes, until it is extremely well broken up.

3. Add mayonnaise, blend well, and mash for another 2 to 3 minutes — until a very smooth paste is formed. Add celery and blend well.

4. Divide the mixture between 2 slices of bread. Smear a little extra mayonnaise on 2 more slices of bread and top the tuna with those (mayo side down, of course). Serve or hold.

NOTE: You can make a tuna salad sandwich with either tuna packed in oil or tuna packed in water (I prefer the oil-packed one, because it has more flavor). But whichever one you choose, please purchase the slightly more expensive "solid white albacore tuna"; the resulting salad is so much firmer, so much better.

If you wish, you can take it one step beyond the supermarket and purchase the very best tuna salad tuna imaginable. There is a fairly new industry that has sprung up in the Pacific Northwest and northern California producing cans of albacore tuna that has been packed in its juices. Now, I wouldn't advise eating this tuna just by itself, as on an antipasto platter, because it's fairly dry. But when you whip it up with a whole lotta mayo, you get the best-textured, best-tasting tuna salad ever.

Here are some brands to look for:

Great American Smokehouse and Seafood Co. Deluxe Albacore Tuna, Brookings, OR

Dave's Home-Style Santa Cruz Albacore Fillets, Santa Cruz, CA

Katy's Smokehouse Very Fancy Hand-Packed Albacore, Prime Solid White Tuna, Trinidad, CA

☆ Tuna Melt with Avocado ☆

A great old-fashioned American lunch at home is the tuna melt, in which tuna salad on toast gets covered with a mantle of cheese, which then gets melted under the broiler. I like it well enough. But modern, stylish retro diners are putting New Wave spins on dishes like these. And in my opinion, the smart addition of avocado to this old dish, making it buttery-creamy rich, sends it soaring toward the Comfort Food Hall of Fame.

Yield: 4 luncheon servings

2 tablespoons finely chopped red onion
2 (6-ounce) cans white tuna in water, drained and flaked
2 tablespoons finely chopped celery
½ cup Hellmann's mayonnaise
2 teaspoons fresh lemon juice
4 slices rye bread
2 teaspoons unsalted butter
1 avocado, peeled, pit removed, thinly sliced, and lightly salted
1 cup shredded sharp cheddar cheese

1. Place the chopped red onion in a small strainer and place strainer in a bowl of ice water. Let sit for 10 minutes. Drain onion and pat dry.

2. In a bowl, combine the onion, tuna, celery, mayonnaise, and lemon juice. Season to taste with salt and pepper.

3. Preheat the broiler. Lightly toast the bread, and spread each slice with butter. Distribute avocado slices evenly over the 4 slices of bread. Spread tuna mixture evenly on top of avocado and sprinkle the cheese evenly on top of tuna. Place under the broiler until cheese melts, approximately 1 to 2 minutes. Serve immediately.

The Sandwich Box

Americans make a lot of sandwiches at home: for lunch, to take to work as lunch, for snacks, for late-night snacks, even for dinner. The following is a list of the seven main categories of headliner sandwich fillings, and a host of ways in which Americans dress up those fillings. Most of them are simple and basic — but if you've missed any of them, when you try them you'll be reminded of how good simple and basic can be.

Turkey

- on a roll with black pepper, lettuce, and lots of mayo
- the club sandwich: three pieces of toast, bacon, lettuce, tomato, lots of mayo
- the club sandwich hero: Italian bread, bacon, lettuce, tomato, provolone cheese, lots of mayo

Salami

- on rye with yellow mustard
- on white bread with yellow mustard and thinly sliced tomato
- sautéed, on white bread, with yellow mustard
- on a hero with rare roast beef, lettuce, and tomato (no dressing)

Ham

- on rye with dark brown mustard and Swiss cheese
- on toasted rye with Gulden's spicy brown mustard
- on fluffy white bread with lots of mayo
- on a hero with salami, provolone cheese, shredded lettuce, tomato, oil and vinegar

Roast Beef

- on white bread with salt, pepper, lettuce, and lots of mayo
- on white bread with lots of butter and Worcestershire sauce
- on a roll (preferably an onion roll) with horseradish-laced mayo

Corned Beef

- steamed on rye with yellow mustard
- the Reuben (see page 271)
- shredded, mixed with mayo and chopped onion, served on white bread or whole wheat bread

Liverwurst

- on a hero with mayo, yellow mustard, and lots of thinly sliced onion

Vegetables

- ripe tomato slices on fluffy white bread with lots of mayo
- mozzarella cheese, tomato, basil, roasted bell pepper, and olive oil on focaccia

☆ Classic ☆
Grilled Cheese Sandwich

Oh, there are lots of fancy grilled cheese sandwiches out there these days, especially in upscale retro American restaurants. They're fun . . . every once in a while. But at midnight . . . staring at your refrigerator . . . wondering what's gonna send you off to bed just right . . . you just can't beat the classic grilled cheese sandwich. There are a few technical bells and whistles in the following recipe, but they're only in service of a better classic. The hardest thing you need to think about is which kind of American cheese to buy. I tested Kraft and Land O'Lakes processed American cheese — and found the Kraft to be sweeter but more processed tasting, the Land O'Lakes to be saltier but more cheeselike. Your move.

Yield: I sandwich

2 slices supermarket white bread (such as
    Wonder Bread)
2 tablespoons butter, melted
2 slices American cheese, each ⅔ to ¾ ounce

I. Place a medium skillet over medium heat.
2. Using a pastry brush, coat both sides of the bread slices with the melted butter. Take care not to compress the bread as you brush. Place the slices of bread in the skillet and cook until lightly golden on one side, about I½ minutes. With a spatula, remove the bread to your work surface, cooked side up, and place the cheese slices on one slice of the bread. Top the cheese with the second slice of bread, cooked side down, and transfer to the skillet with the spatula. Cook the first side until golden brown, about 2 to 2½ minutes, reducing the heat if it threatens to burn. Flip with the spatula and cook the sec-

ond side until golden brown and the cheese has melted, another 2 to 2½ minutes. Remove from the skillet, cut in half, and serve.

☆ Fancy Grilled Cheese ☆
Sandwich with Pullman Loaf,
Emmentaler, Bacon,
and Tomato

The key in this "upscale" version of the grilled cheese sandwich is the same as in any grilled cheese sandwich: you want the bread to reach its beautiful, golden brown color — and no more! — just as the cheese has melted.

Yield: I sandwich

2 slices of best-quality white bread (such as
    from a Pullman loaf), cut ½ inch thick
3 tablespoons unsalted butter, melted
3 ounces Emmentaler cheese (Swiss cheese),
    grated
2 slices bacon, cooked to taste and cut in half
    crosswise
2 (¼-inch-thick) slices tomato, cut in half and
    blotted briefly on a paper towel

I. Place a medium skillet over medium heat.
2. Using a pastry brush, coat both sides of the bread slices with the melted butter. Place the slices of bread in the skillet and cook until lightly golden on one side, about I½ minutes. With a spatula, remove the bread to your work surface, cooked side up, and place half of the cheese on one slice of the bread, spreading it almost to the edges. Top this slice with the bacon and then the tomato,

distributing them evenly. Distribute the remaining cheese on top and place the second slice of bread, cooked side down, on top of the other ingredients, pressing gently to compact it.

3. Remove the skillet from the heat for a minute or two, allowing it to cool briefly before transferring the sandwich to it. Return the skillet to the heat and weight the sandwich with a smaller, heavy skillet (or use a small cutting board topped with a weighty can). Cook the first side until golden brown, about 2 to 2½ minutes, reducing the heat if it threatens to burn. Flip with a spatula, weight the sandwich, and cook the second side until golden brown and the cheese has melted, another 2 to 2½ minutes. Remove from the skillet, cut in half, and serve.

☆ The Ultimate BLT ☆

One of my chief gripes with the usual BLT is not only that the crunchy toast seems a little too dry but that it's not fun to brush your soft palate against all that hard crunch while you're trying to get your mouth around a thick sandwich. On the other hand, the toasting lends a great flavor. The following recipe solves the dilemma: toast the bread slices on one side only! Next come the ingredient choices — and I find that the perfect BLT maintains a balance of tradition and upscaling. I don't want focaccia, I want white bread! But if you can find one that's got a slightly finer, tighter crumb, it adds a little something. Tomatoes *must* be upgraded; I make a BLT only when I have dripping-sweet, intensely scented end-of-summer tomatoes. I'm all for iceberg lettuce, but the softer, tastier leaves of green leaf lettuce give the sandwich a better taste and a more elegant feel. Lastly, of course,

is the bacon — I have finally decided that I do not want thick, smoky, premium bacon for my BLT! A good brand of regularly presliced supermarket bacon is better for the balance of a perfect BLT. Please follow the instructions below . . . for I have carefully worked out exactly what has to touch what in order for the ultimate-BLT sparks to fly.

Yield: I sandwich

6 slices good-quality supermarket bacon
    (not the extra-thick or smoky stuff)
2 slices good white bread
4 to 6 tablespoons Hellmann's mayonnaise
    (or more to taste), not supercold
6 to 8 medium-thick tomato slices
    (each almost ¼ inch)
Kosher salt
2 leaves green leaf lettuce, selected to fit the
    sandwich

I. Fry the bacon (I like the bacon with some malleable tenderness remaining). Reserve on paper towels.

2. Toast the bread under a broiler on one side only. Place one of the slices, toasted side down, on a counter. Slather with I to I½ tablespoons of the mayonnaise.

3. Top with a single layer of tomato slices, approximately 3 to 4. Season with kosher salt and freshly ground pepper. Spread another I to I½ tablespoons of the mayonnaise over the tomato. Lay 3 strips of cooked bacon over the tomato and mayonnaise, evenly spaced to cover the bread. Place both leaves of the lettuce on top of the bacon. Place the remaining 3 slices of bacon across the lettuce; set the slices so that they're perpendicular to the first slices. Slather the bacon with another I to I½ tablespoons of the mayon-

naise. Top the bacon with the remaining tomato slices. Season with kosher salt and freshly ground pepper. Lastly, slather the remaining piece of toast with mayonnaise on the untoasted side and place it, with the mayonnaise side down, on top of the sandwich. Cut in half and serve immediately.

Hearty Main Courses

☆ Tuna Noodle Casserole ☆

Even before Tuna Helper, lots of American moms and dads had long prepared some sort of combination casserole that included chunks of canned tuna and noodles. It's fast, it's easy, it's nutritious, it's inexpensive, and — despite the drubbing it takes from snobby types — it is usually enjoyed by all, even today. There are, however, better and worse examples — and the following béchamel-based casserole, though it has a few more steps than most, is delicious enough to change the mind of any snob about this all-American dish. And it's still easy, nutritious, and inexpensive!

Yield: 8 main-course servings

2 cups plain bread crumbs, preferably
    homemade (see recipe on page 9)
1½ cups grated Parmesan cheese
2 tablespoons chopped parsley
1¾ teaspoons dried thyme
1 small garlic clove, minced
1 teaspoon salt
1¼ teaspoons black pepper
1¾ cups (3½ sticks) unsalted butter
3 (6-ounce) cans solid white tuna in oil
12 ounces wide egg noodles
1 tablespoon olive oil
1¼ cups diced red bell pepper
1¼ cups diced yellow bell pepper
1 cup diced onion
¼ cup finely chopped shallot
12 ounces white mushrooms, thinly sliced
3 tablespoons flour
4 cups whole milk
½ teaspoon celery seeds
¼ teaspoon cayenne

1. In a bowl, mix together bread crumbs, Parmesan cheese, parsley, ½ teaspoon of the thyme, the garlic, the 1 teaspoon of salt, and ¼ teaspoon of the black pepper. Add to work bowl of a food processor. Melt 1½ cups (3 sticks) of the butter. Add melted butter to crumb mixture and pulse on and off, just until crumbs have been moistened. Set bread crumb topping aside.

2. Drain tuna, reserving 2 tablespoons of the canned oil.

3. Cook noodles in boiling, salted water for 2 minutes. Drain noodles immediately, add to large bowl, and toss noodles with the 2 tablespoons reserved tuna oil.

4. Place the olive oil in a large skillet over low heat. Add red bell pepper, yellow bell pepper, and onion. Cook until vegetables are tender, about 10 minutes. Transfer to a bowl.

5. In the same skillet, melt 1 tablespoon of the remaining butter over medium-low heat. Add shallot and sauté for 3 minutes. Add mushrooms and ¼ teaspoon of the remaining thyme. Sauté for an additional 5 minutes. Add mushroom mixture to cooked onion-pepper mixture. Season to taste with salt and pepper.

6. Preheat oven to 350 degrees.

7. In the same skillet, melt the remaining 3 tablespoons of butter over low heat. Add the flour, stirring constantly. This mixture must be absolutely smooth. Cook until the mixture is bubbly, about 1 to 2 minutes. Remove from heat.

8. In a saucepan, bring the milk to a boil. Using a whisk, add the hot milk to the flour-butter mixture in the skillet. Put the skillet back on medium-high heat and bring to a boil, whisking. Reduce heat to a simmer. Add celery seeds, cayenne, the remaining 1 teaspoon of thyme, and the remaining 1 teaspoon of black pepper. Simmer for 10 minutes more, stirring frequently.

9. Add reserved tuna and vegetables to the sauce. Break up large pieces of tuna with a wooden spoon. Remove from heat. Add tuna-vegetable mixture to reserved noodles; combine well using a large spoon. Pour mixture into a 9 by 13 by 2½-inch baking pan. Pat bread crumb mixture evenly over the top. Bake until casserole is bubbly and top is golden brown, about 30 minutes.

☆ Chicken Pot Pie ☆

Many Americans grew up eating chicken pot pie at home — out of the freezer and into the oven, thanks to the good folks at Swanson! Some of those Americans hit midlife in the eighties and nineties, became cook-it-yourselfers, and discovered the joys of making their own chicken pot pies from scratch. The following piecrust contains more butter (it's amazingly flaky-tender!) than any frozen product (other than frozen butter!). And you'll love the deep flavor of this pie's medium-thick filling. As a slight tweak on the classic, there is an herbal dimension to this filling, which I love — but if you're simply seeking to reproduce the chickeny goodness of a plain, old-fashioned pie, by all means leave the herbs out.

Yield: 6 main-course servings

1 teaspoon dried thyme
1 teaspoon freshly ground pepper
1 teaspoon dried rosemary
2 teaspoons crushed bay leaf
1 tablespoon loosely packed dried sage leaf
2 whole chicken breasts with skin and bones
*   attached, each one split in half*
*   (about 3 pounds total)*
¾ cup (1½ sticks) plus 5 tablespoons
*   unsalted butter*
2¾ cups plus 5 tablespoons all-purpose flour
2½ teaspoons salt
¼ teaspoon baking powder
¼ cup vegetable shortening, divided into
*   12 teaspoons*
2 large eggs (1 egg beaten with 3 tablespoons
*   ice water, plus 1 egg yolk beaten with*
*   1 tablespoon water)*
2 tablespoons bacon fat
1 pound carrots, peeled
½ cup chopped onion
½ cup chopped celery
3 cups canned chicken broth
24 fresh, raw pearl onions (see Note)
½ cup plus 2 tablespoons frozen peas
⅛ teaspoon ground nutmeg
¼ cup unseasoned bread crumbs
Finely minced parsley for garnish

1. Mix together thyme, pepper, rosemary, crushed bay leaf, and sage; rub into chicken. Set aside in a bowl.

2. Prepare the dough: Cut the ¾ cup of butter into ¼-inch pieces; keep very cold. Put the 2¾ cups of flour, ½ teaspoon of the salt, and the baking powder in bowl of food processor; pulse to combine. Add cut-up butter and shortening to the flour; pulse for 5 to 8 seconds. You want the flour and fats to be mixed together, but you want pieces of butter and lard to still be visible.

3. Add the egg—ice water mixture to the food processor bowl and process just until the liquid is incorporated, about 8 to 10 seconds. The mixture will look like crumbs.

4. Turn mixture out onto a work surface. To ensure that the dough is homogeneous, take small portions of the dough and crush against work surface with the heel of your hand, moving each portion along the work surface for an inch or two. Then combine all the pieces into one mass and divide in half. Wrap each half in waxed paper and refrigerate for 30 minutes.

5. Melt bacon fat in a 12-inch skillet with a lid. Chop enough carrots to measure ½ cup and add them to the skillet. Add onion and celery and cook over low heat, covered, for 10 minutes, stirring occasionally. Push vegetables to the side of the pan and raise heat to high. Sprinkle chicken with the remaining 2 teaspoons of salt and add to the pan, skin side down. Lower heat to medium-high and cook for 5 minutes. The chicken skin should get dark brown but should not burn. Check occasionally by lifting with a fork to ensure that the chicken is cooking properly. Do not turn chicken over. Remove lid, add chicken broth, and bring to a boil. Reduce heat to

low, cover, and simmer chicken for 15 minutes. Turn heat off and allow chicken to remain in skillet with the lid on for ½ hour.

6. Remove chicken to a bowl; reserve. Pass liquid through a strainer, pressing solids with a spoon against the strainer to extract as much flavor as possible before discarding vegetables and herbs. Reserve broth; you should have about 3½ cups.

7. Soak pearl onions in a bowl of warm water for 5 minutes and then peel. Chop enough carrots to measure 1½ cups: cut carrots in half lengthwise. On an angle, chop carrots into pieces that measure about ¾ inch long.

8. Melt 1 tablespoon of the remaining butter in a small pan with a lid over medium heat. Place the pearl onions in the pan and cook for 5 minutes, shaking the pan occasionally. Add the 1½ cups of carrots and ½ cup of the reserved chicken broth. Bring liquid to a boil, then reduce heat to low. Cover pan and cook for 10 minutes. Add peas and cook with lid on for an additional 3 minutes. Strain out vegetables and reserve. Add vegetable broth to remaining reserved chicken broth.

9. Remove skin and bones from the chicken and chop meat into 1-inch-square pieces. Put chicken pieces and reserved vegetables in a large bowl.

10. Heat the remaining 4 tablespoons of butter in a saucepan over low heat. Add the remaining 5 tablespoons of flour, stirring constantly. Cook for 1 to 2 minutes, until bubbly and smooth. Whisk in the reserved chicken-vegetable broth, making sure to add not more than 3½ cups. Bring to a boil, and

then reduce heat to a simmer. Add nutmeg, and season with salt and pepper to taste. Cook for an additional 10 minutes. Remove from heat and add to reserved chicken and vegetables. Set aside and allow to cool.

11. Preheat oven to 425 degrees.

12. Remove the 2 pieces of pie dough from the refrigerator and roll out each piece into an 11-to-12-inch round. Lay one piece in the bottom of a 9½-inch deep-dish pie plate. Sprinkle bread crumbs on the piece of dough in the bottom of the pie plate. Top with chicken and vegetable mixture. Top with the other crust. Press the edges of the two crusts together to seal. Crimp decoratively, if desired. Brush dough with the egg yolk–water mixture. Cut a few slits in center of crust to allow steam to escape. Place in oven.

13. Bake until crust is golden brown, about 40 to 50 minutes. Remove and let cool 20 minutes before serving. To serve, scoop portions out with a large serving spoon and place each portion (which will probably not hold its shape) in a wide, shallow soup bowl. Sprinkle each portion with finely minced parsley.

NOTE: You may substitute a 10-ounce package of frozen pearl onions for the fresh pearl onions. Add them to the chicken broth when you add the peas.

☆ Super Bowl Chili ☆

On page 359, in the Texas section, is a version of what most food historians consider to be the original chili: no beans, no tomatoes, just chilies and cubes of beef in gravy. Most Americans are not impressed. What follows is the type of chili that gets made in millions of homes, particularly when the guys get together to watch football. Heck, this stuff is so good you could eat it watching a live telecast of *Tristan and Isolde* from the Metropolitan Opera. It's runny, tomatoey, spicy, a little sweet, downright crowd pleasing.

Yield: 4 servings (supplemented
by plenty of beer and tortilla chips)

¼ cup vegetable oil, or more if necessary

1 (28-ounce) can tomatoes, drained

½ pound ground pork

½ pound ground beef chuck

1 medium onion, peeled and coarsely diced

2 fresh hot green chilies, seeded and finely chopped (more or less to taste)

1 tablespoon minced garlic

1¾ cups unsalted chicken broth (homemade or canned), plus more if necessary

¾ cup beer

2 tablespoons plus 1 teaspoon Chili Spice Mixture (recipe follows)

½ teaspoon kosher salt

1 tablespoon tomato paste

8 ounces canned kidney beans, drained

1. Preheat the oven to 350 degrees. Line a baking sheet with aluminum foil and coat with a thin layer of the vegetable oil. Slice all the tomatoes in half lengthwise and place them, cut side up, on the baking sheet. Drizzle a small amount of vegetable oil over each tomato half, place the baking sheet in the oven, and roast them for about 1 hour. They will shrink a bit, concentrating their flavor, but should still be quite moist. Remove them from the oven, chop them coarsely, and reserve.

2. Place a large skillet over medium-high

heat and add 2 tablespoons of the vegetable oil. Just as the oil begins to smoke, add the pork and beef and lightly brown it all over, reducing the heat if the meat threatens to burn, about 5 to 6 minutes (do this in batches if the skillet isn't large enough to hold the meat in one layer). As the meat cooks, break up the larger chunks with a wooden spoon. Transfer the meat to a bowl and reserve.

3. Let the skillet cool slightly and place it over a medium-low heat, adding another 1 tablespoon of oil. Add the onion, chopped chilies, and garlic; cook gently for 4 to 5 minutes, stirring occasionally. Add the chicken broth, beer, 2 tablespoons of the spice mixture, the ½ teaspoon salt, and tomato paste, scraping the bottom of the skillet to loosen any browned bits. Add the reserved roasted tomatoes and reserved meat, raise the heat to medium-high, and bring just to a boil. Immediately reduce to a bare simmer, cover loosely with a lid or foil and cook, very gently, for about 1 hour, stirring occasionally.

4. Stir in the beans and the remaining 1 teaspoon of chili spice mixture, cover loosely, and cook for ½ hour more. When ready, the chili should resemble a stew with a thinnish liquid but shouldn't be at all watery. Stir in additional broth or water if it seems a bit dry. Conversely, if the mixture seems a bit loose and wet, uncover the skillet and allow it to simmer until thickened slightly. Taste for seasoning and add salt and pepper as needed, and serve in individual bowls. Pass extra chili spice for the nose tackles and linebackers.

★ Chili Spice Mixture ★

Yield: About ½ cup

3 tablespoons chili powder
4 teaspoons ground cumin
1 teaspoon ground cinnamon
1 teaspoon sweet paprika
½ teaspoon cayenne
2 teaspoons dried oregano
2 teaspoons firmly packed dark brown sugar

Combine all the ingredients in a small bowl, breaking up any lumps of brown sugar. Store in a dry place in a tightly covered container.

☆ Best-Ever Baked ☆ Chicken Thighs

Lots of home cooks prepare chicken in their ovens — but if you're looking for juicy meat and crisp skin, the results can be uneven. The following recipe is absolutely foolproof.

Yield: 4 main-course servings

8 large chicken thighs, with skin and bone
Dash of freshly grated nutmeg

1. Preheat oven to 300 degrees.
2. Sprinkle thighs with salt, pepper, and a tiny bit of nutmeg. Place chicken skin side down in a roasting pan, cover tightly with aluminum foil, and bake in oven for 45 minutes.
3. Remove from oven, carefully peel back foil, and turn thighs skin side up. Cover tightly again with foil and return to oven. Bake for 1 hour more.

4. Remove thighs from oven. Preheat the broiler. If you wish to debone the thighs, let them cool until easy to handle, then pull the thigh bone out of each and discard. Whether you're serving them with bone in or bone out, place them under a broiler before serving, skin side up, until they're brown and crunchy on top (about 10 minutes). Serve immediately.

NOTE: These simple-as-can-be thighs are great just by themselves — but I like them even better with a few tweaks. Stuffing them, for example, is a great idea; after you have cooled and deboned them, a few tablespoons of stuffing slipped under the skin, prior to broiling, brings a lot of extra excitement. Use your favorite stuffing, already cooked; I like to use roasted and finely chopped mushrooms. Another helper is sauce. Any kind will do. I like to deglaze the roasting pan with a cup or so of dark stock, add a little red wine, thicken with Wondra quick-mixing flour, and finish with a knob of room-temperature butter, whisked in.

☆ Pressure Cooker ☆ Fried Chicken and Gravy

Pressure cooking became a reality for cooks in the United States in 1939, when an American company presented the first home model of a pressure cooker at the New York World's Fair. It's a dream for time-pressed Americans; the super-heated steam under the locked lid cooks food much faster than other methods do. Unfortunately, pressure-cooking hasn't really caught on across the country; it's the rare home cook who makes use of a pressure cooker. The following recipe — which I worked up in my kitchen after learning that the famous Colonel originally cooked

his fried chicken in a pressure cooker — has the power, I hope, to change anyone's opinion about this convenient device. Though the finished chicken does not taste "fried," it has the most golden, gauzy, chickeny taste of any quick-cooked chicken I've ever experienced. It is pure time travel back to a more innocent day; serve it with mashed potatoes (page 448 or 449) and you can go back a few years further.

Warning: This recipe can be very dangerous to prepare if you don't understand the pressure cooker you are using. You must read, fully comprehend, and follow all the guidelines and instructions for your pressure cooker. Each brand, make, and model works a little differently, so you may need to adapt this recipe for use with your pressure cooker. If you are not completely comfortable with your pressure cooker, please pass this recipe by.

Yield: 2 main-course servings

1 cup plus 1 tablespoon flour
¼ teaspoon onion powder
¼ teaspoon garlic powder
¼ teaspoon rubbed sage
¼ teaspoon ground thyme
1 tablespoon salt
1 tablespoon black pepper
2 teaspoons paprika
⅛ teaspoon cayenne
½ cup milk
1 egg
4 boneless skin-on chicken thighs
½ cup Crisco
½ cup plus 2 tablespoons chicken broth

1. In a paper bag, combine the 1 cup of flour, the onion powder, garlic powder, sage, thyme, salt, black pepper, paprika, and cayenne. Shake the bag to combine the flour mixture thoroughly. In a pie plate, using a fork, whisk

together the milk and egg. Using a fork to handle the chicken, coat a piece of chicken in milk-egg mixture and then immediately place it in the bag with the seasoned flour. Shake the chicken in the flour mixture until it is completely coated. Remove it from the bag and place it on a plate. Repeat the process for the other pieces.

2. Place a pressure cooker on the stove over medium-high heat. Add the Crisco. Once the shortening is very hot, add the chicken. Fry the chicken pieces skin side down, just until they are golden brown, about 2 minutes. Flip them over and decrease the heat to low. Place the lid on the pressure cooker and lock it down. Pressure-cook the chicken, using low pressure, for 8 minutes.

3. Run cool water around the edges of the pressure cooker to cool it down. Unlock the lid. Remove the chicken and hold it in a warm oven.

4. Add the ½ cup of chicken stock to the liquids that are already in the bottom of the pressure cooker; bring mixture to a boil. In a small bowl whisk together the remaining 1 tablespoon of flour with the remaining 2 tablespoons of chicken stock; whisk that mixture into the boiling liquid. Simmer over medium heat for 4 minutes. This will thicken the gravy (if it's not thick enough, reduce it until it is). Strain if needed to remove any lumps. Season the gravy with salt and pepper to taste. To serve, remove the chicken pieces from the oven, place them on a platter, and serve them topped with gravy, or alongside a gravy boat filled with the pan gravy.

☆ Thick and Juicy Pork Chops, ☆ Sautéed in the Pan

Lots of Americans come home from work and throw a few pork chops in a pan for dinner. But lots of Americans started getting a nasty surprise about twenty years ago: cowed by consumers' ostensible demand for less fat, the pork industry starting breeding lower-fat animals. The result? Lots of tough and dry pork chops in those pans across America. The following method, which involves a relatively quick brining — have a drink! relax! have dinner an hour later! — is the most reliable method I know of for getting juicy, appealing chops to the table today.

Yield: 4 main-course servings

4 cups cold water
4 tablespoons coarse salt
2 tablespoons sugar
10 whole cloves
2 bay leaves
½ teaspoon oregano
¼ teaspoon celery seeds
½ orange, cut in half again
4 center-cut pork loin rib chops (each about
    ¾ inch thick)
¾ cup self-rising flour
2 teaspoons table salt
1 teaspoon pepper
Vegetable shortening for frying

1. Combine water, coarse salt, sugar, cloves, bay leaves, oregano, and celery seeds in a large bowl. Squeeze juice from orange pieces into the bowl, dropping in the orange skins. Add the pork chops and marinate for 1 hour in the refrigerator.

2. Mix flour, table salt, and pepper together and put into a plastic or paper bag.

3. Remove pork chops from the marinade and allow excess liquid to drip over the bowl. Shake chops in the flour mixture, one at a time, making sure to coat thoroughly. Remove to a plate.

4. Place vegetable shortening in a heavy 12-inch skillet with a lid to a depth of ½ inch. When the shortening is very hot and just beginning to smoke, add the chops to the pan and lower the heat to medium. Cook for 5 minutes. Turn the chops and continue to cook for another 4 minutes. Cover skillet tightly, lower heat to low, and continue to cook for an additional 6 minutes.

5. Remove chops, place on paper towels, and allow to rest for 3 minutes before serving.

☆ Hamburger Tips ☆

Hamburgers are obviously very near and dear to the hearts of Americans. I know they are to mine. Because of this — and because of their ubiquity in the world of American food — it is not easy to give a "hamburger recipe." However, there are a series of hamburger tips that I think may lead to better hamburgers in your house — no matter what special tips of your own you bring to the subject.

✪ When buying hamburger meat, choose ground meat that is at least 20 percent fat.

✪ A loose grind is best; avoid fine grinds.

✪ If you can control what's in the grind, or if you're grinding your own, choose chuck. If you can really control what's in the grind, choose neck meat (technically part of the chuck category).

✪ When shaping your burgers, never squeeze or compact them. Place the ground meat on the counter and gently pry it open, in half (like lifting a lid). Season with salt and pepper. Bring the meat back together loosely and as gently as you can. Shape as gently as you can.

✪ I like burgers neither too thin nor too thick; about one-half inch thick is perfect for me.

✪ Chill burgers before cooking, so that you can get a browner crust before the inside starts to move past rare.

✪ Always remember: beef fat is your friend in cooking burgers. Buy some spare fat when you buy hamburger; toss it in a hot pan to render liquid fat. Reserve to cook hamburgers.

✪ My favorite way to cook a burger at home is under a superhot broiler — but only if I have a superhot broiler, such as a salamander. Drizzle burger, while cooking, with a little melted beef fat.

✪ A hot grill is also good. Once again, drizzle burger with beef fat.

✪ If cooking on your range, heat beef fat over high heat in a thick pan. Cook burger in pan over high heat.

✪ Superimportant: Don't press on your burgers with a spatula while they're cooking!

✪ A grilled burger bun is good, but I like a steamed bun even better — especially after it has been smeared with butter.

✪ There's a whole world of condiments out there. My favorites for a beautiful bunful of beef: ketchup and a slice of sweet onion.

☆ Bacon-Scented Meat Loaf ☆ with Tomato Glaze

Meat loaf is one of those massively American comfort food dishes that most people crave when their inner child starts crying. Me, I crave it any time at all, with mashed potatoes and a boatload of gravy. But there's meat loaf, and there's meat loaf. Some years ago

I decided that the very soft and tender kind of loaf, such as the one in the recipe below, is my favorite. Until recently, however, I was baking it in a loaf pan and not coating it with a tomato glaze. I changed. I now feel that a freestanding loaf, all encrusted on the outside with tomatoey goodness, is about as high as I can take the art.

Yield: 1 meat loaf, a total of 12 thick slices,
enough for 12 main-course servings

2 large eggs, beaten in a large bowl
1 cup milk
7 slices white bread, crusts removed
1½ tablespoons Dijon mustard
2½ teaspoons salt
½ teaspoon pepper
¾ teaspoon dried basil
½ teaspoon dried thyme
⅓ teaspoon nutmeg
1 very large onion (about 1 pound),
*   very finely chopped*
¾ cup chopped celery with leaves
6 tablespoons finely chopped fresh parsley leaves
18 thick slices smoked bacon, lightly cooked
*   and coarsely chopped*
3 pounds ground beef
Tomato Paste Glaze (recipe follows)

1. Spill out one-fourth of the beaten egg (or reserve for another use). Beat milk into remaining egg mixture until well blended. Tear bread into small pieces and drop into bowl. Mix. Let stand until bread absorbs the liquid, about 15 minutes. Mash and stir mixture.
2. Add mustard, salt, pepper, basil, thyme, nutmeg, onion, celery, parsley, and bacon. Mix well. Add ground beef and mix well. Refrigerate overnight, tightly covered.
3. Preheat oven to 350 degrees.

4. Remove meat mixture from refrigerator and place on a baking pan. Mold into a loaf that's about 10 inches long and 5 inches wide. Place in hot oven and cook for 40 minutes. Remove loaf from oven and brush top and sides with tomato paste glaze. Return to oven and cook 15 minutes longer. Remove, and let stand at least 5 minutes before slicing.

★ Tomato Paste Glaze ★

Yield: Enough to glaze 1 meat leaf
½ cup tomato paste
1 tablespoon sugar
3 tablespoons olive oil

Whisk ingredients together. Brush some on meat loaf during the last 15 minutes of baking time; the quantity depends on how tomatoey you like the top of the meat loaf to be.

☆ Swiss Steak ☆

This humble dish is mainline cafeteria food: hunks of beef cooked en casserole for a long time with tomatoes and seasonings. According to preeminent food writer Jean Anderson, the dish has been around since at least 1915, but the tomatoes didn't join the party until the 1930s. More revisionism: according to John Mariani, author of *The Encyclopedia of American Food and Wine*, the name Swiss may have nothing to do with Switzerland; it may instead refer, he speculates, to an English method of smoothing out cloth between rollers (swissing), much like the pounding out of the steak in the recipe. The history, of course, becomes of secondary importance once you taste the dish — and the following version, thick and sweet with tomatoes, shot through with deep, beefy flavor, makes me question my own history, which has left out

Swiss steak for years. Welcome back! This is wonderful nostalgia food of the highest order.

Yield: 4 main-course servings

1½ pounds bottom round steak, cut into
*   4 slices, each about 1 inch thick*
¼ cup all-purpose flour
½ teaspoon paprika
1 tablespoon vegetable oil
2 large onions, thinly sliced
½ cup diced celery
1 clove garlic, finely chopped
1 teaspoon chopped fresh thyme,
*   or ½ teaspoon dried thyme*
1 (14½-ounce) can diced tomatoes, undrained
2 tablespoons tomato paste
1 teaspoon cider vinegar
1 teaspoon sugar
1 bay leaf

1. Preheat oven to 350 degrees.
2. Place one of the steak slices between 2 sheets of waxed paper and pound with a meat mallet until about ¾ inch thick. Repeat with remaining pieces. In a shallow bowl, combine flour and paprika, and season with salt and pepper. Season meat with salt and pepper. Dredge meat on both sides in flour, tapping off excess. Reserve flour mixture.
3. In a large skillet, heat vegetable oil over medium-high heat. Add meat, browning well on both sides, about 2 minutes per side. When the meat is well browned, place steaks in one layer in a baking dish or casserole with a lid. The pieces should fit snugly.
4. In the same steak-browning skillet, add onion slices and celery, sautéing until onion is browned, about 5 minutes. Add garlic and

thyme; cook until garlic is fragrant, about 1 minute. Add 1 tablespoon reserved flour mixture and begin stirring; cook 1 minute to remove raw flour smell. Add tomatoes, tomato paste, vinegar, sugar, and bay leaf. Bring to a simmer and pour over meat. Cover baking dish and bake for 15 minutes; reduce heat to 300 degrees and bake until meat is fork tender, about another 1½ hours. Divide among four dinner plates and serve immediately.

✴ Braised Short Ribs ✴ with Carrots, Parsnips, and Red Wine

Interest in cooking short ribs at home has been rekindled by the short rib boom in trendy restaurants. Americans across the map have rediscovered the comforting deliciousness of collagen-rich cuts of meat, such as short ribs, melting down in a pot over 3 to 4 hours into soft and buttery puddles of protein. The following recipe — with its wine sauce and its carefully cooked vegetables — is a homey version of something you might expect to see in a modern restaurant. Serve, by all means, with mashed potatoes.

Yield: 4 main-course servings

1 large leek (white and pale green part only)
*   washed, quartered, and chopped into*
*   ½-inch pieces*
2 medium shallots, peeled and coarsely chopped
2 large stalks celery, washed, halved lengthwise,
*   and chopped into ½-inch pieces*
2 medium carrots, peeled, quartered, and
*   chopped into ½-inch pieces*
6 large garlic cloves, peeled and thinly sliced
4 large sprigs thyme

1 small sprig rosemary
1 bottle good-quality dry red wine
5 pounds beef short ribs, bone-in, crosscut so
they're about ¾ inch thick (should be
8 rib pieces)
Kosher salt
All-purpose flour for dusting meat
½ cup vegetable oil
3 ounces sliced, unsmoked bacon (such as pancetta),
cut into ⅜-inch pieces (see Note)
2 tablespoons tomato paste
1 (14½-ounce) can beef broth
2 cups water
Glazed Carrots and Parsnips (recipe follows)

1. Combine the leek, shallots, celery, carrots, garlic, thyme, rosemary, a few grindings of black pepper, and the wine in a large nonreactive bowl. Nestle the short ribs in the bowl so they're completely submerged (weight them with a plate if necessary). Cover tightly, refrigerate, and marinate overnight.

2. Remove the short ribs from the marinade, blot them dry on paper towels, and transfer them to a rimmed baking sheet or platter. Strain the marinade into a colander set over a nonreactive bowl and transfer the vegetables to a bowl lined with paper towels to absorb excess moisture. Reserve the marinade and the vegetables.

3. Preheat the oven to 300 degrees.

4. Evenly sprinkle some kosher salt on both sides of the ribs. Dust one side of the ribs with flour. Place a large, heavy stockpot with a tight-fitting lid over high heat, uncovered. Add the vegetable oil (it looks like a lot of oil, but it will help the meat brown better and you'll pour it off later), and just as the oil begins to smoke, carefully add 4 of the rib sections, floured side down. Reduce the heat to medium-high and allow them to brown until deeply colored on the first side, 8 to 10 minutes, regulating the heat if they threaten to burn. Dust the second side with a bit more of the flour, turn the ribs over, and brown them until deeply colored, 6 to 8 minutes more. Return the browned ribs to the baking sheet, repeat with the remaining rib sections, and set aside.

5. Allow the pot to cool slightly and pour off all but 2 tablespoons of the oil. Return the pot to medium heat, add the bacon, and cook until golden brown but still tender. Using a slotted spoon, transfer the bacon to paper towels and reserve. Raise the heat to medium-high and add the reserved marinated vegetables. Immediately scrape the bottom of the pot with a spatula to loosen any browned bits, and cook, stirring occasionally, until the vegetables are lightly browned at the edges, 5 to 7 minutes. Add the tomato paste and cook, stirring regularly, for 1 minute. Add the reserved wine marinade, the beef broth, and the water, scraping the bottom of the pot with a spatula as you did before. Immerse the reserved ribs in the liquid (adding any juices left behind on the baking sheet) and bring just to a simmer. Skim any impurities that rise to the surface. Cover the pot and transfer it to the oven. Let the ribs braise gently until the meat is very tender and falling from the bones, about 3 hours (if your ribs are 1 inch or thicker, cooking time will be closer to 4 hours).

After 20 minutes of braising, check the pot and make sure the meat is just barely simmering. If it's bubbling at more than a bare simmer, reduce the heat to 275 degrees, return the cover, and continue cooking, checking it again after 15 minutes and regulating the heat as necessary.

6. Remove the pot from the oven and let it rest, uncovered, for at least 1 hour, submerging as much of the meat as possible under the remaining liquid. Skim off most of the orangey fat that has risen to the top of the pot and discard. Carefully transfer the ribs to a large dish and cover tightly with foil. Return them to the oven to warm. Pass the braising liquid through a mesh strainer (not superfine mesh) set over a medium saucepan, pressing on the solids to extract the flavor and some of the thickening power of the vegetables. You should have about 3 cups of liquid. Place the saucepan over medium-high heat, bring to a lively simmer, and cook, skimming occasionally, until thickened slightly and reduced in volume by one-fourth (to about 2¼ cups). The consistency should be about halfway between a broth and a sauce that coats the back of a spoon. Season with additional salt if necessary.

7. To serve, gently reheat the glazed carrots and parsnips (see recipe below). Place a spoonful of mashed potatoes (if using) in the center of four dinner plates and top each with 2 pieces of the short ribs. Ladle about ¼ cup of the reduced braising liquid over and around each serving. Arrange a portion of glazed carrots and parsnips attractively over each. Pass the remaining braising liquid at the table.

NOTE: If you're using smoked bacon, immerse it in simmering water before frying for 2 to 3 minutes to lessen the smoky flavor.

★ Glazed Carrots and Parsnips ★

Yield: Enough for 4 servings of Braised Short Ribs with Carrots, Parsnips, and Red Wine

6 medium carrots (about ¾ pound) with
    1 inch of green tops left on, peeled
    and halved lengthwise
4 tablespoons (½ stick) unsalted butter
1 teaspoon kosher salt
1⅓ cups water, plus additional as needed
6 medium parsnips (about ¾ pound),
    peeled and halved lengthwise

1. Place the carrots, cut side down, in a large skillet with 2 tablespoons of the butter, half the salt, and half the water. Repeat with the parsnips and the remaining butter, salt, and water in a second skillet. Cover loosely.

2. Bring the skillets to a boil over high heat and reduce them to a bare simmer, lightly shaking the skillets to distribute the butter and salt. Let the vegetables simmer and steam until they are tender but still a bit firm, turning them after about 5 minutes of cooking. Depending on the thickness and age of the vegetables, the total cooking time for the carrots should be 6 to 10 minutes, and for the parsnips, 8 to 12 minutes. If toward the end of cooking the water has evaporated, add a few tablespoons to keep the vegetables moist, as necessary.

3. When the vegetables are tender but still firm, remove the lids and turn up the heat

slightly to evaporate most of the remaining liquid. As the liquid becomes thickened and buttery, gently shake the skillets, carefully turning the vegetables so that they become glazed and glossy on all sides. Serve immediately, or transfer the vegetables to a plate to cool. When ready to reheat, combine all the vegetables in one skillet (with a tablespoon of water if they seem a bit dry), cover loosely, and warm over medium heat.

✸ Simplest, Beefiest Pot Roast ✸

A real staple of the American home kitchen is pot roast — a piece of beef long-cooked in liquid (that's why it's in a pot), and in the oven for evenness of cooking (that's why it's a roast). But the pot roast memories of some of us are tainted by what Mom did to it. In fact, a perfectly cooked pot roast — tender, melting, primordially beefy, its rich gravy running over a mound of mashed potatoes — can be an absolutely glorious cold-weather

All about Brisket

The brisket is a large (normally twelve to thirteen pounds) rectangle of beef that is taken from the front of the animal, just on top of the legs; above the brisket are the animal's shoulders, from which we get chuck. Brisket has no bones and is quite tough — unless you cook it slowly for a long time. Then its unique blend of lean meat and fatty, spongy meat melts into something spectacular. Corned beef is made from brisket, and I think brisket makes the very best pot roast of all.

Of course, when you buy a chunk of brisket for pot roast, you'll have a big decision to make. You'll usually need only half of a brisket for the pot roast recipe here, which feeds eight — but which half? About two-thirds of the brisket is what butchers refer to as the first cut; it's flat, quite lean, with what fat it has layered on top. The other third is called the second cut; it's thicker and much more irregular, with meat and fat interspersed throughout. It also contains the insanely delicious deckle, which is the most sinfully tasty spot in the whole brisket. For my money, though the second

cut is fattier, and though it requires a little more "cutting away" at the table, it is much more flavorful, juicy, and interesting.

If you are fat phobic, ask the butcher to cut the brisket in half, and take home the six-pound chunk that's all first cut. But if you've made peace with a little fat, as I have, I think the best solution is to take home the other half — the six-pound chunk that has some first cut in it and all the second cut. This way you can serve leaner pieces from the first cut to those who want them . . . and keep the second-cut pieces for the feinschmeckers. Just save the deckle for me.

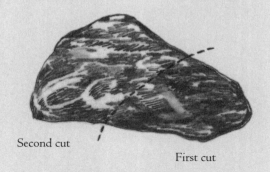

Second cut

First cut

meal. And the sandwiches the next day may be even better.

Many recipes call for beef round or rump of beef. In my kitchen, the best cut of beef for pot roast is brisket (see sidebar on page 441). Next, it is important to brown the meat well before you pour the liquid around it; this helps bring out the depth of beef flavor as you cook it. Lastly, cook the pot roast at a fairly low temperature for a long time. Cooking at 325 degrees or above forces the fat to run out of the meat, leading to a dry result; cooking at 300 degrees or below allows more fat to remain in the meat and the collagens to melt gently and tenderly.

These days it is not uncommon to see hotshot chefs in New American restaurants doing Olympic spins on pot roast: Annatto-Rubbed Pot Roast with Hoja Santo Essence; Tuscan Pot Roast with Sage, White Beans, and Aged Balsamic Vinegar; Hunan Red-Cooked Pot Roast with Star Anise and Hoisin Sauce. Whatever. If you want to add flavors to your pot roast, do that on your own. But please try this recipe as is. Once you know how delicious a pot roast that relies on beef for flavor (with a bass line of onions) can be, you may just feel, as I do, that you don't want to mess with it. Simplicity is a virtue!

Yield: 8 main-course servings

6 tablespoons simple olive oil
3 pounds onions, peeled and thinly sliced
4 teaspoons sweet paprika
1 (6-pound) piece of brisket (see sidebar on page 441)
8 tablespoons flour
¼ cup crushed tomatoes
6 cups rich beef broth at room temperature

1. Place 3 tablespoons of the olive oil in a large pot or sauté pan over high heat (see sidebar for discussion of cooking vessels). When it's hot, add half the onions and cook them until they are nicely browned, just short of burned, and still a little crunchy. Don't stir them until the brownness starts to appear, then stir occasionally. The whole process may take 5 to 8 minutes. Remove onions and reserve. Repeat with remaining half of onions. Remove onions and combine with reserved cooked onions. Evenly stir in 2 teaspoons of the paprika. Reserve.

2. Season the brisket well with salt and freshly ground pepper. Coat evenly with 6 tablespoons of the flour. Add the remaining 3 tablespoons of olive oil to the pan you

Cooking Vessels for Pot Roast

The ideal cooking vessel for pot roast is a large, heavy pot that can accommodate the six-pound piece of brisket. But not everyone has such a creature. You could use a roasting pan for pot roast, as long as the sides are high — but lots of roasting pans are made of thin metal, and they won't be ideal for the initial browning of the onions and the beef. The best solution for most home chefs will be a two-stage solution. Brown the onions and the meat in the largest, heaviest sauté pan that you have. Then transfer the onions and the meat to a roasting pan with high sides before you pop the beef in the oven. The roasting pan I use for braising pot roast is twelve by eighteen inches, with sides that are three and one-half inches high. Use aluminum foil to cover the roasting pan.

used for the onions. Place over high heat. When it's hot, add the beef. Sear well on all sides until the beef is brown black (this should take about 5 minutes per side). Remove beef and sprinkle evenly with the remaining 2 teaspoons of paprika.

3. Preheat oven to 300 degrees.

4. Select a large pan for braising the beef (see sidebar on page 442 for discussion of cooking vessels). Spread the reserved onions out in the bottom of the pan, making a bed that's about the size of the beef. Spread the crushed tomatoes over the onions. Place the beef on the onion-tomato bed.

5. Place the remaining 2 tablespoons of flour in a mixing bowl. Slowly blend in the beef stock, adding just a few tablespoons of stock at first to make a thick slurry. Then beat in the rest of the stock quickly. After you've made sure the flour is blended, pour the mixture over and around the beef. The size of your pan will determine the depth of the liquid in the pan; an ideal depth is anywhere from a quarter to halfway up the side of the beef.

The Day After

There are some good arguments for serving the pot roast the next day. First of all, if you put the gravy in the refrigerator overnight, fat removal is a snap; when the gravy's cold, you simply lift off the congealed fat on top. Second, some people feel that the beef tastes better — deeper, beefier, sweeter — the second day. Lastly, I think pot roast tastes best when it's thinly sliced — and this is easiest to do when the meat is cold.

Here are three great ideas for the day after:

1. *A simple, cold pot roast sandwich.* Slice the cold beef as thinly as you can. Smear something sinful on an Italian hero. Butter's good, mayonnaise is possible. Best of all comes from the Jewish brisket-the-day-after tradition: smear your bread with schmaltz, or chicken fat. Yum! Plenty of salt and pepper, and you're all set for a sublimely simple treat.

2. *A surprisingly wonderful plate of just-warm pot roast.* Slice the cold beef as thinly as you can. Place the slices in a single layer on a microwaveable plate. Pop in the microwave for thirty to forty seconds, or until the beef is slightly warm and just starts to glisten. Serve the plate with a mustard vinaigrette that's loaded with finely minced shallot and parsley (you can use the one on page 71 as a base, eliminating the tarragon). A little horseradish in the vinaigrette wouldn't hurt. It all ends up tasting something like a quintessential French bistro dish.

3. *Reheated pot roast slices.* If you wish to reheat the meat, heat the defatted gravy first. Slice the meat, put it in a roasting pan, cover with the gravy, cover with aluminum foil, and heat in a three-hundred-degree oven until the meat is heated through (about half an hour). If you wish to give it a little extra flair — okay, okay, I can accept a little logical creativity! — you can mix some barbecue sauce in with the gravy (proportions are up to your taste). I have discovered a brand that works insanely well with the pot roast; it's called Show-Me, it's made in a boutique way in Missouri, and you can write for it at 1250 Cedar Grove Boulevard South, Columbia, MO 65201.

6. Cover the pan very tightly with aluminum foil and place in the oven. Baste beef occasionally (once an hour or so) with braising liquid. Cook until beef is very tender. If you've used the first cut of brisket (see sidebar on page 441 for discussion of brisket), this may take 3½ to 4½ hours; if you've used the second cut of brisket, this may take 4 to 5 hours.

7. When the brisket is tender, remove from pan and let rest for a few minutes. Meanwhile, skim as much fat from the gravy as possible. You may strain the onions out, but I prefer to keep them in. Cut the beef — across the grain! — into slices that are about ¼ inch thick. Cover meat with gravy and serve.

Side Dishes

✫ Perfect Restaurant-Style ✫ French Fries

French fries — despite the Gallic moniker — are among America's most beloved treats. But I think of them as restaurant food above all — fast food places, coffee shops, lunch counters, upscale California grill restaurants, bistros of all sorts. Why? Because home cooks are not pleased with the results they get when they haul out the deep fryer. It's frustrating to discover that McDonald's makes fries vastly superior to yours. Restaurant fries are often light, crispy, and airy, with what I call an irregular, "nubbly" texture on the outside. Home fries are usually slick and smooth on the outside, lacking textural interest. Until now. Stealing a secret from the fast-food industry, I have devised the following recipe — in which the fries are actually cooked three times: they are boiled first, to make them more interesting in texture, then fried twice, as per the classic French fry recipe. With so much handling, you must exercise care, lest the potatoes break. But the effort is well worth it; these fries are as good as any restaurant fries in America.

Yield: Enough for 4 servings

5 large russet potatoes
2 tablespoons table salt (plus coarse salt
    for sprinkling)
2 tablespoons sugar
2 quarts vegetable oil

1. Peel potatoes and trim each one into the shape of a rectangle. Cut the potatoes lengthwise into broad slices that are about ⅜ inch thick. Then cut each slice into strips that are about ⅜ inch wide. (It is important for the size of the potatoes to be correct for the cooking process to work perfectly. A French fry cutter that yields ⅜ inch fries is a good investment.) Hold the cut potatoes in a bowl of cold water until ready to use.

2. Place 3 quarts water, the 2 tablespoons of table salt, and the 2 tablespoons of sugar in a large pot. Bring to a boil. Add the cut potatoes to the boiling water, let the water return to a boil, then immediately reduce the heat so that the water comes to a gentle boil. Cook the potatoes for 7 minutes, or until they are quite soft but still holding together. You don't want to make mashed potatoes, so check the potatoes during the last few minutes of the boiling period. Remove them with a wide, slotted utensil (what chefs call a spider would be ideal), and place them on

Cut the potatoes
into blocks

French Fries

Cut the blocks into
French fries

Remove the
potatoes carefully
with a "spider"

paper towels in a single layer. Bring to room temperature (about 10 minutes).

3. When ready to do the first fry, heat vegetable oil in a deep, heavy, straight-sided pot to 250 degrees. Using your hands, carefully place a small batch of potatoes on a spider (or another wide, slotted utensil), making sure not to break them. Slowly lower the spider into the oil, drop the potatoes into the oil, and cook them for 2 minutes. After removing them from the oil with the spider, place them on paper towels in a single layer. This step essentially blanches the potatoes, so there should be very little color. Repeat with the rest of the potatoes, in small batches, until all of them have had a first fry.

4. When ready to serve, heat the oil to 350 degrees. Using your hands, slowly remove a small batch of the fries from the paper towels without breaking them and place them on

the spider. Slowly lower the spider into the oil, drop the fries into the oil, and cook, stirring occasionally to ensure even browning. You want the French fries to have a deep golden brown color and for the surface to be a little crinkly; this should take about 3 minutes. Remove them from the oil with the spider and place them in a single layer on a baking pan lined with paper towels. Sprinkle generously with coarse salt. Repeat with the remaining fries. Serve immediately for maximum crispness — but if you're holding the first batch or two, hold the completed fries in a 300-degree oven.

FREEZING NOTE: After completing step 3 of the process, the first frying, you can place the fries on a baking pan in a single layer and freeze them. Once they are frozen solid, place them in an airtight freezer bag and keep them frozen until you need them. To cook them, thaw the fries in the refrigerator, then fry them using the directions in step 4.

★☆★

✴ Macaroni and Cheese ✴

This American classic probably goes back at least to Thomas Jefferson's time. Over the centuries, many different techniques have been employed to get the perfect bubbly, cheesy casserole. The central issue has always been: How to get the cheese incorporated? Earlier recipes usually used a white sauce and topped the casserole with the cheese; later recipes use a cheese sauce. The following recipe, in the hunt for ever greater flavor, does both. But the cheese is not the only star here. I love the delicious, creamy, fresh-dairy taste of this recipe, lent by the crème fraîche. And I love the texture: rich but not gloppy, almost like a great version of an Italian-American casserole.

Yield: 8 side dish servings

6 tablespoons (¾ stick) butter
2 tablespoons dry bread crumbs
2 tablespoons grated Parmesan cheese
1 tablespoon chopped parsley
1½ teaspoons chopped fresh thyme
    (or ½ teaspoon dried)
1½ teaspoons paprika
¼ cup all-purpose flour
2 teaspoons dry mustard
1 teaspoon salt
¼ teaspoon ground nutmeg
2¼ cups milk
1 garlic clove, peeled
½ cup crème fraîche
8 ounces grated extra-sharp white
    cheddar cheese
4 ounces grated mild cheddar cheese
8 ounces elbow macaroni, cooked al dente,
    drained, and rinsed with cold water

1. Preheat oven to 400 degrees. In a small saucepan, melt 2 tablespoons of the butter. In a small bowl, combine bread crumbs, Parmesan cheese, parsley, thyme, and ½ teaspoon of the paprika; toss with the melted butter. Set aside.

2. In another saucepan, melt remaining 4 tablespoons of butter. Whisk in flour, mustard, salt, nutmeg, remaining 1 teaspoon paprika, and freshly ground pepper, to taste, until smooth. Cook over low heat for 1 to 2 minutes, or until mixture smells "toasty." Add milk, whisking until smooth. Add garlic clove, return to a simmer, and simmer about 10 minutes. Remove saucepan from heat and whisk in crème fraîche. Reserving ½ cup of each cheese for topping, stir the rest of the cheese into the sauce until melted. Remove and discard garlic clove.

3. Place cooked macaroni in a baking dish, add cheese sauce, stirring to coat all the macaroni with the sauce. Sprinkle with half the bread crumb mixture, then remaining cheese, then remaining bread crumbs. Bake uncovered about 20 minutes or until browned and bubbly.

✴ Glazed Carrots ✴ with Orange Zest

If this classic American dish — sweet chunks of tender carrots in a gauzy, buttery sauce — doesn't make you think of Norman Rockwell, nothing will! But for me, the dish did recently creep ever so slightly into the post-Rockwell era when a friend of mine made it for Thanksgiving with some nontraditional orange zest in it. The flavors nicked beautifully, and I now prefer it this way. By the way, the carrots in this recipe are cooked until quite soft, which gives more carroty flavor to the sauce. If you'd like a slightly firmer carrot, start with only one and one-fourth cups of chicken broth and proceed.

Yield: 6 servings

12 medium carrots (about 2½ pounds),
    peeled and cut into large chunks
1½ cups chicken broth
6 tablespoons (¾ stick) unsalted butter
3 tablespoons sugar
1½ teaspoons orange zest

1. In a large skillet, combine the carrots, chicken broth, butter, and sugar. Place over high heat, bring to a boil, and cook, uncovered, stirring occasionally, until all the liquid has reduced and the carrots are glazed, about 12 minutes. Season with salt and pepper and sprinkle with the zest. Toss.
2. Transfer to a serving plate and serve immediately.

✭ Classic Green Bean ✭ Casserole, Judiciously Updated

The canned-soup-with-stuff casserole in general became an American classic in the early part of the twentieth century, thanks to the recipes created and publicized by the Campbell Soup Company. In 1955 Campbell hit the jackpot — creating the most popular casserole of all time, the classic Green Bean Bake, made with Campbell's cream of mushroom soup and topped with fried onions from a can. Things don't become classics because they're bad — and the combination of ingredients in this dish is really quite delicious. That's not to say that a tweak or two can't improve it. Try the following version with fresh-fried shallots and dried tarragon thrown into the mix. It's irresistible! This version respects the fifties taste but is so much brighter and more layered in flavor. The soy sauce, by the way, was part of the original recipe.

Yield: 6 to 8 side dish servings

1½ pounds green beans, trimmed and cut in
    half crosswise
Vegetable oil for deep-frying
¼ cup all-purpose flour
1 teaspoon sweet paprika
6 large shallots, peeled and sliced into thin rings
1 tablespoon butter
½ pound button mushrooms, washed and
    thickly sliced
1 can Campbell's cream of mushroom soup
½ cup milk
½ cup water
1 tablespoon lemon juice
1 teaspoon soy sauce
1 teaspoon dried tarragon

1. Preheat oven to 350 degrees.
2. Bring a pot of salted water to a boil. Add green beans and boil for 3 minutes. Drain beans and immediately plunge into ice water to stop the cooking. Drain well, and set beans aside in a 9 by 13-inch baking dish.
3. In a large saucepan, bring 2 inches of vegetable oil to 365 degrees. In a medium bowl, combine flour and paprika. Season with salt and pepper. Place shallots in the bowl and, using your hands, dredge lightly in the flour mixture. Tap off the excess flour and place half the shallots in the oil. Fry until golden and crispy, about 1 to 2 minutes. Remove and drain on paper towels; season with salt and pepper. Repeat with remaining shallots.

4. Melt the butter in a large skillet over medium heat. Add sliced mushrooms and cook without stirring until browned, about 2 minutes. Add mushroom soup, milk, water, lemon juice, soy sauce, and tarragon to skillet and whisk until smooth. Bring mixture to a simmer, pour over green beans, and stir to combine. Add half the shallots and stir again. Bake until sauce bubbles, about 30 minutes. Top evenly with remaining shallots and bake 5 more minutes. Serve immediately.

☆ Scalloped Potatoes ☆ with Ham

When it comes to potato casseroles, the French get most of the accolades; their creamy potato gratin is certainly worth the international attention it gets. But there's a lot to be said for its American cousin, too — scalloped potatoes. In fact, the following recipe, I'm convinced, could go spud to spud with the French classic in any competition. It is homey, heartwarming, bursting with potato flavor, seasoned perfectly, graced with the wonderfully complementary flavors of ham and cheese. And there's this amazing advantage — it has a kind of lightness to it, so you can enjoy a lot more of it than you can the creamy French gratin.

Yield: 6 to 8 side dish servings

1 tablespoon unsalted butter
2 tablespoons flour
2 teaspoons chopped fresh thyme
1 teaspoon salt
½ teaspoon freshly ground pepper
1¾ cups chicken stock
¾ cup whipping cream
2 tablespoons Dijon mustard

3 pounds red-skinned waxy potatoes, peeled and thinly sliced
½ pound grated Gruyerè cheese
¾ pound ham, cut into ¼-inch cubes
½ cup dried bread crumbs

1. Preheat oven to 375 degrees. Generously grease a 9 by 13-inch baking dish with the butter. In a small bowl, combine flour, thyme, salt, and pepper. In a medium saucepan, bring chicken stock and cream to a simmer; whisk in mustard and remove from heat; set aside.

2. Place one-third of the potatoes in an even layer in the baking dish. Sprinkle with half the flour mixture, one-third of the cheese, and one-third of the ham. Repeat with another layer of potatoes, flour, cheese, and ham. Make a final layer of potatoes, cheese, and ham. Pour cream mixture over and sprinkle with bread crumbs.

3. Place in the oven and bake until potatoes are easily pierced with a knife, about 1 hour to 1 hour and 10 minutes. If top becomes too brown before potatoes are cooked through, cover with foil and continue baking.

☆ Rich Mashed Potatoes ☆

There's only one thing I insist on in a mashed-potato recipe: the use of a ricer or a food mill. Other means of mashing the potatoes lead to variations of lumpiness and glueyness. Beyond that, however, there are many different options for the finished product. The recipe that follows is a modern version of what was served in my house. My mom, as many moms did, liked to make mashed potatoes rich with dairy products; her diary product of choice was canned, evaporated milk. We loved it! But if you're going the dairy route, I suggest that mashed potatoes taste even better with whipping cream and lots of butter. This particular recipe has double greatness in it: the dairy flavor is wonderful, *and* the roasting of the potatoes leads to a massive payload of potato flavor as well.

Yield: 4 servings

4 medium russet potatoes, about 2½ pounds
2 cups whipping cream
½ pound (2 sticks) unsalted butter, cut into
*   16 pieces*
2 teaspoons salt (more or less to taste)
1 teaspoon freshly ground pepper
4 tablespoons finely sliced chives (optional)

1. Preheat oven to 400 degrees.
2. Place the potatoes on the center rack of the oven and bake for about 1 hour, or until the potatoes are soft when squeezed.
3. While the potatoes are cooking, place the cream in a small saucepan over medium heat. As the cream approaches a boil, drop in the butter and cook until it has melted entirely. Turn off the heat and reserve.
4. When potatoes are done, remove them from the oven and allow them to cool for about 2 minutes, or until you can handle them. It is very important that you do not allow the potatoes to cool too much because they will become starchy. Cut the potatoes in half and scoop out the insides.
5. Pass cooked potato pulp through a ricer or a food mill into a large, clean pot. Rewarm the cream-butter mixture if it has cooled down. Over low heat, whip about three-quarters of the cream-butter mixture into the riced potatoes. Check the consistency of the potatoes, and add more cream and butter if you like a richer, creamier texture. Season with salt and pepper; fold in the chives and serve immediately.

☆ Light Mashed Potatoes ☆

Mashed potatoes seem to scream "rich" — but they don't have to. Home cooks who wish to lighten their cooking know that if you coax all the flavor there is out of the potato, then butter and cream seem almost unnecessary. You could say, in fact, that dairy additions reduce the potato flavor! The following recipe makes the most of the potato cooking water — which is whipped with the potatoes to create a delightful light-and-moist mashed potato with nary a lick of dairy. If your main course is already rich — as in this dish's favorite partner, the Pressure Cooker Fried Chicken and Gravy on page 434 — who needs rich?

Yield: 4 servings

2 pounds potatoes, preferably Yukon Gold
3 cups water
1 teaspoon kosher salt, plus more for seasoning

1. Peel the potatoes, then cut them into chunks roughly the size of limes. Wash well. Place them in a small saucepan and add the water; if the potatoes are not just covered by the water, add a little more until they are. Stir in the 1 teaspoon of salt. Place over high heat and bring rapidly to a boil.
2. As soon as the water boils, reduce heat, bring water to a rapid simmer, partially cover pot, and cook until the potatoes are tender, 25 to 30 minutes.
3. Remove potatoes with a slotted spoon,

reserving the cooking liquid, and pass potatoes through a ricer. Stir 1½ cups of hot potato cooking water into the riced potatoes. Whip briefly with a whisk. Season to taste with salt and pepper and serve immediately.

✮ Creamed Spinach ✮

Home cooks in America regularly pop frozen boil-in-bags of creamed spinach into hot water — and the results are actually pretty darned good. You have to admit, however, that the results are even better at great steak houses, where creamed spinach is a classic side dish. A little extra trouble, and the following recipe will bring that steak house difference to your dining room table.

Yield: 4 side dish servings

2 pounds fresh spinach leaves
2 tablespoons plus 1 teaspoon butter
¼ cup finely chopped shallot
1 whole clove
½ teaspoon freshly ground pepper
⅛ teaspoon ground nutmeg
1 cup whipping cream

1. Remove and discard the stems from the spinach. Rinse and drain the spinach thoroughly. (Using a salad spinner is an easy way to eliminate the excess water.) Reserve.
2. Melt the 2 tablespoons of butter in a large nonreactive skillet over low heat. Add shallot and clove and cook slowly for about 10 minutes, stirring occasionally. Remove and discard the clove.
3. Increase heat to medium-high and add the spinach. If all the spinach does not fit into the pan, allow the spinach in the pan to cook

down, stirring constantly. In less than a minute there will be enough room to add the remaining spinach. Continue to cook for an additional 5 minutes. Remove from heat and allow to cool for 10 minutes.
4. Transfer spinach to a food processor and chop fine (I like to stop the chopping just short of a puree). Return spinach to skillet and place on medium heat. Add the pepper and nutmeg. Add the whipping cream, ¼ cup at a time, pouring cream in a steady stream into the spinach, stirring quickly and constantly. As the mixture thickens, continue adding cream in the same manner until all the cream has been incorporated. This will take about 5 minutes.
5. Adjust salt and pepper to taste. Stir in the 1 teaspoon of butter and serve immediately.

✮ The Forget-Steamed- ✮ Broccoli Broccoli

All that hue and cry some years back when we discovered that our president did not like broccoli undoubtedly was the indirect result of someone in the Bush household giving broccoli a long water treatment; steamed or boiled broccoli that has been overcooked really is awful. The following broccoli strategy is almost as easy as the boiling one, and immensely superior in taste. The result, in fact, is highly reminiscent of a side dish in a good and homey Italian-American restaurant (though you rarely see this exact dish there).

Yield: 4 side dish servings

6 tablespoons olive oil
15 large garlic cloves, smashed and peeled
2 pounds fresh broccoli, trimmed (see Note)

Place the oil in a large, wide pot with a cover over medium heat. Add the garlic cloves and sauté for 3 minutes. Add the broccoli and a sprinkle of salt, and toss well with the garlic and oil. Turn heat to medium-high, cover, and cook for 7 minutes, or until broccoli is almost tender. Uncover, stir, reduce heat to medium, and cook, uncovered, until broccoli is at the degree of doneness you like. Season to taste with salt and pepper and serve.

NOTE: Any way you like to cut broccoli should work in this recipe. My preference is to cut away the very end of the stalk (about a half inch), then to divide what's left into two pieces: the stalk and the florets. I cut the stalk into long spears, and I divide the florets into clusters about the size of walnuts. Then, with a small, sharp knife, I remove the dull green peel everywhere and discard it, revealing a wetter, deeper green layer beneath.

Breads

☆ White Bread, ☆ Pullman-Loaf Style

Let's face it — everyone takes the basic white bread for granted. As with vanilla ice cream, however, a white bread can be wonderful and comforting. Confession: I sometimes even love the supermarket white (such as around a good old-fashioned tuna salad sandwich)! But because most of us have succumbed to the convenience of that supermarket white, many have forgotten the pleasures of a white bread with a little more texture and flavor. Such a loaf is the Pullman loaf — so named either (depending on your source) because it used to be served in Pullman dining cars or because its shape resembles a Pullman car. You can find the Pullman loaf, and related serious whites, in good bakeries today. Or best of all, you can make your own. While you're at it . . . why not make three? They freeze well, and there's always canned tuna in the cupboard. . . .

Yield: 3 loaves (8½ by 4½ inches)

6 cups bread flour, plus extra for rolling the dough
4 tablespoons sugar
1½ cups cool water
1 cup whole milk
3 tablespoons plus 1½ teaspoons rapid-rise (instant) yeast
3 tablespoons kosher salt
2½ tablespoons unsalted butter, melted
Olive oil for greasing the bowl and pans
Egg Wash (recipe follows)

1. Place the 6 cups bread flour, sugar, water, milk, yeast, salt, and butter in the large bowl of a stand mixer fitted with a dough hook attachment.

2. Mix the ingredients on very slow speed until all the ingredients are just combined. Increase the mixer speed to medium-high and continue to mix the dough for 6 minutes more. Dough should be a bit sticky.

3. Lightly oil a large bowl. Remove the ball of dough from the mixer and place in the oiled bowl. Cover and place in a warm spot until the dough ball has doubled in size, about 1 hour.

4. Lightly flour a rolling pin and a countertop with a little extra flour. Remove the risen dough to the counter. Using the rolling pin, flatten the dough to expel all the gases that have developed inside.

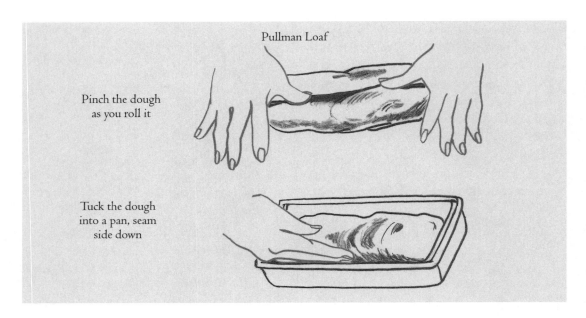

Pullman Loaf

Pinch the dough as you roll it

Tuck the dough into a pan, seam side down

5. Using a serrated knife, divide the dough into 3 equal pieces. Place dough pieces on the countertop so that they are not touching each other and cover the group with a damp cloth. Let rest for 20 minutes.

6. Lightly oil 3 (8½ by 4½ by 2½-inch) loaf pans and set aside. Lightly flour a rolling pin and a countertop with extra flour. Remove 1 piece of the dough to the counter. Using the rolling pin, flatten the dough to expel all the gases that have developed inside; form it into a rectangle approximately 5 inches wide and 8 inches long. Place a 5-inch end in front of you.

7. Using lightly floured hands, pick up the 5-inch end in front of you and roll it toward the other 5-inch end. As you roll, stop frequently and lightly pinch the crease that you're rolling over. Continue rolling forward until you reach the other 5-inch end. The bread you're forming should also spread from side to side as you're rolling; just make sure it doesn't spread out to more than 8 inches or it will not fit into your loaf pans. This process is like rolling a jelly roll without any filling. When you've reach the other end, be sure to seal well by pinching the seam together with your fingers. Place the dough in a loaf pan, seam side down. Make sure the ends of the loaf touch the inside ends of the pan. Repeat with remaining 2 pieces of dough. Cover each pan with a piece of clear plastic wrap and let each one rise in a warm area until it has doubled in size, about 1¼ hours.

8. While dough rises, preheat the oven to 375 degrees. When the loaves are ready to be baked, brush the tops with egg wash (see following recipe).

9. Place the loaf pans in the oven, on the center rack, and bake until they are golden

brown, about 20 to 24 minutes. The internal temperature should be 200 degrees and the loaves should sound hollow when tapped.

10. Remove the loaf pans from the oven and let cool for 5 minutes before using your hands to remove the loaves from the pans. Allow them to cool down to room temperature before serving.

☆ Egg Wash ☆

Many breads traditionally take on a patina of egg wash before they go into the oven. This is principally a visual choice; the chief function of the wash is to give a shine to a loaf of bread. But the wash can also be useful when you're attempting to make seeds adhere to the top and sides of a loaf.

Yield: Enough for approximately 4 large loaves of bread

1 whole egg
½ cup milk
Pinch of sugar

Whisk ingredients together in a bowl.

☆ Parker House Rolls ☆

One of the great staples of old-fashioned American restaurants, these puffy yeast rolls are also very easy to make at home. They were invented — guess where? — at the Parker House hotel, in Boston, in 1855; as in the tarte tatin story in France, the mythology is that they were originally a mistake. They are odd, folded-over as each one is, instead of a continuous whole. But the result of the following recipe is miraculously light, soft, feathery — and will make you dream of an earlier, simpler time.

Yield: About 3 dozen rolls

1 package active dry yeast (¼ ounce)
*3 tablespoons warm water (between
    100 degrees and 115 degrees)*
2 tablespoons sugar, plus an extra pinch
*3 tablespoons butter, plus 3 more tablespoons
    butter, melted and cooled*
2 tablespoons vegetable shortening
1 cup whole milk
1½ teaspoons salt
1 large egg
3½ to 4 cups all-purpose flour
Olive oil for greasing the bowl

1. In the mixer bowl of a stand mixer, combine yeast, warm water, and a pinch of sugar. Let stand about 5 minutes, until yeast is bubbly. Meanwhile, in a small saucepan, melt the 3 tablespoons butter and the shortening together. When melted, add milk, the 2 tablespoons sugar, and the salt. Stir to combine. Cool to about 100 degrees. The mixture should be slightly warm to the touch.

2. Add milk-butter mixture to the mixer bowl, along with the egg. Beat on low speed with the paddle attachment to combine. Add 2 cups of the flour and mix for 30 seconds. Add another cup of flour and mix for another 30 seconds. Add the remaining flour in small increments to get a sticky dough — it should not yet pull away from the sides of the bowl, but it should not be soupy. On a wet or humid day, you will probably need to use all 4 cups of flour.

3. Switch to a dough hook and knead until dough is very smooth and elastic, about 10 minutes.

4. Lightly grease a large bowl with the olive oil. Remove the ball of dough from the mixer and place in the oiled bowl. Cover and place in a warm area until the dough ball has doubled in size, about 1 hour.

5. Punch dough down and let rest, covered, in the refrigerator for about 15 minutes.

6. Punch down again and, using a knife, divide into 2 equal pieces. Lightly flour a rolling pin and countertop. Roll out 1 piece into a rectangle ½ inch thick. Cut rectangle into 18 rounds with a 2½-inch round cookie cutter. Repeat both steps with the second piece of dough. Using the dull side of a knife press down lightly to make a visible crease that's slightly off center of the dough round, brush the marked round with some of the melted and cooled butter, and fold over, so the top is just shy of meeting the bottom. Cover and let rise until doubled again, about 1 hour. Brush tops with remaining melted butter and let rise until doubled, about 1 hour. Meanwhile, preheat oven to 425 degrees.

7. Bake until golden, about 12 minutes, rotating the pan once about halfway through the baking time. These rolls taste best when served warm.

Parker House Rolls

Cut out rounds from the dough with a cookie cutter

Use the dull side of a knife to make an off-center, visible crease

Fold over on the crease, the fold falling short of the edge

✯ Potato Rolls with Dill ✯

Using mashed potatoes in baking bread may have Pennsylvania Dutch origins in the United States, but the idea has now spread widely — as you can see by the lineup of potato rolls, potato hamburger buns, and potato hot dog buns in most supermarkets across the country. The potato doesn't add its subtle flavor to bread, but it does add a delightfully rich texture, and the bread usually emerges from the oven with a fair share of internal moistness. These potato rolls are wonderful as dinner rolls or as sandwich rolls.

Yield: 24 rolls

1½ cups Red Bliss potatoes (or small red new potatoes), unpeeled
6 cups bread flour, plus extra for rolling dough
3 tablespoons sugar
3 tablespoons plus 1 teaspoon kosher salt
3 tablespoons rapid-rise (instant) yeast
1¼ cups buttermilk, room temperature
1¼ cups water, room temperature

7 tablespoons unsalted butter, room temperature
2 tablespoons whole dill seeds (see Baker's note)
½ cup fresh dill, chopped (see Baker's note)
Olive oil for greasing the bowl
Light rye or whole wheat flour for dusting
Handful of ice cubes

1. Preheat oven to 400 degrees. Rinse the potatoes and arrange them on a baking pan. Place the pan in oven and bake until the potatoes are completely cooked, when a knife inserted into the center of a potato comes out easily, about 45 minutes. Let cool completely before using a small knife to slice potatoes into small pieces.

2. Place the roasted potatoes, the 6 cups bread flour, sugar, kosher salt, yeast, buttermilk, water, and butter in a large bowl of a stand mixer fitted with a dough hook attachment.

3. Mix the ingredients on a very slow speed until all the ingredients are just combined. Increase the mixer speed up to medium-high and continue to mix until the dough takes on a shiny appearance and starts to pull away from the bottom of the bowl, about 9 minutes. The ball of dough should be thoroughly kneaded.

4. Begin mixing again on a very low speed before adding the dill seeds and fresh dill. Slowly increase the speed until dill is completely mixed into the dough. Do not overmix the dough.

5. Lightly grease a large bowl with the olive oil. Remove the ball of dough from the mixer and place in the oiled bowl. Cover and place in a warm area until the dough ball has doubled in size, about 45 minutes.

6. Lightly flour a rolling pin and a countertop with extra bread flour. Tip the risen dough onto the counter. Using a rolling pin, flatten the dough to expel all the gases that have developed inside.

7. Using a knife, divide the dough into golf ball–size pieces. With lightly floured hands, place dough on a lightly floured countertop and begin to shape each dough piece into a round roll by cupping your palms over the pieces of dough and moving your hands in a circular motion. Then arrange the dough rolls at 2-inch intervals on a baking pan lined with parchment paper. Cover with plastic wrap and place in a warm area until rolls double in size, about 1½ hours.

8. Arrange a single rack in the center of the oven and place an ovenproof baking pan on the bottom of the oven. Preheat oven to 435 degrees. Just prior to loading the rolls into the oven, dust the tops of them with light rye or whole wheat flour. While loading the bread into the oven, carefully toss a handful of ice cubes into the ovenproof pan on the bottom of the oven. This will slightly steam the rolls.

9. Bake the bread on the center oven rack until golden brown, about 12 to 14 minutes. The internal temperature of the bread should be 200 degrees. Remove the pan from the oven and allow it to cool on a wire rack.

BAKER'S NOTE: The dill and dill seed are added at the end of the mixing process to avoid discoloration of the dough. If added earlier, the fresh dill would start breaking down . . . and the released chlorophyll would turn your dough a nondesirable shade of green. Moreover, because of their shape, the dill seeds would act like tiny razor blades in the dough, slashing the gluten formed by the mixing process. This would cause your dough to become "slack" and lose its shape-retaining properties. As a general rule, whenever a dough recipe calls for seeds, add them toward the end of the mixing process.

☆ Irish Soda Bread ☆

This is an amazing — albeit Americanized — version of Irish soda bread, the most delectable version I've ever tried. Originally, soda bread was a poor man's dish in Ireland. In America — where, due to its simplicity, more and more people are making it at home — we have fattened and sweetened the loaf. It is, in fact, the magical interplay of sugar and caraway — as well as the remarkable contrast between crunchy exterior and fluffy interior — that makes this rendition of Irish soda bread so good.

Yield: 1 loaf (about 6 hearty servings)

2 cups all-purpose flour, plus extra
    for kneading
3 tablespoons sugar
1 teaspoon baking soda
¾ teaspoon salt
4 tablespoons cold unsalted butter,
    cut into small cubes
½ cup dried currants
2 teaspoons toasted caraway seeds
1 cup minus 2 tablespoons buttermilk
Vegetable oil for greasing baking sheet

1. Preheat oven to 375 degrees. In a large bowl, sift together the 2 cups flour, the sugar, baking soda, and salt.
2. Using your fingertips, blend butter into flour until it resembles coarse meal. Add currants and caraway seeds, tossing to coat with flour. Add buttermilk, and use a wooden spoon to stir until just combined. Place dough on a floured surface and knead a few times, just until the dough quickly comes together in 1 piece.
3. Form dough into a round loaf about 8 inches in diameter and place on a greased baking sheet. Using a sharp floured knife, cut a cross into the top of the bread. Bake on the middle rack of the oven until bread is golden brown and a tester inserted in the center of the loaf comes out clean, about 30 to 35 minutes. Cool on a rack about 10 minutes before serving.

Desserts

☆ Apple Pie ☆

Just what is it about this pie that places it right up there on every short list of The Things That Define America? Apples are not indigenous; we have knowledge of their cultivation in Egypt going back four thousand years. The pie itself is not indigenous; English cooks were baking it long before the Pilgrims landed here. But the Pilgrims did bring the first apple seeds to North America . . . and, almost four hundred years later, America is the world's largest producer of apples. Moreover, after the spread of apples across America in the early nineteenth century, pies became the signature American way of cooking them. So, though we are originally responsible for neither fruit nor pie, no country in the world has as much enthusiasm for the apple pie as ours does. The following recipe, I hope, will show you why. Made from Golden Delicious apples (sometimes disrespected, but always my favorite pie choice), and with a tender, flaky, buttery crust, this pie is guaranteed to make it feel like a combination of Mother's Day and the Fourth of July whenever you bake it.

Yield: 8 servings

*⅓ cup all-purpose flour, plus extra for
    rolling dough*
*Superflaky Piecrust (page 458; 2 flat rounds
    of dough)*
*3 pounds Golden Delicious apples, peeled,
    cored, and cut into ⅛-inch slices*
2 tablespoons lemon juice
1 cup plus 1 tablespoon sugar
1 teaspoon ground cinnamon
½ teaspoon salt
2 tablespoons butter, cut into ½-inch cubes
1 egg beaten with 1 tablespoon milk for glaze

1. Preheat oven to 425 degrees.
2. Sprinkle a little flour on a countertop and roll out larger piece of dough into an 11-inch circle. Gently lift and place in a 9-inch pie plate. Trim edges to hang about ½ inch over the edge of the plate. Refrigerate while you prepare the filling.

3. In a large bowl, toss apples with lemon juice. Add the 1 cup sugar, the ⅓ cup flour, the cinnamon, and salt, tossing to coat all the apples well. Dump mixture into prepared crust. Pat down apples with your hands to make sure there are no air pockets. Dot top with butter cubes. Brush edges of crust with a little of the egg glaze.
4. Roll out remaining flat round of dough into an 11-inch circle. Gently lift and place over filling. Trim so crust is even with the edge of the bottom crust. Fold both crust edges under the rim to form a lip, then crimp all around using the index finger of one hand and the index and middle finger of the other hand together. Cut 3 slashes 2 inches long at the twelve o'clock, four o'clock, and eight o'clock positions.
5. Bake pie on the bottom rack of the oven for 20 minutes. It is a good idea to put a large piece of aluminum foil or a sheet pan under the pie to catch the bubbling juices. After 20 minutes, reduce oven temperature to 375 degrees, move pie to the middle rack,

Apple Pie

The bottom crust
without filling

Lay the top crust
over the filling

Crimp the 2 crusts
together

and bake an additional 30 minutes. Remove pie from oven, brush liberally with egg glaze, and sprinkle with the remaining 1 tablespoon of sugar. Bake another 10 minutes, or until crust is golden and you can see the juices bubbling through the slashes in the pie. Cool at least 1 hour before slicing.

☆ Superflaky Piecrust ☆

This is my favorite crust of all: buttery, with the kind of flaking and layering that begin to suggest puff pastry. It could work with light fillings or hearty fillings — but it's the kind of crust that draws attention to itself and therefore might not be the best choice for the kinds of pies (for example, key lime pie) in which the focus is never on the crust.

Yield: Enough for 1 double-crusted pie (9½ inches)

1½ cups all-purpose flour
½ cup cake flour
¼ teaspoon salt
8 tablespoons unsalted butter, cut into
      ½-inch squares
3 tablespoons cold vegetable shortening
⅓ cup ice water mixed with 1 tablespoon
      distilled white vinegar (have an extra
      1 to 2 tablespoons ice water in reserve;
      you may need a bit more)

1. In a medium bowl, gently combine the all-purpose flour, cake flour, salt, and butter. Butter should be left in half-inch squares. Place in the freezer until butter is hard, about 5 minutes. Dump mixture on the counter and roll it over quickly with a rolling pin, scraping off whatever adheres to the pin; repeat 2 or 3 times until the butter forms flat flakes. Scrape mixture back into bowl and add shortening in chickpea-size lumps. Freeze another 5 minutes.

2. Dump mixture on the counter and roll and scrape two more times to incorporate shortening. Return to bowl, freeze 5 minutes more. Add water-vinegar mixture to bowl; toss with a fork. Press a few tablespoons of the mixture in your hand. If it clumps, you are okay; if it crumbles, add water a teaspoon at a time until mixture clumps. Dump onto the counter and bring together with your hands. Knead only once or twice, just to form a mass that sticks together. Divide into 2 flat rounds, one just slightly larger than the other. Wrap each piece in plastic wrap and refrigerate at least 2 hours before rolling.

☆ Lemon Squares ☆

If you're a fan of tart lemon desserts, you'll love these small squares of sweet-and-sour ecstasy, set on a flaky crust.

Yield: 16 (2-inch) squares

FOR THE CRUST:
¼ pound (1 stick) unsalted butter, chilled
      and cut into ½-inch cubes, plus
      2 teaspoons unsalted butter for
      greasing the baking pan
1 cup all-purpose flour
½ teaspoon salt
¼ cup light brown sugar, firmly packed
⅛ teaspoon ground ginger
1 teaspoon finely grated lemon zest

FOR THE FILLING:

3 large eggs
¾ cup granulated sugar
Finely grated zest of 2 lemons
6 tablespoons lemon juice
3 tablespoons all-purpose flour
¼ teaspoon baking powder
Confectioners' sugar for dusting

1. Preheat oven to 350 degrees. Use the 2 teaspoons of butter to grease an 8 by 8-inch baking pan.

2. To make the crust: In a food processor, pulse together the flour, salt, brown sugar, ginger, and lemon zest. Drop the cubes of butter down the feed tube and pulse until the mixture resembles coarse bread crumbs.

3. Place mixture in the buttered baking pan and, using your hands, spread mixture out across the bottom of pan evenly. Tamp down to compact it. Bake until golden, about 15 minutes. Remove from oven and set aside.

4. In the meantime, make the filling: In a medium bowl, whisk together the eggs and granulated sugar until well blended. Add the lemon zest and lemon juice, then the flour and baking powder.

5. Pour mixture onto the baked crust; it's okay if the crust is still warm. Smooth out so the filling is even.

6. Bake in 350-degree oven until the filling is just set, about 20 minutes. Do not overbake. Set on rack to cool.

7. When cool, dust with confectioners' sugar and cut into 2-inch squares. Serve at room temperature.

☆ Chocolate Cake ☆ for All Purposes

One of the handiest things to have in your dessert repertoire is a fast, easy, reliable, delicious chocolate cake — and that's exactly what the following recipe gives you. You can serve it just as it is — or you can embellish it with your favorite frosting. You can make two of these cakes and put a layer of buttercream between them. You can serve the cake with ice cream, with whipped cream, with mascarpone, with fruit. You can also freeze it and serve it next month. One of the secrets to its good nature is the inclusion of mayonnaise — yes, Hellmann's or another good brand! The notion of including mayo in chocolate cake goes back to the First World War, when food companies were encouraging Americans to ration their eggs — and use mayonnaise instead, which was widely available. The strategy arose again as World War II approached. In 1937 Hellmann's themselves published a recipe for mayonnaise chocolate cake — but this time eggs were in and short-supply milk and butter were out. The great news is that mayo, though undetectable as mayo in the finished product, adds a lovely mouth feel to any chocolate cake. The following recipe uses a little butter, milk, egg — *and* mayo — to devastatingly delicious effect.

Yield: 8 servings

1 tablespoon unsalted butter
1 tablespoon all-purpose flour
1 cup sugar
1 cup good-quality mayonnaise,
    such as Hellmann's
2 teaspoons vanilla extract
2 cups cake flour
½ cup cocoa powder
1 teaspoon baking soda
½ teaspoon kosher salt
3 large eggs
1 cup whole milk

1. Preheat oven to 350 degrees. Grease an 8 by 8 by 2-inch baking dish with the butter. Sprinkle evenly with the all-purpose flour. Set aside.

2. In a medium mixing bowl, beat the sugar, mayonnaise, and vanilla with a whisk until blended.

3. In another bowl, sift together the cake flour, cocoa, baking soda, and salt.

4. In another bowl, beat the eggs lightly, then add the milk, whisking to blend.

5. Whisking slowly, add one-third of the flour mixture to the mayonnaise mixture. Add half of the egg-milk mixture, whisking, then another third of the flour mixture. Keep whisking, then finish with the remaining half of the egg mixture and the last third of the flour mixture.

6. Pour into the prepared baking dish and bake for about 40 minutes or until a skewer inserted in the center comes out clean. Let cool on a rack.

Frozen Desserts

The only thing that might be more American than apple pie . . . is an ice cream cone! Tell the truth: do you eat more apple pie every year or more ice cream? We Americans love our frozen confections. The supermarkets have always been loaded with inexpensive gallons of decent-quality ice cream. Twenty years ago, the market selection expanded dramatically, to include products from smaller, more artisanal companies, such as Ben & Jerry's and Häagen-Dazs — still, nationally distributed, mind you! More recently, a wave of very small, local ice cream producers making very small batches of ice cream began appearing. Restaurant chefs have caught the habit, and all kinds of exotic ice creams are being devised in restaurant kitchens. And ice cream making at home — once a favorite American pastime — is surging back, with the appearance on the market of wonderfully easy, high-quality home ice cream machines. Don't forget to make sorbets in those machines as well — for we as a nation, from the Italian ices of old to the shave ice of Hawaii to the rainbow sherbet of the 1950s to the degustation of twelve tropical fruit sorbets in fancy restaurants today, love our flavored ice too.

The following recipes for ice creams do what ice cream recipes always do: they lead you up to the freezing of the confection and then turn you over to the "manufacturer's direction" — the manufacturer of your ice cream machine, that is. Well, there's nothing else to be done; all ice cream machines are different, and each has its own particulars. But I'll take you one step further and recommend a specific machine: the ice cream machine that I've come to love is the Lussino model 4080, made in Italy. It is a compressor-type ice cream machine, which means that it is self-chilling; you do not have to pre-freeze and insert a canister, as many other machines force you to do. That makes the Lussino simplicity itself: you just pop your ice cream mixture into the machine, flip two switches — and a half hour later you have up to one and one-half quarts of ice cream.

The important thing is: you have up to one and one-half quarts of *great* ice cream. It must be the case that this machine whips less air into the ice cream than other machines — because Lussino-made ice creams, in test after test, were richer, silkier, heavier than ice creams made in other machines.

The only bad news is the price: about six hundred dollars. Now, there are more-expensive and less-expensive machines out there — but if you're serious about making ice cream at home, I would highly recommend picking up a Lussino 4080.

The machine is available at good housewares stores around the country. If you have any trouble finding it, contact:

Lello Appliances Corporation
355 Murray Hill Parkway
East Rutherford, NJ 07073
201-939-2555
201-939-5074 (fax)

☆ Double-Vanilla Ice Cream ☆

Americans love ice cream. We have even invented our own type of ice cream: Philadelphia-style ice cream, which eschews the egg custard base of French-style ice cream. Once upon a time we were a nation of home ice cream makers; throwing rock salt on ice and cranking the old wooden machine were part of the American experience. Commercial ice cream ended all that; from ice cream parlors to supermarkets, ice cream became extremely easy to acquire — without all that work! In recent years, however, nostalgic

The Right Temperature for Ice Cream

One of the main differences between ice cream in the United States and ice cream in Italy and France is that Europeans eat ice cream very soon after it's made, when it's still quite soft. With our larger-scale distribution system in the United States, ice cream usually goes into the deep freeze right after it's made. When you buy it at the store, it's usually a solid, frozen block. Some people like it that way — but I far prefer eating ice cream in a softer, more velvety state; the texture is sexier and the flavor's more pronounced.

All the ice creams here may be eaten as soon as they come out of the ice cream machine, European style — or they may be frozen for later eating. If you choose to freeze them, do so in an airtight container. When you're ready to eat the ice cream, please give my way a try: allow the ice cream to sit out of the freezer until it reaches about twenty degrees, approximately ten to fifteen minutes, before eating. You can check the temperature with an instant-read meat thermometer.

Once the ice cream has softened, use a spoon to stir and mash it down; this will give it an old-fashioned, hand-packed, ice cream shop texture. And in the case of fruit ice creams, this motion will help distribute the fruit more evenly.

Americans — helped along by wonderful high-tech electric ice cream machines — have started making ice cream at home again. And it's often nostalgic flavors they make — like the following old-fashioned vanilla, made with no eggs, in the American style. Some feel — as I do — that a flavor as delicate as vanilla comes through better when there are no eggs getting in the way.

Yield: 1 generous pint

2 cups whipping cream
½ cup sugar
1 vanilla bean, split
½ cup vanilla extract, preferably Mexican

1. Put 1 cup of the cream, the sugar, and vanilla bean in a heavy 1-quart saucepan over medium-high heat and cook, stirring, until the milk is just below scalding, approximately 175 degrees. Remove from heat.
2. When cream mixture is cool enough to handle, remove vanilla bean and scrape out seeds into the cream. Discard pod. Stir in the vanilla extract and the remaining 1 cup of cream.
3. Let stand, covered, in refrigerator for at least 4 hours, or overnight.
4. Freeze mixture in an ice cream machine; follow manufacturer's directions.

✹ Burned Chocolate ✹ Ice Cream

Of course, there's a lot of ice cream innovation these days. In the new world of creative, designer ice creams, the plain old chocolate stuff is not good enough for everybody anymore. Is that a bad thing? Not when it leads to the "burned" chocolate ice cream I tasted in Napa Valley recently! Oh, I'm not giving up my basic chocolate — but just wait until you try this haunting, complex stuff that's so rich it demands its own ice cream base. Eat it alone or as a "burned" sundae topped with caramel sauce, toasted nuts, and roasted marshmallows.

Yield: 3 pints

2 cups milk
2 cups whipping cream
⅔ cup sugar
1 vanilla bean, split lengthwise
1 cup egg yolks (from about 14 large eggs)
Ice cubes
1 cup semisweet chocolate morsels (see Note)

1. Combine the milk, cream, ⅓ cup of the sugar, and the split vanilla bean in a large saucepan placed over medium heat. Bring the mixture to a boil.
2. Meanwhile, in a large mixing bowl combine the egg yolks and the remaining ⅓ cup of sugar; with a whisk, mix them together thoroughly.
3. When the mixture in the saucepan comes to a boil, remove it from heat. Very slowly, in a thin stream at first, whisk the hot cream mixture into the bowl with the egg-yolk mixture. When the cream mixture and the egg-yolk mixture are combined, pour into the saucepan.
4. Place the saucepan over medium-low heat. Cook the mixture, stirring constantly, until it starts to thicken (it should take less than 5 minutes); at this stage it will evenly coat the back of a spoon and register about 175 degrees on an instant-read thermometer. Remove mixture from heat and pour it

into a large bowl that is set among ice cubes in a baking pan. Let the mixture cool down for 15 minutes, stirring occasionally.

5. Place the chocolate morsels in a small, heavy-bottomed sauté pan. Place the pan over medium-low heat and cook the morsels for about 5 minutes. Stir them only once every minute, because you want them to burn. This is a very smoky process, but it is worth it. When the melted chocolate has burned — it's black and is smoking — slowly whisk the burned chocolate into the cream mixture in the bowl in the ice pan. The mixture will need to cool once more for 15 minutes. Then cover the bowl with plastic wrap and poke a few holes in it to let the steam out. Refrigerate until it is cold. Finally, strain the mixture through a fine mesh strainer into a medium-size bowl.

6. To freeze the mixture, you will need to follow the manufacturer's directions from your ice cream machine.

NOTE: This is one instance in which you do *not* want to use the best-quality chocolate on the market. Instead, choose something like Nestle Toll House morsels, which have a higher oil content than most good-quality chocolate and will therefore burn more easily, better capturing the burned quality of this unique ice cream.

☆ Coffee Ice Cream ☆

I love coffee ice cream — though I can rarely get enough concentrated coffee flavor. Until now. I can't explain why, but the no-egg base of this stupendous ice cream clears the path for the brightest, most intense coffee flavors I've ever experienced in an ice cream.

Yield: 1 generous pint

1 cup good-quality espresso coffee beans
   (see Note)
2 cups whipping cream
½ cup sugar
½ vanilla bean, split

1. Place the coffee beans in the bowl of a food processor with the chopping blade already in place. Grind the beans for about 1 minute, leaving them slightly chunky.

2. Place 1 cup of the cream, the ground coffee, sugar, and vanilla bean in a 1-quart saucepan. Heat the mixture over medium heat almost to a boil. Turn the heat off and let the mixture come to room temperature.

3. Strain the mixture through a fine mesh strainer into a medium-size bowl. Add the remaining 1 cup of cream to the strained coffee-cream mixture. Then let stand, covered, in the refrigerator for 4 hours, or overnight.

4. Freeze in an ice cream machine; follow manufacturer's directions.

NOTE: It's simple: if you get superlative beans, you'll make superlative ice cream. That's why I think it's worth going to the trouble to secure the very best beans you can in making this ice cream. I would recommend a phone call, or a Web site visit, to Peet's in San Francisco, one of the country's best coffee roasters. Peet's can be reached by calling 800-999-2132, or Peet's beans can be ordered by logging on to: *www.peets.com.* The beans cost about $12 per pound plus shipping (the more you order, the more the per-pound shipping cost goes down). Minimum order is one-half pound. *Note:* Freshness and storage are of paramount importance in the bean game. One of the great things about Peet's is that they guarantee your beans will have been roasted no more than a day before shipping.

Acknowledgments

✩✩✩✩✩✩✩✩✩✩✩

A cookbook of this size is necessarily a collaborative effort. It takes a team to dream up, plan, develop, test, and retest over 400 brand-new recipes. In my view, it would be just about impossible to have "too many cooks" in such an endeavor — and when the team is spectacular, as mine was, the "broth" can never be spoiled, only vastly improved.

Helping me to coordinate the team every step of the way — and contributing mightily himself in the test kitchen — was North Carolina native T. J. Robinson, who runs the office of David Rosengarten Ltd. and *The Rosengarten Report.* I met T. J. a few years ago when I was a guest chef at the Biltmore Estate, in Asheville, North Carolina; T. J., who was then the chef of the Biltmore Estate Winery, was assigned to be my assistant for that cooking weekend. I could immediately see his immense cooking talent and his wonderful sense of all things truly American. He came to work for me in New York and was absolutely instrumental in the development of many recipes in this book — particularly those with Southern themes, those featuring barbecue, and those in the dessert and baking sections of the book.

Another major collaborator was the broadly talented Amy Stevenson, with whom I worked for many years at the Food Network. Amy was one of the marvelous behind-the-scenes kitchen people who make us look so good on TV. For this book, I collaborated with Amy on developing and testing a sizable number of recipes — which was easy to do, since Amy is so gifted in all corners of food preparation. She grew up in Pittsburgh, with a combination of Lithuanian and Pennsylvania German roots — which made her my #1 candidate for work on good, hearty, old-fashioned home food. But her touch with Italian food, Southwestern dishes, jams, jellies, and pickles, as well as many other things, was just as strong.

David Whiteman, a native New Yorker, a French Culinary Institute grad, and an excellent private chef/caterer, was extremely valuable to me because he reminds me so much of myself: absolutely obsessed with anything you can eat or drink. His wonderful work on recipes from Cajun to Asian — with stops in Morocco, Italy, France, and other places along the way — was a key contribution to the book. And his broad store of general food and wine knowledge — with reports from his Land Rover tour of Africa or his time spent in the Italian vineyards — always kept us fascinated and inspired.

Another very international cook at work on the project was the very gifted, very English Wendy Taylor, who grew up in London (her grandmother was a professional chef there). Marriage brought her to the United States, where she trained at the California Culinary

Academy before going on to graduate work in the Food Studies program at NYU. Along the way, she has worked in a wide range of restaurant and catering jobs in the United States, developing a very American perspective on food. She did terrific work with me on American interpretations of French, Caribbean, Korean, and Southeast Asian recipes — and emerged as my key collaborator in the book's dessert recipes.

My key collaborator in the book's bread recipes was Michael John Coe, whom I met on a trip to Phoenix some years ago. Simply put, Coe is the baking wizard of Arizona: co-owner of Tammie Coe Cakes in Phoenix, winner of multiple awards for producing the best bread in Arizona, and the youngest Certified Master Baker in the United States. Coe turns out amazing artisanal breads professionally — but is extremely sensitive to the special challenges that face the home baker.

Mary Macksoud brought something a little different to the party — by dint of her Lebanese in-laws! Mary, who's from a great Italian family with roots in Sicily and Naples, grew up with family foodies who produced much of what they ate and drank (her immigrant grandparents had a New Jersey farm). After raising her own family, she indulged her life-long love of food and received a Grand Diploma from the French Culinary Institute. Her combo of cooking savvy, good taste, stunning Italian-American home food, and extraordinary Middle Eastern delights made her a most valuable collaborator.

I was extremely lucky to have met Susan Bird, and her husband, Rick, at a cooking class in Connecticut. Susan, who works in pharmaceuticals, was the only amateur chef to have collaborated on this book — but when you get to her area of expertise, Louisiana home cookin', it'd be hard to find a more talented cook anywhere. Well, she's got the background: she grew up in a family of fanatic cooks, right in the heart of Cajun country. She helped us all avoid the clichéd perspectives on Cajun food — and worked with us to develop dishes that taste as food does in the Bayou.

Other chefs made less sizable, but nevertheless valuable, contributions. Sarah LaGrotteria, from an Italian family in Chicago, helped a great deal with the dessert recipes while she was working in the pastry kitchen at Mario Batali's Esca. Todd Coleman, now a producer at the Food Network, grew up "all over" with his Air Force dad — and made contributions in a wide range of ethnic cuisines. Tina Prestia has a father from Calabria and a mother from Arkansas — so of course she developed a special interest in, and nifty talent for, Tex-Mex food. Justin Wangler was born in South Dakota, grew up in North Carolina, and today cooks fancy, creative food at restaurants in Sonoma County — giving us great insight into the ways of modern restaurant food. And Lynne Calamia, a Broadway dancer, who decided to switch to a kitchen career — which, via the French Culinary Institute, led her to a great cooking job at new York's famed Jean-Georges — favored us with her family's knowledge of Philippine and Southeast Asian food.

American stories, all. And delicious ones at that.

A few of the recipes in the book were developed from dishes that I tasted at various restaurants, hotels, stores, or homes of friends, or from dishes that I'd heard or read about. For these, I'd like to thank the Hotel Bel-Air and the Beverly Hills Hotel, both in Los Angeles, Gary Greengrass of Barney Greengrass in New York City, Sotirios Karamouzis of the International Grocery in New York City, Joyce Matsumoto of the Halekulani Hotel in Honolulu, Lari Robling (Philadelphia food writer), Jorge Rodriguez of the Chimichurri Grill in New York City, Vincent Scotto of Gonzo in New York City, *Southern Living* magazine, Costas Spiliadis of Milos in New York City, and the globe-trotting writer Anya von Bremzen (who makes New York City her base).

Additionally, great ideas that became recipes in the book were contributed by Laurel Murphy, Christy Rizzo, Carlyne McGee Morrow, Nancy Wood, Blake DeBoest, Sheila Tillman, Sandy Shope, Carolyn White, Ginger Robinson, Vera Evans, and Hanna Lee.

I must also thank my core group of colleagues at the Food Network, with whom I've worked happily for so many years, and with whom I developed recipes that, in one form or another, ultimately led to some of the recipes in this book. Special thanks go to John Jenkins, Georgia Downard, Susan Stockton, and Julia Harrison.

Contributions were also made to the book, both directly and indirectly, by the talented and dedicated folks who work at my office, or with whom I work on my newsletter, *The Rosengarten Report.* This list includes Phil Teverow (the marketing director of *The Rosengarten Report*), Nancy Loseke (the research director of *The Rosengarten Report*), who worked overtime on copyediting, Elizabeth van Italie, Yvette Diamond, Tracy Mattikow, Sara Firebaugh, Scott Tripp, Dana Bowen, Jennifer Noble, Mercedes Johnson, Banu Ogan, Julia Cheiffetz, Catherine Chiu, Courtney Pardue, and Nellia Mikhailiv.

My deep appreciation also goes to the wonderful people who represent me in various ways — keeping my time free for recipe development! Kathy Robbins (my literary agent) makes all things possible. Susan Anderson, my agent at ICM, has contributed much support — as well as a few family recipes! Peter Fairley and Rosalind Evia at Mason & Co. have kept my business affairs as untangled as possible. Lastly, Sharon Bowers and Amy Voll, who represent TV chefs, are always on the prowl for exciting projects in which I may participate.

Thanks go as well to my wonderful editor at Little, Brown, Deborah Baker, and to her assistant, Allison Powell. Deborah supplied the vision that launched this project and kept me steadily on course throughout its execution.

Finally, there's my dad — who passed away before the writing of this book but contributed indirectly in so many vital ways, both culinary and emotional. And I must give the deepest thanks of all to the two people who are my most important food-tasters (they really are!), as well as the real inspiration for everything I do: my daughters, Andy and Sarah.

Index

About the Author

✦✧✦✧✦✧✦✧✦✧✦✧✧

David Rosengarten is a food writer, cookbook author, cooking teacher, TV journalist, wine writer, and travel writer. He is best known for his cooking show *Taste*, which aired on the Food Network from 1994 to 2001. His articles about food, wine, travel, and restaurants have appeared in the *New York Times, Gourmet, Food & Wine*, and *Bon Appétit*, among many other publications. Rosengarten is the editor in chief of *The Rosengarten Report*, an award-winning consumer newsletter that is published every six weeks. He is also the author of several other books, including the bestselling *Dean & DeLuca Cookbook; Taste*, which won the IACP Award for Best International Cookbook; and, most recently, *David Rosengarten Entertains: Fabulous Parties for Food Lovers*. In 2004 Rosengarten received a James Beard Award in the "Cooking of the Americas" category for *It's All American Food*. He lives in New York City.

For more information, or to subscribe to *The Rosengarten Report*, visit www.davidrosengarten.com.